Torts

BY MARC A. FRANKLIN
Stanford University

W. JONATHAN CARDI
University of Kentucky

MICHAEL D. GREEN
Wake Forest University

Twenty-Fourth Edition

EDITORIAL OFFICES: 1 North Dearborn St., Suite 650, Chicago, IL 60602
REGIONAL OFFICES: Chicago, Dallas, Los Angeles, New York, Washington, D.C.

PROJECT EDITOR
Melissa B. Vasich, B.S., J.D.
Attorney At Law

SERIES EDITOR
Elizabeth L. Snyder, B.A., J.D.
Attorney At Law

QUALITY CONTROL EDITOR
Sanetta M. Hister

Summary of Contents

TORTS TEXT CORRELATION CHART **i**
TORTS CAPSULE SUMMARY **I**
GILBERT EXAM STRATEGIES **(i)**
INTRODUCTION **(v)**

I. INTENTIONAL TORTS
▶ Key Exam Issues 1
A. Torts to the Person 1
1. Battery 1
2. Assault 7
3. False Imprisonment 11
4. Intentional Infliction of Emotional Distress 16
CHART: **Torts to the Person—Comparison of Key Elements** **21**
B. Defenses and Privileged Invasions of Personal Interests 22
1. Consent 22
CHART: **Approach to Determining Validity of Consent** **23**
2. Self-Defense 27
3. Defense of Third Persons 30
4. Defense of Land or Chattels 31
5. Force to Recover Possession of Land Wrongfully Withheld 32
6. Force to Effect Recapture of Chattels Wrongfully Withheld 33
7. Privilege of Arrest 35
CHART: **Arrests Without an Arrest Warrant** **38**
8. Privilege of Discipline 38
CHART: **Allowable Force in Defenses to Intentional Torts** **39**
C. Torts to Property 40
1. Trespass to Land 40
2. Trespass to Chattels 43
3. Conversion of Chattels 45
CHART: **Acts of Conversion** **48**
CHART: **Property Torts—Comparison of Key Elements** **49**
D. Defenses and Privileged Invasions of Land and Chattels 50
CHART: **Privileged Invasions of Another's Land and Chattels** **56**

II. NEGLIGENCE
▶ Key Exam Issues 59
A. In General 59

B. Negligence (Based on the "Duty of Due Care") 60
CHART: **Variances in Standards of Negligence** **69**
CHART: **Elements of Res Ipsa Loquitur** **80**
CHART: **Comparison of Rules for Establishing Actual Cause** **100**
CHART: **Recovery of Special (Economic) Damages** **122**
CHART: **Recovery of General Damages** **124**
C. Special Duty Questions 127
CHART: **Approach to Determining Duty to Aid Others in Peril** **130**
CHART: **Liability of Principal for Agent's Torts—An Approach** **145**
CHART: **Failure to Control Third Parties—A Summary** **154**
CHART: **Duty of Land Possessor to Those on Premises—Status Approach** **167**
CHART: **Comparison of Emotional Distress Torts** **181**
D. Defenses to Negligence 182
CHART: **Comparison of Negligence Defenses** **197**
E. Effect of Liability Insurance 198

III. STRICT LIABILITY
▶ Key Exam Issues 203
A. In General 203
B. Animals 204
CHART: **Personal Injuries from Animals—Strict Liability** **205**
C. Abnormally Dangerous Activities 207
D. Extent of Liability 211
E. Defenses 212

IV. PRODUCTS LIABILITY
▶ Key Exam Issues 213
A. In General 213
CHART: **Overview of Products Liability Theories** **214**
B. Liability Based on Intentional Acts 215
C. Liability Based on Negligence 216
D. Strict Liability in Tort 220
CHART: **Tests for Design Defects—A Summary** **225**
CHART: **Defects Creating Strict Liability—A Summary** **230**
CHART: **When Product Is Defective—Examples** **238**
E. Liability Based on Breach of Warranty 245
CHART: **Types of Warranties** **246**

V. NUISANCE
▶ Key Exam Issues 253
A. In General 253
CHART: **Approach to Determining Presence of a Private Nuisance** **254**
B. Plaintiff's Interest 256
C. Defendant's Conduct 256
D. Substantial and Unreasonable Harm to Plaintiff 257
E. Causation 259
F. Remedies 259
G. Defenses 260

VI.	**MISCELLANEOUS FACTORS AFFECTING RIGHT TO SUE**	
▶	Key Exam Issues	263
A.	Survival of Tort Actions	263
B.	Wrongful Death	264
	***CHART:* "True" Type Wrongful Death Actions**	**268**
C.	Injuries to Members of the Family	268
D.	Tort Immunity	275
E.	Release and Contribution Among Joint Tortfeasors	282
F.	Indemnity	284
G.	Statutes of Limitations	286
VII.	**STATUTORY CHANGES IN PERSONAL INJURY LAW**	
▶	Key Exam Issues	287
A.	Changes Targeting Specific Kinds of Tort Claims	287
B.	Changes Affecting Tort Claims Generally	297
VIII.	**DEFAMATION**	
▶	Key Exam Issues	301
A.	In General	302
	***CHART:* Approach to Common Law Defamation**	**303**
B.	Publication to a Third Party	304
C.	Harm to Reputation	308
D.	False Facts	314
E.	Causation	317
F.	Damages and Other Remedies	318
	***CHART:* Categories of Slander Per Se**	**321**
G.	Defenses	323
	***CHART:* Traditional Absolute and Conditional Privileges**	**328**
H.	Constitutional Privileges	333
	***CHART:* Approach to Constitutional Defamation**	**334**
	***CHART:* Fault and Damages Rules in Constitutional Defamation Actions**	**343**
IX.	**WRONGFUL INVASION OF PRIVACY**	
▶	Key Exam Issues	345
A.	Intrusions into Plaintiff's Private Life or Affairs	345
B.	Public Disclosure of Private Facts	349
C.	Appropriation of Plaintiff's Name or Likeness	356
D.	Publicity Placing Plaintiff in a "False Light"	359
	***CHART:* Four Categories of Privacy Torts—A Summary**	**361**
E.	Claims Involving Privacy of Third Persons	362
F.	Important—Related Torts	363
X.	**OTHER TORTS**	
▶	Key Exam Issues	365
A.	Misrepresentation	365
	***CHART:* When Plaintiff May Rely on Misrepresentations—A Summary**	**371**
B.	Injurious Falsehood	377

C. Interference with Economic Relations 382
D. Unjustifiable Litigation 391

REVIEW QUESTIONS AND ANSWERS **399**
EXAM QUESTIONS AND ANSWERS **475**
TABLE OF CITATIONS TO RESTATEMENT OF TORTS **509**
TABLE OF CASES **511**
INDEX **527**

Text Correlation Chart

Gilbert Law Summary TORTS	Christie, Meeks, Pryor, Sanders *Cases and Materials on the Law of Torts* 2004 (4th ed.)	Dobbs, Hayden *Torts and Compensation* 2005 (5th ed.)	Epstein *Cases and Materials on Torts* 2008 (9th ed.)	Franklin, Rabin, Green *Tort Law and Alternatives: Cases and Materials* 2006 (8th ed.)	Goldberg, Sebok, Zipursky *Tort Law: Responsibilities and Redress* 2008 (2nd ed.)	Henderson, Pearson, Kysar, Siliciano *The Torts Process* 2007 (7th ed.)	Keeton, Sargentich, Keating *Tort and Accident Law: Cases and Materials* 2004 (4th ed.)	Schwartz, Kelly, Partlett *Prosser, Wade, and Schwartz's Torts: Cases and Materials* 2005 (11th ed.)
I. INTENTIONAL TORTS								
A. Torts to the Person	Page 32-55, 1151-1185, 1382-1406	Page 37-68, 561-569	Page 4-10, 79-100	Page 884-931	Page 550-587, 610-699	Page 9-37, 681-721	Page 7-11, 30-56, 94-118	Page 29-66
B. Defenses and Privileged Invasions of Personal Interests	62-106, 1386-1391	82-109	35-65	907-908, 931-942	587-610, 635-645	38-93, 98-103	56-93	91-118, 125-128
C. Torts to Property	55-61	68-74	10-35	669-676	773-783, 791-799	385-387, 393-396	119-136	66-90
D. Defenses and Privileged Invasions of Land and Chattels	57, 96-106	100-109	59-79	942-949	783-791, 799-803	93-98	137-152	118-124
II. NEGLIGENCE								
A. In General	107-108	111-114	169-171	31-39	47-50	149-157	11-14	132-145
B. Negligence (Based on the "Duty of Due Care")	108-343, 815-962	114-133, 148-270, 382-440, 855-900	171-326, 449-562, 853-901, 910-927	39-131, 339-439, 698-762	50-73, 137-353, 463-502	105-138, 149-217, 230-300, 545-622	308-440, 563-700	145-359, 519-564
C. Special Duty Questions	457-540, 587-623	133-147, 347-381, 483-559, 569-598, 624-660	261-285, 549-644	17-30, 132-218, 264-305	74-136, 502-513, 699-755	138-148, 177-189, 217-257, 300-321	398-418, 441-483, 771-804	404-438, 450-464, 480-518, 660-685
D. Defenses to Negligence	344-406	272-319	327-401	440-496	389-424	359-377	503-562	586-614
E. Effect of Liability Insurance	963-992	800-804	929-960	762-771, 784-806	527-540	623-646	722-749	297
III. STRICT LIABILITY								
A. In General		661-669	122-168, 645	506	759-773	423	20-25	686
B. Animals	624-630	669-670, 682	645-656		153-154	423-427	807-813	686-691

Gilbert Law Summary TORTS	Christie, Meeks, Pryor, Sanders *Cases and Materials on the Law of Torts* 2004 (4th ed.)	Dobbs, Hayden *Torts and Compensation* 2005 (5th ed.)	Epstein *Cases and Materials on Torts* 2008 (9th ed.)	Franklin, Rabin, Green *Tort Law and Alternatives: Cases and Materials* 2006 (8th ed.)	Goldberg, Sebok, Zipursky *Tort Law: Responsibilities and Redress* 2008 (2nd ed.)	Henderson, Pearson, Kysar, Siliciano *The Torts Process* 2007 (7th ed.)	Keeton, Sargentich, Keating *Tort and Accident Law: Cases and Materials* 2004 (4th ed.)	Schwartz, Kelly, Partlett *Prosser, Wade, and Schwartz's Torts: Cases and Materials* 2005 (11th ed.)
C. Abnormally Dangerous Activities	631-678	676-691	656-675	506-549	825-842	427-450	20-25, 813-837	692-710
D. Extent of Liability		691-693	653, 660-661			429	837-851	710-717
E. Defenses	676-678	693-694	394, 674-675	528-529	840-841	447-449	851-861	714-717
IV. PRODUCTS LIABILITY								
A. In General		695	723-728	550	843-868	451	925-926	718-719
B. Liability Based on Intentional Acts								
C. Liability Based on Negligence	679-690	695-696, 716	728-739	550-555	845-848, 883	452-455, 480-541	926-936, 1001-1026, 1037-1039	719-721
D. Strict Liability in Tort	698-784, 795-811	698-785	739-754, 764-841	556-655	843-985	464-541	951-1099	732-795
E. Liability Based on Breach of Warranty	690-698	697-698	737-739, 745-747, 752, 754-763	555-556, 655-668	853-854, 871, 951	455-464, 480-541	936-951	721-732
V. NUISANCE								
A. In General	1052-1057	670-673, 675-676	675-722	676-682	803-807	387-389	123-136	799-800
B. Plaintiff's Interest	1057-1060, 1067-1068	672-673	678	680-682	803, 805	389	893	800
C. Defendant's Conduct	1060-1061	673-682	684-685	680-682	805-806	389	862-876, 914-918	805-808
D. Substantial and Unreasonable Harm to Plaintiff	1061-1074	673-675	681-682, 694-695	681-682, 693	806, 812-819	389-392	132-136, 910-914	808-815
E. Causation								
F. Remedies	1052-1083	675	700-710	682-697	819-825	392-422	877-910	816-825, 827
G. Defenses	1063, 1080-1083	674-675, 682	697-699	691-692	806	418-419	919-924	825-826
VI. MISCELLANEOUS FACTORS AFFECTING RIGHT TO SUE								
A. Survival of Tort Actions	936-938	612-615	906	18, 726-729	357	609	700	578-585

Gilbert Law Summary TORTS	Christie, Meeks, Pryor, Sanders *Cases and Materials on the Law of Torts* 2004 (4th ed.)	Dobbs, Hayden *Torts and Compensation* 2005 (5th ed.)	Epstein *Cases and Materials on Torts* 2008 (9th ed.)	Franklin, Rabin, Green *Tort Law and Alternatives: Cases and Materials* 2006 (8th ed.)	Goldberg, Sebok, Zipursky *Tort Law: Responsibilities and Redress* 2008 (2nd ed.)	Henderson, Pearson, Kysar, Siliciano *The Torts Process* 2007 (7th ed.)	Keeton, Sargentich, Keating *Tort and Accident Law: Cases and Materials* 2004 (4th ed.)	Schwartz, Kelly, Partlett *Prosser, Wade, and Schwartz's Torts: Cases and Materials* 2005 (11th ed.)
B. Wrongful Death	936-952	611-621	901-906	18, 729-732	354-369	609	700-713	565-578
C. Injuries to Members of the Family	853-870, 952-962	583-585, 599-610, 1011-1013	907-909	301-305, 326-338, 920-925	73, 354-355, 365-367	321-344	713-721	464-479, 1135-1139
D. Tort Immunity	540-587	441-481	1301-1338	218-263	432-462	377-383	483-502	621-659
E. Release and Contribution Among Joint Tortfeasors	406-407, 416-431	166-169, 805-812, 814-825, 833-854	404-428	369-372, 375	513-526	123-124, 369	596-612	371-392
F. Indemnity	413-414	625, 786, 817-818, 821-823, 853	407-408, 436-437	23-24	527-540	144	598-599, 604	383-392
G. Statutes of Limitations	810-814, 951-952, 1214	320-342			424-432			614-621
VII. STATUTORY CHANGES IN PERSONAL INJURY LAW								
A. Changes Targeting Specific Kinds of Tort Claims	809-814, 963-1051	417-431, 772-785, 914-977	961-1018	807-883	251-253, 418, 430, 477-478, 767-773	542-544, 647-679	1125-1214	196-197, 795-798, 1191-1216
B. Changes Affecting Tort Claims Generally	416-424, 815-936	840-842, 871-882	409-420, 881-883, 895-898, 914-927	369-372, 715-717, 732-739, 761-762, 779-784, 809-816	481-483, 520-521, 1000-1020	369, 551-556, 585-586, 623-624	609-612, 749-770, 1136-1151	366-371, 539-543, 556-564
VIII. DEFAMATION								
A. In General	1198-1199		1021-1023		674-675	711, 723-724	155, 158	829-830
B. Publication to a Third Party	1211-1214	983	1023-1034	976-977	674-675	736-738	177-181	858-869
C. Harm to Reputation	1203-1211, 1214-1227	983-984	1034-1048	972-989		724-730	155-166, 172-177	830-850
D. False Facts	1227-1231	985-986, 991, 997-998	1067-1073	997-998		745-747	185-188, 203-204	907-912, 915-923
E. Causation							169-171	
F. Damages and Other Remedies	1186-1205, 1279-1280, 1298-1313	984-985, 997	1048-1067	990-997	674-675	730-736	159-172	850-857, 932-938
G. Defenses	1219-1220, 1227-1254	986-987, 991	1067-1097	997-1027		739-746	202-222	923-932

Gilbert Law Summary TORTS	Christie, Meeks, Pryor, Sanders *Cases and Materials on the Law of Torts* 2004 (4th ed.)	Dobbs, Hayden *Torts and Compensation* 2005 (5th ed.)	Epstein *Cases and Materials on Torts* 2008 (9th ed.)	Franklin, Rabin, Green *Tort Law and Alternatives: Cases and Materials* 2006 (8th ed.)	Goldberg, Sebok, Zipursky *Tort Law: Responsibilities and Redress* 2008 (2nd ed.)	Henderson, Pearson, Kysar, Siliciano *The Torts Process* 2007 (7th ed.)	Keeton, Sargentich, Keating *Tort and Accident Law: Cases and Materials* 2004 (4th ed.)	Schwartz, Kelly, Partlett *Prosser, Wade, and Schwartz's Torts: Cases and Materials* 2005 (11th ed.)
H. Constitutional Privileges	1254-1313	987-999	1097-1129	1027-1120		749-766	181-202	869-923
IX. WRONGFUL INVASION OF PRIVACY								
A. Intrusions into Plaintiff's Private Life or Affairs	1316, 1324-1341	1008	1139-1154	1167-1208		773-783	223-228	952-961
B. Public Disclosure of Private Facts	1341-1364	1009	1154-1170	1123-1158		783-801	223-228, 230-232	961-972
C. Appropriation of Plaintiff's Name or Likeness	8-17, 1317, 1364-1381	1008, 1033-1035	1175-1194	1208-1228		807-815	223-224	940-952
D. Publicity Placing Plaintiff in a "False Light"	1317-1323	1008-1011	1170-1175	1158-1167		801-807	223-230	973-983
E. Claims Involving Privacy of Third Persons	1380-1381		1192-1194	1209	369			950
F. Important—Related Torts		587-588, 1008		1173-1174		803-804		968-970
X. OTHER TORTS								
A. Misrepresent-ation	1102-1137	1040-1059	1195-1240	1229-1252	108-109	817-853	233-279	1022-1077
B. Injurious Falsehood		1014-1018		1269-1270	674-675			1078-1089
C. Interference with Economic Relations	1137-1150	1018-1028	1242-1266	1253-1276		853-874		1089-1134
D. Unjustifiable Litigation	1392-1406	999-1008		906-907	634-635			1004-1021

Capsule Summary

INTRODUCTION

Tort recovery is contingent upon two primary variables: the type of harm alleged by the plaintiff ("P") and the nature of the defendant's ("D's") alleged conduct. Compensable tortious harms are generally divided into personal injury, property damage, and (to a more limited extent) emotional distress, invasion of intangible interests such as reputation and privacy, and economic harm (*i.e.*, financial loss). The nature of D's conduct corresponds to three main bases of liability—***intent, negligence,*** and ***strict liability***. The following summary is keyed to these categories.

I. INTENTIONAL TORTS

A. TORTS TO THE PERSON

1. Battery §1

A ***prima facie case*** involves an act by D, with intent to inflict a harmful or offensive touching, a harmful or offensive touching, and causation.

a. Act by D §2

The term "act" refers to ***volitional*** movement of D's body. Unconscious acts are not "volitional" (*e.g.,* epileptic seizures, persons asleep), and neither are instinctive actions (*e.g.,* blinking). However, stretching out an arm to brace for a fall is volitional. Note that persons not legally competent are capable of volitional acts.

b. Intent §6

D must act with the intent to inflict a harmful or offensive touching. Intent is determined by whether D acted with the ***desire*** to cause the touching or with the ***belief*** that the touching was ***substantially certain*** to occur. P generally need not prove D's intent to offend or injure, merely that D intended a touching that ***might*** be offensive or harmful. Intent is a subjective test. Note that although motives are immaterial to establishing the prima facie case, if malice is present D may be liable for punitive damages.

(1) Transferred intent §10

Under the transferred intent doctrine, if D acts intending to cause a battery, assault, false imprisonment, trespass to land, or trespass to chattels, he will be liable even if the particular harm or P is unexpected.

c. **Harmful or offensive touching** §11

The touching must involve contact with P's person or something closely associated with P (*e.g.,* knocking P's hat off her head). Touching is "harmful" if it injures, disfigures, or impairs the body; it is "offensive" if it would offend a ***reasonable*** person's sense of dignity; a hypersensitive reaction is insufficient. Note that P need ***not*** have knowledge of the touching at the time thereof.

d. **Causation** §17

D's conduct must ***directly or indirectly*** bring about the injury. Setting in motion the force that actually causes the touching suffices.

e. **Damages** §19

Actual damages are not required. Compensatory (*e.g.,* pain and suffering, medical bills, etc.) and punitive damages (if D acted maliciously) are recoverable. However, punitive damages may be found to violate due process if: (i) there is a large disparity between the compensatory award and the punitive award; (ii) the punitive award is much more severe than the criminal or administrative penalties that could have been imposed for D's conduct; and (iii) D's conduct was not unduly reprehensible.

2. **Assault** §27

A ***prima facie case*** involves an act by D, with intent to cause apprehension of an immediate harmful or offensive touching, apprehension, and causation.

a. **Act by D** §28

The "act" must be a volitional movement of the body. ***Words alone*** are ordinarily ***insufficient*** except where surrounding circumstances force P to rely on mere words (*e.g.,* "Don't turn around or I'll shoot").

b. **Intent** §32

Same as battery—*i.e.,* intent to inflict a harmful or offensive touching or cause apprehension of a harmful or offensive touching. The transferred intent doctrine is applicable.

c. **Apprehension** §35

P must be placed in reasonable apprehension of an ***imminent*** harmful or offensive touching of P's (and not someone else's) person and must be subjectively ***aware*** of the threat at the time thereof.

(1) **Source of threatened harm** §41

D is liable if he arouses apprehension of harm from any source (*e.g.,* "Duck! X just threw a rock at you!").

(2) **Imminence of threatened harm** §42

Threat of an ***imminent*** harmful or offensive touching is required. Thus, words may negate the threat (*e.g.,* where threat is of future harm). However, a ***conditional*** threat may be an assault where D is not privileged to make the threat (*e.g.,* "Take back what you said or I'll kill you").

(3) **Nature of P's apprehension** §47

P's apprehension must be ***reasonable***. Fear is ***not*** required; ***apparent*** ability to inflict a touching suffices.

d. **Causation** §52

P's apprehension must be legally caused by D's act or something D set in motion (same as battery).

e. **Damages** §53

Actual damages are not required. Compensatory and punitive damages are recoverable (same as battery).

3. **False Imprisonment** §54

A ***prima facie case*** involves an act by D, with intent to confine P to a specific area, a confinement, and causation.

a. **Act by D** §55

D's act must be volitional, but words alone ***may*** suffice.

b. **Intent** §57

This is measured by the ***desire or belief in substantial certainty*** test (*supra,* §6)—intent to confine is required.

c. **Confinement** §60

P must be restricted to a limited area without knowledge of reasonable means of escape and must be ***aware*** of the confinement at the time thereof or else be harmed by the confinement.

(1) **Cause of confinement** §65

This may be by:

(a) ***Physical force*** exercised against P or a member of P's family;

(b) ***Threats of immediate harm*** to P, P's property, or P's family;

(c) ***Actual or apparent physical barriers*** to escape (includes ***refusing to release*** P when under a duty to do so); or

(d) ***Assertion of legal authority*** and P's submission thereto.

d. **Causation** §76

Confinement must be legally caused by D's intentional act or a force set in motion by D (same as battery).

e. **Damages** §77

Actual damages are not required. Compensatory and punitive damages are recoverable (same as battery). P may also recover for injuries suffered in a reasonable attempt to escape.

4. **Intentional Infliction of Emotional Distress** §79

A ***prima facie case*** involves extreme and outrageous conduct by D, with intent to cause severe emotional distress, causation, and severe emotional distress.

a. **Act by D** §80

D's act must be ***extreme and outrageous***. Words alone may suffice, but simple insults are not actionable. The courts will consider the totality of the circumstances.

(1) **Exceptions** §83

Common carriers and public utilities are held to a stricter standard; they may be liable for insults not ordinarily actionable. Also, cases based on racial or gender attacks or insults may be actionable under state or federal law even if not amounting to a traditional tort.

(2) **Extension—liability to third persons** §85

D's liability also includes emotional distress of members of the ***intended victim's family*** if their presence was known to D.

b. **Intent** §86

D must intend to cause severe emotional distress. However, reckless conduct (*i.e.,* where D disregards a high probability that his act will cause emotional distress) also suffices, and intent is inferred where D ***knows*** P is particularly sensitive. Note that the doctrine of transferred intent is ***not*** applicable here.

c. **Causation** §90

Under the early view, demonstrable physical injuries were required, but under the modern approach, ***distress alone*** suffices—outrageousness of the conduct insures reliability of the claim.

d. **Severe emotional distress** §92

The distress must be more than a reasonable person could be expected to endure. However, D is liable for causing severe distress in a person with ***known sensitivities*** even if a reasonable person would not have been so distressed.

e. **Defenses** §94

Common law defenses to other intentional torts are ***irrelevant*** here. However, the First Amendment protections of free speech and free exercise of religion have been permitted as defenses (*e.g.,* gross insults aimed at public person may be protected; church may denounce member without liability).

f. **Damages** §98

Compensatory and punitive damages are recoverable. (Some states bar punitive damages generally; others do so where speech is involved).

B. DEFENSES AND PRIVILEGED INVASIONS OF PERSONAL INTERESTS

1. **Consent** §100

Most courts treat consent as an affirmative defense; a few require P to show lack of consent as part of the prima facie case.

a. **Types of consent** §101

The basic types of consent are:

(1) ***Actual (express) consent***;

(2) ***Apparent consent***—what the reasonable person would infer from custom or from ***P's conduct***; or

(3) ***Consent implied by law***—if necessary to save a life or other important interest ***and***:

(a) ***P is unconscious or otherwise unable*** to consider the matter;

(b) An ***immediate decision*** is necessary;

(c) There is ***no reason to believe P would withhold consent*** if able; and

(d) A ***reasonable person in P's position would consent.***

b. When consent is not a defense

(1) Acts in excess of consent §105

If the invasion goes beyond the scope of consent, the consent is ineffective.

(2) Fraud §106

Consent is ineffective if procured by fraud (unless the fraud relates to a collateral matter).

(3) Duress §108

Consent given under duress (physical force or threats) is ineffective.

(4) Mistake §109

P's consent is ineffective if due to a mistake ***caused by or known to D***. Mistake may be one of two types:

(a) Mistake of law §110

A mistake of law ***caused by D*** renders P's consent ineffective.

(b) Mistake of fact §111

If P fails to understand the ***nature or consequences*** of the invasion of her person or property, her consent is ineffective.

1) Lack of consent in medical treatment §112

If a patient did not give consent to medical treatment, the doctor may be liable for battery.

2) Lack of informed consent §113

If P alleges that she was not adequately informed of the risks and benefits prior to surgery, the claim is usually treated as ***negligence***, not as an intentional tort.

(5) Incapacity to consent §114

Consent given by a person incapable of consenting (*e.g.,* infant, mental incompetent) is ineffective.

(6) Criminal acts §115

The majority holds consent to a criminal act ineffective if the act involves a ***breach of the peace***. The minority holds consent to a criminal act effective except where P is a member of a class protected by statute.

2. Self-Defense

a. Nondeadly force §119

Nondeadly force may be used if D ***reasonably believed*** P was about to inflict ***imminent bodily harm***, and the force used was ***reasonably necessary*** to prevent the harm. D is under no duty to retreat ***unless*** D recognizes that P acted unintentionally or had mistaken D's identity.

b. Deadly force §123

Deadly force may be used if D ***reasonably believed*** P was about to inflict ***death or serious bodily harm***. Under the majority view, there is ***no*** duty to retreat. The minority view is contra if retreat is safe, unless: (i) D is in her ***own home***, (ii) retreating would endanger D or a third party, or (iii) D is attempting a valid arrest.

c. Threats of force §129

D is privileged to threaten greater force than she could actually use if such threats would do no more than cause apprehension.

d. Limitations on right of self-defense §130

The right to self-defense is limited where:

(1) ***D knows the danger is terminated***;

(2) ***D uses excessive force***—this may give P the right to use force in self-defense;

(3) ***P's conduct is privileged***; or

(4) ***D intentionally injures a third person*** (unintentional injuries create liability only if D is negligent).

e. Reasonableness §136

This is tested objectively (reasonable person standard).

3. Defense of Third Persons §137

A person may be privileged to use deadly force to protect another only to the extent the person defended would have been privileged to use deadly force under the circumstances. The traditional view protects D only if the person protected is ***actually privileged*** to defend herself. The modern view protects the actor's ***reasonable mistake***.

4. Defense of Land or Chattels

a. Nondeadly force §142

D may ***not use deadly force*** to defend land or chattels. He may use nondeadly force if:

(1) ***Intrusion by P is not privileged*** (or P led D to believe this);

(2) ***D reasonably believes force is necessary*** to prevent or terminate the intrusion; ***and***

(3) ***D, prior to the use of force, makes a demand*** that the intruder desist or leave (unless the demand appears futile).

b. **Mechanical devices** §143

Such devices may be used only where (i) ***reasonable and necessary, or customary*** in the locale; ***and*** (ii) ***adequate warning*** is given or posted. If the devices threaten ***death or serious bodily harm***, intrusion must ***in fact*** constitute a threat of death or serious bodily harm to D or D's family.

c. **Threats** §145

The Second Restatement permits D to threaten greater force than he is actually privileged to use, as long as such threats only cause apprehension.

5. **Force to Recover Possession of Land Wrongfully Withheld** §146

The majority view in such a case recognizes ***no privilege***. The minority view permits prompt and reasonable nondeadly force when dispossession is achieved by fraud, force, duress, or without claim of right.

6. **Force to Effect Recapture of Chattels Wrongfully Withheld**

a. **Tortious dispossessions** §150

D is privileged to use ***reasonable nondeadly force*** to recapture chattels of which he was tortiously dispossessed under the following conditions: (i) D is ***in fact*** entitled to immediate possession of the chattel; (ii) demand for return has been made by D and ignored, or the demand appears futile; (iii) D is in "fresh pursuit" (*i.e.*, D was diligent in discovering the loss and in his efforts to retake the chattel); and (iv) recapture is effected from the dispossessor or a third party having knowledge that the property was stolen, etc.

b. **Other dispossessions** §156

In cases of nontortious dispossession, there is no privilege to use force. But in conditional sales contract situations where the buyer defaults, the seller may repossess ***peacefully***.

c. **"Shopkeeper's privilege"** §158

In most states, a shopkeeper is privileged to ***detain temporarily*** for investigation if: (i) there are ***reasonable grounds to suspect the person detained***; (ii) detention is on the ***store premises or in the immediate vicinity***; (iii) ***only reasonable, nondeadly force*** is used; and (iv) the detention is for only as long as is needed to conduct a ***reasonable investigation***.

7. **Privilege of Arrest**

a. **Arrests for felonies without an arrest warrant** §165

A ***police officer*** is privileged to arrest without an arrest warrant if there are ***reasonable grounds to believe*** that a ***felony*** has been committed and this particular person committed it. A ***private citizen*** is privileged to arrest without a warrant only when a felony has ***in fact*** been committed and there are reasonable grounds to believe this person committed it.

b. **Arrests for misdemeanors without an arrest warrant** §166

Under the general view, officers and private citizens ***in fresh pursuit*** are privileged to arrest for a misdemeanor without a warrant if the misdemeanor was a ***breach of the peace*** and committed in their presence. The minority view permits the officer a reasonable mistake.

c. **Arrests under a warrant** §168

Such arrests are privileged if the warrant is ***"fair on its face"*** (*i.e.,* free of defects that a reasonable police officer would discover).

d. **Amount of force privileged** §171

Reasonable ***nondeadly*** force is permitted when making a misdemeanor arrest. For felony arrests, the traditional view permits reasonable use of ***deadly*** force for ***any*** felony, but the modern view limits such force to ***serious*** felonies (*e.g.,* rape, murder). In any case, where arrest is by the government (*e.g.,* the police) the Supreme Court has held that deadly force is reasonable only if necessary to prevent a felon's escape when there is cause to believe that the felon or suspect poses a significant ***threat of death or serious injury***.

e. **Right to invade land** §178

This right is included within the privilege of arrest.

f. **Effect of D's misconduct following arrest** §179

If the initial arrest was privileged but the arresting party subsequently uses excessive force or unreasonably delays arraignment, the modern view is that D is liable only for harm caused by subsequent misconduct.

g. **Resisting arrest** §180

Common law allowed reasonable nondeadly force to resist an unlawful arrest. There is no such privilege under the modern trend, and resisting is itself a crime in some states.

8. **Privilege of Discipline** §181

Parents, teachers, and military supervisors may use reasonable force to preserve order. Note, however, that this common law rule has been rejected by some legislatures and courts in cases of corporal punishment.

C. TORTS TO PROPERTY

1. **Trespass to Land** §182

A ***prima facie case*** involves P in possession of land or entitled thereto, an act by D with intent to invade the land, an intrusion upon the land, and causation.

a. **Act by D** §183

D's act must be volitional (same as battery).

b. **Intent** §184

D must ***intend to intrude*** on the land or ***know with substantial certainty*** that his actions will cause entry, but he need not know the land belongs to another. The transferred intent doctrine applies.

(1) **Distinguish—negligence** §185

D is liable for negligent entry if ***damages*** are shown.

(2) **Distinguish—strict liability** §186

Certain invasions are actionable on a strict liability theory.

c. **Intrusion on land** §188

D must personally enter the land or cause entry by a third person or object. Failure to leave or remove an object after consent is withdrawn is also sufficient. An intrusion of a nonphysical nature (*e.g.,* smoke, vibrations, etc.) is treated as a ***nuisance***.

d. **P in possession or entitled to immediate possession** §190

Any possession (even wrongful possession) is sufficient. However, ***if no one is in actual possession***, a person with the right to immediate possession may maintain the action. Note, however, that although a tenant has possession during a lease, courts usually permit an action by the landlord ***or*** tenant, but each can recover only for damage to his own interest.

(1) **Airspace above land** §196

There is no right to possession of airspace above the normal minimum flight altitude. Below the minimum flight altitude, modern authority limits possession to the ***"immediate reaches"*** of the land. (*Note:* There may be a possibility of a nuisance action even though there is no actionable trespass).

e. **Causation** §202

The invasion must be legally caused by D's act or by a force set in motion thereby. D is liable for any harm caused, even if it was not foreseeable (*e.g.,* trespasser can be liable for causing owner to have heart attack).

f. **Damages** §204

Actual damages generally are not required.

2. **Trespass to Chattels** §206

A ***prima facie case*** involves P in possession of a chattel or entitled thereto, an act by D with intent to invade a chattel interest, an invasion of such interest, and causation. (Regarding damages, *see* below).

a. **Act by D** §207

D's act must be a volitional movement resulting in dispossession of or harm to P's chattel.

b. **Intent** §208

D must have intended to deal with the chattel in the manner in which he did so. D's mistaken belief that he had a right to do so is no defense. The transferred intent doctrine applies.

c. **Invasion of chattel interest** §210

This can be by ***"dispossession"*** (assertion of proprietary interest in chattel, *e.g.,* theft) or ***"intermeddling"*** (a lesser interference, *e.g.,* throwing a stone at P's car).

d. **P in possession or entitled to immediate possession** §213

This is the same as in a trespass to land.

e. **Causation** §214

The invasion must have been legally caused by D's intentional act or a force set in motion by D.

f. **Damages** §215

For ***dispossession***, P can sue for loss of use (*e.g.,* rental value) or for conversion of chattels. If there is only an ***intermeddling***, there is no action unless there is ***actual damage*** to the chattel.

3. **Conversion of Chattels** §216

A ***prima facie case*** involves P in possession or entitled thereto, an act by D with intent to substantially invade a chattel interest, a substantial invasion of such interest, and causation.

a. **Act by D** §217

D's act must be a volitional movement that results in a substantial interference with another's possession of her chattels.

b. **Intent** §218

D must have intended to deal with the chattel in the manner in which he actually did deal with it.

c. **Substantial invasion of chattel interest** §219

This can be accomplished by any of the following: (i) ***substantial dispossession*** (*e.g.*, D takes chattel or bars possessor's access without consent); (ii) ***destruction or material alteration*** of chattel; (iii) ***unauthorized use by bailee*** (use must amount to ***material breach*** of authority); (iv) ***buying or receiving stolen property*** where D intended to acquire ownership rights (good faith is irrelevant); (v) ***selling or disposing of stolen property***; (vi) ***misdelivering a chattel***, even by innocent mistake; or (vii) ***refusing to surrender chattel on demand*** (but carrier or bailee is privileged to make a ***qualified*** refusal to deliver for the purpose of investigating ownership).

d. **P in possession or entitled to immediate possession** §230

Same as in preceding sections.

e. **Causation** §231

Same as in preceding sections.

f. **Remedies** §232

If "dispossession," P has a choice of actions:

(1) **Replevin, detinue, or claim and delivery** §233

P may obtain return of the chattel and collect damages sustained during its detention.

(2) **Forced sale damages** §234

P may recover the value of the chattel plus damages for detention (*i.e.,* ***"forced sale"*** of chattel to D).

(a) **Effect of offer to return** §236

D's prompt offer to return mitigates damages if D acquired the chattel in good faith and did not affect its value or condition. If P accepts D's offer, P no longer has an action for conversion but only for trespass to chattels.

D. DEFENSES AND PRIVILEGED INVASIONS OF LAND AND CHATTELS

1. **Consent** §237

P's valid consent (expressly or by conduct) to the invasion is a defense.

2. **Privileged Invasion of Another's Land to Reclaim Chattels** §238

The scope of the privilege depends on where fault lies for the presence of D's chattels on P's land.

a. **Landowner at fault** §239

If the landowner is at fault, D has a ***complete privilege*** to enter to retake his chattels after ***demand*** (unless demand would be futile or would subject the chattel to harm). D is not liable for damage to P's land if D acted reasonably. However, D cannot enter a building other than that in which his chattels are kept. If P resists, D may use ***reasonable, nondeadly*** force subject to the same conditions attached to the recapture of chattels defense.

b. **Chattel owner at fault** §245

If the chattel owner is at fault, D has ***no*** privilege. Instead, he must bring an action for replevin, detinue, etc.

c. **Act of God** §246

If an act of God (*e.g.,* storm) causes chattels to be on another's land, D has an ***incomplete privilege*** (*i.e.*, is liable for damages caused in process of recapture but not for mere trespass). However, if the underlying causal factor is D's ***negligence*** (*e.g.*, failure to secure chattels), he has ***no*** privilege.

d. **Third party at fault** §250

If chattels are on land because of a third party's act, D has an ***incomplete privilege*** where the landowner is unaware of the tortious dispossession.

e. **Limitation** §251

In all cases, D has ***no*** privilege if D is not ***in fact*** entitled to possession of the chattel; mistake is irrelevant.

3. **Privilege to Exclude or Evict Trespassing Chattels of Another** §252

D is ***completely*** privileged to use reasonable force to exclude chattels of another where ***reasonably believed to be necessary*** to protect D's interests or chattels (*e.g.,* D may shoot neighbor's dog in D's chicken coop). Reasonableness is tested by the need for immediate action, whether the force is excessive, and the comparative values of the property.

4. **Privileged Invasion of Another's Land or Chattels as a Public Necessity**

a. **Averting public disaster** §254

There is a ***complete*** privilege to enter land or interfere with a chattel if it reasonably appears necessary to avert a public disaster. Thus, D can break and enter a dwelling and use whatever force on the property owner is reasonably necessary to effect the privilege.

b. **Detouring around obstructed highway** §258

A traveler on a public road has an ***incomplete*** privilege to enter neighboring lands where the road reasonably appears impassable—unless obstruction is the traveler's fault.

c. **Media** §262

The First Amendment does ***not*** give the media a privilege to enter private land whenever they seek information—even important information.

5. **Privileged Invasion of Another's Land or Chattels as a Private Necessity** §263

There is a privilege to enter land or interfere with chattels where it appears reasonably necessary to protect any person from death or serious harm or to protect land or chattels from injury. The harm prevented must exceed the harm caused by the invasion. The privilege holder may break and enter dwellings and use reasonable, nondeadly force, but is liable for resulting damages. The privilege ***supersedes*** the landowner's privilege to exclude trespassers.

6. **Privileged Invasion of Land or Chattels to Abate a Nuisance** §268

An owner or possessor of land may, after ***demand*** to abate, invade property or chattels of another to abate a nuisance. The privilege is ***complete***, but D must enter at a reasonable time and use only reasonable force (force to person not allowed).

a. **Distinguish—public nuisance** §273

There is ***no*** privilege for abatement of a public nuisance unless the injury is "peculiar in kind."

7. **Effect of D's Misconduct** §274

There is no privilege if D did not act "reasonably" while exercising the privilege. Note that if D's entry is proper initially but he subsequently acts improperly, D is liable for the subsequent misconduct but not for the initial intrusion.

II. NEGLIGENCE

A. IN GENERAL §276

Negligence, the second broad category of tort liability, imposes liability for results that were ***not intended*** by D. D is at fault for failing to perform some legal ***duty***.

B. NEGLIGENCE (BASED ON THE "DUTY OF DUE CARE") §278

A ***prima facie case*** involves an act or omission to act that breaches a duty of care and is the actual and proximate cause of P's injuries.

1. **Act or Actionable Omission by D** §279

This refers to a volitional act or an omission when under an affirmative duty to act.

2. **Duty of Due Care** §280

Duty is determined by the court and requires a two-step inquiry: (i) whether D owed a duty of care, and if so, (ii) what the scope of that duty is.

a. **Default duty to act as a "reasonable person" would** §281

Where D's conduct ***creates a risk of physical harm***, she owes a duty to act as a reasonable person ought to ***under the same or similar circumstances***.

(1) **Objective test** §282

The test is objective; D's subjective good faith belief is immaterial.

(2) **Standard remains same under all circumstances** §284

The circumstances dictate the care required (*e.g.,* "reasonable person" would act differently in emergency). However, the standard never varies.

b. **Variances in the generalized standard of due care** §289

The reasonable person standard applies to all persons.

(1) **Common carriers** §290

Historically, courts held common carriers to a higher standard, but modern courts are moving toward the reasonable person standard.

(2) **Children** §291

Minors are held to the standard of care that would be expected from a child of like age, intelligence, and experience. They may be held to an ***adult*** standard when they engage in a dangerous adult activity (*e.g.,* driving a car).

(3) **Persons with physical disability** §295

Such persons are held to the standard of the reasonable person with that disability. Thus, limitations in ability may require exercise of greater care. *Compare:* Those voluntarily intoxicated are held to the standard of a sober person.

(4) **Adults with mental deficiency** §299

There is no allowance for mental disability in part because of the fear of fraud and in part because of the difficulty in applying a reduced standard.

(5) **Special knowledge and skills** §301

Those engaged in a profession or trade are held to the standard of care exercised by similar professionals in the same or similar communities.

(a) **Medical profession** §305

Some courts held doctors to the standard of doctors in the "same" community. The modern trend expands the standard to "similar" communities. National standards may be imposed for nationally certified medical specialists. P must establish the particular standard for medical care, and generally presents it by expert testimony.

1) **Informed consent** §311

Doctors have a duty to disclose relevant information about benefits and risks, alternatives, etc., to a patient. The courts are split on whether the standard is the level of disclosure customary in the medical profession or that required based on what a reasonable doctor would recognize as material to the patient's decision. There are exceptions where there is an emergency or where disclosure would be detrimental to the patient's health, and a doctor does not need to disclose his inexperience.

c. **The unforeseeable P—to whom is the duty of care owed?** §320
If a reasonable person would not have foreseen injury to ***anyone*** from D's actions, most courts hold that no duty is owed to unexpectedly injured persons. However, views differ when D could have reasonably foreseen danger to ***someone***, but whether injury to the particular P was foreseeable is questionable.

(1) **Broad (Andrews) view** §321
The broad view is that D's duty of due care is owed to ***anyone*** in the world injured as a result of D's breach of duty, leaving the foreseeability of a particular P a matter to be determined in the context of ***proximate cause*** (*Palsgraf* dissent).

(2) **Narrow (Cardozo) view** §322
Under the narrow view, there is a duty of due care owed only to a ***"foreseeable P"*** or class of persons in the ***"zone of danger"*** (*Palsgraf* majority).

(3) **Judge vs. jury** §326
Justice Cardozo felt that judges ought to determine P foreseeability, whereas Justice Andrews wanted to leave such questions to the jury as a matter of proximate cause.

(4) **Application—duty to rescuers** §327
The duty of due care extends to persons injured while making an attempt to rescue the imperiled person. The same result applies where the rescuer injures a third person; *i.e.,* D is liable. However, the original D will not be liable if the rescue attempt was foolhardy under the circumstances.

d. **Limitations on duty** §333
Even if D's actions created a risk of harm, courts sometimes analyze the facts of a case and its policy implications to determine whether and to what extent to impose a duty. Some courts limit a D's duty due to a consideration of the closeness of the connection between D's conduct and P's injury, D's moral blameworthiness for her conduct, whether imposing liability will further the policy of preventing future harm, the extent of the burden imposed and its consequences on the community, etc. Courts also refuse to impose a duty, despite the clear creation of a risk, in the face of special problems of principle or policy.

e. **The line between act and omission** §339
Where P is injured as a result of D's negligent action (***misfeasance***), a duty of reasonable care exists. But where P's injury results from D's negligent failure to act (***nonfeasance***), no duty exists absent a special affirmative duty (*see infra*, §§546 *et seq.*).

(1) **Misfeasance or nonfeasance?** §341
Courts sometimes find the following situations difficult to characterize: (i) negligent entrustment, (ii) negligent/nonnegligent creation of risk, (iii) voluntary undertaking, (iv) negligent misrepresentation, and (v) encouraging dangerous acts.

3. **Breach of Duty** §347

Conduct that exposes others to an unreasonable risk of harm (*i.e.,* conduct falling short of the duty owed) is a breach of duty. A finding of breach includes determination of (i) what in fact happened, and (ii) whether those facts show D acted unreasonably.

a. **Proving what actually happened** §348

This may be shown by direct evidence or circumstantial evidence.

b. **Determining whether conduct proved is unreasonable** §352

Whether D acted reasonably under the circumstances is generally a question for the jury. Some courts indicate that this analysis requires a balancing of the foreseeable severity of harm to P against the foreseeable social value of D's conduct. D's conduct is unreasonable if the magnitude of risk outweighs the benefit. Judge Learned Hand's formula for this analysis is: Breach = Probability × Loss > Burden on D of taking the risk.

c. **Judge vs. jury** §360

A court's finding in favor of the nonmoving party on a motion for summary judgment creates "mini rules" regarding what conduct is reasonable or unreasonable. Thus, leaving the decision to the jury avoids unjust future results.

d. **Res ipsa loquitur ("the thing speaks for itself")** §363

Occurrence of a particular harm may tend to establish what happened and that it was through D's fault.

(1) **Essential elements** §364

Three elements must be established:

(a) **Accident must be of a type that normally does not occur absent someone's negligence** §365

This is most often applied to commonplace and ordinarily safe activities (*e.g.,* bleachers at a ball field do not ordinarily collapse absent negligence); the ultimate issue is one of probabilities.

(b) **Negligence attributable to D** §369

Some courts require a showing that the instrumentality causing injury was under D's "exclusive control." The better view questions whether the injury was one that D owed a ***duty to guard against***.

1) **"Joint control" or "concerted action" theories of control** §373

Some courts find "exclusive control" in a group of physicians and nurses where each had contact with an unconscious patient who is injured (*Ybarra* case).

(c) **Neither P nor a third party contributed to or caused P's injuries** §376

No inference arises if it appears that P's own conduct (or acts of a third person) was the likeliest cause of the accident.

(d) **Third Restatement's single-element approach** §378
The Third Restatement adopts only the first element above because "exclusive control" and "no P contribution" are merely used to determine that D's negligence likely caused P's injury.

(2) **Other factors affecting use of res ipsa loquitur** §379
Most courts hold that if the above three elements are met, the doctrine applies even if D cannot add any evidence on the issue of what happened.

(3) **Effect of establishing res ipsa loquitur** §382
Most courts treat res ipsa loquitur as giving rise to a permissible ***inference*** of negligence. Other courts give it the status of a rebuttable presumption; still others classify it as a presumption that can be dispelled by any counterevidence.

e. **Effect of custom and statutes** §385
Safety-related statutes and customs may be offered as some, but not conclusive, evidence of D's adherence to or departure from the reasonable person standard.

(1) **How custom established** §386
For a custom to be relevant, its purpose must be to avoid the type of harm P suffered. If D is a member of the community in which the relevant custom is practiced, D will be charged with knowledge of it.

f. **Criminal statutes and breach—"negligence per se"** §396
If a common law duty is already owed and a criminal statute provides that specific conduct breaches the duty, courts may use the criminal statute to establish breach. In such situations, breach of the statute constitutes negligence per se.

(1) **Requirements for "negligence per se"** §398
For a criminal statute to constitute breach for purposes of a civil suit, the following requirements must be met:

(a) ***Statutory duty is clear***;

(b) ***Statutory purpose was to protect a class*** of persons of which P is a ***member*** from the ***type*** of injury suffered; and

(c) ***Violation was unexcused***. Statute cannot be used to establish negligence per se if D had a ***legally acceptable excuse*** for its violation (*e.g.*, D is physically disabled or incapacitated, it was safer under the circumstances not to comply, etc.).

(2) **Effect of violation of statute**

(a) **Unexcused violations** §408
If there is no excuse, the majority treats the violation as ***negligence per se***. The minority views treat a violation as a rebuttable presumption or evidence only.

(b) **Excuse offered** §412

If an excuse is offered, the majority defers to the judge's decision on the validity of the excuse; there is negligence per se if the excuse is ***invalid***. If crucial facts are disputed, the jury will determine these. The minority views treat a violation as a rebuttable presumption or evidence only.

4. **Actual Cause ("Cause in Fact")** §415

D's negligent conduct must be the cause in fact of P's injuries; *i.e.,* P would not have been injured ***but for*** D's negligent conduct.

a. **Concurrent liability rule** §418

Where separate negligent acts of D and X concur and P would not have been injured but for the concurrence, ***both*** D and X are actual causes.

(1) **Distinguish—jointly engaged tortfeasors** §419

If several Ds jointly engage in a course of negligent conduct (*e.g.*, participants in a drag race), ***each*** is liable even though only one of them actually inflicted the injury. But note that many courts have limited or abolished this rule.

(2) **Successive tortfeasors** §420

When successive acts of independent tortfeasors produce harm that is difficult to apportion, the tortfeasors must try to disprove their responsibility for the injury.

b. **Multiple sufficient causes—"substantial factor" rule** §421

If either one of two acts was sufficient to cause the injury, both actors are liable if each person's conduct was a substantial factor (*e.g.,* two negligent motorcyclists simultaneously pass P's horse, causing it to run away).

c. **Problem of alternative liability** §423

Where it is not clear which of several negligent Ds caused P's injury, some courts shift the burden to each D to prove he was not the cause (*Summers v. Tice*).

(1) **Market share liability** §427

Where a specific manufacturer of the DES drug cannot be identified, some courts allow P to recover from all manufacturers (but courts vary as to whether, or how, a particular D can be relieved from a share of liability). Note that courts have been reluctant to use market share liability in cases not involving DES.

d. **Risk of future harm** §433

If P is more likely to suffer a future harm as the result of the present injury caused by D's negligence, the majority allows recovery. The minority views permit delayed or partial recovery.

e. **Loss of chance** §436

Traditionally, P could not recover for such loss unless she could prove she was more likely than not to have received something. However, in medical cases some courts allow suits for loss of recovery chances that are less than 50%, and damages for emotional distress can be awarded if physical injury is present.

f. **Where D's negligence has deprived P of proof** §440

In such a case, the burden may shift to D to show that he was not the cause.

5. **Proximate Cause ("Scope of Liability")** §442

Proximate cause is actually a policy decision as to who should bear the loss for unexpected injuries or for expected injuries caused in unexpected ways.

a. **Basic tests**

(1) **Foreseeability test** §445

Proximate cause exists if the ***type, extent, and manner*** of injury to the ***particular P*** were the foreseeable result of D's negligent conduct. This is the most commonly used approach.

(2) **Directness/remoteness test** §446

Proximate cause exists for ***all*** harm (regardless of how unforeseeable) that is a ***direct result*** of D's negligent conduct as long as it is ***not too remote***.

(3) **Risk rule** §447

Proximate cause exists if P's ***harm*** is ***within the scope of the risks*** that made D's conduct negligent. This approach is gaining ground.

(4) **Substantial factor test** §448

Proximate cause exists if D's conduct was a ***more (or the most) substantial factor*** in causing P's harm than other factors.

(5) **Andrews factors** §449

Establishing proximate cause requires a consideration of all of the above factors.

b. **Direct vs. indirect causation** §453

Direct causation means that there were ***no intervening forces*** operating between D's conduct and P's injury. Indirect causation means that an intervening force extended the result of D's negligence or combined with D's act to produce P's injury.

(1) **Intervening act** §455

This can be an "act of God," act of a third person, or act of an animal (if P's own conduct contributed to her injury, it will be analyzed under a different doctrine—contributory negligence or assumption of the risk, *infra*). "Intervening act" does ***not*** include a force set in motion by D, a preexisting condition, or a third person's omission to act.

c. **Direct causation** §461

If there are no intervening acts, the case is one of direct causation and D will be deemed the proximate cause of most foreseeable results.

(1) **Exceptions** §464

Public policy may limit liability. *Example:* Where D fails to control a flame in a populated area, New York courts hold that expansion of the fire beyond the first building is not foreseeable. Also, some courts hold that a highly extraordinary chain of events excuses D from liability. Other courts following the risk rule impose liability as long as the ***result*** is foreseeable.

(2) Unforeseeable results ("set stage") §467

Courts are split where direct causation yields an unforeseeable ***type*** of injury (*Polemis* view—D liable for all direct consequences vs. *Wagon Mound* majority view—unfair to hold D liable for unforeseeable result). All courts hold D liable where unforeseeability goes only to the ***extent*** of injury ("thin-skulled P" cases).

d. Indirect causation

(1) Rules focusing on nature of intervening act

(a) Dependent intervening force §478

This is a ***normal response*** to a situation created by D's negligent act. The response arises because of D's act and is held to be foreseeable. D is liable if the ***result is foreseeable***.

1) Checking forces §479

Negligent treatment in response to D's injury to P is deemed foreseeable. (But reckless or intentional medical misconduct is not.)

2) Rescue forces §481

Infliction or aggravation of an injury by a rescuer is deemed foreseeable.

3) Escape forces §482

Infliction or aggravation of injuries through escape efforts is deemed foreseeable.

4) Caution §484

The crucial element in the above cases is that response be ***normal*** (not highly unusual).

(b) Independent intervening force §485

This is an agency that operates upon the situation created by D's act but is ***not a response or reaction*** thereto (*e.g.,* the act of a third person, an animal, or nature). D remains liable for the foreseeable results of his act unless the force is an unforeseeable intentionally tortious or criminal act.

1) Intervening tortious or criminal acts §486

These terminate liability if the intervening acts are ***unforeseeable***. However, if D's negligent conduct has increased the risk that another's negligent, intentional, or criminal act will occur, the intervening force will be found to be foreseeable (*e.g.*, landlord's failure to install locks on common areas of apartment building in high-crime area).

(2) **Rules focusing on results of D's negligence**

(a) **Foreseeable results produced by unforeseeable intervening forces** §488

Liability is generally imposed here, but some courts relieve D of liability if the intervening act is the intentional or reckless conduct of a third person; the apparent guideline is moral responsibility.

1) **Acts of God** §489

These will not prevent liability where they lead to the result threatened by D's original negligence.

2) **Distinguish—unforeseeable criminal or tortious acts** §490

Generally, a court will hold that the moral culpability of one who intentionally or recklessly commits a harm overwhelms the moral responsibility of a negligent D. Thus, unforeseeable intentional or criminal acts are held by some courts to relieve D from liability, but negligent conduct will not prevent liability unless "highly extraordinary."

a) **Abnormal rescue attempts** §493

Foolhardy rescues are deemed unforeseeable and thus cut off liability even if they lead to foreseeable results.

3) **Third person's failure to prevent harm** §494

This will not relieve D from liability unless so extraordinary as to "neutralize" the original risk.

(b) **Unforeseeable results produced by foreseeable intervening forces** §497

There is a split of authority, some courts holding D not liable for an unforeseeable ***result***, while other courts impose liability on the basis that the intervening force was foreseeable.

(c) **Unforeseeable results produced by unforeseeable intervening forces** §498

Ordinarily there is ***no*** liability—except common carriers may be held liable for any loss due to delay in transit.

(d) **Ultimate result depends on degree of foreseeability** §500

Keep in mind that the ultimate decision on proximate cause depends on the degree of ***emphasis a court places on foreseeability***.

e. **Unforeseeable P** §501

The Cardozo approach rejects an unforeseeable P at the duty stage. The Andrews view considers several factors, including P foreseeability, at the causation stage (*see supra,* §449).

6. **Damages** §510

Actual damages are required.

a. **Types of damages recoverable**

(1) **"Special" damages** §512

These include past, present, and future economic losses (*e.g.,* medical bills, loss of wages or profits, etc.). Future economic loss must be discounted to present value, unlike awards for pain and suffering (below). Recently, however, a few courts permit P to recover the full award, with no discount.

(2) **"General" damages** §522

These are deemed inherent in the injury itself—*e.g.,* past, present, and future pain and suffering, disfigurement, disability, etc.

(3) **Punitive damages** §529

These are ***not*** recoverable for negligence, but some states permit them for "reckless" conduct (*e.g.,* drunk driving).

b. **"Avoidable consequences" rule** §531

Any ***additional*** damages caused by P's failure to act reasonably in minimizing loss are ***not*** recoverable (*e.g.,* unreasonable refusal to submit to medical care).

(1) **Anticipatory avoidable consequences** §534

This means unreasonable behavior prior to an accident (*e.g.,* a few courts hold that the failure to wear safety belts may reduce damages).

c. **"Collateral sources" rule** §539

There is no deduction against P's recovery for benefits received from sources collateral to the tortfeasor (*e.g.,* victim's insurance benefits, Social Security disability compensation). However, an insurance company usually has subrogation rights (automatic assignment of P's claim against D).

C. SPECIAL DUTY QUESTIONS

1. **Duties and Breach Measured by Statute**

a. **Nature of statute**

(1) **Civil statutes** §546

If a statute governs conduct and provides a civil remedy for violations, common law negligence actions are not needed; the statute is used.

(2) **Criminal statutes and duty** §547

If a criminal statute regulates conduct, the courts use the statute to determine whether D breached his common law duty of care. If there was no preexisting common law duty with regard to the conduct, courts are reluctant to create a new duty.

b. **Means by which statute gives rise to tort duty** §548

A statute may give rise to a tort duty by expressly or impliedly authorizing a private right of action (***"statutory tort"***) or by supplying the reason for a court to impose a ***common law tort duty***.

2. **Duty to Aid Others in Emergency** §551

There is ***no duty*** at common law to warn, protect, or rescue a stranger where D is not at fault.

a. **Duty owed where special factors present** §552

The law may impose a duty under certain circumstances:

(1) ***Duty to aid one with whom D is in a special relationship*** (*e.g.*, parent-child, employer-employee). §553

(2) ***Duty to aid if P's injury is caused by D.*** The modern trend holds D to same duty even where D innocently caused P's peril. §554

(3) ***Statutes may impose a duty.*** For example, it may be a crime for a driver not to aid one involved in an accident with his car, even though the driver was not at fault. §556

(4) ***Duty where D has a special relationship to the harmer*** (*e.g.*, psychotherapist-patient). This may impose a duty to use due care to avoid the harm. §557

b. **Duty owed where D undertakes to aid P ("Good Samaritan obligation")** §560

If D voluntarily undertakes to aid P, D must exercise due care. D can abandon her efforts, but the condition in which she may leave P varies among the states, with some requiring that P be left in no worse condition, others in no comparable peril, and still others in no imminent peril of serious bodily harm. Many states exempt physicians rendering aid in an emergency from negligence liability.

3. **Affirmative Duty to Prevent Harm** §567

Courts increasingly find a duty of care owed by Ds who share a special relationship with P to prevent harm inflicted by another actor (*e.g.*, innkeeper-guest, school district-pupil), but generally government does not owe a duty to protect any particular person and motorists do not owe a duty to protect others from harm by third parties.

4. **Duty to Perform Promises—Nonfeasance vs. Misfeasance**

a. **Gratuitous promises** §572

Generally, there is no tort liability for failure to perform a noncontractual promise because tort liability can be predicated only on ***misfeasance***. However, once D embarks on performance, she must exercise reasonable care.

(1) **Minority view** §574

The minority hold D liable where she knew or should have known that P was refraining from obtaining other necessary assistance in reliance on D's promise.

b. **Contractual promises** §575

Rules for gratuitous promises (above) ordinarily apply in contractual situations as well. Once D undertakes performance, failure to use due care may be both a breach of contract and an actionable tort. D may be liable to third parties for ***misfeasance*** if the harm is foreseeable.

5. **Duty Owed by Common Carrier** §582

Modern authorities impose only the general duty of care on common carriers. However, older courts held that one charged with the safety of another person, or another's property, must exercise a high amount of care.

a. **"Highest degree of care"** §583

Common carriers must always choose a course of conduct least likely to expose passengers to harm. Moreover, carrier employees have an affirmative duty to aid passengers in distress.

b. **Distinguish—liability of auto driver to "guest" or "passenger"**

(1) **Common law rule** §588

A driver must exercise due care to warn any rider of known dangers not reasonably apparent and must use due care in operating the car.

(2) **"Guest statutes"** §589

A few jurisdictions hold a driver liable to a ***guest*** only for ***"wanton" or "gross"*** misconduct. A rider is ***not*** a "guest" if payment is made that serves as a motivating influence for the driver's furnishing the ride. *Example:* Sharing of expenses may qualify the rider for "passenger," not "guest," status.

6. **Duty to Control Third Persons** §591

D may be liable for failure to control third persons over whom she had the power of control.

a. **Bailment cases** §593

The owner of bailed chattel is liable for failure to exercise due care to prevent the bailee's tortious acts committed ***in her presence***. Also the owner is liable for failure to use ***due care in selecting the bailee***.

(1) **Vicarious liability** §601

Even though not negligent herself, the owner of a car may be vicariously liable for the driver's negligence under the ***"family purpose doctrine"*** or ***"permissive use statutes."***

(2) **Products liability** §604

A bailor may also be responsible for injury caused by defective chattel. (*See* "Products Liability," *infra*, §§925 *et seq.*)

b. **Master-servant cases** §605

An employer is directly liable for failure to prevent her employee's tortious acts committed in her presence and for failure to exercise due care in hiring a reliable employee, training the employee, or supervising the employee.

(1) **Doctrine of respondeat superior—vicarious liability** §609

An employer is vicariously liable for tortious acts committed by an employee ***within the scope of employment***. Note that intentional torts often are held to be ***outside*** the scope of employment unless they are committed in furtherance of the employer's business (*e.g.,* injuries inflicted by a bodyguard). Moreover, a company may not shield itself from liability for an employee's tortious conduct (*e.g.*, drunk driving) with rules forbidding such conduct. Note also that no vicarious liability exists unless it is first shown that the employee in fact acted tortiously, but an employee's immunity from liability is immaterial.

c. **Independent contractor cases** §614

An employer who fails to use due care in selecting a competent independent contractor may be directly liable for torts of that independent contractor.

(1) **Vicarious liability** §615

Vicarious liability can be imposed on an employer if the independent contractor is an ***apparent or ostensible agent*** or is hired to perform ***nondelegable duties*** (*e.g.,* maintaining an automobile in safe condition, keeping premises safe for business visitors) or an activity so intrinsically dangerous that the employer should realize it involves a ***peculiar risk of physical harm*** (*e.g.,* blasting, use of fire to clear land).

(2) **Contractor's assumption of liability** §626

This does not insulate the employer from liability to third persons, but it does create rights of indemnification.

(3) **Limitation—collateral negligence** §627

The employer is not liable if the contractor's negligence is deemed "collateral" to the risk that gives rise to vicarious liability in the first place (*e.g.,* employer might be liable for injuries resulting from contractor's blasting, but not for injury that contractor negligently causes while driving to the blast site).

d. **Partners and joint venturers** §628

One member of a joint enterprise is vicariously liable to outsiders for conduct of other members within the scope of the enterprise if there is a ***mutual right to control*** operation of the enterprise. Some jurisdictions also require a ***common business purpose***.

(1) **Automobile trips** §630

Some courts hold that a driver and rider who agree on an itinerary, to take turns driving, and to split all costs are engaged in a joint enterprise, while others hold that the mere sharing of expenses without a business purpose is not enough.

e. **Liability of parent for torts of child** §633

Parents are ***not*** vicariously liable at common law (limited liability under some modern statutes) for torts of their children, but may be liable for their ***own*** negligence where they: (i) ***fail to control*** the child's acts committed in their presence; (ii) ***fail to exercise reasonable care to protect*** against the child's ***known*** dangerous tendencies; (iii) ***fail to warn*** others of such tendencies; (iv) ***fail to prevent*** the child's foreseeable use of inherently dangerous instrumentalities; or (v) ***negligently entrust*** chattels to the child.

f. Liability of tavernkeeper §636

A tavernkeeper has ***no*** liability at common law for consequences of a purchaser's intoxication.

(1) "Dram Shop Acts" §637

Such acts impose liability on ***commercial establishments*** in favor of third persons injured by an intoxicated patron.

(2) Judicial rejection of common law rule §642

Even without a statute, some courts have found a tavernkeeper liable if risk to third persons is foreseeable. If the patron is already intoxicated, furnishing liquor may be a crime—possible "negligence per se." Recovery is usually limited to third parties. Social hosts are generally not liable except in cases where liquor is served to minors.

(3) Distinguish—liability of tavernkeeper as land occupier §649

As a land occupier, a tavernkeeper owes a duty to prevent dangerous patrons from injuring other patrons on the premises.

7. Duties Owed by Land Occupiers §650

A majority of states substitute a special duty of care for land occupiers in place of the general duty rule.

a. "Land occupier" §651

This is a person in possession of the land (*e.g.,* owner, tenant, adverse possessor).

b. Duties owed to persons outside the land

(1) Natural conditions §653

At common law, there is no duty of care owed to persons outside the land for natural conditions on the land, except a land occupier in an urban area owes a duty to prevent native trees from creating an unreasonable risk of harm to persons on the adjacent street. However, a large minority holds that the occupier owes a duty of due care to protect those outside the land from natural conditions on the land.

(2) Artificial conditions §656

At common law, there is no duty owed to persons outside the land for artificial conditions on the land, with two exceptions:

(a) ***If a portion of a structure abuts adjacent land***, there is a duty to inspect and maintain it in a reasonably safe condition.

(b) ***If the conditions "substantially adjoin" a public road***, there is a duty to protect users of the road from harm.

(3) Activities on land **§659**

There is a duty not to create an unreasonable risk of harm.

c. Duties owed to persons coming onto the land

(1) Ordinary trespassers **§660**

An "ordinary trespasser" is anyone coming onto the land without consent or privilege. Generally, there is ***no duty*** to ***unknown*** trespassers, but if the occupier ***knows or should know*** of a trespasser's presence, there is a duty to (i) warn of or make safe ***artificial conditions*** involving a risk of death or ***serious*** bodily harm that the trespasser is unlikely to discover, and (ii) carry on ***all activities*** involving ***any*** risk of harm. However, many states impose on occupiers the same duty to known trespassers as they owe to licensees (*see infra*, §692).

(2) Constant trespassers upon a limited area (habitual intruders) **§666**

Generally, if a land occupier knows or has reason to know that persons are habitually trespassing, there is a duty to warn of or make safe known ***artificial conditions***, and to carry on ***all activities***, involving a risk of death or ***serious*** bodily harm that are unlikely to be discovered. However, many states impose on occupiers the same duty to habitual intruders as they owe to licensees (*see infra*, §692).

(3) Child trespassers—"attractive nuisance doctrine" **§674**

A child trespasser is a child so immature as to be unable to recognize the danger involved.

(a) Artificial conditions **§677**

Where the land occupier discovers children trespassing or is charged with such knowledge, there is a duty owed to warn or protect them from ***artificial conditions*** involving risk of death or ***serious*** bodily harm, ***provided:***

1) The place is one where children are ***known or likely to trespass***;

2) The land occupier ***knows or has reason to know*** that dangerous conditions exist;

3) The ***risk to children outweighs the utility*** to the land occupier and the burden of eliminating the danger; and

4) The condition is such that children, because of their youth, do ***not discover or realize danger*** is involved.

(b) Activities **§683**

An occupier's duty regarding activities on the land depends on whether the child is an undiscovered, discovered, or habitual trespasser (*see supra*).

(c) **Child trespasser doctrine as defense to trespass** §688
A few courts extend the doctrine to bar actions by land occupiers against children for trespass.

(4) **Licensees** §689
This refers to persons coming onto the land for ***their own purposes*** with express or implied permission of the land occupier (*e.g.,* social guests, salespeople, etc.).

(a) **Duties owed** §692
There is a duty to warn of or make safe ***natural or artificial conditions***, and to carry on ***all activities***, involving ***any*** risk of harm known to the land occupier and not obvious to a reasonable person, including threats of harm by ***third parties*** already on the land. There is ***no duty to inspect***.

1) **Warning** §694
A land occupier may usually discharge the duty by posting effective warning signs.

2) **Knowledge of licensee's presence** §695
There is no duty to discover licensees, but a land occupier must keep in mind the possibility of their presence and conduct himself accordingly.

(5) **Invitees** §696
This refers to persons coming onto the land with the land occupier's express or implied permission for some purpose related to the ***activities or interests of the land occupier***. A ***"public invitee"*** enters land for the purpose for which the land was held open to the public (*e.g.,* library patron). A ***"business invitee"*** enters primarily for business dealings with the land occupier (*e.g.,* store customer)—the entrant need only have a reasonable belief business dealings would transpire.

(a) **Caution—change of status** §703
An invitee retains that status only if he remains on that part of the premises to which he was invited.

(b) **Duties owed** §704
There is a duty owed to ***inspect and discover*** dangerous conditions and activities and to warn thereof or make safe.

1) **Warning enough?** §705
Under the modern trend, a warning may not suffice if it would not make the premises safe.

2) **Safeguarding activities of third persons** §707
There may also be a duty to warn or protect invitees from foreseeable tortious or criminal acts of third persons.

3) **Safeguarding chattels** §710

There is a duty to inspect and make safe tools or equipment supplied to an invitee.

(6) **Public entrants** §711

This refers to ***public employees*** entering land under legal privilege (*e.g.,* firefighters, police officers, tax assessors, etc.). "Private persons" entering in exercise of the privilege are deemed licensees. A public entrant is treated as an invitee if entry involves business dealings with the land occupier or if on business premises during normal business hours; otherwise a public entrant is treated as a licensee.

(7) **Recreational land** §717

By statute in most states, landowners are protected against lawsuits of persons injured while using the land for recreational purposes unless the owner has engaged in willful or wanton conduct.

d. **Alternative view** §718

In about half the states, the duty of a land occupier generally is determined by the ***reasonable person standard*** regardless of the entrant's status; *i.e.,* P's status is only one factor relevant to determining the "reasonableness" of D's conduct. Some states apply a separate standard when the entrant is a trespasser.

e. **Open and obvious dangers** §721

Courts are split on whether a land occupier owes a duty to protect against open and obvious dangers, with some finding a duty to ***mitigate*** the risk and others holding P ***comparatively negligent***.

8. **Duties Owed by Entrants on Another's Land** §722

Most courts apply a general standard of due care. The Second Restatement gives land occupier status to those working for or under the land occupier's orders.

9. **Duties Owed by Lessors of Land**

a. **Duties owed to persons outside the land** §725

For a reasonable time after a lessor transfers possession to a lessee, the lessor's duty of care to those outside the land continues. During this time, the lessor has a duty to repair or warn the lessee of known dangerous artificial conditions or of conditions that may become dangerous. The duty continues only until the lessee has a ***reasonable opportunity*** to discover the condition and remedy it. But if the lessor actively concealed the danger, the duty continues until the lessee actually discovers and has time to remedy it.

b. **Duties owed to lessee** §733

There is a duty to repair or warn of known latent dangerous conditions. If the condition is reasonably apparent, no duty is owed.

(1) **Dangerous conditions arising after transfer** §737

There is ***no duty*** with respect to conditions arising after the lease period begins ***except:*** (i) a lessor may be liable for making ***negligent repairs***; and (ii) under the modern trend, a lessor is liable in tort for failure to make ***repairs covenanted in the lease***.

c. **Duties owed to third persons coming onto the land with lessee's consent** **§745**

Generally, a lessor owes the same duty to a tenant's visitors as is owed to the tenant (*see* above).

d. **Duties owed where lessor retains control of common areas** **§751**

As to common areas (*e.g.,* elevators, stairways, hallways), the lessor is regarded as the land occupier—thus, there is a duty to discover and remedy dangerous conditions. Moreover, several courts impose a duty to take reasonable precautions against foreseeable criminal acts of third parties.

e. **Duty owed where lessor has right to control dangerous activity or condition created by tenant** **§753**

If the lessor has actual knowledge of a danger plus the right to terminate it, there is a duty to prevent injuries therefrom to third persons.

10. **Duties Owed by Sellers of Land** **§754**

Generally, ***no*** duty is owed to those injured on or outside the premises after possession is transferred. However, (i) sellers must disclose ***known latent*** dangerous conditions; and (ii) if the property contained an ***unreasonable risk*** of harm to persons outside the premises, the seller is liable for a reasonable time after transfer. Absent active concealment, the duty terminates when the buyer has had a reasonable time to discover and repair.

11. **Duties Owed by Bailors of Chattels** **§758**

A duty is owed to all persons within the foreseeable scope of use of the bailed goods. If the bailment is ***gratuitous***, there is a duty to warn of ***known, concealed*** defects. If the bailment is for hire, there is a duty to ***inspect*** and warn of defects. However, warning might not discharge the duty to third persons.

12. **Duties Relating to Emotional Distress**

a. **Duty owed** **§762**

Under the early view, there is a duty to exercise due care not to subject others to a risk of physical injury, through physical impact or threat thereof, that might foreseeably result in emotional distress and consequent physical injuries. Most courts have broadened the duty.

b. **Actual or threatened physical impact** **§764**

Under the early view, D must have subjected P to physical impact. Today, a ***threat*** of impact (*i.e.,* P is within the "zone of danger") is sufficient.

(1) **Exposure cases** **§767**

Mere exposure to a toxic substance or infectious disease is not "impact" unless P knows of the exposure and has a serious fear that she will likely develop the harm. However, contact with someone with AIDS is "impact" only if P is actually exposed to the virus.

(2) **Exception** §769

In some cases (*e.g.*, mishandled corpses, erroneous reports of death), P need not establish that she was within the "zone of danger" to recover for emotional distress.

c. **Injury or threat of injury to another (bystander recovery)** §771

The older view requires P to be within the "zone of danger," but the newer view allows recovery where D's negligence injures or threatens a member of P's family.

(1) **Determinative factors under broader view** §773

There are three requirements:

(a) P and the victim must be ***closely related***;

(b) P must be ***"present"*** at the scene of the accident and must be aware the victim is suffering;

(c) P must suffer ***direct emotional impact*** (beyond that of an unrelated bystander) from contemporaneous personal observance of the accident ("within moments" after accident suffices).

(2) **Limitation** §779

P's right of action is dependent on the imperiled person's right to recover. Thus, if D is not liable for the harm to the victim, P cannot recover for emotional distress.

d. **Damage to property** §780

Most cases deny recovery for emotional distress and consequential injuries when property interests (including pets) are negligently damaged or threatened.

e. **Resulting physical manifestation required** §782

Emotional distress must result in tangible physical manifestation, although a growing minority allows recovery for ***severe*** emotional distress without physical manifestation.

f. **"Severe" emotional distress required** §785

Recovery is generally limited to what a ***normally constituted person*** would have suffered. But if D ***knew or should have known*** of P's special vulnerability ("eggshell psyche"), P may recover even if a normally constituted person would not have so suffered. Moreover, if D's conduct would have caused severe distress to a normally constituted person, P may recover the ***full extent*** of her emotional distress, even if beyond what a normally constituted person would have suffered.

13. **Duty Not to Cause Purely Economic Loss** §789

Although generally D has no duty not to cause purely economic loss, courts permit recovery in limited circumstances (*e.g.*, defamation, misrepresentation).

D. **DEFENSES TO NEGLIGENCE**

1. **Contributory Negligence** §791

This is conduct on the part of P that is a contributing cause of his own injuries and that falls below the standard of care to which he is required to conform for his own protection.

a. **Prima facie case** §792

The prima facie case is similar to that of negligence except the actor owes a duty to himself.

(1) **Statutory standards** §798

Where P, without excuse, violates a statute designed for his own protection as well as that of others and the violation is a contributing cause of his injury, the violation may establish duty and breach. Note, however, that there is no contributory negligence where P is a member of a special class sought to be protected by the statute.

b. **Effect of contributory negligence** §802

Traditionally, contributory negligence was a ***complete bar*** to P's recovery for ***negligence***. But it is not a defense to intentional torts.

c. **Exception—last clear chance doctrine** §804

If immediately before an accident D had the last clear chance to avoid the accident, P's contributory negligence will not bar recovery.

(1) **"Helpless peril" cases** §805

P has placed himself in a position from which he is powerless to extricate himself. If D had ***actual knowledge*** of P's peril (or should have had such knowledge) and could have avoided the harm but failed to do so, most courts allow P to recover.

(2) **"Inattentive peril" cases** §806

P could have extricated himself but fails to do so because P was unaware the accident was about to occur. Last clear chance is applied only if D had ***actual knowledge*** of P's peril.

d. **Imputed contributory negligence** §807

Generally, one person's contributory negligence will be imputed to another in only three situations:

(1) **Master-servant** §808

An employee's negligence is imputed to the employer.

(2) **Joint enterprise** §809

The negligence of one member of a joint enterprise is imputed to others to bar recovery against a third person.

(3) **Suit based on injury to third persons** §810

In actions for wrongful death, loss of consortium, or for bystander emotional distress, the negligence of the victim is imputed to P by most courts.

(4) **Distinguish—bailees and spouses** §811

Negligence of a bailee is ***not*** imputed to the bailor as against third parties. Negligence ordinarily is not imputed between spouses (a few community property states are contra).

2. **Comparative Negligence** §815

Virtually all states reject the rule that contributory negligence is an absolute bar to recovery and base liability on the comparative fault of P and D.

a. **"Pure" comparative negligence** §817

Under a pure comparative negligence scheme, P may recover the percentage of damages for which D is liable even where P's negligence exceeds D's.

b. **"Partial" comparative negligence** §818

Under a partial comparative negligence scheme, P may recover the percentage of damages for which D is liable only if ***P's own negligence is less than a certain threshold level***. If there is more than one D, most states require that P's negligence be less than the ***combined*** negligence of all Ds. A few states compare P's fault with ***each*** D's, and permit recovery against that D only if P's negligence is less.

c. **Impact of comparative negligence doctrine on other rules**

(1) **Last clear chance** §824

Under comparative negligence, the last clear chance doctrine is generally abolished.

(2) **Wanton or reckless conduct by D** §825

Such conduct apparently will not affect the comparative negligence doctrine; *i.e.,* P's recovery can still be reduced. But the majority do not recognize P's negligence as a factor if D acted ***intentionally***.

(3) **Avoidable consequences** §831

Total relevant fault is apportioned; thus, failure to mitigate damages is no longer charged solely to P.

(4) **Jury instructions** §833

There is a split of opinion as to whether a jury in a comparative negligence case should be told how its apportionment will affect recovery.

(5) **Imputation of comparative negligence** §834

The availability of comparative negligence has led some courts to more freely impute negligence.

(6) **Rescuers** §835

Most courts do not allow a rescuer's negligence to result in a reduction in the rescuer's award.

(7) **Intoxicated Ps** §836

Some states have concluded that allowing partial recovery to an intoxicated P against a negligent tavernkeeper or liquor seller will serve to discourage negligence.

(8) **Res ipsa loquitur** §837

Most states no longer require Ps to show freedom from contributory negligence as part of a res ipsa case.

(9) **Punitive damages** §838

P may not recover punitive damages where the jury has attributed more fault to P than to D.

3. Assumption of the Risk §839

If P expressly or impliedly consents to confront harm from a particular risk, this bars recovery in negligence provided P (i) ***recognized and understood*** the danger, and (ii) ***voluntarily chose*** to encounter it.

a. **By agreement—"exculpatory clauses"** §842

Enforceability of such clauses turns on contract law.

(1) **Offer and acceptance problem** §843

P must have been aware of the provision at the time of the agreement (*e.g.,* "fine print provisions" may be unenforceable). The provision must be part of the contract, although the words "negligence" and "breach of warranty" need not appear.

(2) **Scope of the contract** §844

The provision must encompass P's injury. Ambiguities are construed against the drafter (usually D).

(3) **Limitation—adhesion contract** §845

The provision cannot be part of an "adhesion contract." Where parties are in ***unequal bargaining positions***, an exculpatory clause may violate public policy.

(4) **Limitation—intentional torts** §849

Enforceability of exculpatory clauses is limited to ***negligence*** claims; they are ***no*** defense to intentional or wanton or reckless torts.

b. **Implied assumption of the risk by conduct** §850

D must show P's knowledge of the particular risk and her voluntary choice to encounter the risk. P is not required to surrender a legal right to avoid danger.

c. **Exception** §858

If P is a member of a statutorily protected class, she is deemed legally incapable of assuming the risk.

d. **Distinguish—P's negligence** §859

There may be both negligence by P and assumption of the risk by P in the same case (*e.g.,* P uses staircase that he knows is dangerous because D has negligently failed to replace a light bulb). Under comparative negligence, P's negligence generally will be compared to D's negligence in such cases.

e. **Abolition of implied assumption of risk** §860

A number of jurisdictions have abolished the implied assumption of risk defense. It is treated as a question of duty or contributory negligence. A few states taking this same basic approach speak of "primary" and "secondary" assumption of risk.

E. EFFECT OF LIABILITY INSURANCE

1. Present "Third Party" Liability Insurance System §865

Insurance protects the insured against legal liability to others.

a. General operation §866

The suit is defended by the insurer in the name of the insured. Most policies cover only negligent conduct by D or strict liability. Generally, there is no direct action by P against the insurer until P obtains a judgment against D.

b. Insured's duty of "cooperation" §870

The insured must cooperate with the insurer.

c. Insurer's duty of "good faith" in settlement §871

An insurer is obligated to make a good faith effort to settle the case within the policy limits. For failure to exercise good faith, the insurer is liable for the full amount of the judgment. The insurer's duty generally runs only to the insured; the insurer does not owe the duty to third persons who might also be affected.

III. STRICT LIABILITY

A. IN GENERAL §880

Torts that are neither intentional nor the result of negligence may still create liability simply because a certain type of injury occurs—even if no one is at fault. A ***prima facie case*** consists of an act or omission to act that breaches an ***absolute*** duty to make safe and is the actual and proximate cause of P's injuries.

B. ANIMALS

1. Trespassing Livestock §882

The possessor of livestock is strictly liable for the trespass itself and any harm done.

2. Domestic Animals (Including Livestock) with Known Dangerous Propensities §884

The possessor is strictly liable for all harm done as a result of that dangerous propensity. If a domestic animal is of a class that normally has dangerous propensities (*e.g.,* a bull), the possessor is not strictly liable for injuries caused by the normal dangerous propensity.

3. Domestic Animals Without Known Dangerous Propensities §887

The possessor generally is ***not*** strictly liable. However, several state statutes hold the possessor liable for all dog bites even if there was no prior knowledge of the propensity to bite.

4. Wild Animals §889

The possessor is liable for harm done as a result of a wild animal's ***normally*** dangerous propensity. However, where the wild animal is kept under a ***public***

duty (*e.g.,* by a zoo), strict liability does not apply; P must show negligence (but D is held to a high amount of care).

5. **Persons Protected Where Injury Occurs on D's Premises** §893
Invitees and licensees are protected. A trespasser whose presence is not known or anticipated is ordinarily not protected. But a landowner must warn of ***vicious watchdogs***.

C. ABNORMALLY DANGEROUS ACTIVITIES

1. **General Rule** §898
One who maintains an abnormally dangerous condition on his premises, or engages in an activity presenting an unavoidable risk of harm to others, may be liable for harm caused even though reasonable care was exercised.

2. **"Abnormally Dangerous" Activities**

   a. **Origin—*Rylands v. Fletcher*** §900
   A force, brought by D onto his land, that involves a "nonnatural" use of the land and is likely to cause substantial damage if it escapes renders D strictly liable if it escapes and does harm.

   b. **First Restatement—"ultrahazardous" activity** §901
   An ultrahazardous activity is any activity necessarily involving a risk of serious harm to others such that it cannot be eliminated by utmost care and that is not a matter of common usage.

   c. **Second Restatement—"abnormally dangerous" activity** §902
   Six factors are considered:

   (1) Whether the activity ***involves a high degree of risk***;

   (2) The ***gravity*** of that risk;

   (3) Whether the risk can be ***eliminated by the exercise of reasonable care***;

   (4) Whether the activity is a ***matter of common usage***;

   (5) Whether the activity is ***appropriate to the locale***; and

   (6) The ***value*** of the activity ***to the community***.

   d. **Third Restatement standard** §905
   An activity is considered abnormally dangerous if it creates a foreseeable and highly significant risk even when reasonable care is exercised and is not a matter of common usage.

3. **Products Liability Cases** §912
Strict liability is imposed against suppliers of ***defective*** products.

D. EXTENT OF LIABILITY

1. **Scope of Duty Owed** §914
An absolute duty is owed to make safe abnormally dangerous animals, activities, and conditions. The duty is owed ***only to foreseeable Ps*** and only for

harm that ***flows from the normally dangerous propensity*** of the condition or activity involved.

2. **Actual Cause** **§918**
All courts use the same rules as in negligence cases.

3. **Proximate Cause** **§919**
Virtually all courts apply the same rules as in negligence cases.

E. DEFENSES

1. **Contributory Negligence** **§920**
This is ***no defense*** unless P knew of the danger and negligently caused the activity to miscarry.

2. **Comparative Negligence** **§921**
This ***reduces*** recovery in most comparative negligence jurisdictions.

3. **Assumption of Risk** **§922**
The voluntary encountering of a known risk may prevent P's recovery. Consent to a risk is implied to bar strict liability where D acted for P's benefit (*e.g.*, water line maintained partially for use by P).

IV. PRODUCTS LIABILITY

A. IN GENERAL **§925**

The liability of a supplier of a product for ***physical harm to person or property*** caused by ***defective*** products is the basis for products liability.

B. LIABILITY BASED ON INTENTIONAL ACTS **§929**

A manufacturer or supplier who sells a chattel ***known to be defective***, without adequate warning, may be liable for battery. Punitive damages are potentially recoverable.

C. LIABILITY BASED ON NEGLIGENCE

1. **Background—Gradual Abrogation of "Privity" Requirement** **§932**
Early decisions limited liability to cases where there was "privity" between the product supplier and the injured party, but this requirement was gradually eroded.

2. **Impact of *MacPherson v. Buick Motor Co.*—Liability Based on Foreseeability of Harm** **§933**
Today, if a reasonable person would foresee a risk of harm if the product is not carefully made or supplied, the manufacturer or supplier owes a duty of due care to all foreseeable users.

3. **General Scope of Negligence Liability Today** **§934**
The *MacPherson* rule has been adopted in all states and now covers negligent design, foreseeable bystanders, and property damage. Most courts also extend the rule to design and construction of real property.

   a. **Assembler of components manufactured by others** **§940**
   A supplier who markets a product under the supplier's name and who

has only assembled component parts negligently manufactured by others is liable for a defect in the components whether or not discoverable.

b. Proving negligence—res ipsa loquitur §942

Res ipsa loquitur frequently applies in products liability cases based on negligence.

4. Role of Dealer or Middleman §943

There is ***no duty to inspect or test*** products manufactured by others ***unless*** there is a reason to know of the defect.

a. Where dealer has reason to know of danger §945

If a dealer or middleman has reason to know of the danger (*e.g.*, because of previous complaints, source of supply is unreliable, manufacturer failed to label properly, etc.), he must inspect or at least warn, but failure to do so will ***not*** affect the manufacturer's liability.

b. Where dealer actually knows of danger §947

If a dealer or middleman actually knows of the danger and fails to warn the purchaser, the manufacturer is relieved of liability for unintended harm because the dealer or middleman's failure to warn will be treated as a superseding cause.

5. Damages §949

P can recover for personal injury and property damage but not purely economic loss in most states. Punitive damages may be recovered where recklessness is shown.

6. Defenses §951

Contributory negligence, assumption of the risk, and comparative negligence may apply.

D. STRICT LIABILITY IN TORT §952

Most courts hold manufacturers and suppliers of defective products strictly liable in tort to consumers and users for injuries caused by the defect.

1. Rationale for Strict Liability §953

D is better able to insure against loss; increased safety incentive; difficulty of proving negligence—all these are bases for a public policy imposition of liability without fault.

2. Caution—Liability Not Absolute §957

Liability is strict, but not absolute. P must still prove that the defect that caused her injury is attributable to D.

3. Caution—Liability May Not Even Be "Nonfault" §958

The type of "defect" involved may control whether strict liability or negligence is applicable.

a. Three kinds of defects

(1) Manufacturing defects §960

A manufacturing defect occurs where a product is ***not in the condition the manufacturer intended*** at the time it left the manufacturer's control. Liability for this type of defect is "strict."

(2) Design defects §961

Design defects occur where the product is designed in such a way that it ***presents an undue risk of harm in normal use***. Although courts speak of strict liability in such cases, the same result is almost always reached by a negligence analysis, because the undue risk should have been discovered and prevented by due care.

(a) Crashworthiness §965

A manufacturer can be held liable for failure to design a product so as to minimize foreseeable harm caused by other parties or conditions (*e.g.,* design of automobile for safety in collisions).

(b) Approaches to design defects

1) Risk/utility test §967

Under this prevailing approach, the question is whether the product's risks outweigh its utility—*e.g.,* whether D could have removed the danger without serious adverse impact on the product's utility and price.

2) Consumer expectation test §969

Under this approach, P must prove that the product did not perform as safely as an ordinary consumer would have expected. This test is often used in defective food cases.

3) Combined approach §972

Under this approach, recovery is permitted if P satisfies either the risk/utility test or the consumer expectation test.

4) Reasonable alternative design test §975

The Second Restatement was based on consumer expectations and did not allow recovery for patent dangers. Under the Third Restatement approach (not applied in cases involving food), D's design is defective if the greater safety of a reasonable alternative design outweighs its disadvantages.

(c) Dangers not foreseeable at time of marketing §976

The majority of courts follow the Restatement and deny strict liability where the manufacturer could not have guarded against the danger by the application of reasonable developed human skill and foresight.

(d) Discovery of danger §978

When a scientifically unknowable risk becomes discoverable, the manufacturer or supplier becomes liable. The manufacturer has a duty to eliminate the danger, if feasible. Otherwise she must warn consumers or discontinue distribution. There is a duty to take reasonable steps to warn those who bought before the risk was discovered.

(3) **Inadequate warnings** §979
Defects may arise from packaging and inadequate instructions, warnings, or labels. Inadequate warnings may make a product defective when the dangers are not apparent to consumers and users.

(a) **Unexpected dangers** §980
The danger must be something that a reasonable user would have no reason to expect or anticipate in the product. The means of harm may also be unexpected and require specific warning. If the danger is unexpected by D because it could not be anticipated, most courts will analyze it as a negligence question.

(b) **Unavoidably unsafe products** §983
Many useful products are unavoidably unsafe (*e.g.,* knives), but this does not render them defective, because there is no safer way to make them. To create liability for failure to warn of such danger, the danger must be not reasonably apparent (*e.g.,* danger from short-burning dynamite fuse).

(c) **Testing adequacy of warning** §986
A warning may be inadequate if it is incomplete, is inconsistent with how the product is used, or does not give the reason for the warning.

(d) **Testing who must receive warning** §989
Usually the warning must reach the person at risk from the danger (*e.g.,* supplier of glue to bookbinding plant must warn workers who come in contact with glue of its dangers).

1) **Learned intermediary exception** §990
Most courts hold that as to pharmaceuticals, an adequate warning need reach only the prescribing physician.

4. **Scope of Liability**

a. **Parties liable—commercial suppliers** §992
All participants in the marketing of the product may be held liable.

(1) **Sellers** §993
Liability applies to manufacturers, retailers, and distributors.

(2) **Lessors** §994
Liability applies to commercial bailors and lessors.

(3) **Assemblers of components** §997
Liability applies to manufacturers of components and to assemblers of the finished product.

(4) **Contractors** §998
A contractor who provides a defective product may be liable.

(5) **Successors in interest to manufacturers of defective products** §999
Such persons are generally ***not*** liable ***unless*** there was a merger of

companies, the buying company agreed to assume the seller's liability, or the sale was a fraudulent attempt by the seller to avoid liability.

(6) **Sellers of used products** §1000

Some courts hold used product sellers liable for safety defects attributable to the design or manufacture if the product fails to meet the purchaser's reasonable expectations; other courts bar strict liability unless the seller makes representations of quality.

(7) **Franchisors** §1002

Franchisors may be liable if they retain some control over franchisees.

(8) **Trademark licensors** §1003

Trademark licensors may be liable if they participate in product design and marketing.

b. **Distinguish—noncommercial supplier** §1004

Only those regularly engaged in the business of manufacturing, selling, or leasing can be held strictly liable.

c. **Parties who may invoke liability**

(1) **Ultimate user or consumer** §1008

The ultimate user of a product as well as the purchaser may invoke the doctrine.

(2) **Bystanders** §1009

Most states permit suit by bystanders.

(3) **Rescuers** §1010

Some case authority permits suit by rescuers.

(4) **Business firms** §1011

Courts are split over whether business entities may recover from each other for property damage under strict liability.

d. **Liability extends only to "products"** §1012

This is an expansive view that includes: (i) ***products in their natural state*** (*e.g.,* poisonous mushrooms), and (ii) ***defective mass-produced buildings*** (modern trend). But ***services are not covered***. Nevertheless, courts find a "product" furnished in cases involving defective food or hair treatment. Note that most states bar such suits in cases involving transfused blood; Ps must seek to recover on a negligence basis.

e. **Liability extends only to "defective" products**

(1) **Basic approaches**

(a) **Restatement view** §1023

The product must be ***"unreasonably dangerous" due to a defect***—*i.e.,* something other than what a reasonable person would expect in normal use.

(b) **Alternative approach—"defect" alone** §1027

Under this view, an action lies for injuries from a defect that may not be unreasonably dangerous in terms of foreseeability.

(2) **Misuse** §1028

The defect must arise in the ***normal*** or ***foreseeable*** use of the product. However, a certain amount of misuse, carelessness, and modification is foreseeable, so that a product may be deemed defective if safety measures are not taken.

(3) **Abnormal reactions** §1032

Highly unusual reactions do ***not*** render a product defective. But if the reaction is shared by even a small percentage of the population (*e.g.,* 3-4%), a defect may be found. Under the modern trend, if there is a known risk to ***any*** number of potential users, a manufacturer owes a duty to warn.

f. **Proof required** §1035

P has the burden to prove (i) the product was ***defective when it left D's control***, and (ii) a ***causal relationship*** to the injuries exists.

(1) **Circumstantial evidence of "defect" admissible** §1036

A defect may be ***inferred*** where the product functions improperly in normal use.

(2) **Causation** §1037

P must prove her injuries were caused by a defect ***existing*** at the time the product was marketed by D.

(a) **Cause in fact (actual cause)** §1039

The defect must be a ***substantial*** factor in causing the injury (*e.g.,* an adequate warning would have made a difference; or an omitted safety device would have decreased severity of the inevitable accident).

(b) **Proximate cause** §1043

Proximate cause must be shown; the effect of intervening causes is the same as in negligence.

g. **Kinds of losses recoverable** §1048

Damages for pain and suffering, medical expenses, lost wages, property damages, etc., are recoverable. Recovery for purely economic loss is ***not*** generally allowed, but a minority is contra.

5. **Defenses to Strict Tort Liability**

a. **Contributory negligence** §1054

This is not per se a valid defense. However, the product is not "defective" when the injury is caused by an unreasonable misuse of the product.

b. **Comparative fault** §1057

This is used in most states. P's recovery is ***reduced*** to reflect her own carelessness.

c. **Assumption of the risk** §1059

Assumption of the risk can be a ***valid defense***—*e.g.,* voluntary use after "adequate" warning. However, most courts hold that if a dangerous situation confronts a person who unreasonably chooses to encounter it, the defense is not assumption of the risk, but rather ***comparative fault***.

d. **Disclaimers** §1065

These have been held invalid in ***consumer*** transactions as against public policy, but may be upheld between business concerns.

e. **Statute of limitations** §1067

The period is that of tort rather than contract.

f. **Preemption** §1068

A few courts have concluded federal legislation has impliedly preempted state tort law (*e.g.,* airbag in automobile, warning on cigarettes).

E. LIABILITY BASED ON BREACH OF WARRANTY

1. Express Warranties §1070

If a seller makes a representation about the product, an express warranty arises, and breach of the warranty gives rise to contract liability.

2. Implied Warranties

a. **Fitness for particular purpose** §1073

Where the seller should know that the buyer is purchasing for a particular purpose and that the buyer is relying on the seller's expertise to choose suitable goods, the product is warranted to be fit for that particular use.

b. **Merchantability** §1074

A seller who deals in goods of that kind warrants that the goods are generally ***fit for normal use***.

c. **Transactions covered** §1076

The U.C.C. applies only to ***sales of goods***.

(1) **Bailments** §1077

Bailments are covered by analogy to the U.C.C.

(2) **Sale of real property** §1078

Some courts extend warranties to the construction and sale of a new home.

(3) **"Goods" vs. "services"** §1079

Warranties are ***not*** implied in contracts for services, although sometimes it is difficult to distinguish goods from services (*e.g.,* sale of food in restaurant is "sale of goods," but most states treat blood transfusions as "services").

(4) **Dealers** §1082

Generally, only those who "deal" regularly in the product are subject to warranty liability.

3. **Effect of Breach of Warranty** §1083
Warrantors are liable regardless of fault or negligence.

4. **Requirement of "Privity of Contract"**

a. **Former rule** §1085
Implied warranties would run only to those in privity with the manufacturer (*i.e.*, distributors, wholesalers). Thus, purchasers and consumers had no direct action against the manufacturer.

b. **Modern law** §1088
Under U.C.C. alternatives, privity extends to:

(1) ***Members of family and guests*** who are injured; or

(2) ***Any individual reasonably expected to use*** or be affected by goods who is injured; or

(3) ***Any person reasonably expected to use*** or be affected by goods who is injured.

c. **Abandonment of "privity" as to dangerous products** §1091
Historically, certain products, such as foodstuffs and firearms, were excluded from the "privity" requirement. Today, due to public policy considerations, this concept has been expanded by many courts to encompass ***any dangerous product*** and extends to all persons within the ***foreseeable scope of use***.

d. **Consumer protection statutes** §1094
Some states have abolished the privity requirement between the manufacturer and the purchaser of ***all*** consumer goods.

e. **Causation** §1095
D is not liable where, because of an independent superseding event, its breach is not the proximate cause of the damage. Note that if the danger of the product is apparent to an ordinary purchaser, warranty liability will not lie.

f. **Damages** §1097
Damages are generally the same as in a strict liability tort action, although a few states bar damages for wrongful death on a warranty theory.

5. **Defenses to Warranty Actions** §1098
Although contributory negligence is not formally a defense to a breach of warranty action, most courts have developed an analogous defense to parallel the tort developments; *i.e.,* comparative fault. If P discovers a defect and unreasonably uses the product in its defective condition, ***assumption of the risk*** is a complete defense in warranty actions. Under limited conditions, disclaimers may limit liability.

V. NUISANCE

A. IN GENERAL

1. **Prima Facie Case** §1107
A ***prima facie case*** consists of an act by D that constitutes a nontrespassory

interference with P's interest in the use and enjoyment of P's land and that causes substantial and unreasonable harm.

2. **Private Nuisance vs. Public Nuisance**

a. **Private nuisance defined** §1108

A private nuisance is an unreasonable interference with the possessory interest of an individual in the use or enjoyment of her land. Distinguish trespass, which requires ***entry*** of a person or thing onto P's property. For example, the casting of invisible chemical particles onto P's land may be a trespass; an intrusion by means of noise, odor, or light can only be nuisance. (*But note:* Some acts may be ***both*** trespass and nuisance; *e.g.,* blasting that causes rocks to fall on P's land).

b. **Public nuisance defined** §1110

A public nuisance inconveniences the public at large. A private individual may maintain the action for a public nuisance only if she suffered an injury "peculiar in kind"—*i.e.,* apart from that suffered by the public. However, the lawful sales of lawful products (*e.g.*, handguns, fast food) do not give rise to a public nuisance claim.

B. PLAINTIFF'S INTEREST §1114

P must be in actual ***possession*** or have the right to immediate possession. Some courts extend nuisance to interference with business interests as well as land.

C. DEFENDANT'S CONDUCT §1118

D's act can be intentional, negligent, or actionable under strict liability rules; the distinction is necessary to ascertain available defenses.

D. SUBSTANTIAL AND UNREASONABLE HARM TO PLAINTIFF

1. **"Substantial"** §1123

This refers to something that would offend a reasonable person.

2. **"Unreasonable"** §1124

This means the harm outweighs justification for D's conduct.

a. **Factors** §1125

Factors to consider are the neighborhood, values of respective properties, cost to cure, social benefits, etc.

b. **Aesthetic considerations** §1126

Most courts have held that aesthetic considerations may not ordinarily create a nuisance.

c. **Prior occupation** §1128

"Coming to the nuisance" (*i.e.,* D was there first) may be relevant but not conclusive.

d. **Effect of zoning** §1129

Zoning ordinances permitting D's activity are not conclusive (presumptive defense in some states).

3. **Minority Rule—Intentional Substantial Interference Enough** §1130

A number of courts hold that substantial interference suffices regardless of reasonableness if D acted intentionally.

E. CAUSATION §1132

Same as battery if D acted intentionally; same as negligence if conduct is inadvertent.

F. REMEDIES §1134

Compensatory damages are available. An injunction may lie if the nuisance is continuing in nature, and the self-help remedy of abatement may be available.

G. DEFENSES

1. **Contributory or Comparative Negligence** §1138

   D may reduce or escape liability for ***inadvertent*** conduct by proving P was negligent. However, where the nuisance is intentional, contributory or comparative negligence is ***not*** a defense.

2. **Assumption of the Risk** §1142

   Assumption of the risk may also be available to relieve D of liability. However, the fact that the activity existed before P came (*i.e.,* coming to the nuisance) is ***not*** necessarily a defense.

VI. MISCELLANEOUS FACTORS AFFECTING RIGHT TO SUE

A. SURVIVAL OF TORT ACTIONS

1. **Common Law—No "Survival"** §1150

   Traditionally, tort actions did not survive the death of either the tortfeasor or victim.

2. **Survival Statutes** §1151

   Such statutes, enacted in almost all states, usually provide for survival of personal injury or property actions. However, most states do not allow actions to survive where the tort involves recovery for invasion of intangible personal interests (*e.g.,* defamation, right of privacy). Also there is usually ***no*** recovery of punitive damages from the decedent's estate.

B. WRONGFUL DEATH §1156

At common law, there was ***no*** cause of action for wrongful death. Today, wrongful death statutes exist in every jurisdiction.

1. **"Survival" Type** §1158

   Some jurisdictions provide that any action the decedent might have maintained ***himself*** survives, plus recovery for damages to his estate (including pain and suffering, loss of future earnings).

2. **"True" Type (Majority)** §1159

   Most jurisdictions have statutes that create a new cause of action for the benefit of certain relatives to recover their pecuniary loss. (The decedent's estate maintains a separate action for the decedent's losses.)

   a. **Computing pecuniary loss**

(1) **Wage earners** §1162

If the decedent was a ***wage earner***, damages are based on estimated earnings over his life expectancy.

(2) **Children** §1163

Probable earnings of a child are only speculative; the award is fixed on the "pecuniary value" of the child's life.

(3) **Non-wage earners** §1164

If the decedent was not a wage earner, recovery is generally the cost to replace the services of the deceased, including advice and companionship.

(4) **Retired persons** §1165

If the decedent was a retired person, his survivors are entitled to some recovery despite the speculative nature.

b. **Effect of remarriage** §1166

Most courts bar evidence of remarriage.

c. **No punitive damages** §1167

The general rule is that even where punitive damages could have been awarded had the victim survived, they are not awardable in a wrongful death action.

3. **Defenses**

a. **Victim's negligence, etc.** §1168

D may use all defenses she could have asserted against the decedent (*e.g.,* contributory negligence).

b. **Victim's inter vivos recovery** §1169

The majority view holds that recovery during the victim's life bars any action after death.

c. **Beneficiary's negligence** §1170

Contributory negligence reduces or negates recovery (if one beneficiary, no recovery; if more than one, proportional reduction); comparative negligence reduces recovery.

C. INJURIES TO MEMBERS OF THE FAMILY

1. Loss of Consortium and Services

a. **Common law** §1172

The ***husband's*** right to recover for loss of his wife's services and consortium was recognized. Also, a ***parent*** could recover for a child's labor and expenses of care, but no action was allowed for loss of a child's consortium.

b. **Modern law** §1175

Under modern law, ***either spouse*** may recover for loss of services or consortium (must be complete loss of companionship and intercourse for some definite time). If a spouse is ***killed***, the surviving spouse has only the remedies of the survival and wrongful death statutes.

(1) **Parent-child** §1181

Traditionally, a parent could recover only economic losses for a child; the modern rule allows recovery for loss of the child's society and comfort.

(2) **Children** §1185

Children may ***not*** recover for injuries to their parents. A few states are contra.

c. **Effect of victim's negligence** §1186

Defenses assertable against the victim may be asserted against P.

d. **Joinder requirement** §1187

Claims must be joined with the victim's claim to avoid double recovery.

2. **Prenatal Injuries to Child** §1188

Traditionally, no recovery was allowed to a child for prenatal injuries. In most states today, a child can recover for prenatal injuries if the child was "viable" at the time of injury. Some states permit recovery for injuries sustained even before viability.

a. **Wrongful death** §1192

There is a split of authority. Many states allow recovery for wrongful death if the child was viable.

b. **"Wrongful birth"** §1193

In wrongful birth cases (*e.g.,* negligent unsuccessful vasectomy resulting in unwanted child), the ***mother*** may recover for pain and suffering during pregnancy and delivery, and for related medical expenses and loss of consortium during this time. Most courts also permit recovery for extraordinary medical and related expenses if the child has genetic defects. The modern trend is to permit recovery for costs of raising an unwanted healthy child (but benefits of the birth are usually offset against recoverable expenses). Almost all states bar suit by the child.

3. **Intentional Interference with Family Relationships**

a. **Alienation of affections** §1201

The states are split as to whether a spouse can bring such an action. In the states where it has not been abolished, ***either*** spouse may bring suit (contrary to the common law).

(1) **Parent-child claims rejected** §1204

Modern courts ***reject*** claims brought by either parent or child (*e.g.,* suits by parents against religious groups are rejected).

b. **Criminal conversation** §1207

The early view permitted a husband to sue for damages if he could prove that D had had sexual relations with the husband's wife. Today, most states have ***abolished*** this action because of its potential for blackmail.

c. **Intentional interference with custodial rights** §1209

Recently, several states have recognized a cause of action for intentional interference with a parent-child custodial relationship.

d. **Emotional distress claims** §1210

Courts are split over whether to permit an action for intentional infliction of emotional distress where the action closely resembles one for alienation of affections or criminal conversation that has been barred by the state.

D. TORT IMMUNITY

1. Intrafamily

a. **Husband-wife** §1211

At common law, spouses could ***not*** sue each other in tort. However, virtually all states have abolished spousal immunity altogether.

b. **Parent-child** §1214

Traditionally, only causes of action pertaining to property were permitted. The modern trend rejects or restricts immunity. Some states that have abolished the immunity relax the duty of care owed; others impose a normal duty of care on the parent.

c. **Other relationships** §1221

There is no tort immunity for other family relationships. However, some states bar suit by one child for harm caused by a sibling's negligent supervision.

2. Governmental Tort Immunity (Sovereign Immunity) §1222

At common law, the state was held to be immune from tort liability.

a. **State and federal** §1223

State and federal governments and agencies are immune (*e.g.,* hospitals, schools, etc.).

b. **Municipalities** §1224

"Proprietary" or ***"private"*** functions performed by municipalities are ***not*** immune (*i.e.,* functions that could have been provided by a private corporation) but ***"governmental"*** functions are.

c. **Status of doctrine today** §1228

Many courts have abolished sovereign immunity, and some legislatures reacted by reenacting limited governmental immunity. The Federal Tort Claims Act abolishes immunity for negligence of government employees and for most intentional torts by federal investigative or law enforcement officers.

d. **Liability of governmental officers** §1235

Judges, legislators, and high ranking members of the executive branch are immune from tort liability for acts carried out within the scope of their duties. Lower level administrative officers are immune from claims of negligence under federal law and some states' laws.

(1) **No immunity for "ministerial" functions** §1238

Other states grant immunity to lower level officers who act honestly and in good faith when performing ***"discretionary"*** functions (*i.e.,* functions involving personal judgment or decisionmaking).

(2) **Statutory changes** §1241

A person acting under color of state law who deprives P of a federal right is liable for damages. [42 U.S.C. §1983]

(a) **Basis of liability** §1242

The action requires that the deprivation be caused by malicious and intentional behavior or deliberate indifference.

(b) **Interests protected** §1243

The action clearly includes physical well-being and freedom from improper incarceration.

(c) **Defenses** §1244

The statute is silent and no general rules have emerged regarding defenses.

(d) **Distinguish—federal agents** §1246

Violation of federal constitutional rights by federal agents gives rise to civil liability.

3. **Charitable Immunity** §1248

Charities traditionally were immune from liability for acts of employees; however, this immunity has been ***abolished*** in almost all states.

E. RELEASE AND CONTRIBUTION AMONG JOINT TORTFEASORS

1. **Introduction** §1252

Joint tortfeasors are jointly and severally liable for harm they cause. This applies to persons ***acting in concert*** or those whose independent acts cause ***indivisible injury***.

2. **Judgment and Satisfaction** §1254

An ***unsatisfied*** judgment against one joint tortfeasor is no bar against others. A ***satisfied*** judgment against one prevents recovery for any additional amount against others.

3. **Releases** §1255

Traditionally, a release of one releases all; however, the rule is avoided in some states by contractual provisions reserving rights against others or by statute.

4. **Contribution** §1258

At common law, there was no contribution between joint tortfeasors; *i.e.,* one who pays may not recover from others. Modern statutes permit contribution among ***nonintentional*** joint tortfeasors.

a. **Impact of comparative negligence** §1260

A number of states retain joint and several liability, but contribution is allowed between joint tortfeasors on a comparative fault basis. Where D is liable on a market share basis, most versions of market share liability hold that liability is only several, not joint.

F. INDEMNITY §1262

A D who is ***secondarily*** liable for P's injury but is forced to pay a judgment is entitled to indemnification against the ***primary*** tortfeasor. Indemnity shifts the ***entire loss***. In contrast, contribution requires each party to pay a proportionate share. Indemnity is appropriate in vicarious liability (*e.g.,* respondeat superior) situations, and where one D is more culpable (*e.g.,* retailer held under strict liability is entitled to indemnity from negligent manufacturer). An originally negligent tortfeasor is entitled to be indemnified by the person who aggravates damages.

G. STATUTES OF LIMITATIONS §1268

The typical limitations period for negligence cases is two or three years. The period begins to run when P's claim ***accrues***—in some states when P suffers a legally cognizable injury, and in others upon D's act. Today, most states provide that the clock does not begin to run until P ***discovers*** his injury.

VII. STATUTORY CHANGES IN PERSONAL INJURY LAW

A. CHANGES TARGETING SPECIFIC KINDS OF TORT CLAIMS

1. Workers' Compensation §1272

Before the passage of workers' compensation laws, workers were generally barred from recovering for work-related injuries under tort principles because of the doctrines of contributory negligence and assumption of the risk, in addition to the fellow-servant doctrine. Today, well over 80% of workers are covered by comprehensive, mandatory workers' compensation laws that allow them to recover for all claims for personal injuries arising out of and in the course of their employment, ***regardless of fault***. These statutes provide the ***exclusive remedy*** for an employee against the employer. However, the worker can usually still sue a third party in tort.

2. "No-Fault" Auto Insurance §1285

No-fault insurance is designed to alleviate problems arising from a "fault" basis—*e.g.,* uncompensated victims, high premium rates, etc. It eliminates "fault" as the basis for liability in auto accident cases in about half of the states. The essential provisions of the various plans include: (i) insurance for all car owners is ***mandatory***; (ii) coverage includes ***all claims*** arising from the ***use or operation of any motor vehicle***; (iii) injured car occupants make claims against the policy covering the cars they were riding in; and (iv) damages are limited to ***economic losses*** (no pain and suffering).

a. Impact of "no-fault" plans §1292

The plans limit some of the traditional negligence actions. Also, there is automatic subrogation for payments by other insurers (no double recovery).

3. Medical Malpractice §1297

Rapidly escalating malpractice insurance rates have resulted in controlling legislation. These laws include provisions that shorten the applicable statute of limitations, limit pain and suffering awards, require periodic rather than lump sum payments if an award exceeds some minimum figure, limit legal fees, allow deduction of collateral sources from awards, and establish malpractice panels.

4. **Products Liability** §1305

Manufacturers and retailers have encouraged legislation to lessen their financial burden created by common law decisions. About half of the states have enacted more moderate laws regarding strict liability, the most common change being the enactment of ***statutes of repose***, which limit the time during which an action on a defective product may be brought. Also, Congress has enacted a limited no-fault compensation scheme for injuries caused by certain vaccines.

5. **Miscellaneous Statutory Changes to Personal Injury Law** §1313

A few states have a broad statutory ***duty to rescue*** others exposed to grave physical harm, and many states have enacted ***dram shop laws*** concerning liability of tavern owners and social hosts for actions of intoxicated people. Most states have laws compensating ***victims of violent crimes***. Many nations, including the United States, have joined the ***Warsaw Convention***, which provides victims of international air mishaps with strict liability recovery of a ***limited*** amount. Federal legislation provides limited no-fault compensation to ***nuclear accident victims***, miners afflicted with ***black lung disease***, and victims of the ***September 11th attacks***. As to certain risks (*e.g.*, cigarettes, airbags), federal law may expressly or impliedly ***preempt*** state law.

B. CHANGES AFFECTING TORT CLAIMS GENERALLY

1. **Motivation** §1329

In the mid-1980s, some perceived the tort system to be in a state of crisis, *e.g.,* excessive damages awards, disproportionate payments by joint tortfeasors, and high insurance premiums. In response, a large majority of the states have adopted legislation to reduce these problems.

2. **Joint and Several Liability** §1330

About 10 states have abolished this. A number of other states have limited damages based on a D's degree of fault. Other limitations are based on the nature of the tort (*e.g.,* no joint and several liability unless Ds acted with a common plan or the action involves toxic substances).

3. **Limitations on Damages** §1334

More than a quarter of the states have restricted noneconomic damages (*e.g.,* pain and suffering), and many states provide for periodic payments (instead of a lump sum) for future damages awards. Approximately half of the states now restrict punitive damages (*e.g.,* caps on awards, higher standards of proof).

4. **Collateral Sources Rule** §1344

Some states have limited the rule by permitting setoffs of funds obtained from collateral sources from the damages award.

5. **Miscellaneous** §1349

Other recent changes include regulation of attorneys' fees, required arbitration, and sanctions for frivolous claims.

VIII. DEFAMATION

A. IN GENERAL §1352

A ***prima facie case*** at common law required the publication to a third person of a statement that harmed P's reputation, thereby causing P to suffer damages. On First Amendment grounds, the Supreme Court has eroded the common law framework, thus prohibiting states from following their common law rules on strict liability and burdens of proof in certain actions for defamation. Any problem involving defamation may also involve the ***right to privacy*** or the ***wrongful causing of emotional distress***.

B. PUBLICATION TO A THIRD PARTY

1. Language Uttered Only to Plaintiff Not Actionable §1357

The defamation must be "published" (communicated) to someone other than P.

2. Any Third Person Sufficient §1358

Publication to ***any*** third person is sufficient regardless of the relationship between the parties.

3. Manner of Publication §1360

Publication can be by words, gesture, or conduct.

4. Publication Must Have Been Intentional or Negligent §1362

Publication must at least be negligent; D must have reason to foresee that a third party would overhear or see the statement. Cases are split on whether there is a publication when the defamed person is forced by circumstance to repeat the defamation (*e.g.,* a job applicant who tells a prospective employer his former employer's reason for firing him).

5. Who Is a Publisher?

a. Original publishers §1367

This includes anyone having any part in the original publication. Respondeat superior applies.

b. Republishers §1370

At common law, the republisher of a defamatory statement could be held liable equally with the original publisher (subject to certain exceptions for privileged communications).

(1) Slander or libel §1371

If the original defamation is libel (*e.g.,* written), republication is libel even if the republication is oral (*i.e.*, slander). If the original publication was oral (slander), a written republication is libel.

(2) Failure to remove defamation §1373

Failure to remove defamation posted on one's premises by someone else may be negligent republication by the owner (*e.g.,* failure to remove graffiti from men's room wall).

(3) Effect of republication on liability of original publisher §1374

The original defamer's liability is increased by whatever harm is caused by republication if republication was intended by the original defamer or reasonably foreseeable.

(4) **Legal duty to republish** §1375

One who is under a legal duty to publish has an absolute privilege to do so (*e.g.,* executor is privileged to probate a will containing defamatory remarks).

c. **Disseminators** §1376

Persons who circulate, sell, or otherwise deal with the physical embodiment of defamatory matter are liable ***only if*** they had reason to know of the defamatory nature of the material they handle.

(1) **Distinguish—printers** §1378

Independent contract printers have no duty to inspect a publication for libelous content.

(2) **Distinguish—computer bulletin boards** §1379

The majority view relieves computer bulletin board providers from liability.

C. HARM TO REPUTATION

1. **Defamatory Meaning** §1380

To be actionable, a statement must have the potential to injure P's reputation.

a. **Is the alleged meaning defamatory?** §1381

The statement must tend to lower P's reputation in the estimation of the community where published, or deter others from associating with her. Some states require that P be exposed to hatred, contempt, or ridicule.

(1) **Community standards control** §1383

Whichever standard is used, the statement must injure P in the eyes of a substantial and respectable minority of the community.

(2) **Defamatory effect** §1384

The focus is on how the words were reasonably understood by some third person to whom the statement was published, rather than on what the speaker meant. If the statement was in a foreign language which the third party did not understand, the statement cannot be defamatory.

(3) **"Libel-proof plaintiffs"** §1387

At common law, some courts dismiss cases brought by persons with reputations so bad that a false statement could not really hurt them. This rule is not required by the First Amendment.

b. **Can the words carry the suggested meaning?** §1389

In determining the meaning attached to a statement, courts look at the fair and natural meaning the statement will be given by reasonable persons of ordinary intelligence. Publications are generally read as a whole in light of the context in which the statement appears.

(1) **Defamation by implication and insinuation** §1393

The form of language used by D is not controlling, as long as third

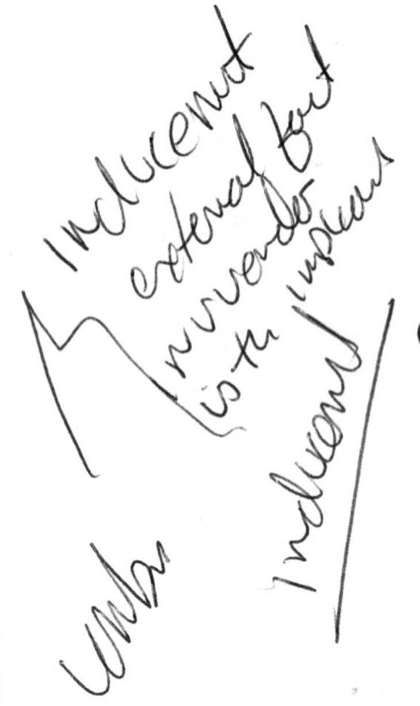

persons could ***reasonably*** interpret it as defamatory to P (*e.g.,* article stating that protestor died of heart attack while doctor he was protesting against was in nearby building could be taken to mean that doctor knew of the protestor's problem and chose not to help him).

(2) Incomplete defamation §1395

If the defamatory meaning arises only when the words are combined with extrinsic facts (*e.g.,* report that P had twins is defamatory when combined with extrinsic fact she had been married only one month), P must allege and prove the extrinsic facts (the ***"inducement"***), that these facts were known to a third person who heard the statement, and that the implication (***"innuendo"***) of the statement, when combined with those facts, is defamatory.

2. "Of and Concerning" P §1396

Some third person must have reasonably interpreted the statement to refer to P.

a. Defamed person unnamed—colloquium §1397

Where a publication is clearly defamatory of somebody, yet on its face does not refer to P, P must establish the ***colloquium***; *i.e.,* that some persons reasonably interpreted it as applying to P.

b. Who may be defamed—in general §1400

Any living person, corporation, partnership, or other legally recognized entity may be defamed. Fraternities and unincorporated associations, on the other hand, do not possess sufficient status as an entity to sue for defamation. Similarly, no action will lie for defamation of a dead person. However, most states following the usual tort rule provide for survival of a claim when P dies after being defamed but before suit or trial.

c. Individual claims arising from group defamations §1405

Most states hold that no member of a defamed group may bring an action unless the group is so small that the statement may reasonably be interpreted as applying to each member. However, some courts hold that group size is not the sole consideration, and consider other factors that affect the intensity of suspicion cast upon the group. Note that if a group is small enough, a charge against "some" may be a charge against all.

3. Strict Liability §1408

Although "publication" requires intent or negligence, "harm to reputation" at common law is based on strict liability; *e.g.,* it is irrelevant whether D anticipated that some readers would understand an article as it is now claimed they did. However, constitutional law restricts strict liability (*see infra*, §§1503 *et seq*.).

D. FALSE FACTS

1. **Falsity** §1409

At common law, the burden was on D to prove the statement was true. D was strictly liable for defamatory statements, regardless of D's knowledge of the statement's falsity. However, some states have moved to a negligence standard, and stricter standards apply where the First Amendment is involved (*e.g.*, public figures, matters of public concern). The general view is that truth of the defamatory matter is a ***complete*** defense.

2. **P's Burden to Prove Falsity** §1414

At least where the statement involves a ***matter of public concern,*** the First Amendment requires P to bear the burden of proving the statement is false.

3. **Statement Cannot Be False Unless it Contains Assertions of Fact** §1416

To meet the burden of proving falsity, P must show that the alleged defamation contained statements of fact or implied unstated facts that were false.

   a. **No automatic protection for "opinion"** §1417

   An opinion may be defamatory if it can be reasonably interpreted by the recipient as being based on underlying defamatory facts.

   b. **Specificity of language** §1421

   The more specific the language, the more likely it is to be reasonably interpreted as either a statement of fact or a statement based on underlying facts.

E. CAUSATION §1422

Same as for negligence, except recovery of special damages is limited to ***foreseeable*** damages.

F. DAMAGES AND OTHER REMEDIES §1423

The scope of damages under common law depends on the ***form*** of the publication—libel or slander—as well as on the ***motives*** with which it was uttered. Also, there may be constitutional limitations for Ds protected by the First Amendment.

1. **"Libel" and "Slander" Distinguished**

   a. **"Libel"** §1424

   Libel is a defamation reduced to some ***permanent physical embodiment***—usually written or printed (representation to the eye).

   b. **"Slander"** §1425

   Slander is ***oral*** defamation—less permanent (representation to the ear).

   c. **Borderline cases** §1426

   In borderline cases consider the permanence of the form, area of dissemination, and deliberate or premeditated character of the publication.

      (1) **Broadcasting** §1427

      Under the newer view, all radio and TV publications are libel, but state statutes are split.

2. **Damages Rule for Slander** §1429

Slander is not actionable without a showing of ***special damages***, unless deemed "actionable per se."

a. **Compensatory damages recoverable**

(1) **"Special damages"** §1430

Special damages are pecuniary damages actually suffered and not presumed by law. Once some special damages are proved, P may recover general damages.

(2) **"General damages"** §1431

General damages compensate for harm to P's reputation. Even if not provable, their existence can be presumed based on the likely effect of the defamation considering the number of persons likely to hear it, the nature of the charge, and the identity of the speaker and P.

(3) **Emotional damages** §1433

Emotional damages are allowed in many states, but others limit recovery for emotional damages if P also qualifies for presumed damages.

b. **Slander per se—special damages not required** §1434

Proof of special damages is ***not*** required in four situations:

(1) Where D charges that P committed a serious, ***morally reprehensible crime***, or that P has been ***incarcerated*** for such a crime;

(2) Where D imputes to P a presently existing ***loathsome communicable disease*** (*e.g.,* venereal disease or leprosy);

(3) Where D imputes to P conduct, associations, or characteristics ***incompatible with proper performance of P's business, trade, office, or profession***; and

(4) Where D imputes ***unchastity to a female P*** (some states extend this to include males and to allegations of homosexuality).

3. **Damages Rule for Libel** §1443

Where the statement is defamatory on its face, in most jurisdictions special damages need ***not*** be shown; general damages are ***presumed***.

a. **Libel per quod** §1444

Where the matter is innocent on its face, the courts are split:

(1) Special damages need ***not*** be shown; or

(2) Damages are presumed only where the libel falls into one of the "slander per se" categories.

4. **Punitive Damages** §1445

Most states allow punitive damages if the defamation can be shown to have been made with common law malice, such as hatred, ill will, or spite.

a. **Federal constitutional restrictions** §1446

The First Amendment prohibits punitive damages for defamations involving ***matters of public concern***, where the falsity is attributable only to ***negligence***. The U.S. Supreme Court has not ruled on whether the First Amendment provides special protection against punitive damages in libel cases where a public figure has proved actual malice (state courts have rejected this claim). However, the Court has held that where the defamation involved a confidential report to a few people, it does not involve a matter of public concern and punitive damages are recoverable even for negligent defamations.

b. **State constitutional restrictions** §1448

Some states disallow punitive damages under state constitutional law.

5. **Retraction** §1449

Several states by statute preclude recovery of general damages from news media if a retraction is promptly published.

6. **Injunctions** §1450

Courts traditionally have refused to enjoin defamatory speech because of First Amendment concerns.

G. DEFENSES

1. **Consent** §1451

Consent is a complete defense.

2. **Truth** §1452

Truth is generally a complete defense. Also, most states impose upon P the burden of proving falsity in almost all cases.

3. **Common Law Absolute Privileges** §1453

Absolute privileges are complete defenses regardless of malice or abuse:

a. **Participation in the processes of government**

(1) **Legislative privilege** §1454

Federal and state legislative members are constitutionally privileged to utter defamations while on the floor or in committee sessions, etc. There is ***no*** relevancy requirement.

(2) **Judicial privilege** §1456

Any participant in a judicial proceeding is privileged as to matter ***relevant*** to the issue at hand. Judicial proceedings include hearings, depositions, etc. Some authority extends the privilege to communications preliminary to a proposed judicial proceeding. The privilege also includes administrative hearings.

(3) **Executive privilege** §1460

Top-rank, policymaking executive officers are privileged if the matter is ***relevant*** to performance of official duties. Some states include lesser-ranking officials.

b. **Domestic privilege** §1461

Either spouse is privileged to utter defamations of third parties to the other spouse.

4. **Common Law Conditional or Qualified Privileges**

a. **Recognized conditional privileges**

(1) **Inferior legislative bodies and inferior executive and administrative officers** §1463

The modern view gives such bodies and officials absolute privilege, but some states retain conditional privilege.

(2) **Protection of private interests** §1464

Requirements for the privilege are:

(a) A reasonable belief that an ***important interest is threatened*** (interest can be own interest, interest of third person, or interest of person to whom statement is published);

(b) The statement is ***reasonably relevant*** to the interest protected;

(c) A reasonable belief that the ***person to whom the statement is published can protect the interest***; and

(d) There must be ***some relationship*** between the publisher and the person to whom the statement is published. If no relationship, then it must be in response to a request.

(3) **Protection of public interest** §1473

A statement is privileged if D reasonably believes utterance is necessary to protect a public interest and the person to whom it is published is empowered to protect the interest (*e.g.,* statement to police).

b. **Conditional privilege may be lost through bad faith or abuse** §1475

There is ***no privilege*** where: (i) the statement is motivated solely by malice and intent to injure P, (ii) there is excessive publication (*i.e.,* beyond that necessary to accomplish purpose of privilege), or (iii) there is a lack of honest belief in the statement's truth (minority requires reasonable belief as well if assertions are made in credit standing cases; some courts also hold that a speaker seeking to protect the public interest must reasonably believe the statement).

5. **Fair Comment Privilege** §1483

Before constitutional case development, the majority protected critics of matters of public interest if their criticism was based on true facts and expressed honestly believed opinion. The minority extended the privilege even if facts were incorrectly stated—which played a role in the constitutional developments discussed *infra.*

6. **Record Libel Privilege** §1486

Reports of judicial, legislative, or executive proceedings are privileged if ***fair and accurate***.

a. **Nonofficial proceedings** §1487

Some courts extend the privilege to reports of nongovernmental public meetings in which there is a general interest (*e.g.,* political or medical conventions).

b. **Official but nonpublic documents** §1488

Some courts extend the privilege to nonpublic official documents (*e.g.,* government files), but at least one court has refused to extend it to reports of foreign governments.

c. **How privilege is lost** §1490

The privilege is lost when D's report is inaccurate. D need not believe that the statement was truthful (*e.g.,* accurate report of an official's lies is privileged).

7. **Federal Preemptive Privileges** §1493

Radio and TV stations are ***not*** liable for defamation in a campaign speech. Also, labor laws are held to preempt state defamation laws as to defamatory statements published during labor disputes.

8. **Defenses of Republishers** §1498

Each republisher must establish his own defense.

a. **Exception—intermediary** §1499

Those under a duty to dispatch messages (*e.g.,* telegraph company) are privileged to transmit defamations whether or not they believe them.

b. **Media reliance on usually reliable source** §1500

Most states have granted newspapers a conditional privilege to reprint wire service stories and syndicated features.

c. **Media reports of statements made by others** §1501

Some courts have granted the media a constitutional privilege called "neutral reportage" to permit the media to cover a story in which important persons or groups accuse others of improprieties.

9. **SLAPP Suits** §1502

Some states have adopted laws requiring courts to dismiss on motion libel complaints in cases involving public issues unless the court concludes that there is a probability that P will prevail.

H. CONSTITUTIONAL PRIVILEGES

1. **In General** §1503

Under the First Amendment, in certain instances the interest in freedom of expression is held to ***outweigh*** the interest in protecting reputation, and hence the defamation is ***privileged***. The constitutional protection available in defamation cases depends on the status of P (*i.e.,* whether P is a: (i) public official, (ii) public figure, or (iii) private person).

2. **Public Ps** §1507

The highest level of protection has been granted for statements concerning public officials or public figures.

a. **"Public officials"** §1508

Public officials are persons who have substantial responsibility over government affairs.

b. **"Public figures"** §1513

A person who is not a public official may be deemed a public figure: (i) if she has achieved such pervasive fame or notoriety that she becomes a public figure for ***all purposes*** and contexts; or (ii) if she voluntarily enters or is drawn into a particular public controversy, and thereby becomes a public figure ***for that limited range of issues***.

(1) Limited purpose public figures §1514

Courts tend to use three steps in identifying "limited purpose" public figures: (i) isolating the particular public controversy; (ii) deciding if P has voluntarily assumed a central role in that controversy; and (iii) finding the alleged defamation germane to P's participation in the controversy. Not every person who seeks government aid or draws attention by some voluntary behavior becomes a "public" P (*e.g.,* scientist applying for federal grant does not become a public figure by applying for the grant).

(a) Involuntary public figures §1516

The Supreme Court has indicated that it might be possible for people to become public figures through no purposeful action of their own, but considers such instances to be exceedingly rare.

c. Constitutional standard in cases involving public Ps §1517

Ps who are public officials or public figures must prove that the false defamatory statement was published with ***actual malice***; *i.e.,* ***knowledge of falsity*** or ***reckless disregard for the truth***.

(1) What constitutes "knowing or reckless falsity" §1518

P must show that D was ***subjectively aware*** that the statement was false, or that he was ***subjectively reckless*** in making the statement.

(a) Motive to harm insufficient §1519

It is not enough that D is shown to have acted with spite, hatred, ill will, or intent to injure P.

(b) Negligence insufficient §1520

"Reckless" conduct is not measured by a reasonable person standard. There must be a showing that D ***in fact entertained serious doubts*** as to the truthfulness of the publication.

(2) Proving "knowing or reckless falsity"

(a) Burden of proof §1523

P must prove actual malice with ***convincing clarity*** (*e.g.,* show that D relied on an extremely questionable source, but mere failure to investigate or reporting on a story known to be incomplete might not be sufficient).

(b) Discovery §1528

To prove D's state of mind, P may ask D about it, even if D is a reporter or editor; *i.e.,* the First Amendment does not protect a reporter or editor from inquiries about his motives for reporting, belief in the accuracy of his sources, etc.

d. **Damages** §1530

When P establishes "knowing or reckless falsity" against a media D, she may recover any damages permitted under state law.

3. **Private Ps** §1531

A P who is neither a public official nor a public figure is a private person. A lower constitutional standard applies in such cases.

a. **Constitutional limitation** §1532

Liability without fault cannot be imposed, at least where a matter of public concern is involved. Where the statement is such that substantial danger to reputation would be apparent to a reasonably prudent editor or broadcaster, P must prove either knowledge of falsity, recklessness as to truth, or negligence as to falsity.

(1) **Caveat—matters of private concern** §1534

If the matter is of purely private concern, a private P may recover presumed and punitive damages without proving actual malice.

b. **Applicable standard of liability** §1535

The Supreme Court has left it to the states to determine standards for liability to private Ps (in matters of public concern), as long as they do not apply strict liability. Almost all states have set the standard for liability at the level of negligence. A few states require knowledge of falsity or reckless disregard for the truth.

c. **Burden of proving falsity** §1539

A private P has the burden of proving falsity, at least where the speech is of public concern.

d. **Damages** §1540

If D was negligent in ascertaining or reporting the truth (but had neither actual knowledge of falsity nor reckless disregard for the truth), a private P can recover damages, which are limited to ***actual injury***. Actual injury is not limited to out-of-pocket losses. If the defamation was deliberate or reckless, P is entitled to whatever recovery is permitted under state law.

IX. WRONGFUL INVASION OF PRIVACY

A. INTRUSIONS INTO P'S PRIVATE LIFE OR AFFAIRS

1. **Prima Facie Case** §1544

P must prove an intentional or negligent and highly offensive intrusion by D into P's private life, and causation.

2. **Protected Area of Seclusion** §1545

There are areas of P's life that P can ***reasonably*** expect will not be intruded upon.

a. **Distinguish—no privacy for corporations** §1547

Corporations do not have traits of a highly personal and sensitive nature and so cannot be Ps in such cases.

3. **Types of Intrusion** §1548

This may include ***any*** behavior that is intrusive including:

a. ***Intrusion onto P's property***; and

b. ***Nonphysical intrusions*** (*e.g.,* secretly photographing tanning salon patrons while they are nude).

4. **Intrusion Must Be Highly Offensive** §1552

The conduct must be highly offensive to a reasonable person.

5. **Intent** §1553

The conduct must be ***intentional***, although D need not have intended it to offend P.

6. **No Publication Necessary** §1556

The interest protected is P's "right to be let alone" and not P's interest in not having the information disseminated.

7. **Causation** §1557

D's conduct must have been the cause in fact and the proximate cause of the invasion of P's interest and the ensuing damage.

8. **Defense—Consent** §1558

There is no cause of action if the intrusion is authorized or permitted unless the intrusion falls outside P's actual or implied consent.

9. **Damages** §1560

Pure emotional distress or mental anguish ***are*** sufficient damages; P need not prove special damages.

10. **Constitutional Protection** §1561

State law may not impose liability on a third party who uses the fruits of proscribed intrusion and publishes true statements of public interest.

B. PUBLIC DISCLOSURE OF PRIVATE FACTS

1. **Prima Facie Case** §1562

P must show a highly offensive public disclosure by D of private facts about P, no legitimate public interest, fault in making the disclosure, and causation.

2. **What Are "Private Facts"?** §1563

The details must be private facts; they cannot appear as a matter of public record or occur in public.

3. **Publication Must Be Highly Offensive** §1568

The details must be highly offensive to reasonable person (*e.g.,* a newspaper article on P's recent, private sex change operation).

4. **Must Be a "Public" Disclosure** §1569

Disclosure must be to the public at large or to enough individuals that it is likely to reach the general public.

5. **No Public Interest ("Newsworthiness")** §1570

Even if D publicizes private facts about P, the publication is ***privileged*** if the facts are "newsworthy." This includes any matter as to which there is a legitimate public interest. This may be very broad when concerning voluntary public figures and even involuntary public figures.

6. **Fault** §1577
D must have been at fault for the action that gave rise to the highly offensive disclosure.

7. **Causation** §1578
Actual and proximate causation are required.

8. **Defenses**

   a. **Truth is no defense** §1579
   The gist of the tort is embarrassment; truth is irrelevant.

   b. **Consent** §1580
   Consent is a complete defense, but consent may be withdrawn before publication. Note that if P voluntarily divulged facts to D, she will be barred from bringing suit; failure to "keep secrets" is not a tort.

   c. **Constitutional privilege for media** §1584
   There is an ***absolute privilege*** regarding matters taken from official court records that are accurately stated. If the matter was lawfully obtained from the government, is truthful, and prohibition is not necessary to further a state interest of the highest order, D is privileged to publish information (*e.g.,* publication of deceased rape victim's name that was obtained through inadvertent release by the police).

9. **Damages** §1587
Same as for intrusions, *supra*.

10. **Privacy Action Rejected** §1588
A few states do not recognize this action where true facts are involved.

C. APPROPRIATION OF P'S NAME OR LIKENESS

1. **Prima Facie Case** §1590
This involves the unauthorized use of P's name or likeness for advertising or for other commercial purpose, and causation. Some courts extend protection to items beyond name or likeness (*e.g.,* a robot that acted too much like TV quiz show assistant Vanna White).

2. **Right of Publicity vs. Right of Privacy** §1595
If P is a celebrity, she is entitled to damages not so much for invasion of privacy but for interference with her right of publicity.

3. **Causation** §1597
Actual and proximate causation are required.

4. **Defense—Newsworthiness** §1598
Where P is a public figure or currently newsworthy, publication is not actionable where D does not use the publication for commercial gain. However, the media has no right to film or broadcast an entire commercial performance (interference with right of publicity).

5. **Damages** §1601
For ***celebrity*** Ps, P may recover the reasonable value of the use of P's name or likeness. For ***private*** Ps, emotional harm is likely to be the main element.

D. **PUBLICITY PLACING P IN A "FALSE LIGHT"**

1. **Prima Facie Case** §1602
P must show a publication by D that places P in a false light in the public eye, knowing or reckless falsity if a newsworthy matter, and causation.

2. **Publication** §1604
Dissemination to a reasonable number of third persons is required.

3. **Falsity Required** §1605
The false light in which P is placed must be ***highly offensive*** to a reasonable person.

4. **Distinguish—Defamation** §1606
If the false light would affect P's community reputation, a defamation action may also lie.

5. **Fault** §1607
Newsworthy statements that put P in a false light are not actionable unless the "knowing or reckless falsity" standard is met.

6. **Causation** §1610
Actual and proximate causation are required.

7. **Damages** §1611
P may recover damages to reputation, emotional distress, and pecuniary damages.

E. **CLAIMS INVOLVING PRIVACY OF THIRD PERSONS**

1. **Publications Regarding Living Persons** §1612
P cannot recover for an invasion of privacy based on publicity concerning ***another*** living person.

2. **Publications Concerning a Dead Person** §1613
There is no right of recovery by survivors (invasion of their interests) or by the decedent. Note that if the invasion occurred during the decedent's ***lifetime***, then her estate may be able to sue depending upon the survival statute in effect.

   a. **Celebrity's right of publicity** §1617
   A celebrity's right to exploit her name must be exercised during the person's lifetime.

F. **RELATED TORTS** §1619
Torts related to invasion of privacy include ***defamation*** and ***wrongful infliction of emotional distress***.

1. **Breach of Confidential Relationship** §1620
A preexisting relationship may be relied on by courts instead of using a privacy approach (*e.g.,* doctor breaches patient's confidence).

2. **Limitation on Causes of Action Under Uniform Act** §1621

The Uniform Single Publication Act limits recovery to one single cause of action for damages arising from a single publication (whether defamation or privacy claim).

X. OTHER TORTS

A. MISREPRESENTATION

1. **Intentional Misrepresentation ("Fraudulent Misrepresentation" or "Deceit")** §1623

The ***prima facie case*** requires a false, material representation of fact, known to be false, made with intent to induce P's reliance, with justifiable reliance to P's damage.

a. **Misrepresentation by D**

(1) **Affirmative misrepresentation** §1624

A false, material representation of past or present ***fact*** is required.

(a) **"Material" misrepresentation** §1625

"Material" means a representation that would influence a reasonable person in P's position, as well as any representation that D knew this specific P considered important.

(b) **"Fact"** §1626

A ***present state of mind or intention*** is a fact (however, failure to perform a promise does not by itself prove that the promisor did not intend to perform when she made the promise).

(c) **"Representation"** §1628

The representation may be oral, written, or by conduct (*e.g.*, turning back mileage indicator).

(2) **Fraudulent concealment of facts** §1629

This is sufficient misrepresentation except where the transaction is marked "as is" or where P is charged with knowledge of concealed facts.

(3) **Failure to disclose facts** §1630

This is ***not*** a misrepresentation, ***except***:

(a) **Fiduciary relationship** §1632

Where P and D are in a fiduciary relationship.

(b) **Half-truths** §1633

Where D knowingly made an incomplete, ambiguous, or half-true statement.

(c) **New information** §1634

Where D later finds a prior statement to be false and knows P is relying on the earlier statement.

(d) **Reliance** §1635

If D knowingly makes a false statement with no intent to induce reliance but later finds out P is about to act on it.

(e) **Sale of property (modern trend)** §1636

Where the seller fails to disclose material facts unknown and not readily accessible to the buyer (*e.g.,* house is infested by termites).

b. **Scienter** §1637

Scienter refers to D's knowledge of the falsity, or knowledge that she had an insufficient basis for determining the truth of the representation. The enormity of an unreasonable belief may allow a jury to infer lack of honest belief. Most courts require Ps to prove fraud by clear and convincing evidence.

c. **Intent to induce reliance** §1640

Generally, D must have intended to induce reliance of P or a class of persons to which P belongs. However, there is no need to show intent to induce P's particular reliance where there is "continuous deception" (*e.g.,* mislabeling of product).

d. **Causation** §1642

The misrepresentation must play a substantial part in inducing P to act as he did (*i.e.,* actual reliance).

e. **Justifiable reliance by P**

(1) **Reliance must be foreseeable** §1643

P's reliance must be ***intended*** by D ***or reasonably foreseeable***.

(2) **Whether reliance is "justified" depends on type of representation**

(a) **Representations of fact** §1645

Reliance on material misrepresentations of ***fact*** is always justified except where obviously false; P is under ***no duty to investigate***.

(b) **Representations of opinion** §1647

Reliance on misrepresentations of opinion, value, or quality is ***not*** justified ***except*** where: (i) ***D has superior knowledge*** not available to P; (ii) ***D owes a fiduciary duty*** to P; (iii) ***D has secured P's confidence*** by reason of special relationship or affiliation; or (iv) ***D is apparently a disinterested third party*** offering advice on the transaction P is contemplating with another without disclosing that D has a financial interest in the deal.

(c) **Representations of law** §1652

P's reliance on misrepresentations of ***law*** is justified when the representation is in the nature of a fact rather than opinion.

f. **Damages** §1654

Actual damages must be shown.

2. **Negligent Misrepresentation** §1655

The ***prima facie case*** requires negligent misrepresentation by D toward a particular group and P's justifiable reliance to his damage.

a. **Misrepresentation—made in business or professional capacity** §1656

This is the same as in intentional misrepresentation but must normally be made by one in the ***business of supplying information*** for others in business transactions. Where volunteered by a nonprofessional or in a noncommercial setting, liability results only if the representation is not honestly made.

b. **Negligence toward particular P** §1659

If D provides information with intent that P rely on it in a business transaction or knows that such reliance is likely, D is under a duty to exercise reasonable care to discover the truth or falsity of representations.

(1) **To whom duty owed** §1660

D must have contemplated the reliance of a particular P or group of persons to which P belongs. It is sufficient if D knew the recipient would communicate to a specific P or group.

(2) **Professional liability** §1663

Although professionals are always liable to clients for negligently prepared reports and documents, there is disagreement as to how far liability may be extended to third parties.

(a) **Traditional view** §1664

Under the traditional view, an accountant was not liable to third parties for negligently prepared statements unless there was essentially privity between the accountant and the third party.

(b) **Modern views** §1665

Three different approaches have emerged:

1) **New York ("linkage") view** §1666

Under the New York view, for an accountant (D) to be liable to a noncontractual party (P), D must be aware that a known party intended to rely on the financial statement, and some conduct must link D to P in a way suggesting the accountant's willingness to incur a duty to the creditor.

2) **California ("specific foreseeability") view** §1667

Under the California view, an accountant is liable if she knows that a specific third party plans to rely on the statement for a transaction whose nature and extent are known to the accountant.

3) **New Jersey ("general foreseeability") view** §1668

A few states follow the New Jersey view and hold that an accountant may be liable if the third party (P) belongs to a class who could generally be foreseen to receive and rely on the statement.

(c) **Distinguish—liability based on statute** §1669

Apart from common law negligence, liability to third persons may be based on D's violation of statutory duties to provide accurate information. Such duties run to the general public, so it is not necessary to show D's knowledge that a particular P would rely.

c. **Cause in fact (actual reliance)**
This is the same as in negligence.

d. **Justifiable reliance** §1670
This is the same as in intentional misrepresentation, except unreasonable failure to investigate may be contributory negligence.

e. **Proximate cause**
This is the same as in negligence.

f. **Damages**
See infra.

3. **Misrepresentation Predicated on Strict Liability ("Innocent Misrepresentation")** §1671
Some courts impose strict liability in connection with the sale of land or chattels, even if the representation was "innocent." Liability is analogous to breach of warranty and unjust enrichment situations. There must be a false representation made with intent to induce P's reliance in a business transaction, and P must justifiably rely thereon to her financial detriment and to D's gain.

4. **Defenses**

a. **Contributory negligence** §1675
This is a defense to ***negligent*** misrepresentation but not to intentional or strict liability misrepresentation.

b. **Assumption of risk** §1676
This is a defense to ***strict liability*** and ***negligent*** misrepresentation.

c. **Exculpatory contracts** §1677
Such contracts for intentional conduct are ***void*** in most states.

5. **Measure of Damages**

a. **Benefit-of-bargain rule (majority)** §1679
P recovers the value of the property as contracted for, less the actual value received.

b. **Emotional distress** §1682
Some states allow damages for emotional distress if it is a natural and proximate consequence of the misrepresentation.

c. **Punitive damages** §1683
These may be awarded for intentional misrepresentations made with malice (intent to harm).

B. INJURIOUS FALSEHOOD

1. **Prima Facie Case** §1684
P must prove a false statement by D disparaging P's business, property, etc., intentionally made to others about P causing P injury, and special damages.

2. **False Statement** §1685
P must prove D published a harmful statement and that the statement was false.

3. **Publication to Third Persons** §1686
This is the same as for defamation. It may be oral or written.

4. **Statement Disparaging P's Business, Property, Etc.** §1688
The statement must be reasonably likely to discourage others from dealing with P or must otherwise interfere with P's relations with others to P's disadvantage.

   a. **Statements denying P's ownership ("slander of title")** §1689
   A statement casting doubt on title is sufficient.

   b. **Statements denying quality of P's property ("trade libel")** §1690
   A statement attacking the quality of property is sufficient.

   c. **Statements derogatory of P's business in general ("trade libel")** §1691
   Statements derogatory of P's business without reflecting on title or quality of property (*e.g.,* "service in P's restaurant is poor") are sufficient.

   d. **Statements interfering with nonbusiness relations** §1692
   Statements that do not affect any commercial enterprise may still be actionable.

   e. **Statement need not be defamatory** §1693
   The statement need not be defamatory as long as it is false. But not every imputation against a business or its product implies ***personal*** inefficiency in P.

5. **Intent** §1695
D must intend to cast doubt on P's property or financial interests. Motive is irrelevant, and under the modern view scienter is required.

6. **Causation and Damages** §1699
Actual and proximate causation are required. Actual ("special") damages must be shown.

   a. **Slander of title** §1700
   P can recover lost profits from a contemplated sale and expenses of legal proceedings to remove the cloud on title.

   b. **Trade libel** §1701
   Loss of profit from specific customers is recoverable. If not provable, courts may permit P to show a general decline in business. Consequential and parasitic damages (*e.g.,* for mental distress) are ***not*** recoverable.

7. **Defenses**

   a. **Consent** §1702
   Consent is a defense.

   b. **Truth** §1703
   The prima facie case requires falsity; thus, it is not necessary to consider truth as a defense.

c. **Privilege** §1704

The same privileges to defamation are recognized as privileges to disparagement (*see supra,* §§1453 *et seq.*).

(1) **Judicial proceedings** §1705

The recording of a "lis pendens" is absolutely privileged.

(2) **Protection of private interests** §1706

There is a conditional privilege to protect one's own interests or those of another.

(a) **Competitors** §1707

D is privileged to make general claims about her own product but cannot make specific false claims about P's product or business.

(b) **Noncompetitors** §1708

D is protected if she honestly believed the truth of the statement in a situation covered by defamation privileges.

C. INTERFERENCE WITH ECONOMIC RELATIONS

1. **Interference with Contract—Prima Facie Case** §1711

P must prove words or action by D intentionally undertaken to interfere with existing contract of P, causing P injury, and special damages.

a. **Nature of contract** §1712

This action applies to any type of contract (except contracts to marry).

(1) **Illegal contracts** §1713

Contracts that are illegal or contrary to public policy do not qualify for protection.

(2) **Unenforceable contracts** §1714

Unenforceable contracts (*e.g.,* contracts that run afoul of the Statute of Frauds) can be the subject of this tort. A few courts are contra.

(3) **Contracts terminable at will** §1715

These can be the subject of this tort under the general view. However, issues of damages and privilege may be affected.

b. **D's interference** §1716

The interference must be active.

(1) **Breach not required** §1717

Breach is ***not*** required; it is sufficient if performance is made more difficult.

(2) **Collective action** §1718

Concerted action by a group (*e.g.,* boycott) may give rise to liability, subject to a possible privilege.

(3) **Whether D may be a party** §1719

Generally, if D is a party to the contract, the action will not lie. But an officer who induces his corporation to breach a contract may be liable.

(a) **Minority allows action for tortious breach of contract** §1721
A few states permit a party to a contract to sue the other party in tort for a breach motivated by an interest other than the contract relationship (*e.g.,* to help D acquire a competitive benefit over P in some other matter). Also, some states recognize a tort action for breach of the implied covenant of good faith and fair dealing where there is a special relationship between the contracting parties.

(b) **Majority allows suit for wrongful discharge** §1723
The majority view is that a tort action lies for discharging P for an improper reason (*e.g.,* refusal to participate in an illegal price-fixing scheme) even though the hiring was at will.

c. **Intent** §1724
D must be aware of the contract and ***intend to cause interference*** therewith. The cases have refused to impose liability for mere negligent interference with contractual relationships.

(1) **Master-servant cases** §1725
A few courts permit recovery by an employer for ***negligent*** injury to an employee.

d. **Causation and damages** §1726
Actual and proximate cause are required. The modern view seems to allow P to recover for actual and consequential damages, harm to reputation, mental suffering, and punitive damages.

(1) **Offset recovery for breach of contract** §1728
Any recovery against the breaching party must be offset against damages recoverable from D who induced the breach.

e. **Defenses—privilege** §1729
To be privileged, D must use ***reasonable means and*** have a ***justifiable purpose***.

(1) **Ends must be valid**

(a) **Furtherance of nonpersonal interests** §1731
If D has no financial interest, she is privileged if predominantly acting for a social good or to protect a third person's interest.

(b) **Furtherance of D's own financial interest** §1733
If D has a financial interest, she may further her own interests only if seeking to protect ***existing*** economic interests rather than a prospective advantage.

1) **Exception** §1736
A competitor is privileged to induce third persons to end contracts ***terminable at will***.

(2) **Means must be proper** §1737

D is limited to honest persuasion—no lies or violence. Unreasonable and coercive economic persuasion defeats the privilege. Improper means may support liability for defamation or injurious falsehood, as well as wrongful interference with contractual relations.

(3) **Burden of proof** §1740

Most courts require D to show proper justification and P to show D's conduct was wrongful by showing more than the interference itself.

2. **Intentional Interference with Prospective Economic Advantage** §1741

The right to pursue business without unjustifiable interference is protected.

a. **Prima facie case** §1742

This is the same as interference with contract except ***no existing contract*** need be shown.

(1) **D's act** §1743

The interfering act consists of: (i) inducing a third party not to enter into a prospective relationship with P, or (ii) preventing P from acquiring the prospective relationship.

b. **Privilege** §1745

D is privileged to use any ***bona fide competitive means*** to solicit customers.

c. **Distinguish—interference with noncommercial expectancies (*e.g.,* prospective gifts)** §1748

The modern trend allows recovery where there is a strong probability that the expectancy would have been realized (*e.g.,* fraudulently inducing testator to disinherit).

3. **Negligent Interference with Prospective Economic Advantage** §1751

A ***prima facie case*** consists of the same elements as in a negligence case. ***Duty*** is the critical factor because P's interest in protection from economic harm has been considered too remote to impose a duty of due care.

a. **Modern trend** §1754

Some courts impose a duty of care when D can ***reasonably foresee*** harm to a ***specific*** P.

(1) **Attorney liability** §1755

Most courts hold that attorneys may owe duties of due care to persons other than their clients in a negotiated deal.

(2) **Limitation** §1756

A duty of due care is imposed ***only*** where a D knows his conduct will affect a pinpointed P.

b. **Other elements** §1757

Once duty is found, the other elements are analyzed as in regular negligence cases.

D. UNJUSTIFIABLE LITIGATION

1. Malicious Prosecution—Prima Facie Case §1759

P must prove initiation of criminal proceedings against P that terminated in P's favor and for which there was no probable cause and an improper purpose, all to P's damage.

a. Instigation of proceedings by D §1761

Proceedings may be begun by a charge to police that causes issuance of a warrant or indictment; it is sufficient if D caused a third person to institute malicious prosecution. However, merely providing full and truthful information to a public officer is ***not*** instigation of proceedings.

b. Proceedings terminated favorably to P §1764

There must be a decisive termination in P's favor (*e.g.,* P's acquittal after trial, case is dismissed for lack of evidence).

c. Lack of probable cause §1766

There must be a lack of honest or reasonable belief in the truth of the charge. An attorney is not liable if a reasonable attorney would have brought the claim.

(1) Lack of probable cause ***cannot be inferred from an improper purpose***; it must be proved independently.

(2) An ***indictment or commitment by a magistrate is prima facie evidence*** of probable cause.

(3) A ***conviction is usually conclusive evidence*** of probable cause ***even if*** overturned on appeal.

(4) ***Reliance on advice of counsel conclusively establishes*** probable cause if there was ***full disclosure*** of facts.

d. Improper purpose §1773

D must have acted for some purpose other than bringing a guilty person to justice. An improper purpose may be inferred from a lack of probable cause.

e. Causation and damages §1775

P can recover for the cost of defending the criminal suit, embarrassment, etc., and punitive damages.

f. Defenses §1776

Valid defenses include guilt of P. There is an absolute privilege for judges, prosecutors, and other law enforcement officers.

2. Malicious Institution of Civil Proceedings §1778

This action requires the same elements as malicious prosecution but has been extended to civil actions in many states. (Many courts reject this action to encourage resort to courts.)

a. Nature of proceedings §1779

This tort extends to any noncriminal proceeding (recordation of lis pendens suffices even though privileged regarding slander of title).

b. **Effect of prior verdict** §1783

A prior verdict in favor of P is res judicata.

c. **Causation and damages** §1785

The same rules apply as when the unfounded case was a criminal prosecution. A minority view is that P must show special damages to person or property. Under this view, there is no claim when P seeks to recover only attorney's fees.

3. **Malicious Defense** §1787

A few states have created a tort mirroring malicious institution cases for instances where D raises a totally unjustified defense.

4. **Spoliation of Evidence** §1788

Most courts facing the issue have created a cause of action where a party hides or destroys evidence.

5. **Abuse of Process** §1791

This tort is committed by the intentional use of a court process for a purpose for which it was not intended. A ***prima facie case*** involves only an ***intentional misuse*** and damages to P.

(i) P need ***not*** show D lacked probable cause.

(ii) Proceedings need ***not*** have terminated in P's favor.

(iii) When process has been abused, P may ***counterclaim in the same action for damages*** arising from the abuse.

a. **Who may sue** §1796

The action may be maintained by any third party whose property was injured by the proceedings (*e.g.,* suit causing attachment of X's property) as well as by the other party to the proceedings.

Gilbert Exam Strategies

A course in Torts deals with a number of distinct and separate legal problems that are to a large extent governed by dissimilar principles and doctrines. For example, the rules governing liability in a battery case are entirely different from those governing liability in a case involving the sale of contaminated foodstuffs; yet both are "torts" problems. In the battery case, the applicable rules reflect a policy judgment to deter the defendant's wrongful conduct, even though the plaintiff may not have been physically injured. In the foodstuffs case, the principles governing liability seem to reflect a policy judgment to provide compensation to an injured consumer, with less attention to whether the defendant was at fault.

This interplay between the policies of ***providing adequate compensation*** to an injured plaintiff, and of ***deterring wrongdoers*** underlies much of the law of Torts. In effect, when the reasons for taking money from the defendant and giving it to the plaintiff coincide, tort liability will follow. When either reason is missing, the question of liability is likely to be difficult. In determining the relative strength and applicability of these policies, you need to consider certain factors.

Use the following analytical approach to focus on these factors and determine the key issues for you to analyze in answering an exam question. (Also review the key exam issues found at the beginning of each chapter and the Exam Tips interspersed throughout the Summary.)

1. **Identify the Tort**

   The nature and scope of liability that may be imposed, as well as the matters that may be considered by way of defense, vary significantly depending upon which particular tort is involved. Consequently, the first thing you need to do is to determine from the facts ***which particular tort (or torts) may be a possible basis*** for liability.

   Keep in mind that there is no fixed, rigid classification of recognized torts. While there are a number of "classic" tort situations (*e.g.,* battery, false imprisonment, defamation, etc.), there are also many cases that do not fit into the "classic torts" but may still be actionable (*see infra,* §§1622 *et seq.*). In such cases, and indeed with all tort problems, the nature and scope of liability depend on your determination of the following two factors:

   a. **The nature of plaintiff's interest that has been injured**

      There are many different types of protectable interests—one's person, property, reputation, emotional well-being, advantageous business relationships, etc. You must determine exactly which interests have been injured, because the scope of liability may vary radically (*e.g.,* the scope of liability that will be imposed on a defendant for a negligent injury to the plaintiff's body is greater than that imposed for negligent injury to the plaintiff's economic well-being).

Gilbert Exam Strategies

b. The nature of defendant's conduct

The second crucial factor in identifying the tort is the concept of fault: Did the defendant act intentionally to cause the result that occurred? Or was the conduct negligent? Or was the defendant's conduct blameless under the circumstances? As you might expect, the greater the defendant's "fault" in causing the plaintiff's injuries, the greater the extent to which liability will usually be imposed on the defendant for his acts and the fewer the matters that may be permitted by way of defense. For example, if the defendant ***intentionally*** injures the plaintiff's person, the defendant will almost certainly be held liable for all resulting harm, whether or not foreseeable; whereas if the defendant's conduct was merely ***negligent***, liability may be limited to foreseeable injuries (*infra,* §§442 *et seq.*).

2. Apply the Prima Facie Case

After you have identified each interest of the plaintiff that has been invaded, and evaluated the defendant's conduct with regard to that interest, you can establish the particular area of tort liability involved—*e.g.,* was there an intentional invasion of the plaintiff's real property ("trespass to land"), negligent injury to the plaintiff's person ("negligence"), etc. Don't go into any more elaborate "definition" of the particular tort involved. Rather, focus your attention on the ***prima facie case*** of that tort—*i.e.,* the ***essential elements*** that the plaintiff must establish as a basis for liability. These essential elements "define" the tort.

In answering your question, analyze the facts given to make sure that ***each element*** of the prima facie case is present. Remember that, in some situations, a single wrongful act by the defendant (*e.g.,* false publication regarding the plaintiff's private life) may conceivably be the basis for ***several entirely different tort theories*** (*e.g.,* defamation, invasion of privacy, infliction of emotional distress). Hence, consider the ***prima facie case of each tort*** that could conceivably be in issue. In close cases, weigh the policy factors of compensating the plaintiff and deterring the defendant in the particular tort involved.

3. Consider Defenses or Limitations on Liability

After you have found all elements of the prima facie case, look for any defenses that might be available to the defendant. Remember that the matters that may be asserted by way of defense, or to mitigate or limit liability, will vary with the two factors that "identify" the tort—the ***nature of the plaintiff's interest*** and the ***nature of the defendant's conduct.*** For example, where the defendant negligently causes physical injury to the plaintiff's person, the defendant may prove by way of complete or partial defense that the plaintiff was also negligent; whereas, if the defendant had intentionally caused the same injuries, this might not be a permissible defense.

4. Note—Evaluate the Facts

Often, the rules of law in Torts are easier to state than they are to apply. This is because Torts problems invariably involve difficult ***factual*** issues that must be resolved before the applicable rules of law can be determined. For example, the prima facie case of certain torts requires a finding of "unreasonable" conduct by the defendant; the rules of causation may be based on determinations of "foreseeability" of harm; various privileges and defenses are lost by "excessive" or "unreasonable" acts; etc. However, these are all ultimate ***conclusions*** that can be reached only after careful evaluation of the facts given in the particular problem. For a good answer, avoid discussing these matters in the abstract, or making snap judgments as to the outcome. Rather, consider all operative facts in the problem, together with the logical inferences to be drawn from them. Be sure to make each step of this reasoning explicit in your answer. Remember, a conclusion concerning "reasonableness," "foreseeability," etc., will be only as good as the factual analysis upon which it is based.

5. Other Considerations

a. Parties

Be sure of the parties. Be certain you know who is the plaintiff and who is the defendant. In fact situations involving multiple parties, consider the rights and liabilities of ***each*** party. As to each plaintiff, consider and analyze separately each ***interest*** that has been invaded; and, as to each defendant, analyze separately the ***nature of that person's conduct*** and responsibility for the plaintiff's injuries.

b. Relationship

Check the relationship, if any, between the parties. This may be important for these reasons:

(1) There may be a basis for ***imputing liability*** from one to another (*e.g.*, master-servant cases; *see infra*, §609);

(2) If there is a marital or family relationship between the plaintiff and the defendant, there may be possible ***immunity*** from suit (*see infra*, §§1211 *et seq.*);

(3) The relationship may ***increase the amount of care*** owed by one party to the other (*e.g.*, a common carrier's higher standard of care owed to a passenger; *see infra*, §582); or

(4) The relationship may ***decrease the standard of care*** owed (*e.g.*, a landowner's limited duty to social guests; *see infra*, §§650 *et seq.*).

c. Effect of death of party

Whenever any party—plaintiff or defendant—has died subsequent to commission of the tort, consider problems of ***survival*** of causes of action and the applicability of ***wrongful death*** (*see infra*, §§1150 *et seq.*).

d. Statutes

Although the law of Torts is primarily judge-made, in certain areas (*e.g.*, "guest" statutes, wrongful death statutes, survival statutes, comparative negligence statutes), legislative enactments are found so frequently that any analysis of a problem in such areas must include a discussion of the effect of the relevant statutes.

6. Caution—One Fact May Raise (and Influence) Several Issues

Perhaps the greatest danger in Torts problems lies in treating the various issues and elements as separate, when they are usually interrelated. For example, if P decides to cross a street in the face of oncoming traffic, this single fact bears significantly on a number of legal doctrines that may be applicable—*e.g.*, D's duty under the circumstances, P's own negligence, and P's assumption of the risk. A correct analysis will emphasize that these various issues are related and dependent on each other: Whether P assumed the risk or was negligent is related to and dependent on what duty, if any, D is held to owe to P under the circumstances. Keep in mind, then, that a single fact may influence more than one issue in the case, and that each issue should be treated as interrelated with others in the problem.

Introduction

This Summary is organized around two main themes. First, it considers the basic clusters of tortious ***harms***—personal injury, property damage, and invasion of other interests such as reputation. Second, it dicusses the three main ***bases of liability***—intentional harm, negligent harm, and torts based on strict liability. Thus, the progression is from intentional infliction of personal injury and property damage, to negligent infliction of such harm, and then to situations in which strict liability will lie. The Summary then considers protection of the plaintiff's other interests: reputation, privacy, economic interests such as freedom from interference with contract relationships, and protection from unjustified litigation.

Remember that tort law is always concerned with both subjects at once—*i.e.*, ***what interests of the plaintiff*** should be protected from what kinds of ***interferences by the defendant.***

Chapter One: Intentional Torts

Outline

CONTENTS

▶	Key Exam Issues	
A.	Torts to the Person	§1
B.	Defenses and Privileged Invasions of Personal Interests	§100
C.	Torts to Property	§182
D.	Defenses and Privileged Invasions of Land and Chattels	§237

Key Exam Issues

The following basic framework should be used to analyze intentional torts, which are among the most basic instances of the imposition of tort liability.

1. ***First identify all the possible torts.*** Oftentimes, a fact situation creates the possibility of many different torts. You may immediately see one tort (*e.g.,* a battery), but don't stop there. Consider what other torts are suggested by the facts. In other words, sort the facts out into the various cubbyholes of intentional torts.

2. ***Then consider the prima facie case*** of each tort and see whether you have all the elements of each tort. The prima facie case is usually quite simple—the only common problem may be the element of ***intent.*** Remember to apply the term "intent" to the ***result*** that occurred, ***not*** to the act the defendant engaged in; *i.e.,* the defendant must have desired that a particular result occur or have been substantially certain that such a result would occur.

3. ***After you have found that the defendant has committed a particular tort,*** think about whether the defendant had a ***privilege or defense*** for his action. (Note that if there is no plausible privilege or defense, the defendant has behaved very badly indeed.) Issues in this area may present analytical difficulties by overlapping in a particular fact situation. For example, if you are attacked on the street, you are privileged to engage in appropriate self-defense, but what kind of force can you use without losing the privilege? If you disarm your assailant, has the privilege ended? Before the attack, did the assailant challenge you to a fight and did you "consent" to the fracas? The facts may slide back and forth among the various privileges. Be sure to remain flexible in your thinking about which privilege or privileges apply to the facts.

A. Torts to the Person

1. Battery [§1]

Prima facie case:

- *Act by Defendant*
- *Intent*
- *Harmful or Offensive Touching*
- *Causation*
- (*Lack of Consent*—discussed as a defense, *see infra,* §§100 *et seq.*)

a. Act by defendant [§2]

The word "act" as used in intentional torts means an external manifestation of the actor's will; it refers to some ***volitional movement*** by the actor of some part of his body. Thus, if the defendant intentionally drove his automobile into the plaintiff, the "act" complained of would not be the driving of the automobile, but rather the movement by the defendant of his ***arms and legs*** in setting the automobile into motion and directing it at the plaintiff. [Restatement (Second) of Torts ("Rest. 2d") §2 (1965)]

(1) Unconscious acts [§3]

Because of the requirement of a "volitional" movement, the movements of persons having an epileptic seizure or of persons asleep or under the influence of drugs are not generally sufficient "acts" for the purpose of establishing liability for intentional torts. [**Lobert v. Pack,** 9 A.2d 365 (Pa. 1939)]

(2) Reflex actions [§4]

Instinctive action, when there is no time to think and choose, does not constitute volitional movement and therefore cannot be wrongful conduct. [**Collette v. Boston & Manchester Railroad,** 140 A. 176 (N.H. 1928)] Thus, if a person blinks her eyelids when a stone is thrown at her, the blinking is not an "act" because it is purely reflexive. But if someone, finding himself about to fall, stretches his hand out to save himself, the stretching out of his hand ***is*** an "act"; his mind has grasped the situation and dictated a muscular contraction in an effort to prevent the fall.

(3) Acts by incompetents [§5]

Persons who are not legally competent are still capable of volitional conduct; *i.e.,* insane persons or minors may be held liable for their acts. [**Goff v. Taylor,** 708 S.W.2d 113 (Ky. 1986); **McGuire v. Almy,** 8 N.E.2d 760 (Mass. 1937)]

b. Intent [§6]

To make out a case for battery, the plaintiff generally must show that the defendant did the "act" with the intent ***to inflict a harmful or offensive touching*** on the plaintiff or a third person. [Rest. 2d §13(a)]

EXAM TIP **gilbert**

Note that everyone is "capable" of intent. Incapacity is not a good defense. Thus, young children and persons who are mentally incompetent ***will be liable*** for their intentional torts.

(1) Test—desire or belief in substantial certainty [§7]

Whether the defendant had the requisite intent is measured by whether he acted with the ***desire*** to cause the touching or ***believed that a touching was substantially certain*** to result from his act. Courts are split on whether the plaintiff must also prove that the defendant intended offense or harm or merely that the defendant intended to cause a touching, which ***might*** be offensive or harmful. [**Frey v. Kouf,** 484 N.W.2d 864 (S.D. 1992); **Garratt v. Dailey,** 279 P.2d 1091 (Wash. 1955)]

---

e.g. **Example:** D shoved P, a young child, to get her out of the area in which some boys were playing. P fell and broke her elbow; D has committed a battery. Even if D did not desire the touching, he believed that an offensive (if not harmful) touching was substantially certain to occur. [**Baldinger v. Banks,** 26 Misc. 2d 1086 (1960)]

(a) Test is subjective [§8]

The issues of "desire" and what the defendant "believed" to be substantially certain to occur turn on the subjective consideration of what was in the defendant's mind when he acted. Although juries may make inferences about the defendant's state of mind from objective facts, the basic question is ***not*** what a reasonable person would have desired or believed, but what the particular defendant ***in fact*** desired or believed.

(2) Motives immaterial [§9]

The defendant's motive for acting generally is immaterial to the question of whether the act was sufficient to establish a prima facie case. As in criminal law, a distinction must be made between "malice" and "intent." "Malice" refers to the defendant's ***motives*** (***why*** the defendant acted as he did). Tort law is concerned only with whether the defendant had the requisite ***intent*** under the "desire or belief in substantial certainty" test, above.

(a) But note

If "malice" (intent to injure) exists, the defendant may be held liable for ***punitive*** damages (*see* below).

(3) Transferred intent doctrine [§10]

For historical reasons, in certain circumstances a different intent is sufficient to make out a prima facie case for battery. Battery arose out of the old common law form of action called "trespass." Trespass gave rise to four other modern actions: assault, false imprisonment, trespass to land, and trespass to chattels. Under the doctrine of transferred intent, if the defendant acts intending to cause any one of these harms to a person, the defendant will be liable on an intentional tort theory if ***any*** of the five harms occurs to that person or to ***another person*** (the plaintiff)—even though the other person is unexpected and the harm is unexpected.

---

e.g. **Example:** D attempted to strike X, who ducked. The blow hit P, who had unexpectedly appeared. *Held:* Because D had committed an assault on P, D has committed a battery on P. [**Carnes v. Thompson,** 48 S.W.2d 903 (Mo. 1932)]

Example: D unlawfully shot at X's dog (trespass to chattels) and hit P. Even though D had no reason to know that anyone might be in the area, D committed a battery on P. [**Corn v. Sheppard,** 229 N.W. 869 (Minn. 1930); *and see* **Alteiri v. Colasso,** 362 A.2d 798 (Conn. 1975)—attempted assault on X led to battery on P]

(a) Comment

Although the justification is phrased as involving "intent," the better explanation for the doctrine is that the courts are imposing strict liability on D because of his serious misbehavior in directing the initial act against X or X's property.

c. Harmful or offensive touching [§11]

To make out a case for battery, the plaintiff must show that the defendant's intentional act resulted in the infliction of a harmful or offensive touching of the plaintiff's person, or something so closely associated with the plaintiff as to make the touching tantamount to a physical invasion of the plaintiff's person. Things "closely associated" with the plaintiff's person would cover situations where the defendant knocks the plaintiff's hat off his head, grabs a plate out of his hand, etc. [**Fisher v. Carrousel Motor Hotel, Inc.,** 424 S.W.2d 627 (Tex. 1967); Rest. 2d §18] *Note:* There must be ***actual physical contact***—"coming close" is not enough to constitute a battery.

(1) "Harmful" touching [§12]

A touching is "harmful" if it injures, disfigures, impairs, or causes pain to any bodily organ or function.

(2) "Offensive" touching [§13]

A touching is "offensive" if it would offend a ***reasonable person's sense of personal dignity.***

(a) Plaintiff's hypersensitive reaction insufficient [§14]

A touching that would not cause a reasonable person to take offense, but at which the plaintiff does take offense, is not sufficient to impose liability for battery. [Rest. 2d §19]

Example: P, a mortician who embalmed the deceased, sued Hospital for battery because Hospital did not tell P that the deceased had died of AIDS. P had worn protective gear during the embalming process and therefore had not been exposed to the AIDS virus. *Held:* P's claim was based on fear that was unreasonable and thus insufficient to constitute a battery. [**Funeral Services by Gregory, Inc. v. Bluefield Community Hospital,** 413 S.E.2d 79 (W. Va. 1991)]

---

e.g. **Example:** P, a patient of D dentist, sued for battery because D performed a procedure upon P while D was infected with HIV. The risk of actual infection from the procedure was tiny and there was no evidence of actual exposure. D had not created a reasonable basis for P's fear and thus was not liable. [**Brzoska v. Olson,** 668 A.2d 1355 (Del. 1995)]

---

1) Exception—knowledge of hypersensitivity [§15]

This rule might ***not*** apply in a situation in which the defendant knows of the plaintiff's hypersensitivity but proceeds anyway. Thus, under circumstances where it might generally be acceptable to gain someone's attention by tapping him lightly on the back, the defendant may be liable for a battery if he lightly taps the plaintiff on the back knowing that the plaintiff does not wish such contact. [Rest. 2d §27]

(3) Plaintiff unaware of touching [§16]

The plaintiff need not have knowledge of the touching at the time thereof. Thus, if the defendant kisses the plaintiff while the plaintiff is asleep, but does not waken or harm the plaintiff, the kiss may be a sufficiently "offensive" touching to establish liability—even though the plaintiff does not learn of the contact until a later time. [Rest. 2d §18 cmt. d] Similarly, batteries may occur while a plaintiff is unconscious during an operation.

d. Causation [§17]

The harmful or offensive touching must be caused by the defendant's act or some force that the act sets in motion. This causation element is satisfied if the defendant's conduct "directly or indirectly" results in the injury. [Rest. 2d §13]

---

e.g. **Example:** D throws a piece of wood at P, intending to injure her. The wood misses the mark but strikes a pile of rocks, setting loose an avalanche of rocks that kills P. D's act directly or indirectly brought about the injuries that led to P's death by setting loose the rocks. D is therefore liable for battery.

---

(1) Distinguish—negligence liability [§18]

The law holds an ***intentional*** wrongdoer liable for the direct and indirect consequences of his acts, ***whether or not foreseeable.*** [Rest. 2d §13] However, in ***negligence*** cases, proximate cause rules may operate to terminate liability so that a negligent tortfeasor may be excused from liability for injuries for which an intentional tortfeasor would be held liable (*see infra,* §§442 *et seq.*).

e. **Damages [§19]**

A battery is complete upon commission of the harmful or offensive touching. Even if no physical harm is suffered—as in the case of some offensive touchings—the court will award at least ***nominal*** damages. This is sometimes a symbolic amount of one dollar.

(1) **Compensatory damages [§20]**

In the alternative to nominal damages, the plaintiff may recover damages to ***compensate*** her for the harm suffered. Compensatory damages may include amounts for general damages and special damages.

(a) **General damages [§21]**

"General damages" are nonpecuniary damages deemed to result from the touching—such as embarrassment at being hit in the face with a pie, pain or suffering, disfigurement or disability, etc.

(b) **Special damages [§22]**

"Special damages" are specific, identifiable economic losses—such as medical bills or lost wages.

(2) **Punitive damages [§23]**

If it appears that the defendant's act was motivated by an intent ***to injure or harm the plaintiff,*** most courts also permit juries to award ***punitive*** ("exemplary") damages against the defendant.

(a) **Jury discretion [§24]**

Even if the defendant's conduct would justify a punitive award, the jury is not required to make one. The jury must be instructed as to the criteria to consider in deciding whether to award punitive damages.

(b) **Review of jury award [§25]**

If the jury does make an award, state law usually requires careful post-trial review and appellate review of the amount of the award.

(c) **Constitutional concerns [§26]**

The Eighth Amendment prohibition on excessive fines does not apply to punitive damages awards in tort cases between private parties. [**Browning-Ferris Industries of Vermont, Inc. v. Kelco Disposal, Inc.,** 492 U.S. 257 (1989)] Punitive damages awards can, however, violate the Due Process Clause if the defendant did not have adequate notice of the possible severity of the penalty. The Supreme Court has indicated it will look to the following factors in determining whether the defendant had adequate notice that a severe penalty might be imposed:

(i) The ***reprehensibility*** of the conduct by the defendant toward the plaintiff under the governing state law;

(ii) The *disparity* between the compensatory award and the punitive award; and

(iii) The *difference* between the punitive award and ***possible criminal and administrative penalties for such conduct.***

Although the Court has resisted limiting punitive damages to a particular multiplier of compensatory damages, it has strongly suggested that a ratio greater than 9:1 would likely prove unconstitutional. Lower courts have largely treated a 9:1 ratio as the de facto constitutional limit. [**State Farm Mutual Automobile Insurance Co. v. Campbell,** 538 U.S. 408 (2003); **BMW of North America, Inc. v. Gore,** 517 U.S. 559 (1996)]

---

e.g. **Example:** P purchased a new car that was manufactured by D. Unbeknownst to P, the car had been damaged before it was sold and it was repainted. When P discovered these facts, he demanded that D replace his vehicle. When D refused, P brought suit to recover damages. The jury awarded $4,000 in compensatory damages and $2 million in punitive damages. The Supreme Court found that the punitive award violated the Due Process Clause because the only harm threatened was economic and not related to safety, there was a great disparity between the compensatory award and the punitive award, and the criminal penalties that could have been applied to D for D's conduct were minor fines. [**BMW of North America, Inc. v. Gore,** *supra*]

---

2. Assault [§27]

Prima facie case:

- *Act by Defendant*
- *Intent*
- *Apprehension*
- *Causation*
- (*Lack of Consent*—discussed as a defense, *see infra,* §§100 *et seq.*)

a. Act by defendant [§28]

The act required to make out a prima facie case for assault is the same type of act as is required for battery—*i.e.,* a ***volitional*** movement of some portion of the body.

(1) Words alone not sufficient [§29]

Because of the requirement that the act create in the plaintiff an apprehension of an ***immediate*** touching (*see* below), words alone are generally not enough to constitute an assault. There must also be some volitional movement of the body, however slight. [**Western Union Telegraph Co. v. Hill,** 150 So. 709 (Ala. 1933); Rest. 2d §31]

Example: If D says to P, "You are about to die," there is no assault. But if D accompanies the statement with the slightest movement of his hand toward a pistol on the table, this act may be sufficient to constitute an assault. [**Cullison v. Medley,** 570 N.E.2d 27 (Ind. 1991)—entry without permission plus reaching for pistol in holster sufficient]

(a) Exception for certain threats [§30]

Occasionally, the ***impact*** of the words alone may create a sufficient apprehension of immediate harm to constitute an assault. [Rest. 2d §31 cmt. d]

Example: Verbal threats of imminent harm to a blind person may constitute an assault.

Example: D comes up behind P saying, "Don't turn around or I'll shoot you." This may be an assault because the surrounding circumstances force P to rely on the words alone—*i.e.,* it is unsafe for P to turn around to see if D really has a gun.

(b) Distinguish—emotional distress [§31]

Note that words alone, even if insufficient for an assault, may be sufficient to impose liability for intentional infliction of emotional distress (*see infra,* §80).

b. Intent [§32]

To make out the prima facie case for assault, the plaintiff must show that the defendant intended to: (i) ***inflict*** a harmful or offensive touching on the plaintiff or a third person, ***or*** (ii) ***put*** the plaintiff or a third person ***in apprehension of*** an imminent harmful or offensive touching.

(1) Test [§33]

Again, the defendant's intent is measured by the ***"desire or belief in substantial certainty"*** test (*see supra,* §7). No malice need be shown. [**Langford v. Shu,** 128 S.E.2d 210 (N.C. 1962)]

(2) Transferred intent [§34]

The transferred intent doctrine is likewise applicable (*see supra,* §10).

c. Apprehension [§35]

The defendant's intentional act must have placed the plaintiff in apprehension of an ***imminent*** harmful or offensive touching of her person. [**Proffitt v. Ricci,** 463 A.2d 514 (R.I. 1983)]

(1) Plaintiff's awareness of threat [§36]

The apprehension requirement means that the plaintiff cannot complain of an assault unless she was aware of the threat ***at the time thereof.*** [Rest. 2d §22]

 **Example:** There is no actionable assault if all D did was silently point a gun at P while her back was turned.

(a) Distinguish—battery [§37]

The rule is different in battery, where apprehension is not required, and where the plaintiff need not have knowledge of the touching at the time thereof (*see supra,* §16).

EXAM TIP **gilbert**

Be sure to remember this important difference between assault and battery. For ***assault***, the victim ***must be aware*** of the assault at the time it is committed or the action will fail. For ***battery***, the victim ***need not know*** that he was touched; indeed, the victim may even have been unconscious at the time of the touching.

---

(2) Nature of harm threatened [§38]

Moreover, the plaintiff must be apprehensive of a touching ***to her own person.*** Threats to her home or property, or to the person or property of any third person (even members of her own family), are not enough. [Rest. 2d §26]

(a) Distinguish—emotional distress [§39]

But such threats may be sufficient to impose liability for emotional distress (*see infra,* §80).

(b) Distinguish—false imprisonment [§40]

Threats to a member of the plaintiff's family may create a false imprisonment (*see infra,* §67).

(3) Source of threatened harm [§41]

In assault cases, normally the source of the harm threatened is the defendant himself, or some force the defendant sets in motion. However, this is not essential. The defendant may be liable for an assault where he arouses apprehension of harm ***from someone else*** (or even from an act of God). [Rest. 2d §25]

---

e.g. **Example:** For the purpose of making P apprehensive, D falsely says, "Watch out! A snake is about to bite you!" or "Duck! X just threw a rock at you!" D may be liable for assault. (These are also examples in which "words alone" are sufficient; *see supra,* §30.)

---

(4) Imminence of threatened harm [§42]

The plaintiff must be placed in apprehension of an imminent harmful or offensive touching. Thus, even if menacing gestures are involved, if the defendant's words ***negate*** any immediate threat, there is no actionable assault.

---

e.g. **Example:** If D shakes his fist at an elderly man saying, "If you weren't such an old fool, I'd break your neck," the words negate the immediacy of the threat.

(a) Threats of future harm insufficient [§43]

Likewise, if the defendant's words make it clear that some significant interval of time remains before the harm will be inflicted, there is no assault. [Rest. 2d §29(2)]

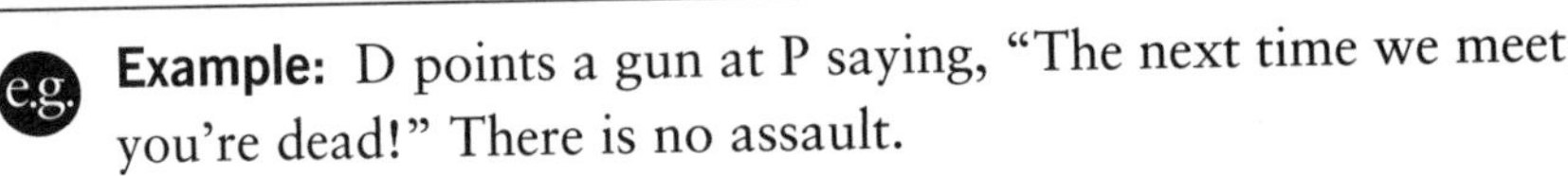

e.g. **Example:** D points a gun at P saying, "The next time we meet, you're dead!" There is no assault.

---

e.g. **Example:** Threatening phone calls to P were not sufficiently imminent because callers were not close enough to inflict damage. [**Brower v. Ackerley,** 943 P.2d 1141 (Wash. 1997)]

---

1) Distinguish—emotional distress [§44]

Again, however, threats of future harm may be sufficient for the tort of intentional infliction of emotional distress (*see infra,* §80).

(b) Conditional threats may be sufficient [§45]

A threat of imminent harm may constitute an assault even if the threat is conditional, provided the condition is one that the defendant is not privileged to assert. [Rest. 2d §30]

---

e.g. **Example:** D points a gun at P saying, "Take back what you said about my sister, or I'll kill you!" D is liable for an assault because no privilege exists for him to force a retraction in this manner.

---

1) What is privileged [§46]

As to the circumstances under which one person is privileged to use or threaten harm against another, *see* self-defense (*infra,* §§119 *et seq.*) and privilege of arrest (*infra,* §§165 *et seq.*).

(5) Nature of plaintiff's apprehension

(a) Reasonable apprehension [§47]

Many courts require that a plaintiff's apprehension have been reasonable.

(b) Fear not required [§48]

The plaintiff need only be placed in apprehension of a touching; she need ***not*** be frightened. Thus, it is immaterial that the plaintiff may be able, and knows that she is able, to escape or prevent the threatened touching. [Rest. 2d §24]

---

e.g. **Example:** A frail, five-foot tall, 90-pound weakling may commit an assault against a powerful, six-foot tall, 250-pound linebacker by threatening to strike the linebacker, even if the linebacker knows that he can overpower the weakling or can step away before the weakling can possibly touch him.

---

1) **Subjective test [§49]**
It is also immaterial that a reasonable person would not have been placed in apprehension by the defendant's act. ***Actual*** (*i.e.,* subjective) apprehension is the test. [Rest. 2d §27]

(c) **Apparent ability sufficient [§50]**
It is sufficient if the defendant had the actual ***or apparent*** ability to inflict the touching. [**Allen v. Hannaford,** 244 P. 700 (Wash. 1926); Rest. 2d §27]

---

e.g. **Example:** If D intends to make P apprehensive by appearing to menace her with a loaded gun from 50 feet away, an assault has been committed even if the gun is in fact unloaded.

---

1) **Distinguish—criminal assault [§51]**
The rule may be different for a criminal assault. (*See* Criminal Law Summary.)

d. **Causation [§52]**
The plaintiff's apprehension must have been caused by the defendant's act or something the defendant set in motion. As to what is sufficient causation, *see* discussion of this element in battery, *supra,* §17.

e. **Damages [§53]**
The damages rules discussed under battery (*supra,* §19) generally apply to assault as well. The plaintiff need not have suffered any emotional distress, physical injuries, or other damages (although, again, these are recoverable if sustained). In addition to compensatory damages, punitive damages might also be recoverable (subject to the limitations described *supra,* §§23-26).

3. **False Imprisonment [§54]**
Prima facie case:

- *Act by Defendant*
- *Intent*
- *Confinement*

- *Causation*
- (*Lack of Consent*—discussed as a defense, *see infra,* §§100 *et seq.*)

a. **Act by defendant [§55]**
To make out a prima facie case of false imprisonment, the plaintiff must show some act by the defendant that ***caused the confinement of the plaintiff.*** As in battery and assault, the act required is usually a volitional movement by the defendant of some part of his body.

(1) **Words alone sufficient [§56]**
In false imprisonment, words alone ***may be*** a sufficient act. Thus, ***threats*** of physical force (*see* below), or words asserting legal authority ("I arrest you"), may result in actionable imprisonment without any accompanying physical movement. [**Martin v. Houck,** 54 S.E. 291 (N.C. 1906)]

b. **Intent [§57]**
The act must have been done by the defendant with the intent ***to confine*** the plaintiff or some third person.

(1) **Test [§58]**
Again, intent is measured by the ***"desire or belief in substantial certainty"*** test (*supra,* §7).

(2) **Transferred intent [§59]**
The transferred intent doctrine applies (*see supra,* §10).

c. **Confinement [§60]**
The defendant's intentional act must result in the confinement of the plaintiff within boundaries fixed by the defendant for some period of time, however short. "Confinement" requires that the plaintiff be ***restricted to a limited area without knowledge of a reasonable means of escape.***

(1) **What constitutes "confinement"**

(a) **Area of confinement [§61]**
Normally, there must be some ***specific area*** in which the plaintiff is ***completely*** confined by the defendant's acts.

---

e.g. **Example:** Where P is prevented from going in a certain direction (*e.g.,* by D's blocking a highway), there is ***not*** a sufficient confinement to constitute false imprisonment because P is not bounded and can go in other directions. [**Bird v. Jones,** 115 Eng. Rep. 668 (1845)]

(b) **No means of escape available [§62]**
There is no confinement if ***reasonable*** means of escape are available

and known to the plaintiff. [**Davis & Allcott Co. v. Boozer,** 110 So. 28 (Ala. 1926)]

1) **But note**

The plaintiff is under no duty to search for a means of escape or to run any risk of harm to her person or property (*e.g.,* clothing) by attempting to escape. [Rest. 2d §36]

2) **Unlawful demand [§63]**

If the defendant asserts that he will free the plaintiff if the plaintiff complies with some unlawful condition (*e.g.,* payment of money which the plaintiff is under no obligation to pay), compliance is ***not*** deemed a "reasonable" means of escape.

(c) **Plaintiff's awareness [§64]**

There can be no confinement unless the plaintiff ***knows*** that she is confined ***at the time*** of the confinement ***or*** is ***harmed*** by the confinement. [Rest. 2d §42]

Example: A baby locked in a bank vault for several days may have an action for false imprisonment if she was harmed by the confinement, even if she was not aware of it.

---

(2) **How confinement caused [§65]**

The plaintiff's confinement may be caused by any of the following:

(a) **Physical force [§66]**

The defendant's use of physical force against either the plaintiff or a member of the plaintiff's ***immediate family*** constitutes confinement. The reasonableness of the plaintiff's submission thereto is immaterial. [Rest. 2d §39]

Example: A football player may be confined by a frail nun who grabs the player's coat, intending to detain him.

(b) **Threats or duress**

1) **Threats to plaintiff or plaintiff's family [§67]**

Confinement may be effected by submission to threats of ***imminent*** physical harm to the plaintiff or a member of her ***immediate family***. [Rest. 2d §40A]

Example: D may confine P by threatening to shoot P's child standing beside her if P tries to leave the room.

---

a) **Distinguish—future harm [§68]**
There is no actionable confinement where the plaintiff submits to threats of ***future*** harm. [Rest. 2d §40 cmt. b]

---

e.g. **Example:** D says to P, "Unless you stay with me, I'll kill your husband when he gets off work." There is not a sufficient confinement to constitute false imprisonment. (However, P may succeed in claiming intentional infliction of emotional distress; *see infra,* §80.)

---

2) **Threats to plaintiff's property [§69]**
Threats to inflict immediate harm on the plaintiff's property may also be sufficient. [Rest. 2d §40A]

---

e.g. **Example:** Without any privilege to do so, D removes a valuable stamp from P's stamp collection and threatens to tear it in half unless P stays in the room. This is an effective confinement.

---

3) **Threats to plaintiff's economic well-being [§70]**
Submission to words of another usually does not constitute false imprisonment where the plaintiff stays to avoid losing her job. [**Faniel v. Chesapeake & Potomac Telephone Co.,** 404 A.2d 147 (D.C. 1979)]

---

e.g. **Example:** Where D led P employee to believe that if P left the room during questioning about drug deals and thefts, D would terminate P's employment, the threat was insufficient to support a false imprisonment claim. [**Johnson v. United Parcel Services,** 722 F. Supp. 1282 (D. Md. 1989)]

(c) **Actual or apparent physical barriers to escape [§71]**
Physical barriers may be in the form of an enclosure, fence, walls, etc. Similarly, acts that deprive the plaintiff of the ability to escape may cause confinement by physical barrier (*e.g.,* taking away the crutches or wheelchair from a crippled person; or, where P is down a well, taking away the ladder that is the only way up). [Rest. 2d §38]

1) **Refusing to release [§72]**
In addition, the barriers may consist of refusing to release the plaintiff or to assist her in leaving ***when under a duty to do so.*** [Rest. 2d §45]

a) **Limitation [§73]**
Of course, absolute freedom of movement at all times cannot be expected.

---

e.g. **Example:** When a passenger boards a commercial airliner or bus, she impliedly agrees to abide by the rules of entrance and exit at scheduled stops only. There is no actionable confinement if the passenger is denied permission to depart at a nonscheduled stop.

---

cf. **Compare:** On the other hand, if the plaintiff submits herself to the defendant's care or custody (*e.g.*, by boarding defendant's pleasure yacht) with the implicit understanding that the defendant will assist her in leaving any time she wishes, if the defendant subsequently refuses to allow the plaintiff to leave, and it is actually or apparently impossible for the plaintiff otherwise to escape, there is a sufficient confinement to establish false imprisonment. [**Whittaker v. Sandford,** 85 A. 399 (Me. 1912)]

(d) Arrest [§74]

A confinement may also be effected by ***the defendant's assertion of legal authority*** (*i.e.*, an arrest) ***and submission thereto by the plaintiff.*** [**Martin v. Houck,** *supra,* §56; Rest. 2d §41]

1) Filing complaint is not basis for false imprisonment [§75]

A private citizen who does no more than file a complaint with the police regarding another is ***not*** liable for false imprisonment because it is the police who assert legal authority and confine the person against whom the complaint is made. [**Baker v. Coon,** 166 N.W. 555 (Neb. 1918)]

a) But note

A citizen who files a ***false*** complaint may be liable for malicious prosecution (*see infra,* §1759).

d. Causation [§76]

The confinement must have been caused by the defendant's intentional act or some force set in motion thereby (*see* discussion of this element, *supra,* §17).

e. Damages [§77]

The tort of false imprisonment is complete upon the confinement, and recovery may be had even though the plaintiff suffers no special damages—*e.g.*, injuries, loss of earnings, etc. (However, if sustained, these damages are also recoverable.) In addition to compensatory damages, punitive damages might also be recoverable (subject to the limitations described *supra*, §§23-26).

(1) Injuries while attempting escape [§78]

"False imprisonment invites escape"; thus, a plaintiff can also recover for any injuries sustained in a ***reasonable*** attempt to escape. [*But see* **Sindle v.**

New York City Transit Authority, 33 N.Y.2d 293 (1973)—no recovery for injuries suffered in ***unreasonable*** escape attempt]

---

e.g. **Example:** P was a passenger on a bus. Several students defaced the bus during their ride home from school. The driver announced that he was departing from the normal route and driving the bus to the police station. To escape, P jumped out of a window as the bus turned a corner and was severely injured. P could not recover for false imprisonment because he acted unreasonably in jumping out of the window. [**Sindle v. New York City Transit Authority,** *supra*]

---

4. Intentional Infliction of Emotional Distress [§79]

Prima facie case:

- *Act by Defendant—"Extreme" and "Outrageous" Conduct*
- *Intent*
- *Causation*
- *Severe Emotional Distress*

a. Act by defendant—extreme and outrageous conduct [§80]

Unlike the intentional tort of assault (*see supra,* §27), ***words alone*** may be a sufficient "act" to make out a prima facie case of intentional infliction of emotional distress. Or liability may be predicated on any other gesture, conduct, or action by the defendant. However, courts generally require that the conduct be ***"extreme" and "outrageous"***—*i.e.,* the conduct must exceed "all bounds of decent behavior." [Rest. 2d §46]

---

e.g. **Example:** *Threatening language by bill collectors,* bullying tactics of landlords seeking their rent, insults hurled in public, and deliberately killing P's pet dog are typical cases of extreme and outrageous conduct. [**Sherman v. Field Clinic,** 392 N.E.2d 154 (Ill. 1979)]

---

cf. **Compare:** Leaving collection agency business cards on P's door and contacting P's neighbors, apartment manager, and former employer did ***not*** amount to "extreme and outrageous" conduct when debtor, P, would not respond to the agency. [**Munley v. ISC Financial House, Inc.,** 584 P.2d 1336 (Okla. 1978)]

---

e.g. **Example:** *An insurance company's refusal to pay benefits clearly owing* (for purpose of forcing a policyholder to settle a claim for less than the amount due) has been held sufficiently "outrageous" that the policyholder could recover for emotional distress. [**Fletcher v. Western National Life Insurance Co.,** 10 Cal. App. 3d 376 (1970)]

---

e.g. **Example:** ***A moving company's failure to deliver*** P's household goods until several months after the date promised, coupled with the company's ***knowingly false assurance*** to her during the interim that delivery was imminent, and its ***knowledge*** that P's emotional state was at the breaking point over the delivery problem, has been held sufficiently "outrageous" conduct. [**Hanke v. Global Van Lines, Inc.,** 533 F.2d 396 (8th Cir. 1976)]

---

e.g. **Example:** ***A doctor's having sexual relations*** with his nurse, knowing that he had an active case of herpes and was likely to infect her, was extreme and outrageous because the doctor was aware that the disease was painful and incurable. [**B.N. v. K.K.,** 538 A.2d 1175 (Md. 1988)]

---

e.g. **Example:** ***A psychologist's initiation of affair*** with his patient's wife, knowing that his patient was emotionally unstable, was sufficiently outrageous that the patient could recover for emotional distress. [**Figueiredo-Torres v. Nickel,** 584 A.2d 69 (Md. 1991)]

---

e.g. **Example:** ***A single racial epithet from an employer*** (county sheriff) to an employee may suffice. [**Taylor v. Metzger,** 706 A.2d 685 (N.J. 1998)]

---

cf. **Compare:** A doctor's act in telling P, the mother of a deceased patient, that he "had her son's brain in a jar" for autopsy purposes did ***not*** amount to extreme and outrageous conduct even though she had asked that a brain examination not be performed. [**Burgess v. Perdue,** 721 P.2d 239 (Kan. 1986)]

---

cf. **Compare:** Making 340 "hang-up" phone calls to P over a two-month period after P refused to date D a second time was ***not*** sufficient for the tort. [**Russo v. White,** 400 S.E.2d 160 (Va. 1991)]

---

(1) Totality of the circumstances [§81]

In determining whether conduct is extreme and outrageous, courts will consider the "totality of the circumstances," not each isolated individual incident.

(2) Petty insults [§82]

There is no redress for simple insults, annoyances, or petty indignities (*e.g.*, where a frustrated telephone user curses at the operator). [Rest. 2d §46 cmt. d]

(a) Exception—special carrier/utility rule [§83]

Common carriers and public utilities have been held liable for gross insults that would not otherwise be actionable under the common law requirement of extreme and outrageous conduct.

(b) **Exception—harassment [§84]**
Cases involving insults or attacks based on race or gender may be actionable harassment claims pursuant to state or federal statute even if not amounting to the traditional tort of intentional infliction of emotional distress. [**Franklin v. Gwinnett County Public Schools,** 503 U.S. 60 (1992)—sexual harassment of high school student by teacher may create private remedy under Title IX of Educational Amendments Act of 1972; **Meritor Savings Bank v. Vinson,** 477 U.S. 57, *on remand,* 801 F.2d 1436 (D.C. Cir. 1986)—unwelcome sexual advances that create hostile working environment violate Title VII of 1964 Civil Rights Act]

(3) **Extension—liability to third persons [§85]**
Even if the defendant's conduct was aimed only at a particular person, the defendant will also be liable for infliction of emotional distress to ***members of that person's family*** present at the time of the conduct—if the defendant knew of their presence. *Rationale:* Under the circumstances, the defendant must have known that his conduct toward the first person was substantially certain to hurt the plaintiff (family member), or the conduct was at least reckless toward the plaintiff. [**Grimsby v. Samson,** 530 P.2d 291 (Wash. 1975)] This is ***not*** transferred intent (*see infra,* §88).

b. **Intent [§86]**
The defendant must have intended ***to cause severe emotional distress or mental anguish*** to the plaintiff. ***Reckless*** conduct will also suffice (*i.e.,* where the defendant acts in deliberate disregard of a high probability that his actions will cause emotional distress). [*See* **Womack v. Eldridge,** 210 S.E.2d 145 (Va. 1974)]

(1) **Inference of intent [§87]**
Such intent or recklessness may be inferred if ***the defendant knows that the plaintiff is particularly sensitive*** or susceptible to emotional distress, but acts in disregard of the probability that such harm is likely to occur (*e.g.,* abusive words used to persons who are ill or elderly, to pregnant women, or to children). [*See* **Hanke v. Global Van Lines, Inc.,** *supra,* §80]

(2) **No transferred intent among torts [§88]**
If the defendant intended to cause bodily harm or property damage to the plaintiff but did not succeed, and ***only*** unintended and unexpected emotional distress resulted, the defendant is ***not*** liable for intentional infliction of the emotional distress because transferred intent does not apply to this tort. (Negligent infliction of emotional distress is discussed *infra,* §§762 *et seq.*)

(3) **Distinguish—assault [§89]**
Intentional infliction of emotional distress must be distinguished from assault. In assault, the defendant must have intended to harmfully or offensively ***touch*** the plaintiff or a third person or to place the plaintiff or third

person *in apprehension* of such a touching. Also, liability in assault is complete upon occurrence of the apprehension—whether or not any mental anguish, emotional distress, or physical injury results.

c. **Causation**

(1) **Early view—physical injuries required [§90]**
Early cases held that the defendant's intentional act had to cause a severe emotional disturbance in the plaintiff, which in turn caused ***demonstrable physical injuries.*** (This was to assure against fraudulent claims.) [**Clark v. Associated Retail Credit Men,** 105 F.2d 62 (D.C. Cir. 1939); **Wilkinson v. Downton,** 2 Q.B.D. 57 (1897)]

(2) **Modern approach—distress alone suffices [§91]**
However, the modern view is that if the defendant intentionally and successfully causes severe emotional distress to the plaintiff, recovery is allowed even if the plaintiff suffered no demonstrable physical injuries. *Rationale:* The ***outrageous nature*** of the defendant's conduct may be a more reliable indication of damage to the plaintiff than actual physical injury. [**State Rubbish Collectors Association v. Siliznoff,** 38 Cal. 2d 330 (1952); Rest. 2d §46]

(a) **Note**
Whether the defendant's conduct is sufficiently "outrageous" to cause mental anguish is a fact question in each case. Changing attitudes and social conditions are relevant to this issue. [**Alcorn v. Anbro Engineering, Inc.,** 2 Cal. 3d 493 (1970)—racial slurs held actionable without physical injuries]

d. **Severe emotional distress [§92]**
Although much passes as emotional distress for purposes of recovery in other torts (*e.g.,* embarrassment, humiliation, shame, fright, and grief), the distress must be ***severe*** to recover for intentional infliction of emotional distress. It must be more than a reasonable person could be expected to endure. [**Harris v. Jones,** 380 A.2d 611 (Md. 1977)]

---

e.g. **Example:** If D attempts to carry out a cruel practical joke, but P is aware of the joke and thus is only angered at D, rather than humiliated, P has not suffered severe emotional distress—even though D's conduct may well have been extreme and outrageous.

---

e.g. **Example:** Where P is a corporation, P could not have suffered severe emotional distress no matter how extreme and outrageous D's conduct. [**Chamberlaine & Flowers, Inc. v. Smith Contracting, Inc.,** 341 S.E.2d 414 (W. Va. 1986)]

---

(1) **Known sensitivity—"eggshell psyche" rule [§93]**
Generally, the defendant's conduct must be sufficient to cause severe emotional distress in an ordinary person. [**Taylor v. Metzger,** *supra*, §80] However, pursuant to the "eggshell psyche" rule, a defendant who has knowledge of the plaintiff's fragile condition is liable even if the defendant's conduct would not have caused a reasonable person severe distress but—due to the plaintiff's preexisting mental or emotional state—did inflict such distress upon the plaintiff. [**Stockdale v. Baba,** 795 N.E.2d 727 (Ohio 2003)]

EXAM TIP **gilbert**

Intentional infliction of emotional distress is the only intentional tort to the person that requires actual damages (***severe*** emotional distress). Thus, if the plaintiff has suffered ***only nominal*** damages, you can cross intentional infliction of emotional distress off your list of possible torts.

e. **Defenses**

(1) **Common law defenses [§94]**
Although theoretically the common law defenses available to other intentional torts (*see* below) should apply here, in reality these defenses are not available because the prima facie case requires such an extreme level of misbehavior. Therefore, defenses based on good faith or reasonable mistake are not relevant to this tort.

(a) **Note**
Some courts will not allow a claim for emotional distress if the same facts would have supported a claim for criminal conversation, which has been abolished in most states (*see infra,* §§1207-1208). [**Koestler v. Pollard,** 471 N.W.2d 7 (Wis. 1991)] *Rationale:* To permit this action would undermine the policies that led to abolition of the criminal conversation tort.

(2) **Constitutional defenses [§95]**
The First Amendment may be a defense to intentional infliction of emotional distress where allowing the suit would curb the freedom of speech and press or the free exercise of religion.

(a) **Freedom of speech [§96]**
If the defendant's act is a ***statement*** that injures the plaintiff, the act may be protected speech even though the act constitutes extreme and outrageous behavior. [**Hustler Magazine v. Falwell,** 485 U.S. 46 (1988)—gross insults aimed at public person not actionable unless defamatory or an invasion of privacy] The contours of this limitation mirror First Amendment limitations to defamation (*see infra*, §§1503 *et seq.*).

TORTS TO THE PERSON—COMPARISON OF KEY ELEMENTS

gilbert

	BATTERY	ASSAULT	FALSE IMPRISONMENT	EMOTIONAL DISTRESS (INTENTIONAL)
ACT	Volitional movement of body resulting in ***harmful or offensive touching***	Volitional movement of body causing ***apprehension*** of imminent harmful or offensive touching (words alone generally not enough)	Volitional movement of body causing ***confinement*** of plaintiff (words alone usually not enough)	Volitional movement of body constituting ***extreme and outrageous conduct*** (words alone ***may*** be enough)
INTENT	Desire to inflict ***harmful or offensive touching*** (or belief that conduct is substantially certain to cause that result)	Desire to inflict ***apprehension of imminent harmful or offensive touching*** (or belief that conduct is substantially certain to cause that result)	Desire to ***confine victim*** (or belief that conduct is substantially certain to cause that result)	Desire to inflict ***severe emotional distress***, or deliberate disregard of a high probability that conduct will cause severe emotional distress (*i.e.*, ***recklessness***)
RESULT	Harmful or offensive touching; contemporaneous knowledge of touching not required	Apprehension of imminent harmful or offensive touching; fear is not required	Restriction to a limited area without a reasonable means of escape; victim usually must be aware of confinement while confined	***Severe*** emotional distress

(b) **Free exercise of religion [§97]**
If the defendant is a church or other religious organization, and the act is part of a religious activity, some courts have held that the Free Exercise Clause bars recognition of this tort. [**Paul v. Watchtower Bible & Tract Society,** 819 F.2d 875 (9th Cir. 1987)—Jehovah's Witnesses' practice of "shunning" a disassociated church member is protected from suit for outrageous conduct; **Molko v. Holy Spirit Association for the Unification of World Christianity,** 46 Cal. 3d 1092 (1988)—threats of divine retribution made by church members were protected religious speech and could not form the basis for emotional distress claim; **Murphy v. International Society for Krishna Consciousness of New England,** 571 N.E.2d 340 (Mass. 1991)—no claim of emotional distress by mother of child who became involved with defendant group because claim could only be proved by testimony about the group's religious beliefs]

f. **Damages [§98]**
In addition to compensatory damages, punitive damages may be recoverable in states that permit them because of the nature of the defendant's act (subject to the limitations described *supra*, §§23-26).

(1) **Exception—conduct entirely speech [§99]**
Because of free speech concerns, some states that usually permit punitive damages may bar them if the tortious conduct is entirely speech. [**Huffman & Wright Logging Co. v. Wade,** 857 P.2d 101 (Or. 1993)]

B. Defenses and Privileged Invasions of Personal Interests

1. **Consent [§100]**
The plaintiff's consent to the defendant's conduct may be a defense to an intentional tort. Most courts require the ***defendant*** affirmatively to plead and prove that the plaintiff consented. A few make ***lack of consent*** an element of the prima facie case that the plaintiff must plead and prove.

a. **Types of consent [§101]**
There are two basic types of consent: consent based on the plaintiff's behavior and consent implied by law.

(1) **Consent based on plaintiff's behavior [§102]**
The plaintiff may consent by:

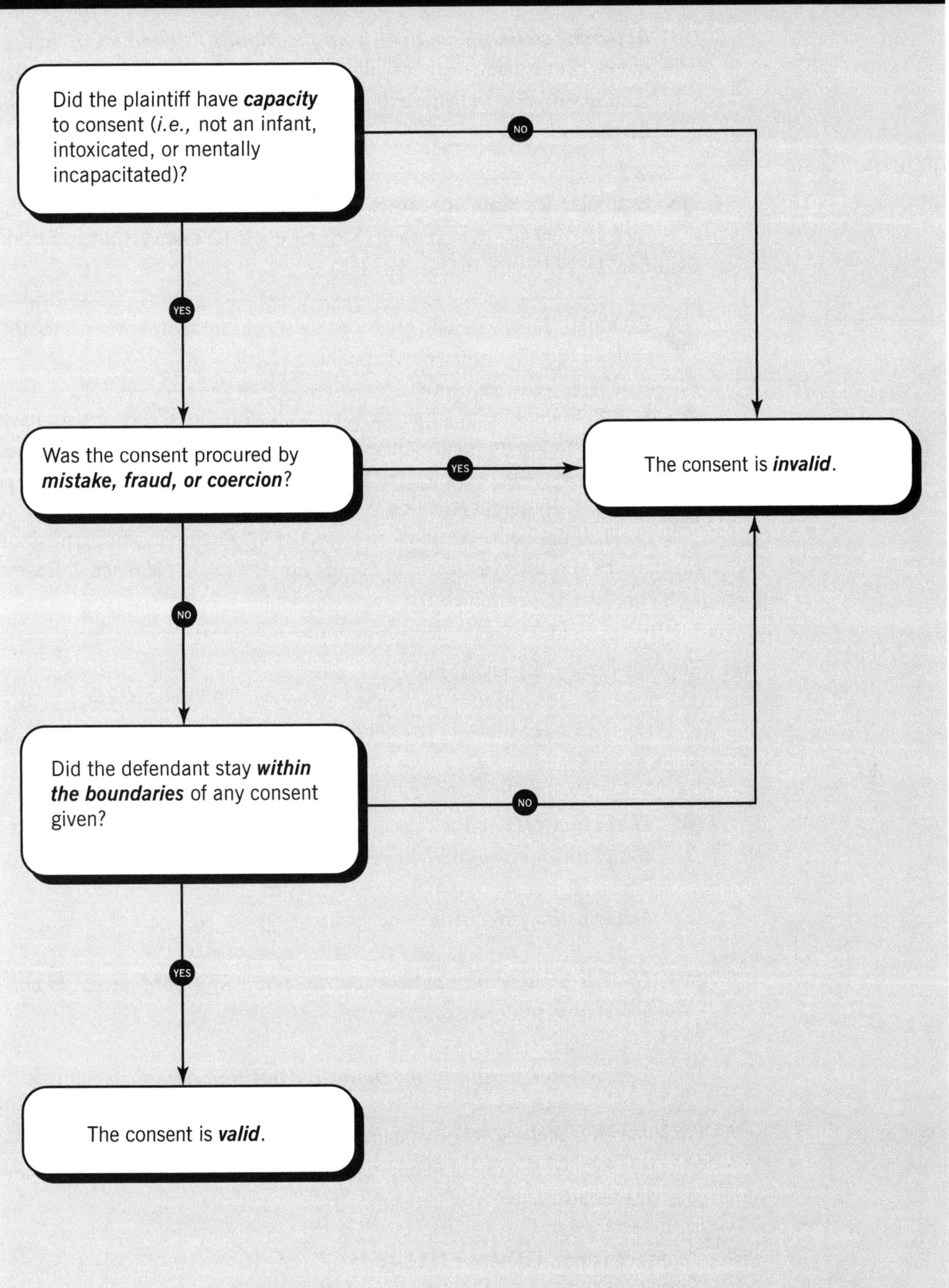
APPROACH TO DETERMINING VALIDITY OF CONSENT
gilbert
Did the plaintiff have capacity to consent (i.e., not an infant, intoxicated, or mentally incapacitated)?
NO
YES
Was the consent procured by mistake, fraud, or coercion?
YES
The consent is invalid.
NO
Did the defendant stay within the boundaries of any consent given?
NO
YES
The consent is valid.

(i) ***Actual express consent***—when the plaintiff actually ***communicates*** to the defendant a willingness to submit to the defendant's conduct; or

(ii) ***Apparent consent—implied from the plaintiff's conduct*** in light of the circumstances; *i.e.*, the plaintiff, by conduct, has led the defendant reasonably to believe that the plaintiff is willing to submit to the defendant's act.

---

e.g. **Example:** P's failure to object to a vaccination that P sees D preparing for P conveys apparent consent to the injection. [**O'Brien v. Cunard Steam-Ship Co.,** 28 N.E. 266 (Mass. 1891)]

---

e.g. **Example:** A person who enters into a sport impliedly consents to normal contacts by other participants.

---

e.g. **Example:** Similarly, someone who walks on the streets or uses mass transportation impliedly consents to taps on the shoulder or brushings.

---

e.g. **Example:** A parent standing in the middle of a stairwell during a school fire drill impliedly consents to a teacher's "placing her fingertips" on the parent's shoulder in an attempt to get her attention. [**Wallace v. Rosen,** 765 N.E.2d 192 (Ind. 2002)]

---

(2) Consent implied by law [§103]

The plaintiff's consent may be implied by law to a bodily contact (*e.g.*, surgery) that is necessary to save her life or some other cardinal interest in person or property *if*:

(i) ***The plaintiff is unconscious*** or otherwise ***unable*** to consider the matter and grant or withhold consent;

(ii) ***An immediate decision*** is necessary;

(iii) ***There is no reason to believe that the plaintiff would withhold consent*** if able to do so; ***and***

(iv) ***A reasonable person in the plaintiff's position would consent.***

[Rest. 2d §62; **Miller v. Rhode Island Hospital,** 625 A.2d 778 (R.I. 1993)—emergency room personnel may dispense with consent where patient is unable to give it due to intoxication]

b. When consent is not a defense [§104]

Consent is ***not*** effective in the following circumstances:

(1) **Acts in excess of consent given [§105]**

There is no effective consent if the invasion goes beyond the limits of the consent given.

---

e.g. **Example:** P consents for D, a doctor, to remove a uterine tumor. In the middle of the operation, D decides to remove P's diseased appendix. D's removal of P's appendix is an unprivileged battery because it went beyond the limits of the consent given. [***In re*** **Johnson's Estate,** 16 N.W.2d 504 (Neb. 1944)]

---

(2) **Fraud [§106]**

The plaintiff's consent to the invasion is ineffective if procured by fraud. [*See* **Bartell v. State,** 82 N.W. 142 (Wis. 1900)—magnetic healer taking indecent liberties with young woman while purporting to treat her]

---

e.g. **Example:** If P allows D to take blood from P's arm because D represents that this is necessary to save P's life, and D knew that these representations were untrue, the consent is void.

(a) **Distinguish—collateral fraud [§107]**

If the fraud is only with respect to a ***collateral matter,*** the consent is effective.

---

e.g. **Example:** If P consented to D's taking blood from P's arm because D had given P a $20 bill, the consent is effective even if the bill is counterfeit. [**Desnick v. American Broadcasting Cos.,** 44 F.3d 1345 (7th Cir. 1995)]

---

(3) **Duress [§108]**

The plaintiff's consent is ineffective if given under duress (physical force or threats thereof) against the plaintiff or a member of the plaintiff's family. [**Neibuhr v. Gage,** 108 N.W. 884 (Minn. 1906)]

(4) **Mistake [§109]**

The plaintiff's consent is also ineffective if given due to a mistake and either: (i) the mistake was caused by the defendant, or (ii) the defendant was aware of the mistake. [Rest. 2d §892]

(a) **Mistake of law [§110]**

A mistake of law caused by the defendant may render the plaintiff's consent ineffective.

---

e.g. **Example:** P is hurt while leaving a train, and the conductor tells P that P must file an accident report before he can get medical aid. Although P stays, his consent does not bar a subsequent suit for false imprisonment because it was given under a mistake of law caused by the conductor. [**Whitman v. Atchison, Topeka & Santa Fe Railway,** 116 P. 234 (Kan. 1911)]

(b) Mistake of fact [§111]

The plaintiff's mistake as to the ***essential nature or consequences*** of the invasion of her person or property is treated as a mistake of fact and voids any consent to the invasion if the mistake was caused by the defendant or the defendant was aware of it.

e.g. **Example:** For a fee, Owner consented to allow Lessee to build an earthen pit on Owner's property to dispose of waste salt water resulting from Lessee's operation of oil wells on the property. Salt water percolated down out of the pit and contaminated Owner's fresh water supply, which Owner relied on for farming purposes. Testimony showed that Lessee may have been aware of similar problems at other pits in the area and Lessee admitted that if he thought seriously about the pollution issue, he would have devised a different system of disposal. On the other hand, nothing in the facts showed that Owner knew or should have known that the salt water would percolate into the fresh water supply. Therefore, Owner's consent was void. [**Brown v. Lundell,** 344 S.W.2d 863 (Tex. 1961)]

1) Lack of consent in medical treatment [§112]

It is on this very basis that a patient's consent to surgery or other medical treatment is sometimes held ineffective, thereby exposing the doctor to liability for battery (*see supra,* §105). [**Gray v. Grunnagle,** 223 A.2d 663 (Pa. 1966)]

2) Lack of informed consent [§113]

Where the plaintiff asserts that she consented to the surgical procedure performed, but that she had not been adequately informed of the risks and benefits of the procedure, the claim is generally treated as one for negligence rather than an intentional tort (*see infra,* §311). [**Cobbs v. Grant,** 8 Cal. 3d 229 (1972)]

(5) Incapacity to consent [§114]

There is no valid consent if the plaintiff is known to be a person ***incapable*** of giving consent (*e.g.,* is an infant, or is drunk or mentally incapacitated). [**Hollerud v. Malamis,** 174 N.W.2d 626 (Mich. 1969)]

EXAM TIP **gilbert**

This requirement of capacity differs from the rule for the intent element of intentional torts, where incapacity is no defense; *i.e.,* everyone (even a young child) has the capacity to ***commit*** a tort, but not everyone has the capacity to ***consent*** to a tort.

(6) **Criminal acts [§115]**
There is a split of authority on whether the plaintiff's consent is effective if the act consented to is a ***crime.***

(a) **Majority view [§116]**
Most cases distinguish between criminal acts that involve ***breaches of the peace,*** and those that do not: If no breach of the peace was involved (*e.g.,* an illegal abortion), the plaintiff's consent is effective. On the other hand, if the consented-to act involved a breach of the peace (*e.g.,* a fight in the streets), these courts hold the plaintiff's consent ***not*** effective, thus permitting the plaintiff to recover from the defendant for any injuries sustained. [**Teeters v. Frost,** 292 P. 356 (Okla. 1930)]

1) **Rationale**
If a breach of the peace is involved, there is a public interest in seeing that the participants bear full liability—criminal and *civil*—for their acts.

(b) **Minority view [§117]**
Some courts hold the plaintiff's consent ***effective in any case***, thus barring any later claims by the plaintiff based on the illegal act. [**Hart v. Geysel,** 294 P. 570 (Wash. 1930); Rest. 2d §60]

1) **Rationale**
No reason is seen to invalidate the plaintiff's consent (and thus allow a cause of action) merely because the act consented to was a crime. Moreover, participants in criminal acts should be left in the status quo; if they are allowed to recover from each other, one might "profit" from her own wrongdoing. [**Sayadoff v. Warda,** 125 Cal. App. 2d 626 (1954)]

2) **Exception—plaintiff is a member of protected class [§118]**
Even under the minority view, however, the plaintiff's consent will be disregarded if the plaintiff is a member of the particular class of persons for whose benefit the statute was enacted.

---

e.g. **Example:** If a statute forbids boxing matches unless licensed by the state boxing commission, and also demonstrates a concern for the safety of participants, a boxer who is hurt in an unlicensed match may sue the promoter. [**Hudson v. Craft,** 33 Cal. 2d 654 (1949)]

---

2. Self-Defense

a. Using nondeadly force [§119]
When acting in self-defense, a defendant is privileged to use force that is ***not***

likely to cause death or serious bodily harm, subject to the following conditions [Rest. 2d §63]:

(1) Reasonable apprehension of any bodily contact [§120]
The plaintiff must have acted in a way that led the defendant to ***reasonably*** believe (either correctly or by reasonable mistake) that the plaintiff was about to inflict an ***imminent*** harmful or offensive contact upon him; and

(2) Reasonable means used [§121]
The defendant used only those means that appeared reasonably necessary to avoid or prevent the contact threatened.

(3) Retreat [§122]
The defendant must not have had a duty to retreat. There is ***generally no duty*** to retreat or comply with any demand made by the person threatening the force, ***except that:***

(a) ***If the defendant recognizes that the plaintiff is not intentionally creating the risk,*** there is a duty to retreat if he can safely do so; and

(b) ***If the defendant recognizes that the plaintiff has mistaken the defendant's identity,*** the defendant must make reasonable efforts to resolve the matter instead of using force in self-defense.

b. Using deadly force [§123]
The defendant is privileged to use force ***likely to cause death*** or serious bodily harm when acting in self-defense, subject to the following conditions [Rest. 2d §65]:

(1) Reasonable apprehension of serious bodily harm [§124]
The plaintiff must have acted in a way that led the defendant to reasonably believe that the plaintiff was about to inflict an imminent harmful or offensive contact upon him, ***and*** the defendant reasonably believed that such contact would inflict ***death or serious bodily harm.***

(2) Duty to retreat [§125]
There is a split over whether, as an alternative to using deadly force in self-defense, the defendant must retreat if it is safe to do so.

(a) Majority view [§126]
Most courts hold that there is ***no duty*** to retreat as an alternative to using deadly force that would otherwise be permissible. [*See* **People v. Bush,** 111 N.E.2d 326 (Ill. 1953)]

1) Rationale
When one is threatened with deadly force, the feasibility of retreat should not be second-guessed by courts after the event. Also,

as between the actor and the person threatening him, the actor has the "right" to be where he is. [**People v. Estrada,** 60 Cal. App. 477 (1923)]

(b) Minority view [§127]

A minority of courts impose a duty to retreat before using deadly force if this can be done safely. [Rest. 2d §65]

1) Rationale

The social interest in preventing deadly affrays outweighs the actor's "right" to stand his ground when threatened. [Joseph H. Beale, Retreat from a Murderous Assault, 16 Harv. L. Rev. 567 (1903)]

a) But note

Where ***guns*** are involved, there is rarely a means of safe retreat; thus, the minority view will not apply.

2) Exceptions [§128]

Even under the minority view, there is ***no duty*** to retreat if: (i) the defendant ***is in his own home*** (or also, in some states, his ***place of business***); (ii) retreating would endanger a third party; ***or*** (iii) the defendant is attempting a lawful arrest. [Rest. 2d §65(2)]

c. Threats of force [§129]

The defendant is privileged to ***threaten*** more force than he would in fact be privileged to use in self-defense, provided he has no reason to believe his threats will do more than place the plaintiff in apprehension. (This protects the defendant from liability for assault based on such threats.) [Rest. 2d §70(2)]

d. Limitations on right of self-defense [§130]

The privilege to act in self-defense is not unlimited.

(1) Danger terminated [§131]

There is no privilege of self-defense if the ***defendant knows that the danger has terminated.*** [**Germolus v. Sausser,** 85 N.W. 946 (Minn. 1901)—D continued to whip P after P was disarmed]

(2) Excessive force used [§132]

Neither is there any privilege to use force ***in excess of*** that which the defendant is privileged to use to defend himself (*e.g.,* P slaps D across the face; D could easily prevent further harm by holding plaintiff's arms, but instead stabs P with a knife). When excessive force is used:

(i) ***The defendant is liable*** for whatever amount of the force is excessive; ***and***

(ii) ***The plaintiff then has a privilege of self-defense*** to protect herself against the degree of force being inflicted by the defendant. (In the example above, P might become privileged to use deadly force to defend against D's knife attack.)

[Rest. 2d §71]

(3) Plaintiff using privileged force [§133]

There is no privilege of self-defense against ***privileged*** action by another (*e.g.,* a lawful arrest). [Rest. 2d §72; **Ellis v. State,** 596 N.E.2d 428 (Ohio 1992)—trespasser not entitled to assert self-defense to justify assault on another who had legitimately used nonlethal force to exclude trespasser from property]

(4) Third person intentionally injured [§134]

Finally, the privilege of self-defense does not justify the defendant's ***intentional*** use of harmful force ***against a third person.*** [Rest. 2d §73]

---

e.g. **Example:** X threatens D with serious bodily harm. If, in attempting to escape from X, D intentionally runs over P, causing her injury, D is liable to P for battery.

(a) Distinguish—unintentional harm [§135]

But if the defendant ***unintentionally*** injures a third person while reasonably attempting to defend himself, he will be liable only if he was ***negligent*** toward the third person. [**Helms v. Harris,** 281 S.W.2d 770 (Tex. 1955)]

e. "Reasonableness" [§136]

Self-defense rules are couched in terms of "reasonableness." This is an ***objective test—i.e.,*** how the situation would have looked to the reasonable person in the same or similar circumstances, ***not*** how the defendant actually perceived it ***or*** how it actually was.

3. Defense of Third Persons [§137]

The defendant may also be privileged to use force to defend another person. However, the force the defendant may use is limited to that which the person defended would have been privileged to use in self-defense under the circumstances. Use of force in this situation raises certain additional issues:

a. Who may be defended [§138]

Under modern law, the policy is to encourage a person to go to the aid of ***anyone*** who is endangered—even if the person defended is a complete stranger to the defendant.

b. Effect of defendant's mistake in intervening [§139]

Nevertheless, the courts are split on whether the defendant is privileged if the person defended was not actually entitled to defend himself. For example, undercover police officer P attempts to arrest X; D does not realize P is a police officer, thinks P is beating up X, and goes to X's aid, injuring P.

(1) Older view [§140]

Traditionally, courts held that if D intervenes, he must "stand in the shoes" of the person he is defending, so that ***unless the person being helped was actually privileged*** to defend himself, D is subject to tort liability (*e.g.*, battery). Thus, the privilege could not be based on the defendant's mistake, no matter how reasonable.

(2) Modern view [§141]

The Restatement and recent cases allow a reasonable mistake in exercise of the privilege. Hence, D is privileged to use force to defend a third person as long as the actor correctly or reasonably believes that:

(i) The ***third person (X) was privileged*** to defend himself and to use the ***means*** of defense (deadly vs. nondeadly) and ***amount*** of force that D used; and

(ii) D's intervention was ***necessary*** to protect the third person.

[Rest. 2d §76; **Clark v. Ziedonis,** 513 F.2d 79 (7th Cir. 1975)]

4. Defense of Land or Chattels

a. Use of nondeadly force [§142]

A defendant may ***not use deadly force*** (force likely to cause death or serious bodily harm) to defend his land or chattels. He is privileged to use force ***not likely*** to cause death or serious bodily harm, but only ***if***:

(i) ***The intrusion by the plaintiff is not privileged,*** or is conducted so as to lead the defendant to reasonably believe that it is not privileged; ***and***

(ii) ***The defendant reasonably believes that force is necessary*** to prevent or terminate the plaintiff's intrusion; ***and***

(iii) ***The defendant, prior to the use of force, demands that the plaintiff desist or leave,*** and the demand is ignored. (No demand need be made, however, where it reasonably appears that it would be futile or would further endanger the defendant's property.)

[Rest. 2d §77; **Daniels v. Dillard Department Stores, Inc.,** 881 F. Supp. 505 (D. Kan. 1995)—officers privileged to use force where plaintiff was loud, profane, disruptive, and hostile toward officers, was told she would have to leave store or be arrested for trespass if she did not calm down, and she did not comply]

EXAM TIP gilbert

Remember that this defense is ***not available against someone with a privilege***. Whenever an actor has a privilege to enter onto the land of another because of necessity, recapture of chattels, etc. (see *infra*), that privilege will ***supersede*** the privilege of the land possessor to defend her property.

EXAM TIP gilbert

There is a common misperception that deadly force may be used to protect one's home. This is not strictly true. Many of the "home defense" cases are really ***self-defense*** cases. Thus, deadly force can only be used when a ***person***, not just property, is threatened.

b. Use of mechanical devices [§143]

The defendant is privileged to use mechanical devices (high-voltage fences, spring traps, etc.) in defense of his land or chattels ***only if:***

(i) ***The use of such means*** to protect property is ***reasonable and necessary*** under the circumstances, or ***customary*** in the locale; ***and***

(ii) ***Adequate warning*** of the use thereof is given or posted.

[Rest. 2d §84; **Allison v. Fiscus,** 100 N.E.2d 237 (Ohio 1951)]

(1) Deadly mechanical devices [§144]

If the devices employed threaten ***death or serious bodily harm,*** their use is privileged only if the intrusion ***in fact constitutes*** (not just reasonably appears to constitute) a threat of death or serious bodily harm to the defendant or his family. [Rest. 2d §85]

(a) Rationale

Simple trespass, vandalism, or theft is ***not*** sufficient justification for use of deadly devices. [**Katko v. Briney,** 183 N.W.2d 657 (Iowa 1971)—spring gun; *but see* Alaska Stat. §09.65.210 (1987)—no recovery for personal injury or death sustained in the commission of a felony]

c. Use of threats [§145]

A defendant is privileged to ***threaten*** a ***greater*** amount of force than he would actually be privileged to use in defense of his property (*e.g.*, farmer pointing shotgun at trespasser crossing field)—provided that he has no reason to believe that such threats would cause anything more than fright or apprehension in the plaintiff. [Rest. 2d §81]

5. Force to Recover Possession of Land Wrongfully Withheld

a. **Majority view [§146]**

Under the present majority rule, there is ***no privilege*** to use force to recover possession of land wrongfully withheld even if the owner has been "tortiously dispossessed" (below). An owner who uses force to retake possession will be liable for the resulting harm (*e.g.*, battery). The owner's title or right to possession of land is ***no defense*** to the tort. [**Daluiso v. Boone,** 71 Cal. 2d 484 (1969)]

(1) **Rationale**

In practically all states today, there are judicial procedures (*e.g.*, ejectment, unlawful detainer, etc.) that provide a quick and effective remedy for the recovery of land wrongfully withheld. Such procedures are supported by public policy favoring resort to courts, rather than self-help, to settle land disputes.

b. **Minority view [§147]**

A minority of jurisdictions follow the Restatement rule that a person who is entitled to possession of land, and who has been "tortiously dispossessed" therefrom, may use ***reasonable, nondeadly force*** to regain possession—provided he acts promptly upon discovering the dispossession. [**Shorter v. Shelton,** 33 S.E.2d 643 (Va. 1945); Rest. 2d §§89, 91]

(1) **"Tortious dispossession" [§148]**

The term "tortious dispossession" means that the plaintiff obtained possession ***by force, fraud, or duress,*** or without any claim of right (*e.g.*, is a trespasser).

(2) **Distinguish—other dispossessions [§149]**

If there was ***no tortious dispossession,*** there is no privilege to use ***any*** force to recover possession of land, on the rationale that the owner's right to possession is less important than avoidance of the affrays and violence which the use of force might entail. [Rest. 2d §88]

---

e.g. **Example:** P cannot use force against a tenant who overstays the lease, or a person who moves onto property in the honest but mistaken belief that he owns it.

---

6. **Force to Effect Recapture of Chattels Wrongfully Withheld**

a. **Tortious dispossession cases [§150]**

A defendant who has been ***tortiously dispossessed*** of chattels (*e.g.*, by a robber, pickpocket, shoplifter, or defrauder) is privileged to use ***reasonable, nondeadly force*** in recapture of those chattels. [**Rogers v. Kabakoff,** 81 Cal. App. 2d 487 (1947)] This privilege, however, is subject to the following conditions [Rest. 2d §§101-106]:

(1) **Immediate right to possession [§151]**
The defendant must in fact be ***entitled to the immediate possession*** of the chattel. (No mistake, however reasonable, is permitted.)

(2) **Demand [§152]**
The defendant must ***demand return*** of the chattel and the demand must be ignored (but if demand would be futile or dangerous, no demand is required).

(3) **Fresh pursuit [§153]**
The recapture must be effected promptly—*i.e.,* the defendant must be in ***"fresh pursuit."*** This encompasses two factors: (i) the defendant must have been reasonably diligent in ***discovering*** the loss; and (ii) following discovery, the defendant must have been reasonably diligent in his ***efforts*** to retake the chattel. Both of these requirements are measured by a "reasonable person" standard.

(4) **Holder at fault [§154]**
The defendant must effect the recapture from the person who tortiously dispossessed him, or from a third party who has notice that the chattels involved were stolen, etc.

(a) **Distinguish—transfer to innocent person [§155]**
If the thief has sold or given the chattels to an innocent party, this cuts off the defendant's privilege to use force to effect their recapture, even if he can show "fresh pursuit."

b. **Other dispossessions [§156]**
If the defendant has ***not*** been tortiously dispossessed of chattels (*i.e.,* no fraud, force, etc.), the general rule is that he is ***not privileged to use any force*** to effect their recapture. Redress must be in the courts.

---

e.g. **Example:** B borrows A's book and later decides not to return it; or A parks his car in B's parking lot, and B later refuses to release the car. In either case, A has no privilege to use force to get back his property.

---

(1) **Conditional sales contracts [§157]**
When a buyer defaults on a conditional sales contract, the seller is entitled to ***peacefully*** repossess; neither force nor fraud is permitted. [**Stallworth v. Doss,** 194 So. 2d 566 (Ala. 1967)] In fact, even if the sales contract purports to allow for a forceful recapture, most courts will find such a provision void as against public policy. [**Girard v. Anderson,** 257 N.W. 400 (Iowa 1934)]

c. **"Shopkeepers' privilege" [§158]**
Most states today recognize a privilege, usually limited to shopkeepers, to ***detain temporarily*** for investigation anyone whom they reasonably suspect of having

tortiously taken their goods. [**Teel v. May Department Stores Co.,** 155 S.W.2d 74 (Mo. 1941); Rest. 2d §120A]

(1) Rationale

This privilege has been justified by the very practical need for some degree of protection for shopkeepers in their dealings with suspected shoplifters. Absent such privilege, a shopkeeper would be faced with the dilemma of either allowing suspects to leave without challenge or acting upon his suspicion and risking a false arrest if mistaken.

(2) Requirements [§159]

Proper exercise of the privilege requires that *all* of the following conditions be satisfied [**Collyer v. S.H. Kress,** 5 Cal. 2d 175 (1936)]:

(a) Investigation on or near premises [§160]

The detention itself must be effected either on the store premises or in the *immediate vicinity* thereof.

(b) Reasonable suspicion [§161]

The shopkeeper must have *reasonable grounds to suspect* the *particular person* detained.

(c) Reasonable force [§162]

Only *reasonable, nondeadly* force may be used to effect the detention.

(d) Reasonable period and manner of detention [§163]

The detention itself may be only for the period of time necessary for reasonable investigation (usually very short) and must be conducted in a reasonable manner.

(3) Effect—reasonable mistake protected [§164]

Where these conditions are established, the shopkeeper is immune from liability for false arrest, battery, etc.—even though it turns out that the person detained was innocent of any wrongdoing. [**Teel v. May Department Stores Co.,** *supra*]

7. Privilege of Arrest

a. Arrests for felonies without an arrest warrant [§165]

There is a distinction between felony arrests made by the police and those made by private citizens.

(1) *A police officer* is privileged to arrest for a felony without a warrant if he reasonably suspects that a felony has been committed *and* that the person he arrests committed it. [Rest. 2d §121; **United States v. Watson,** 423 U.S. 411 (1976)—requiring "reasonable grounds" for warrantless arrest]

(2) ***A private citizen*** is privileged to arrest for a felony without a warrant only if a felony has ***in fact*** been committed, and he reasonably suspects that the person he arrests committed it. [Rest. 2d §119]

b. Arrests for misdemeanors without an arrest warrant [§166]

According to the general view, both police officers and private citizens are privileged to arrest for misdemeanors without a warrant if the misdemeanor involves a ***breach of the peace*** that has ***in fact*** been committed in the presence of the arresting party, who makes the arrest in ***fresh pursuit.***

(1) Minority view [§167]

Under a minority view, a ***police officer*** is privileged to arrest for a misdemeanor based on the ***reasonable belief*** that the misdemeanor was being committed ***in his presence*** and that the ***party arrested is guilty***. [**Coverstone v. Davies,** 38 Cal. 2d 315 (1952)]

c. Arrests under arrest warrant [§168]

An arrest made under a warrant "fair on its face" is privileged—even if it develops that the warrant was improperly issued and the person arrested is innocent of any crime.

(1) "Fair on its face" [§169]

A warrant is "fair on its face" as long as ***its face*** is free of defects that a reasonable police officer would discover. (*See* Criminal Procedure Summary regarding warrant requirements.)

(2) Distinguish—search warrant [§170]

An arrest made without an arrest warrant and without probable cause while the officer is executing a ***search*** warrant gives rise to an action for false arrest. [**Barr v. County of Albany,** 50 N.Y.2d 247 (1980)]

d. Amount of force privileged

(1) Misdemeanors [§171]

If the arrest is for a misdemeanor, both the police officer and the private person are privileged to use that degree of force necessary to effect the arrest, but ***never deadly force.*** [**Noback v. Town of Montclair,** 110 A.2d 339 (N.J. 1954)]

(2) Felonies [§172]

If the arrest is for a ***felony,*** there is a split of authority as to the permissible use of deadly force:

(a) Traditional view [§173]

The traditional common law rule (still followed in a number of states) provides that in a lawful arrest for ***any*** felony, ***deadly*** force may be used by police officers or private persons, if reasonably necessary to effect the arrest. [Rest. 2d §131]

(b) Modern view—deadly force limited to "serious" felonies [§174]
Some states now limit the right to use deadly force to arrests for "serious" felonies (*e.g.*, murder, rape, robbery, etc.) and do ***not*** permit deadly force in arrests for other felonies, such as larceny. [**Peterson v. City of Long Beach,** 24 Cal. 3d 238 (1979)]

1) Rationale
There are far more felonies today than there were at common law and many modern felonies are not as "serious" as common law felonies, so the mere fact that a felony is implicated does not establish that the social interest in apprehending a suspect is sufficient to outweigh the potential for harm to innocent parties resulting from the use of deadly force.

2) Fourth Amendment requirement [§175]
The Supreme Court has held that use of deadly force by police officers is reasonable under the Fourth Amendment only if it is necessary to prevent a felon's escape (or to capture a suspect) ***and*** there is probable cause to believe that the felon or suspect poses a ***significant threat of death or serious injury*** to the officer or others. [**Tennessee v. Garner,** 471 U.S. 1 (1985); *and see* Model Penal Code §3.07]

a) Effect on state tort law [§176]
States are free to define defenses to a state tort claim. Therefore, a state statute may privilege a defendant's use of force in the plaintiff's state tort claim, even if the same action is a violation of the plaintiff's constitutional rights under the *Garner* standards for deadly force. [**Brown v. City of Clewiston,** 848 F.2d 1534 (11th Cir. 1988)]

b) Effect on constitutional torts [§177]
However, in a federal civil action where the plaintiff sues the defendant for violating the plaintiff's constitutional rights, the defendant's force is privileged only if it meets the *Garner* standards.

e. Right to invade land [§178]
The privilege of arrest carries with it the privilege of entering another's land for the purpose of effecting an arrest. [Rest. 2d §204]

f. Effect of defendant's misconduct following arrest [§179]
What happens if the initial arrest was privileged, but the defendant subsequently uses excessive force against the arrestee or unreasonably delays arraignment (so

that the arrestee is held an unreasonably long time without being able to get out on bail)? The modern view is that the person making the arrest is liable only for such harm as is attributable to his misconduct following the arrest—*i.e.*, only for the force or detention exceeding the amount that was otherwise privileged. [**Dragna v. White,** 45 Cal. 2d 469 (1955); Rest. 2d §136]

g. **Resisting arrest [§180]**

Although the traditional view allowed a person unlawfully arrested to use reasonable force to resist, the modern trend has been to deny such a privilege. [**State v. Koonce,** 214 A.2d 428 (N.J. 1965)] Moreover, in some states, failure to submit to asserted legal authority is itself a crime [*see, e.g.*, Cal. Penal Code §834a] so that even though the original arrest was improper, the officer may use reasonable force to arrest for the ***crime of resisting arrest.***

ARRESTS WITHOUT AN ARREST WARRANT **gilbert**

	FELONY ARREST BY POLICE OFFICER	FELONY ARREST BY PRIVATE CITIZEN	MISDEMEANOR ARRESTS
WHEN PRIVILEGED	The officer must ***reasonably suspect*** that a felony has been committed ***and*** that the person he arrests has committed it	The felony must have ***in fact*** been committed and the citizen must reasonably suspect that the person he arrests has committed it	The misdemeanor must be a ***breach of peace*** committed in the arresting party's ***presence*** (minority allows police to arrest on ***reasonable belief*** that a misdemeanor was committed in his presence and that person arrested is guilty)

8. **Privilege of Discipline [§181]**

Parents and teachers are recognized as having the privilege to use such "reasonable" force or confinement as they believe "reasonably" necessary for the proper control, training, and education of children in their care. [Rest. 2d §147] A similar privilege is recognized in military service. [Rest. 2d §146]

a. **But note**

Some legislatures and courts have rejected the common law approach as applied to corporal punishment. [*See* **Rodriguez v. Johnson,** 132 Misc. 2d 555 (1986)—school bus matron who slapped rowdy child was liable for battery although the slap was not excessive use of force]

ALLOWABLE FORCE IN DEFENSES TO INTENTIONAL TORTS **gilbert**

	AMOUNT OF FORCE ALLOWED	
DEFENSE	NONDEADLY FORCE	DEADLY FORCE
SELF-DEFENSE	If reasonably necessary to protect self and ***no duty to retreat***	Only if faced with threat of imminent ***death or serious bodily harm***
DEFENSE OF OTHERS	If reasonably necessary to protect third person	Only if third person faced with threat of imminent ***death or serious bodily harm***
DEFENSE OF PROPERTY	If reasonably necessary to defend one's property ***after demanding*** (unless futile) that P desist or leave	Never
RECOVER LAND	If reasonably necessary to regain possession of ***tortiously dispossessed*** land	Never
RECAPTURE CHATTELS	If reasonably necessary to recapture ***tortiously dispossessed*** chattels ***after demanding*** their return and while in ***hot pursuit***	Never
EFFECTUATE ARREST		
• **POLICE**	If reasonably necessary to arrest for felony or misdemeanor	**Felony:** Modern view allows deadly force only for ***serious*** felonies, such as murder, rape, etc. *But note:* Police use of deadly force may be a ***constitutional*** violation unless reasonably necessary to arrest suspected felon who threatens death or serious bodily harm **Misdemeanor:** Never
• **PRIVATE CITIZEN**	If reasonably necessary to arrest for felony or misdemeanor	**Felony:** Modern view allows deadly force only for ***serious*** felonies, such as murder, rape, etc. **Misdemeanor:** Never
DISCIPLINE	If reasonably necessary for proper control, training, and education of children or military personnel	Never

C. Torts to Property

1. Trespass to Land [§182]

Prima facie case:

- *Act by Defendant*
- *Intent*
- *Intrusion upon Land*
- *Plaintiff in Possession or Entitled to Immediate Possession*
- *Causation*

a. Act by defendant [§183]

To make out a prima facie case for trespass to land, the plaintiff must show a volitional movement by defendant of some part of his body that results in an ***intrusion onto another's land*** or that sets in motion a force resulting in such intrusion.

---

e.g. **Example:** If D pushes X onto P's land, there is an invasion of P's land—but D and not X is the trespasser (because there was no volitional movement by X).

---

b. Intent [§184]

The defendant must have intended ***to do the act that causes the intrusion*** onto the land or have ***known with substantial certainty*** that his actions would cause entry. However, he need not realize that the land belongs to another; he is liable for an intentional entry even though he acts in good faith, believing himself to be the owner.

(1) Distinguish—negligence [§185]

If it appears that the defendant's invasion of the land was not intentional, he might still be liable on a negligence theory (*see infra,* §§276 *et seq.*).

---

e.g. **Example:** D drives his automobile down the highway with knowledge that his luggage rack is not fastened securely, and the rack flies off the car and onto P's land. D might very well be held liable for negligence—*if* P can show ***damages.*** (Damages are required where liability is based on negligence, but ***not*** where the trespass is intentional; *see infra,* §510.)

(a) Note

Although authorities differ as to whether such an action is properly described as "trespass" or "negligence," because the plaintiff must prove actual damages and punitive damages are not available, the distinction seems semantic.

(2) Distinguish—strict liability [§186]

Alternatively, certain invasions may be actionable on the theory of strict liability (*see infra,* §§881 *et seq.*)—*e.g.,* rocks hurled onto P's land as the result of D's exploding dynamite on neighboring property.

(3) Transferred intent [§187]

The transferred intent doctrine applies to trespass (*see supra,* §10).

c. Intrusion upon land [§188]

The defendant's intrusion may be by personal entry onto the plaintiff's land or by causing some third person or thing to enter (*e.g.,* D obstructs a stream so that water flows onto P's land). Alternatively, it may be found in the defendant's failure either to leave the land, or to remove property therefrom, after permission to remain has expired. [**Rogers v. Board of Road Commissioners,** 30 N.W.2d 358 (Mich. 1948); Rest. 2d §158]

(1) Intrusion by intangibles [§189]

Where the intrusion consists of intangible things such as dust particles, smoke, vibrations, noise, odors, etc., some courts treat the intrusion as a ***nuisance*** (*see infra,* §§1107 *et seq.*) rather than a trespass. Other courts allow liability either pursuant to trespass or nuisance, or both. [**Martin v. Reynolds Metals Co.,** 342 P.2d 790 (Or. 1959)]

d. Plaintiff in possession or entitled to immediate possession [§190]

At the time of the trespass, the plaintiff's interest in the land must be either actual possession or the right to immediate possession.

(1) "Actual possession" [§191]

The person actually in possession may bring an action for trespass because any possession is a legal possession as against a trespasser. Thus, even a wrongful occupier (*e.g.,* adverse possessor) may maintain a trespass action against a wrongful intruder. [Rest. 2d §157]

(2) "Right to immediate possession" [§192]

If no one is in actual possession, the person who has the ***right to immediate possession*** may maintain the action. ("Immediate" means the holder of some present possessory estate, as contrasted with a future interest; *see* Property Summary.)

(a) Dispossessed owner cannot sue [§193]

If an owner has been ousted from possession by another (*e.g.,* by an adverse possessor), the owner ***cannot*** maintain a suit for trespass because the ***dispossessor*** is in "actual possession." The owner must bring suit to ***eject*** the person who dispossessed her and make him account for any damage to the property during the time he held it. [**Kelman v. Wilen,** 283 A.D. 1113 (1954)]

(b) Lease cases [§194]

During the term of a lease, the tenant has ***both*** actual possession and the right to immediate possession. The landlord has neither (*i.e.,* he has only a future interest—a reversion).

1) Modern rule [§195]

Under the modern rule, ***either*** the landlord or the tenant can maintain trespass. However, the ***recovery*** available depends on who sues:

a) ***If the tenant sues,*** some courts allow recovery only for interference with the tenant's interest (*i.e.,* the right to exclusive possession until the end of the term). Other courts allow the tenant to also recover for any permanent injury to the property, but these latter damages must be held in trust for the landlord.

b) ***If the landlord sues,*** most courts allow recovery ***only*** for the damages to the ***landlord's*** interest (*i.e.,* for permanent injury to the property).

(3) Extent of possession—airspace above land [§196]

There has never been much doubt that a certain amount of the airspace above land is deemed part of the occupant's "actual possession," so that an intrusion thereof (*e.g.,* by telephone lines or by an overhanging building) can constitute an actionable trespass. But the question is ***how high*** the right to exclusive possession extends. This issue is of particular importance where the intrusion is by aircraft.

(a) Above normal flight altitude [§197]

Under modern authority, a landowner has no right to possession of that portion of the airspace that extends ***above*** the minimum altitudes for normal aircraft flights (excluding landing and takeoff). In effect, such upper airspace is a "public highway" in which no private possessory rights exist; hence, no trespass action will lie for its invasion. [**United States v. Causby,** 328 U.S. 256 (1946)]

(b) Beneath normal flight altitude [§198]

On the other hand, the landowner may have a protectable right to the airspace below minimum flight altitude.

1) Modern view—"immediate reaches" standard [§199]

Modern authority holds that a landowner's right to possession extends to the airspace within the ***"immediate reaches"*** of the land, but at the same time, invasions of such lower airspace are often deemed ***privileged*** as long as they do not "interfere substantially with the landowner's use and enjoyment of his land"—

i.e., as long as they do not constitute a nuisance. [Rest. 2d §159(2)—based on **United States v. Causby,** *supra*]

a) **What constitutes "immediate reaches" [§200]**
The term "immediate reaches" of the land has yet to be defined, but the Restatement suggests that any flight under 50 feet is clearly within the "immediate reaches," while any flight over 500 feet clearly is not. Indeed, any flight within 500 feet of a person or structure, except for landing and takeoff, would violate Federal Aviation Administration regulations. [14 C.F.R. §91.119]

(c) **Distinguish—nuisance [§201]**
Even if the landowner has no right to possession of the airspace involved (*e.g.*, flights through upper airspace or in airspace not directly over landowner's premises), the landowner may be entitled to protection against unreasonable interference (through noise, fumes, vibrations, etc.) with the use and enjoyment of the land on a ***nuisance*** theory (*see infra,* §§1107 *et seq.*). [**Nestle v. City of Santa Monica,** 6 Cal. 3d 920 (1972)]

e. **Causation [§202]**
Finally, for trespass to land the invasion must be caused by the defendant's intentional act or some force set in motion thereby. (As to what is sufficient causation, *see* discussion of this element, *supra,* §17.)

(1) **Unforeseeable harm [§203]**
A trespasser is liable for harm to person or property caused to the owner even if the harm was not foreseeable. [**Baker v. Shymkiv,** 451 N.E.2d 811 (Ohio 1983)—confrontation with trespasser caused owner to have heart attack]

f. **Damages [§204]**
It is immaterial whether any actual damages were caused. [Rest. 2d §163] Trespass to land is complete upon the defendant's intentional intrusion, and the defendant will be liable for at least nominal damages for harm to the plaintiff's right to exclusive possession. *Rationale:* The defendant's conduct if repeated might otherwise ripen into a ***prescriptive right*** (*see* Property Summary). (As to punitive damages, *see supra,* §§23-26.)

(1) **Exception—chemical pollutants [§205]**
If there is a continuing trespass by intrusion of chemical pollutants, the plaintiff may be required to plead actual and substantial damages. [**Bradley v. American Smelting & Refining Co.,** 709 P.2d 782 (Wash. 1985)]

2. **Trespass to Chattels [§206]**
Prima facie case:

- *Act by Defendant*
- *Intent*
- *Invasion of Chattel Interest*
- *Plaintiff in Possession or Entitled to Immediate Possession*
- *Causation*
- *Damages* (where only intermeddling involved)

a. **Act by defendant [§207]**
To make out a prima facie case for trespass to chattels, the plaintiff must show a volitional movement by the defendant of some part of his body that results in ***dispossession of or damage to the chattels of another.*** (Note that "chattel," as used herein, includes any tangible identifiable object (*e.g.*, computer memory), but does not include a purely monetary debt. [*See* **CompuServe Inc. v. Cyber Promotions, Inc.,** 962 F. Supp. 1015 (S.D. Ohio 1997)])

b. **Intent [§208]**
It is necessary only that the defendant have intended ***to deal with the chattel in the manner in which he did deal***; the fact that he may have been acting under a mistaken claim of right, thinking the chattel belonged to him all the time, is immaterial.

(1) **Note**
If intent to deal with the chattel cannot be shown, ***negligence*** or ***strict liability*** may possibly be a basis for an alternative cause of action.

(2) **Transferred intent [§209]**
The transferred intent doctrine applies (*see supra*, §10).

c. **Invasion of chattel interest [§210]**
The defendant's volitional act (or some force set in motion thereby) must have resulted in either a ***"dispossession" or*** an ***"intermeddling"*** with the chattel of another. [Rest. 2d §217] (The principal reason for this distinction concerns the damages requirement, below.)

(1) **"Dispossession" [§211]**
"Dispossession" refers to conduct amounting to the defendant's assertion of a proprietary interest in the chattel over the interests of the rightful owner. Examples include theft or destruction of the chattel, or even a barring of the rightful owner's access to it.

(2) **"Intermeddling" [§212]**
"Intermeddling" embraces conduct by the defendant that does ***not*** challenge the rightful owner's interest in the chattel, although the defendant may have gone so far as to carry the chattel away. "Intermeddling" includes throwing a stone at another's automobile, beating another's animals, or stampeding another's herd of cattle.

d. **Plaintiff in possession or entitled to immediate possession [§213]**
The plaintiff must either be in actual possession or must have the right to immediate possession; this is the same as in a trespass to land (*see supra,* §§191-192). [**John A. Artukovich & Sons, Inc. v. Reliance Truck Co.,** 614 P.2d 327 (Ariz. 1980)]

e. **Causation [§214]**
As with a trespass to land, the invasion must have been legally caused by the defendant's intentional act or a force set in motion thereby. (Again, for further discussion of this element, *see supra,* §17.)

f. **Damages [§215]**
If the defendant's conduct amounts to a ***"dispossession,"*** or the defendant otherwise deprives the plaintiff of the chattel's use, the plaintiff can recover for loss of possession (*e.g.,* rental value) even if the chattel itself has not been damaged. In cases of dispossession, the plaintiff may choose to sue for conversion of chattels (*see infra*). But if the defendant's act accomplishes only an ***"intermeddling"*** short of interfering with plaintiff's possession, a trespass action will not lie absent a showing of ***actual damage*** to the chattel. [**Glidden v. Szybiak,** 63 A.2d 233 (N.H. 1949)] (As to punitive damages, *see supra,* §23.)

3. **Conversion of Chattels [§216]**
Prima facie case:

- *Act by Defendant*
- *Intent*
- *Substantial Invasion of Chattel Interest*
- *Plaintiff in Possession or Entitled to Immediate Possession*
- *Causation*

a. **Act by defendant [§217]**
To make out a prima facie case for conversion, the plaintiff must show a volitional movement by the defendant of some part of his body that results in a ***substantial interference with another's possession*** of her chattels.

b. **Intent [§218]**
The defendant need only have intended ***to deal with the chattel in the manner in which he actually did deal with it.*** Thus, if the defendant did to the chattel what he intended to do, it is no defense that he was ***not*** a conscious wrongdoer (as where he mistakenly thought he was the owner). [Rest. 2d §244]

---

e.g. **Example:** A towing company is liable for conversion when it refuses to deliver an impounded car until outstanding charges are paid—even though it mistakenly believes it has a lien on the car for such charges. [**Murrell v. Trio Towing Service, Inc.,** 294 So. 2d 331 (Fla. 1974); *but see* **Simonian v. Patterson,** 27 Cal. App. 4th 773 (1994)—no conversion in helping daughter move belongings that appeared to be hers]

---

(1) **Note**

Remember the possibility of invoking ***negligence*** or ***strict liability*** as bases for other actions where the requisite intent to establish a conversion cannot be shown.

c. **Substantial invasion of chattel interest of another [§219]**

The invasion required for a conversion claim is greater than that required for a trespass to chattels claim. The following invasions will suffice:

(1) **Substantial dispossession [§220]**

If the defendant takes a chattel from another without the other's consent, bars the possessor's access to the chattel, or obtains possession of a chattel by fraud, there is a conversion. [**Russell-Vaughn Ford, Inc. v. Rouse,** 206 So. 2d 371 (Ala. 1968)]

(a) **Distinguish—trespass to chattels [§221]**

However, if the defendant merely intermeddles with the owner's rights in the chattel or if the defendant's interference with the owner's rights is not "substantial," the owner has at most a trespass claim against the defendant. [**Zaslow v. Kroenert,** 29 Cal. 2d 541 (1946)—no conversion where defendant tenant-in-common took plaintiff's goods and placed them in storage but did not otherwise exercise dominion over them; no showing of permanent ouster of possession]

(2) **Destroying or altering [§222]**

If the defendant destroys or materially alters a chattel, there is a conversion.

(3) **Unauthorized use by bailee [§223]**

If the defendant receives possession of the chattel as bailee and uses it in such a manner as to constitute a ***material breach*** of his authority, there is a conversion. [Rest. 2d §228]

(a) **Note**

An important factor is whether any harm to the chattel was caused by ***or during*** the improper use (*e.g.,* car rented in Boston for trip to Baltimore, driven instead to Miami, where it is seriously damaged in a collision). This is usually enough to constitute a conversion—even if the harm was entirely accidental and ***not the fault of the bailee!*** [**Perham v. Coney,** 117 Mass. 102 (1875)]

(4) **Buying or receiving stolen property [§224]**

If the defendant buys or receives stolen property, even though he acts in good faith, there is a conversion because this still involves the requisite intent to assert ownership rights and to deal with the chattel in a manner inconsistent with the rights of the true owner. [Rest. 2d §229]

(5) **Selling or disposing of stolen property [§225]**
If the defendant sells or otherwise disposes of the stolen property, even though acting in good faith, there is a conversion.

(6) **Misdelivering a chattel [§226]**
If the defendant misdelivers a chattel, there is a conversion even though the defendant acts in good faith. This covers the situation where a bailee, acting under an innocent mistake, delivers the chattel to the wrong person; or where he violates some condition in delivering it, even though he did deliver to the right person. [Rest. 2d §§234, 235]

---

e.g. **Example:** If Bailor says, "Give this ring to X if he pays you $10," and Bailee delivers the ring without receiving $10, there is a conversion. [**Baer v. Slater,** 158 N.E. 328 (Mass. 1927); **Marshall & Michel Grain Co. v. Kansas City, Ft. Scott & Memphis Railroad,** 75 S.W. 638 (Mo. 1903)]

---

(7) **Refusing to surrender a chattel on demand [§227]**
Where the acquisition itself was not wrongful, there must be a demand for return of the chattel before there can be a conversion. [Rest. 2d §237; *and see* **Sporting Goods Distributors, Inc. v. Whitney,** 498 F. Supp. 1088 (N.D. Fla. 1980)]

(a) **Exception—qualified refusal in order to identify claimant [§228]**
A carrier or bailee (*e.g.*, finder) in possession of the chattel is privileged to make a ***qualified*** refusal to deliver, for the purpose of investigating the claimant's right to the chattel. [Rest. 2d §239]

(8) **Application—multiple acts of conversion [§229]**
Note that a defendant's (or multiple defendants') conduct may result in ***several*** distinct invasions of the plaintiff's interest—*i.e.*, several different acts of conversion.

---

e.g. **Example:** D steals the chattel, sells it to an innocent purchaser, later buys it back, and then refuses to give it to P on demand. D has committed four separate acts of conversion.

---

d. **Plaintiff in possession or entitled to immediate possession [§230]**
The plaintiff must be in actual possession or have the right to immediate possession; this is the same as in a trespass to land. (*See supra,* §§191-192.)

e. **Causation [§231]**
This is also the same as in preceding sections (*see supra,* §§202, 214).

ACTS OF CONVERSION 

THE FOLLOWING INVASIONS OF ANOTHER'S CHATTEL INTEREST ARE SUFFICIENT ACTS OF CONVERSION:

- ☑ ***Substantial dispossession*** of chattel (*e.g.,* theft, embezzlement)
- ☑ ***Destruction or material alteration*** of chattel
- ☑ ***Unauthorized use*** of chattel causing ***substantial interference*** with owner's rights
- ☑ ***Purchase or receipt*** of ***stolen*** property
- ☑ ***Sale or disposal*** of ***stolen*** property
- ☑ ***Misdelivery*** of chattel
- ☑ ***Refusal to surrender*** chattel on demand

f. **Remedies [§232]**

If the defendant's conduct amounts to a "dispossession" (*i.e.,* an assertion of ownership rights in the chattel inconsistent with the rights of the true owner), the plaintiff will often have a choice of actions:

(1) **Replevin, detinue, or claim and delivery [§233]**

The plaintiff may obtain return of the chattel and collect damages sustained during its detention. This remedy is typically governed by state statute and is often available in the form of pretrial, temporary return of the chattel as well as permanent relief.

(2) **Forced sale damages [§234]**

The plaintiff may recover the ***value*** of the chattel ***plus damages*** for the dispossession. Hence, satisfaction (*i.e.,* payment) of the judgment operates as a ***forced sale of the chattel to the defendant.*** (*See* Remedies Summary.)

(a) **Measure of value [§235]**

The measure of recovery is ordinarily the market value of the goods at ***the time of the conversion*** (plus interest to date of suit). [**Nephi Processing Plant, Inc. v. Talbott,** 247 F.2d 771 (10th Cir. 1957)]

1) ***If the property has a fluctuating value,*** some courts allow the plaintiff to recover the highest value between the time of the conversion and the time of trial. [**United States v. Merchants Mutual Bonding Co.,** 242 F. Supp. 465 (N.D. Iowa 1965)]

2) ***If the property has no market value,*** resort may be had to replacement value or to the actual value of the property to the

plaintiff. [**Jensen v. Chicago & Western Indiana Railroad,** 419 N.E.2d 578 (Ill. 1981)—spare rods for antique steam locomotives]

(b) Effect of offer to return [§236]

An offer by the defendant to return the chattel does not affect the defendant's basic liability, but it will ***mitigate*** damages recoverable if the defendant acquired the property innocently and in good faith—provided the defendant made the offer to return promptly after learning that the plaintiff was the rightful owner, and provided the chattel was not impaired in value or condition since originally converted. [Rest. 2d §922] Should the plaintiff accept the defendant's offer to return the property, the plaintiff no longer has an action for conversion (but only for trespass to chattels).

EXAM TIP gilbert

There are two key differences between the actions for trespass to chattels and conversion: First, a trespass need not (but might) amount to a ***substantial*** interference with the owner's property rights; second, an action for trespass does not result in a ***forced sale*** of the property. Thus, if a plaintiff seeks to recover the full value of the property, ***but not the property itself***, the better action is ***conversion***. If the plaintiff seeks to recover an amount that is typically less than the full value of the property and ***wishes to retain title***, the better action is ***trespass***.

PROPERTY TORTS—COMPARISON OF KEY ELEMENTS gilbert

	TRESPASS TO LAND	TRESPASS TO CHATTELS	CONVERSION OF CHATTELS
ACT	Volitional movement by defendant causing ***intrusion onto another's land***	Volitional movement by defendant resulting in ***dispossession*** of ***or damage*** to chattels of another	Volitional movement by defendant resulting in a ***substantial interference*** with another's possession of her chattels
INTENT	Intent to do the act that causes intrusion on plaintiff's land	Intent to deal with the chattel in the manner in which it was dealt	Intent to deal with the chattel in the manner in which it was dealt
RESULT	Intrusion onto plaintiff's land; no other damages needed	Dispossession or intermeddling (*e.g.*, joyriding, smashing car windows)	Substantial dispossession (*e.g.*, destruction of chattels, selling chattels after they are stolen, refusing to surrender chattels on rightful demand)

D. Defenses and Privileged Invasions of Land and Chattels

1. **Consent [§237]**
The plaintiff's consent (expressly or by conduct) to the invasion of her land or chattels operates as a defense, so that no action by her to impose liability for the invasion will lie. (*See supra,* §§100-103.) However, consent may not be effective: as to trespasses that go beyond the scope of the consent; if consent was obtained through fraud, duress, or apparent mistake; if the person giving consent lacked capacity; etc. (*see supra,* §§104-118). [*See* **Copeland v. Hubbard Broadcasting, Inc.,** 526 N.W.2d 402 (Minn. 1995)—fact question whether consent given for educational purposes extended to secret videotaping for later broadcast; *but see* **Desnick v. American Broadcasting Cos.,** *supra,* §107—consent given to reporters posing as patients extended to their later reporting on what they observed]

2. **Privileged Invasion of Another's Land to Reclaim Chattels [§238]**
The scope of this privilege depends on where the fault lies for the presence of the defendant's chattels on plaintiff's land:

   a. **Landowner at fault [§239]**
   If the defendant's chattels are on the plaintiff's land because the ***plaintiff has tortiously dispossessed the defendant*** of them (or has received the chattels from some third person whom she ***knows*** has tortiously dispossessed the defendant), the defendant has a ***complete*** privilege to enter the land for the purpose of retaking possession.

      (1) **Demand generally required [§240]**
      Before entry, the defendant must make a demand for permission to enter the land for the purpose of reclaiming the chattel—***unless*** it appears that the demand would be futile or that delay would subject the property to danger of harm.

      (2) **Reasonable entry [§241]**
      The defendant must effect the entry at a reasonable time and in a reasonable manner. [Rest. 2d §198]

      (3) **Extent of privilege [§242]**
      The privilege is ***"complete"***—meaning the defendant cannot be held liable for any harm done to the plaintiff's land in the reasonable exercise of the privilege.

         (a) **Limitation—no mistake [§243]**
         The defendant is liable for trespass if he breaks and enters a building

other than that in which his chattels are kept. An ***honest*** mistake will ***not*** justify a trespass.

(b) Force to person of landowner [§244]

If the plaintiff resists the defendant's lawful attempts to come onto the plaintiff's land, the defendant is privileged to use ***reasonable, non-deadly force*** to the plaintiff's person, subject to the same conditions as in the exercise of the privilege of recapture of the chattel (*see supra,* §§150-155). In other words, it must appear not only that the defendant was tortiously dispossessed by the plaintiff or some third party in complicity with the plaintiff, and that a demand for return of the chattel was made or was unnecessary, but also that the recapture is effected promptly—***"fresh pursuit."*** [**Arlowski v. Foglio,** 135 A. 397 (Conn. 1926)]

b. Chattel owner at fault [§245]

If the defendant's chattels are on the plaintiff's land through the ***defendant's own fault*** (*e.g.,* where the defendant negligently allows his cattle to wander), the defendant has ***no privilege of any type*** to go onto the plaintiff's property to recover possession. Rather, he must bring an action for replevin, detinue, claim and delivery, etc. [Rest. 2d §200]

c. Act of God [§246]

If the defendant's chattels are on the plaintiff's land through the fault of ***neither the plaintiff nor the defendant,*** but rather because of "an act of God" (*e.g.,* storm, wind, flood, etc.), the defendant has an ***incomplete*** privilege to enter the land to reclaim the chattel.

(1) Extent of privilege [§247]

The privilege is ***"incomplete"*** in that the defendant is liable for actual damage done to the plaintiff's land in the process of recapturing the chattel, although the defendant is not liable for damage caused solely from the chattel being deposited there. [Rest. 2d §198 cmt. k]

---

e.g. **Example:** A freak windstorm causes D's tower to fall onto P's land, where it crashes into P's house. In removing the tower, D tramples P's flower beds. D is liable for the damage to the flower beds but not to the house.

---

(2) Conditions of privilege [§248]

Other than the fact that the privilege is "incomplete," the conditions and scope of privilege are the same as where the landowner is at fault (above); *i.e.,* entry must be made at a reasonable time and in a reasonable manner, and ordinarily a request for permission to enter is required.

(3) Caution—necessity to determine underlying causal factor [§249]
If the defendant's chattels are deposited on the plaintiff's land through flood, storm, etc., it is always a question of fact whether the reason was the storm or flood ("act of God") or the ***defendant's negligence*** in failing to secure his chattels, properly construct his property, etc. If the cause is the defendant's negligence, the defendant has ***no*** privilege (*see supra,* §245).

d. Third party at fault [§250]
If the defendant's chattels are on the plaintiff's land because of the tortious dispossession ***by a third party,*** but the plaintiff is not aware of the presence of the chattels on the land (or if she does know of their presence, is not aware that the third party tortiously dispossessed the defendant), the defendant again has an ***incomplete*** privilege to enter the land to reclaim the chattel. [Rest. 2d §198]

e. Limitation—privilege cannot be based on mistake [§251]
In all of the above cases, the defendant must ***in fact*** be entitled to possession of the chattels, both at the time he was dispossessed and at the time he seeks to enter the plaintiff's land for the purpose of reclaiming the chattels. If the defendant is ***not*** in fact entitled to possession of the chattels, he cannot claim the privilege—even if he reasonably and in good faith believes that he is the owner of the chattels. Here again, an ***honest*** mistake will ***not*** excuse a trespass.

3. Privilege to Exclude or Evict Trespassing Chattels of Another

a. Conditions of privilege [§252]
A defendant is ***completely*** privileged to use reasonable force to evict or exclude the chattels of another when such force is ***reasonably believed to be necessary*** to protect the defendant's interest in the exclusive possession of his land or chattels (*e.g.,* defendant's shooting a neighbor's dogs in defendant's chicken coop). [Rest. 2d §260]

b. Determining reasonableness [§253]
The "reasonableness" of the force used should be judged by (i) the ***necessity for immediate action*** to prevent the injury or destruction threatened by the invading chattels; (ii) whether the ***force used was excessive*** or only that necessary to terminate or prevent the intrusion; and (iii) the ***comparative values*** of the property threatened and the chattels to which the force is applied—*i.e.,* in the above example, are the dogs worth more than the chickens?

4. Privileged Invasion of Another's Land or Chattels as a Public Necessity

a. Averting public disaster [§254]
A person is ***completely*** privileged to enter land or interfere with chattels in the possession of another if necessary—or if it ***reasonably appears*** necessary—to avert a ***public disaster.*** [**South Dakota Department of Health v. Heim,** 357 N.W.2d 522 (S.D. 1984)—state's destruction of P's diseased elk herd was privileged where

necessary to avert public health risk; Rest. 2d §196] The term "person" here includes both public officials and private citizens.

(1) Extent of privilege [§255]

This is a ***complete*** privilege; *i.e.*, the defendant is not liable for any damage or destruction to the land or chattels involved, as long as the destruction or damage was done in the proper exercise of the privilege.

(a) Damage to improvements [§256]

The defendant is also completely privileged to break and enter fences and any buildings, ***including dwellings.***

(b) Force to the person [§257]

Moreover, if the property owner resists the defendant's attempt to enter the land or deal with the chattels, the defendant may use whatever force is reasonably necessary to effect the privilege, including ***deadly*** force if necessary.

b. Detouring around obstructed highway [§258]

A traveler on a public road that is, or ***reasonably appears*** to be, impassable has an ***incomplete*** privilege to enter neighboring lands in the possession of another, "as a matter of public right" in continuing the journey. [Rest. 2d §195]

(1) Conditions of privilege—reasonable need [§259]

The privilege exists only if the entry "reasonably appears" to be necessary. Courts consider: (i) the availability of alternate routes; (ii) the urgency of the traveler's business; and (iii) whether the obstruction on the road could have been removed by the traveler with reasonable efforts.

(2) Extent of privilege [§260]

This is an ***incomplete*** privilege—meaning the defendant is liable for any ***actual*** harm caused to the land during proper exercise of the privilege.

(3) Limitation—traveler at fault [§261]

There is no privilege if the obstruction on the road was caused by the ***fault of the traveler.***

c. Media [§262]

The First Amendment does ***not*** give the media a privilege that allows reporters to enter private land whenever they seek information—even important information. [**Green Valley School, Inc. v. Cowles Florida Broadcasting, Inc.,** 273 So. 2d 810 (Fla. 1976); **Le Mistral, Inc. v. Columbia Broadcasting System,** 61 A.D.2d 491 (1978)]

5. Privileged Invasion of Another's Land or Chattels as a Private Necessity

a. Conditions of privilege [§263]

A person is privileged to enter land or interfere with chattels in the possession of another if the entry or interference is—or reasonably appears to be—necessary to protect ***any person*** (the actor, the owner of the land or chattels, or some third person) from ***death or serious bodily harm***; or if it is—or reasonably appears to be—necessary to protect ***any land or chattels*** from ***destruction or injury***. [Rest. 2d §§197, 263]

(1) **"Reasonableness" limitation [§264]**
The entry or interference must be reasonable considering the harm that it is intended to prevent, as compared with the harm to land or chattels that it is likely to cause.

b. **Extent of privilege**

(1) **Force to person or property [§265]**
The defendant may break and enter fences and buildings, ***including dwellings***. Similarly, if the owner of the land or chattels resists the invasion, the defendant may use "reasonable" force to effect the privilege. (However, it is doubtful that deadly force would be privileged because the policy factors in cases where the invasion is a ***public*** necessity would not be present here.)

(2) **Privilege incomplete [§266]**
The privilege is ***incomplete***; the defendant is liable for all harm done to the land or chattels in exercise of this privilege. [**Vincent v. Lake Erie Transportation Co.,** 124 N.W. 221 (Minn. 1910)—D liable for damages to P's dock resulting from D's tying his boat to P's dock to ride out a storm]

c. **Supersedes owner's privilege to exclude trespassers [§267]**
The privilege to invade another's land or chattels as a private necessity ***supersedes*** the privilege of the possessor of land or chattels to use reasonable force to protect her property from invasion. Hence, any force used by the landowner to exclude the entrant is wrongful and subjects the landowner to liability. Moreover, the landowner is liable to the entrant for the harm the entrant suffers as a result of being denied entry (*e.g.*, loss of boat, etc.). [**Ploof v. Putnam,** 71 A. 188 (Vt. 1908)]

(1) **Note**
This same principle applies to ***all of the entry privileges*** discussed in this section.

6. **Privileged Invasion of Land or Chattels to Abate a Nuisance**

a. **Conditions of privilege [§268]**
A "nuisance" is any unreasonable interference with the use or enjoyment of another's property (*see infra,* §§1107 *et seq.*). A defendant is ***completely*** privileged to invade the land or chattels of another for the purpose of abating a

private nuisance (*i.e.*, a nuisance that affects one or only a few landowners as opposed to the public at large) created or maintained on the land or chattels of the other, subject to the following conditions:

(1) Ownership or possessory interest [§269]
The entrant must be the owner or possessor (*e.g.*, tenant) of land or chattels injuriously affected by the nuisance.

(2) Demand [§270]
The entrant must first make a demand that the nuisance be abated, unless it reasonably appears that a demand would be impractical or useless.

(3) Reasonableness [§271]
The entrant must enter at a reasonable time and use only ***reasonable force*** to effect the abatement. [Rest. 2d §201]

b. Extent of privilege [§272]
Because this is a ***complete*** privilege, the defendant is not liable for any harm resulting to land or chattels in the proper exercise of the privilege. But the privilege does ***not*** extend to using force against a resisting property owner. [Rest. 2d §201 cmt. k]

(1) Rationale
There is less urgency here than in the "public necessity" or "private necessity" privileges—so that if the owner resists, the entrant should withdraw and seek judicial relief.

c. Distinguish—public nuisance [§273]
The privilege discussed in this section applies only to the abatement of a ***private nuisance***. If the nuisance is a public one (affecting all persons or property in substantially the same manner), a private individual generally has ***no*** privilege of abatement unless the public nuisance is causing him some injury "peculiar in kind"—so that as to him it is a private nuisance as well. (*See infra,* §§1110-1113.)

7. Effect of Misconduct by Actor

a. While exercising privilege [§274]
As noted above, many of these privileges are conditioned on "reasonableness"; *i.e.*, the defendant must enter at a reasonable time, in a reasonable manner, etc. If the defendant is unreasonable in coming onto the land (using excessive force, etc.), the required conditions do not exist and the defendant's entry is not privileged. [Rest. 2d §214(1)]

b. Subsequent to exercise of privilege [§275]
A related problem is the effect of misconduct by an entrant ***subsequent*** to an initially privileged intrusion. For example, if after properly entering through an

PRIVILEGED INVASIONS OF ANOTHER'S LAND AND CHATTELS

gilbert

PRIVILEGE	CONDITIONS OF PRIVILEGE	EXTENT OF PRIVILEGE	AMOUNT OF FORCE ALLOWED
TO RECLAIM CHATTELS			
• **LANDOWNER AT FAULT**	D's chattels are on P's land because P has ***tortiously dispossessed*** D of them	Complete (*i.e.,* D ***not liable*** for any damage to P's land in reasonable exercise of privilege)	Reasonable, nondeadly force
• **CHATTEL OWNER AT FAULT**	D's chattels are on P's land because of D's ***own fault*** (*e.g.,* negligence)	None	None
• **ACT OF GOD**	D's chattels are on P's land through the ***fault of neither*** P nor D (*e.g.,* storm)	Incomplete (*i.e.,* D ***is liable*** for actual damage to P's land in recapture of chattels)	Reasonable, nondeadly force
• **THIRD PARTY AT FAULT**	D's chattels are on P's land through the fault of a ***third party***	Incomplete	Reasonable, nondeadly force
TO EXCLUDE OR EVICT ANOTHER'S TRESPASSING CHATTELS	P's chattels are on D's land and D ***reasonably believes*** that force is ***necessary*** to protect his land or chattels	Complete	Reasonable force
AS A PUBLIC NECESSITY			
• **AVERT PUBLIC DISASTER**	***Necessary*** (or reasonably appears necessary) for D to enter P's land or interfere with P's chattels to avert a ***public disaster***	Complete	Reasonable force, ***including deadly force***
• **DETOUR AROUND HIGHWAY OBSTRUCTION**	***Public road*** is (or reasonably appears to be) ***impassable*** so D enters P's land to detour around obstruction	Incomplete	Reasonable, nondeadly force
AS A PRIVATE NECESSITY	***Necessary*** (or reasonably appears necessary) for D to enter P's land or interfere with P's chattels to protect (i) any person from ***death or serious bodily harm*** or (ii) any land or chattels from ***destruction or injury***	Incomplete	Reasonable force, ***including deadly force***
TO ABATE A NUISANCE	After ***demand*** (unless futile), D enters P's land to ***abate nuisance*** affecting ***D's*** land or chattels	Complete	Reasonable, nondeadly force

open gate to reclaim his chattels, the entrant unnecessarily tears down the landowner's fences to leave, the modern view is that the entrant does ***not*** lose the entire privilege by virtue of his subsequent tortious conduct. Thus, the entrant is liable only for damages caused by his subsequent misconduct, and no damages can be recovered for the initially privileged intrusion. [Rest. 2d §214(2)] (The old view held the entrant liable for the entire episode under the doctrine of "trespass ab initio.")

Chapter Two: Negligence

CONTENTS

▶	Key Exam Issues	
A.	In General	§276
B.	Negligence (Based on the "Duty of Due Care")	§278
C.	Special Duty Questions	§545
D.	Defenses to Negligence	§791
E.	Effect of Liability Insurance	§865

Key Exam Issues

Negligence is the most important area of tort law. It is also the most frequent subject of exam questions, both because of its importance and because it requires special care in applying the bare rules to the varied fact situations. Whereas intentional torts tend to be a series of cubbyholes and categories—both in the prima facie case and in the privileges—this is not true in negligence. Here, there are a few critically important standards and some rules. Your task is not so much remembering them as it is ***applying*** them to the facts.

Some general guidelines for you to follow:

1. The most important habit to acquire is to go through the ***sequence of elements*** methodically in every case. This means, *e.g.*, finding an appropriate act or actionable omission ***before*** turning to the issue of "duty," or concluding that there was a breach of duty ***before*** considering causation. Analyzing each element in turn allows you to identify the troublesome issue and to address each issue in the terms set out in this chapter.

2. Be sure to look at the defendant's allegedly wrongful act(s) and potentially the relationship between the plaintiff and the defendant in identifying the ***appropriate duty*** to impose on the defendant. You must ***never assume*** that the defendant owes a duty of care. Even though that is usually the case, you must explain why a duty exists in each case.

3. Remember that the plaintiff must show actual cause ("cause in fact") ***and*** proximate cause ("scope of liability"), and you should discuss each of these elements.

4. Finally, determine whether the facts suggest any ***defense*** to the negligence (*e.g.*, contributory negligence, etc.). Defenses are usually less important in negligence cases; the focus is almost always on the prima facie case.

A. In General

1. Introduction [§276]

The second broad basis for tort liability is negligence. Here, liability may be imposed for results that were ***not intended*** by the defendant. However, this is ***not*** "liability without fault" (strict liability). It must be shown in every case that the defendant was ***at fault***—*i.e.*, that the defendant failed to perform some ***duty*** that the law required of the defendant under the circumstances.

2. Duty [§277]

Depending on the circumstances, there may be either (or both) of two types of duties owed: (i) the duty to conduct oneself as a reasonable person would under the same or similar circumstances—the so-called default duty of due care; or (ii) some special duty, imposed by statute or case law, which may be ***in addition to, or in place of***, the default duty of due care (*see infra*, §§545 *et seq.*).

B. Negligence (Based on the "Duty of Due Care")

1. Elements of Negligence [§278]

Prima facie case:

- *Act or Actionable Omission by Defendant*
- *Duty of Due Care*
- *Breach of Duty* (Lack of due care)
- *Actual Cause* ("Cause in fact")
- *Proximate Cause* ("Scope of liability")
- *Damages*

a. Note

Courts most often describe negligence as having five or even four elements. The requirement of an act or omission is typically analyzed as part of the duty analysis, and many courts (unfortunately) lump the actual cause and proximate cause inquiries into a unified element called variously "causation," "legal cause," or "proximate cause."

2. Act or Actionable Omission by Defendant [§279]

In addition to the type of "act" required for intentional torts (*i.e.*, a volitional movement by defendant of some part of his body), liability for negligence may be predicated on a willful omission to act ***when under an affirmative duty to act.*** Thus, as discussed in the "special duties" section, *infra*, the law imposes certain affirmative duties of care (*e.g.*, the duty of a person charged with the care of another to aid that person in an emergency). Failure to perform such a duty is ordinarily not a sufficient "act" for intentional tort purposes, but it may be sufficient for purposes of negligence. [**L.S. Ayres & Co. v. Hicks,** 40 N.E.2d 334 (Ind. 1942)]

3. Duty of Due Care

a. Duty requires two-step inquiry [§280]

Duty is the only element of negligence decided in the first instance by the court. (Each of the other elements is left to the jury, unless the court decides the element as a matter of law.) A court's determination of duty consists of a two-step inquiry: First, the court decides ***whether the defendant owed a duty of care.*** If so, the court must then define the ***scope of the duty***—*i.e.*, the standard by which the jury will determine whether the defendant breached its duty.

b. Default duty to act as a "reasonable person" would [§281]

If the defendant's ***conduct creates a risk of physical harm***, the defendant owes a duty to "do the conduct" with due care. [Restatement (Third) of Torts: Liability for Physical Harm ("Rest. 3d-PH") §7(a) (Proposed Final Draft No. 1, 2005)] The scope of this duty is defined by the "reasonable person" standard: Each person owes a duty to act as a reasonable person would ***under the same or similar circumstances***. [**Brown v. Kendall,** 60 Mass. 292 (1850); Rest. 2d §283]

(1) Objective test [§282]

This is an objective standard, and it is therefore immaterial that the defendant believed in good faith (subjectively) that he was being careful. The issue is ***not*** what the defendant believed or intended, but rather how the ***"reasonable person of ordinary prudence"*** would have acted. [**Vaughan v. Menlove,** 132 Eng. Rep. 490 (1837)]

(2) Test reflects moral judgment [§283]

This standard is aspirational in the sense that it asks not what the ordinary person in fact does, but what the ordinary person ***ought to do*** under the relevant circumstances.

---

e.g. **Example:** Many people dial numbers on their cell phones while driving. A jury might conclude, however, that although such conduct is "ordinary," it is nevertheless unreasonable because it results in inattention and the creation of undue risk.

EXAM TIP **gilbert**

The ramifications of the objective "reasonable person" standard are important and could sneak in on an exam question. For example, because the test is not based on how any specific individual or group would have acted, it is ***improper*** to instruct the jurors in a negligence trial to decide the case by asking themselves how ***they*** as individuals would have acted. The question is how the ***reasonable person*** would have acted under the circumstances (although jurors no doubt consider themselves "reasonable persons").

(3) Standard remains same under all circumstances [§284]

Although the amount of care and the kind of conduct required will vary with the circumstances, the ***standard itself never varies***. It is always whatever care the reasonable person would have exercised ***under the circumstances*** that existed at the time of the defendant's conduct (*e.g.*, the location of the parties, the conditions of traffic, etc.). [**Triestram v. Way,** 281 N.W. 420 (Mich. 1938)]

(a) Application—risk of harm [§285]

The greater the foreseeable risk of harm involved and the greater the amount of that harm, the greater the care required (*e.g.*, the reasonable person no doubt handles chemicals more carefully than less dangerous products). Whatever the situation, the amount of care required is determined by the reasonable person standard. [**Stewart v. Motts,** 654 A.2d 535 (Pa. 1995)—single standard of due care applies to handling of gasoline]

(b) Application—emergency [§286]

Likewise, certain conduct may be acceptable in ***emergency*** but not in nonemergency situations because the need for immediate action justifies acts that otherwise could be considered unreasonable. However, the standard still remains the same—*i.e.*, how the reasonable person would have acted under the circumstances (*i.e.*, in the emergency). [Rest. 2d §296; **Rivera v. New York City Transit Authority,** 77 N.Y.2d 322 (1991)]

1) Emergency instructions [§287]

Because the standard always remains the same (*i.e.*, how the reasonable person would have acted under the circumstances), many states find a separate emergency instruction unnecessary or superfluous. [**Lyons v. Midnight Sun Transportation Services, Inc.,** 928 P.2d 1202 (Alaska 1996)] A minority, however, require an instruction reminding the jury that the defendant should be judged according to what would be reasonable under the specific ***emergency*** circumstances. [**Levey v. DeNardo,** 725 A.2d 733 (Pa. 1999)]

(4) Distinguish—special duty situations [§288]

It is important to understand that this "duty of due care" is only applicable where the defendant's ***affirmative conduct creates a risk of physical harm*** (*e.g.*, the defendant drives her car into the plaintiff or pollutes the plaintiff's drinking water). Because injuries caused by affirmative conduct provide the most common factual scenario for negligence cases, courts often presume the existence of a duty without discussion. (On your exam, however, you should always address and analyze the existence of a duty.) In the following scenarios, courts decide the existence and scope of a duty pursuant to a ***different*** set of rules: (i) where the plaintiff alleges that it was the defendant's "nonfeasance," or failure to act, that caused the plaintiff's harm; (ii) where the plaintiff asserts purely emotional or economic injury; or (iii) where the status of the defendant (*e.g.*, as a government entity or landowner) raises additional policy considerations. (*See infra*, §§545 *et seq.*)

c. Variances in the generalized standard of due care [§289]

The reasonable person standard applies to all persons—it is flexible enough to cover any individual or class of individuals. There are several exceptions to this rule, however:

(1) Common carriers [§290]

Although courts have long held that common carriers owe a "higher standard of care" than do others [**Widmyer v. Southeast Skyways, Inc.**, 584 P.2d 1 (Alaska 1978)—"the highest degree of care"], modern courts are moving in the direction of imposing the typical reasonable person standard in such cases [*see* **Bethel v. New York City Transit Authority**, 92 N.Y.2d 348 (1998)].

(2) Children [§291]

Minors are held to the reasonable person standard, with the age, intelligence, and experience of the individual being considered as *part of the circumstances*. Thus, the question is: What is to be expected of the reasonable person having this child's actual age, actual intelligence, and actual experience, with regard to such matters as judgment, memory, and risk perception? [**Peterson v. Taylor**, 316 N.W.2d 869 (Iowa 1982)]

(a) Minimum age [§292]

The general view is that below some age, usually around four, a child simply cannot make the calculations needed to establish negligence. [**Mastland, Inc. v. Evans Furniture, Inc.**, 498 N.W.2d 682 (Iowa 1993)—three-year-old could not be negligent]

1) Minority approach [§293]

Some states declare children under seven conclusively incapable of committing negligent acts. These same minority states often create a rebuttable presumption that children between seven and 14 are incapable of being negligent.

(b) Exception—adult activities [§294]

If children engage in dangerous activities normally undertaken only by adults (*e.g.*, operating cars, airplanes, motorboats, etc.), *no special allowance is made* for their immaturity or limited experience. They are held to the same standard as an adult, even if they are beginners. [**Stevens v. Veenstra**, 573 N.W.2d 341 (Mich. 1997)—14-year-old participating in a driver's education course; **Robinson v. Lindsay**, 598 P.2d 392 (Wash. 1979)—13-year-old driving a snowmobile]

(3) Persons with physical disability [§295]

Persons with physical disabilities (crippled, blind, deaf, etc.) are held to the reasonable person standard, with their disability *as one of the circumstances*. [*See*, *e.g.*, **Hill v. City of Glenwood**, 100 N.W. 522 (Iowa 1904); Rest. 2d §283C]

(a) Knowledge of disability one of the "circumstances" [§296]

Thus, such persons are charged with knowledge that they have a disability, and may be found negligent for engaging in any activity that a ***reasonable person with the same disability*** would not have attempted.

Example: If D has poor vision, she is held only to the standard of care that a reasonable person with such vision would exercise. But if a reasonable person would realize that it was unreasonably unsafe to drive a car with poor vision, D's driving under normal circumstances would be negligent. [**Roberts v. Ring,** 173 N.W. 437 (Minn. 1919)]

---

1) **Distinguish—treated conditions [§297]**
Even with knowledge, if the defendant is using due care to treat his condition, he will not necessarily be held liable for injuries resulting from the condition. [**Hammontree v. Jenner,** 20 Cal. App. 3d 528 (1971)—epileptic carefully treating his condition, which was under control, was not liable for crashing his car into a storefront during an unanticipated epileptic seizure]

(b) **Distinguish—voluntary intoxication [§298]**
If the physical impairment results from voluntary intoxication, it is ***disregarded*** in determining liability; *i.e.*, a person who uses alcohol or drugs is held to the same standard as would be expected if she were not under their influence. [Rest. 2d §283C]

(4) **Adults with mental deficiency [§299]**
Adults with mental deficiencies are judged by the reasonable person standard ***without any allowance*** for their mental deficiency. Hence, although a ***child's*** intelligence is taken into account in determining whether he was negligent (*supra*), an adult's is not! This is true whether the defendant's limitation is subnormal intelligence or outright insanity. [**Breunig v. American Family Insurance Co.,** 173 N.W.2d 619 (Wis. 1970); Rest. 2d §283B]

(a) **Rationale**
The fear of fraud, the difficulty of determining what kind of mental aberration will lessen the care owed, the difficulty of applying any reduced standard, and the fear of complicating tort law the way the insanity defense has complicated criminal trials are some of the reasons for this rule. (*See* Criminal Law Summary.)

(b) **Distinguish—contributory negligence [§300]**
Note, however, that a few cases have allowed evidence of the ***plaintiff's*** low intelligence in determining whether his conduct was ***contributorily*** negligent (*see infra*, §797). [**Lynch v. Rosenthal,** 396 S.W.2d 272 (Mo. 1965)]

(5) **Special knowledge and skills [§301]**
All persons are held to certain ***minimum*** standards in their activities. [**Delair**

v. McAdoo, 188 A. 181 (Pa. 1936)] If they have acquired special competence, they are held to a standard that takes account of their ***superior*** knowledge or skills. [Rest. 2d §289(b)] As opposed to particular knowledge or skill, higher-than-average natural abilities such as intelligence or athleticism are typically not considered.

(a) **Learners or beginners [§302]**
An inexperienced person who engages in activities involving a known risk of harm to others (*e.g.*, driving a car on a public street) is held to the same standard of care as an experienced reasonable person. *Rationale:* Those who engage in such activities—rather than the innocent victim—should bear the risk of loss. [**Stevens v. Veenstra,** *supra,* §294—14-year-old participating in a driver's education course; **Dellwo v. Pearson,** 107 N.W.2d 859 (Minn. 1961)—operation of motorboat; Rest. 2d §299 cmt. d]

(b) **Profession or trade [§303]**
If the defendant undertakes to render any service in a recognized profession or trade (builder, attorney, plumber, etc.), she is held, at a ***minimum***, to the standard of care customarily exercised by members of that profession or trade—whether or not she personally possesses such skills. [**Heath v. Swift Wings, Inc.,** 252 S.E.2d 526 (N.C. 1979); Rest. 2d §299A]

1) **General rule—"same or similar" community standard [§304]**
Generally, persons engaged in a trade or profession—except physicians, *see infra,* §306—are required to exercise the degree of care that would be exercised by members of their profession nationwide. [Rest. 2d §299A cmt. g]

a) **Rationale**
As the dissemination of knowledge and information increases, professionals and those in the trades in most localities are not only confronting the same problems, but also have the same knowledge at their disposal to solve those problems. This means that the standard will be "national" (when there are no significant differences among communities).

2) **Medical profession**

a) **Older view—local standard [§305]**
Some early cases limited the standard of care for physicians to that of other physicians in the ***same*** community or locality.

b) **Modern trend—"same or similar" community standard [§306]**
However, this distinction is disappearing in modern cases so that, as with other professionals, courts are holding that

physicians must meet ***at least*** the standard of care existing in the "same ***or similar***" communities—and experts from such communities may testify as to the appropriate standards (*i.e.*, country doctors will be held to the same standard of care as other country doctors, but not necessarily to the same standard as big-city doctors). [**Tallbull v. Whitney,** 564 P.2d 162 (Mont. 1977)]

1/ Nationally certified physicians [§307]

A growing number of courts impose a ***national*** standard of care on ***nationally certified*** medical specialists. [**Robbins v. Footer,** 553 F.2d 123 (D.C. Cir. 1977)—board-certified obstetrician; **Sheeley v. Memorial Hospital,** 710 A.2d 161 (R.I. 1998)—allowing expert testimony of New York doctor in case involving defendant Rhode Island doctor]

c) Establishing a standard [§308]

To prevail, the plaintiff must establish the particular standard of medical care that is required ***and*** show a departure from that standard. Because the standard is measured in relation to professional understandings, the plaintiff must generally present expert testimony to establish the standard.

1/ Note

The modern trend permits experts in one specialty to testify against those in another field of medicine if they have sufficient knowledge of the other field. [**Melville v. Southward,** 791 P.2d 383 (Colo. 1990)—orthopedic surgeon may testify if shown to be familiar with standards of podiatry or if the standards of the two are shown to be substantially identical]

2/ Obvious occurrence exception [§309]

If a physician's conduct is so egregious and obvious that a layperson could identify the breach of duty, no expert testimony is needed to establish the duty of care and the breach. [**Heimer v. Privratsky,** 434 N.W.2d 357 (N.D. 1989)—allowing toxic substance to come in contact with patient's eye obviously negligent to layperson]

d) Controversial techniques [§310]

If respectable medical opinions differ as to the best technique, courts will allow a doctor to follow either view [**Furey v. Thomas Jefferson University Hospital,** 472 A.2d 1083 (Pa.

1984)] or even one followed by a "reputable and respected" minority of the medical profession [**Gala v. Hamilton,** 715 A.2d 1108 (Pa. 1998)].

e) **Informed consent [§311]**

Doctors have a duty to disclose relevant information about benefits and risks inherent in proposed treatment, alternatives to that treatment, and the likely results if the patient remains untreated (*see supra,* §113). [**Canterbury v. Spence,** 464 F.2d 772 (D.C. Cir. 1972)] That duty may extend to informing the patient about noninvasive options. [**Matthies v. Mastromonaco,** 733 A.2d 456 (N.J. 1999)—failure to alert patient to all plausible options is actionable] This obligation is not extended to hospitals or nurses, but extends only to the physicians and surgeons themselves. [**Wells v. Storey,** 792 So. 2d 1034 (Ala. 1999)]

1/ **Standard of disclosure [§312]**

The courts are split between those that require only the level of disclosure customary in the medical profession [**Woolley v. Henderson,** 418 A.2d 1123 (Me. 1980)] and those that require disclosure of what the doctor should reasonably recognize would be material to the patient's decision [**Korman v. Mallin,** 858 P.2d 1145 (Alaska 1993)].

a/ **Applications**

Disclosure of a 1-3% chance of pregnancy has been required. [**Hartke v. McKelway,** 707 F.2d 1544 (D.C. Cir. 1983)] But a trier of fact could conclude that a chance of death of 8.6 in one million need not be disclosed. [**Smith v. Shannon,** 666 P.2d 351 (Wash. 1983)]

2/ **Exceptions [§313]**

Three exceptions to the doctor's duty of disclosure are recognized:

a/ **Emergencies [§314]**

There is no duty of disclosure in an emergency situation (*e.g.*, where the patient is unconscious or unable to comprehend, and prompt medical treatment is required).

b/ **Therapeutic privilege [§315]**

If the patient is so distraught or unstable that the physician ***reasonably*** concludes that full disclosure would be ***detrimental*** to the patient's well-being, there may be no duty to disclose. (But the burden of proving these facts is on the doctor.) [**Canterbury v. Spence,** *supra*] But the fact that an adult may decline lifesaving treatment does ***not*** justify imposing treatment over objection. [**Shine v. Vega,** 709 N.E.2d 58 (Mass. 1999)]

c/ **Lack of experience [§316]**

An inexperienced physician does not have a duty to inform his patient that he has never before performed the procedure he is recommending. [**Whiteside v. Lukson,** 947 P.2d 1263 (Wash. 1997)] Similarly, a cosmetic surgeon has no duty to inform his patient that he is not a plastic surgeon and does not have hospital privileges where he did not claim to be anything more than he was. [**Ditto v. McCurdy,** 947 P.2d 952 (Haw. 1997)]

3/ **Causation [§317]**

In informed consent cases, most courts follow the ***objective*** view and hold that the patient must show that if properly informed ***neither*** the patient ***nor a reasonable person*** in similar circumstances would have undergone the procedure. [**Reikes v. Martin,** 471 So. 2d 385 (Miss. 1985); **Largey v. Rothman,** 540 A.2d 504 (N.J. 1988)]

a/ **Minority view [§318]**

Some jurisdictions adopt a ***subjective*** standard by which plaintiffs establish causation by persuading the trier of fact that the plaintiff personally would not have consented to the procedure. [**Scott v. Bradford,** 606 P.2d 554 (Okla. 1980); **Arena v. Gingrich,** 748 P.2d 547 (Or. 1988)]

4/ **Revoking consent [§319]**

As long as viable medical options remain, a patient may revoke her consent. If she does so (or if there is a substantial change in circumstances, either medical or legal), a physician is required to have a new informed consent discussion. [**Schreiber v. Physicians Insurance Co. of Wisconsin,** 588 N.W.2d 26 (Wis. 1999)—patient may revoke consent to vaginal delivery after four hours of labor]

VARIANCES IN STANDARDS OF NEGLIGENCE gilbert

TYPE OF PERSON	STANDARD
COMMON CARRIERS	Early cases held common carriers to a higher standard of care, but the modern trend is to impose the ***reasonable person*** standard.
CHILDREN	Most states consider children under age 4 ***incapable*** of negligence. A few have a ***conclusive*** presumption that children under age 7 are incapable of negligence and also a ***rebuttable*** presumption that children between ages 7 and 14 are not capable of negligence.
PERSONS WITH PHYSICAL DISABILITIES	Reasonable person standard applies but the disability is treated as ***one of the circumstances*** in deciding how a reasonable person would act.
ADULTS WITH MENTAL DEFICIENCIES	Reasonable person standard applies ***without regard to the mental deficiency.***
LEARNERS/BEGINNERS ENGAGING IN RISKY ACTIVITIES	Reasonable person standard applies ***without regard to their status.***
PROFESSIONALS	A professional (other than a physician) is held at a minimum to the standard of care ***customarily exercised nationwide*** by members of that profession.
MEDICAL PROFESSIONALS	Early cases held medical professionals to the standard of care of other medical professionals in the same community; modern trend expands to care used in ***same or similar community***, and requires nationally certified specialists to meet a national standard.

d. **The unforeseeable plaintiff—to whom is the duty of care owed? [§320]**

If a reasonable person would ***not*** have foreseen injury to ***anyone*** from the defendant's conduct, most courts hold that there is no duty owed to a person who is unexpectedly hurt by the defendant's actions. There is a split of authority, however, in cases where the defendant could reasonably have foreseen danger to ***someone***, but there is some question as to whether injury to the ***particular plaintiff*** was foreseeable. The split is embodied by the majority and dissenting opinions in the *Palsgraf* case, discussed below.

(1) **Broad view—if duty owed to anyone, duty owed to all [§321]**

The broad view is that the defendant's duty of due care is owed to ***anyone*** in the world who suffers injuries as a result of the defendant's breach of duty, leaving the foreseeability of a particular plaintiff a matter to be determined in the context of ***proximate cause***. [Rest. 3d-PH §7 cmt. j; **Gipson v. Kasey,** 150 P.3d 228 (Ariz. 2007)—foreseeability not a relevant consideration in court's duty analysis] (As to what constitutes "proximate cause," *see infra*, §§442 *et seq.*)

(a) **Note**

This is the "***Andrews view,***" referring to the dissenting opinion written by Justice Andrews in the famous *Palsgraf* case. [**Palsgraf v. Long Island Railroad,** 248 N.Y. 339 (1928)]

(2) **Narrow view—duty owed only to "foreseeable plaintiffs" [§322]**

The contrasting view is the "***foreseeable plaintiff***" or "***zone of danger*** ***doctrine***" espoused by Justice Cardozo in his majority opinion in the *Palsgraf* case: Defendant owes a duty of care only to those persons as to whom the reasonable person would have foreseen a risk of harm under the circumstances. Therefore, before the court may impose a duty of care on the defendant, it must determine that the reasonable person would have ***foreseen a risk of harm to the plaintiff or a class of persons to which the plaintiff belongs***—*i.e.*, that plaintiff was a "foreseeable plaintiff," located in a foreseeable "zone of danger." [*See also* Rest. 2d §281(b)]

---

e.g. **Example:** A wife's paramour owes her husband a duty not to transmit to him a sexually transmitted disease because a spouse is a foreseeable victim of adultery. [**Mussivand v. David,** 544 N.E.2d 265 (Ohio 1989)]

---

(3) **Application**

(a) ***Palsgraf* facts [§323]**

The circumstances of the *Palsgraf* case clearly illustrate the two views. X, a passenger, was running to catch one of D's trains that was beginning to move. In helping X board the train, one of D's employees dislodged an innocent-looking package from X's arms. The package contained fireworks, which exploded so violently that the concussion knocked over some heavy scales, 25 to 30 feet away at the other end of the platform. The scales fell upon and injured P.

1) **"Cardozo view" [§324]**

Under the "Cardozo view," D breached no duty to owed P. Although a risk of harm to X or X's package might have been foreseeable (or even a risk to persons near X if he should trip while being helped or drop the package on someone's feet), a reasonable person would not have foreseen any risk to P (who was a considerable distance away). Hence P was not within the "zone of danger," and D owed her ***no relevant duty*** of due care. (X, since he knew he was carrying explosives, would owe a duty of due care to a wider group.)

2) **"Andrews view" [§325]**

Under the "Andrews view," however, D owed P a duty of due care. In helping a passenger board the moving train, D had a duty to that passenger, those nearby, and anyone else in the world who might be injured because of D's careless conduct. (Remember that finding a duty is only one element of the tort. Andrews still had to consider proximate causation questions, among others.)

3) **Judge vs. jury [§326]**

The judge/jury issue is at the heart of the *Palsgraf* debate. Justice Cardozo felt that judges ought to determine the foreseeability of the plaintiff, whereas Justice Andrews wanted to leave such questions to the jury as a matter of proximate cause. The matter is made more complicated in Cardozo jurisdictions because it is often difficult to discern whether a case involves plaintiff foreseeability or foreseeability of the type or manner of injury. For example, is the issue in *Palsgraf* best characterized as whether harm to P was foreseeable, or whether harm by means of an explosion was foreseeable? This characterization can be important in Cardozo jurisdictions because if the issue is characterized as ***plaintiff*** foreseeability, it is a duty question to be decided by the ***court***. If the issue is characterized as ***risk*** foreseeability, it is likely to be decided by the ***jury*** as part of proximate cause.

EXAM TIP **gilbert**

Although many courts have purported to follow or distinguish *Palsgraf*, in real life, harm is rarely caused to an unforeseeable plaintiff. Indeed, there are so few comparable cases that it is not possible to identify either view as being the majority or minority position. Nevertheless, the issue can easily come up on an exam question (since exam questions are not limited to real life). To keep the two views straight, it may help to remember:

Andrews—**A**nyone
Cardo**zo**—**Zo**ne

Andrews took the broad view that the ***duty of care runs to anyone*** whose injury was proximately caused by a negligent defendant, while Cardozo took the narrower view that a duty is owed only to those ***in the foreseeable zone of danger***.

(b) **Rescuers [§327]**

If the defendant owes a duty to someone, it generally follows that the duty is also owed to any other person who goes to the rescue of the person imperiled. The theory is that "danger invites rescue."

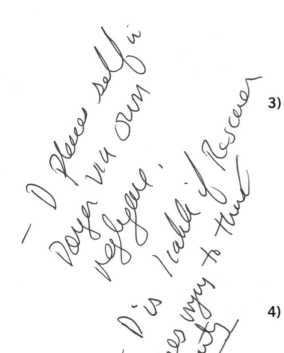

1) **Foreseeable plaintiffs [§328]**

Even under the narrow "Cardozo view," the "zone of danger" includes any person who comes to the rescue of one imperiled by the defendant's negligent conduct. The rescuer, therefore, is as much a foreseeable plaintiff as the person actually imperiled, and hence is within the scope of the defendant's duty. [**Wagner v. International Railway,** 232 N.Y. 176 (1921)]

2) **Harm caused by rescuer [§329]**

Likewise, the above result and reasoning apply where the rescuer ***causes*** injury to another in a reasonable rescue attempt.

---

e.g. **Example:** D negligently imperils X. Y attempts to come to X's aid, and in so doing injures P. D's duty of due care extends to P. (Same result where the rescuer injures or aggravates the injury to X.)

---

3) **Defendant in peril from own negligence [§330]**

The same result and reasoning also apply even though the person imperiled by the defendant's conduct is the ***defendant himself.***

---

e.g. **Example:** D (through his own negligence) places himself in a position of peril. P, seeing this, reasonably attempts to come to D's aid and is injured in so doing. D's duty of due care extends to P. [**Lowrey v. Horvath,** 689 S.W.2d 625 (Mo. 1985)]

---

4) **Limitation—reasonableness [§331]**

Keep in mind, however, that in every case the rescue attempt must not be foolhardy under the circumstances (*see infra*, §794). If the attempt was foolhardy, the original defendant may not be liable for the resulting injuries (*see infra*, §493). In a comparative negligence state, the defendant's liability may be reduced by the plaintiff-rescuer's fault in acting rashly. [**Bridges v. Bentley,** 769 P.2d 635 (Kan. 1989)]

5) **Limitation—professional rescuers [§332]**

Where professionals undertake rescue operations, it is generally held that the person whose negligence occasioned the need for rescue is ***not*** liable for harm suffered by the rescuers. [**Maltman v. Sauer,** 530 P.2d 254 (Wash. 1975)] This situation is analogous to the case in which a person's carelessness requires the services of firefighters, who injure themselves putting out the fire (*see infra*, §841).

e. **Limitations on duty [§333]**

Even if a person's actions created a risk of harm, courts sometimes analyze the generalized fact pattern of a case and its various policy implications to decide whether to impose a duty and, if so, to determine its scope. This is also true where the defendant's actions did not create a risk, but where an affirmative duty might exist (*see infra*, §§551 *et seq.*). "No-duty" decisions typically follow one of two patterns of reasoning:

(1) **California factors [§334]**

A growing number of courts, beginning with California, have been explicit in identifying the considerations that go into deciding whether to impose a duty. These include, ***in addition to foreseeability*** of harm to the plaintiff: (i) the closeness of the connection between the defendant's conduct and the injury; (ii) the moral blame attached to the defendant's conduct; (iii) the policy of preventing future harm; and (iv) the extent of the burden to the defendant and the consequences to the community of imposing a duty of care. [**Randi W. v. Muroc Joint Unified School District,** 14 Cal. 4th 1066 (1997)—based on list of factors, court held that victim of sexual assault could maintain action against school districts which, despite knowing prior charges of sexual misconduct had been leveled against former employee, positively recommended him for job in school district where he assaulted victim; **Knoll v. Board of Regents,** 601 N.W.2d 757 (Neb. 1999)—list of factors; **Hopkins v. Fox & Lazo Realtors,** 625 A.2d 1110 (N.J. 1993)] Other courts impose similar limitations on duty but may do so by focusing on the relationship that exists between the parties.

(2) **Special problems of principle or policy [§335]**

Courts sometimes decline to impose a duty, even if the defendant's actions created a risk of harm, due to some compelling consideration of principle or policy. The following is a nonexhaustive list of such considerations. Further examples and discussion may be found *infra*, §§545 *et seq.*

(a) **Crushing liability [§336]**

Some courts fear crushing liability in situations that do not involve privity relationships even though the victims are foreseeable. [**Strauss v. Belle Realty Co.,** 65 N.Y.2d 399 (1985)—fear of extended liability of a public utility led court to deny duty for injuries incurred during blackout by tenant in a common area; *and see infra*, §581]

(b) **Conflict with other duties [§337]**

If a doctor negligently performs an abortion, the physical injury to the mother might foreseeably cause birth defects in a child yet to be conceived. But because the doctor's duty to a child not yet conceived would be difficult to define and might create a conflict with the duty owed the patient, and any such duty might last for generations, a court may hold that a duty to a future child does not exist. [*See* **Albala v. City** of **New York,** 54 N.Y.2d 269 (1981); **Grover v. Eli Lilly & Co.,** 591 N.E.2d 696 (Ohio 1992); *but see* **Renslow v. Mennonite Hospital,** 367 N.E.2d 1250 (Ill. 1977)—duty to child born nine years after D negligently transfused blood to mother]

(c) Concern for social institutions [§338]

Some courts refuse to impose a duty, despite the clear creation of a risk, due to a concern for the continuance of important social institutions. [**Thompson v. McNeill,** 559 N.E.2d 705 (Ohio 1990)—no duty owed by golfer whose errant ball struck another golfer's head because to do so "might well stifle the rewards of athletic competition"; **Zurla v. Hydel,** 681 N.E.2d 148 (Ill. 1997)—same regarding hockey injury]

f. The line between act and omission [§339]

In some cases, it is difficult to judge whether the plaintiff's injury stemmed from the defendant's negligent action (***misfeasance***) or negligent failure to act in the face of a duty to do so (***nonfeasance***). The distinction is important because if the court considers the case to be one of misfeasance, the default rule is that a duty of reasonable care exists. If the court concludes that the facts implicate a claim of nonfeasance, the default rule is that no duty exists (absent a special affirmative duty, *see infra*, §§545 *et seq.*).

(1) Note

The Third Restatement has drawn the line rather precisely and in favor of misfeasance. Pursuant to that standard, the default duty of due care arises when the actor's conduct is a ***factual cause of physical harm*** or when the actor's conduct ***creates a risk of harm.*** [Rest. 3d-PH §§6, 7] Considering the ease with which factual causation is satisfied, this standard is indeed inclusive.

(2) Misfeasance or nonfeasance? [§340]

The following is a nonexhaustive list of scenarios that courts sometimes find difficult to categorize as misfeasance or nonfeasance:

(a) Negligent entrustment [§341]

When a defendant ***provides the instrumentality of harm*** to another, courts sometimes characterize such conduct as having created a risk of harm; others characterize the claim as a negligent failure to carry out an affirmative duty to warn or protect the injured party (*see infra*, §597).

---

e.g. **Example:** D's relative, who provides D with money to purchase a vehicle despite knowing of D's poor driving record and substance abuse, may be held liable for negligent entrustment if D's passenger is injured. [**Vince v. Wilson,** 561 A.2d 103 (Vt. 1989)]

---

e.g. **Example:** A service station owner who sells gasoline to a six-year-old child owes a duty to the child and her playmates because entrusting a child with a dangerous substance creates a risk of harm. [**Jones v. Robbins,** 289 So. 2d 104 (La. 1974)]

(b) Negligent/nonnegligent creation of risk [§342]

If a defendant's conduct harms the plaintiff or puts the plaintiff in a position of danger, the defendant has a ***duty to warn*** the plaintiff of ***or rescue*** the plaintiff from her predicament (*see infra*, §§554-555). A court might determine that such a duty is within the scope of the defendant's duty of "reasonable care" that arises from the defendant's creation of a risk, or a court might consider the duty to be of the affirmative, nonfeasance type.

---

e.g. **Example:** When D's train nonnegligently severs P's arm, D has a duty to render assistance. [**Maldonado v. Southern Pacific Transportation Co.,** 629 P.2d 1001 (Ariz. 1981)]

---

1) Note

Whether the defendant's conduct in fact created a risk is sometimes a difficult conclusion. [**Harper v. Herman,** 499 N.W.2d 472 (Minn. 1993)—refusing to impose on boat captain an affirmative duty to warn guest not to dive into shallow water even though captain may have created a risk of harm by choosing to moor in shallow water]

(c) Voluntary undertaking [§343]

Although a person does not owe a duty to warn of or rescue another from a risk arising from a third source, if a defendant ***voluntarily undertakes to warn or rescue***, the defendant owes a duty to do so with reasonable care (*see infra*, §§560-568). Although some courts consider such a duty to be an affirmative duty to rescue, it seems better characterized as part of the defendant's duty of reasonable care arising from the defendant's conduct. [**Farwell v. Keaton,** 240 N.W.2d 217 (Mich. 1976)]

(d) Negligent misrepresentation [§344]

Where a plaintiff charges a defendant with ***negligently misrepresenting some fact*** on which the plaintiff ***relied to her detriment***, whether the defendant's duty arises as a result of misfeasance or nonfeasance is often a difficult call. [**Randi W. v. Muroc Joint Unified School District,** *supra*, §334]

---

e.g. **Example:** D recommends X for a job at P's company. If the recommendation reads, "X was always on time for work," then P's claim is more easily characterized as one of nonfeasance—*i.e.*, D should have warned of X's shortcomings, but did not. However, if the recommendation reads, "X is an excellent employee in every respect," then X's words (*i.e.*, affirmative conduct) might have themselves created the risk of harm.

1) **Distinguish—misrepresentation [§345]**
Negligent misrepresentation that results in ***physical*** harm must be distinguished from a misrepresentation resulting in purely ***economic*** injury (*see infra*, §§1622 *et seq.*).

(e) **Encouraging dangerous acts [§346]**
A defendant has a duty not to create an ***unreasonable risk of harm from third parties***. Thus, a radio station has been held liable for the death of a motorist whose car was forced off the road by a teenager racing to win a radio contest by being the first to locate a "traveling disc jockey." [**Weirum v. RKO General, Inc.**, 15 Cal. 3d 40 (1975)] Although a court might conclude that the risk was created by the teenager, it seems clear that the defendant also participated in creating the risk and therefore also owed a duty to do so with reasonable care.

EXAM TIP — gilbert

Remember that the "duty of due care" is only applicable where the defendant's ***affirmative conduct creates a risk of physical harm*** (e.g., the defendant cuts down a tree that falls on the plaintiff). Although the existence of a duty is often presumed by courts in affirmative conduct cases, do not make this mistake on an exam—***always address and analyze the existence of a duty***.

4. **Breach of Duty [§347]**
Once it is shown that the defendant owed a duty of due care to the plaintiff, it must then be shown that the defendant breached this duty through an act or omission exposing others to an ***unreasonable risk of harm***. These three elements—*i.e.*, an act or omission by the defendant, a duty of due care owed to the plaintiff, and a breach of duty by creation of an unreasonable risk of harm—together constitute a ***"negligent act."*** (However, the elements of ***factual causation, proximate cause,*** and ***damages***, *infra*, must also be satisfied in order to establish ***liability*** for the negligent act—*i.e.*, to establish "negligence.") Whether the defendant has breached a duty of due care requires a two-step demonstration: (i) proof of what actually happened, and (ii) a showing that the defendant acted unreasonably under those circumstances.

a. **Proving what actually happened [§348]**
There are two basic methods of proof available for the plaintiff to establish what in fact occurred:

(1) **Direct evidence [§349]**
In some cases, direct evidence may be available.

e.g. **Example:** A broken ladder rung in a negligence case against the ladder's manufacturer can be used as direct evidence of negligence.

e.g. **Example:** N, a neighbor, observes D throw a brick from his second floor window and sees the brick strike P in the street below; N's testimony as to what occurred is direct evidence.

(2) Circumstantial evidence [§350]

In other situations, the plaintiff may rely on circumstantial evidence to create an inference of what occurred.

e.g. **Example:** P is injured when she trips over something in D's darkened theater. If P can show that a pipe was lying near the place at which she tripped and that a scuff mark on her shoe was made by a pipe-like object when she fell, a jury could infer that P fell over the pipe.

e.g. **Example:** If P, a customer who slips in the supermarket, must show that the slippery substance was on the floor long enough for a reasonable market to find it and remedy the condition, P may do this by showing that the product on the floor was "dirty and messy." [**Negri v. Stop and Shop, Inc.,** 65 N.Y.2d 625 (1985)]

(a) Limitation—similar accidents [§351]

Parties may ***not*** introduce evidence of similar accidents or occurrences (or the absence thereof), unless the past acts occurred under substantially similar circumstances. As a result, the owner of an office building may not defend himself against a suit brought by a pedestrian who slipped on a wet floor within the building, by presenting evidence of the building's safety record. Such a record would not be relevant to the specific circumstances on the day in question. [**Moody v. Haymarket Associates,** 723 A.2d 874 (Me. 1999); *and see* Evidence Summary]

b. Determining whether conduct proved is unreasonable [§352]

The second step in determining whether there was a breach of duty by the defendant (*i.e.*, a negligent act) is whether the defendant acted unreasonably under the circumstances present at the time of the defendant's conduct. This determination is highly fact-specific and is therefore reserved for the jury [**Stagl v. Delta Airlines, Inc.,** 52 F.3d 463 (2d Cir. 1995)] unless, on a motion for summary judgment or the like, a court can rule as a matter of law that "no reasonable jury" could find in favor of the nonmoving party (*see infra*, §360). Courts do not typically give juries precise instructions on how to analyze reasonableness, leaving juries to apply their own moral judgment, common sense, and understanding of community norms. Some courts have indicated that reasonableness requires a ***balancing of the risks and benefits*** of the conduct. [Rest. 2d §291] This manner of reasoning was reduced to an algebraic formula by Judge Learned Hand in **United States v. Carroll Towing Co.,** 159 F.2d 169 (2d Cir. 1947).

(1) Risk—"magnitude of the risk" [§353]

The risk of the defendant's conduct is a combination of (i) the foreseeable *severity* of damage that might occur, and (ii) the foreseeable ***probability*** that the damage will occur. Thus, in each situation, consider the social value that the law attaches to the interests endangered by the defendant's conduct, the foreseeable likelihood of an actual injury by the conduct, and the foreseeable extent or degree of injury threatened (including the number of individual interests imperiled). [**United States v. Carroll Towing Co.,** *supra*]

(2) **Benefit—"utility of the conduct" [§354]**
The benefit of running the risk is usually measured by the expense or inconvenience spared in not taking safety precautions. In determining whether the defendant's conduct is otherwise justified, consider the social value that the law attaches to the type of conduct involved, the foreseeable likelihood that the conduct will achieve some desirable end, the availability of safer alternative methods, and the costs of such methods. [**United States v. Carroll Towing Co.,** *supra*]

(3) **Application of balancing test—risks vs. benefits analysis [§355]**
The defendant's conduct will be considered unreasonable—and therefore negligent—if the magnitude of the risk that would be perceived in advance by a reasonable person in the defendant's position ***outweighs*** its utility. Judge Hand stated this analysis as a formula: Breach = Probability × Loss > Burden on the defendant of taking the risk (commonly abbreviated PL > B). [**United States v. Carroll Towing Co.,** *supra*] Obviously, this determination will vary in each case, depending on the specific circumstances involved.

(a) **General rule [§356]**
Where the risk of injury is low and the cost of alternative (safer) methods is high, the defendant's conduct is more likely to be considered reasonable (*i.e.*, nonnegligent). [**McCarty v. Pheasant Run, Inc.,** 826 F.2d 1554 (7th Cir. 1987)]

(b) **Distinguish [§357]**
Where the utility of the conduct is slight and less dangerous alternatives are available at little cost or effort, it is more likely that negligence will be found—especially if the risk of injury is significant. [**Pease v. Sinclair Refining Co.,** 104 F.2d 183 (2d Cir. 1939)—D provided demonstration kit with water in bottles labeled "kerosene"; a simple warning or an accurate label would have avoided the accident that occurred when P used what was thought to be "kerosene"]

(c) **Cost of safeguarding [§358]**
The costs of safeguarding against the risk must always be measured by the foreseeable ***likelihood*** and ***gravity*** of damage. The more probable and more grievous the harm, the greater the effort and expense that must be undertaken to avoid that harm. And conversely, the less likely the harm, the less effort and expense that need be undertaken.

(This explains why shooting a gun in a densely populated city is more likely to be negligent than engaging in the same activity in a sparsely populated area.)

(d) Limited use of the standard [§359]

In some circumstances (*e.g.*, where factors other than economic risk and benefit enter reasonableness determinations), strict application of a risk-benefit analysis leads to counterintuitive, and likely unacceptable, results. For this and other reasons, trial courts generally do not instruct the jury on the Learned Hand Formula, leaving them only with the general "reasonable care under the circumstances" standard. Appellate courts are more likely to invoke the Hand Formula in assessing whether there was sufficient evidence of negligence, although use by appellate courts is by no means pervasive.

---

e.g. **Example:** An auto manufacturer locates the gas tank of a particular car next to the car's rear bumper, knowingly exposing the car to a substantial risk of explosion on rear impact. If the design saves millions of dollars in manufacturing costs, and if the dollar value of the inevitable fatalities does not exceed (or equal) such savings, then the manufacturer's actions would be deemed reasonable pursuant to the Hand Formula. Nonetheless, a reasonable jury might conclude that the manufacturer's knowing trade of human life for cost savings is unreasonable. [*See* **Grimshaw v. Ford Motor Co.,** 119 Cal. App. 3d 757 (1981)]

EXAM TIP **gilbert**

Professors sometimes test a natural extension of the Learned Hand Formula in which ***no*** reasonable safety precaution would ***completely*** avoid harm, but where alternative measures would only ***reduce the risk*** that harm would occur. In such cases, the Hand Formula becomes slightly more complicated. Reformulated, it would be:

PL ***without*** safety precaution – PL ***with*** safety precaution > B.

In other words, the defendant's failure to take the safety precaution would be unreasonable if the ***risk prevented by the precaution outweighs the burden of preventing it***. For example, if there is a 10% risk of causing $100,000 in damages without the safety precaution, and a 1% risk of causing $100,000 in damages with the safety precaution, the risk prevented by the precaution is $10,000 – $1,000 = $9,000. Thus, if the burden of taking the precaution is less than $9,000, the defendant must take it to avoid being negligent.

---

c. Judge vs. jury

(1) Decision as matter of law creates "mini-rules" [§360]

Although the breach issue is typically reserved for the jury, on a motion for summary judgment (or directed verdict, or the like) a court may decide the issue by holding that no reasonable jury could find in favor of the nonmoving party. Each time that a court makes a breach decision "as a matter of law," it creates a "mini-rule" regarding what conduct is reasonable or unreasonable in a given set of facts. Some courts find this attractive in light of the collective experience the court gains over many trials regarding community norms of conduct. [*See, e.g.*, **Baltimore & Ohio Railroad v. Goodman,** 275 U.S. 66 (1927)—holding, as a matter of law, that reasonableness dictates that a motorist must get out of his car and look both ways before crossing railroad tracks]

(2) Jury decision avoids unjust future results [§361]

Most courts, however, feel reluctant to take the breach question from the jury in all but the clearest cases, largely because creating "mini-rules" intrudes on the province of the jury and runs the danger of producing unjust results as those rules are applied to future cases with slightly different facts. [*See, e.g.*, **Pokora v. Wabash Railway,** 292 U.S. 98 (1934)—limiting *Goodman, supra*, to its facts, particularly where to get out and look both ways would actually increase the danger to the motorist]

(3) Breach is fact-specific [§362]

At the very least, courts agree that decisions of breach as a matter of law should be narrowly limited to the facts of the case.

d. Res ipsa loquitur ("the thing speaks for itself") [§363]

In certain cases, ***the very fact that a particular harm has occurred*** may itself tend to establish ***both*** parts of the breach requirement: what happened and that it was through the defendant's unreasonable conduct. In such cases, the law may permit an ***inference or a presumption*** that the defendant was at fault under the doctrine of res ipsa loquitur.

(1) Essential elements [§364]

Three essential factors must be established to invoke res ipsa loquitur. [*See, e.g.*, **Hull v. L. & A. Montagnard Social Club, Inc.,** 498 A.2d 597 (Me. 1985); **Anderson v. Service Merchandise Co.,** 485 N.W.2d 170 (Neb. 1992)] They are set out in the chart below.

ELEMENTS OF RES IPSA LOQUITUR — **gilbert**

FOR RES IPSA LOQUITUR:

- ☑ The accident must be of a type that ***normally does not occur*** in the absence of someone's negligence;
- ☑ The negligence can be ***attributed to the defendant*** because the accident is of a type that the defendant had a ***duty to guard against***; and
- ☑ Neither the plaintiff nor any third person ***contributed to or caused*** the plaintiff's injuries (*but see infra*, §837).

(a) **Accident of a type that normally does not occur without negligence [§365]**

If the accident is one that normally does not occur in the absence of negligence, the courts hold that the ***occurrence itself*** will permit the conclusion that ***someone*** was negligent. [**Brannon v. Wood,** 444 P.2d 558 (Or. 1968)]

---

e.g. **Examples:** Injuries suffered from eating canned spinach containing large chunks of glass, or from the collapse of bleachers at a baseball game, or from a barrel falling from an upper floor of a building are all examples of events that normally do not occur unless someone is negligent. [*See, e.g.,* **Byrne v. Boadle,** 159 Eng. Rep. 299 (1863)]

---

e.g. **Example:** Similarly, a spare tire coming loose from its cradle underneath a tractor-trailer and crashing into the vehicle following the tractor-trailer is the type of accident that does not occur but for the failure of someone to exercise reasonable care. [**McDougald v. Perry,** 716 So. 2d 783 (Fla. 1998)]

---

1) **Distinguish—accidents without fault [§366]**

However, many accidents can occur without anyone's fault—*e.g.*, a tire blowout, injuries resulting from a falling tree or from fires of unknown origin. [**Klein v. Beeten,** 172 N.W. 736 (Wis. 1919)] In these cases, without further evidence, res ipsa loquitur ***cannot*** be applied.

2) **Necessity for expert testimony [§367]**

Sometimes, expert testimony is required to determine whether negligence can be inferred from the happening of the accident.

---

e.g. **Example:** In medical malpractice cases involving ***complex care*** or treatment, expert testimony is usually required to establish the probability that the injuries resulted from someone's negligence, the rationale being that lay jurors are not competent to infer negligence merely from the occurrence of injury in the course of complicated medical treatment. [**Connors v. University Associates,** 4 F.3d 123 (2d Cir. 1993); **Hightower-Warren v. Silk,** 698 A.2d 52 (Pa. 1997)]

---

a) **But note**

Even in medical malpractice cases, expert testimony is ***not*** required where the ***occurrence is so bizarre*** that someone's negligence is obvious even to a lay juror [**Kambat v. St. Francis Hospital,** 89 N.Y.2d 489 (1997)—18-inch pad left in patient's body], or where the medical ***procedure itself*** is so ***routine*** that common knowledge may be relied upon to determine whether the accident could occur in the absence of someone's negligence [**Bardessono v. Michels,** 3 Cal. 3d 780 (1970)—cortisone injection to treat tendonitis].

3) **Analysis—ultimate issue of probabilities [§368]**
Whether the accident is of a type that normally does not occur in the absence of someone's negligence is ultimately a matter of ***probabilities***; it must appear that the trier of fact could reasonably conclude that, on the whole, it is more likely than not that negligence was associated with the harm.

(b) **Negligence attributable to defendant [§369]**
This element requires that it appear more likely than not that the inference of negligence arising from proof of the first factor (above) can be *focused on the defendant.*

1) **Defendant's control over source of harm [§370]**
Whether a showing of "control" by the defendant is essential for res ipsa loquitur purposes, and if so, what the nature of that control must be, is a subject of divergent views:

a) **"Exclusive control" standard [§371]**
Some courts require that the instrumentality causing the plaintiff's injury be shown to have been under the defendant's "***exclusive control***" at the time of the injury.

---

e.g. **Example:** Pedestrian P is struck by a sign that falls from D's store building. D is deemed in "control" of the sign, and res ipsa loquitur is applied. [**Both v. Harband,** 164 Cal. App. 2d 743 (1958)]

---

e.g. **Example:** Passenger P is injured when D's bus goes out of control and turns over; D is deemed to be in "control" of the instrumentality causing injury for purposes of res ipsa loquitur. [**Whitney v. Northwest Greyhound Lines, Inc.,** 242 P.2d 257 (Mont. 1952)]

---

cf. **Compare:** Hotel guest P is injured when water in D's hotel shower suddenly turns hot. There is evidence that P adjusted the faucets before the incident. P has not shown that D is in "control" of the water. [**Malvicini v. Stratfield Motor Hotel, Inc.,** 538 A.2d 690 (Conn. 1988)]

---

cf. **Compare:** If D leaves his car parked on a hill, and it starts rolling and injures P, res ipsa applies—at least if there was only a short interval between the time D left his car and the time it started rolling. But after a ***long*** time interval has elapsed, other causes—for which D was ***not*** responsible—might appear to be more likely. [**Hill v. Thompson,** 484 P.2d 513 (Okla. 1971)—time lapse of four hours held not enough to prevent inference of D's negligence]

cf. **Compare:** Shopper was injured when an escalator on which she was riding suddenly stopped. There was no evidence on why the escalator stopped, but there were emergency stop buttons at the top and bottom landings that could be pushed by anyone in an emergency. Res ipsa loquitur does not apply because the department store owner was not in exclusive control of the escalator. [**Holzhauer v. Saks & Co.,** 697 A.2d 89 (Md. 1997)]

b) **"Control" only one factor to consider [§372]**

The better view is that showing the defendant's "control" over the instrumentality that caused the injury is only one way of proving the defendant's responsibility. The essential question is whether the injury to the plaintiff was one ***that the defendant owed a duty to guard against.*** [**Corcoran v. Banner Super Market, Inc.,** 19 N.Y.2d 425 (1967)]

e.g. **Example:** A tire manufacturer may be liable under res ipsa loquitur for injuries to a consumer who was mounting a tire for the first time when it exploded, even though the tire had been purchased over a year before. D was no longer realistically in "control" of the tire, but the type of injury was one that D owed a duty to guard against. [**Baker v. B.F. Goodrich Co.,** 115 Cal. App. 2d 221 (1953)]

e.g. **Example:** The same result and reasoning apply in the ***"bursting bottle"*** cases (*i.e.*, plaintiff injured by explosion of defendant's bottled beverage purchased from retailer), as long as it appears that the bottle was not subjected to unusual treatment by the plaintiff, retailer, or any other customer. [**Zentz v. Coca-Cola Bottling Co.,** 39 Cal. 2d 436 (1952)]

c) **"Joint control" or "concerted action" theories of control [§373]**

Some courts have extended the "exclusive control" concept to a ***group*** of physicians and nurses when an unconscious patient, with whom each defendant had some contact, suffers harm of a type that might be found attributable to someone's negligence. Rather than nonsuit the plaintiff for failure to identify the specific person whose negligence caused the harm, the courts—sympathizing with the plaintiff's inability to obtain such proof—have treated the individual defendants potentially as members of a ***joint enterprise*** and imposed responsibility for the harm upon each defendant who cannot exculpate himself. [**Ybarra v. Spangard,** 25 Cal. 2d 486 (1944); **Kolakowski v. Voris,** 415 N.E.2d 397 (Ill. 1980); *but see* **Hoven v. Rice Memorial Hospital,** 396 N.W.2d 569 (Minn. 1986)—questioning *Ybarra*]

---

e.g. **Example:** In *Ybarra*, P, while under an anesthetic, sustained a shoulder injury during an appendectomy. Res ipsa loquitur was held applicable against all doctors and hospital employees connected with the operation, even though there was no proof when the injury occurred or which defendants were present at that time. *Rationale:* Each defendant was charged with a duty to guard against injury to P.

1/ **Limitation—no joint enterprise [§374]**

The doctrine will not be invoked where multiple defendants lack the cohesiveness of a unit. [**Fireman's Fund American Insurance Cos. v. Knobbe,** 562 P.2d 825 (Nev. 1977)—res ipsa loquitur not invoked against four social friends for fire negligently started in a hotel room by one of them (who cannot be identified)]

2/ **Limitation—tortfeasor cannot be identified [§375]**

Where P is unable to identify the tortfeasor, and it is not certain that the tortfeasor is among a large number of defendants sued, courts refuse to make defendants prove their nonculpability. [**Clift v. Nelson,** 608 P.2d 647 (Wash. 1980)—when only one in crowd caused injury, and 10 of 30 members of crowd were sued, P had to identify the tortfeasor]

(c) **Plaintiff or any third party did not contribute to or cause plaintiff's injuries [§376]**

There is no inference of negligence if it appears that the plaintiff's own conduct (or that of some third person for whom the defendant is not responsible) was as likely a cause of the accident as was the defendant's conduct. [A.M. Swarthout, Annotation, Res Ipsa Loquitur Doctrine as Affected by Injured Person's Control Over or Connection with Instrumentality, 169 A.L.R. 953 (1947)]

1) **Distinguish—contributory negligence [§377]**
This requirement must be distinguished from the issue of contributory negligence (*see infra*, §791).

---

e.g. **Example:** Res ipsa loquitur is inapplicable in the crash of a dual-control airplane where human error was the cause and the student pilot (whose family was seeking damages) was at one of the controls and could have been the party at fault. [**Udseth v. United States,** 530 F.2d 860 (10th Cir. 1976)]

(d) **Third Restatement's single-element approach [§378]**
Although most courts adopt a two- or three-element test for res ipsa loquitur, the Third Restatement adopts a single-element approach. It states: "The factfinder may infer that the defendant has been negligent when the accident causing the plaintiff's physical harm is a type of accident that ordinarily happens as a result of the negligence of a class of actors of which the defendant is the relevant member." [Rest. 3d-PH §17]

1) **Rationale**
The Restatement explains that it has dropped the requirements of "exclusive control" and "no plaintiff contribution" because they are merely imperfect proxies for determining that the injury was likely due to the negligence of the defendant. For example, one day after the purchase of a car, the brakes fail, and the car hits a pedestrian. In such case, the driver of the car was in sole control, and yet the element of "sole control" does not capture the fact that the driver likely had nothing to do with the faulty brakes. [**Smoot v. Mazda Motors of America, Inc.,** 469 F.3d 675 (7th Cir. 2006)]

(2) **Other factors affecting use of res ipsa loquitur**

(a) **Accessibility of evidence [§379]**
Most courts hold that if the above three elements are met, the doctrine will apply even if the defendant cannot add any evidence on the issue of what happened. [**Judson v. Giant Powder Co.,** 107 Cal. 549 (1895)—explosion of nitroglycerine factory destroyed all evidence, but res ipsa loquitur was still applied]

1) **Note**
Some courts rely on the defendant's special access to information in denying motions for nonsuits where the plaintiffs have done the best they can to identify the cause of the accident—***even if*** the traditional elements of res ipsa are absent. This is probably the explanation for the unconscious patient cases (*see supra*, §373),

though, as seen, courts often try to force such cases into the three-part test of the basic res ipsa doctrine.

(b) Effect of proving specific acts of negligence [§380]

A plaintiff who attempts to prove specific acts of negligence to explain what happened may still use res ipsa loquitur as long as the three-part test is met. (The jury may reject the plaintiff's specific proof but may accept the general inference of negligence from the happening of the accident.) [**Ward v. Forrester Day Care, Inc.,** 547 So. 2d 410 (Ala. 1989)—P tried to prove D negligent in supervision of day care center; P could also use res ipsa because introduction of evidence on how accident could have happened does not preclude application of res ipsa loquitur if evidence does not clearly resolve culpability; **Abbott v. Page Airways, Inc.,** 23 N.Y.2d 502 (1969)—P tried to prove that helicopter fell from sky because pilot flew too slowly and was not paying attention; P also allowed to use res ipsa because helicopters do not usually fall without some negligence]

1) Minority view [§381]

A few states hold that a plaintiff may be denied the benefit of res ipsa if too much specific evidence of negligence has been presented. [**Malloy v. Commonwealth Highland Theatres, Inc.,** 375 N.W.2d 631 (S.D. 1985)—P presented too much direct evidence to be allowed to rely also on res ipsa loquitur]

(3) Effect of establishing res ipsa loquitur

(a) Majority view—inference [§382]

Most courts treat res ipsa loquitur as creating only a permissible ***inference*** of negligence—*i.e.*, a conclusion that the trier of fact ***may*** (or may not) choose to draw from the facts, the strength of the inference depending on, and varying with, the circumstances of each case. [**Gardner v. Coca-Cola Bottling Co.,** 127 N.W.2d 557 (Minn. 1964)]

---

e.g. **Example:** D's truck veered over onto P's side of the road and rolled over onto P's vehicle during a storm. D produced testimony about a sudden wind to explain the event. The jury was properly charged that the burden of persuasion remained on P. [**Bauer v. J.B. Hunt Transport, Inc.,** 150 F.3d 759 (7th Cir. 1998)]

---

1) But note

Even in inference states, facts may be so strong that an inference ***must*** be drawn if not rebutted. [**Farina v. Pan American World Airlines, Inc.,** 116 A.D.2d 618 (1986)—plane ran off runway while landing]

(b) **Minority view—presumption [§383]**

A few courts, however, give res ipsa loquitur the status of a ***rebuttable presumption*** of breach of duty owed; *i.e.*, it shifts the burden of going forward with the evidence to the defendant (to give a satisfactory explanation of how the injuries occurred, by a ***preponderance*** of evidence), and if the defendant fails to do so, the plaintiff would be entitled to a directed verdict on liability. [**Weiss v. Axler,** 328 P.2d 88 (Colo. 1958)] (*See* Evidence Summary for further discussion of inferences and presumptions.)

(c) **Minority view—"disappearing" presumption [§384]**

In still other states, res ipsa is classified as a presumption, but one that is dispelled by counterevidence. [Cal. Evid. Code §646] Thus, if the defendant can simply produce evidence sufficient to sustain a finding of fact in his favor (*see* Evidence Summary), the presumption has no further evidentiary effect; the burden of proof is back on the ***plaintiff*** to persuade the trier of fact that the defendant breached his duty of care under the circumstances.

EXAM TIP **gilbert**

You may encounter an exam question involving res ipsa loquitur that has the defendant making a motion for a directed verdict. You don't need to memorize the rules of civil procedure for this type of question, but you do need to remember the following:

(i) ***Deny*** the defendant's motion for a directed verdict if the plaintiff has established res ipsa loquitur or presented some other evidence of breach of duty (such as the defendant's violation of a statute); or

(ii) ***Grant*** the defendant's motion for a directed verdict if the plaintiff has failed to establish res ipsa loquitur and failed to present some other evidence of breach of duty.

e. **Effect of custom and statutes [§385]**

A safety-related statute or custom in a community or industry arguably reflects collective notions of whether the relevant conduct is safe and feasible. For this reason, courts typically admit evidence of safety-related statutes and customs as some, but not conclusive (with one rather large exception, *see infra*, §394), evidence of the defendant's adherence to or departure from the reasonable person standard of care. [Rest. 2d §295A]

(1) **How custom established**

(a) **Purpose must be to avoid harm [§386]**

For a custom to be relevant to the standard of care, its purpose must be to avoid the ***type of harm*** suffered by the plaintiff.

---

e.g. **Example:** Some churches have a custom not to burn candles. The origin of the custom is likely tied to a theological departure from Catholic traditions and not to a desire to avoid church fires. Therefore, the custom will not be admissible as evidence that keeping candles in a particular church breached the standard of care.

(b) Need not be universal [§387]

Conduct need not be universal in order to constitute a custom, but only need be "fairly well-defined" or "widespread" within the relevant community or industry. [**Trimarco v. Klein,** 56 N.Y.2d 98 (1982)]

(c) Defendant must be member of relevant community [§388]

For a custom to be applicable, the defendant (and sometimes the plaintiff) must be a member of the industry or community in which the relevant custom is practiced. If such a member, the defendant may be charged with knowledge of the custom even if actual knowledge is lacking.

(2) Effect of custom [§389]

Custom in the community is admissible as ***evidence*** of the standard of care owed, but it is ***never conclusive*** (indeed, some customs may themselves be found to be negligent). The fact that the defendant has acted (or failed to act) as others in the community customarily do may provide a clue as to the reasonableness or unreasonableness of the conduct. The test remains whether the reasonable person would have so acted under the same or similar circumstances. [**Texas & Pacific Railway v. Behymer,** 189 U.S. 468 (1903); **The T.J. Hooper,** 60 F.2d 737 (2d Cir.), *cert. denied*, 287 U.S. 662 (1932); Rest. 2d §295A]

(a) Application—expert witnesses [§390]

When the most qualified expert witnesses are ***all*** employed by the specific defendant industry (*e.g.*, airport terminal designers or baggage claim systems experts), courts will apply a more lenient standard for qualifying expert witnesses. Otherwise, the defendant industry could, through unchallenged expert testimony, use custom to define what is reasonable. [**Stagl v. Delta Air Lines, Inc.,** 117 F.3d 76 (2d Cir. 1997)]

(b) Proof of compliance with custom [§391]

Although not binding on courts, proof of a defendant's ***compliance*** with custom may indicate to the court that an adverse decision will affect many people (*i.e.*, an entire industry may have to alter its behavior). It may also suggest that there is no better way to perform the task in question. [**Low v. Park Price Co.,** 503 P.2d 291 (Idaho 1972); **Williams v. New York Rapid Transit,** 272 N.Y. 366 (1936)]

---

e.g. **Example:** P, a motel guest, claimed that D, the motel owner, had a duty to provide emergency lighting in each room in case of a power failure. Evidence that no motel or hotel provided such emergency lighting was properly admitted, because although industry custom is not conclusive as to what is reasonably prudent conduct in a given case, it may be a useful guide, unless it is apparent that under the circumstances of the case, no reasonable person would conform to industry-wide custom. [**LaVallee v. Vermont Motor Inns, Inc.,** 569 A.2d 1073 (Vt. 1989)]

(c) **Proof of deviation from custom [§392]**

Showing of the defendant's ***deviation*** from customary conduct in the community may aid the plaintiff because it shows the court that a determination of negligence in the case will ***not*** upset the practices of an entire industry or group of people. Moreover, the fact that others perform the task in a safer manner suggests that an alternative not only was feasible, but that the defendant knew or should have known of the custom. [**Levine v. Russell Blaine Co.,** 273 N.Y. 386 (1937); Clarence Morris, Custom and Negligence, 42 Colum. L. Rev. 1147 (1942)]

(3) **Effect of compliance with statute [§393]**

Where the defendant's duty exists pursuant to the common law duty of reasonable care, the fact that the defendant complied with applicable statutes governing the conduct is admissible on the question of whether the defendant's conduct was negligent, but again, it is ***not conclusive.*** The standard of "due care" is still the reasonable person test, and the statute may or may not have demanded such a level of conduct. [**Clinkscales v. Carver,** 22 Cal. 2d 72 (1943)] Compliance with a statute setting only a minimal level of conduct may not be enough to establish reasonable care under the circumstances.

---

e.g. **Example:** A landlord who complied with a statute requiring that apartment windows be guarded "by a barrier at least eight inches high" might still be found negligent because a jury could find that it was reasonable to have the barrier 12 or more inches high under the circumstances.

(a) **Exception [§394]**

If the court concludes that the statute's standard is reasonable (rather than minimal) and the facts closely resemble those contemplated in the statute, the court may declare that compliance satisfies the duty of care. [Rest. 2d §288C; **Josephson v. Meyers,** 429 A.2d 877 (Conn. 1980); **Espinoza v. Elgin, Joliet & Eastern Railway,** 649 N.E.2d 1323 (Ill. 1995)—administrative approval of precise configuration of grade crossing is conclusive in tort action]

(b) **Distinguish—conduct in violation of statute [§395]**

If the defendant's conduct ***violated*** some applicable safety statute (the conduct fell below the statutory standard), the plaintiff may be able to establish negligence simply by proving the violation. (*See infra*, §§546-550.)

EXAM TIP gilbert

Remember the basics regarding compliance with custom and statute:

Custom: The defendant's compliance with or deviation from industry custom ***never conclusively proves*** whether the defendant's conduct was reasonable. However, compliance with custom aids the defendant's case because finding the defendant's behavior negligent can upset the practices of the entire industry. Deviation from industry custom aids the plaintiff's case because it shows that a safer alternative was available and that the defendant either knew or should have known of the custom.

Statute: In a case in which duty exists pursuant to the common law duty of reasonable care, the defendant's compliance with a statute ***never conclusively proves*** that his behavior is reasonable. If the statutory duty is minimal, more care may be required. But if the facts of a case (or an exam question) closely resemble those contemplated by the statute, a court may find that compliance satisfies the duty of care. Also, violation of a safety statute may itself establish breach of the duty of care.

f. **Criminal statutes and breach—"negligence per se" [§396]**

Where a common law duty of care is ***already*** owed, and a statute provides that specific conduct breaching that duty is subject to criminal penalties, under appropriate circumstances, courts may use violation of the criminal statute to establish ***breach*** of duty in a civil negligence action. In such situations, breach of the statute constitutes negligence per se. [**Osborne v. McMasters,** 41 N.W. 543 (Minn. 1889)]

(1) **Not applicable to children [§397]**

Under the majority rule, the doctrine of "negligence per se" is not invoked against children engaged in children's activities. [**Bauman v. Crawford,** 704 P.2d 1181 (Wash. 1985)] The children's standard is discussed *supra*, §291.

(2) **Requirements for "negligence per se" [§398]**

For a criminal statute to establish a breach for civil negligence purposes the following must appear:

(a) **Statutory duty clear [§399]**

The statute itself must be clear and unambiguous. It must specify exactly what conduct or duty is required, of whom it is required, and what constitutes a breach of that duty.

(b) **Violation within statutory purpose [§400]**

It must also appear that in enacting the statute, the legislature was seeking to accomplish two separate objectives: (i) to ***prevent the particular***

type of injury involved in the current tort action, and (ii) to ***protect the particular class of plaintiff*** involved in the current tort action.

1) **To prevent type of injury [§401]**
The legislative purpose must have been to prevent the type of injury actually suffered by the plaintiff. [**Matomco Oil Co. v. Arctic Mechanical, Inc.,** 796 P.2d 1336 (Alaska 1990); **Darmento v. Pacific Molasses Co.,** 81 N.Y.2d 985 (1993)]

---

e.g. **Example:** A statute makes it unlawful for auto owners to leave their vehicles parked with the keys in the ignition. Auto owner D violates this statute and thief X steals D's car, drives it negligently, and injures P. Does the statute create a duty of due care on D? Probably not. It is doubtful that the legislature intended to prevent ***this type*** of injury. More likely, the legislative intent was to make auto theft more difficult or to protect innocent purchasers of stolen cars. [**Anderson v. Theisen,** 43 N.W.2d 272 (Minn. 1950); **Pendrey v. Barnes,** 479 N.E.2d 283 (Ohio 1985); *but see, e.g.,* **Ney v. Yellow Cab Co.,** 117 N.E.2d 74 (Ill. 1954)—contra]

---

e.g. **Example:** D gas station sells gas to arsonists in violation of a statute forbidding the sale of gas in plastic containers. Arsonists use the gas to accelerate a fire that kills and injures P. Courts will not use this statute to create a duty of due care because it was designed to make the transport and storage of gas safer, not to make it harder to buy untanked gas. [**Morales v. City of New York,** 70 N.Y.2d 981 (1988); *and see* **Di Ponzio v. Riordan,** 89 N.Y.2d 578 (1997)—P hurt when D customer illegally failed to turn off engine at gas station and car rolled into P; P could not use violation of statute in the case because statute's purpose was to prevent fires]

---

2) **To protect class of persons [§402]**
The legislature must also have intended to protect a class of persons of which plaintiff is a member. [**Kelly v. Henry Muhs Co.,** 59 A. 23 (N.J. 1904)]

---

e.g. **Example:** D makes an illegal left-hand turn in violation of the Vehicle Code, collides with an oncoming car, and crashes into P's building on the side of the road. Courts will probably not use this statute to create a duty of due care because P was not among the ***class of persons*** sought to be protected by the statute; *i.e.,* its apparent objective is to protect other motorists on the highway, not owners of property along the roadside. [**Erickson v. Kongsli,** 240 P.2d 1209 (Wash. 1952)]

---

3) **Licensing statutes [§403]**

Courts often conclude that a violation of licensing statutes does ***not*** establish negligence per se. [**Brown v. Shyne,** 242 N.Y. 176 (1926)—chiropractor who performed service that only physicians were permitted to perform by law held not per se negligent] This is because failure to comply with a licensing statute is not necessarily relevant to one's safety or competence in performing the licensed activity—*e.g.*, one might have failed to pay one's licensing dues or simply forgotten to fill out a timely renewal of license form.

(c) **No excuse [§404]**

Often a violation of statute is reasonable. Although the reasonableness of a defendant's conduct will not alone excuse the violation of a safety statute, a statute can be invoked to establish negligence per se only if the defendant has no ***legally acceptable excuse*** for its violation.

1) **Legally acceptable excuses [§405]**

Courts and the Third Restatement [Rest. 3d-PH §15] have recognized several categories of legally acceptable excuses:

a) Where the violation is reasonable in light of the defendant's ***tender years, physical disability, or physical incapacitation***;

b) Where the defendant ***neither knows nor should know of the factual circumstances*** that render the statute applicable;

c) Where the defendant's violation is due to the ***confusing way in which the statute's requirements are explained*** to the public;

d) Where it was ***safer, under the circumstances, to disobey*** the statute than to follow it; and

e) Where the defendant ***exercised reasonable care to comply*** with the statute.

2) **Application [§406]**

If the defendant had no good reason for the infraction, this presents the clearest case for a finding of negligence per se. [**Robinson v. District of Columbia,** 580 A.2d 1255 (D.C. 1990)—proof of custom of crossing street outside crosswalk cannot excuse violation of traffic regulation] On the other hand, although a person failed to comply with a statute's mandate where it was safer, under the circumstances, not to comply, it may be that such conduct was reasonable. In such cases, she has not been negligent and should not be held liable for violating the statute. [**Tedla v. Ellman,** 280 N.Y. 124 (1939)—walking on highway with back to traffic may be illegal but is not negligent if traffic is much heavier in facing direction]

---

e.g. **Example:** It has been held not to be negligence where D disobeys the letter of a statute because of physical circumstances beyond his control, as where his lights unexpectedly fail on the highway at night or where he is forced to drive on the left because the right is blocked. [**Brotherton v. Day & Night Fuel Co.,** 73 P.2d 788 (Wash. 1937)]

---

a) **Rationale**

Violations of statute permit the court to use a ***specific*** breach to replace the more general duty of care already discussed. However, this can be justified only if the basic assumption that it is reasonable to obey the criminal law holds; *i.e.*, when a reasonable person would violate the law, the theory fails.

3) **Excuses must be heard [§407]**

Unless the legislature intended to foreclose consideration of excused violations (which is rarely the case), the court is bound to hear excuses offered by the defendant; to do otherwise would be tantamount to imposing strict liability (*i.e.*, liability regardless of fault).

(3) **Effect of violation of statute**

(a) **Unexcused violations [§408]**

If the defendant makes no effort to justify or excuse his prima facie violation of a criminal statute that was enacted to protect a class of persons of which the plaintiff is a member from the type of injury the plaintiff actually suffered, liability will be analyzed under one of three views:

1) **Majority view—"negligence per se" [§409]**

Under the widely followed majority view, such a showing will lead the trial judge to conclude that the defendant was negligent ***as a matter of law***; there will be no question for the jury on the question of breach. [**Martin v. Herzog,** 228 N.Y. 164 (1920)—driving wagon without lights after dark is negligence per se; Rest. 2d §288B]

2) **Minority view—rebuttable presumption [§410]**
One minority view holds that the violation creates only a rebuttable presumption of negligence and does not establish negligence per se. But this view significantly differs from that of the majority ***only*** when the defendant offers an ***excuse*** for his behavior. Absent such a showing, the presumption of negligence cannot be rebutted, and negligence will be found as a matter of law, just as under the majority view. [**Satterlee v. Orange Glenn School District,** 29 Cal. 2d 581 (1947)]

3) **Minority view—evidence only [§411]**
A second minority view holds that violation of a statute or ordinance is never more than ***evidence*** of breach of duty and is not binding on the trier of fact. Thus, subject to the usual limits on the jury's role, a jury might find even an unexcused violation to be nonnegligent behavior. [**French v. Willman,** 599 A.2d 1151 (Me. 1991)—car crossing center line on road is "evidence of negligence"]

(b) Where excuse offered for violation

1) **Majority view [§412]**
Where the defendant attempts to justify his behavior, in the majority of jurisdictions the trial judge will decide the validity of the offered excuse. If the excuse is found valid (and supported by the facts), the judge will rule for the defendant. (If crucial facts are disputed, the jury will determine these.)

a) **But note**
If the excuse is ***unacceptable***, even if supported by the facts, the excuse will not justify the violation.

2) **Minority view—rebuttable presumption [§413]**
Under the "rebuttable presumption" approach, the apparent violator has the burden of persuading the trier of fact that the behavior was reasonable even though it may have violated a statute. If the defendant does not meet this burden, the plaintiff will prevail.

3) **Minority view—evidence only [§414]**
Under the "evidence only" approach, the jury is instructed that the burden is on the plaintiff to establish negligence as in the usual common law case. The asserted statutory violation is treated as one of the circumstances of the case and will have whatever effect the jury decides to give it (operating within the usual limits on jury power).

EXAM TIP **gilbert**

Negligence fact patterns involving a criminal statute are fairly common on law school exams. Don't rush to apply the statute. First, be sure that ***there is an existing common law duty***. Then use the statute to determine whether there was a breach. While violating a statute can result in a finding of ***negligence per se*** (*i.e.*, as a matter of law), don't rush to this conclusion. Remember to check first for the three prerequisites to finding negligence per se: (i) the statute must clearly specify the ***duty and conduct that violates it***, (ii) the purpose of the statute must have been to ***prevent the particular type of injury*** involved and to ***protect the particular type of plaintiff*** involved, and finally, (iii) violation of the statute must be ***without any legally acceptable excuse*** (be sure that the defendant's conduct actually violated the statutory command). If any of these prerequisites is missing, the conduct is not negligence per se. Also remember that even if all of the prerequisites are met, some courts will treat the violation only as a rebuttable presumption of negligence, and a few will treat it only as evidence of negligence.

5. Actual Cause ("Cause in Fact") [§415]

The defendant's negligent act must be a cause of the plaintiff's injuries in order to impose liability. Some courts include, within the element of "causation," both the "actual cause" (or "cause in fact" or "factual cause") and "proximate cause" (or "scope of liability") inquiries, thus describing the negligence action as having only four elements: duty, breach, causation, and damages. In other courts, the term "proximate cause" is confusingly used to mean the combined causation element ("legal cause" is another term used to mean both elements, although sometimes it is used only to mean proximate cause). Many other courts, the Third Restatement, and this Summary describe actual cause and proximate cause as distinct concepts. ***Actual cause*** is the factual inquiry into whether the defendant's negligent conduct was a cause of the plaintiff's injuries. ***Proximate cause*** (discussed *infra*, §§442 *et seq.*) requires a judgment by the jury about whether, even if all the other elements of a negligence claim are satisfied, the type, manner, or extent of the plaintiff's injury calls for the imposition of liability.

a. "But for" rule [§416]

The defendant's negligent act must have been the ***cause in fact*** of the plaintiff's injuries. If the plaintiff would ***not*** have been injured ***but for*** the defendant's negligent act, that act is a cause in fact of the injury. [**Chaney v. Smithkline Beckman Corp.**, 764 F.2d 527 (8th Cir. 1985)—Arkansas would not permit recovery when expert said "20 to 80% chance" that D caused P's injury]

(1) Defendant's act must be negligent [§417]

It is not enough that the plaintiff's injury would not have occurred but for the defendant's conduct. The plaintiff must prove that the injury would not have occurred but for the defendant's ***negligence.***

e.g. **Example:** P can prove that her injury would not have occurred but for having taken a particular drug of which D negligently prescribed too large a dose. P has not yet proven cause in fact—it may be, for instance, that prescribing the drug at any dosage would have caused the injury (but that D had no reason to know of this risk). P must prove that it was D's excess dose, ***which occurred due to D's negligence***, that was the factual cause of the injury. [**Zuchowicz v. United States,** 140 F.3d 381 (2d Cir. 1998)]

EXAM TIP **gilbert**

On your exam, it is important to remember that if the plaintiff would have sustained the same injury regardless of the defendant's act, the act is ***not the cause in fact*** of the injury and the defendant is not liable to the plaintiff. Thus, *e.g.*, actual cause is missing where the plaintiff's land is flooded after the defendant's negligently maintained railroad embankment collapsed if it appears that the storm was severe enough to have caused the collapse of even a reasonably maintained embankment.

b. **Concurrent liability rule [§418]**

Where the separate negligent acts of the defendant and a third party concur to cause a single injury, and it appears that the plaintiff would ***not*** have been injured ***but for the concurrence***, then ***both*** the defendant and the third party are actual causes. [**Hill v. Edmonds,** 26 A.D.2d 554 (1966)]

e.g. **Example:** Where a collision of two vehicles injures a pedestrian, and the collision was caused by the negligence of ***both*** drivers (*i.e.*, "but for" the negligence of both, the accident would not have occurred), the pedestrian can recover from either or both for any indivisible injuries suffered. *But note:* Many states have recently abolished the traditional common law rule of joint and several liability or limited its applicability (*see infra*, §1331).

(1) **Distinguish—jointly engaged tortfeasors [§419]**

Similar rules apply where the injury is inflicted by one of several defendants ***jointly engaged*** in a course of negligent conduct. In such a case, ***each defendant*** is liable even though only one of them (who ***can*** be identified) actually inflicted the injury (*see infra*, §1252). [Rest. 2d §876]

e.g. **Example:** All participants in an illegal "drag race" on a public highway are liable to bystanders who are consequently injured, even though the accident involved only one of the racing cars. [**Bierczynski v. Rogers,** 239 A.2d 218 (Del. 1968)]

(2) **Successive tortfeasors [§420]**

When successive acts of unrelated independent tortfeasors produce harm that is difficult to apportion, the tortfeasors must try to disprove their responsibility for the injury.

Example: A woman suffering from arthritis is injured in an auto accident. The injuries are worsened by another accident several weeks later. Although each negligent defendant is responsible only for the portion of the injury that each caused, the burden of allocating that causation is placed on the defendants. [**Phennah v. Whalen,** 621 P.2d 1304 (Wash. 1980)]

c. **Multiple sufficient causes—"substantial factor" rule [§421]**
If the plaintiff sustains injury as the result of the negligent conduct of two tortfeasors, and it appears that the conduct of ***either one*** alone would have been sufficient to cause the injury, ***both*** are nevertheless liable if each of their acts was a "substantial factor" in causing the injury. [**Anderson v. Minneapolis, St. Paul & Sault Ste. Marie Railway,** 179 N.W. 45 (Minn. 1920)]

Example: Where two negligent motorcyclists simultaneously pass P's horse, thereby frightening it and causing it to run away, and either motorcyclist ***alone*** would have caused the fright, the conduct of each of them is a "substantial factor." [**Corey v. Havener,** 65 N.E. 69 (Mass. 1902)]

(1) **Analysis—distinguish "but for" and concurrent liability rules [§422]**
In this type of case, it is really ***not*** the concurrence that causes the damage, because either force by itself would have resulted in the same injuries. Moreover, if the "but for" rule (above) were strictly applied, both the defendant and the third party would escape liability, because in testing the defendant's liability one would find that the injuries would have occurred ***despite*** the defendant's acts; and the same would apply to the third party's liability. That is why courts have worked out the "substantial factor" rule to cover this type of case. [Rest. 2d §§431-433A]

d. **Problem of alternative liability [§423]**
If a plaintiff has been injured through the negligence of one of several possible defendants, and it is not clear which one caused the injury—***but it is clear that only one of them did***—how can causation be established?

Example: D1 and D2 are ***both negligent*** in firing their rifles near P. P is struck by a bullet from one of the rifles, but it is impossible to tell from which rifle the bullet came.

EXAM TIP **gilbert**

Be careful not to confuse multiple sufficient causes with alternative causes. Under the ***multiple sufficient causes*** approach, ***each party was a cause of the harm.*** Under the ***alternative causes*** approach, although more than one party acted negligently, ***only one caused the harm.***

(1) **"But for" rule would exclude liability [§424]**
Application of the "but for" rule will not work; because it cannot be shown which defendant's fault caused the harm, it is impossible to ascertain whether the injury would have occurred "but for" that defendant's acts.

(2) **Better view shifts burden to each defendant [§425]**
Only a few courts have recently dealt with this problem. These decisions hold that where P cannot show whether D1's or D2's negligence was the actual cause of P's injuries, ***the burden of going forward with the evidence shifts to each defendant*** to show that his negligence was ***not*** the actual cause. [**Summers v. Tice,** 33 Cal. 2d 80 (1948); Rest. 2d §433B(3)]

(3) **Shifting burden where only one defendant negligent [§426]**
The above view may be an eminently desirable result when there is some evidence that ***both*** defendants were acting negligently, even if not acting jointly. However, where there is no evidence as to where culpability lies, and it appears from the facts that ***only one*** of the two defendants ***could*** have been negligent—although the plaintiff does not know which one—application of the "shifting burden" rule may impose a hardship on the innocent defendant because he must assume the burden of proving his innocence, which he may be unable to do unless he can effectively prove the culpability of the other defendant. [**Garcia v. Joseph Vince Co.,** 84 Cal. App. 3d 868 (1978)—P who cannot show which saber caused fencing accident cannot shift burden]

(4) **Market share liability [§427]**
Suits against manufacturers of the pregnancy drug diethylstilbestrol ("DES") have led to a theory of causation called market share liability. This theory is useful in situations where even if all the defendants are assumed negligent, it is uncertain which one of them actually caused the plaintiff's injury due to the passage of time and the fact that the defendants' drugs were generally indistinguishable. Courts have agreed that burden shifting (*supra,* §425) does not apply because there are too many tortfeasors or because not all the tortfeasors are before the court. Several views have emerged that vary both as to scope of the doctrine and whether it involves joint or several liability.

(a) **New York view [§428]**
Under the New York view, all defendants are liable based on their culpability. Culpability is measured by the risk each defendant imposed on the public at large; *i.e.,* the risk each defendant caused is measured by its ***national*** market share of the product. Defendants cannot exculpate themselves from liability, even if they can show that they could not have caused the plaintiff's injury, unless they demonstrate that they did not produce the product for the use that injured the plaintiff (in this case, as a pregnancy drug). Liability is several (*i.e.,* each

defendant is liable only for the injuries attributable to that defendant). [**Hymowitz v. Eli Lilly & Co.,** 73 N.Y.2d 487, *cert. denied*, 493 U.S. 944 (1989)]

(b) **Washington view [§429]**

Under the Washington view, after the plaintiff makes out a prima facie case against at least one defendant, all others joined may then exculpate themselves by showing that they could not have caused the injuries. The remaining defendants may then rebut the presumption of equal market shares by showing their true market shares. Plaintiffs may recover less than full damages if every defendant can prove its true market share and some absent possible causes exist. Liability is several. [**George v. Parke-Davis,** 733 P.2d 507 (Wash. 1987); **Martin v. Abbott Laboratories,** 689 P.2d 368 (Wash. 1984)]

(c) **California view [§430]**

Under the California view, if the defendants in the action represent a ***substantial share*** of the market for the product, they will be liable for a percentage of the plaintiff's injuries equal to their market share. Defendants can exculpate themselves if they can show that they could not have caused the plaintiff's injuries. Liability is several. [**Brown v. Superior Court,** 44 Cal. 3d 1049 (1988); **Sindell v. Abbott Laboratories,** 26 Cal. 3d 588, *cert. denied*, 449 U.S. 912 (1980)]

(d) **Rejection of market share liability [§431]**

Some jurisdictions have rejected market share liability in any form and rely on traditional notions of causation. [**Smith v. Eli Lilly & Co.,** 560 N.E.2d 324 (Ill. 1990)]

(e) **Extension beyond DES cases [§432]**

Most states willing to use market share analysis for DES cases have been reluctant to extend the doctrine to other products—sometimes because of fact differences. [**Santiago v. Sherwin Williams Co.,** 3 F.3d 546 (1st Cir. 1993)—proof inadequate to permit theory to apply against defendants who marketed lead paint over a 30-year period; **Goldman v. Johns-Manville Sales Corp.,** 514 N.E.2d 691 (Ohio 1987)—because asbestos products can be distinguished from one another in terms of harmfulness, market share theory was rejected; *but see* **Wheeler v. Raybestos-Manhattan,** 8 Cal. App. 4th 1152 (1992)—market share theory applied to manufacturers of brake pads because they used asbestos fibers that were very similar in harmfulness; **Smith v. Cutter Biological, Inc.,** 823 P.2d 717 (Haw. 1991)—applying theory to blood-coagulating factor used by hemophiliacs]

COMPARISON OF RULES FOR ESTABLISHING ACTUAL CAUSE	gilbert
"BUT FOR" RULE	Plaintiff would ***not*** have been injured ***but for*** defendant's ***negligent*** act.
CONCURRENT CAUSES RULE	Plaintiff would ***not*** have been injured ***but for the combination of*** defendant's and a third party's ***negligent*** acts.
SUBSTANTIAL FACTOR RULE	Plaintiff is injured as a result of several causes, ***any one of which would have been sufficient*** to cause the injury, and defendant's negligent act was a ***substantial factor*** in causing the injury.
ALTERNATIVE CAUSES RULE	Plaintiff is injured by the negligent act of one of several possible defendants, ***but it is not known which one***. Burden of proof ***shifts*** to defendants to show each one's negligence is ***not*** the actual cause.

e. **Risk of future harm [§433]**

If the onset of an injury brings with it the likelihood of future harm, courts have split over whether to award damages for that chance of future harm. Most courts have allowed recovery if the plaintiff can show that it is more likely than not to occur. [**Mauro v. Raymark Industries, Inc.,** 561 A.2d 257 (N.J. 1989)]

(1) **Minority view—no recovery at this time [§434]**

Some states hold that although the plaintiff is now more likely than not to suffer a future harm as the result of the defendant's negligence that has already caused the present injury, the plaintiff must wait until the second condition comes into existence in order to recover for it. [**Simmons v. Pacor, Inc.,** 674 A.2d 232 (Pa. 1996)—the "two-suit" rule]

(2) **Minority view—some recovery possible [§435]**

A few states permit the plaintiff to recover a partial amount now even if the risk is less than even that the future harm will occur. [**Petriello v. Kalman,** 576 A.2d 474 (Conn. 1990)—where defendant's negligence caused harm and exposed plaintiff to 8-16% risk of future harm, plaintiff could recover that 8-16% now]

f. **Loss of chance [§436]**

Traditionally, a plaintiff could not recover for a loss unless she could prove that she had lost something that she was ***more likely than not*** to have acquired or retained but for the defendant's conduct.

(1) **Medical exception [§437]**

In medical cases, courts have recently begun to allow suits for loss of recovery chances that are less than 50%. [**Wendland v. Sparks,** 574 N.W.2d 327

(Iowa 1998)—allowing recovery for loss of chance where plaintiff able to show only loss of a less-than-even chance; **Alberts v. Schultz,** 975 P.2d 1279 (N.M. 1999); *but see* **Fennell v. Southern Maryland Hospital Center, Inc.,** 580 A.2d 206 (Md. 1990)—refusing to recognize action for loss of a 40% chance of survival; **Kramer v. Lewisville Memorial Hospital,** 858 S.W.2d 397 (Tex. 1993)]

(a) Damages [§438]

Courts are split on the issue of damages in loss of recovery cases. Where the lost chance was greater than 50%, some courts have awarded damages for the entire lost chance (*i.e.*, as if the patient had lost a 100% chance of recovery). In states that recognize the medical exception, the recovery for a lost chance less than 50% is the value of that percentage to the total damages. In some of these states, even plaintiffs who prove that they lost a chance greater than 50% may recover only that percentage of their loss, rather than 100%. [*See* **DeBurkarte v. Louvar,** 393 N.W.2d 131 (Iowa 1986)]

(2) Distinguish—emotional distress [§439]

When physical injury is present, courts allow recovery for fear of further harm, such as cancer. [**Mauro v. Raymark Industries, Inc.,** *supra*] But where there is no present physical injury, recovery for ***fear*** about future developments is much less likely. [**Potter v. Firestone Tire & Rubber Co.,** 6 Cal. 4th 965 (1993)—prolonged exposure to toxic landfill does not permit recovery for emotional distress without a showing that it is "more likely than not that the plaintiff will develop the cancer in the future due to the toxic exposure"]

g. Problem where defendant's negligence has deprived plaintiff of proof [§440]

A similar approach may be taken in cases where the plaintiff finds herself unable to prove "but for" causation because the defendant's negligence has ***deprived the plaintiff of evidence*** of the actual cause. In such cases, the burden may be shifted to the defendant to prove that his negligence was ***not*** the cause in fact of the plaintiff's injuries.

---

e.g. **Example:** D, the owner of a hotel, negligently fails to provide a lifeguard at the swimming pool, as required by statute. P's husband drowns while using the pool, but P is unable to show how the drowning occurred ***because*** no lifeguard (or other witness) was present; *i.e.*, the absence of the required lifeguard not only was negligence as to P's husband, but deprived P of the means of establishing the cause of death. Under such circumstances, the burden of proof may be shifted to D to show that its failure to provide lifeguard service was ***not*** the cause of death. [*See* **Haft v. Lone Palm Hotel,** 3 Cal. 3d 756 (1970)]

---

(1) **Rationale**

This is an extension of **Summers v. Tice,** *supra,* §425; *i.e.,* unless the burden is shifted to the defendant, the defendant's negligence would go unredressed because the plaintiff ***would otherwise have no way to prove causation.***

(2) **Extension [§441]**

In a few cases, this rationale has been extended to include instances in which negligence by its nature does not become apparent until many years later. [*See* **Sindell v. Abbott Laboratories,** *supra,* §430]

6. Proximate Cause ("Scope of Liability") [§442]

Although every negligent act produces consequences that (at least hypothetically) extend into infinity, an actor cannot be held liable for all of those infinitely extending consequences. (Imagine holding Eve liable for all of the harm that has befallen humankind since people were ejected from the Garden of Eden over the forbidden fruit.) ***Proximate cause*** is the element of a negligence claim by which juries (or courts, as a matter of law) decide whether the actual consequences of a defendant's conduct were so bizarre or far-removed from the risks that made the actor's conduct negligent that the defendant, although blameworthy, should not be held liable for the resulting harm.

a. Policy judgment [§443]

"Causation" is actually a misleading term here because all issues of cause and result have already been considered under "actual cause," above. Rather, proximate cause is a policy determination: Under some circumstances, it is deemed unfair to hold the defendant legally responsible for all consequences of his wrongful conduct, hence the question, ***"How far does the defendant's liability extend for consequences caused by his negligent acts?"*** (This accounts for the term used by the Third Restatement, "scope of liability.")

b. Basic tests [§444]

Because proximate cause represents a difficult policy judgment, courts have not settled on a single approach to analyzing the question. Instead, several general tests continue to be used, depending on the jurisdiction.

(1) **Foreseeability test [§445]**

Proximate cause is established if the injury ***to the plaintiff*** and the ***type, extent, and manner of the plaintiff's injury*** were the foreseeable result of the defendant's negligent conduct under the circumstances. If the plaintiff or the type, extent, or manner of injury was not foreseeable, then a jury or court would deny liability. Under this approach, troublesome proximate cause questions fall into three basic patterns (and will be analyzed in this order):

(i) *Unforeseeable manner*—A foreseeable result occurs but it has come about in an unforeseeable manner.

(ii) *Unforeseeable result*—The foreseeable plaintiff has been injured, but an unexpected extent or type of harm has occurred.

(iii) *Unforeseeable plaintiff*—Although the defendant's act exposed a certain group of potential victims to a foreseeable risk, the person hurt was not a member of that group.

(a) Note

The foreseeability test for proximate cause is different from foreseeability considered in the context of breach in the following respects. Breach foreseeability is a question of general focus—that some range of injuries, of some range of severity of injury might occur—and one that helps to define the blameworthiness of a defendant's conduct. The foreseeability test for proximate cause is not general but specific to the ***particular injury*** suffered by the ***particular plaintiff*** at hand (*i.e.*, it asks whether the plaintiff's particular type of injury was foreseeable).

(2) Directness/remoteness test [§446]

Proximate cause is established for all harm that flows from the defendant's negligent conduct, ***regardless of how unforeseeable***, as long as the harm was a ***direct result*** of that conduct and was ***not too remote***. [***In re* Polemis,** 3 K.B. 560 (1921)] This approach is generally less restrictive than foreseeability (*i.e.*, it allows more claims to survive proximate cause), but it also provides less guidance to juries. It seems clear that injuries indirectly caused by the defendant's conduct will not survive under this test (*see infra*, §§454-460). Injuries that occur in some remote place or time, or perhaps pursuant to some remote twist of events also seem likely to fail (*see infra*, §469).

(3) Risk rule [§447]

Proximate cause is established if the plaintiff's harm is ***within the scope of the risks*** that made the defendant's conduct negligent. Conversely, proximate cause does not exist if the plaintiff's harm is different from the harms whose risks made the defendant's conduct negligent. [Rest. 3d-PH §29; **Doe v. Manheimer,** 563 A.2d 699 (Conn. 1989)] This approach instructs the jury to think of the risks it considered when determining whether the defendant acted unreasonably—if the risk of what actually happened to the plaintiff was part of what made the defendant's conduct unreasonable, the defendant is liable for the plaintiff's injury. The essence of this test is arguably the same as a general foreseeability of harm test.

(4) Substantial factor test [§448]

Many courts purport to use what they refer to as a "substantial factor" test to decide proximate cause. This terminology is unfortunate for two reasons: (i) "substantial factor" is the name of a test used to determine actual cause, not proximate cause (*see supra*, §421); and (ii) in most cases in which courts use a test they call "substantial factor" to decide proximate cause, the substance of the test is typically either foreseeability, directness/remoteness, or the risk rule. [*See, e.g.*, **Doe v. Manheimer**, *supra*—court spoke of "substantial factor," but actually applied the risk rule] If there exists a "substantial factor" test for proximate cause, it likely inquires as to whether the defendant's conduct was a ***more (or perhaps the most) substantial factor*** in causing the plaintiff's harm than other factors. Or perhaps the "substantial factor" test for proximate cause makes most sense when a jury is instructed in terms provided in the Second Restatement: "[T]he defendant's conduct has such an effect in producing the harm ***as to lead reasonable men to regard it as a cause,*** using that word in the popular sense . . . ." [Rest. 2d §431 cmt. a]

(5) Andrews factors [§449]

In his dissent in *Palsgraf*, Justice Andrews stated that proximate cause is a matter of "practical politics," "convenience," "common sense," "public policy," and "a rough sense of justice" and is established on consideration of a ***number of factors***, including: (i) foreseeability of the harm, (ii) directness of the connection between the defendant's act and the plaintiff's harm, (iii) whether there was a natural and continuous sequence between the two, (iv) whether the act was a substantial factor in causing the harm, and (v) whether the harm was too remote in time and space. (*See infra*, §§502-503.)

c. Common issues in determining proximate cause [§450]

Of the five tests, the foreseeability approach is the most commonly used today, although the risk rule is gaining ground. The following sections examine the various factual and conceptual problems that courts face when deciding proximate cause. The sections primarily apply the foreseeability test, although other approaches are discussed where particularly relevant.

(1) Cross-refer—duty [§451]

Remember that the proximate cause discussion assumes that the ***duty question*** has already been resolved in the plaintiff's favor. Thus, under the Cardozo view of duty (*see supra*, §324), an unforeseeable plaintiff loses at the duty stage. Because the defendant owed no duty to the plaintiff, there is no need to reach the issue of proximate cause at all.

(a) But note

If a duty is found owing to the plaintiff under the Cardozo view, and breach is established, two issues remain: was the manner of occurrence foreseeable, and was the result foreseeable? Under the Andrews approach (*supra*), foreseeability of manner, result, and plaintiff are among the factors considered in deciding whether the negligent defendant proximately caused the plaintiff's injury.

(2) Terminology [§452]

If the manner, result, or plaintiff was unforeseeable, this may be either because the defendant had no reason to know the nature of the situation on which his negligence would operate or because an unexpected new force has come into play.

(a) Direct causation—no intervening forces [§453]

"Direct causation" means that there was no intervening force or agency operating between the defendant's negligent act and the occurrence of the harm to the plaintiff. In other words, the defendant acts upon a "set stage"—*i.e.*, all of the contributing factors are already in place on the stage as the defendant acts. (Visualize knocking over a row of dominoes.)

(b) Indirect causation—intervening factors present [§454]

"Indirect causation" means that some force or agency ***intervened*** between the defendant's negligent act and the occurrence of the plaintiff's harm, and either ***extended*** the results of the defendant's negligence or ***combined*** with the defendant's act to produce the injury. Some intervening forces are foreseeable and some are unforeseeable. Note, however, that although sometimes the nature of the intervening force may be crucial, the existence of intervening forces does not necessarily terminate the defendant's liability. The determinative factor in each case is usually whether, at the time the defendant acted, it was ***reasonably foreseeable that the result*** that occurred would in fact occur.

1) What is an "intervening act"? [§455]

An intervening act can consist of an "act of God" (*e.g.*, storm, flood, etc.), an act of a third person, or an act of an animal.

a) Distinguish—contributory negligence [§456]

Acts of the ***plaintiff*** should ***not*** be analyzed as intervening forces. The plaintiff's conduct may establish contributory negligence or assumption of the risk, but these are affirmative defenses to a negligence action (*see infra*, §§791 *et seq.*) and do not affect the prima facie case of negligence.

2) Factors that are not "intervening acts"

a) Preexisting conditions [§457]

Contributing factors that are already in operation when the

defendant acts (*i.e.*, the "set stage," above) are not intervening acts. For example, the plaintiff's physical condition, which may combine with the defendant's negligence to cause an unexpected injury, is ***not*** an intervening act—"defendant takes his victim as he finds him."

b) **Forces set in motion [§458]**

Similarly, a force set in motion by the defendant's conduct is not deemed an intervening act.

---

e.g. **Example:** Where D (driving negligently) runs into a garbage truck, causing debris to fly through the air and injure P, the debris is a force set in motion by D.

---

c) **Omissions to act [§459]**

Although a third person's failure to act may have contributed to the plaintiff's injury, such omission is not deemed to be an intervening act—even though the third person may have been under a legal duty to act; however, in extreme cases, this may nonetheless affect the defendant's liability (*see infra*, §§494-495).

(c) **Caution—ultimate issue is foreseeability [§460]**

Although some courts still give important weight to the difference between direct and indirect causation when deciding proximate cause issues, this is generally an outmoded view. The causal sequence may help sort out the various fact patterns that present themselves, but the ultimate issue is ***foreseeability***.

---

e.g. **Example:** P was injured when he fell on broken glass that D city negligently allowed to remain on a playground. Even though P's fall was caused by some boys pushing P, D's negligence was a proximate cause of the harm because falling in a playground—from whatever cause—was foreseeable. [**Parness v. City of Tempe,** 600 P.2d 764 (Ariz. 1979)]

---

d. **Direct causation [§461]**

If there are no intervening acts operating on the particular fact situation, the case is one of direct causation. Whether the defendant should be deemed the proximate cause of the plaintiff's injury turns on the "foreseeability" of the results.

(1) **What is the "result"? [§462]**

The definition of "result" is one developed on a case-by-case basis through judicial use of common sense. For example, where the defendant carelessly drives her automobile through a crosswalk, she should reasonably expect to run down a pedestrian and break his leg. If the broken bones are wrapped around each other in a bizarre "figure eight pattern," the defendant may try to avoid liability by asserting that the extent to which the bones were broken was not foreseeable. However, it is clear that the ***"result"*** is the broken leg (due to impact from the car)—not the figure eight pattern. Results would seldom be foreseeable if so narrowly defined.

(2) Foreseeable results lead to liability [§463]

If the defendant causes a foreseeable injury, this presents such a clear case of liability that proximate cause is rarely in issue. Thus, in the example above, had the defendant negligently failed to keep her eyes on the road, thereby running over a pedestrian and breaking his leg, this would be a clear case of a foreseeable result occurring to a foreseeable plaintiff in a foreseeable manner—and the defendant would be liable for the damages resulting from the broken leg.

(a) Exceptions—no liability for certain foreseeable results

1) Unusual manner [§464]

Some courts, and the Second Restatement, refuse to impose liability on the negligent defendant where the ***result***—although foreseeable—has come about in a ***"highly extraordinary" manner.*** [Rest. 2d §435(2)]

---

e.g. **Example:** D takes her eyes off the road while driving her small car. She returns her eyes to the road just in time to see P carefully crossing the street in a marked crosswalk. D has no time to stop, so she swerves to the right. The car hits a parked truck and ricochets to the other side of the street, where it bounces off another truck and back into the street, knocking P down and breaking his leg. Because of the bizarre sequence of events, courts following the Restatement might protect D from liability to P because of the bizarre chain of events.

---

a) Distinguish—risk rule [§465]

Other courts think it fair that the defendant be held liable as long as the result was foreseeable—no matter how odd the sequence. The "risk rule" of the Third Restatement takes this approach, stating that proximate cause exists when the harm was within the scope of risks created by the defendant's conduct, ***regardless of the manner in which that harm came about*** (*see supra*, §447).

2) "New York fire rule" [§466]

Suppose the defendant carelessly fails to control a flame or sparks in a populated area. Although it is foreseeable that such negligence can cause a fire that may spread to adjoining buildings, the New York courts have held that expansion of the fire beyond burning of the first building is not "foreseeable." [**Rose v. Pennsylvania Railroad,** 236 N.Y. 568 (1923)—limiting liability to owner of first structure burned; **Ryan v. New York Central Railroad,** 35 N.Y. 210 (1866)]

a) **Rationale**

Because potential liability for this type of carelessness could extend almost indefinitely, public policy requires an arbitrary cut-off point.

b) **But note**

Most other states treat fire cases under a general foreseeability approach on a case-by-case basis. [**Osborn v. City of Whittier,** 103 Cal. App. 2d 609 (1951)]

(3) **Unforeseeable results [§467]**

In some cases, the defendant's negligence, although occurring on a "set stage," causes unexpected results. Here, two types of cases must be distinguished: unforeseeable type of injury cases and unforeseeable extent of injury cases.

(a) **Unforeseeable type of injury [§468]**

Where one type of injury to the plaintiff was foreseeable, but an entirely different injury occurred without any intervening force, there is no clear consensus; courts split over whether the defendant should be held liable.

1) ***"Polemis"* view—liability for unforeseeable consequences [§469]**

Some courts hold the defendant liable for ***all direct*** consequences of his wrongful conduct—despite the occurrence of an unforeseeable type of injury to plaintiff. *Rationale:* The plaintiff is an innocent victim and thus the defendant, having acted negligently, should bear the loss.

---

e.g. **Example:** While unloading P's ship, worker D negligently knocked a plank into the hold. (This was negligent because of the unreasonable danger posed to cargo, to anyone working below, and to the ship's hull.) Unknown to D, gas fumes were present in the hold. When the plank hit the bottom, it created a spark that ignited an unforeseeable fire, which in turn destroyed the ship. D was held liable, primarily on the theory that a negligent defendant should be liable for all harm he has ***directly*** caused; the fact that the actual risk created by D (explosion) differed from that reasonably to be anticipated (minor impact damage or plank hitting person) was deemed immaterial. [*In re* **Polemis,** *supra*, §446]

---

2) ***"Wagon Mound"* view—no liability for unforeseeable consequences [§470]**

Most courts reject the approach of the *Polemis* court and its rigid reliance on direct causation. The majority emphasize ***foreseeability*** and assert that when an unforeseeable result occurs, it is unfair to hold the defendant liable—no matter what causation pattern has transpired. [**Wagon Mound No. 1,** 1961 A.C. 388 (1961)] (*See* further discussion, *infra*, §497.)

---

e.g. **Example:** In *Wagon Mound*, D negligently discharged furnace oil into the bay. A fire resulted and P's dock was burned. D was held ***not*** liable because, under the circumstances, only minor cloggage damage to P's dock could have been foreseen; fire was not a foreseeable risk created by the negligence.

(b) Unforeseeable extent of injury—"thin-skulled plaintiffs" [§471]

The most common example of a defendant's negligent act directly causing an unforeseeable result involves cases in which the nature of the plaintiff's injuries is unexpected. This is the so-called thin-skulled plaintiff (or "eggshell skull" or preexisting condition) situation. In these cases, ***all courts*** hold the defendant liable for the ***full extent*** of the plaintiff's injuries (*i.e.*, even courts following the *Wagon Mound* approach). *Rationale:* ***"A tortfeasor takes his victim as he finds him."*** [**Steinhauser v. Hertz Corp.,** 421 F.2d 1169 (2d Cir. 1970); **Freyermuth v. Lufty,** 382 N.E.2d 1059 (Mass. 1978); **McCahill v. New York Transportation Co.,** 201 N.Y. 221 (1911)]

---

e.g. **Example:** P suffered a bruised chest and fractured ankle when the car in which he was a passenger was struck by D. P had a history of heart disease and died from a heart attack six days after the accident. At trial, the jury should be given a thin-skulled plaintiff instruction—*i.e.*, instructed that if it finds that P's death was the result of the accident, D can be liable despite P's unusual susceptibility to heart attacks. [**Benn v. Thomas,** 512 N.W.2d 537 (Iowa 1994)]

---

1) But note

A latent condition such as heart disease would almost certainly have lowered the plaintiff's life expectancy, thus reducing the damages that the defendant must pay for future years, or, should plaintiff die, for wrongful death. [**Steinhauser v. Hertz Corp.,** *supra*]

2) **Only applies to preexisting condition of plaintiff [§472]**
The thin-skulled plaintiff rule only applies to preexisting conditions ***of the plaintiff***. It does ***not*** apply to property. For example, in *Polemis* (*supra*), the preexisting condition of gas fumes in the hold did not trigger the thin-skulled rule.

e. **Indirect causation**

(1) **In general [§473]**
As noted, indirect causation exists when an intervening force has come into play after the defendant has acted and has either extended the plaintiff's injuries or combined with the defendant's act to produce the plaintiff's injuries. Among such situations, factors to consider are:

(a) **Unforeseeable intervening force with foreseeable result [§474]**
Even though an ***unforeseeable force*** has intervened, the defendant will generally be liable for the harm where the negligent act produces a ***foreseeable result.***

1) **Exception—intentional or criminal act [§475]**
Exceptions to this general rule sometimes apply where the intervening conduct is an ***intentional or criminal act***, but not when the intentional conduct was foreseeable.

(b) **Unforeseeable intervening force with unforeseeable result [§476]**
In a few exceptional cases, the defendant may be found to be the proximate cause of the plaintiff's harm even though ***both*** the intervening force and result are unforeseeable.

(c) **Intervening force of third party [§477]**
Even if proximate cause exists despite an intervening force, where the intervening force is the ***negligent act of another***, the defendant will likely—pursuant to rules of factual causation and apportionment (*see infra*, §§1252-1261, 1330-1333)—pay ***only a portion of the damages*** suffered after the intervening negligence.

---

e.g. **Example:** D negligently set fire to a ship moored to a dock. Just when the firefighters arrive, the dock owner negligently unties the moorings, causing the ship to go adrift and burn to the water. In such case, D will be held 100% responsible for the damages that the ship would have suffered but for the dock owner's negligence, and—assuming a finding of proximate cause—some smaller percentage (perhaps 50%) of the damages caused in part by the dock owner.

EXAM TIP **gilbert**

It is crucial to keep in mind the interplay between the presence of intervening forces and the foreseeability of results; *i.e.,* although both the nature of the intervening act and the nature of the result will affect the proximate cause determination, the ***result*** is the more important factor.

(2) Rules focusing on nature of intervening act

(a) Dependent intervening forces [§478]

A "dependent" intervening force is an act of a third person or an animal that is a ***normal response*** to the situation created by the defendant's negligent act. Because such forces are responses arising because of the defendant's negligence, they are deemed foreseeable and will ***not*** relieve the defendant of liability for the harm caused if they lead to foreseeable results.

1) Main types of cases involving dependent intervening forces

a) "Checking forces" [§479]

D's negligence causes P serious harm, and P is taken to a hospital. The surgeon improperly diagnoses P's case and performs an unnecessary operation (or, after proper diagnosis, performs a necessary operation carelessly). It is reasonably foreseeable both that P would have to go to the hospital as a result of the injuries inflicted by D, and that P would receive unsuccessful medical treatment, whether or not the result of negligence. (This is deemed a normal risk incurred in hospitalization.) Hence, D is liable for the additional harm sustained by P in the hospital. [**Atherton v. Devine,** 602 P.2d 634 (Okla. 1979)—ambulance accident on way to hospital after initial injury; **Thompson v. Fox,** 192 A. 107 (Pa. 1937)]

1/ Exception—recklessness [§480]

This analysis does ***not*** apply to reckless medical conduct or to deliberate efforts to maim the plaintiff—*e.g.*, operation by a drunk surgeon or performance of an operation completely unrelated to P's condition. [**Upham's Case,** 139 N.E. 433 (Mass. 1923)]

b) "Rescue forces" [§481]

D's negligence has imperiled P or P's property. X sees the situation and attempts to go to the aid of P or P's property. In doing so, X is acting reasonably, but nevertheless inadvertently aggravates P's injuries and also injures himself.

Because "danger invites rescue" (*see supra*, §327), the reasonable person should have foreseen the rescuer's attempts and also that the attempts might cause further harm. Thus, D is liable for both the aggravated injuries to P and the injuries to X. [Rest. 2d §445; *but see* **Snellenberger v. Rodriguez,** 760 S.W.2d 237 (Tex. 1988)—no liability on original tortfeasor where police officer-rescuer's heart attack was not foreseeable result of automobile driver's negligence]

c) **"Escape forces" [§482]**

Because of D's negligence, an elevator crashes to the bottom of the shaft. The passengers panic and in rushing to the exit, push P to the ground and trample him. The attempts of individuals threatened with harm to escape are reasonably foreseeable, as is the possibility that such attempts may endanger others. Hence, D is liable for P's injury. [**Crow v. Colson,** 256 P. 971 (Kan. 1927); **Griffin v. Hustis,** 125 N.E. 387 (Mass. 1919)]

d) **Other "response" forces [§483]**

Other reactions by animate forces may also be held foreseeable:

---

e.g. **Example:** D negligently explodes a firecracker, frightening the horse P is riding. The horse throws P to the ground, injuring P and Y's dog that was trotting alongside. D is liable for both injuries because the horse's reaction is held a normal, and thus foreseeable, response. [**Quinlan v. City of Philadelphia,** 54 A. 1026 (Pa. 1903)]

---

e.g. **Example:** D's negligence causes P such serious injury that P becomes insane and ***further injures or kills*** himself or a third party. P's reaction is held foreseeable (a "normal" response to the situation created by D), so that D's negligence is the proximate cause of such injuries. [**Fuller v. Preis,** 35 N.Y.2d 425 (1974)—suicide by P seven months after accident, caused by mental breakdown resulting from accident; *but see* **District of Columbia v. Peters,** 527 A.2d 1269 (D.C. 1987)—no causal link without showing that D's act produced an "irresistible or uncontrollable impulse to commit suicide"]

---

2) **Caution—response must be normal [§484]**

The crucial requirement in all of the above cases is that the response to the situation created by the defendant's negligent act be a ***normal*** one. If the response or reaction is ***highly unusual***, it is held ***not*** to be a dependent intervening force (*see infra*, §488).

(b) Independent intervening forces [§485]

An "independent" intervening force is one that operates upon the situation created by the defendant's negligent act but which is ***not a response or reaction thereto***. (Such force may be the act of a third person or an animal, or an "act of God.") Where such is the case, the defendant will remain liable for the foreseeable results of his act unless the force is an unforeseeable intentionally tortious or criminal act. [Rest. 2d §442B] (However, unforeseeable intervening forces may also lead to liability; *see infra*, §488.)

---

e.g. **Example:** D negligently causes an automobile collision in which a bystander, P, is injured. Surgery for P is required, and, in the course of surgery, bacteria from the air (foreseeable intervening force) enter the open wound and infect it, eventually causing P's death. D may be held liable for P's death. [**Hastie v. Handeland,** 274 Cal. App. 2d 599 (1969)]

---

e.g. **Example:** D negligently causes a collision with a truck carrying noxious gas. The truck overturns, discharging the gas into the air, and the wind carries the gas onto P's nearby land, damaging P's crops. Because wind is reasonably foreseeable, D is liable for the crop damage.

---

1) Problem—intervening tortious or criminal acts [§486]

Ordinarily, criminal acts on the part of others are not reasonably foreseeable. However, if the defendant's negligent conduct has created a situation in which a reasonable person would have foreseen that negligent, intentional, or even criminal acts might be committed by others (*i.e.*, if defendant has ***increased the risk*** that this type of act will occur), then the occurrence of such acts is held a ***foreseeable intervening force*** that does not terminate the defendant's liability.

---

e.g. **Example:** Because D negligently blocks the area alongside a road, P is forced to walk in a roadway, where he is struck by a truck. It is reasonably foreseeable that negligent motorists may strike persons forced into the street by D; thus, D is liable if P is run down. [**Grainy v. Campbell,** 425 A.2d 379 (Pa. 1981)—careless act by third party, if foreseeable, does not foreclose D's liability]

Example: D's train fails to stop at the station and the conductor negligently tells P to walk home. To get home, P must walk back through a hobo encampment. The criminal rape of P by a hobo is foreseeable, and D would be civilly liable for the rape. [**Hines v. Garrett,** 108 S.E. 690 (Va. 1921)]

Example: A landlord who fails to install proper locks on entrances to the common areas of an apartment building in a high-crime neighborhood may be held liable to a tenant for injuries inflicted by a mugger in the hallway of the building (*see infra*, §§707-709—lessor's general duty to safeguard premises against crime). [**Trentacost v. Brussel,** 412 A.2d 436 (N.J. 1980)]

(3) **Indirect causation—rules focusing on results of defendant's negligence [§487]**
As alluded to earlier, there remain three fact situations calling for special consideration: (i) what if a ***foreseeable*** result is caused by an ***unforeseeable*** intervening force; (ii) what if an ***unforeseeable*** result is caused by a ***foreseeable*** intervening force; and (iii) what if an ***unforeseeable*** result is caused by an intervening force that is itself ***unforeseeable***?

(a) **Foreseeable results produced by unforeseeable intervening forces [§488]**
The fact that an intervening force was not reasonably foreseeable under the circumstances does ***not*** usually excuse the defendant from liability as long as the ***result was foreseeable.*** If the ultimate result was reasonably foreseeable under the circumstances, liability is usually imposed even though the harm occurred in a totally unexpected manner.

1) **Acts of God [§489]**
Extraordinary and unprecedented floods, storms, or other weather conditions are usually held to be unforeseeable intervening forces. But they are ***not*** considered "superseding causes" where they lead to the ***result threatened by the defendant's original negligence.***

Example: D negligently allowed gas vapors to accumulate in the hold of its ship. The resulting explosion and damage to nearby persons and property (the results) were foreseeable, and D was therefore held liable—even though the explosion was actually set off by an unprecedented stroke of lightning (the intervening force) that was ***not*** foreseeable. [**Johnson v. Kosmos Portland Cement Co.,** 64 F.2d 193 (6th Cir. 1933)]

2) **Distinguish—unforeseeable criminal or tortious acts [§490]**
Where a third person's criminal or tortious conduct was not reasonably foreseeable (*i.e.*, defendant's conduct has ***not*** enhanced the risk that such acts will occur; *see supra*, §486), but the ultimate ***result*** was nonetheless foreseeable, the defendant's liability may turn on the ***culpability*** of the intervening act.

a) **Rationale**
For some courts, the moral culpability of a person whose misconduct was intentional or reckless overwhelms the moral responsibility of a defendant who was merely negligent.

b) **Intentional or criminal acts [§491]**
If the defendant had no reason to expect intentionally tortious or criminal acts by a third person, some courts hold the defendant ***not*** liable for harm caused thereby, even though his negligence afforded an opportunity for such conduct, and foreseeable harm resulted. [Rest. 2d §448]

---

e.g. **Example:** P was pulled from a lake in an unconscious condition. Firefighters arrived on the scene. To warm P, firefighter T gave the nurse at the scene a heating block made and sold by defendant D. The block did not properly warn that insulation was needed before the block was applied to a body. There was evidence that T knew of this need but handed the block to the nurse without insulation and watched as she applied it in that manner—causing serious burns to P. If the jury found those facts, then the outrageousness of T's behavior would supersede D's negligent labeling. [**McLaughlin v. Mine Safety Appliances Co.,** 11 N.Y.2d 62 (1962)]

---

cf. **Compare:** D hotel failed to maintain its fire escape routes. In a fire started by an arsonist, guests were injured when they had to jump from upper floor windows. The court rejected D's claim that its negligence was superseded by the criminal act of the arsonist. The hotel's obligation was to anticipate fires from whatever cause. [**Addis v. Steele,** 648 N.E.2d 773 (Mass. 1995)]

---

c) **Negligent acts [§492]**
On the other hand, a third person's negligent conduct does ***not*** relieve the defendant of liability—even though such conduct was unforeseeable—if it causes a ***result*** similar to that

threatened by the defendant's conduct, unless the action was ***"highly extraordinary"*** under the circumstances (*i.e.*, ***more than*** unforeseeable). [Rest. 2d §447(b)]

---

e.g. **Example:** D negligently allows its telephone pole to become rotten with termites. The pole falls and injures P, but only after having been jarred by a careening automobile negligently driven by X. D would be held liable for P's injuries because the pole's toppling and injuring a passerby was the ***foreseeable result*** of D's original negligence. The fact that this result was brought about by X's negligent driving is ***not*** so highly extraordinary as to cut off causation. [**Gibson v. Garcia,** 96 Cal. App. 2d 681 (1950)]

1/ Abnormal rescue attempts by third persons [§493]

An abnormal or foolhardy effort by a third person to avert a risk created by the defendant is deemed an ***unforeseeable*** intervening force, and ***relieves the defendant from liability*** for injuries—even if it leads to a foreseeable result. This would be a "moral responsibility" decision as discussed above.

---

e.g. **Example:** P was driving on a two-lane road. D negligently attempted to pass P. While the cars were abreast of one another, a truck appeared ahead in the road, traveling in the opposite direction. To avoid a potential crash, P steered his car toward the right shoulder, but a passenger in P's car grabbed the steering wheel and turned the car sharply to the left, so that the car crossed the road, ran into a ditch, and overturned. The passenger's actions were a superseding cause of P's damages. [**Robinson v. Butler,** 33 N.W.2d 821 (Minn. 1948)]

---

3) Third person's failure to prevent harm [§494]

Although not actually deemed an "intervening act" (*see supra*, §459), proximate cause issues involving a third person's omission to act generally are treated in the same manner as affirmative negligence by a third person. Thus, the failure of a third person to act so as to prevent the harm threatened by the defendant's negligent conduct does ***not*** relieve the defendant of liability, even where the third person is under some legal duty to act (and is therefore negligent in failing to avert the harm). [Rest. 2d §452]

Example: Where D negligently allows poisonous gas to escape from its pipeline, it is liable for injuries to workers in the vicinity (foreseeable result), even though the workers' employer, X, ***knew*** of the danger and was negligent in failing to protect them. X's negligence was foreseeable and did not supersede D's liability. [**Ewart v. Southern California Gas Co.,** 237 Cal. App. 2d 163 (1965)]

a) Limitation—"neutralization of the risk" [§495]

In certain cases, the third person's failure to act may be deemed so culpable or extraordinary that it will be held to have "neutralized the risk" created by the defendant's original negligence, and the failure to act will be treated as the superseding cause of the harm suffered by the plaintiff. [Rest. 2d §452 cmt. f]

Example: D negligently leaves dynamite caps on the ground and a young child, P, picks one up and shows it to his father. If P's father recognizes what it is but fails to take it away, the father's negligence will be considered so "highly extraordinary" as to have "neutralized the risk" created by D's original negligence so that if the cap subsequently explodes and injures P or a third person, D is not liable. [**Kingsland v. Erie County Agricultural Society,** 298 N.Y. 409 (1949)]

4) Application of the "risk rule" [§496]

In a jurisdiction that applies the "risk rule," as adopted by the Third Restatement (*see supra*, §447), proximate cause exists where the harm is ***within the scope of the risk*** that made the defendant's conduct negligent. This is true ***even if*** an unforeseeable intervening act, including an unusual force of nature or independent culpable or nonculpable human act, is also a factual cause of the harm. [Rest. 3d-PH §34]

Example: D city negligently leaves an open pit in the sidewalk without surrounding barriers or warnings. Proximate cause exists against D under the risk rule when P is injured by a passerby who intentionally pushes P into the pit. The harm (landing in the pit) was within the scope of the risk that made D's conduct negligent, although the manner (P pushed in by another) was unexpected.

a) Rationale

With the adoption of comparative responsibility rules (*see infra*, §§815-822, 1330-1333), there is little reason to completely bar a plaintiff's recovery against a defendant simply due to the intervening act of another potential defendant.

(b) **Unforeseeable results produced by foreseeable intervening forces [§497]**
Even though an intervening force may be foreseeable, some courts will terminate the defendant's liability if the ***result*** was unforeseeable, while others would nevertheless impose liability. This presents a variation on the *"Polemis-Wagon Mound"* debate (*see supra*, §§469-470).

---

e.g. **Example—"narrow" view:** P's father had heated a pot of water on the kitchen stove because D landlord negligently failed to provide hot water to the apartment. P collided with his father, who was carrying the water to the bathroom, and was burned when the water spilled on him. *Held:* No liability because the kind of injury was unlike that reasonably expected, such as illness, from D's original negligent act. [**Martinez v. Lazaroff,** 48 N.Y.2d 819 (1979); *but see* **Enis v. Ba-Call Building Corp.,** 639 F.2d 359 (7th Cir. 1980)—contra (on almost identical facts)]

---

e.g. **Example—"broad" view:** D negligently moored its ship in the river. The ship was set adrift by current (foreseeable intervening force) and was carried downstream, where it struck and collapsed a bridge. The collapse created an ice jam, which caused water to back up and flood P's factory on the riverbank (unforeseeable result). (The foreseeable damage to P's factory was being crashed into by the ship.) D was liable for the flooding. [***In re* Kinsman Transit Co. (No. 1),** 338 F.2d 708 (2d Cir. 1964)]

(c) **Unforeseeable results produced by unforeseeable intervening forces [§498]**
As a general rule, whether courts emphasize the foreseeability of the result or the foreseeability of the intervening force, where ***both*** are unforeseeable, all courts agree that defendant is ***not liable.***

---

e.g. **Example:** D negligently blocked a road, forcing P to take a detour along a more dangerous path. While P was on the detour, he was struck by a falling airplane. The court denied liability. [**Doss v. Town of Big Stone Gap,** 134 S.E. 563 (Va. 1926)] *But note:* If the path were more dangerous because of the risk of falling rocks, and a rock fell on P, D would be liable (foreseeable result).

---

1) **Common carrier exception [§499]**
Some courts that impose a high standard of care on common carriers may hold a defendant carrier liable for ***any*** loss or damage that occurs to goods delayed in transit, even though the damage

(the result) was unforeseeable and caused by an unforeseeable flood or other "act of God" (the manner). [**Green-Wheeler Shoe Co. v. Chicago, Rock Island & Pacific Railway,** 106 N.W. 498 (Iowa 1906)]

(d) Comment—ultimate result depends on degree of emphasis on foreseeability [§500]

Note again that every case involving an unforeseeable result is by definition a bizarre situation involving some aspect that the defendant could not reasonably expect. This factor favors the defendant; but on the other hand, the fact that the defendant has been negligent and the actual cause of the plaintiff's harm also enters into the court's determination. The choice depends ultimately on the importance the court gives to foreseeability.

f. Unforeseeable plaintiff [§501]

This situation recalls the **Palsgraf v. Long Island Railroad** case (*see supra*, §321) involving the falling scales. Courts following the ***Cardozo*** approach would reject an unforeseeable plaintiff at the duty stage. But those courts following the ***Andrews*** view must still face the proximate cause question and may consider the plaintiff's unforeseeability simply as a factor favoring the defendant in the proximate cause issue.

(1) Uncommon applicability [§502]

Probably because of the unusual sequences involved, few courts have faced a true *Palsgraf* situation; *i.e.*, the occasion of a potentially unforeseeable plaintiff is not all that common. Most jurisdictions have found cause to address the question, however. When analyzed as a question of ***duty***, most courts ***deny*** liability where the plaintiff was not foreseeable. But when analyzed as ***proximate cause*** issue, courts either deny liability ***or leave the issue to the jury***.

---

e.g. **Example:** X is struck by D bus and tossed in the air so as to hit P, who had been in what appeared to be a safe spot. The court found no liability. [**Dahlstrom v. Shrum,** 84 A.2d 289 (Pa. 1951)]

---

e.g. **Example:** D negligently ran down X. Seven years later, X, who had suffered brain damage from the accident, shot and wounded P. The court denied liability against D because the passage of time permitted the intervention of many other possible factors. [**Firman v. Sacia,** 7 A.D.2d 579 (1959)]

---

(2) Andrews view [§503]

Because Justice Andrews would permit a jury to find liability in *Palsgraf*, he must reject the majority's total reliance on foreseeability. Instead, he determined that several factors should be considered in deciding whether a jury could properly find that a defendant's negligence was the proximate cause of a plaintiff's harm (*see supra*, §449).

g. Summary of proximate cause

(1) Role of foreseeability [§504]

Although the concept of foreseeability is playing a role at three points in proximate cause analysis, the term probably plays a different role at each point.

(a) Manner [§505]

Generally, it is irrelevant whether a particular manner of occurrence was foreseeable as long as the result was. Rather, the test is a negative one: ***Manner of occurrence is irrelevant unless*** the sequence was "highly extraordinary"—in which case courts split over the result. Some courts conclude that it is unfair to hold a defendant responsible for such sequences. Others conclude that if the defendant's negligence led to a foreseeable result, this is enough to create liability, and a highly extraordinary manner raises no moral argument to relieve the defendant from liability that would otherwise exist.

1) Intervening intentional or criminal acts [§506]

If intervening intentional or criminal acts are foreseeable, liability will follow. But if they are unforeseeable, the greater moral blameworthiness of the third party's act leads some courts to hold that it supersedes the defendant's liability, even when a foreseeable result occurs.

(b) Result [§507]

Courts are split over how important it is that the result that befalls the plaintiff have been reasonably foreseeable. Although courts that follow *Wagon Mound* (*see supra*, §470) give foreseeability great weight (except in "thin-skull" cases), courts following *Polemis* (*see supra*, §469) reject it in "direct" cases, and courts following *Kinsman Transit* (*see supra*, §497) deemphasize it in "indirect" cases.

(c) Plaintiff [§508]

Foreseeability of the plaintiff is absolutely central to the courts following the majority in *Palsgraf*, while other courts give it some weight when considering proximate cause.

(2) Distinguish—duty [§509]

Remember that the duty element involves the question of who is owed a duty of due care. Foreseeability is used in that analysis under both the Cardozo view (foreseeability of plaintiff or group to which plaintiff belongs) and the Andrews view (foreseeability of harm to anyone).

7. Damages [§510]

Once a negligent act and causation are established, the plaintiff must show damages resulting therefrom in order to impose liability on the defendant. Unlike intentional torts, in every case where liability is based on ***negligence***, there must be a showing of ***actual damages*** to person or property.

a. **Types of damages recoverable [§511]**

The basic purpose of awarding damages in negligence cases is compensatory, rather than punitive—*i.e.*, to restore the plaintiff insofar as possible to her condition before she was injured, rather than to punish the defendant.

(1) **"Special" damages [§512]**

The plaintiff is entitled to recover ***all economic losses and expenses*** ("special" damages) she has suffered as a result of the injury—*e.g.*, medical bills, lost wages or business profits, cost of hiring household help, etc. This includes expenses already incurred, and expenses that the plaintiff proves she probably will incur in the ***future*** (as where she remains under medical care or is unable to return to work).

(a) **Computing lost wages—the tax question**

1) **Traditional rule [§513]**

Until recently, the uniform practice was to measure wage loss by gross earnings before income tax deductions. [John E. Theuman, Annotation, Propriety of Taking Income Tax into Consideration in Fixing Damages in Personal Injury or Death Action, 16 A.L.R.4th 589 (1982)]

2) **Federal rule [§514]**

In cases under the Federal Employers' Liability Act [45 U.S.C. §§51 *et seq.*], and perhaps other federal actions, the wage loss must be calculated on an after-tax basis unless the difference between the two methods would be trivial. [**Norfolk & Western Railway v. Liepelt,** 444 U.S. 490 (1980)]

a) **Rationale**

Under federal tax laws, damages for physical injuries, including awards for lost wages resulting from physical injuries, are exempt from federal income taxes.

3) **State rule [§515]**

Although many states have adhered to the traditional rule [*see, e.g.,* **Johnson v. Manhattan & Bronx Surface Transit Operating Authority,** 71 N.Y.2d 198 (1988)], others have insisted that after-tax income is the only permissible basis for assessing the loss [*see, e.g.,* **Caldwell v. Haynes,** 643 A.2d 564 (N.J. 1994)].

(b) **Future economic losses [§516]**

The recovery for future loss of earnings, medical expenses, etc., can take into account whatever period of time the plaintiff's disability is expected to last.

1) **Child's loss of earning capacity [§517]**

If a child has suffered a severe injury with lasting or permanent effects that will likely impair the child's ability to earn, a number of jurisdictions allow juries to consider the child's loss of income-earning capacity even without specific quantifying evidence. [*See, e.g.,* **Lesniak v. County of Bergen,** 563 A.2d 795 (N.J. 1989)]

2) **Effect of inflation [§518]**
If the plaintiff's disability is expected to continue over a period of years, modern courts allow the jury to take into consideration expert testimony as to probable future inflation rates in computing the plaintiff's loss of future earnings and future medical expenses. [*See* **United States v. English,** 521 F.2d 63 (9th Cir. 1975)]

3) **Award must be discounted to present value [§519]**
After factoring in the inflation rate (if any), most courts require the award for future economic losses to be discounted to its ***present*** value, *i.e.*, the amount of money that if now invested at reasonable rates would defray the economic losses that the plaintiff is expected to sustain in the future. [**Jones & Laughlin Steel Corp. v. Pfeifer,** 462 U.S. 523 (1983)]

a) **Distinguish—pain and suffering [§520]**
Most courts do ***not*** discount awards for future pain and suffering (below) because such awards are not really mathematically computable. [**Brant v. Bockholt,** 532 N.W.2d 801 (Iowa 1995); *but see* **Metz v. United Technologies Corp.,** 754 F.2d 63 (2d Cir. 1985)—contra]

4) **Minority rule—offsetting factors [§521]**
Some courts have concluded that the discount factor and the inflation rate are likely to be about the same, so that there is no need to take account of either factor. The plaintiff should be awarded the full amount awarded by the jury without discount. [**Beaulieu v. Elliott,** 434 P.2d 665 (Alaska 1967)]

RECOVERY OF SPECIAL (ECONOMIC) DAMAGES — gilbert

TYPE OF LOSS	RECOVERY
LOST WAGES	Modern rule calculates wage loss on an after-tax basis.
FUTURE ECONOMIC LOSSES	Recoverable for the period of time disability will last. Most courts will take inflation into consideration but will discount award to present value; some hold these two items cancel out each other.

(2) "General" damages [§522]

In addition to all special damages incurred, the plaintiff is entitled to recover those damages deemed ***inherent in the injury itself***—*e.g.*, pain and suffering (past, present, and future), and any disfigurement (loss of limb, scars, etc.) or disability (loss of mobility, etc.) attributable to the injury. These are "general" damages.

(a) Pain and suffering before death [§523]

A defendant is liable for the pain and suffering experienced by a plaintiff before death from an accident the defendant negligently causes, even when the plaintiff lives only a very short time. Thus, an award of $30,000 for the two minutes a 14-month-old infant suffered while drowning was appropriate [**Landreth v. Reed,** 570 S.W.2d 486 (Tex. 1978)], and $70,000 was not excessive when the plaintiff was conscious for 60 minutes after she was hit by a train [**Juiditta v. Bethlehem Steel Corp.,** 75 A.D.2d 126 (1980); *but see* Cal. Civ. Proc. Code §377.34—contra].

1) Victim conscious [§524]

Courts require that the victim be sufficiently conscious to experience the pain and suffering. [**McDougald v. Garber,** 73 N.Y.2d 246 (1989)]

(b) Pre-impact fear and post-impact pain [§525]

Most courts award damages for fear caused by apprehension of impending death. [**Haley v. Pan American World Airways, Inc.,** 746 F.2d 311 (5th Cir. 1984)—$15,000 for four to six seconds of fear felt by passenger who sensed impending fatal crash; **Beynon v. Montgomery Cablevision Ltd. Partnership,** 718 A.2d 1161 (Md. 1998)—upholding $350,000 award for emotional distress suffered during two seconds before deadly automobile accident; *but see* **St. Clair v. Denny,** 781 P.2d 1043 (Kan. 1989)—no recovery for pre-impact distress where skid marks from P's car were only 60 feet long]

(c) Loss of enjoyment of life [§526]

Most courts have refused to recognize a separate item of damages called loss of enjoyment of life that would cover such matters as the inability to be active or to play the violin. These items are properly considered as a component of pain and suffering. [**Leiker v. Gafford,** 778 P.2d 823 (Kan. 1989)—plaintiff must be conscious that such a loss occurred; **McDougald v. Garber,** *supra*; *but see* **Fantozzi v. Sandusky Cement Products Co.,** 597 N.E.2d 474 (Ohio 1992)—concluding that separate measurement of lost enjoyment would achieve greater precision in measurement as long as duplication of items was avoided]

(d) **Unexpected damages included [§527]**
Remember that "the tortfeasor takes his victim as he finds him" (*see supra*, §471) so that the defendant is liable for all injuries actually sustained by the plaintiff even if they are due to the plaintiff's abnormal sensitivities, to aggravation of some preexisting illness or condition (*e.g.*, a minor impact that causes a previously dormant condition to "flare up," resulting in permanent disability), or if they make the plaintiff susceptible to an illness or condition that she otherwise would not have suffered (*e.g.*, complications following surgery required by the original injury).

RECOVERY OF GENERAL DAMAGES gilbert

TYPE OF LOSS	RECOVERY
PAIN AND SUFFERING	***Recoverable in most courts***, even if victim lived only a short time, but victim must have been conscious to experience.
PRE-IMPACT FEAR	***Recoverable in most courts***, even if victim lived only a short time, but victim must have been conscious to experience.
LOSS OF ENJOYMENT OF LIFE	***Not recoverable in most courts*** as a separate item, but may be considered ***as part of damages for pain and suffering***.
UNEXPECTED DAMAGES	Plaintiff can recover ***to full extent of injury*** even if, because of plaintiff's preexisting condition or abnormal sensitivity, injury is much worse than would be expected under the circumstances.

(3) **Damages for destruction of personal property [§528]**
When personal property has a ***market value***, that value is the measure of damages for its destruction. If it has no market value but can be reproduced or replaced, the ***cost of reproduction or replacement*** is the measure. If the property has no market value and can be neither replaced nor reproduced, damages are measured by its ***value to the owner***, but "unusual sentimental value" is not included. [**Mieske v. Bartell Drug Co.,** 593 P.2d 1308 (Wash. 1979)—loss of treasured family movie film]

(4) **Punitive damages not recoverable [§529]**
As indicated above, damages in a negligence case are intended to be compensatory only. Hence, punitive damages—sometimes allowed for intentional torts (*see supra*, §23)—are ***not*** recoverable for negligent conduct.

(a) **Distinguish—"reckless conduct" [§530]**
Many states do permit punitive damages when the defendant has engaged in conduct that courts consider "reckless"—*e.g.*, ***drunk driving***. *Rationale:* The voluntary act of driving while intoxicated evinces

a sufficiently reckless attitude to support an award of punitive damages. [**Taylor v. Superior Court,** 24 Cal. 3d 890 (1979); **Johnson v. Rogers,** 763 P.2d 771 (Utah 1988)]

b. "Avoidable consequences" rule [§531]
Some courts refer to the "avoidable consequences" rule as "the plaintiff's duty to mitigate damages": An injured party must act reasonably to minimize her loss or injury, and where the damages are unnecessarily aggravated or increased through her failure to do so, the ***additional*** damages are ***not recoverable.*** [**Zimmerman v. Ausland,** 513 P.2d 1167 (Or. 1973)]

---

e.g. **Example:** P unreasonably refuses to submit to medical care following a personal injury caused by D's negligence. D is liable only for the damages originally inflicted and those likely to have occurred after reasonable treatment—not for any added pain, suffering, or disfigurement that could have been avoided had P sought medical attention. [**Withrow v. Becker,** 6 Cal. App. 2d 723 (1935)]

---

(1) Burden of proof [§532]
Although the plaintiff always has the burden of proving her damages, the burden is on the ***defendant*** to prove that the plaintiff unreasonably failed to mitigate those damages (as by refusing to submit to surgery or other medical treatment).

(2) What constitutes "unreasonableness" [§533]
Factors considered in determining the reasonableness of the plaintiff's failure to mitigate damages include: (i) the ***risk*** involved in the mitigating conduct; (ii) the ***probability of success***; (iii) the ***pain and effort*** involved; and (iv) whether ***the plaintiff could financially afford*** the course of action (*e.g.*, medical treatment, etc.). [**Hall v. Dumitru,** 620 N.E.2d 668 (Ill. 1993)—no duty to undergo any surgery whether major or minor]

(3) "Anticipatory" avoidable consequences [§534]
Although most avoidable consequences cases involve the plaintiff's unreasonable conduct ***after*** an accident (*e.g.*, failure to get proper medical attention after injury), the issue also may arise where the plaintiff acted unreasonably ***prior to*** an accident.

(a) Application—failure to wear safety belts [§535]
Thus, the refusal to wear a safety belt may be an unreasonable failure to minimize harm from a future automobile collision—on the theory that had the safety belt been used, the plaintiff's injuries might not have been as severe (or may have been avoided entirely).

1) Judicial opinion [§536]
However, only a few courts faced with the issue (*e.g.*, New York, California), applying the reasonable person standard (*i.e.*,

whether a reasonable person would have worn the belts), have concluded that such neglect is to be considered in determining the plaintiff's damages. [*See, e.g.*, **Spier v. Barker,** 35 N.Y.2d 444 (1974)]

2) **Legislation [§537]**

Although most states now have statutes requiring the use of safety belts, many of these laws bar (or limit the effect of) evidence of failure to use the belts to establish the plaintiff's contributory negligence or to establish an unreasonable failure to mitigate damages.

(4) **Impact of comparative negligence [§538]**

As to the effect of comparative negligence on the avoidable consequences rule, *see infra*, §831.

c. **"Collateral sources" rule [§539]**

In most states, the plaintiff is entitled to recover the full amount of her damages from the defendant without any deduction for benefits that she may have received from sources "collateral" to the tortfeasor, such as insurance protection or a benefits program that the victim has provided for herself, or that has been provided for the victim by her employer or the government. [**Montgomery Ward & Co. v. Anderson,** 976 S.W.2d 382 (Ark. 1998)]

(1) **Rationale**

The defendant's liability should not be lessened by the fact that the plaintiff (or her employer or the government) was prudent enough to provide insurance against the kind of loss that the defendant caused. [**Helfend v. Southern California Rapid Transit District,** 2 Cal. 3d 1 (1970); **Bandel v. Friedrich,** 584 A.2d 800 (N.J. 1991)]

(2) **Criticism—"double recovery" [§540]**

This result has been criticized as permitting the plaintiff to recover twice for the same losses, so that awarding those items of damages against the defendant is inefficient and is more punitive than compensatory in nature.

(a) **Answer to criticism—subrogation [§541]**

However, insurance law and written policies increasingly provide for ***subrogation*** (below) or otherwise require the injured party to ***refund*** to the insurer any benefits paid upon ultimate recovery from the tortfeasor and so, in practice, there is often no "double recovery."

(3) **Subrogation rights of plaintiff's insurer [§542]**

To whatever extent the plaintiff's own insurance company has paid any benefits to the plaintiff (*e.g.*, for medical expenses or property damage to her car), legal rules and most policies today provide that the insurance company is "subrogated" to the claims the plaintiff may have against the person who caused those losses—*i.e.*, an automatic ***assignment***.

(a) **Right to reimbursement [§543]**
Usually, insurance policies give the insurance company the right to sue the defendant in the name of the insured (plaintiff). In practice, however, the plaintiff more frequently maintains her own action against the defendant (for pain and suffering and whatever other damages or losses she has sustained), while her insurance company asserts a right to ***reimbursement*** out of any settlement or judgment plaintiff obtains.

(b) **Defenses may be asserted against insurer [§544]**
The insurance company, as subrogee (assignee), "stands in the plaintiff's shoes" with respect to its right to recover from the defendant. Thus, whatever defenses could be asserted against the plaintiff—*e.g.*, contributory negligence—can likewise be asserted against her insurance company.

C. Special Duty Questions

1. **Introduction [§545]**
This section deals with the circumstances under which the defendant may owe some special duty of care to the plaintiff. Usually, this will be a duty owed ***in addition to*** the general duty of due care the defendant owes under the "reasonable person" standard, *supra*. However, in a few instances (*e.g.*, when dealing with land occupiers, *see infra*), the special duty of due care is ***in place of*** the general duty of due care. As a matter of analysis, if the circumstances indicate that some special duty of care may be on point, consider first whether the defendant created a risk of physical harm and therefore owed a duty of reasonable care. Then, even if the defendant owed a duty of reasonable care, consider whether a special duty might also apply.

2. **Duties and Breach Measured by Statute**

a. **Nature of statute**

(1) **Civil statutes [§546]**
Some statutes regulating conduct expressly provide a ***civil*** remedy for their violation. In such cases, the plaintiff can ***sue directly under the statute*** and usually need not be concerned with common law negligence.

(2) **Criminal statutes and duty—no preexisting general duty of care [§547]**
If a criminal statute regulates the conduct involved in a tort (*e.g.*, traffic codes), courts usually rely on the statute only to determine whether the defendant has breached his common law duty of care (*see supra*, §§396 *et seq.*). If there is no preexisting common law duty of care, as in the case of

statutes that criminalize failure to protect or aid others, courts are reluctant to use the criminal statute to ***create*** a new duty. [**Perry v. S.N.,** 973 S.W.2d 301 (Tex. 1998)—no tort duty created where defendants violated criminal statute requiring them to report suspected instances of child abuse]

---

e.g. **Example:** Although a few states have statutes requiring citizens to attempt "easy" rescues of those in peril, no state has created a civil duty to rescue.

---

b. Means by which statute gives rise to tort duty [§548]

Whether the statute is civil or criminal in nature, the statute might give rise to a tort duty in one of two ways: (i) by leading a court to recognize a legislatively-created ***"statutory tort,"*** or (ii) by supplying the reason for a court to impose a ***common law tort duty.***

(1) "Statutory torts," or "private enforcement actions" [§549]

Whether or not a common law duty might otherwise apply, a statute could ***expressly*** or ***impliedly*** impose a tort duty. If the court rules that the statute creates a statutory tort (or "private enforcement action"), the scope of the defendant's duty is defined wholly by the statute—if the defendant complied with the statute, there is no breach of duty; if the defendant violated the statute, a breach exists. If the statute does not expressly authorize a private right of action, a court may hold that the statute impliedly does so. [**Alexander v. Sandoval,** 532 U.S. 275 (2001)—concluding that the disparate-impact regulations of Title VI of the Civil Rights Act do not imply a private right of action] Courts consider the following factors in deciding whether a statute impliedly creates a statutory tort:

(i) Whether the plaintiff is ***one of the class for whose particular benefit the statute was enacted***;

(ii) Whether recognition of a private right of action would ***promote the legislative purpose***; and

(iii) Whether creation of such a right would be ***consistent with the legislative scheme.***

---

e.g. **Example:** A statute requires that schools conduct periodic scoliosis screenings. D school fails to do the required screening, and P's parents sue under the statute alleging that had D tested for scoliosis, P would have been diagnosed and received timely treatment. The court determined that although P was one of the class for whose benefit the statute was enacted, the legislature clearly contemplated administrative enforcement of the statute (*e.g.*, withholding funding for noncompliance), and an implied private right of action would be inconsistent with the legislative scheme. [**Uhr v. East Greenbush Central School District,** 94 N.Y.2d 32 (1999)]

---

(2) Common law duty by reference to statute [§550]

If the defendant would not otherwise owe a common law duty—most commonly because there exists no affirmative duty to rescue, warn, or protect another (*see infra*, §551)—and even if the court determines that a statute does not expressly or impliedly authorize a statutory tort, a court may still impose an affirmative common law tort duty ***by reference to the statute.*** [Rest. 3d-PH §38] The reasoning behind such decisions is that the statute represents some evidence of a community norm that counsels in favor of recognizing a common law tort duty.

---

e.g. **Example:** A criminal statute requires citizens to report suspected child abuse. By reference to the statute, a court may impose a common law affirmative duty on D for failure to protect neighbor P's children from abuse by D's husband. [**J.S. v. R.T.H.,** 714 A.2d 924 (N.J. 1998)] *But note:* Courts are not unified in their willingness to impose a common law duty based on such child-protection statutes.

---

3. Duty to Aid Others in Emergency

a. General rule—no duty [§551]

Under the general common law rule, a defendant owes ***no*** duty to warn, protect, or rescue a stranger from a risk of harm—at least if the defendant was in no way responsible for that person's risk or injury. *Rationale:* Tort law is not concerned with purely moral obligations. [**Bishop v. Chicago,** 257 N.E.2d 152 (Ill. 1970)]

b. Exceptions—duty owed where special factors present [§552]

Where certain factors are present, the law imposes upon a defendant an ***"affirmative duty"*** to act:

(1) Special relationship to plaintiff [§553]

Courts recognize that a defendant owes a duty to go to the aid of another in an emergency where some ***special relationship*** exists between them—*e.g.*, parent-child, employer-employee, host-guest, carrier-passenger, jailer-prisoner, etc. [**Carey v. Davis,** 180 N.W. 889 (Iowa 1921); *and see* **Farwell v. Keaton,** 240 N.W.2d 217 (Mich. 1976)—extending duty to "companions on a social venture"; *but see* **H.B. & S.B. v. Whittemore,** 552 N.W.2d 705 (Minn. 1996)—trailer park manager has no duty to tell parents of resident children who told manager about abuse by another resident; **Donaldson v. YWCA,** 539 N.W.2d 789 (Minn. 1995)—YWCA desk clerk has no duty to check on reportedly distraught resident] This duty may extend beyond emergencies (*see infra,* §567).

APPROACH TO DETERMINING DUTY TO AID OTHERS IN PERIL

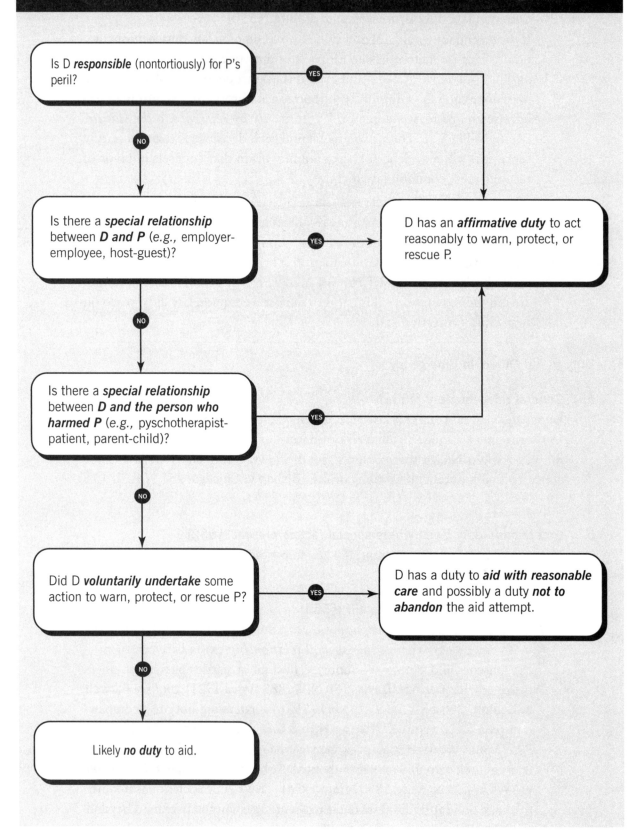

Is D ***responsible*** (nontortiously) for P's peril?

YES → D has an ***affirmative duty*** to act reasonably to warn, protect, or rescue P.

NO ↓

Is there a ***special relationship*** between ***D and P*** (*e.g.,* employer-employee, host-guest)?

YES → D has an ***affirmative duty*** to act reasonably to warn, protect, or rescue P.

NO ↓

Is there a ***special relationship*** between ***D and the person who harmed P*** (*e.g.,* pyschotherapist-patient, parent-child)?

YES → D has an ***affirmative duty*** to act reasonably to warn, protect, or rescue P.

NO ↓

Did D ***voluntarily undertake*** some action to warn, protect, or rescue P?

YES → D has a duty to ***aid with reasonable care*** and possibly a duty ***not to abandon*** the aid attempt.

NO ↓

Likely ***no duty*** to aid.

(2) **Responsibility for plaintiff's peril [§554]**
A defendant who is responsible for the plaintiff's injury or peril is under a duty to go to the plaintiff's aid ***and*** to exercise reasonable care in so doing.

(a) **What if defendant not at fault? [§555]**
Although earlier decisions found a duty to aid only where the defendant's responsibility was tortious, current decisions recognize a duty to aid a person in peril even where the defendant's original conduct was ***innocent*** but has nevertheless created a perilous situation (*e.g.*, where D's golf ball strikes P on the head and no risk to P had been foreseeable, D still owes a duty to render assistance). [Rest. 2d §321]

EXAM TIP — **gilbert**

If you encounter an exam question in which the defendant's conduct created a risk of harm, remember that the defendant owed a normal duty of care ***with regard to that conduct***—*i.e.,* the defendant owed a duty to do that conduct with reasonable care. Your analysis doesn't end there, however. An additional issue in such cases, if the defendant acted reasonably in creating the risk, is whether the defendant owes a ***second, affirmative duty*** to warn, protect, or rescue the plaintiff from that risk.

(3) **Statutory exceptions [§556]**
The no-duty rule has also been limited in several states by statutes requiring persons to assist others in certain emergency situations.

e.g. **Example:** Several states have statutes making it a criminal offense for the driver of an automobile to fail to go to the aid of any person involved in an accident with his car, even though the driver was in no way at fault in causing the accident. [*See* Cal. Veh. Code §20003] Civil liability may also be imposed.

(a) **Note**
By statute, a few states impose ***criminal*** liability for failure to go to the aid of anyone whom the defendant recognizes to be in serious peril, provided this would not greatly endanger the defendant. [*See* 12 Vt. Stat. Ann. §519] However, no state has created a civil duty of easy rescue.

(4) **Special relationship to harmer [§557]**
If the defendant has some relationship with the person who does the harm, courts may use that to recognize an affirmative duty to use due care to avoid the harm. (*See infra*, §§591 *et seq.*) Thus, if a doctor or psychotherapist has reason to know that a patient is likely to harm a ***specific*** third party, the doctor owes a duty to use reasonable care on behalf of the intended victim. [**Tarasoff v. Regents of the University of California,** 17 Cal. 3d 425 (1976)]

---

e.g. **Example:** A physician who fails to keep a patient under observation after he loses consciousness twice in the physician's office owes a duty of care to the victim of a subsequent automobile collision. [**Cram v. Howell,** 680 N.E.2d 1096 (Ind. 1997)]

---

e.g. **Example:** A psychiatrist who knows or should know that a schizophrenic child poses a serious danger of violence to others owes a duty to the child's parents even in the absence of specific threats against them. [**Hamman v. County of Maricopa,** 775 P.2d 1122 (Ariz. 1989)]

---

e.g. **Example:** Despite the absence of a doctor-patient relationship, a doctor has a duty to warn an infant's father about dangers of contracting polio from coming into contact with feces of the recently immunized infant. [**Tenuto v. Lederle Laboratories,** 90 N.Y.2d 606 (1997)]

---

cf. **Compare:** A psychotherapist who knows that an outpatient is schizophrenic owes no duty to warn when the outpatient has not shown any violent tendencies and the psychotherapist has no reason to know the identity of the outpatient's friends (and in particular, the friend the outpatient eventually stabbed to death). [**Fraser v. United States,** 674 A.2d 811 (Conn. 1996)]

---

cf. **Compare:** There is no duty to warn a misdiagnosed patient's future husband of Hepatitis C, where, at the time of the misdiagnosis, neither the doctor nor the patient knows of the (future) husband. [**Hawkins v. Pizarro,** 713 So. 2d 1036 (Fla. 1998)]

---

cf. **Compare:** A physician reviewing a surgery team at the behest of a hospital has no duty to intervene when he observes malpractice occurring. [**Clarke v. Hoek,** 174 Cal. App. 3d 208 (1985)]

(a) Failure to warn patients about risks to others [§558]

Most courts emphasize foreseeability in imposing a duty on a physician to those who might be injured by the patient if the physician does not adequately warn them or the patient about a condition. The outcomes of these cases vary widely according to facts and jurisdiction.

---

e.g. **Example:** A physician who discovers a congenital condition in a patient that is likely to arise in the patient's children has a duty to warn the patient about the dangers her children may face. [**Pate v. Threlkel,** 661 So. 2d 278 (Fla. 1995)]

---

cf. **Compare:** A physician who fails to warn a patient against driving when his epilepsy is not under control does not owe a duty to victims of a subsequent accident. [**Praesel v. Johnson,** 967 S.W.2d 391 (Tex. 1998)—court reluctant to extend liability beyond the relationship even though the harm might be deemed foreseeable]

(b) **Congenital diseases [§559]**

When a physician diagnoses a patient with a genetically transferable disease, the physician owes a duty to the children to warn them of the dangers they face, but this duty can be fulfilled by warning the patient. [*See* **Pate v. Threlkel,** *supra*; *but see* **Safer v. Estate of Pack,** 677 A.2d 1188 (N.J. 1996)—dicta suggesting that there may be situations in which the duty requires warning to persons other than the patient]

c. **Distinguish—duty owed where defendant undertakes to aid plaintiff ("Good Samaritan obligation") [§560]**

Note that where the defendant clearly owed no duty to aid the plaintiff initially (*i.e.*, where the defendant was not responsible for the plaintiff's predicament and no special relationship existed between them), if the defendant ***voluntarily undertakes*** to aid the plaintiff, he must do so carefully. That is, the defendant need not act at all, ***but if he does, he owes a duty of reasonable care.*** [**Zelenko v. Gimbel Bros.,** 158 Misc. 904 (1935)] This is often characterized as an affirmative duty, but may also be thought of as part of a person's duty to conduct his actions with reasonable care.

e.g. **Example:** D finds a stranger (P) lying unconscious in the street and decides to take her to a hospital. In doing so, D owes a duty to exercise reasonable care in moving P and driving to the hospital. If D acts unreasonably, he will be liable for any injuries attributable to his lack of care.

(1) **Effect of abandonment [§561]**

The fact that the defendant has undertaken to aid the plaintiff does not necessarily require the defendant to continue his efforts. However, the condition in which the defendant may leave the plaintiff without incurring liability varies among the states.

(a) **No worse condition [§562]**

In some states, the defendant may terminate his efforts at any time without liability ***provided*** the subsequent abandonment leaves the plaintiff in ***no worse condition*** than that in which the defendant found her. [**Miller v. Arnal Corp.,** 632 P.2d 987 (Ariz. 1981)]

e.g. **Example:** Same facts as in the above example, except that on the way to the hospital D decides he does not want to become involved and abandons P by the side of the road. D will not be liable as long as he has not thereby placed P in greater peril ***or*** deprived P of the chance of aid by others.

(b) **No comparable peril [§563]**

In some states, the defendant must exercise due care at least to the extent of not shifting the plaintiff to a position of peril ***comparable to that from which she was rescued.*** [**Parvi v. City of Kingston,** 41 N.Y.2d 553 (1977); Rest. 2d §324 cmt. g]

(c) **No imminent peril of serious harm [§564]**

In still other states, a defendant is free to abandon a voluntary rescue effort unless to do so would leave the person in ***"imminent peril of serious bodily harm."*** [Rest. 3d-PH §44]

(2) **Extension to other voluntary actions [§565]**

Some cases have extended this duty to those who have taken some other action—not attempted rescue—and who are then sued because of a subsequent accident. [**Union Park Memorial Chapel v. Hutt,** 670 So. 2d 64 (Fla. 1996)—funeral director assumed duty of due care to mourners when he voluntarily organized a funeral procession; *but see* **Tavarez v. Lelakis,** 143 F.3d 744 (2d Cir. 1998)—no duty on D who held ladder while P was cleaning D's high shelves where P fell after D had stopped holding the ladder to answer the telephone and P kept cleaning and fell; D did not leave P worse off than she was in her original position]

(3) **Statutory exception for physicians [§566]**

So as not to discourage physicians (who may be concerned about malpractice liability should the due care standard apply) from assisting others in emergencies, so-called Good Samaritan statutes have been adopted in virtually all states, ***exempting physicians*** who render aid in an emergency from liability for negligence. [*See* Frank B. Mapel & Charles J. Weigel, Good Samaritan Laws—Who Needs Them?: The Current State of Good Samaritan Protection in the United States, 21 S. Tex. L.J. 327 (1981)] This statutory exemption extends even to physicians who render aid in a hospital to patients to whom they owed no prior duty of care. [**Hirpa v. IHC Hospitals, Inc.,** 948 P.2d 785 (Utah 1997)—extending Good Samaritan protection to physician who assisted in emergency that occurred in a hospital but for which the physician had no preexisting duty to lend aid]

4. **Affirmative Duty to Prevent Harm [§567]**

In addition to the special duties imposed under the specific categories below, courts increasingly are finding a duty of care owed by defendants who share a special relationship with the plaintiff to prevent harm, whether or not inflicted by another person. Such a duty builds on situations in which the defendant may be liable even though an intervening negligent or intentional act by a third party separates the defendant's act or omission from the injury to the plaintiff. (Examples of such relationships are carrier and passenger, innkeeper and guest, school district and pupil, etc.) [*See, e.g.,* **Nova Southeastern University v. Gross,** 758 So. 2d 86 (Fla. 2000)—school sending student into dangerous neighborhood for clinical placement owes duty of care to student] But not every relationship suffices. [*See* **Harper v. Herman,** *supra*, §342—captain owes no affirmative duty to warn guest of danger in diving off side of pleasure boat]

a. **Voluntary assumption of care [§568]**
The defendant may assume a special duty voluntarily by certain acts that cause the plaintiff to be more vulnerable to injury from a third person than had the defendant not acted at all.

---

e.g. **Example:** Where D, the owner of a building in a high-crime neighborhood, hires an attendant to watch the lobby, a visitor might reasonably be lulled into a false sense of security and neglect normal safety precautions. If P is attacked by a third person while the attendant is inexcusably absent, D may be liable. [**Nallan v. Helmsley-Spear, Inc.,** 50 N.Y.2d 507 (1980); *and see* **Cross v. Wells Fargo Alarm Services,** 412 N.E.2d 472 (Ill. 1980)—municipal housing authority that provided part-time security guard service increased danger to tenants during hours when guards not present]

---

b. **Governmental entities' duty to protect [§569]**
The general rule is that in protective capacities, absent special circumstances, the government's duty is owed to the public generally, not to any particular members of the public, and so recovery is barred. [*See* **Davidson v. City of Westminster,** 32 Cal. 3d 197 (1982)—police in stakeout owed no duty to victim hurt before police closed in; **City of Rome v. Jordan,** 426 S.E.2d 861 (Ga. 1993)—no duty to protect P, who had sought police aid because she feared harm from disappointed suitor who had threatened her; **Riss v. City of New York,** 22 N.Y.2d 579 (1968)]

(1) **Exceptions [§570]**
Although the general rule is that governmental entities do not owe an affirmative duty to protect, courts have imposed a duty under the following circumstances:

(a) Where there is a ***separate legal basis for arrest*** of a third person who has threatened harm [**Sorichetti v. City of New York,** 65 N.Y.2d 461 (1985)];

(b) Where a ***statute*** creates a duty to particular plaintiffs [**Busby v. Municipality of Anchorage,** 741 P.2d 230 (Alaska 1987)—statutory obligation of police to assist persons apparently incapacitated by alcohol];

(c) Where the governmental entity's ***promise or conduct induces reliance*** on the part of the plaintiff [**DeLong v. County of Erie,** 89 A.D.2d 376 (1982)—dispatcher's promise to send help "right away" enough to constitute an undertaking and support a duty];

(d) Where the governmental entity has a ***special relationship*** with the plaintiff or the person who injured the plaintiff [**Jackson v. City of Kansas

City, 947 P.2d 31 (Kan. 1997)—police custody of plaintiff in handcuffs gave rise to a duty to protect him]; or

(e) Where it is the governmental entity's ***action*** (*e.g.*, high-speed police chase), rather than inaction, that injured the plaintiff.

(2) Note

Even if a court imposes a duty on the defendant governmental entity, the court might still withhold liability due to governmental immunity (*see infra*, §§1222-1247). This area of the law is particularly confusing because courts often mingle duty and immunity analyses. Specifically, they sometimes refer to a "public duty" analysis as a consideration of immunity, or discuss matters of governmental immunity as part of the duty analysis.

c. Motorists' duty to prevent harm [§571]

Most courts have found that motorists do not have a duty to drive in such a way as to prevent injury from the negligence of ***others***. For example, a driver need not swerve onto the shoulder unless it will assist that driver in avoiding a collision. There is no duty to help others avoid colliding. [**Ratliff v. Schiber Truck Co.,** 150 F.3d 949 (8th Cir. 1998); *and see* **Monreal v. Tobin,** 61 Cal. App. 4th 1337 (1998)]

5. Duty to Perform Promises—Nonfeasance vs. Misfeasance

a. Gratuitous promises [§572]

In general, a defendant's ***failure to perform a gratuitous promise*** to render service or assistance does not give rise to a basis for tort liability—even if the defendant knew that the plaintiff would suffer damage as a result of nonperformance. [**Thorne v. Deas,** 4 Johns. 84 (1809)]

---

e.g. **Example:** D voluntarily promises to obtain insurance on P's building but fails to do so, and the building is then destroyed by fire. D is not liable in tort to P. [**Brawn v. Lyford,** 69 A. 544 (Me. 1907)]

---

(1) Rationale—distinction between misfeasance and nonfeasance

It is a deep-rooted principle that, absent some legal duty to act, tort liability is predicated only on ***misfeasance—not on nonfeasance***. Thus, a promisor's failure to perform his promise is not by itself a sufficient basis for tort liability. (*But see infra*, §1626, imposing liability where the defendant makes a promise with no intention of fulfilling it.)

(2) Distinguish—duty owed where defendant begins performance [§573]

However, even where the promise is gratuitous, a defendant-promisor who "enters upon its performance" in any manner must perform with reasonable care. Failure to do so is "misfeasance," and is a sufficient basis for tort liability.

Example: Although the federal government need not publish aviation charts, it will be held liable for any injuries caused by inaccuracies in charts it does publish. [**Reminga v. United States,** 631 F.2d 449 (6th Cir. 1980)]

---

(3) Minority view—duty owed based on foreseeable reliance [§574]

A number of cases have held a defendant liable for failing to perform his promise where he knew or should have known that plaintiff was ***refraining from obtaining other necessary assistance in reliance*** on the promise.

Example: Sheriff D, under no legal obligation to do so, promised to warn P before X was released from jail, because X had threatened to kill P. D failed to do so; X killed P, and D was held liable to P's heirs. [**Morgan v. Yuba County,** 230 Cal. App. 2d 938 (1964); **Hartley v. Floyd,** 512 So. 2d 1022 (Fla. 1987)]

---

b. Contractual promises [§575]

Generally, the rules for gratuitous promises apply to contractual promises.

(1) Nonfeasance [§576]

Tort liability normally ***cannot*** be predicated solely on the defendant's failure to perform a contract. Where the defendant simply fails or refuses to begin ***any*** performance under the contract, the plaintiff's remedy is strictly in contract. [**Louisville & Nashville Railroad v. Spinks,** 30 S.E. 968 (Ga. 1898)—carrier failed to furnish transportation for goods as agreed]

(2) Misfeasance [§577]

On the other hand, a defendant who undertakes performance of a contract owes a duty of reasonable care; improper performance may constitute ***both*** a breach of contract and an actionable tort, allowing the plaintiff to bring either action.

Example: P hires D to erect a windmill on P's property. If D never shows up on the job, he may be liable for breach of contract, but not in tort. However, once he starts the construction, he must exercise due care; and if, as the result of improper design or construction, P's property is damaged or some other loss ensues, D may be liable either in contract or in tort. [**Flint & Walling Manufacturing Co. v. Beckett,** 79 N.E. 503 (Ind. 1906)]

(a) Proof in medical cases [§578]

A plaintiff who alleges that a medical doctor breached a contract to achieve a certain medical result may find it hard to establish the existence of a contract promising a particular result. *Rationale:* Doctors rarely can, in good faith, promise specific results, and patients have a tendency to transform their doctor's optimistic statements into firm promises. [**Clevenger v. Haling,** 394 N.E.2d 1119 (Mass. 1979)]

(b) Application to other contractual relationships [§579]

Similarly, other relationships, contractual in the first instance, impose a tort obligation once performance is undertaken—*e.g., carrier-passenger; innkeeper-guest; bailor-bailee.*

(3) Liability to third parties [§580]

A defendant's ***misfeasance*** in the performance of a contract with one person may involve a foreseeable risk of harm to others (*e.g.*, a railroad worker who throws the wrong switch may cause harm to passengers and others nearby). In such cases, the defendant's liability to any third persons injured thereby is judged on straight negligence standards—foreseeability of harm—and no privity or contractual relationship need be established. But, again, no tort liability can be predicated solely on ***nonfeasance.***

(a) Exception—water company cases [§581]

However, most courts have held that a private company that contracts with a city to furnish water is ***not liable*** to a private citizen when the service fails at a critical moment—*e.g.*, when water pressure drops and a house is destroyed by fire. [**H.R. Moch Co. v. Rensselaer Water Co.,** 247 N.Y. 160 (1928); *but see* **Weinberg v. Dinger,** 524 A.2d 366 (N.J. 1987)—contra where the loss is uninsured]

1) Judicial rationale

The failure of water service is deemed only "nonfeasance," on the theory that the private utility had not undertaken any direct performance to the private citizen; hence, there is no tort liability.

a) Note

Private citizens cannot recover on a contract theory, because these courts hold the citizens to be only "incidental beneficiaries" of the utility's contract with the city. (*See* Contracts Summary.)

2) Underlying rationale

Although the above rationale has been criticized for years, the rule is still generally followed. The explanation may be that virtually all improved property is insured against loss by fire, so that this suit is really one by a subrogated fire insurer against a liability insurer. This is thought to be an administratively wasteful suit, especially because one result might be to raise the price of water. [**Libbey v. Hampton Water Works Co.,** 389 A.2d 434 (N.H. 1978)]

6. Duty Owed by Common Carrier [§582]

Modern authorities treat the duty owed by one legally charged with the care of others as simply a duty of due care; the fact that a carrier is involved is only one of the circumstances to be considered in determining whether the duty was breached. [*See* **Bethel v. New York City Transit Authority,** *supra,* §290] However, older courts treated the duty of a common carrier as imposing a ***separate, affirmative standard of care,*** demanding the "utmost care consistent with the nature of his undertaking." [**Gardner v. Boston Elevated Railway,** 90 N.E. 534 (Mass. 1910)] In any case, wherever a person is legally charged with the safety of another (*e.g.,* carrier transporting passengers) or protecting the property of another (*e.g.,* bailee in possession of bailor's chattels), a high ***amount*** of care—if not a different standard of care—is clearly called for. [**Acosta v. Southern California Rapid Transit District,** 2 Cal. 3d 19 (1970)]

a. "Highest degree of care" [§583]

A common carrier must ***always*** choose the course of action ***least likely to expose its passengers to harm.*** [**Spalt v. Eaton,** 192 A. 576 (N.J. 1937)—bus driver's use of force to eject boisterous passenger was negligent because it endangered other passengers, even though driver was otherwise privileged to use such force; *see supra,* §290]

(1) Affirmative duty [§584]

Carrier employees have an affirmative duty to use due care to aid passengers when they become ill or are attacked by robbers. [**Lopez v. Southern California Rapid Transit District,** 40 Cal. 3d 780 (1985)]

(2) Intervening forces [§585]

Courts sometimes impose liability on common carriers notwithstanding ***intervening forces*** that would excuse other defendants (*see supra,* §499).

(3) Ending the special relationship [§586]

Once a carrier has finished providing services to a passenger, the special relationship and resulting duty end. [**McGettigan v. Bay Area Rapid Transit District,** 57 Cal. App. 4th 1011 (1997)—no duty owed to passenger after he disembarked from train at last stop, even though he was so inebriated that staff had to carry him off train]

b. Distinguish—liability of auto driver to "guest" or "passenger" [§587]

The high degree of care owed by a common carrier to its passengers (above) has not been imposed on the driver of a private automobile with respect to riders therein.

(1) Common law rule [§588]

The driver of an automobile owes any rider therein a duty to exercise reasonable care to warn of any known dangers or defective conditions that are not reasonably apparent, and to exercise reasonable care in operating the car. [**Higgins v. Mason,** 255 N.Y. 104 (1930)]

(a) **Rationale**

This common law duty developed by analogy to the duty owed by a ***land occupier*** to guests or licensees (*see infra*, §692).

(2) **"Guest statutes" [§589]**

A few jurisdictions still have statutes (known as "guest statutes") that eliminate ordinary negligence liability of the driver of an automobile to some riders therein. Guest statutes provide that a driver is liable to a "guest" rider only for ***"wanton" or "gross" negligence***, or for accidents due to intoxication or willful misconduct.

(a) **"Guest" vs. "passenger" [§590]**

The most frequent problem in applying these statutes is to determine whether the injured rider is a "guest" (subject to the statute) or a "passenger," as to whom the general common law duty of due care applies (by analogy to an invitee on land, *see infra*, §696). [**Davis v. Davis,** 622 So. 2d 901 (Ala. 1993)] Generally, if there has been some payment (money, services, or property) that motivates the driver's furnishing the ride, the rider is a passenger and may recover for ***ordinary negligence***. [**Bozanich v. Kenney,** 3 Cal. 3d 567 (1970)] Note that sharing expenses ***may*** be sufficient by itself to qualify the rider for "passenger" status.

7. **Duty to Control Third Persons [§591]**

This section considers situations in which the defendant may be held liable for injuries that were caused by the conduct of third persons over whom the defendant had some influence or power of control. In many of these scenarios, the plaintiff's claim is one of ***nonfeasance***—*i.e.*, where the plaintiff argues that the defendant failed affirmatively to warn, protect, or rescue the plaintiff from the third person's conduct. In other scenarios, the plaintiff's claim more closely resembles ***misfeasance***—*i.e.*, where the plaintiff's claim is that the defendant's conduct enabled the third person's conduct or increased the risk from the third person.

a. **Distinguish direct liability from vicarious liability [§592]**

If the defendant is ***present*** at the time of the third person's wrongful conduct, his failure to exercise control to stop the conduct may be an act of negligence on his own part. However, if the defendant is ***not*** present, he may be charged with liability for the acts of third persons only in limited situations. These latter cases include ***imputing*** the third person's acts to the defendant, who is said to be ***vicariously liable*** therefor (master-servant cases, etc.; *see* below).

b. **Bailment cases**

(1) **Liability based on bailor's negligence [§593]**

If the bailor of chattels permits the bailee to use them, the bailor has a right to control the use and will be liable in two situations for failure to exercise due care to prevent the intentional or negligent acts of the bailee while using the bailed chattel:

(a) **Committed in bailor's presence [§594]**
The bailor will be held directly liable when the bailee's wrongful conduct is committed in the bailor's presence (*e.g.*, D permits X to drive D's car at an excessive speed while D rides beside him).

1) **Exception—owner-passenger [§595]**
In some jurisdictions, the presence of the owner in the car as a passenger does not necessarily impose a duty to control the driver, but it may be a factor to consider. [*See, e.g.*, **Bauer v. Johnson,** 403 N.E.2d 237 (Ill. 1980)]

2) **Distinguish—nonowner-passenger [§596]**
Generally, automobile passengers owe no duty to the driver or to third parties to advise the driver in the operation of the vehicle. [**Hale v. Allstate Insurance Co.,** 639 P.2d 203 (Utah 1981)]

(b) **"Negligent entrustment doctrine" [§597]**
Even if the tortious act has not been committed in the bailor's presence, he will be liable if he has failed to exercise reasonable care in ***selecting*** the bailee; *i.e.*, he knows or should know that the bailee is likely to cause harm to others. A negligent entrustment claim is a claim of ***misfeasance*** because by providing the instrument of harm, the defendant's conduct participated in creating the risk. [Rest. 2d §390]

---

e.g. **Example:** Entrusting his car to an inexperienced driver, or to a driver known to be irresponsible or likely to become intoxicated, may make the bailor liable. [**Mitchell v. Churches,** 206 P. 6 (Wash. 1922); *but see* **Suiter v. Epperson,** 571 N.W.2d 92 (Neb. 1997)—an auto dealer has no duty to check whether a prospective buyer has a driver's license before permitting a test drive, unless there is some reason to doubt the buyer's ability]

---

e.g. **Example:** Parents have been held liable for negligently entrusting a vehicle to a child with known reckless propensities [*see, e.g.*, **Allen v. Toledo,** 109 Cal. App. 3d 415 (1980)], even where title to the car is in the child [**Kahlenberg v. Goldstein,** 431 A.2d 76 (Md. 1981)—parents helped child buy car]. Note, however, that some states limit negligent entrustment to cases involving ***minor*** children. [*See, e.g.*, **Broadwater v. Dorsey,** 688 A.2d 436 (Md. 1997)]

---

e.g. **Example:** An airplane rental company was liable for allowing a legally qualified pilot who had not completed his "high altitude checkout" to fly out of a high altitude airport. The defendant knew that the pilot was inexperienced, and the industry standard was not to rent to such individuals. [**White v. Inbound Aviation,** 69 Cal. App. 4th 910 (1999)]

---

e.g. **Example:** A gun seller was found liable when its clerk sold a gun and ammunition to a drunk customer, helping him fill out the required forms that the customer was too drunk to complete. [**Kitchen v. K-Mart Corp.,** 697 So. 2d 1200 (Fla. 1997)]

---

1) **Distinguish—no liability where no right to control [§598]**
A few cases have held that where the defendant had no right to control the instrument of harm, the defendant owed no duty of care in providing it to the third person.

---

e.g. **Example:** A service station operator who sells gasoline to a recognizably intoxicated motorist is not liable for harm caused by the motorist. *Rationale:* The service station operator is a ***seller***, not a bailor; *i.e.*, he has no right to control the use of the gasoline he sells. [**Fuller v. Standard Stations, Inc.,** 250 Cal. App. 2d 687 (1967)] This is by no means a universal ruling, however. [*See* **Vince v. Wilson,** 561 A.2d 103 (Vt. 1989)—auto seller may be liable for selling car to driver with known poor driving record, and person providing money for purchase may also be liable]

---

a) **Stolen property [§599]**
Likewise, individuals are generally not liable when their property (such as a gun) is stolen and then used to commit a crime. [*See, e.g.,* **McGrane v. Cline,** 973 P.2d 1092 (Wash. 1999); *but see* **Estate of Strever v. Cline,** 924 P.2d 666 (Mont. 1996)—imposing a duty owed to the general public not to leave a loaded gun in an unlocked truck] States are split over whether thefts due to leaving keys in the ignition create duties to innocent persons run into by the thieves. [*See* **Kozicki v. Dragon,** 583 N.W.2d 336 (Neb. 1998)—action lies if thieves more likely to drive negligently than others; **Cruz v. Middlekauff Lincoln-Mercury, Inc.,** 909 P.2d 1252 (Utah 1996)—action lies if theft is foreseeable; *compare* **Poskus v. Lombardo's of Randolph, Inc.,** 670 N.E.2d 383 (Mass. 1996)—court retreats from bar on such actions but concludes that police officer hurt running after car thief has no action against person who permitted theft]

(2) **Liability where bailor not negligent [§600]**
The general rule is that a bailor who has exercised reasonable care in the selection of the bailee (thus avoiding the "negligent entrustment doctrine") is ***not liable*** for negligent or intentional harm inflicted by the bailee outside the bailor's presence.

(a) Exceptions—vicarious liability in automobile cases [§601]

However, there are two exceptions, both involving automobiles, in which the owner may be held liable for harm inflicted by the bailee ***without any showing of negligence*** on the part of the owner (*i.e.*, even though the owner was ***careful*** in selecting the bailee and was ***not present*** at the time of the bailee's tortious conduct). In these two cases, the owner is held ***vicariously liable*** for the torts committed by the bailee:

1) "Family purpose doctrine" [§602]

Some jurisdictions by statute or case law hold an automobile owner liable for injuries resulting from the bailee's negligent operation of the vehicle, even outside the owner's presence, if the bailee is a member of the owner's immediate ***family or household and*** is driving with the ***express or implied permission*** of the owner. [*See, e.g.*, **Nelson v. Johnson,** 599 N.W.2d 246 (N.D. 1999)]

2) "Permissive use statutes" [§603]

Legislation in many states goes even further. So-called permissive use statutes render the owner of an automobile liable for damages (sometimes in a limited amount) caused by the negligence of ***anyone*** (not just family members) driving an automobile with the owner's express or implied consent. [*See, e.g.*, Cal. Veh. Code §17150]

(3) Distinguish—duties with respect to condition of bailed chattel [§604]

In addition to whatever liability a bailor may have for wrongful conduct by the bailee in use of the bailed chattel, a bailor also owes certain duties as to the safety of the bailed chattel itself. Thus, where the bailee was using the chattel properly, but the chattel itself was defective, the bailor may be liable to third persons injured thereby (as well as to the bailee). (*See* detailed discussion *infra*, §§925 *et seq.*)

c. Master-servant cases

(1) Liability based on employer's own negligence [§605]

If an employee's torts cannot be imputed to the employer under respondeat superior (*e.g.*, because outside scope of employment; *see* below), consider whether the employer can be held liable on the basis of the ***employer's own negligence***. (This, of course, is not vicarious liability.) There are three possible theories:

(a) Failure to control acts in employer's presence [§606]

An employer owes an affirmative duty to use due care to control the conduct of his employees in his presence. Therefore, if an employee's tortious acts were committed in the employer's presence, the employer may be held ***directly*** liable for negligence. [**Hogle v. H.H. Franklin Manufacturing Co.,** 199 N.Y. 388 (1910)]

(b) **Negligent hiring of employee [§607]**

An employer may be held liable for willful or criminal actions of an employee if the employer should reasonably have foreseen such tortious action by the employee, even if the action was outside the scope of the employee's job duties. [**J. v. Victory Tabernacle Baptist Church,** 372 S.E.2d 391 (Va. 1988)]

---

e.g. **Example:** Hospitals can be negligent for failing to use reasonable care in keeping facilities safe and in failing to hire (or grant hospital privileges to) only the most competent physicians. [**Welsh v. Bulger,** 698 A.2d 581 (Pa. 1997)—hospital negligent for failing to have a qualified surgeon available during delivery]

(c) **Negligent supervision [§608]**

If an employer is aware of dangerous behavior by an employee, the employer will be held to an affirmative duty to supervise the employee with reasonable care. [**Trahan-Laroche v. Lockheed Sanders, Inc.,** 657 A.2d 417 (N.H. 1995)—truck driver who ran into P, while on D's property and under D's supervision and control, negligently attached his trailer and used inadequate safety chains]

(2) **Doctrine of respondeat superior—vicarious liability [§609]**

An employer is ***vicariously*** liable for any tortious acts committed by his employee ***within the scope of the employment.*** This fundamental rule of agency law applies whether the acts were committed in the presence of the employer or otherwise; *i.e.*, whether or not the employer had the actual ability to control the employee's conduct. (*See* Agency, Partnership & Limited Liability Companies Summary.)

(a) **Crucial requirement—"scope of employment" [§610]**

The doctrine of respondeat superior does not apply to torts committed by the employee ***outside*** the scope of employment. Thus, if the defendant's employee leaves the place of employment and while pursuing some private objective injures the plaintiff, the defendant cannot be held liable under respondeat superior. [*See, e.g.,* **Bussard v. Minimed, Inc.,** 105 Cal. App. 4th 798 (2003)—discussing and refusing to apply the "coming and going rule," the general rule that an employee is outside the scope of her employment when commuting to and from work; **Christensen v. Swenson,** 874 P.2d 125 (Utah 1994)—holding that reasonable minds could differ about whether employee who used 15-minute break to drive to pick up lunch from nearby cafe was acting within scope of her employment]

LIABILITY OF PRINCIPAL FOR AGENT'S TORTS—AN APPROACH

gilbert

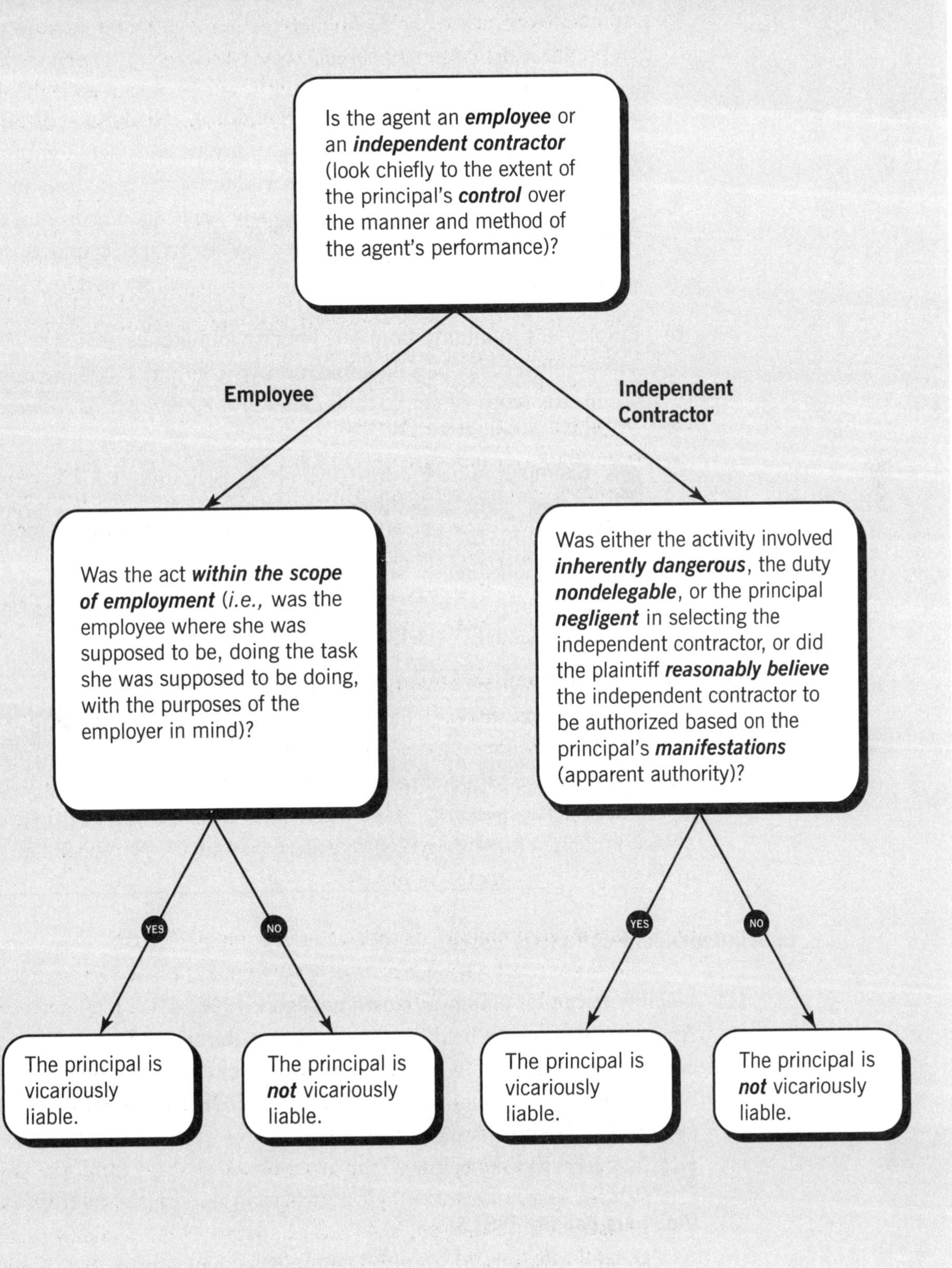

Is the agent an ***employee*** or an ***independent contractor*** (look chiefly to the extent of the principal's ***control*** over the manner and method of the agent's performance)?
Employee
Independent Contractor
Was the act ***within the scope of employment*** (*i.e.,* was the employee where she was supposed to be, doing the task she was supposed to be doing, with the purposes of the employer in mind)?
Was either the activity involved ***inherently dangerous***, the duty ***nondelegable***, or the principal ***negligent*** in selecting the independent contractor, or did the plaintiff ***reasonably believe*** the independent contractor to be authorized based on the principal's ***manifestations*** (apparent authority)?
YES
NO
YES
NO
The principal is vicariously liable.
The principal is ***not*** vicariously liable.
The principal is vicariously liable.
The principal is ***not*** vicariously liable.

1) **Application—intentional torts [§611]**
Batteries and other intentional torts committed by an employee ***may*** be within the scope of employment if the employee's duties involve the use of physical force on others (*e.g.*, bodyguards, bouncers) or force to further the employer's interests (*e.g.*, to collect debt due employer).

2) **Application—company rules forbidding activity [§612]**
An employee's tortious conduct ***may*** be considered within the scope of employment even if it violates a company rule prohibiting such conduct (*e.g.*, a company's rule against driving while intoxicated will not allow it to escape liability if an employee drives drunk while otherwise within the scope of her employment).

(b) **Employee's immunity from tort liability immaterial [§613]**
The employer may be held liable for torts committed by his employee within the scope of employment ***even if the employee is immune***!

e.g. **Example:** Where a husband negligently injures his wife while acting in the scope of his employment, the wife may hold the employer liable for the husband's negligence, even if she cannot maintain an action directly against the husband because of interspousal tort immunity (*see infra*, §§1211-1213). [**Fields v. Synthetic Ropes, Inc.**, 215 A.2d 427 (Del. 1965)]

EXAM TIP gilbert

Keep in mind that the employer's liability under respondeat superior is strictly vicarious; *i.e.*, it must always be shown first that the employee ***was acting tortiously*** before the employer can be held liable. If the employee is exonerated, no judgment can be returned against the employer.

d. **Independent contractor cases**

(1) **Liability based on employer's own negligence [§614]**
An employer may be held directly liable for the torts of an independent contractor if the employer has failed to exercise due care in selecting a competent contractor. This is liability imposed for the employer's ***own*** negligence, and it is immaterial whether there is also a basis for imposing vicarious liability (*see* below).

(2) **Vicarious liability [§615]**
As a general rule, one who employs an independent contractor will ***not*** be held vicariously liable for the negligent conduct of the independent contractor—even while the independent contractor is acting within the scope

of the contract. *Rationale:* The employer has ***no right to control the manner*** in which an independent contractor performs the contract. (*See* Agency, Partnership & Limited Liability Companies Summary.)

(a) Exceptions [§616]

But an increasing number of "exceptions" to this no-liability rule are recognized:

1) "Apparent" or "ostensible" agency [§617]

The employer will be vicariously liable for conduct by an independent contractor if:

(i) The principal (employer) by its actions or words ***manifests that the independent contractor has authority*** to act for the principal; and

(ii) The plaintiff ***reasonably believes*** that the independent contractor was an employee or agent of the principal.

[Rest. 3d of Agency §3.03; *and see* **Roessler v. Novak,** 858 So. 2d 1158 (Fla. 2003); **Petrovich v. Share Health Plan of Illinois, Inc.,** 719 N.E.2d 756 (Ill. 1999)]

2) Nondelegable duties [§618]

If the employer's duty is ***nondelegable*** as a matter of law, the employer cannot avoid liability by hiring an independent contractor to perform. [Rest. 2d §424]

a) Duty to maintain automobile [§619]

It is generally recognized that an automobile owner is under a duty to maintain the car in a safe condition. (Frequently this is required by statute. [*See, e.g.,* Cal. Veh. Code §26453]) Because of the substantial risk of harm inherent in the operation of automobiles, a few courts hold this duty to be ***nondelegable.*** Thus, *e.g.,* the owner is liable if his brakes prove defective—even though he had employed a reputable garage to service his car, and had no independent ability to do the work himself or to inspect to see that it was done properly! [**Maloney v. Rath,** 69 Cal. 2d 442 (1968)]

1/ Note

Most courts, however, have ***not*** found the duty to maintain one's automobile nondelegable. [*See* **Hackett v. Perron,** 402 A.2d 193 (N.H. 1979); Allan E. Korpela, Annotation, Automobiles: Liability of Owner Property

Damage Resulting from Defective Brakes, 40 A.L.R.3d 9 (1971)]

b) **Duty to maintain public premises [§620]**

The duty to keep premises safe for business visitors has also been held nondelegable. Hence, D, a shopping center landlord, is vicariously liable where his independent contractor negligently repairs leased premises, resulting in injuries to the business invitee of D's tenant. [*See, e.g.,* **Valenti v. NET Properties Management, Inc.,** 710 A.2d 399 (N.H. 1998)]

c) **Health care providers [§621]**

A health care provider may be held vicariously liable to a client or patient for negligence by an independent contractor. *Rationale:* A patient has no choice in the provider's selection of a contractor, and the contractor may be judgment-proof or underinsured. [**Marek v. Professional Health Services, Inc.,** 432 A.2d 538 (N.J. 1981)—x-ray film negligently read by contractor; *but see* **Baptist Memorial Hospital System v. Sampson,** 969 S.W.2d 945 (Tex. 1998)—hospital not vicariously liable for conduct of independent contractor emergency room physician]

1/ **"Captain-of-the-ship" doctrine [§622]**

Under the "captain-of-the-ship" doctrine, most states impute the negligence of nonemployees to surgeons [**Ravi v. Coates,** 662 So. 2d 218 (Ala. 1995); **Rudeck v. Wright,** 709 P.2d 621 (Mont. 1985)], although a minority require a showing that the surgeon was personally negligent [**Anglin v. Kleeman,** 665 A.2d 747 (N.H. 1995)].

2/ **Liability based on health care provider's own negligence [§623]**

Even a state that rejects vicarious liability on a hospital for the negligence of an independent contractor may hold the hospital liable for its own negligence in granting staff privileges to unqualified persons. [**Strubhart v. Perry Memorial Hospital Trust Authority,** 903 P.2d 263 (Okla. 1995)—hospital's obligation includes checking before granting privilege in first place, and also checking after reports of complaints or problems; *but see* **St. Luke's Episcopal Hospital v. Agbor,** 952 S.W.2d 503 (Tex. 1997)—according to state statute, hospitals have no duty to use due care in accrediting surgeons]

d) **Other nondelegable duties [§624]**
Other duties deemed to be nondelegable include the duty to provide employees with a safe place to work, to refrain from obstructing a public highway, and to afford lateral support to adjacent land, as well as the duty of a carrier to transport its passengers carefully and that of a landlord to maintain common passageways. Thus, an employer will be vicariously liable for the negligence of an independent contractor in connection with the performance of any of these obligations.

3) **Dangerous activities—"peculiar risk" doctrine [§625]**
If the activity involved is so intrinsically ***dangerous*** that the employer should realize that it involves a peculiar risk of physical harm, the employer cannot avoid liability by hiring an independent contractor to perform. Examples of such dangerous activities include blasting, use of fire to clear land, etc. [Rest. 2d §416]

4) **Contractor's assumption of liability does not overcome exception [§626]**
If the case comes within the nondelegable duty or dangerous activity exceptions, the fact that the independent contractor has (by contract) "assumed all risks" in connection with performance does ***not*** insulate the employer from liability ***to third persons*** injured by the contractor's negligence. But it does give express recognition to the employer's cause of action against the contractor for ***indemnification*** (*see infra*, §§1262-1263). [**Van Arsdale v. Hollinger,** 68 Cal. 2d 245 (1968)]

(b) **Collateral negligence—exception to exception [§627]**
An employer who would otherwise be liable under the nondelegable duty or dangerous activity exceptions may nevertheless escape liability if the independent contractor's negligence is considered "collateral" to the special risk that gives rise to vicarious liability in the first place.

---

e.g. **Example:** Carelessly dropping a paint bucket from a window while painting inside a private room with poisonous paint would be collateral negligence (collateral to the poison hazard).

---

cf. **Compare:** Dropping the bucket while painting a sign over a sidewalk would not be collateral because the very risk that made the duty nondelegable (danger to the public below) is what occurred.

---

e. **Partners and joint venturers [§628]**
Persons who engage in a joint enterprise are vicariously liable for the conduct of the other members within the scope of the enterprise. *Rationale:* Those engaged in such an enterprise have an ***equal right to control*** its operation, and whether or not all members in fact exercise such control is immaterial.

(1) **Requirements [§629]**
A joint enterprise requires: (i) a ***mutual right to control*** the management or operation of the enterprise; and (ii) in some jurisdictions, a ***common business purpose*** in which all persons involved have a mutual interest.

(2) **Application—automobile trips [§630]**
Courts are split on whether there is a joint enterprise between the owner of an automobile and a rider when they have embarked on a "share the expenses" trip, having reached some sort of agreement that they will take turns driving, will mutually agree on an itinerary, and will split all costs.

(a) **Joint enterprise [§631]**
Some courts hold this to be a joint enterprise; if there is an accident, an injured third person can hold liable either of the persons in the car, no matter who was driving at the time of the accident.

(b) **Mere sharing of expenses not enough [§632]**
Other states refuse to find a joint enterprise unless a ***business purpose*** is involved (*see* above). In such jurisdictions, sharing the expenses on vacation or pleasure trips does ***not*** amount to a joint enterprise. [**Winslow v. Hammer,** 527 N.W.2d 631 (Neb. 1995)—no joint enterprise without pecuniary interest and thus husband and wife in van were not in joint enterprise]

f. **Liability of parent for torts of child**

(1) **Common law rule—no vicarious liability [§633]**
Under the general common law rule, parents are ***not*** vicariously responsible for torts committed by their child. The rationale is that parents simply do not have sufficient control to justify imputing liability where they were not otherwise negligent.

(a) **Statutory changes [§634]**
However, the common law rule has been modified by statute in many states today, so that vicarious liability will be imposed under certain circumstances. [*See, e.g.*, Cal. Civ. Code §1714.1—making parents liable up to $25,000 (adjusted biennially for cost-of-living) for any "willful misconduct" of child; Cal. Veh. Code §17708—making parents liable for damages caused by negligence of child driving a car on public highways with parents' express or implied permission]

(2) Liability based on parent's own negligence [§635]
Even if not vicariously liable for a child's torts (above), a parent—or anyone else having care or custody of a child—can be held liable for injuries caused by the child ***if the parent himself was negligent.*** In other words, these are cases based on the parent's ***own liability***—and not any imputed or vicarious liability. Thus, the parent may be liable for:

(a) ***Failing to control the acts of the child committed in the parent's presence.*** [Rest. 2d §316; **Richards v. Soucy,** 610 A.2d 268 (Me. 1992)—negligent supervision]

(b) ***Failing to exercise reasonable care*** to protect against ***the child's known dangerous tendencies*** (*e.g.*, allowing child who had previously caused fires to have access to matches). [**Linder v. Bidner,** 50 Misc. 2d 320 (1966)]

(c) ***Failing to warn*** others with whom the child is likely to come into contact about the child's known dangerous tendencies. [**Ellis v. D'Angelo,** 116 Cal. App. 2d 310 (1953)—babysitter injured by violent four-year-old]

(d) ***Failing to prevent child's foreseeable use of inherently dangerous instrumentalities*** (*e.g.*, leaving dynamite caps or loaded firearms in child's presence). [**Kuhns v. Brugger,** 135 A.2d 395 (Pa. 1957)]

(e) ***Negligent entrustment*** (*see supra*, §597).

g. Liability of tavernkeeper

(1) Common law rule—no liability [§636]
At common law, the seller of intoxicating beverages was not liable for injuries resulting from the purchaser's intoxication—whether the injuries were sustained by the purchaser or by another as the result of the purchaser's subsequent conduct. [**Quinnett v. Newman,** 568 A.2d 786 (Conn. 1990)]

(2) Statutory undermining of common law rule—"Dram Shop Acts" [§637]
To alter the common law rule, many states have passed "Dram Shop Acts." [*See, e.g.*, Minn. Stat. Ann. §340A.801] These statutes create a cause of action against the tavernkeeper in favor of ***third parties*** injured by an intoxicated patron.

(a) Nature of tavernkeeper's fault [§638]
Some of these statutes allow recovery only if the tavernkeeper had ***prior notice*** of a danger in selling to such a patron.

(b) Recovery limited to injured third person [§639]
Recovery under the statutes is generally limited to injured third parties. Only a few statutes allow the intoxicated patron to recover for his

own injuries, but many allow the intoxicated person's ***spouse*** to recover for ***loss of support*** resulting from injuries to or death of the intoxicated person. [**Kiriluk v. Cohn,** 148 N.E.2d 607 (Ill. 1958)—allowing patron's widow to recover for the loss of his support, even where she had killed him, the killing being in self-defense against his drunken rage]

(c) Who can be held liable? [§640]
Most statutes are restricted to ***commercial establishments—i.e.***, those in the business of furnishing liquor (taverns or liquor stores).

(d) Defenses [§641]
Some jurisdictions do not recognize contributory negligence, comparative negligence, or assumption of risk defenses in a dram shop action. (These defenses will be discussed *infra.*) [*See, e.g.,* **Feuerherm v. Ertelt,** 286 N.W.2d 509 (N.D. 1979)]

(3) Judicial rejection of common law rule [§642]
A growing number of courts have reevaluated the common law rule and have imposed liability on tavernkeepers for injuries inflicted by their intoxicated patrons on others, even ***without*** a "Dram Shop Act." [*See, e.g.,* **Nazareno v. Urie,** 638 P.2d 671 (Alaska 1981); **Vesely v. Sager,** 5 Cal. 3d 153 (1971)] *But note:* California's legislature rejected *Vesely* and declared that the act of the intoxicated person was the proximate cause of harm except in situations involving minors. [Cal. Bus. & Prof. Code §25602]

(a) Rationale—common law negligence [§643]
From a ***duty*** standpoint, the question is whether the risk to third persons was reasonably foreseeable and, if so, whether any policy factors suggest rejecting a duty. Breach depends, of course, on what knowledge the bartender had or should have had as to the patron's propensities, how intoxicated the patron appeared to be, etc. From a ***proximate cause*** standpoint, the intoxicated patron's negligent acts must be held ***foreseeable***, and thus do ***not*** bar the tavernkeeper's liability. Indeed, the likelihood that the patron may inflict such injuries is the very hazard that makes the tavernkeeper negligent in the first place! [**Rappaport v. Nichols,** 156 A.2d 1 (N.J. 1959); Rest. 2d §449]

(b) Possible "negligence per se" [§644]
If it appears that the patron was ***already intoxicated***, the furnishing of the liquor is generally made a crime by statute—and negligence per se may exist (*see supra,* §§396 *et seq.*)—because such statutes are designed to protect the public from this kind of harm.

(c) Scope of liability

1) **Recovery by intoxicated patron for his own injury? [§645]**
So far, most courts following this view have allowed recovery only for injuries sustained by ***third parties.*** [*See, e.g.,* **Kindt v. Kauffman,** 57 Cal. App. 3d 845 (1976)] However, a few courts permit recovery by the intoxicated patron for ***his own*** injuries. [*See, e.g.,* **Soronen v. Olde Milford Inn, Inc.,** 218 A.2d 630 (N.J. 1966); *but see* **Wright v. Moffitt,** 437 A.2d 554 (Del. 1981)—contra]

2) **Recovery against social host? [§646]**
Also, virtually all courts have allowed recovery only against ***commercial*** dispensers of alcoholic beverages, rejecting liability on a private individual who serves liquor to an obviously intoxicated guest. [*See, e.g.,* **Klein v. Raysinger,** 448 A.2d 620 (Pa. 1982)]

a) **Exception—intoxicated minors [§647]**
However, several courts have imposed liability against a social host for furnishing liquor to a ***minor*** who became intoxicated and later caused injury to another in a traffic accident—at least where it is shown that the host ***knew*** that the minor would be driving a car after consuming the liquor. [*See, e.g.,* **Brockett v. Kitchen Boyd Motor Co.,** 24 Cal. App. 3d 87 (1972); Cal. Bus. & Prof. Code §25602.1; *but see* **Slicer v. Quigley,** 429 A.2d 855 (Conn. 1980)—passenger in car not liable for giving beer to 19-year-old driver, in violation of statute, because driver's voluntary consumption of the beer was proximate and superseding cause of accident; **Charles v. Seigfried,** 651 N.E.2d 154 (Ill. 1995)—denying action against social host who served alcohol to minor who then hurt herself]

b) **New exception—adults [§648]**
A few courts have extended liability to social hosts whose intoxicated adult guests have injured the plaintiff. [*See, e.g.,* **Kelly v. Gwinnell,** 476 A.2d 1219 (N.J. 1984); *but see* **Ferreira v. Strack,** 652 A.2d 965 (R.I. 1995)—contra] *But note:* A New Jersey statute has substantially limited the *Kelly* case. [N.J. Stat. Ann. §§2A:15-5.1 *et seq.*]

(4) **Distinguish—liability of tavernkeeper as land occupier [§649]**
Even in states that have retained the common law rule of no liability, a tavernkeeper may be held liable if she fails to exercise the duties required of her as a ***land occupier*** to ***business visitors*** on the premises (*see infra,* §704). Thus, if the tavernkeeper knows that one patron may become belligerent and dangerous if drunk, she must exercise due care to prevent that

person from injuring the person or property of *other patrons on the premises*, or at least warn them of the danger. [**Priewe v. Bartz,** 83 N.W.2d 116 (Minn. 1957)]

FAILURE TO CONTROL THIRD PARTIES—A SUMMARY	gilbert
TYPE OF PERSON	**LIABILITY**
BAILORS	Liable where bailee misuses goods ***in bailor's presence*** or where bailor ***negligently selected*** bailee; may also be liable for injuries involving use of an automobile under the ***family use doctrine*** or a ***permissive use statute***, even if not present or not negligent in allowing bailee to use automobile.
MASTERS (EMPLOYERS)	
• AS TO EMPLOYEES	Liable for failure to control acts done ***in employer's presence***; liable for acts performed by employee when employer ***should have foreseen*** resulting injury; liable for any act of an employee committed ***within the scope of employment***.
• AS TO INDEPENDENT CONTRACTORS	Liable for acts performed by independent contractor if act performed was ***nondelegable*** (*e.g.,* duty to maintain public premises), activity was ***dangerous***, or independent contractor was an ***apparent or ostensible agent***.
PARTNERS AND JOINT VENTURERS	Liable for conduct of others within scope of the enterprise.
PARENTS	Liable for acts of children ***only if*** statute so provides or parent was negligent in failing to: control child while ***in parent's presence***, protect or warn against child's ***known dangerous tendencies***, or prevent child from using ***inherently dangerous instrumentalities***.
TAVERNKEEPERS	Liable for acts of patrons injuring third parties if ***Dram Shop Act*** so provides or courts in jurisdiction have abandoned common law rule against such liability.

8. Duties Owed by Land Occupiers [§650]

The common law rule, and still the weight of authority, is that the general duty of due care under the circumstances does ***not*** apply to occupiers of land. Rather, land occupiers are accorded a special status that ***limits*** their liability for injuries to others arising from conditions or activities on their land. In short, land occupiers in most states do ***not*** have to conduct themselves as "reasonable persons under the circumstances"; it is sufficient that they comply with the limited duties and standards of care discussed below. (*But see* the alternative view *infra*, §718.)

a. **"Land occupier" defined [§651]**
"Land occupier" refers to the person ***in possession of the land***, whether the owner, tenant, adverse possessor, or any other type of possessor. [**Merritt v. Nickelson,** 287 N.W.2d 178 (Mich. 1980)]

b. **"Foreseeable risk" defined [§652]**
The "foreseeability" element in all the cases below is a risk of harm to either person or property interests, with the same proximate cause complexities as discussed previously where the risk foreseeable was to one type of interest (person or property) and the actual harm sustained was to the other type.

c. **Duties owed to persons outside the land**

(1) **Natural conditions [§653]**
No duty of care is owed with respect to natural conditions, such as native trees or boulders in place, in rural areas. [Rest. 2d §363]

(a) **Exception—urban areas [§654]**
A land occupier in an ***urban*** area owes a duty of due care to prevent ***native trees*** growing on her land from creating an unreasonable risk of harm to travelers on adjacent public streets. [*But see* **Meyers v. Delaney,** 529 N.W.2d 288 (Iowa 1995)—no liability to neighbor for fall of decayed tree without actual or constructive notice of danger]

(b) **Minority view [§655]**
A large minority of states hold that in both rural and urban areas, the occupier owes a duty of care to protect those outside the land from natural conditions on the land. [**Sprecher v. Adamson Cos.,** 30 Cal. 3d 358 (1981)]

(2) **Artificial conditions [§656]**
No duty is owed as to artificial conditions (buildings, excavations, fences erected, etc.) beyond what is owed for natural conditions.

(a) **Exception—conditions dangerous to adjacent occupiers [§657]**
If portions of any building, fence, etc., protrude onto or abut adjacent land, there is a duty to exercise due care to ***inspect and maintain*** the structures. [Rest. 2d §370]

(b) **Exception—conditions dangerous to users of adjacent public road [§658]**
If the conditions "substantially adjoin" a ***public road***, there is a duty to exercise due care to protect users of the road from harm; this may involve a duty to erect and maintain fences, prune plantings, etc. [Rest. 2d §368]

(3) **Activities on land [§659]**
A land occupier owes a duty not to engage in any activities (business or any

other use to which land is put) that a reasonable person would foresee as involving an unreasonable risk of harm to persons or property outside the land. Hence, a land occupier owes the same duty of due care as if she were conducting her activities in some ***neutral place.*** [**Baisley v. Missisquoi Cemetery Association,** 708 A.2d 924 (Vt. 1998)]

d. Duties owed to persons coming onto the land

(1) Ordinary trespassers

(a) "Ordinary trespassers" defined [§660]

An "ordinary trespasser" is anyone coming onto the land without the express or implied permission of the land occupier or without a legal privilege. [**Blakely v. Camp Ondessonk,** 38 F.3d 325 (7th Cir. 1994)] (*But note:* "Child trespassers" are given greater protection; *see infra*, §§674-688.)

(b) Duties owed to ordinary trespassers

1) Presence unknown [§661]

There is ***no duty*** of reasonable care owed to a trespasser whose presence on the land is unknown, nor is there a duty to discover the presence of trespassers. This is true with respect to both natural and artificial conditions, and all activities on the land. [*See, e.g.,* **Amblo's Administratrix v. Vermont Associated Petroleum Corp.,** 144 A. 460 (Vt. 1929)] There does, however, exist a duty not to *intentionally* or *wantonly* cause injury. [**Micromanolis v. The Woods School, Inc.,** 989 F.2d 696 (3d Cir. 1993)]

2) Presence known [§662]

However, if the land occupier ***knows***—or from known facts should reasonably realize—that there is a trespasser on the land, the land occupier is under a duty to exercise reasonable care (i) to warn the trespasser of, or make safe, ***artificial conditions*** that involve ***a risk of death or serious bodily harm*** and that the trespasser is unlikely to discover (*e.g.*, a concealed pit), and (ii) in carrying on ***all activities that involve any risk of harm.*** [Rest. 2d §§333, 336-338]

a) Duty to aid trespasser in peril [§663]

In addition, should a land occupier discover a trespasser trapped or injured and helpless on the occupier's land, the occupier has an ***affirmative duty*** to use reasonable efforts to aid the trespasser.

b) Same duty as that owed to licensees [§664]

Many jurisdictions impose on land occupiers the same duty

to known trespassers as they owe to licensees—*i.e.*, a duty to exercise reasonable care to warn licensees of, or make safe, ***natural or artificial conditions***, and in carrying on ***any activities***, involving ***any risk of harm known*** to the land occupier and not obvious to the reasonable entrant, including threats of harm by ***third persons*** already on the land.

3) Minority view—foreseeable trespassers [§665]

A small, but growing minority of jurisdictions are beginning to treat foreseeable trespassers as if they were "known trespassers."

(2) Constant trespassers upon a limited area ("CTULA")

(a) "CTULA" defined [§666]

CTULA refers to persons habitually intruding upon the land or a certain portion of the land—*e.g.*, those who cut across a portion of the land occupier's fields as a shortcut to town. [**Louisville & Nashville Railroad v. Spoonamore's Administrator,** 129 S.W.2d 175 (Ky. 1939)]

1) Knowledge of land occupier [§667]

The land occupier must be shown to know (or have reason to know) that persons are in the habit of cutting across her fields, etc. Physical evidence on the land ("the beaten path") will usually be sufficient to charge the land occupier with knowledge.

2) Prevention of CTULAs [§668]

The land occupier may prevent intruders from obtaining CTULA status by acts showing that she objects to the intrusion. Thus, if the land occupier posts "No Trespassing" signs on the area in which the intrusion occurs, this may be sufficient to ***convert*** persons who would otherwise qualify as CTULAs into ordinary trespassers (to whom a lower standard of care applies; *see* above), ***unless*** the intrusions still continue, and the land occupier knows this but fails to do anything further about it.

(b) Duties owed to CTULAs [§669]

A CTULA is afforded a higher duty of care than an "ordinary trespasser" on the theory that if the land occupier knows that persons are in the habit of trespassing on a section of her land and does nothing about it, their presence is at least tolerated; *i.e.*, the land occupier has given a ***type of implied consent*** to their presence.

1) Duty to discover [§670]

The land occupier owes a duty ***to discover*** whether or not CTULAs as a class are intruding.

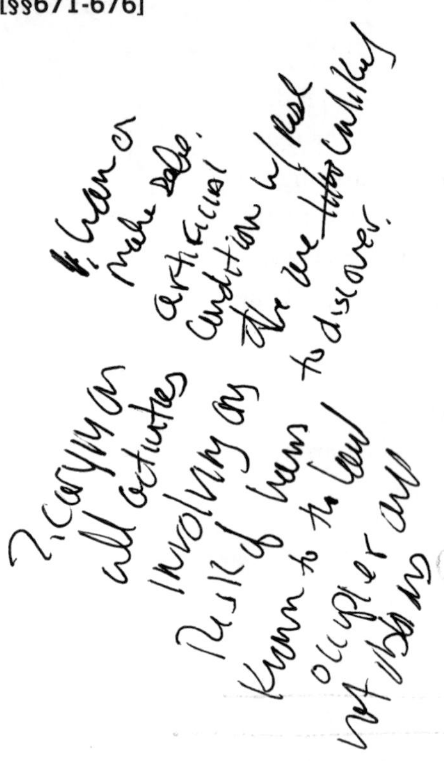

2) **Activities and artificial conditions within scope of duty [§671]**
If charged with knowledge that CTULAs are intruding, the land occupier owes a duty to exercise reasonable care (i) to warn them of, or make safe, ***artificial conditions*** that involve ***a risk of death or serious bodily harm*** and that they are unlikely to discover, and (ii) in carrying on ***all activities*** that involve ***a risk of death or serious bodily harm.*** [Rest. 2d §§334, 335]

3) **No duty regarding other conditions and activities [§672]**
With respect to ***natural conditions*** involving any risk of harm, and artificial conditions and activities threatening less than death or serious bodily injury, there is ***no duty*** owed.

4) **Same duty as that owed to licensees [§673]**
A growing minority of jurisdictions impose on land occupiers the same duty to CTULAs as they owe to licensees—*i.e.*, a duty to exercise reasonable care to warn licensees of, or make safe, ***natural or artificial conditions***, and in carrying on ***any activities***, involving ***any risk of harm known*** to the land occupier and not obvious to the reasonable entrant, including threats of harm by ***third persons*** already on the land.

(3) **Child trespassers—"attractive nuisance doctrine" [§674]**
The "attractive nuisance doctrine" imposes a special duty of care on a land occupier with respect to conditions on the land that involve a risk of harm to ***children*** unable to recognize the danger involved. [**McKiddy v. Des Moines Electric Co.,** 206 N.W. 815 (Iowa 1926); Rest. 2d §339]

(a) **Rationale**
Society has a greater interest in the safety of children than in a land occupier's right to do as she pleases with her land.

(b) **Minority view [§675]**
A few courts still reject the attractive nuisance doctrine. A few others apply the doctrine only to a hazard that has attracted the child onto the land. [**Johnson v. Bathey,** 376 So. 2d 848 (Fla. 1979); **Logan v. Old Enterprise Farms, Ltd.,** 564 N.E.2d 778 (Ill. 1990)]

(c) **"Child trespasser" defined [§676]**
To be a "child trespasser," the child must be ***so immature as to be unable to recognize the danger involved.*** In practice, beyond age 14, there are fewer conditions for which there can be recovery; and at some point (probably beyond age 16) the "child trespasser" doctrine no longer applies. [**O'Keefe v. South End Rowing Club,** 64 Cal. 2d 729 (1966)]

(d) **Duties owed to child trespassers**

1) **No obligation to discover [§677]**
A land occupier does *not* owe a duty to exercise due care to discover trespassing children on her property.

2) **Artificial conditions within scope of duty [§678]**
If a land occupier discovers children trespassing, or is charged with such knowledge, she then owes a duty to exercise due care to ***warn or protect*** them from ***artificial conditions*** involving a risk of ***death or serious bodily harm*** to children, ***provided*** [Rest. 2d §339]:

a) **Foreseeability of trespass [§679]**
The place where the condition is maintained is one where children are ***known or likely*** to trespass; ***and***

b) **Foreseeability of harm [§680]**
The land occupier knows, or has reason to know, of the existence of the artificial condition on the land, and realizes (or should realize) that it involves an ***unreasonable risk*** of death or serious bodily harm to such children; ***and***

c) **Risk outweighs utility of condition [§681]**
The ***utility to the possessor*** of maintaining the condition and the ***burden of eliminating*** the danger are ***less*** than the risk to children; ***and***

d) **Child unaware of danger [§682]**
The condition is such that children, because of their youth, will not discover it or ***will not realize the danger involved***. In other words, the condition or device that causes the injury must be unfamiliar to children of similar age—*i.e.*, "in the nature of a trap" for such children. [**Reynolds v. Willson,** 51 Cal. 2d 94 (1958)] This is usually the central dispute in litigation. [**Merrill v. Central Maine Power Co.,** 628 A.2d 1062 (Me. 1993)—nine-year-old trying to cook eel on D's live wire understood the risk]

EXAM TIP — gilbert

The question of whether a child is capable of realizing the danger is ultimately one of ***fact***. The younger the child, the more likely a condition will be held to be an "attractive nuisance." Thus, if a child is actually too young to realize the danger, even a swimming pool may be an attractive nuisance.

3) **Activities [§683]**
A land occupier's duty owed to a child trespasser regarding activities on the land depends on the child's status as an undiscovered

trespasser (***no duty***; *see supra*, §661), discovered trespasser (duty of reasonable care as to activities involving ***any risk of harm***; *see supra*, §662), or CTULA (duty of reasonable care as to activities involving ***a risk of death or serious bodily harm***; *see supra*, §671). [Rest. 2d §339 cmt. a]

4) **Application [§684]**

Using the foregoing yardstick, unattended vehicles, machinery, explosives, etc., have been held to qualify as "attractive nuisances."

a) **Distinguish—"ordinary risks" [§685]**

On the other hand, ordinary risks involved in fire, bodies of water, or falling from a height or onto an excavation or sandpile are known to young children and therefore ordinarily do ***not*** qualify. [**Holland v. Baltimore & Ohio Railroad,** 431 A.2d 597 (D.C. 1981)—moving train is a known risk to a nine-year-old child]

1/ **But note**

Even a body of water may become an attractive nuisance if some other dangerous condition is involved—*e.g.*, concealed high-suction drain at bottom of pond, or swimming pool maintained at deceptively low water level. [**Reynolds v. Willson,** *supra*]

b) **Removal of hazardous object [§686]**

Some states extend the doctrine to any harm that results when a trespassing child carries a hazardous object away from a land occupier's property. [*See, e.g.,* **Christians v. Homestake Enterprises, Ltd.,** 303 N.W.2d 608 (Wis. 1981)—blasting cap taken by child from defendant's premises later explodes]

no duty for natural conditions

5) **Distinguish—no similar duty regarding natural conditions [§687]**

A land occupier owes the above duty with respect to highly dangerous ***artificial*** conditions. No such duty is owed with respect to ***natural*** conditions. [**Loney v. McPhillips,** 521 P.2d 340 (Or. 1974)—no duty to 13-year-old who drowned in dangerous ocean cove; *but see* Rest. 2d §339—questions this limitation]

(e) **Child trespasser doctrine as defense to trespass [§688]**

The child trespasser doctrine has also been extended by a few courts to bar any action by a land occupier ***against the children*** (or their parents, where they would otherwise be liable) for damages the children cause to the property. [**Aetna Insurance Co. v. Stringham,** 440 F.2d 103 (6th Cir. 1971)—children attracted onto P's land to play in empty barn toyed with matches and burned down barn] (Compare the extraordinary liability of adult trespassers, *supra*, §203, for harm done during the trespass.)

(4) **Licensees**

(a) **"Licensee" defined [§689]**

A "licensee" is a person coming onto the land, with the express or implied ***permission*** of the land occupier, for the ***entrant's own purposes***, conferring no particular benefit on the land occupier or on any use to which the land occupier is putting the land. [**Barmore v. Elmore,** 403 N.E.2d 1355 (Ill. 1980); **Carter v. Kinney,** 896 S.W.2d 926 (Mo. 1995); Rest. 2d §330]

1) **Illustration—persons held to be "licensees" [§690]**

Licensees generally include ***social guests*** and ***visiting relatives***. [**Hall v. Duke,** 513 S.W.2d 776 (Tenn. 1974)] It also covers business visitors (*infra*, §700) or privileged entrants (*infra*, §703) who have strayed from that part of the premises to which they were invited or authorized to enter, door-to-door salespersons (unless the property is posted otherwise), and process servers. [**Prentiss v. Evergreen Presbyterian Church,** 644 So. 2d 475 (Ala. 1994)—member of local chorus allowed to use church for its rehearsals is licensee of church; **Young v. Paxton,** 873 S.W.2d 546 (Ark. 1994)—son-in-law hurt trimming trees during social visit is licensee]

2) **"Permission to enter" broadly interpreted [§691]**

The courts construe "implied permission" broadly and thus accord licensee status to many who would otherwise be outright trespassers.

---

e.g. **Example:** Persons who solicit money for charity, who come to borrow tools, or who come on personal business dealings with employees of the land occupier (*e.g.*, child bringing lunch to his father) are all held to enter with at least the implied permission of the land occupier.

(b) **Duties owed to licensees [§692]**

A land occupier owes a duty to exercise reasonable care to warn licensees of, or make safe, ***natural or artificial conditions***, and in carrying on ***activities***, involving ***any risk of harm known*** to the land occupier and not obvious to a reasonable person coming onto the land—including threats of harm by ***third persons*** already on the land. [Rest. 2d §§341, 342; *and see* **Indianapolis Street Railway v. Dawson,** 68 N.E. 909 (Ind. 1903)—where D invited P onto his premises, ***knowing*** that X was already there and that X intended to attack P, D owed duty to warn P of danger]

1) **No duty to discover danger [§693]**

Note that a land occupier is under no duty with respect to dangerous conditions or activities of which she is not actually aware. ***Nor is the land occupier under a duty to inspect*** the land to discover such dangers. [Rest. 2d §342 cmt. d]

2) **Warning usually sufficient [§694]**

A land occupier may effectively discharge the duty to licensees by posting signs, etc., warning of the danger, unless she knows such signs to be ineffective.

3) **Knowledge of licensee's presence [§695]**

Although a land occupier owes no duty to discover licensees generally, she must conduct her activities as though some licensees ***may have accepted the occupier's permission*** and entered the premises; *i.e.*, the defendant's lack of knowledge that a particular licensee was actually present is no defense, as the defendant must use reasonable care in the exercise of all activities.

(5) Invitees

(a) **"Invitee" defined [§696]**

An invitee is a person who enters by the express or implied invitation of the land occupier for some purpose ***related to the activities or interests of the land occupier.*** An invitee may be either a "public invitee" or a "business visitor," and sometimes is both. [Rest. 2d §332]

1) **"Public invitee" [§697]**

A "public invitee" is a person who is "invited" to enter or remain upon land as a member of the public for a purpose for which the land is held open to the public. [**Dowd v. Portsmouth Hospital,** 193 A.2d 788 (N.H. 1963)]

a) **"Invitation" defined [§698]**

A personal and express invitation is not required. The fact that the property is held open to the public suffices. A person who is on the land pursuant to some ***legal privilege***, however (*e.g.*, police on land under warrant, firefighter, etc.), is ***not*** an invitee (*see infra*, §§711-716).

b) **Premises need not be public [§699]**

Note that the premises involved may be either public or private: A person entering a public library (public premises) to borrow a book is an invitee, as is a person entering a drugstore (private premises) to use the public telephone. [*See, e.g.,* **Clark v. Moore Memorial United Methodist Church,** 538 So. 2d 760 (Miss. 1989)—parishioner who slips and falls while leaving Sunday School class is a public invitee]

2) **Business invitee [§700]**

A business invitee is one who enters upon the premises of another for a purpose ***connected with the business conducted on the land,*** or where it can reasonably be said that the visit may confer a business, commercial, monetary, or other tangible benefit to the landowner. [**Peterson v. Romine,** 960 P.2d 1266 (Idaho 1998)]

a) **Illustration—who is a "business invitee" [§701]**

The term "business invitee" generally covers store customers, as well as any person entering premises held open for admission (free or paid) to the general public—*e.g.,* theatres, hotels, airports, etc. [**Dickau v. Rafala,** 104 A.2d 214 (Conn. 1954)] It also covers workers, garbage collectors, etc., who come onto the land to further the use to which the land occupier is putting the premises—as well as building inspectors and similar persons, who are concerned with regulating the use. [**Holzheimer v. Johannesen,** 871 P.2d 814 (Idaho 1994)—fact question whether farmer borrowing boxes or buying them at cost was business visitor or licensee obtaining a favor from neighbor]

b) **Immaterial that business dealings fail to materialize [§702]**

The entrant need only have a ***reasonable belief*** that he is going onto the land for the purpose of business dealings with the land occupier. Even if it turns out that no such business dealings are possible, he will still qualify as an invitee. [**Chatkin v. Talarski,** 193 A. 611 (Conn. 1937)—P came into D's mortuary to inquire about engaging D's services for a friend; it later turned out the friend was alive, but P still qualified as a business visitor in the mortuary]

3) **Caution—change of status [§703]**

An invitee retains the status of an invitee ***only when he is on that part of the premises that he was invited to enter.*** If he wanders elsewhere, he becomes a licensee or perhaps even a trespasser (*e.g.,* when a store customer enters area marked "employees only").

Example: When P exceeded the scope of a limited invitation by not complying with D's request that P notify D as to when P was coming to D's home, P became a trespasser when he came onto D's land without notice. [**Buzzell v. Jones,** 556 A.2d 106 (Vt. 1989)]

(b) **Duties owed to invitees [§704]**

A land occupier owes invitees a duty to use reasonable care to ***inspect and discover*** the presence of any dangerous ***natural or artificial conditions or activities*** and to exercise due care to warn invitees of such dangers ***or make the conditions or activities safe.*** [Rest. 2d §§341A, 343; *but see* **Fleming v. Arrington,** 610 So. 2d 1160 (Ala. 1992)—no need to warn where invitee saw ants four hours before they attacked her]

1) **Warning enough? [§705]**

Traditionally, a warning will satisfy the duty owed. However, a modern trend requires the land occupier to actually make the premises safe where, under the particular facts, a warning would ***not*** render the condition or activity reasonably free from danger; *i.e.*, in some cases a mere warning will not suffice. [**Tharp v. Bunge Corp.,** 641 So. 2d 20 (Miss. 1994)—step down from building to sloping ground below was more than 30 inches, enough to be dangerous even though visible to invitee-inspector who had to maneuver down the step; **Wilk v. Georges,** 514 P.2d 877 (Or. 1973)—garden nursery operator held liable when customer slipped and fell on wet plank despite posted sign stating that area was slippery where operator had covered some planks with asphalt material but not others]

a) **Condition must present sufficient danger [§706]**

No warning at all is needed if the condition is not one that presents sufficient danger. [**Howe v. Stubbs,** 570 A.2d 1203 (Me. 1990)—no need to warn invitee of danger that car might crash into shop located on a "T" intersection at the foot of the hill where this had happened only three times in 25 years]

2) **Safeguarding activities of third persons [§707]**

A land occupier may be required to exercise reasonable care to warn or protect invitees from ***foreseeable tortious or criminal acts of third persons.***

---

e.g. **Example:** Those holding their premises open to the public for commercial purposes are charged with a duty to use due care to protect their customers—as well as licensees (*see supra*, §692)—from foreseeable injuries at the hands of third persons. [**Taco Bell, Inc. v. Lannon,** 744 P.2d 43 (Colo. 1987)—restaurant in high crime area has duty to take ***reasonable measures*** to protect patrons from consequences of armed robbery by third parties; **Delta Tau Delta v. Johnson,** 712 N.E.2d 968 (Ind. 1999)—fraternity owed female party guest a duty to take reasonable care to protect her from a foreseeable sexual assault; *but see* **Williams v. Cunningham Drug Stores, Inc.,** 418 N.W.2d 381 (Mich. 1988)—merchant in high crime area has no duty to provide armed, visible security guards to protect customers from armed robbery by third parties]

---

a) **Role of foreseeability [§708]**
In an effort to limit the liability of land occupiers for third-party crime, many courts have adopted narrow definitions of "foreseeability." In some jurisdictions, a land occupier owes a duty to protect patrons only if "he is aware of specific, imminent harm about to befall them." In others, a duty exists only in light of "evidence of previous crimes on or near the premises." In still others, the owner owes a duty to protect customers against any harm that is foreseeable under a "totality of the circumstances." [**Posecai v. Wal-Mart Stores, Inc.,** 752 So. 2d 762 (La. 1999)—P was mugged in D's parking lot and sued D for negligently failing to have a security guard posted outside the store; court held no duty because crime was not foreseeable]

b) **Specific no-duty rules [§709]**
In a further effort to limit the liability of business owners for third-party crime, some courts have adopted specific no-duty rules. Thus, a business may have no duty to comply with the demands of a thief who threatens harm to the business's patrons if his demands are not met. [**Kentucky Fried Chicken v. Superior Court,** 14 Cal. 4th 814 (1997)]

3) **Safeguarding chattels [§710]**
A land occupier who undertakes ***to supply equipment, tools, or other chattels*** to persons coming onto the premises for business purposes owes a duty to exercise due care to inspect and discover any defective condition in the chattels that she supplies. [**The Student,** 243 F. 807 (4th Cir. 1917)—D liable for furnishing unsafe scaffolding to workers on the premises]

(6) **Public entrants**

(a) **"Public entrants" defined [§711]**
"Public entrants" refers to any public employee entering land under a privilege recognized by law and irrespective of any express or implied

consent from the land occupier—*i.e.*, someone whose entry the land occupier has ***no right to prevent.***

---

e.g. **Examples:** Firefighters, police officers, sanitation inspectors, postal workers, meter readers, tax assessors, etc., are all public entrants—as long as they are acting in the scope of their official duties.

---

1) **Distinguish—private entrants [§712]**
Any "private person" entering under one of the recognized entry privileges—*e.g.*, to recapture chattels, etc. (*supra*, §238)—is treated as a ***licensee.*** [Rest. 2d §345(1)]

(b) **Duties owed to public entrants [§713]**
The duty owed to public entrants depends on the ***purpose*** of their entry.

1) **Business purpose [§714]**
If a public entrant enters for some purpose involving business dealings with the land occupier (*e.g.*, postal workers, garbage collectors, meter readers, sanitation inspectors, tax assessors, etc.), the public entrant is owed the same duties as ***invitees.*** [Rest. 2d §345 cmt. c]

2) **Nonbusiness purpose but privileged entry [§715]**
If the public entrant's entry is not for a business visit with the land occupier, but under some other privilege afforded by law (*e.g.*, entry by police to chase a burglar), most courts hold that the public entrant is entitled only to the status of ***a licensee.*** [Rest. 2d §345 cmt. c] A few consider the entrant an invitee. [**Dini v. Naiditch,** 170 N.E.2d 881 (Ill. 1960)]

a) **Distinguish—entry on business premises [§716]**
Keep in mind, however, that if the entry is on ***business premises*** (held open to the public) during normal business hours, the entrant would be treated as an ***invitee***—the same as any other member of the public. [**Meiers v. Fred Koch Brewery,** 229 N.Y. 10 (1920)—police officer entering store during business hours to make routine investigation]

(7) **Recreational land users [§717]**
Virtually every state has enacted legislation that protects owners of land against lawsuits brought by persons who have been using the land for recreational purposes, unless the owner has engaged in willful or wanton conduct. [*See, e.g.,* Cal. Civ. Code §846; **Ornelas v. Randolph,** 4 Cal. 4th 1095 (1993)]

DUTY OF LAND POSSESSOR TO THOSE ON PREMISES—STATUS APPROACH

gilbert

STATUS OF ENTRANT	DUTIES OWED: ARTIFICIAL CONDITIONS	NATURAL CONDITIONS	HARMFUL ACTIVITIES
UNDISCOVERED TRESPASSER	No duty, but may not intentionally or wantonly injure trespasser	No duty	No duty, but may not intentionally or wantonly injure trespasser
DISCOVERED OR ANTICIPATED TRESPASSER	Duty to warn of or make safe known conditions if nonobvious and ***highly*** dangerous	No duty	Duty of reasonable care
CONSTANT TRESPASSER UPON A LIMITED AREA ("CTULA")	Duty to warn of or make safe known conditions if nonobvious and ***highly*** dangerous	No duty	Duty of reasonable care
CHILD TRESPASSER (IF PRESENCE ON LAND FORESEEABLE)	Duty to warn of or protect from if foreseeable risk to child outweighs expense of eliminating danger and child would not appreciate danger	No duty	Duty of reasonable care unless undiscovered trespasser (*see supra*)
LICENSEE (INCLUDING SOCIAL GUEST)	Duty to warn of or make safe known conditions if nonobvious and dangerous	Duty to warn of or make safe known conditions if nonobvious and dangerous	Duty of reasonable care
INVITEE (*e.g.*, MEMBER OF PUBLIC, BUSINESS VISITOR)	Duty to make reasonable inspections to discover nonobvious dangerous conditions and warn of or make them safe	Duty to make reasonable inspections to discover nonobvious dangerous conditions and warn of or make them safe	Duty of reasonable care
PUBLIC ENTRANT	If on business purpose, same as invitee; otherwise, same as licensee	If on business purpose, same as invitee; otherwise, same as licensee	Duty of reasonable care (*but see* firefighter's rule, *infra*, §841)
RECREATIONAL LAND USER	No duty	No duty	Avoid willful or wanton injurious conduct

e. Alternative view—duty of land occupiers determined by reasonable person standard [§718]

About half the jurisdictions today reject all or most of the common law rules discussed above and hold that a land occupier's duty does not depend entirely on the entrant's status (*e.g.*, trespasser, licensee, invitee). Rather, the test is whether the occupier has acted as a ***reasonable person in the management of her property in view of the likelihood of injury to others*** (*i.e.*, the general duty of due care under the circumstances). [*See, e.g.,* **Rowland v. Christian,** 69 Cal. 2d 108 (1968); **Jones v. Hansen,** 867 P.2d 303 (Kan. 1994); *but see* **Carter v. Kinney,** *supra*, §689—adhering to traditional categories]

(1) Rationale

Under modern law, human safety is at least as important as a land occupier's right to act as she chooses on her land. Consequently, there is no longer any reason to immunize landowners from general negligence liability. [**Smith v. Arbaugh's Restaurant, Inc.,** 469 F.2d 97 (D.C. Cir. 1972); *but see* **Musch v. H-D Electric Cooperative, Inc.,** 460 N.W.2d 149 (S.D. 1990); **Younce v. Ferguson,** 724 P.2d 991 (Wash. 1986)—adhering to traditional analysis]

(2) Analysis—plaintiff's status only one of the "circumstances" [§719]

Under this view, the status of the plaintiff (as trespasser, licensee, invitee, etc.) may be considered, but it is no longer conclusive on the scope of duty owed by the defendant land occupier. Rather, the defendant's duty depends on all the pertinent circumstances, including—in addition to the plaintiff's status—the foreseeability of harm, the relation between the defendant's conduct and the plaintiff's injury, the moral blameworthiness attached to the defendant's conduct, the availability of insurance, and the like. [**Pagelsdorf v. Safeco Insurance Co.,** 284 N.W.2d 55 (Wis. 1979)]

(3) Note—split over trespassers [§720]

About 12 of the states that have rejected the common law status-based duties in favor of the duty of due care under the circumstances, have done so only with respect to licensees and invitees and have retained the common law duty rules with respect to trespassers (*see supra,* §§660 *et seq.*). [*See, e.g.,* **Sheets v. Ritt, Ritt & Ritt, Inc.,** 581 N.W.2d 602 (Iowa 1998)—adopting limited approach after categorizing state positions; **O'Leary v. Coenen,** 251 N.W.2d 746 (N.D. 1977)]

f. Open and obvious dangers [§721]

Some courts hold that a land occupier owes no duty to protect against dangers that are open and obvious to visitors (*e.g.*, an obviously ice-covered sidewalk). Other courts reject this rule, considering instead whether the risk was great enough that the land occupier had a ***duty to mitigate*** the risk (rather than merely warning about it) or that the entrant was ***comparatively negligent.*** [**Tharp v. Bunge Corp.,** *supra*, §705] The Second Restatement is consistent with the latter approach, stating that an occupier does not owe a duty to warn of an obvious danger (because any warning of an obvious danger is superfluous) ***unless*** the occupier should foresee harm despite the obviousness of the danger. [Rest. 2d §343A(1)]

9. Duties Owed by Entrants on Another's Land [§722]

The issue here is whether an invitee or licensee can "stand in the shoes of the land occupier" with respect to duties owed to other persons coming onto the land.

---

e.g. **Example:** D, a postal worker who is delivering a parcel to O (the land occupier) on O's premises (D thus being an invitee), negligently backs up his truck while on the land and injures P, a trespasser whose presence is not known to anyone. Is D held to the general standard of due care under the circumstances, or can he claim the restricted duty that O might assert if the trespasser were injured through O's negligence?

---

a. Prevailing view—general duty of due care applies [§723]

Although there is authority to the contrary, most courts hold that those not in possession of the land are ***not*** entitled to the advantage of the occupier's limited duty—even if the entrants have entered with the occupier's consent. The rationale is that the special policy considerations given to possessors of land do not extend to persons on the land of others. [**Musch v. H-D Electric Cooperative, Inc.,** *supra; but see* **Robbins v. Minute Tapioca Co.,** 128 N.E. 417 (Mass. 1920)—contra]

b. Restatement view—middle position [§724]

The Second Restatement provides that those on the land working for the occupier, or acting under the occupier's orders, need only meet whatever limited duty the occupier has; but others, although legally on the land, are not entitled to such protection (*i.e.,* they are subject to the general standard of due care). [Rest. 2d §§383-387]

10. Duties Owed by Lessors of Land [§725]

One who has leased possession of land to another may owe certain duties with respect to dangerous conditions on the property. And the duties may be owed not only to the lessee, but also to persons who come onto the property or pass outside it. In any case, however, the lessor's liability is ***generally limited.*** This reflects the fundamental rationale that tort liability for hazardous conditions on land is based on ***control*** of the land—so that where the defendant has transferred control to another (by lease or conveyance), special circumstances must exist to justify imposing tort liability on the lessor. [**Borders v. Roseberry,** 532 P.2d 1366 (Kan. 1975)]

a. Duties owed to persons outside the land [§726]

Suppose the lessor leases a building to a tenant. One month later, a passerby on the street is struck by an awning falling off the side of the building. Who is liable to the passerby?

(1) Dangerous conditions existing at time of transfer [§727]

Those duties that the lessor would have owed as a land occupier to persons outside the land had she retained possession *continue* for a reasonable length of time after she leases it. (*See supra*, §§653 *et seq.*)

(a) Duty to repair or warn lessee [§728]

Thus, the lessor of land owes a duty to exercise due care to discover and repair ***existing*** dangerous conditions on the land of which she has reason to know, ***or at least warn the lessee thereof***, prior to transferring possession. [**Both v. Harband**, *supra*, §371]

1) "Dangerous conditions" [§729]

"Dangerous conditions" refers to ***artificial*** conditions on the land involving ***any*** risk of harm. Most courts impose no duty with respect to natural conditions (except as to trees in urban areas adjoining public roads).

2) "Existing" dangerous conditions [§730]

"Existing" dangerous conditions include conditions that may be only ***potentially dangerous*** at the time of transfer, if they are likely to develop into actual dangers later on (*e.g.*, awning support badly rusted but not yet broken at time of transfer).

(b) Duration of duty limited [§731]

The lessor's duty to persons outside the land continues only until the lessee has had a ***reasonable opportunity*** to discover the condition and remedy it (*e.g.*, if the transferor warned the transferee at the time of transfer, the duty continues only through that period of time required to repair). After such period, the lessee's own negligence—as a land occupier—is regarded as a ***superseding cause*** of any injury suffered by persons outside the land from that condition.

1) Distinguish—deliberate concealment [§732]

However, if the lessor actively concealed the danger, her liability continues until the lessee ***actually discovers*** the danger and has a reasonable time to remedy it.

b. Duties owed to lessee

(1) Dangerous conditions existing at time of transfer [§733]

Whether the lessor owes any duty to the lessee depends on whether the dangerous condition is apparent (patent) or concealed (latent).

(a) Patent dangers—no duty [§734]

With regard to dangerous conditions (artificial or natural) that are reasonably apparent, there is ***no duty*** owed; *i.e.*, the lessor has no obligation to repair the condition or even warn the lessee of its existence. And if the condition is such that a reasonable person would have been aware of it (*e.g.*, excavation in backyard, missing banister on stairway, etc.), the lessee will be charged with such knowledge. [**Kearns v. Smith,** 55 Cal. App. 2d 532 (1942)]

(b) Latent dangers—duty to repair or warn [§735]

However, as to concealed or hidden dangerous conditions (artificial or natural) that involve ***any*** risk of harm and that are ***known to the lessor,*** there is a ***duty to repair or warn*** the lessee. [**Smith v. Green,** 260 N.E.2d 656 (Mass. 1970)]

1) No duty to investigate [§736]

Note that the duty here is limited to conditions of which the lessor was aware at the time of transfer. The lessor is under no duty to inspect or investigate for defects in the absence of some reason to believe that there is a danger. [**Newman v. Golden,** 144 A. 467 (Conn. 1929)]

(2) Dangerous conditions arising after transfer [§737]

Having transferred possession of the premises to the lessee, the lessor owes ***no duty*** with respect to dangerous conditions arising after the transfer—subject to the exceptions noted below.

(a) Exception—lessor negligent in making repairs [§738]

To the extent that the lessor has undertaken to repair dangerous conditions that arose after transfer, and has done so negligently, she is liable for any injuries attributable to that negligence (*e.g.*, where landlord attempts to repair water heater, but does so negligently, causing scalding water to injure tenant). Note that liability will be imposed whether the lessor undertook the repairs gratuitously, pursuant to an obligation under the lease, or because of a statutory duty to repair.

(b) Exception—lessor fails to make repairs as covenanted in lease

1) Traditional view—no tort liability [§739]

Until recently, most courts followed the "***nonfeasance vs. misfeasance***" distinction (discussed *supra*, §§572, 576-577) in cases where a lessor failed to make repairs as covenanted in the lease—so that the landlord's total failure to repair was considered "***nonfeasance,***" which would not support tort liability. [*See, e.g.,* **Jacobson v. Leventhal,** 148 A. 281 (Me. 1930)]

2) Modern trend—tort liability applies [§740]

Today, many courts allow recovery in tort against a landlord who has failed to undertake repairs required by the lease. [**Faber v. Creswick,** 156 A.2d 252 (N.J. 1959); Rest. 2d §357]

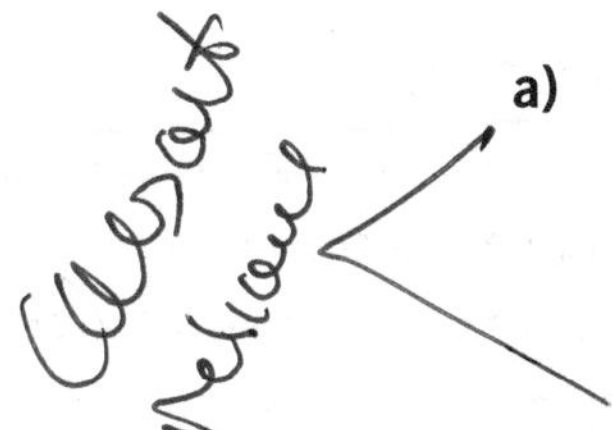

a) **Rationale**

The lessor's covenant to repair is the kind of promise upon which the lessee had a ***right to rely*** in refraining from making the needed repairs himself.

b) **Statutory developments [§741]**

Moreover, statutes increasingly require a landlord to maintain rented premises in a safe condition, and some courts hold that the landlord's failure to make repairs is a violation of her statutory duty (*i.e.*, "negligence per se"). [**Daniels v. Brunton,** 80 A.2d 547 (N.J. 1951)]

c) **Distinguish—gratuitous promises [§742]**

However, if the landlord's promise to repair was ***gratuitous*** (not required by lease or statute), most courts will ***not*** impose tort liability, on the ground that the tenant's reliance here is not as justifiable as where the landlord was legally obligated to make the repairs. [Rest. 2d §357 cmt. b]

d) **Caution—knowledge and opportunity to repair required [§743]**

Remember that even if there is a basis for allowing recovery in tort, any landlord's liability is always contingent on showing that she ***knew or should have known*** of the defective condition (*e.g.*, as by tenant complaints), ***and*** that she had a ***reasonable opportunity*** prior to the injury to make the repairs.

(c) **Minority view—general duty of care [§744]**

A number of states hold that a lessor owes a lessee a duty of ordinary care in all cases. Issues of notice of a defect, its obviousness, and control of the premises are considered in these states only in defining the care that is owed. [*See, e.g.,* **Pagelsdorf v. Safeco Insurance Co.,** *supra,* §719]

c. **Duties owed to third persons coming onto land with lessee's express or implied consent [§745]**

Suppose the lessor leases land to the tenant, who invites the plaintiff onto the premises, and the plaintiff is injured by a dangerous condition on the land.

(1) **Traditional view—no tort liability for lessor [§746]**

The early view held that with the exception of leases contemplating the entry of many people, the lessor owed ***no duty*** to third persons coming onto the premises, on the theory that there was no "privity" between the lessor and the injured party. [**McKenzie v. Cheetham,** 22 A. 469 (Me. 1891)]

(2) Modern trend—same duty as owed to lessee [§747]
Today, many courts treat third persons who enter the premises with the express or implied consent of the lessee as falling within the scope of the lessor's general tort liability. Thus, to the extent the lessor owes a duty of care to the lessee (*supra*), she also owes a similar duty to persons entering the premises with the lessee's express or implied consent.

(a) Latent dangers [§748]
Hence, a landlord's liability with respect to ***known, latent defects*** (*see supra*, §735) would extend to both the tenant and the tenant's guests or visitors, if injured thereby. [**Scholey v. Steele,** 59 Cal. App. 2d 402 (1943); Rest. 2d §358]

1) Duration of liability [§749]
The lessor's liability terminates when the tenant has had sufficient opportunity to discover and remedy the dangerous condition. At that point, the tenant's own breach of duty (as land occupier) to visitors is regarded as a ***superseding cause*** of injuries suffered by the visitors. [Rest. 2d §353(2); *and see* **Borders v. Roseberry,** *supra*, §725—lessor not liable to tenant's social guest who fell on icy steps because tenant knew of condition and should have warned guest]

(b) Failure to make promised repairs [§750]
Moreover, jurisdictions that hold the lessor liable in tort for failing to make repairs as required by the lease or statute (above), generally hold the lessor liable to third persons coming onto the leased premises with the tenant's consent. [**Krieger v. Ownership Corp.,** 270 F.2d 265 (3d Cir. 1959)]

EXAM TIP **gilbert**

If the tenant's guest is injured by a dangerous condition on the premises, the landlord may be liable as ***lessor*** of the premises. But don't stop your analysis there—remember that the ***tenant may also be liable*** to the guest because of the tenant's status as the ***occupier*** of the premises (*see supra*, §§650 *et seq.*).

d. Duties owed where lessor has retained control of common areas [§751]
Where the leased premises consist of multiple units (*e.g.*, office building, apartment house, etc.), the lessor normally retains control of common areas (*e.g.*, lobbies, hallways, elevators, stairways, restrooms). As to such areas, the lessor is regarded as the ***land occupier*** and owes whatever duties of care a land occupier would owe—both to tenants in the building ***and*** to persons entering the premises as guests or business visitors of the tenants. [**Taneian v. Meghrigian,** 104 A.2d 689 (N.J. 1954)]

(1) **Duty to safeguard against crime? [§752]**
Several courts have enlarged this duty to include taking ***reasonable precautions against foreseeable criminal acts of third parties***—*e.g.*, installing a security guard service to protect against muggings and robberies in hallways of an apartment house where criminal acts had occurred frequently, or replacing faulty deadbolt locks. [**Kline v. 1500 Massachusetts Avenue Apartment Corp.,** 439 F.2d 477 (D.C. Cir. 1970); *but see* **Rowe v. State Bank of Lombard,** 531 N.E.2d 1358 (Ill. 1988)—no duty unless landlord voluntarily assumes it]

e. **Duty owed where lessor has right to control dangerous activity or condition created by tenant [§753]**
If the landlord has ***actual knowledge*** that a tenant has created a dangerous condition or activity on the premises, ***plus*** the right to terminate the dangerous condition or activity, the landlord is under a duty to exercise due care to prevent the condition or activity from injuring third persons.

---

e.g. **Example:** A landlord has been held liable for failure to remove a tenant's vicious dog, which attacked a young child playing with the tenant's children. The court found that the landlord knew of previous attacks by the dog. The landlord's right to terminate a tenant's lease on two weeks' notice was deemed a sufficient right to remove the dog. [**Uccello v. Laudenslayer,** 44 Cal. App. 3d 504 (1975); *and see* **Gallick v. Barto,** 828 F. Supp. 1168 (M.D. Pa. 1993)—landlord had duty to begin eviction proceedings against tenant whose ferret later bit plaintiff; *but see* **Frobig v. Gordon,** 881 P.2d 226 (Wash. 1994)—no duty on landlord to protect third person from tenant's dangerous tiger]

---

11. **Duties Owed by Sellers of Land [§754]**
Under the same rationale that justifies limiting a lessor's liability—*i.e.,* that control has been transferred to another (*see supra*, §725)—the general rule is that after possession has been transferred, sellers of land are ***not*** liable for harm suffered by those on or outside the premises. [**Preston v. Goldman,** 42 Cal. 3d 108 (1986)]

a. **Exception—failure to disclose latent dangerous conditions [§755]**
However, a seller who fails to disclose ***known*** dangerous conditions is liable to those harmed thereby—including the buyer, the buyer's family, and third persons entering the land with the buyer's consent. [Rest. 2d §353] *Rationale:* Failure to warn is tantamount to a type of fraud.

b. **Exception—persons outside the premises [§756]**
And if the property sold contained an unreasonable risk of harm to persons outside the premises, the seller will remain liable for a reasonable period after the transfer of possession. [**Derby v. Public Service Co.,** 119 A.2d 335 (N.H. 1955)]

c. **Duration of liability under exceptions [§757]**
Generally, the seller's liability lasts only until the buyer has had a reasonable

time to discover and remedy the condition. But if the seller ***actively concealed*** the hazardous situation, liability continues until the buyer ***actually discovers*** the danger and has a reasonable opportunity to remedy it. [**Narsh v. Zirbser Bros.,** 268 A.2d 46 (N.J. 1970)]

12. Duties Owed by Bailors of Chattels [§758]

Although this is really part of "Products Liability," discussed *infra*, §§925 *et seq*., it is worth noting at this point that the bailor of a chattel owes a certain duty of care (negligence liability) with respect to the condition of the chattel. The duty is owed both to the bailee and to all other persons within the foreseeable scope of use of the chattel (*e.g.*, pedestrians on the streets where a bailed auto may be driven). The ***scope*** of the bailor's duty depends on the ***nature*** of the bailment, and in this regard, it is analogous to that owed by a land occupier (*supra*).

a. Gratuitous bailment [§759]

If the bailment is gratuitous, the bailor owes a duty only to ***warn of known***, ***concealed*** defects (analogous to the duty owed by a land occupier to a licensee). [**Hills v. Lyons Plumbing & Heating Co.,** 457 S.W.2d 503 (Ky. 1970)]

b. Bailments for hire [§760]

A greater duty is owed in the case of bailments for hire. Here, the bailor must exercise due care not only to warn of known, concealed defects, but also to make a ***reasonable inspection*** of the chattel before bailing it in order to determine its safety (analogous to the duty owed by a land occupier to an invitee). [**Collette v. Page,** 114 A. 136 (R.I. 1921)]

(1) Warning may not discharge duty [§761]

Unlike gratuitous bailment cases, the bailor's warning to the bailee may ***not*** be enough to discharge this duty to third persons injured by the bailee's use of a defective chattel. Indeed, a number of modern courts impose ***strict liability*** in tort against commercial bailors (*see infra*, §994). [**Price v. Shell Oil Co.,** 2 Cal. 3d 245 (1970)]

13. Duties Relating to Emotional Distress

a. Traditional view—nature of duty owed [§762]

The traditional view rejects a duty of due care to prevent infliction of emotional distress on others as such. Rather, the duty owed is to exercise due care not to subject others to a risk of physical injury, through physical impact or threat thereof, that might foreseeably result in emotional distress *and* consequent physical injuries to them. [**Battalla v. State,** 10 N.Y.2d 237 (1961)] In most jurisdictions, however, the duty has been broadened (*see infra*).

(1) Distinguish—recovery as parasitic damages [§763]

Remember that where physical injury (*e.g.*, battery) is ***accompanied by*** emotional distress, damages for the distress are recoverable as part of the action for personal injury. In the usual negligence case, pain and "suffering" may include emotional distress related to the physical injury.

EXAM TIP **gilbert**

Keep in mind that the torts for infliction of emotional distress are not the only means of recovering damages for emotional distress. If physical injury has been caused by commission of another tort, plaintiff can ***"tack on" damages for emotional distress*** as a "parasitic" element of his physical injury damages, without the need to consider the elements of the emotional distress torts.

b) **Actual or threatened physical impact [§764]**

The early view required the plaintiff to show that the defendant, by failing to exercise the due care required above, subjected the plaintiff to *actual* physical impact. Today, however, in most states a *threat* of impact to the plaintiff (*i.e.*, plaintiff is within the "zone of danger" from defendant's negligent conduct) will suffice. [**Falzone v. Busch,** 214 A.2d 12 (N.J. 1965); **Battalla v. State,** *supra*]

(1) **Minority view—impact; physical injuries [§765]**

A few states continue to adhere to some version of the impact rule. [*See, e.g.,* **Ruttger Hotel Corp. v. Wagner,** 691 So. 2d 1177 (Fla. 1997)—guests pushed back into their rooms by armed robbers could not recover for emotional distress against hotel for its lack of security because of failure to meet impact rule; **Ross v. Cheema,** 716 N.E.2d 435 (Ind. 1999)—loud pounding on front door, opening of screen door, and attempting to turn knob on main door do not provide required impact; *but see* **Conder v. Wood,** 716 N.E.2d 432 (Ind. 1999)—pedestrian who pounded on side of truck to alert driver that he had run over pedestrian's companion met the state's "modified impact" rule] Moreover, some states require some physical injury to ground an action for negligent infliction of emotional distress. But even these states do not require that this physical injury be shown to have caused the emotional distress. [*See, e.g.,* **Roling v. Daily,** 596 N.W.2d 72 (Iowa 1999)—truck driver who suffered some physical injury when negligent driver crashed into truck may recover for emotional distress at seeing mangled body of the negligent driver, even though emotional distress was not related to the truck driver's physical injury]

(2) **Distinguish—intentional cases [§766]**

Intentional infliction of emotional distress does not require physical impact, or even threat of physical impact, to the plaintiff. (*See supra,* §§79-99.)

(3) **Limitation—exposure cases [§767]**

"Mere exposure" to a toxic substance or infectious disease does ***not*** qualify as "impact," ***unless***—in some jurisdictions—the plaintiff accurately knows of the exposure and has a "serious fear" that she is "more likely than not" to develop the harm caused by the substance or disease. [**Metro-North Commuter Railroad v. Buckley,** 521 U.S. 424 (1997)—asbestos exposure not adequate; **Potter v. Firestone Tire & Rubber Co.,** 6 Cal. 4th 965 (1993)—fear of cancer from asbestos exposure insufficient without proof that cancer was more likely than not to occur]

(a) AIDS cases [§768]

If a plaintiff comes in contact with someone with AIDS, there will be a sufficient threat of impact only if the plaintiff was ***actually exposed*** to the virus. It is not enough that the plaintiff fears that the contact resulted in transmission. [**Brzoska v. Olson,** 668 A.2d 1355 (Del. 1995)—treatment of plaintiff patient by an AIDS-infected physician or dentist is not enough; **K.A.C. v. Benson,** 527 N.W.2d 553 (Minn. 1995); *but see* **Faya v. Almaraz,** 620 A.2d 327 (Md. 1993)—permitting recovery for emotional distress during window of uncertainty before negative test results received; **Williamson v. Waldman,** 696 A.2d 14 (N.J. 1997)—rejecting a requirement of actual exposure to HIV in favor of asking what reasonable well-informed citizens might fear]

(4) Exception—no "zone of danger" requirement [§769]

In a few categories of cases, courts have allowed claims for stand-alone emotional distress to go forward without the "zone of danger" limitation. [*See, e.g.,* **Corgan v. Muehling,** 574 N.E.2d 602 (Ill. 1991)—court imposed a duty on defendant psychologist who had sexual relations with a patient, although the patient never felt a threat to her safety]

(a) False death reports and corpse cases [§770]

Some states following the general view allow recovery for emotional distress without requiring that the plaintiff be within the zone of danger under two circumstances: erroneously reporting a relative's death or mishandling the corpse of a relative. *Rationale:* These cases involve a special likelihood of genuine and serious mental distress, which guarantees that the plaintiff's claim is not fictitious.

---

e.g. **Examples—false death report:** D hospital negligently notifies P, a close relative of a living patient, that the patient has died. P may recover for emotional distress. [**Johnson v. State,** 37 N.Y.2d 378 (1975); *but see* **O'Brien v. Western Union Telegraph Co.,** 113 F.2d 539 (1st Cir. 1940)—most states following the general rule do not recognize this exception]

---

e.g. **Examples—corpse mishandling:** Court imposed a duty where D's lack of due care caused the corpse of P's deceased husband to be mutilated or injured in public. [**Cohen v. Groman Mortuary, Inc.,**

231 Cal. App. 2d 1 (1964); *but see* **Dunahoo v. Bess,** 200 So. 541 (Fla. 1941)—rejecting this rule] Courts have also imposed a duty of reasonable care on a mortuary that sent a stranger's leg to P in the package that was supposed to contain the personal effects of P's deceased father. [**Gammon v. Osteopathic Hospital of Maine, Inc.,** 534 A.2d 1282 (Me. 1987)]

---

c. Injury or threat of injury to another (bystander recovery)

(1) Older view rejects duty [§771]

The older view requires a showing that the defendant's negligence endangered the plaintiff personally. The plaintiff must be in the "zone of danger" to recover for physical manifestations resulting from emotional distress. [**Bovsun v. Sanperi,** 61 N.Y.2d 219 (1984)—requiring zone of danger but not physical manifestation] This rule prevents plaintiffs from recovering in cases in which they were not personally at risk. [**Williams v. Baker,** 572 A.2d 1062 (D.C. 1990)—mother could not recover for harm she sustained after witnessing effect of malpractice D committed on her young son]

(2) Broader view [§772]

But a growing and substantial number of states permit the plaintiff to recover for severe emotional distress—with or without physical manifestation—where the defendant's negligence injures or threatens a member of the plaintiff's family, but not the plaintiff. [**Dillon v. Legg,** 68 Cal. 2d 728 (1968)—mother may recover for emotional distress and consequent physical injury resulting from seeing her child run over in a traffic accident]

(a) Determinative factors under broader view [§773]

Under this view, the plaintiff must meet three requirements [**Thing v. La Chusa,** 48 Cal. 3d 644 (1989)—these are requirements, not just guidelines]:

1) Close relationship [§774]

The plaintiff and the victim must have been closely related. [**Elden v. Sheldon,** 46 Cal. 3d 267 (1988)—no recovery for seeing injury to long-term live-in lover; *but see* **Dunphy v. Gregor,** 642 A.2d 372 (N.J. 1994)—contra; **Leong v. Takasaki,** 520 P.2d 758 (Haw. 1974)—recognizing family relationship between child and stepfather's mother]

2) Physical proximity and contemporaneous observance [§775]

The plaintiff must be at the scene of the accident that injures the victim and must be aware at that time that the victim is suffering from injuries. [**Thing v. La Chusa,** *supra*—no recovery to mother who was not present at scene when accident occurred]

a) **"Contemporaneous" [§776]**

In some states, this need not mean simultaneous. [**Corso v. Merrill,** 406 A.2d 300 (N.H. 1979)—father viewed injured daughter after wife's screams summoned him to scene]

b) **Note**

In some states, the other person need not in fact have been seriously hurt. It is enough if the plaintiff reasonably believes that the type of accident observed would seriously harm those involved. [**Barnhill v. Davis,** 300 N.W.2d 104 (Iowa 1981)]

3) **Suffer extraordinary emotional distress [§777]**

The plaintiff must suffer distress beyond that likely to be suffered by an unrelated bystander who sees the accident. [**Thing v. La Chusa,** *supra*]

(b) **Foreseeability (minority) [§778]**

A few jurisdictions analyze the specific circumstances for foreseeability in a traditional negligence review rather than requiring the three determinative elements set out above. [**Ferriter v. Daniel O'Connell's Sons, Inc.,** 413 N.E.2d 690 (Mass. 1980)—allowing recovery to children who first viewed father's injuries at hospital where he was taken following industrial accident; *but see* **Stockdale v. Bird & Son, Inc.,** 503 N.E.2d 951 (Mass. 1987)—denying recovery to mother who did not learn of accident for several hours and did not see body for 24 hours]

(c) **Limitation [§779]**

The plaintiff's rights may be derivative only. Even where recovery by a third person (parent) is permitted, the right of action is generally *derivative*; *i.e.*, it is dependent upon the imperiled person's (child's) right to recover. Thus, if the defendant was found not liable for the harm to the child (*e.g.*, because of the child's contributory negligence), the parent would not be permitted to recover for emotional distress in witnessing the child's injury. [**Dillon v. Legg,** *supra*]

d. **Damage to property [§780]**

Most cases deny plaintiff recovery for emotional distress *and* consequential injuries when property interests are negligently damaged or threatened. [*See, e.g.,* **City of Tyler v. Likes,** 962 S.W.2d 489 (Tex. 1997)—adopting "overwhelming majority" view that recovery for property damages and economic harm suffices where D's negligence has harmed P's home, and that damages for emotional distress are not recoverable; **Erlich v. Menezes,** 21 Cal. 4th 543 (1999)—same; *but see* **Rasmussen v. Benson,** 280 N.W. 890 (Neb. 1938)—P's cattle were fed poisoned bran through D's negligence; P suffered emotional distress *and* subsequent heart trouble from fear that he had sold poisoned milk to customers and that it would ruin his dairy business]

(1) **Pets [§781]**

Most courts deny recovery for emotional distress caused by the death of a pet. [*See, e.g.,* **Nichols v. Sukaro Kennels,** 555 N.W.2d 689 (Iowa 1996)—death of dog; **Fackler v. Genetzky,** 595 N.W.2d 884 (Neb. 1999)—death of two horses; *but see* **Campbell v. Animal Quarantine Station,** 632 P.2d 1066 (Haw. 1981)—recovery to family that learned over telephone that pet dog had been killed]

e. **Resulting physical manifestation required [§782]**

The general view requires that the emotional distress be shown by ***tangible physical manifestation*** in the plaintiff (*e.g.,* miscarriage, nervous breakdown, paralysis, etc.). [**Nancy P. v. D'Amato,** 517 N.E.2d 824 (Mass. 1988); **Muchow v. Lindblad,** 435 N.W.2d 918 (N.D. 1989); **Reilly v. United States,** 547 A.2d 894 (R.I. 1988)—identifying as majority rule; Rest. 2d §436A]

(1) **Rationale**

Proof of physical manifestation is insisted upon by most courts to preclude the likelihood of fraudulent claims (*i.e.,* simulated emotional distress) and unlimited liability.

(2) **Minority view—no resulting physical manifestation [§783]**

A growing minority view allows recovery for severe emotional distress ***without*** physical manifestation or threat of injury to the plaintiff. [**Johnson v. Ruark Obstetrics & Gynecology Associates,** 395 S.E.2d 85 (N.C. 1990)—negligence producing foreseeable and actual "severe" emotional distress suffices without proof of physical manifestation in suit against physician by parents of stillborn fetus; **Bowen v. Lumbermens Mutual Casualty Co.,** 517 N.W.2d 432 (Wis. 1994)—no requirement of physical manifestation where mother sues for distress when child was killed]

(3) **Minority view—property damage [§784]**

A small minority permits recovery of emotional distress without physical manifestation for negligent destruction of a plaintiff's property. [**Rodrigues v. State,** 472 P.2d 509 (Haw. 1970)—recovery permitted for emotional distress alone where D's negligence permitted six inches of water to enter house that P had just finished building with his own hands; *but see* **Day v. Montana Power Co.,** 789 P.2d 1224 (Mont. 1990)—emotional distress alone insufficient in suit by restaurant owner for negligent destruction of his restaurant]

f. **"Severe" emotional distress required [§785]**

In most states, courts permit a plaintiff to succeed in a claim of negligent infliction of emotional distress only if a ***normally constituted person would have suffered,*** and the plaintiff actually did suffer, *severe* emotional distress. [**Bovsun v. Sanperi,** *supra,* §771]

(1) **"Eggshell psyche" plaintiffs [§786]**

The requirement that a normally constituted person would have suffered severe emotional distress does not preclude consideration of a plaintiff's *particular emotional vulnerability* in two respects:

(a) **Defendant's knowledge of special vulnerability [§787]**

If the defendant knew or should have known that the plaintiff is especially vulnerable, the defendant will be liable even though a normally constituted person would not have suffered severe distress. [**Corgan v. Muehling,** *supra*, §769]

(b) **Damages [§788]**

If the defendant's conduct would have caused severe emotional distress to a normally constituted person, the plaintiff may recover the *full extent* of her emotional distress injuries, even if beyond what a normally constituted person would have suffered. This rule is an extension of the "thin-skull" or "eggshell skull" rule for proximate cause (*see supra*, §471).

COMPARISON OF EMOTIONAL DISTRESS TORTS — gilbert

	INTENTIONAL INFLICTION OF EMOTIONAL DISTRESS	NEGLIGENT INFLICTION OF EMOTIONAL DISTRESS
CONDUCT REQUIRED	***Extreme and outrageous*** conduct by defendant	Subjecting plaintiff to ***physical impact*** or threat of impact
FAULT REQUIRED	***Intent*** to cause severe emotional distress or recklessness as to the effect of conduct	***Negligence*** in creating risk of physical injury to plaintiff
CAUSATION AND DAMAGES	Defendant's conduct must cause ***severe emotional distress***	In most jurisdictions, defendant's conduct generally must cause ***tangible physical manifestation*** (*e.g.*, nervous breakdown, miscarriage)
BYSTANDER RECOVERY WHEN ANOTHER PHYSICALLY INJURED	Plaintiff bystander must be ***present*** when injury occurs and be a ***close relative*** of the injured person, and defendant must ***know*** these facts when he intentionally injures the other person (or defendant must have ***intended*** to cause plaintiff distress)	Under older view, plaintiff bystander must be within the ***"zone of danger"*** created by defendant's negligent conduct (*i.e.*, must be subjected to threat of impact). Broader views allow recovery to plaintiffs who are present and perceive harm to ***family members*** caused by defendant's conduct even when the plaintiff was never endangered

14. **Duty Not To Cause Purely Economic Loss [§789]**

The general rule is that a defendant owes no common law tort duty of care not to cause purely economic loss to another. This is commonly referred to as the ***"economic loss rule."***

a. **Limited exceptions [§790]**

Courts do, however, allow such recovery in limited circumstances. This Summary discusses these circumstances in sections covering the torts of defamation (*see infra*, §§1352 *et seq.*), wrongful invasion of privacy (*see infra*, §§1544 *et seq.*), misrepresentation (*see infra*, §§1622 *et seq.*), injurious falsehood (*see infra*, §§1684 *et seq.*), and interference with economic relations (*see infra*, §§1710 *et seq.*).

> e.g. **Example:** P airport is forced to close due to D railroad's negligence in wrecking a train carrying toxic chemicals. P may not recover economic damages resulting from the closure. [**People Express Airlines, Inc. v. Consolidated Rail Corp.,** 495 A.2d 107 (N.J. 1985)]

D. Defenses to Negligence

1. **Contributory Negligence**

a. **"Contributory negligence" defined [§791]**

Contributory negligence is conduct on the part of a plaintiff that is a ***contributing cause to her own injuries***, and that falls below the standard to which she is required to conform for her own protection. [Rest. 2d §463]

> **EXAM TIP** — **gilbert**
>
> Be careful to note the difference between contributory negligence and the doctrine of avoidable consequences. As previously discussed (*see supra*, §531), a plaintiff is required to exercise reasonable care to mitigate damages and cannot recover for "avoidable consequences"—*e.g.*, aggravated or increased injuries that could have been avoided by seeking reasonable medical care. But this is a ***rule of damages***; it has nothing to do with contributory negligence because the plaintiff's failure to mitigate damages ***in no way caused or contributed to the original accident***. Avoidable consequences operates only to reduce the ***amount*** of damages that the plaintiff can recover, whereas contributory negligence may be a ***complete defense*** to the plaintiff's claim (*see below*).

b. **Prima facie case [§792]**

The prima facie case for contributory negligence is similar to the prima facie case for negligence, except that the duty here is not owed to any other person; rather, it is a duty to exercise due care in the circumstances to avoid ***one's own*** injury at the hands of another. Also, there is ***no*** requirement of an "act"; the duty of self-protection always exists and is often violated by ***unreasonable inaction*** in the face of danger.

(1) **General standard of care [§793]**

The plaintiff's conduct is always measured by what the reasonable person would have done ***under the same or similar circumstances.*** [**Solgaard v. Guy F. Atkinson Co.,** 6 Cal. 3d 361 (1971)]

(a) **Application—emergency cases [§794]**

Thus, if the plaintiff is confronted with an emergency not of her own making, her conduct is compared to what a reasonable person would do in such an emergency. For example, where the plaintiff is faced with ***imminent peril*** to herself (or to a third person), she may assume extraordinary risks or perform dangerous acts in attempting to avoid the peril (or to rescue the third person) without being held contributorily negligent. [**Eckert v. Long Island Railroad,** 43 N.Y. 502 (1871)]

(b) **Application—children [§795]**

Courts differ over whether acts of children may be examined for contributory negligence. Most modern courts instruct the jury to consider the behavior of the plaintiff in light of her age and other circumstances [**Lester v. Sayles,** 850 S.W.2d 858 (Mo. 1993)—child age 4.75 years may be found contributorily negligent], while others follow the rule that assigns presumptions, varying with age, that a child is incapable of negligence [*see, e.g.,* **Glorioso v. YMCA,** 556 So. 2d 293 (Miss. 1989)—nine-year-old child presumptively incapable of contributory negligence; **Price v. Kitsap Transit,** 886 P.2d 556 (Wash. 1994)].

(c) **Application—forgetfulness [§796]**

Momentary forgetfulness is not contributory negligence as a matter of law but is a question for the jury. [**Cohen v. St. Regis Paper Co.,** 65 N.Y.2d 752 (1985)]

(d) **Exception [§797]**

In some states, an adult plaintiff who is unstable need only act reasonably within her limits. [**Tobia v. Cooper Hospital University Medical Center,** 643 A.2d 1 (N.J. 1994)—where duty includes exercise of care to prevent elderly patient from engaging in self-damaging conduct, patient's engaging in such conduct cannot be raised as contributory negligence]

(2) **Statutory standards of care [§798]**

Another significant factor is whether the plaintiff has complied with statutes enacted for her own protection, and if not, whether the violation of such statutes will necessarily affect her claim.

(a) **"Contributory negligence per se" [§799]**

Where the plaintiff has violated a statute designed for her own protection as well as the protection of others (*e.g.*, speed or traffic laws), the violation by itself may establish duty and breach. [Rest. 2d §469]

(b) **Violation must be contributing cause [§800]**

In any case, however, the violation must be a contributing cause to the accident; *e.g.*, driving without a valid driver's license is ***not*** contributory negligence. [**Moore v. Hart,** 188 S.W. 861 (Ky. 1916); **Crawford v. Halkovics,** 438 N.E.2d 890 (Ohio 1982)]

(c) **Exception—plaintiff member of class needing special protection [§801]**

If it is shown that the plaintiff is a member of a special class sought to be protected by the statute—so that the statutory objective would be defeated if the plaintiff's fault were held to be a defense—the plaintiff's violation of the statute may be ***disregarded.*** [**Chainani v. Board of Education,** 87 N.Y.2d 370 (1995)—school bus driver violating statute requiring use of lights and waiting until passenger has crossed the street may not use child's contributory negligence as defense]

c. **Common law effect of contributory negligence [§802]**

At traditional common law, a plaintiff's contributory negligence was an ***absolute and complete bar*** to any recovery for the negligence of the defendant. And this was true even if the plaintiff's negligence was very slight when compared to the negligence of the defendant. [Rest. 2d §467]

(1) **Defense only to negligence [§803]**

Contributory negligence was a defense ***only to negligence.*** It was no defense at all to intentional torts [**Tratchel v. Essex Group, Inc.,** 452 N.W.2d 171 (Iowa 1990)] or to recklessness. (As to its role in strict liability, *see infra*, §920.)

(2) **Note**

By judicial or legislative action, almost every state has adopted comparative negligence. (*See infra*, §815.)

d. **Exception—last clear chance doctrine [§804]**

To soften the "complete defense" rule for contributory negligence, courts held that a plaintiff's contributory negligence would not bar or reduce recovery if the defendant, immediately prior to the accident, had the "last clear chance" to avoid the accident and failed to do so (*but see infra*, §824). [**Davies v. Mann,** 152 Eng. Rep. 588 (1842)] *Rationale:* In these cases, the plaintiff's contributory negligence placed her in a position of either "***helpless***" or "***inattentive***" peril.

(1) **"Helpless peril" cases [§805]**

In a "helpless peril" situation, the plaintiff—through her contributory negligence—had placed herself in a position of danger from which she was ***powerless to extricate*** herself by the exercise of reasonable care. In other words, even though the plaintiff was aware of the danger, the only remaining opportunity to avert the peril rested with the defendant (*e.g.*, while plaintiff was carelessly running across a busy street she fell and sprained her ankle). Most courts allowed recovery if the defendant had ***actual knowledge*** of the plaintiff's peril or should have had such knowledge—and was negligent thereafter.

(2) **"Inattentive peril" cases [§806]**

In an "inattentive peril" case, the plaintiff, through contributory negligence, placed herself in a situation of peril, but from which she ***could*** have extricated herself by the exercise of reasonable care practically up to the moment of injury but did not because she was unaware that the harm was about to occur (*e.g.*, she crossed the street without looking for oncoming cars; had she been paying attention, she would have discovered defendant motorist's approach and could have averted the imminent peril). In these situations, the overwhelming weight of authority required that the defendant have had ***actual knowledge*** of the plaintiff's presence in time to have avoided the accident by due care before last clear chance applied.

e. **Imputed contributory negligence [§807]**

Although contributory negligence was frequently imputed in older cases to bar the plaintiff's recovery, today, in the few states retaining contributory negligence, it is imputed in only three major situations: (i) ***master-servant***, (ii) ***joint enterprise***; and (iii) cases in which the plaintiff is suing because of an ***injury to someone else***. [Rest. 2d §485; **LaBier v. Pelletier,** 665 A.2d 1013 (Me. 1995)—mother's negligence not imputed to child]

(1) **Master-servant [§808]**

A servant's negligence may be imputed to the master. For example, Chauffeur is driving Employer to work in Employer's car. A collision occurs between the cars driven by Chauffeur and D, due to the negligence of both Chauffeur and D. Employer is injured. Chauffeur's negligence will be imputed to Employer in any suit that she brings against D. [**Smalich v. Westfall,** 269 A.2d 476 (Pa. 1970)]

(2) **Joint enterprise [§809]**

Similarly, if P and X are engaged in a joint enterprise (*see supra*, §628) and due to the combined negligence of both X and a third person (D) P is injured, X's negligence will be imputed to P to bar her recovery against D. *But note:* This rule applies only where one joint enterpriser sues a person ***other than*** the negligent joint enterpriser. Thus, should P sue **X**, P will ***not*** be barred from recovery by X's negligence. [Rest. 2d §491 cmt. k]

(3) **Suit based on injury to third persons [§810]**

In actions brought for ***wrongful death*** (*see infra*, §§1156 *et seq.*), for ***loss of consortium*** (*see infra*, §§1172 *et seq.*), or for ***bystander emotional distress*** (*see supra*, §§771 *et seq.*), most courts will impute to the plaintiff the negligence of the person killed or injured. [Rest. 2d §494; **Lee v. Colorado Department of Health,** 718 P.2d 221 (Colo. 1986)]

(4) **Distinguish—bailees [§811]**

Most courts do ***not*** impute the negligence of a bailee in suits brought by the bailor against a third party (D) for negligence. For example, the bailor may sue D for damages to the bailor's car caused by the joint negligence of the bailee and D, and the bailee's negligence will ***not*** be imputed to the bailor in that action. But the negligence ***will be*** imputed if D sues the bailor. [**York v. Day's, Inc.,** 140 A.2d 730 (Me. 1958)]

(a) **Note**

The same refusal to impute contributory negligence appears in family purpose cases (*see supra*, §602). [**Bartz v. Wheat,** 285 S.E.2d 894 (W. Va. 1982)]

(5) **Distinguish—spouses [§812]**

Ordinarily, negligence or assumption of the risk (below) by one spouse is ***not*** imputed to the other so as to bar recovery for injuries received in an accident in which both the first spouse and a third party (D) were negligent. [Rest. 2d §487]

(a) **Intrafamily tort immunity [§813]**

This is important because one spouse may not be able to sue the other for injuries due to intrafamily tort immunity (*see infra*, §§1211-1213), but may still be able to recover by suing the third party.

(b) **Community property states [§814]**

In some community property states, one spouse's negligence ***is*** imputed to the other to bar recovery (or reduce it under comparative negligence) against the defendant. *Rationale:* Such states view the recovery as community property in which the negligent spouse would have an interest, and thus, to prevent the negligent spouse from profiting by his own wrong, the negligence is imputed to the innocent spouse. (*See* Community Property Summary.)

2. Comparative Negligence [§815]

This doctrine—***now adopted by virtually all states*** by statute or judicially—***rejects*** the notion that contributory negligence is always a complete bar to recovery by the plaintiff. Instead, the comparative negligence approach attempts to individualize accident recoveries by placing the economic "sting" on the parties ***in proportion to their fault***. In every case where contributory negligence is shown, the trier of fact must make a special finding on the degree of fault of each party's negligence, and the plaintiff's damages are reduced accordingly, or sometimes barred. [**Li v. Yellow Cab Co.,** 13 Cal. 3d 804 (1975)]

---

e.g. **Example:** If P suffered $50,000 worth of injuries and the jury finds that D was 80% at fault in causing the accident and P was 20% at fault, P would recover 80% of her damages, or $40,000.

---

a. **"Pure" vs. "partial" comparative negligence [§816]**

There are two basic types of comparative negligence formulae for assessing liability:

(1) **"Pure" [§817]**

A number of jurisdictions (*e.g.*, California and New York) have "pure" comparative negligence, which allows the plaintiff to recover a percentage of her damages even if her own negligence ***exceeds*** that of the defendant (*e.g.*, if a jury determines that the plaintiff was 90% at fault, she can still recover 10% of her damages).

(2) **"Partial" [§818]**

Most states, however, recognize only "partial" comparative negligence, in that they ***deny any recovery*** to a plaintiff whose own negligence passes some threshold level.

(a) **"49% limit" plans [§819]**

Some states deny recovery to the plaintiff if her negligence ***equals or exceeds*** that of the defendant. Thus, if the plaintiff is 49% to blame, she can recover 51% of her damages, but if the breakdown is 50-50, she gets nothing. [**Bevan v. Vassar Farms, Inc.,** 793 P.2d 711 (Idaho 1990)]

(b) **"50% limit" plans [§820]**

Some jurisdictions turn this around and allow the plaintiff to recover if the ***defendant's*** negligence equals or exceeds that of the plaintiff (the "equal to or less than" or "50% limit" plans). Under this approach, if the jury finds that the plaintiff was 50% at fault, she can still recover half her damages.

(c) **Multiple defendants [§821]**

If multiple defendants are negligent, almost all states compare the plaintiff's negligence with the ***combined*** negligence of all defendants. [**Elder v. Orluck,** 515 A.2d 517 (Pa. 1986)] Wisconsin and perhaps one or two other states compare the plaintiff's fault with ***each defendant's***, and unless the plaintiff's fault is less than (or equal to) ***any*** defendant's fault, the plaintiff cannot recover from that defendant. [**Delvaux v. Vanden Langenberg,** 387 N.W.2d 751 (Wis. 1986)]

1) Absent parties [§822]

In jurisdictions that retain joint and several liability, absent parties cannot be considered in the apportioning of comparative fault. However, many jurisdictions have modified the rule of joint and several liability (*see infra*, §§1330-1333). In those jurisdictions, there is a split over whether a defendant may seek to cast blame on an absent party. Sometimes the result depends on the wording of the comparative negligence statute. [*Compare* **Baldwin v. City of Waterloo,** 372 N.W.2d 486 (Iowa 1985), *and* **Brown v. Wal-Mart Discount Cities,** 12 S.W.3d 785 (Tenn. 2000)—prohibiting attribution of fault to absent person unless defendant identifies the person sufficiently to permit plaintiff to serve process on that person, *with* **American Motorcycle Association v. Superior Court,** 20 Cal. 3d 578 (1978), *and* **Bowman v. Barnes,** 282 S.E.2d 613 (W. Va. 1981)—permitting attribution of fault to absent persons]

b. Impact of comparative negligence doctrine on other rules [§823]

A comparative negligence standard (of whatever type) affects certain other rules:

(1) Last clear chance [§824]

Under any comparative negligence system, the defendant's negligence *as a whole* is compared to that of the plaintiff. It should make no difference, therefore, whether the defendant's negligence occurred before or after discovering the plaintiff's predicament. Consequently, almost all courts hold that the doctrine of last clear chance is ***abolished*** under comparative negligence. [**Bokhoven v. Klinker,** 474 N.W.2d 553 (Iowa 1991)]

(2) Wanton or reckless conduct by defendant [§825]

Most comparative negligence states that have ruled on the issue have held that a negligent plaintiff's damages can be reduced even if the defendant's conduct was "reckless," "wanton," or "grossly negligent." [**Sorensen v. Allred,** 112 Cal. App. 3d 717 (1980)]

(a) Distinguish—intentional tort by defendant [§826]

Most courts do ***not*** permit a comparison of a plaintiff's negligence with a defendant's intentionally tortious conduct. [**Billingsley v. Westrac Co.,** 365 F.2d 619 (8th Cir. 1966)] In recent years, however, a small but increasing number of courts have been willing to permit such comparisons, at least for some intentional torts, *e.g.*, when the victim of a battery acts to instigate it. [**Bonpua v. Fagan,** 602 A.2d 287 (N.J. 1992)—permitting comparison of plaintiff's negligence in provoking fight with defendant's intentional battery]

(b) Distinguish—intentional act by one party combined with negligence by other party [§827]

In the very common situation in which one defendant's negligence has facilitated an intentional tort or crime by a third party, the courts are split. This issue has become very important because states have begun altering the rule of joint and several liability, *supra*, §418.

1) **Better view—noncomparison [§828]**
If a negligent landlord facilitates attacks on his tenants, the landlord should ***not*** be permitted to reduce his share of liability by arguing that the attacker deserves the overwhelming percentage of fault. [*See* **Whitehead v. Food Max of Mississippi, Inc.,** 163 F.3d 265 (5th Cir. 1998)—reviewing state positions] *Rationale:* The defendant's negligence encompassed the very risk of attack and should not be reduced when the foreseeable risk comes to pass. [Rest. 3d of Torts: Apportionment of Liability ("Rest. 3d-AL") §14 (2000)]

2) **Other view—comparison [§829]**
Some states think it unfair to compare only negligent conduct while leaving the intentional acts out of consideration. [**Reichert v. Atler,** 875 P.2d 379 (N.M. 1994)—allocating liability one-third to bartender, who failed to protect patron from foreseeable killing by another patron, and two-thirds to the killer] But note that even a court that compares in this situation may allocate more fault to the negligent party than to those who commit intentional criminal acts. [**Hutcherson v. City of Phoenix,** 961 P.2d 449 (Ariz. 1998)—allocating 25% fault to boyfriend who murdered plaintiff and 75% to city for negligent 911 operator who assigned victim's call a low priority]

(c) **Distinguish—reckless plaintiff [§830]**
In a "pure" comparative negligence state, a reckless plaintiff may recover some damages from a negligent defendant. [**Zavala v. Regents of the University of California,** 125 Cal. App. 3d 646 (1981); *but see* **Barker v. Kallash,** 63 N.Y.2d 19 (1984)—totally barring claim by 15-year-old who was hurt while making pipe bomb]

(3) **Avoidable consequences [§831]**
The plaintiff's unreasonable failure to mitigate damages caused by the defendant's negligence will serve to decrease the plaintiff's damages, rather than bar recovery. [**Ostrowski v. Azzara,** 545 A.2d 148 (N.J. 1988)—plaintiff's unreasonable postoperative conduct in malpractice case merely decreased her damages]

(a) **Failure to wear safety belt [§832]**
In states with statutes mandating the use of safety belts, evidence of failure to wear one can be admitted (unless the statute bars use in civil proceedings). [**Dahl v. Bayerische Motoren Werke,** 748 P.2d 77 (Or.

1987)] Where no such mandate exists, most courts have held evidence of failure to wear a safety belt inadmissible on the issue of comparative negligence or avoidable consequences. [**Swajian v. General Motors Corp.,** 559 A.2d 1041 (R.I. 1989)]

(4) **Jury instructions [§833]**
Courts are split over whether the jury in a comparative negligence case should be told about how the law works (so that the jurors will know the consequences of their apportionment). [*See* **H.E. Butt Grocery Co. v. Bilotto,** 985 S.W.2d 22 (Tex. 1998)—asserting that growing number of courts are declining to inform juries; *but see* **Wheeler v. Bagley,** 575 N.W.2d 616 (Neb. 1998)—jury should be instructed]

(5) **Imputation of comparative negligence [§834]**
The availability of comparative negligence has led some courts to alter rules to permit imputation of negligence (*compare supra,* §§807-814). [**Mist v. Westin Hotels, Inc.,** 738 P.2d 85 (Haw. 1987)—victim's negligence imputed to spouse for loss of consortium]

(6) **Rescuers [§835]**
Although some states have concluded that rescuers no longer need any special protection, in light of comparative negligence, most courts have retained the earlier rule. [**Ouellette v. Carde,** 612 A.2d 687 (R.I. 1992)—comparative negligence rule does not fully protect underlying policy of rescuer doctrine; rescuer's conduct that is negligent at most should not permit reduction in award]

(7) **Intoxicated plaintiffs [§836]**
Some states have concluded that allowing partial recovery to a drunk plaintiff against a negligent tavernkeeper or liquor vendor will serve to discourage defendants' negligence in these cases. [**Estate of Kelley v. Moguls, Inc.,** 632 A.2d 360 (Vt. 1993)—because neither party will be made whole, both will be deterred; *but see* **Estate of Kelly v. Falin,** 896 P.2d 1245 (Wash. 1995)—contra, because allowing suit would encourage drunk driving]

(8) **Res ipsa loquitur [§837]**
Most states have concluded that after the introduction of comparative negligence, the plaintiff need no longer show freedom from contributory negligence as part of the res ipsa case. [**Giles v. City of New Haven,** 636 A.2d 1335 (Conn. 1994)]

(9) **Punitive damages [§838]**
A plaintiff may not recover punitive damages where the jury has attributed more fault to the plaintiff than to the defendant. Permitting punitive damages in this situation would undermine the purpose of comparative negligence. [**Tucker v. Marcus,** 418 N.W.2d 818 (Wis. 1988)]

3. Assumption of the Risk

a. General rule [§839]

If the plaintiff expressly or impliedly consents to confront the harm from a particular risk created by the defendant, the plaintiff is held to have assumed that risk and thus is barred from any recovery for negligence (or strict liability, *infra*, §§922-924). In every case, however, it must be shown that the plaintiff (i) ***recognized and understood*** the particular risk or danger involved; and (ii) ***voluntarily chose*** to encounter it.

(1) Note—consent to risk of harm essential [§840]

Mere heedlessness of or indifference to the risk is insufficient to establish assumption of the risk; the plaintiff must actually consent for the defense to succeed. [**Thomas v. Holliday,** 764 P.2d 165 (Okla. 1988)—security guard thrown from fleeing suspect's car had not consented to risk of injury]

(2) Application—firefighter's rule [§841]

When police or firefighters are hurt while responding to some emergency or when in some dangerous situation, they are almost universally barred from suing the persons whose acts brought about the emergency. One rationale is that the very nature of their jobs exposes police and firefighters to these risks of harm. [*See, e.g.,* **England v. Tasker,** 529 A.2d 938 (N.H. 1987)—police officer hurt while attempting to pull person from auto wreck cannot sue allegedly negligent driver who caused accident; **Day v. Caslowitz,** 713 A.2d 758 (R.I. 1998)—no recovery for officer who slipped on defendant homeowner's snow- and ice-covered walkway while investigating an activated home-security alarm on the premises]

b. Assumption of risk by agreement—"exculpatory clauses" [§842]

Where the relationship between the plaintiff and defendant arises out of a contract, the defendant may attempt to limit or exclude liability in advance by the use of so-called exculpatory provisions—*e.g.*, a notice printed on a railroad ticket stating that "carrier shall not be liable for injury to person or property" (or limiting liability to a specified dollar amount). Whether the plaintiff is barred or limited by assumption of risk in this situation depends on the enforceability of the provisions both as a matter of ***contract law*** and ***tort law.*** [**Barnes v. New Hampshire Karting Association,** 509 A.2d 151 (N.H. 1986)—race participant barred by release]

(1) Offer and acceptance problem [§843]

First of all, it must be determined that the provision *is* part of the contract—*i.e.*, that a prudent person would have been aware of it at the time the agreement was entered into, so that it would be part of the offer and acceptance. This usually requires a showing that the provision was printed in large type, or that there were large signs posted calling attention to the limitation on liability. Therefore, "fine print provisions" on the backs of tickets or receipts may be totally unenforceable because not deemed part of the parties' contract. (*See* Contracts Summary.)

(a) **Note**
Explicit use of the terms "negligence" and "breach of warranty" is ***not*** necessary for an exculpatory agreement to shield a party from claims based on negligence and breach of warranty; the intent of the parties guides interpretation of the agreement. [**Heil Valley Ranch, Inc. v. Simkin,** 784 P.2d 781 (Colo. 1989)]

(2) **Scope of the contract [§844]**
Second, the court must determine whether the terms of the contract *encompass the plaintiff's injury*. Courts tend to construe exculpatory contracts narrowly and resolve any ambiguities ***against the drafter*** (usually the defendant).

Example: An exculpatory clause covering a rafting trip reads: "The participant releases Extreme Rafting, Inc., from all injuries occurring during the rafting trip." If P is injured while in the rafting company's office, the contract might be construed not to cover the injury.

---

(3) **Limitation—adhesion contract [§845]**
Assuming the provision is deemed part of the contract, its enforceability may depend on the ***bargaining position of the parties***:

(a) **Equal bargaining positions [§846]**
If the parties are in an equal bargaining position (*e.g.*, a merchant ordering goods from a manufacturer), exculpatory provisions are usually upheld. There is no public policy that prevents the parties from limiting liability for ***negligence***; and indeed, the limitation of liability was probably one of the factors relied upon in fixing the contract price.

(b) **Unequal bargaining positions—public policy limitations [§847]**
However, if it appears that one party set all terms to the contract and the other had no opportunity to negotiate—so-called ***adhesion contracts***, such as exculpatory clauses in employment agreements and contracts for public utility services or public transportation—provisions that would exclude or limit liability may be held ***invalid*** as a violation of ***public policy***. [Rest. 2d of Contracts §195; Rest. 2d of Torts §496B cmt. b]

1) **Public policy factors [§848]**
Courts have struggled to develop a useful formula for analyzing the public policy issue. One leading decision holds an exculpatory agreement invalid if: (i) it concerns a type of business generally thought suitable for public regulation; (ii) the party seeking

exculpation is performing an essential service to the public; (iii) the party holds itself out as willing to perform this service for any member of the public who seeks it or falls within certain established standards; (iv) as a result of the essential nature of the service, the party seeking exculpation possesses a superior bargaining power; (v) the party confronts the public with a standardized adhesion contract of exculpation, with no provisions allowing a purchaser to pay additional reasonable fees and obtain protection against negligence; and (vi) as a result of the transaction, the purchaser's person or property is placed under the seller's control, subject to the seller's (or his agent's) risk of carelessness. [**Tunkl v. Regents of the University of California,** 60 Cal. 2d 92 (1963); *and see* **Dalury v. S-K-I, Ltd.,** 670 A.2d 795 (Vt. 1995)—using a similar "totality of the circumstances" test to render unenforceable the exculpatory agreement of a ski resort]

---

e.g. **Example:** A release of liability contained in a ***hospital admission form*** purporting to "waive" any claim the patient might have for medical malpractice against the hospital or attending physicians is contrary to public policy. [**Tunkl v. Regents of the University of California,** *supra*]

---

e.g. **Example:** A provision in a *form lease* whereby an apartment house tenant purported to waive any claim he might ever have against the landlord for injuries arising out of the landlord's failure to maintain common areas for which the landlord was responsible (*e.g.*, elevators, stairways, etc.) is contrary to public policy. [**McCutcheon v. United Homes Corp.,** 486 P.2d 1093 (Wash. 1971)]

---

e.g. **Example:** A release relieving a school district from liability for students' injuries, signed as a condition of participation in interscholastic athletics, is contrary to public policy. [**Wagenblast v. Odessa School District,** 758 P.2d 968 (Wash. 1988)]

---

cf. **Compare:** A release signed by a new member of a fitness club does ***not*** violate public policy because such facilities are not an "essential public service" such that an exculpatory clause would be "patently offensive." [**Seigneur v. National Fitness Institute, Inc.,** 752 A.2d 631 (Md. 2000)]

---

(4) Limitation—intentional torts [§849]

Even where valid, exculpatory provisions are enforceable only with respect to ***negligence*** claims. They can never be used to excuse a tortfeasor from liability for ***intentional*** or wanton or reckless torts. [Rest. 2d of Contracts §195(1); *and see, e.g.*, **Thomas v. Atlantic Coast Line Railroad,** 201 F.2d 167 (5th Cir. 1953); **Sommer v. Federal Signal Corp.,** 79 N.Y.2d 540 (1992)]

c. Implied assumption of the risk by conduct [§850]

In the absence of any contract, the issue is whether the plaintiff, by conduct, can be held to have ***voluntarily*** assumed the ***particular*** risk involved. This is the more common (and more difficult) issue in negligence cases. [**Dillard v. Little League Baseball Inc.,** 55 A.D.2d 477 (1977)—umpire hit in groin by pitch]

(1) Subjective test [§851]

The plaintiff's knowledge of the danger and voluntary exposure to it are measured ***subjectively***—*i.e.*, by what the plaintiff personally was aware of and intended, and ***not*** by what a reasonable person would know and do. However, the plaintiff's subjective state of mind may be determined from ***external manifestations***—words, conduct, etc. [**Hildebrand v. Minyard,** 494 P.2d 1328 (Ariz. 1972)]

---

e.g. **Example:** If P attends a baseball or hockey game, most courts hold that in seeking admission, P must be regarded as having chosen to encounter the well-known risk of flying baseballs or hockey pucks, which attend such sports. [**Kennedy v. Providence Hockey Club, Inc.,** 376 A.2d 329 (R.I. 1977); *and see* **Maddox v. City of New York,** 66 N.Y.2d 270 (1985)—professional baseball player assumed risk of muddy field]

(a) Limitation—plaintiff must fully appreciate risk [§852]

On the other hand, there is no assumption of the risk where, due to ***age or inexperience***, the plaintiff does not in fact comprehend the danger—even though a reasonable person might have.

(b) Distinguish—extraordinary risks [§853]

Moreover, one who participates in sporting events does not impliedly assume the risk of an opponent's flagrant violations of the rules that result in serious injuries. [**Nabozny v. Barnhill,** 334 N.E.2d 258 (Ill. 1975)—soccer goalie kicked in head]

(2) Knowledge of specific danger [§854]

It must also be shown that the plaintiff was aware of the ***particular risk*** by which she was injured, not merely of danger generally.

---

e.g. **Example:** The fact that P was aware that the car in which she was riding was being driven at an excessive speed does not mean that she assumed the risk that another car would rear-end it when the driver stopped short.

---

(3) Voluntary assumption [§855]

The plaintiff's conduct must likewise manifest a ***voluntary choice*** to encounter the risk involved (and implicitly relieve the defendant from the duty of due care); *i.e.*, the risk is not assumed if the plaintiff has no reasonable alternative.

(a) Involuntary acts [§856]

If it appears that the plaintiff's decision was dictated by ***necessity, force, or fraud***, there is no assumption of the risk.

---

e.g. **Example:** Those who dash into a dangerous situation to save their own property or the lives or property of others do not "voluntarily" assume the risk unless the risk is out of all proportion to the value of the interest sought to be protected. [**Cote v. Palmer,** 16 A.2d 595 (Conn. 1940)]

(b) Exception—surrender of legal right [§857]

Generally, the plaintiff is not required to surrender a valuable legal right (such as the use of her own property as she sees fit) simply because the defendant's conduct has threatened her with harm if the right is exercised.

---

e.g. **Example:** P does not "assume the risk" where—to get to work—she attempts to drive her car out of a driveway that D has negligently excavated, even though P knows of the danger. (But P's conduct may be contributory negligence; *see* below.) [**Conroy v. Briley,** 191 So. 2d 601 (Fla. 1966)]

---

d. Exception—no assumption of risk where plaintiff is member of statutorily protected class [§858]

Where the defendant's negligence consists of violation of a statute designed for the ***protection*** of a certain class of persons, a plaintiff who is a member of that class is deemed legally incapable of assuming the risk—either expressly or by implication. [Rest. 2d §496F]

---

e.g. **Example:** A factory's violation of safety regulations instituted for protection of employees is not excused by an employee's continuing to work there, even though the employee knowingly and "voluntarily" chooses to subject herself to the risk. [**Suess v. Arrowhead Steel Products Co.,** 230 N.W. 125 (Minn. 1930)]

---

(1) **Rationale**

The fundamental purpose of such statutes is to protect specific persons against their own inability to protect themselves (*e.g.*, because of lack of judgment or unequal bargaining power), and if the plaintiff were held to assume the risk, this purpose would be defeated.

e. **Distinguish—plaintiff's negligence [§859]**

There may be *both* negligence by the plaintiff and assumption of the risk by the plaintiff in the same case. Under comparative negligence most courts hold that if the defendant has been negligent, any negligence by the plaintiff is to be compared to that of the defendant—even if the plaintiff's negligence is deliberate. [**Davenport v. Cotton Hope Plantation Horizontal Property Regime,** 508 S.E.2d 565 (S.C. 1998)—if plaintiff uses a stairway that he knows is dangerous due to defendant landlord's negligent failure to replace a bulb, the negligence of the two parties should be compared under the state's regime, even though plaintiff knowingly used the dangerous stairway when he may have had an alternative; *but see* **Muldovan v. McEachern,** 523 S.E.2d 566 (Ga. 1999)—recognizing that it is in the minority in treating plaintiff's assumption of risk as a complete bar to recovery in all torts even though the state has adopted comparative negligence]

Example: Jaywalkers who cross against a traffic light do not voluntarily assume the risk that drivers will run them down. (Quite the contrary, it is probably assumed that the drivers will slow down and let them through.)

Example: Accepting a ride with a driver known to be drunk might be unreasonable depending on the circumstances, but it is not assumption of risk. [**Gonzalez v. Garcia,** 75 Cal. App. 3d 874 (1977)—comparative negligence applies to this situation]

---

f. **Abolition of implied assumption of risk [§860]**

In recent years, a growing number of states have concluded that implied assumption of risk is *not* a useful doctrine and have therefore *abolished* it. [**Meistrich v. Casino Arena Attractions, Inc.,** 155 A.2d 90 (N.J. 1959); **Rutter v. Northeastern Beaver County School District,** 437 A.2d 1198 (Pa. 1981)] Instead, what some states analyze as assumption of risk, others handle as a question of duty or contributory negligence.

Example: Where P is hurt by a foul ball at a baseball game, some states deny recovery on the theory that D has met its limited duty (*e.g.*, to provide some seats behind a screen). Note that under this view, D would win regardless of the extent of P's knowledge about the dangers of baseball. [**Brown v. San Francisco Ball Club,** 99 Cal. App. 2d 484 (1950)]

---

(1) **Effect—defenses limited [§861]**

In these states, once the prima facie case of negligence is established against

COMPARISON OF NEGLIGENCE DEFENSES

gilbert

	CONTRIBUTORY NEGLIGENCE	PURE COMPARATIVE NEGLIGENCE	PARTIAL COMPARATIVE NEGLIGENCE	CONTRACTUAL ASSUMPTION OF RISK	IMPLIED ASSUMPTION OF RISK
DEFINED	Plaintiff's ***own negligence*** contributes to her injury	Plaintiff's ***own negligence*** contributes to her injury	Plaintiff's ***own negligence*** contributes to her injury	Plaintiff signed contract with an enforceable ***exculpatory clause***	Plaintiff knew of a risk of injury and ***voluntarily assumed*** it
EFFECT	Plaintiff's claim ***completely barred***	Plaintiff's damages award ***reduced*** by percentage of fault attributable to her	Plaintiff's damages award ***reduced if*** her fault is below the threshold level; otherwise, plaintiff's claim is barred	Plaintiff's claim ***completely barred***	Plaintiff's claim ***completely barred***
DEFENSE NEGATED BY DEFENDANT'S "LAST CLEAR CHANCE"?	Yes	Not applicable	Not applicable	Not applicable	Not applicable
DEFENSE APPLIES TO WANTON OR RECKLESS TORTIOUS CONDUCT?	No	Yes	Yes	No	Yes

the defendant, the only defense available is that the plaintiff behaved ***unreasonably*** (was contributorily negligent). There is no longer room for discussion about voluntarily encountering a known risk.

(2) "Primary" and "secondary" assumption of risk [§862]
A few states tend to follow the approach just stated but instead of speaking directly of "duty" and "contributory negligence," they speak instead of "primary" and "secondary" assumption of risk. The issues are ***exactly the same*** despite the different language.

(a) Primary assumption of risk [§863]
This involves a determination that the defendant has met whatever duty the court thinks appropriate to impose—and thus there is no basis for any liability.

---

e.g. **Example:** In a friendly touch football game, D, trying to defend against a pass, accidentally knocked P over and stepped on her hand. Recovery was denied. The court held that a person hurt by an inherent risk of a sport loses because of "primary" assumption of the risk; the defender did not owe a duty of due care in this case but only a duty not to recklessly or intentionally hurt P. [**Knight v. Jewett,** 3 Cal. 4th 296 (1992)] *Rationale:* In participant sports cases, a duty of due care would chill the fervor of athletic competitions. [**Crawn v. Campo,** 643 A.2d 600 (N.J. 1994); *but see* **Lestina v. West Bend Mutual Insurance Co.,** 501 N.W.2d 28 (Wis. 1993)—adopting negligence as the governing principle in sports injury cases]

(b) Secondary assumption of risk [§864]
Here the court has found a duty of due care and breach. If the defendant asserts that the plaintiff has also acted unreasonably in the accident, the issue is one of contributory negligence. Although some courts refer to this issue as "secondary" assumption of the risk, it operates *exactly* as does comparative negligence in that state—either to reduce or possibly bar recovery. [*See* **Davenport v. Cotton Hope Plantation Horizontal Property Regime,** *supra*, §859]

E. Effect of Liability Insurance

1. Present "Third Party" Liability Insurance System [§865]
At present, most car owners carry insurance against whatever liability (up to the policy's maximum coverage) they may incur to third parties in connection with the operation of their vehicles (hence, known as "third party" or "liability" insurance). Such insurance is also carried for homeowner's liability, products liability (*infra*), and malpractice, and the same principles apply.

a. **General operation of "third party" insurance system [§866]**

When an accident covered by third party insurance occurs, the defendant's insurance carrier investigates the claims of the injured party and defends any lawsuit that is filed. The insurer has a duty to defend any lawsuit that might be covered by the policy, regardless of the claim's actual merit. Note that the duty exists even if there may be doubts as to whether the claim is covered by the policy; *i.e.*, the duty to defend is broader than the duty to pay any judgment. [**Voorhees v. Preferred Mutual Insurance Co.,** 607 A.2d 1255 (N.J. 1992)]

(1) **Insurance carrier's role in lawsuit [§867]**

In most states, the suit is defended in the name of the insured defendant (rather than in the name of the insurance company), and the jury generally is not told whether the defendant is, or is not, insured. (*See* Evidence Summary.)

(a) **Direct action against insurer? [§868]**

Most liability insurance policies insure the defendant only against liability established by a ***judgment*** against her in a legal action (or a settlement agreed to by the insurer). Therefore, until a judgment is returned, most states provide that the injured party (the plaintiff) has ***no direct action*** against the defendant's insurance company. (A very few states are contra by statute.)

1) **But note**

Once a judgment is returned, however, the plaintiff is treated as a ***third-party beneficiary*** of the defendant's insurance company's promise to pay any judgments against the defendant, and hence the plaintiff can sue the defendant's insurer directly if it fails to discharge the judgment against the defendant.

(2) **Effect of intentional or "wanton and reckless" conduct [§869]**

Most liability insurance policies cover only ***negligent*** conduct by a defendant or strict liability. Hence, in cases where the plaintiff alleges that the defendant was acting "wantonly and recklessly" (usually in an attempt to claim punitive damages), the defendant's insurance carrier may be liable for the compensatory part of any award but not for the punitive part. If the act was intentional, the insurer may not be liable for any part of the award.

(a) **Note**

If the policy terms cover punitive damages, most courts require the insurer to pay them. [**Harrell v. Travelers Indemnity Co.,** 567 P.2d 1013 (Or. 1977)] However, some states statutorily prohibit insurance company payment of punitive damages by forbidding coverage of losses caused by the insured's willful acts. [Cal. Ins. Code §533; **J.C. Penney Casualty Insurance Co. v. M.K.,** 52 Cal. 3d 1009 (1991)]

b. Insured's duty of "cooperation" [§870]

An express or implied provision of every liability insurance contract is that the insured party will "cooperate" with the insurer, so that if the defendant acts collusively with the plaintiff, fails to testify when required, etc., the insurance carrier may be able to deny coverage as to any judgment against the defendant.

c. Insurer's duty of "good faith" in settlement [§871]

Every liability insurance policy has a maximum limit (*e.g.*, $25,000 for injuries to any one person), and should a judgment be returned that exceeds the limit, the defendant is personally liable for the excess. Hence, courts today recognize that an insurance company owes at least a ***duty of good faith*** to its insured (the defendant) to attempt to settle any claims against her within the policy limits, so as to avoid the risk of her being held personally responsible for satisfying part of the judgment. [**Pavia v. State Farm Mutual Automobile Insurance Co.,** 82 N.Y.2d 445 (1993)]

(1) Stricter standard imposed by some courts [§872]

Some courts have imposed a more stringent standard of liability on insurers than the "good faith" rule. Thus, for example, it has been held that the insurer has a duty to use ***due care*** to attempt to settle within policy limits whenever there is a substantial likelihood of a recovery exceeding those limits. ***Unreasonable*** failure to settle under these circumstances violates the insurer's duty, even if bad faith is not shown. [**Comunale v. Traders & General Insurance Co.,** 50 Cal. 2d 654 (1958)]

(2) Effect of insurer's breach of duty [§873]

If the insurance carrier is held liable for failure to settle within the policy limits, it may be held liable for the ***full amount*** of any judgment subsequently returned against the defendant (including the excess over policy limits). [*See, e.g.,* **Crisci v. Security Insurance Co.,** 66 Cal. 2d 425 (1967); **Comunale v. Traders & General Insurance Co.,** *supra*]

(a) Special damages also recoverable [§874]

Many states also permit the defendant to recover ***any special damages*** incurred as a result of the insurer's failure to settle—*e.g.*, the value of property taken in satisfaction of the excess judgment, or the defendant's mental suffering caused by the insurer's misconduct. [**Crisci v. Security Insurance Co.,** *supra*]

(b) Insured may assign claim against insurer [§875]

It is further recognized that the defendant's cause of action against her insurance company for failing to make a "good faith" effort to settle is ***assignable***. Hence, where the plaintiff recovers a judgment in excess of the defendant's insurance limits, the defendant (to avoid personal liability for the excess) will usually assign to the plaintiff her cause of action against her insurance company. [**Critz v. Farmers Insurance Group,** 230 Cal. App. 2d 788 (1964)]

(3) Distinguish—no duty to third persons [§876]

Most courts hold that the insurer's duties regarding settlement run only to the insured, and consequently no third person can sue—even where it was foreseeable that failure to settle would result in damages (*e.g.*, emotional distress) to such third person. [**Moradi-Shalal v. Fireman's Fund Insurance Cos.,** 46 Cal. 3d 287 (1988)]

(4) Distinguish—tort claims in "first party" insurance [§877]

Some states extend tort claims for "bad faith" to health, fire, accident, and life insurance, so-called "first party" insurance. [**Gruenberg v. Aetna Insurance Co.,** 9 Cal. 3d 566 (1973)] Other states refuse to do so. [**Spencer v. Aetna Life & Casualty Insurance Co.,** 611 P.2d 149 (Kan. 1980); **Lawton v. Great Southwest Fire Insurance Co.,** 392 A.2d 576 (N.H. 1978)]

(a) Arguments favoring tort claim [§878]

States adopting the tort action rely on the unequal bargaining power of the parties, the value of delay to the insurer who can earn interest on the money that is owed, and the analogy of the third party insurance cases.

(b) Argument against tort claims [§879]

States rejecting the tort claim stress the purely contractual aspect of first party insurance and the existence of statutory and administrative penalties for failure to settle claims properly.

Chapter Three: Strict Liability

CONTENTS

▶ Key Exam Issues

A. In General §880

B. Animals §882

C. Abnormally Dangerous Activities §898

D. Extent of Liability §914

E. Defenses §920

Key Exam Issues

In most fact situations, the plaintiff claims that the defendant has intentionally (Chapter I) or negligently (Chapter II) caused some harm. Occasionally, though, a defendant may be liable ***without any fault*** on his part. In other words, the defendant is strictly liable.

Your task in a strict liability situation is not like your task in a negligence situation. In a negligence situation, you must determine whether the elements of a prima facie case are present. In contrast, your task in a strict liability situation usually is to determine whether the facts involved fall into one of the recognized categories of cases in which courts are willing to impose strict liability. In spotting strict liability situations, especially look for the following facts:

(i) ***Defendant's animals cause an injury***; or

(ii) ***Defendant is involved in an abnormally dangerous activity*** (*e.g.*, using explosives).

When you find a strict liability situation, be sure to consider the ***limitations on strict liability*** (foreseeability of plaintiff and foreseeability of hazard) and the possibility of a ***defense*** (assumption of risk).

A. In General

1. Basis of Liability [§880]

The third broad basis for tort liability involves torts that are neither intentional nor the result of negligence. Rather, liability is imposed simply ***because certain types of injuries happen***—even though no one is at fault. The justification for this policy of strict liability is based on the nature of the activity that caused the harm; if these certain activities cause harm, the view is that liability should rest on the party best able to avoid its recurrence—*i.e.*, the defendant.

2. Prima Facie Case [§881]

Prima facie case (the same as for negligence, except as to duty):

- *Act or Omission by Defendant*
- *Duty to Avoid Harm*
- *Breach of Duty*
- *Actual Cause (Cause in Fact)*
- *Proximate Cause (Legal Cause)*
- *Damages*

B. Animals

1. Domestic Animals

a. Trespassing livestock [§882]

The possessor of livestock trespassing on the land or chattels of another is strictly liable for the trespass itself and any harm done by the trespass. [Rest. 2d §504]

(1) "Livestock" [§883]

The term "livestock" is defined as any animal of domestic value that is relatively easy to control. This includes, *e.g.*, horses, cattle, pigs, and sheep, but ***not household pets.***

b. Domestic animals (including livestock) with known dangerous propensities [§884]

The possessor of a domestic animal with a known dangerous propensity not shared by most members of the animal's class (*e.g.*, a dog that bites) is strictly liable for all harm done ***as the result of that dangerous propensity.*** The rationale is that the social utility of keeping an animal known to have atypical dangerous tendencies is outweighed by the magnitude of the risk involved. [Rest. 2d §509]

(1) Distinguish—normally dangerous domestic animals [§885]

The possessor of a domestic animal belonging to a class of animals that normally has dangerous propensities (*e.g.*, a bull) is ***not strictly liable*** for injuries caused by that animal's normal dangerous propensity. Here, the rationale is that the social utility in keeping these somewhat dangerous animals outweighs their normal risk and thus ***possession should not be discouraged*** by strict liability. Note however that the possessor of such an animal will be liable for ***negligence*** if he does not use adequate care in keeping the animal. [Rest. 2d §509 cmt. e]

(2) Limitation—harm must result from a known dangerous propensity [§886]

Where strict liability applies, the possessor is liable only for injuries ***attributable*** to the animal's known dangerous propensity (*e.g.*, knowledge that a horse is difficult to control may not be sufficient to impose strict liability when the horse bites someone). [**Greeley v. Jameson,** 164 N.E. 385 (Mass. 1929)]

c. Domestic animals without known dangerous propensities [§887]

The general view is that the possessor of animals that have not in the past exhibited dangerous characteristics is ***not*** held to strict liability for their acts. It is therefore said that "every previously well-behaved dog is entitled to one free

PERSONAL INJURIES FROM ANIMALS—STRICT LIABILITY

gilbert

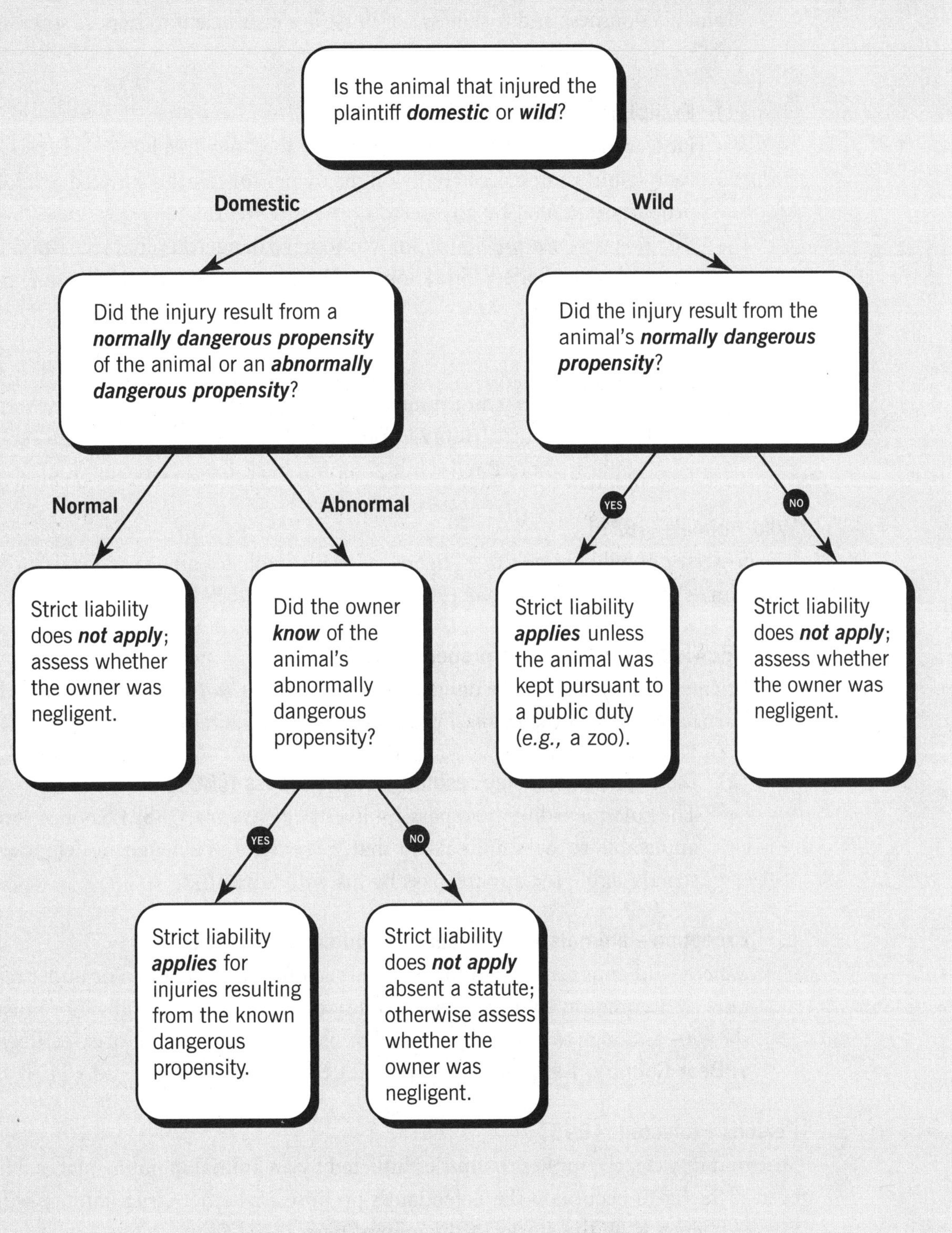

bite"—*i.e.*, only when the owner has reason to know that the dog has vicious tendencies will strict liability apply. [**Gehrts v. Batteen,** 620 N.W.2d 775 (S.D. 2001)—St. Bernards are normally gentle dogs and owners had no reason to know of dangerous propensities; **Jividen v. Law,** 461 S.E.2d 451 (W. Va. 1995)—"rambunctiousness and friskiness" of horse are insufficient to impose strict liability]

(1) Exception—dog bite statutes [§888]

However, statutes in several states reject the "one free bite" rule as to ***dogs*** (only), imposing strict liability on the owner for injuries suffered (excluding property damage) by any person bitten by the owner's dog, even though that dog was ***not*** previously known to have dangerous characteristics. [*See, e.g.*, Cal. Civ. Code §3342] Some other states have reached the same result by case law.

(a) Note

If the statute is not limited to "biting," it may apply even where no contact occurs. [**Henry v. Brown,** 495 A.2d 324 (Me. 1985)—statute applies where P fell while stepping back from charging dog]

2. Wild Animals [§889]

The possessor of wild animals (*e.g.*, tigers) is strictly liable for any harm resulting from the animals' ***normally dangerous*** propensities. [Rest. 3d-PH §21]

a. Knowledge of dangerous propensity [§890]

Scienter (knowledge of the dangerous propensity) is ***not*** necessary, provided the harm results from the ***normal*** propensities or characteristics of the animal.

(1) Distinguish—damage resulting from trespass [§891]

The rule regarding "trespass by livestock" (*supra*, §882) has been made applicable to wild animals so that, regardless of scienter, a defendant is strictly liable for any trespass by his wild animal.

b. Exception—animals kept pursuant to public duty [§892]

Where wild animals are kept under a public duty (*e.g.*, in a zoo or under transport by a common carrier), strict liability does ***not*** apply. Negligence must be shown—although the defendant would be held to a high amount of care. [**Cowden v. Bear Country, Inc.,** 382 F. Supp. 1321 (D.S.D. 1974); Rest. 2d §517]

3. Persons Protected [§893]

Strict liability clearly applies to injuries inflicted by an animal in public places. However, if the harm occurs on the defendant's premises, whether strict liability will be invoked depends on the ***status*** of the injured person:

a. Invitees, licensees [§894]

If a plaintiff enters private property with the express or limited consent of the land occupier (*e.g.*, as a guest or business visitor), strict liability clearly is applied. [**McLane v. Northwest Natural Gas Co.,** 467 P.2d 635 (Or. 1970)]

b. **Trespassers [§895]**
On the other hand, most courts hold that strict liability does not extend to trespassers whose presence the owner had ***no reason to know of or anticipate,*** and thus, no recovery may be had for injuries inflicted by the animal. [Rest. 2d §511] (Of course, if the trespasser's presence was known, negligence liability would apply; *see supra*, §662.)

(1) **Limitation—vicious watchdogs [§896]**
However, even though a trespasser's presence is ***unknown,*** a landowner may be liable for injuries by a ***vicious watchdog***—unless adequate warnings of the dog's presence were posted. [Rest. 2d §516]

(a) **Rationale**
The landowner's privilege to use such dogs for protection of property is similar to the privilege to use mechanical devices under the same circumstances (*supra*, §143)—*i.e.*, absent adequate warnings, the landowner is liable for the harm done, unless the intruder was ***in fact*** threatening death or serious bodily harm.

(2) **Limitation—foreseeable trespassers [§897]**
Moreover, the no-liability rule also does ***not apply*** if the landowner had ***reason to anticipate*** trespassing upon the property (*e.g.*, where injured person is a CTULA, or a child trespasser whose presence the owner had reason to foresee; *supra*, §§666, 674). In such cases, strict liability will be imposed unless ***adequate warnings*** of the animal's presence were given. [Rest. 2d §512]

C. Abnormally Dangerous Activities

1. **General Rule [§898]**
One who maintains an abnormally dangerous condition or activity on his premises or engages in an activity that presents an unavoidable risk of harm to the person or property of others may be liable for the harm caused even if the defendant has exercised reasonable care to prevent the harm. [Rest. 2d §519]

2. **"Abnormally Dangerous" Activities [§899]**
The problem in these cases is to determine what constitutes an "abnormally dangerous" activity so as to give rise to strict liability.

a. **Origin of rule [§900]**
The landmark case of **Rylands v. Fletcher,** L.R. 3 H.L. 330 (1868), held that a

person who brings something onto his land that involves a "*nonnatural* use" of the land and is *likely to cause substantial damage* if it escapes will be strictly liable if it in fact escapes and causes harm.

b. **Application under First Restatement—"ultrahazardous activities" [§901]**
Under the First Restatement, the key term was *"ultrahazardous."* An activity fits that description if it necessarily involved a risk of serious harm to the person, land, or chattels of others that could not be eliminated by the exercise of utmost care and was not a matter of common usage. [Rest. §520]

---

e.g. **Example—"ultrahazardous":** Ultrahazardous activities include blasting, manufacturing explosives, drilling oil wells (in some states), fumigation [**Old Island Fumigation, Inc. v. Barbee,** 604 So. 2d 1246 (Fla. 1992)], and setting off public fireworks [**Klein v. Pyrodyne Corp.,** 810 P.2d 917 (Wash. 1991)].

---

cf. **Compare—"dangerous":** Dangerous activities that are *not* ultrahazardous in nature—usually because they are commonly used—include use of fire, automobiles, firearms, and boilers. [**Beck v. Bel Air Properties, Inc.,** 134 Cal. App. 2d 834 (1955)]

---

c. **Basis for liability under Second Restatement—"abnormally dangerous" activities [§902]**
The Second Restatement changed the critical term to *"abnormally dangerous"* activity because the drafters thought the prior term gave too little weight to the *context* in which the activity was being carried on. [Rest. 2d §519]

(1) **Determinative factors [§903]**
Instead of defining when an activity is abnormally dangerous, the Second Restatement lists the following six factors to be considered and balanced:

(i) Whether the *activity involves a high degree of risk* of harm;

(ii) The *gravity* of that risk;

(iii) Whether the *risk can be eliminated by the exercise of reasonable care*;

(iv) Whether the *activity is a matter of common usage*;

(v) Whether the *activity is appropriate to the place* where it is being carried on; and

(vi) The *value* of the activity *to the community*.

[Rest. 2d §520; *and see* **Langan v. Valicopters, Inc.,** 567 P.2d 218 (Wash. 1977)—applying this section to crop dusting; *but see* **Indiana Harbor Belt**

Railroad v. American Cyanamid Co., 916 F.2d 1174 (7th Cir. 1990)—rejecting section in case against shipper of hazardous chemical that leaked from rail car]

(2) **Impact of new terminology? [§904]**
It is clear that the Second Restatement offers escapes from strict liability in its fifth and sixth factors that were not available under the First Restatement—appropriateness to location and value to the community. [**New Meadows Holding Co. v. Washington Water Power Co.,** 687 P.2d 212 (Wash. 1984)—natural gas pipeline] This might affect such extreme cases as a dangerous mine that supports the economy of an entire town or region.

(a) **But note**
Several courts have shown reluctance to adopt the Second Restatement's softening of strict liability. [*See, e.g.,* **Yukon Equipment, Inc. v. Fireman's Fund Insurance Co.,** 585 P.2d 1206 (Alaska 1978)—per se rule of strict liability for explosion of stored explosives; **Koos v. Roth,** 652 P.2d 1255 (Or. 1982)—field burning warrants strict liability because society "has other ways to lighten the burdens of costly but unavoidable accidents on a valued industry than to let them fall haphazardly on the industry's neighbors"]

d. **Third Restatement standard [§905]**
The Third Restatement adopts a two-element approach, deeming an activity abnormally dangerous if: (i) the activity creates a ***foreseeable and highly significant risk*** of physical harm ***even when*** all actors exercise ***reasonable care***; and (ii) the activity is ***not a matter of common usage.*** [Rest. 3d-PH §20]

e. **Applications**

(1) **Airplane ground damage [§906]**
Early cases deemed flying to be so dangerous that owners of aircraft were strictly liable for all harm caused by aircraft flight to persons and property on the ground.

(a) **Modern cases split on this question [§907]**
Some courts now hold that aviation has reached such a stage of safety, and is of such common usage, that the activity should be regulated by negligence principles. [**Crosby v. Cox Aircraft Co.,** 746 P.2d 1198 (Wash. 1987)] However, other courts and the Second Restatement still adhere to the earlier view. [Rest. 2d §520A]

(b) **Distinguish—unconventional aviation [§908]**
But even those courts that no longer impose strict liability for conventional flying still impose strict liability for stunt flying, crop dusting, test flights, etc. [**Loe v. Lenhardt,** 362 P.2d 312 (Or. 1961)]

(2) **Common carriers [§909]**
Although the Restatement and early cases refused to impose strict liability on a common carrier required to carry abnormally dangerous cargo [Rest. 2d §521], recent cases have imposed strict liability in such cases [*see, e.g.*, **National Steel Service Center, Inc. v. Gibbons,** 319 N.W.2d 269 (Iowa 1982)].

(3) **Handguns [§910]**
Appellate courts are virtually unanimous that handguns do not come within the abnormally dangerous activity doctrine. [**Burkett v. Freedom Arms, Inc.,** 704 P.2d 118 (Or. 1985)]

(a) **Exception—"Saturday Night Specials" [§911]**
One court has held that cheap guns that have little accuracy or reliability have so little social utility that they may become the subject of strict liability. [**Kelley v. R.G. Industries, Inc.,** 497 A.2d 1143 (Md. 1985)—strict liability for all in the chain of distribution of cheap, unreliable, inaccurate guns to all persons shot by criminals; *but note:* this case was sharply limited by statute]

EXAM TIP **gilbert**

Exam questions testing on strict liability may include a statement in the facts or in an answer choice that the defendant exercised reasonable care. But don't be fooled by that—***no amount of due care*** on the part of the defendant will relieve him of liability in a ***strict liability*** situation.

3. **Products Liability Cases [§912]**
As will be discussed *infra* (§§952 *et seq.*), strict liability has been extended to some claims against suppliers of defective products.

a. **Showing of "defect" required [§913]**
But note that the liability imposed on the manufacturer or supplier of defective products is different from that in cases of abnormally dangerous activities: It must appear that the product *was* defective. When dealing with damages arising from blasting cases, impounded water, etc., liability is imposed whether or not there was any defect.

EXAM TIP **gilbert**

Perhaps the easiest way to remember most of the rules concerning strict liability in tort (outside the products liability context, which will be discussed in the next chapter) is to remember that strict liability is imposed for injuries or damages arising from ***abnormal dangers***. Thus, strict liability for injuries from a ***domestic animal*** generally is imposed only for injuries arising from ***propensities that one should not expect*** in the domestic animal. Strict liability is imposed for ***wild animals*** who hurt victims by their ***normally dangerous propensities*** simply because it is abnormal to keep such animals. Strict liability is imposed for ***ultrahazardous activities*** simply because they are ***abnormally dangerous*** when compared to other activities.

D. Extent of Liability

1. Scope of Duty Owed [§914]

Unlike negligence, the duty owed here is a duty to avoid harm from the animal or the activity that is classified as "abnormally dangerous." Liability is therefore imposed for resulting injuries to person or property, regardless of whether anyone was at fault.

a. Duty owed only to foreseeable plaintiffs [§915]

The duty is owed only to ***"foreseeable plaintiffs"***—*i.e.*, persons to whom a reasonable person would have foreseen a risk of harm under the circumstances. [**Whitman Hotel Corp. v. Elliott & Watrous Engineering Co.,** 79 A.2d 591 (Conn. 1951)]

(1) Distinguish—negligence cases [§916]

Although the courts are split over the "foreseeable plaintiff doctrine" in negligence cases (*supra*), the doctrine is the majority view in strict liability cases.

b. Duty extends only to foreseeable hazards [§917]

The harm that occurs must result from the kind of danger foreseeable from the abnormally dangerous animal or activity. Thus, as indicated in the animal cases (*supra*), it must flow from the ***"normally dangerous propensity" of the condition or thing involved.***

---

e.g. **Example:** Blasting operations conducted by D on his land frightened P's minks on adjoining property, causing them to kill their kittens. Although strict liability would extend to the hurling of rocks or debris from the blasting (foreseeable harm), it does not apply to the minks' killing their young, because the result is not ordinarily expected to occur from blasting operations. [**Foster v. Preston Mill Co.,** 268 P.2d 645 (Wash. 1954)]

---

2. Actual Cause [§918]

All courts use the same rules regarding actual cause as in negligence cases (*see supra,* §§415 *et seq.*).

3. Proximate Cause [§919]

Virtually all courts apply the same rules of proximate causation in strict liability as they do in negligence (*see supra,* §§442 *et seq.*). [**Golden v. Amory,** 109 N.E.2d 131 (Mass. 1952)—unforeseeable flood bars liability]

E. Defenses

1. **Contributory Negligence Traditionally No Defense [§920]**
The plaintiff's own lack of care is not a defense to strict liability, ***unless*** he knew of the danger and his contributory negligence was the very cause of the activity's miscarrying.

---

e.g. **Example:** P, knowing he was following D's dynamite truck, negligently tried to pass it; a collision ensued, turning the truck over and causing it to explode. P cannot recover because his negligence was the very reason for the explosion. [**Burke v. Fischer,** 182 S.W.2d 638 (Ky. 1944)]

---

2. **Comparative Negligence [§921]**
Most courts in comparative negligence jurisdictions have reduced the plaintiff's recovery in strict liability cases where his injury was caused in part by his own carelessness. (*See* further discussion, *infra,* §1057.)

3. **Assumption of Risk Is a Valid Defense [§922]**
Any ***voluntary*** encountering of a ***known*** risk may prevent the plaintiff's recovery.

---

e.g. **Example:** P cannot recover for injuries sustained where, knowing the danger, she teases a leopard or voluntarily puts herself within its reach. [**Lehnhard v. Robertson's Administratrix,** 195 S.W. 441 (Ky. 1917)]

---

a. **Determining "voluntariness" [§923]**
Where the defendant's activity is carried on in part for the ***plaintiff's benefit*** (*e.g.*, water or gas pipes maintained partially for his use), the plaintiff's consent to the risk (seepage, overflow, etc.) is usually ***implied***—but only to bar strict liability.

(1) **"Voluntary" [§924]**
There is no "voluntary" assumption where the plaintiff attempts to run from his house to his car in the driveway, knowing the defendant's vicious hog is outside. *Rationale:* The plaintiff's remaining a prisoner inside his house would have meant surrendering his right to move freely on his own property—not a reasonable alternative. [**Marshall v. Ranne,** 511 S.W.2d 255 (Tex. 1974)]

Chapter Four: Products Liability

CONTENTS

▶	Key Exam Issues	
A.	In General	§925
B.	Liability Based on Intentional Acts	§929
C.	Liability Based on Negligence	§931
D.	Strict Liability in Tort	§952
E.	Liability Based on Breach of Warranty	§1069

Key Exam Issues

Products liability questions basically come down to an issue of which theory of recovery is best for the plaintiff. When a defective product causes injury, the manufacturer of the product, as well as the distributor, wholesaler, and retailer who sold it, may be liable to the injured person on a number of distinct legal theories—some in tort and some arising from contract. You will need to consider how well each theory fits your specific fact situation.

Products liability may be based on any of the three previously considered tort bases for liability: intent, negligence, or strict liability. Also, there are the contract bases (breach of various warranties). Depending on the nature of the defendant's conduct, the same injury may be ***actionable on several theories***. So do not stop analyzing until you have considered all of the following bases of products liability:

1. Liability based on ***intentional torts*** (a battery).
2. Liability based on ***negligence*** (harm must be foreseeable and defendant's conduct must be unreasonable).
3. Liability based on ***strict liability*** (***defective*** product that ***caused injury***).
4. Liability based on ***breach of an express or implied warranty*** (especially Uniform Commercial Code ("U.C.C.") warranties of ***fitness*** for a particular purpose and ***merchantability***), which is also "strict" in that it does not require fault.

Determining which bases for liability are involved in your exam question is vitally important because it affects such key issues as:

—***Scope of duty*** owed;

—***Defenses*** assertable (*e.g.,* contributory negligence is no defense to intentional torts);

—***Damages*** recoverable (*e.g.,* punitive damages are not recoverable for negligence or for behavior without fault); and

—***Liability insurance coverage*** (which may exclude some intentional torts).

A. In General

1. Introduction [§925]

The law of products liability focuses on the liability of a supplier of a product for ***physical harm to person or property*** caused by defects in the product. (If the product

OVERVIEW OF PRODUCTS LIABILITY THEORIES **gilbert**

	NEGLIGENCE	STRICT LIABILITY	IMPLIED WARRANTIES
WHO CAN SUE?	Any foreseeable plaintiff	Any foreseeable plaintiff	Under most restrictive U.C.C. alternative, purchaser and her family, household, and guests
WHO CAN BE SUED?	Any commercial seller (*e.g.,* manufacturer, wholesaler, retailer)	Any commercial seller	**Merchantability:** A merchant dealing in the kind of goods sold **Fitness for a Particular Purpose:** Any seller of the goods
WHAT CONSTITUTES BREACH?	Negligent conduct that results in the supplying of a defective product	The supplying of a defective product	**Merchantability:** Sale of goods not generally acceptable or fit for ordinary purposes **Fitness for a Particular Purpose:** Sale of goods not fit for purpose that seller knows or has reason to know of (and knows that buyer is relying on seller's judgment)
WHAT DAMAGES CAN BE RECOVERED?	Personal injury and property damage (no recovery for economic loss standing alone)	Personal injury and property damage (no recovery for economic loss standing alone)	Personal injury and property damage (recovery solely for economic loss also permitted)
WHAT DEFENSES ARE AVAILABLE?	Same defenses that are available in an ordinary negligence case (contributory negligence, comparative negligence, assumption of risk)	Same defenses that are available in an ordinary strict liability case (unreasonable misuse, comparative fault, assumption of risk)	Disclaimers may be possible. Also: **Contributory Negligence States:** Assumption of the risk, unreasonable misuse, and failure to give reasonable notice of breach **Comparative Negligence States:** Any type of fault (under state's comparative negligence rules)

simply does not perform as well as expected, causing purely economic loss to the buyer (*see infra*, §1050), this is primarily a "sales" problem and is covered in detail in the Sale and Lease of Goods Summary.)

2. **Background [§926]**

At early common law, a manufacturer or supplier of a chattel could be held liable for injuries sustained through its use only to those with whom he was in "privity of contract." If there was no "privity," there was no liability—either in tort or contract. Thus, an injured person who was not the purchaser of the product could not recover, no matter how negligent the supplier's conduct. [*See, e.g.,* **Winterbottom v. Wright,** 10 M. & W. 109 (1842)—passenger who was injured when stagecoach collapsed had no cause of action against contractor who agreed with coach owner to keep it in repair, because "no privity of contract"]

a. **Rejection of privity requirement [§927]**

Later, courts began to reject the strict "privity" requirement when dealing with specific types of chattels: first, with bailed goods (*see supra*, §§758-761), then with foodstuffs and ***any*** inherently dangerous chattel. Manufacturers and suppliers of such products were held to owe a tort duty of due care (*i.e.,* liability for negligence) respecting the condition of the chattel, even as to persons with whom they were not in "privity of contract" (*i.e.,* users, consumers, bystanders injured through another's use of the product, etc.).

b. **Modern view [§928]**

As discussed below, the courts have now gone beyond negligence concepts and almost all impose some form of strict liability for any injury sustained through the use of defectively manufactured products. In a few jurisdictions, this result is reached through imposition of implied warranty liability (a contract action), but in most it is regarded as a tort concept. The scope of liability, measure of damages, available defenses, etc., will vary according to the theory on which liability is imposed.

B. Liability Based on Intentional Acts

1. **General Principle [§929]**

A manufacturer or supplier who sells a chattel that he ***knows*** is defective or dangerous, without warning of the danger, may be held liable for ***battery*** to any person injured through use or consumption of the product. As long as the manufacturer or supplier believed the injuries were "substantially certain" to result from the use of the chattel, he will be held to have ***intended*** the consequences of his acts. [**Huset v. J.I. Case Threshing Machine Co.,** 120 F. 865 (8th Cir. 1903)]

2. **Significance—Greater Recovery Potentially Available [§930]**

While intent is difficult to establish, it may (if shown) justify a higher recovery; *i.e.,* the defendant may be liable for ***punitive damages*** in addition to damages for the plaintiff's physical injuries (*see supra*, §23). Also the injured party's contributory negligence would be no defense.

C. Liability Based on Negligence

1. **Introduction [§931]**
Few products liability cases involve intentional misconduct. The more typical problems concern the scope of liability to be imposed on a manufacturer or supplier for ***unintentional*** injuries caused by the use or consumption of its products.

2. **Background—Gradual Abrogation of "Privity" Requirement [§932]**
As already discussed, early decisions limited liability to cases in which there was "privity" between the supplier and the injured party, but this requirement was gradually eroded and replaced with standard negligence concepts.

3. **Impact of MacPherson v. Buick Motor Co.—Liability Based on Foreseeability of Harm [§933]**
Despite earlier inroads on the "privity" requirement, the real establishment of liability for simple negligence came with Judge Cardozo's landmark decision in **MacPherson v. Buick Motor Co.,** 217 N.Y. 382 (1916). There, the plaintiff purchased from a dealer a car that had been manufactured by the defendant. The car had a defective wheel, which had been manufactured by a subcontractor. The court: (i) rejected the defendant manufacturer's claim that it could not be held liable because there was no privity between the plaintiff and the defendant, and (ii) held that if a reasonable person would ***foresee*** that the chattel would create a ***risk of harm to human life or limb*** if not carefully made or supplied, the manufacturer or supplier of the chattel is under a duty of care in its manufacture and supply—and this duty is owed to ***all foreseeable users***.

4. **General Scope of Negligence Liability Today [§934]**
The *MacPherson* rule has been adopted in all states and has been extended in several important respects:

   a. **Negligent design [§935]**
   First of all, the doctrine applies not only to negligence in manufacture, but also to negligence in design—including failure to adequately test, install safety features, and the like. [**Boeing Airplane Co. v. Brown,** 291 F.2d 310 (9th Cir. 1961)] (*See* detailed discussion of design defects, *infra,* §§961 *et seq.*)

      (1) **Limitation—contractors following specifications [§936]**
      A contractor owes no duty to third persons to judge the plans, specifications, or instructions that he has contracted to follow, unless they are so obviously dangerous that no reasonable contractor would follow them. [**Hunt v. Blasius,** 384 N.E.2d 368 (Ill. 1978)]

b. **Bystanders [§937]**

Although *MacPherson* held the manufacturer or supplier liable only to foreseeable users, courts extended liability to ***all persons foreseeably within the scope of use*** of the defective product (*e.g.*, pedestrian injured by defective automobile). [**Flies v. Fox Bros. Buick,** 218 N.W. 855 (Wis. 1928)]

c. **Property damage [§938]**

Furthermore, courts extended the doctrine to ***property*** damage—even when there was no risk of personal injuries. [**Dunn v. Ralston Purina Co.,** 272 S.W.2d 479 (Tenn. 1954)—manufacture of defective animal food that involved foreseeable risk of harm only to animals and to owner's business interests]

d. **Real property [§939]**

Most courts have extended the *MacPherson* rule to the design and construction of ***real property***. [**Wright v. Creative Corp.,** 498 P.2d 1179 (Colo. 1972)—home builder liable for negligence as to defective sliding glass door]

e. **Liability of assembler of components manufactured by others [§940]**

Most courts hold a supplier who markets a product under the supplier's name liable for negligence even though the supplier has only assembled components produced by others, and a negligently manufactured ***component*** has caused the injury. [Rest. 2d §400]

---

e.g. **Example:** If Ajax Motors, a car manufacturer, assembles into its cars a steering control negligently manufactured by XYZ Co., and the defective steering wheel causes an accident, Ajax is liable for XYZ Co.'s negligence.

---

(1) **Undiscoverable defect [§941]**

This rule applies even if the defect could ***not*** have been discovered by the defendant assembler in the exercise of due care. "One who puts out ***as his own*** product a chattel manufactured by another is subject to the same liability ***as though he were its manufacturer.***" [**Ford Motor Co. v. Mathis,** 322 F.2d 267 (5th Cir. 1963)]

f. **Proving negligence—res ipsa loquitur [§942]**

If a manufacturing defect (*e.g.*, missing part) is involved, the injured party may invoke res ipsa loquitur simply by showing that the defect is of a kind that does not usually occur in the absence of negligence of the manufacturer or someone for whom the manufacturer is liable.

---

e.g. **Example:** P is injured when his dump truck tips over during dumping operations because of a missing part in the hoist. D, the truck manufacturer, is ***presumed*** to be at fault because the defect is one that does not usually occur in the absence of the manufacturer's negligence. [**Rennick v. Fruehauf Corp.,** 264 N.W.2d 264 (Wis. 1978)]

---

5. Role of Dealer or "Middleman" [§943]

There may be situations in which the manufacturer or supplier ("D") and the dealer or "middleman" ("X") will owe ***concurrent duties*** of care to the consumer or user ("P").

a. Where dealer has no reason to know of danger [§944]

A dealer or "middleman" owes ***no duty to inspect or test*** chattels manufactured by another before selling them if she has no reason to know that the chattels may be dangerous in normal use. [Rest. 2d §402]

---

e.g. **Example:** A retailer generally owes no duty to inspect or test *packaged* goods from a ***reputable*** manufacturer prior to their sale, in the absence of a reason to suspect that something is wrong (although she cannot blind herself to anything that becomes apparent while she is preparing the goods for sale). [**Kirk v. Stineway Drug Store Co.,** 187 N.E.2d 307 (Ill. 1963)]

---

b. Where dealer has reason to know of danger [§945]

However, a dealer or "middleman" who has reason to know that the product may be dangerous in normal use owes a ***duty to inspect and test*** the goods, or at least to ***warn*** the purchaser of the potential danger. [E.L. Kellett, Annotation, Seller's Duty to Test or Inspect as Affecting His Liability for Product-Caused Injury, 6 A.L.R.3d 1 (1966); Rest. 2d §401]

---

e.g. **Examples:** A dealer has at least a duty to warn when:

(i) *Goods are purchased from an unreliable source of supply—e.g.,* dealer who buys unknown brand of hair dye from bankrupt company. [**Outwater v. Miller,** 3 A.D.2d 670 (1957)—duty to warn of uncertain quality]

(ii) *Danger is not labeled by the manufacturer—e.g.,* dealer who resells poisonous insecticide purchased in bulk from manufacturer.

(iii) *Complaints are received from other customers* as to the very same goods. [**Catlin v. Union Oil Co.,** 31 Cal. App. 597 (1916)]

(iv) *Goods are those as to which the purchaser normally relies on dealer inspection prior to purchase*, and nature of goods makes it likely that defects will lead to serious injury—*e.g.,* in purchasing an automobile, something more than a casual examination may be required. [**Williams v. Steuart Motor Co.,** 494 F.2d 1074 (D.C. Cir. 1974)]

---

(1) Effect of dealer's failure to inspect—manufacturer not excused [§946]

Note, however, that a dealer's negligence does ***not*** supersede the manufacturer's liability. The dealer's failure to inspect or test is regarded as a *foreseeable intervening force*, and hence does not affect the liability of the manufacturer. [**Ellis v. Lindmark,** 225 N.W. 395 (Minn. 1929)]

(2) Distinguish—if dealer actually knows of danger [§947]
On the other hand, if the dealer ***actually knew*** that the product was defective and dangerous, but nevertheless sold it to the purchaser without a warning, most courts hold that this ***will*** relieve the manufacturer of liability for unintended harm. The dealer's failure to warn under such circumstances is regarded as so culpable that it is treated as an ***unforeseeable*** intervening force—*i.e.*, a ***superseding cause*** of the ultimate injury which "neutralizes the risk" created by the manufacturer's original negligence. [**Stultz v. Benson Lumber Co.,** 6 Cal. 2d 688 (1936)]

(a) Caution—result differs from general rules of proximate cause [§948]
In general negligence cases (*supra,* §§488 *et seq.*), it is often foreseeable that a third party might take criminal advantage of D's actions; *e.g.,* D's careless action renders P unconscious, after which T steals P's wallet. But in the products area, it would be extraordinary for a retailer who discovers a product defect to sell the product nonetheless.

EXAM TIP **gilbert**

Products can pass through a number of hands before they reach the market, fail in the hands of the consumer, and injure someone. Different liability rules apply to each type of person in the supply chain. Some of the less obvious rules that you should remember are:

- An ***assembler*** can be held liable for the negligence of a supplier, even if the assembler ***could not have discovered*** the defect with a reasonable inspection.
- A ***dealer or "middleman"*** usually will ***not be liable*** for defects ***unless it has reason to know of them*** (e.g., because the goods were not purchased from a reliable source, the manufacturer did not label the product, prior customers have complained about the same defect, etc.).
- Although a ***manufacturer*** generally remains liable for a dealer's or middleman's negligence in selling defective goods, if the dealer or middleman ***actually knows*** of the defect and sells the goods anyway without at least warning purchasers of the danger, the ***manufacturer is relieved of liability***.

6. Damages [§949]

In a negligence action, the plaintiff can recover for personal injury or property damage caused by the product. In most states, however, ***purely economic*** loss (*e.g.,* product does not work properly, needs repairs, etc.) is ***not*** recoverable in a negligence action; economic loss can be recovered only in an action for breach of warranty (*see infra,* §§1069 *et seq.*).

a. Punitive damages [§950]

Even in an action initially brought as one for "negligence," the plaintiff may recover punitive damages upon showing recklessness (if the plaintiff has given appropriate notice of her intentions). The same is true even if the case is initially brought as one for "strict liability." [**Fischer v. Johns-Manville Corp.,** 512 A.2d 466 (N.J. 1986)]

7. **Defenses [§951]**
As in any other negligence action, the injured party's ***contributory negligence*** or voluntary ***assumption of the risk*** can be asserted as a defense. Thus, if the plaintiff knowingly or recklessly exposes herself to the danger created by the product, she cannot recover for her injuries. Similarly, ***comparative negligence*** would reduce the plaintiff's recovery if the plaintiff is also at fault.

D. Strict Liability in Tort

1. **Introduction [§952]**
In recent years, most courts have entirely bypassed warranty and negligence concepts, and have held manufacturers and suppliers of ***defective*** products ***strictly liable in tort to consumers and users for injuries*** caused by the defect. [**Greenman v. Yuba Power Products, Inc.,** 59 Cal. 2d 57 (1963); Rest. 2d §402A] Almost all strict liability claims are based on common law principles; however, statutes may explicitly or implicitly create a strict liability cause of action. [**Bencosme v. Kokoras,** 507 N.E.2d 748 (Mass. 1987)—liability for failure to remove lead paint from premises despite defendant's lack of notice]

2. **Rationale for Strict Liability Action—Maximum Protection Demanded by Interest in Human Life and Safety [§953]**
"Liability without fault" is imposed here as a matter of public policy, due to the grave risk of harm in placing ***defective*** products in the "stream of commerce."

   a. **Defendant better able to bear risk [§954]**
   A defendant manufacturer is usually better able to distribute (or insure against) the risk of loss than is the innocent consumer; *i.e.,* the manufacturer can better estimate the risks and spread the cost over his operations or pass it on to the public in the form of higher prices. [**Greenman v. Yuba Power Products, Inc.,** *supra*]

   b. **Negligence action may not be adequate remedy [§955]**
   Negligence is often too difficult to prove in product cases to be an adequate remedy. [**La Rossa v. Scientific Design Co.,** 402 F.2d 937 (3d Cir. 1968)]

   c. **Incentive for safer products [§956]**
   Moreover, imposing strict liability may increase the incentive for the manufacture and supply of safer products.

3. **Caution—Liability Not Absolute [§957]**
Note that the strict liability doctrine requires the plaintiff to prove both a ***defect*** in

the product that is ***attributable*** to the manufacturer or supplier, ***and*** that the ***defect caused the injury***. Hence, although liability is strict, it is not absolute. [**Kerr v. Corning Glass Works,** 169 N.W.2d 587 (Minn. 1969)]

4. Caution—Liability May Not Even Be "Nonfault" [§958]

Although the courts and commentators generally speak of this area as one involving "strict" or "nonfault" liability, this almost certainly is ***not*** an accurate description of the state of the law. The type of "defect" involved may control whether the applicable law is that of strict liability or of negligence. It appears that the law of strict liability applies uniformly to "manufacturing" defects; but that "design" defect and "warning" defect cases are in fact decided as negligence cases, even though the courts rarely discuss the difference. This is addressed in the following sections.

a. Three kinds of defects [§959]

A product may be defective in manufacture, in design, or in the sufficiency of the warnings accompanying it.

(1) Manufacturing defects [§960]

In a manufacturing defect case, the product is ***not in the condition that the manufacturer intended*** at the time it left his control; *i.e.,* the product does not conform to the manufacturer's own production standards. Liability for this type of defect is indeed "strict."

---

e.g. **Example:** This covers the usual "assembly line" errors in production—cases in which negligence also would lie, bolstered by res ipsa loquitur. [**Welge v. Planters Lifesavers Co.,** 17 F.3d 209 (7th Cir. 1994)—glass peanut butter jar that shattered "must have contained a defect"]

---

e.g. **Example:** It also covers situations where there may be no negligence—*e.g.,* flaws or impurities in the product that were ***not*** the result of lack of due care.

---

(2) Design defects [§961]

In a design defect case, the product was in the condition intended by the manufacturer or supplier, but was ***designed*** in such a way that it ***presented an undue risk*** of harm in normal use. Although courts speak of strict liability in these cases, the identical result would almost always be reached by a negligence analysis, because the undue risk should have been discovered and prevented by due care. In the few cases in which this is not true, courts have ***denied*** strict liability. (*See infra,* §§1022 *et seq.*)

(a) Variety of defects [§962]

A product may be defective by posing an unreasonable risk to consumers [**Matthews v. Lawnlite Co.,** 88 So. 2d 299 (Fla. 1956)—folding arm of metal rocking chair slices off occupant's fingers], or by not protecting against foreseeable risks, such as inadequate safeguards on an industrial machine.

1) **Limitation—normal wear and tear [§963]**
The defendant will not be held liable, however, for manufacturing or selling a product that simply wears out with normal use. [**Savage v. Jacobsen Manufacturing Co.,** 396 So. 2d 731 (Fla. 1981)—nonskid surface on tractor dismounting platform worn away]

2) **Application—handguns [§964]**
A product, such as a handgun, that functions as intended and is dangerous in its ordinary use, has no defect and cannot give rise to liability based on defect. [**Kelley v. R.G. Industries, Inc.,** *supra*, §911]

(b) **"Crashworthiness" [§965]**
A manufacturer can be held liable for failure to design its product so as to minimize foreseeable harm ***caused by other parties or conditions***. For example, an auto manufacturer may be liable for not designing its cars to withstand at least some highway crashes caused by ***negligent drivers*** (including the buyer). [**Larsen v. General Motors Corp.,** 391 F.2d 495 (8th Cir. 1968)]

---

e.g. **Examples:** Manufacturers have been held liable for designing a gearshift lever that impaled the driver upon collision [**Mickle v. Blackmon,** 166 S.E.2d 173 (S.C. 1969)]; a fuel tank that caught fire following a "rear-end" collision [**Nanda v. Ford Motor Co.,** 509 F.2d 213 (7th Cir. 1974)]; and a horn cap that came off the steering wheel, exposing sharp prongs that caused injuries greater than the driver otherwise would have received from a collision [**Horn v. General Motors Corp.,** 17 Cal. 3d 359 (1976)].

---

e.g. **Example:** Motorcycles may be defective for lack of crash bars to protect the driver's legs. [**Camacho v. Honda Motor Co.,** 741 P.2d 1240 (Colo. 1987)]

(c) **Approaches to design defects [§966]**
The elements of a design defect case depend on the standard used.

1) **"Risk/utility" test [§967]**
Under the prevailing approach, called a "risk/utility" test, the question for the jury is whether the product's ***risks outweigh its utility***. A significant aspect of this inquiry is whether the defendant could have removed the danger without serious adverse impact on the product's utility and price. [**Phillips v. Kimwood**

Machine Co., 525 P.2d 1033 (Or. 1974); *and see* **Dawson v. Chrysler Corp.,** 630 F.2d 950 (3d Cir. 1980), *cert. denied,* 450 U.S. 959 (1981)]

a) **Factors [§968]**
Among the determinative factors are:

(i) *Usefulness* of the product;

(ii) *Type and purpose of the product* (functional utility of design);

(iii) *Style, attractiveness, and marketability* of the product (psychological utility);

(iv) *Number and severity of injuries* actually resulting from the current design (social cost);

(v) *Cost of design changes to alleviate the problem* (safety cost—measured in both price and reduced utility of the product);

(vi) *User's anticipated awareness of inherent dangers* in the product and their avoidability; and

(vii) *Feasibility of spreading the loss* by adjustments in the product's price.

[**Dawson v. Chrysler Corp.,** *supra*; **Dreisonstok v. Volkswagenwerk, A.G.,** 489 F.2d 1066 (4th Cir. 1974); **Volkswagen of America, Inc. v. Young,** 321 A.2d 737 (Md. 1974)]

b) **Note**
In California, the ***manufacturer*** has the burden of proving that the benefits of a product's design outweigh the risks of danger inherent in that design. [**Barker v. Lull Engineering Co.,** 20 Cal. 3d 413 (1978)]

2) **"Consumer expectation" test [§969]**
Under an alternative approach, plaintiffs must prove that the product did not perform as safely as an *ordinary consumer* would have expected. [**Toney v. Kawasaki Heavy Industries, Ltd.,** 975 F.2d 162 (5th Cir. 1992)—claim barred because ordinary consumer would have realized danger of motorcycle without leg guards; *but compare* **Camacho v. Honda Motor Co.,** *supra*, §965—claim for same danger was allowed under the "risk/utility" test]

a) **Applicability to bystanders [§970]**
The courts are split over whether the consumer expectation

test is relevant when the victim was not the buyer or user. [*Compare* **Ewen v. McLean Trucking Co.,** 706 P.2d 929 (Or. 1985)—pedestrian struck by truck claimed to have poor visibility, *with* **Batts v. Tow-Motor Forklift Co.,** 978 F.2d 1386 (5th Cir. 1992)—because danger was obvious to ordinary buyer, product is not defective and no suit lies by bystander whether or not bystander knew or should have known of danger]

b) **Food cases [§971]**

The consumer expectation test is widely applied in food cases to test for defects. [**Jackson v. Nestle-Beich, Inc.,** 589 N.E.2d 547 (Ill. 1992)—whether chocolate-covered pecan-caramel candy with hard pecan shell inside was defective depends on the reasonable expectation of buyers; *but see* **Mexicali Rose v. Superior Court,** 1 Cal. 4th 617 (1992)—if tooth broke on foreign substance (*e.g.,* glass) inside chicken enchilada P need not prove negligence, but if tooth broke on natural substance (*e.g.,* chicken bone) P must prove negligence]

3) **Combined approach [§972]**

Some courts explicitly adopt a combined view under which recovery is permitted if the plaintiff establishes ***either:*** (i) that the product failed to perform as safely as an ordinary consumer would expect when it is used in an intended or reasonably foreseeable manner; ***or*** (ii) that the product's design was defective under the risk/utility analysis, above. [**Welch v. Outboard Marine Corp.,** 481 F.2d 252 (5th Cir. 1973)]

a) **Limitation—everyday experience [§973]**

Some courts permit the plaintiff to choose between the two approaches ***only*** when the "everyday experience of the product's users permits a conclusion that the product's design violated minimum safety assumptions." [**Soule v. General Motors Corp.,** 8 Cal. 4th 548 (1994)—consumer expectation theory ***not*** available concerning to what extent a car's left front quadrant will collapse in a crash because not within the consumer's everyday experience] In such a case, the plaintiff must pursue the risk/utility theory.

b) **Handguns [§974]**

The impact of a court's choice between the consumer expectation and risk/utility tests is illustrated by some of the recent handgun cases. For example, where a child is killed by the accidental discharge of a handgun, application of the risk/utility test might result in liability of the manufacturer—

the benefits of child safety features might be found to outweigh their costs. Many courts, however, have decided instead to apply the consumer expectation test to handguns, holding that guns that fire when the trigger is pulled are working exactly as consumers expect them to work. [**Halliday v. Sturm, Ruger & Co.,** 792 A.2d 1145 (Md. 2002)]

4) **"Reasonable alternative design" test [§975]**

The Second Restatement, drawing heavily on warranty analysis, was based on consumer expectations. This meant that patent dangers were not actionable. As noted above, the courts have tended to move away from that position to one that evaluates risk/utility and the feasibility of alternatives. The Third Restatement has moved more sharply in that direction by using ***only*** the "reasonable alternative design" approach (except in cases involving food, in which the consumer expectation test applies). [Rest. 3d of Torts: Products Liability ("Rest. 3d-PL") §2 & cmt. h (1998)] Under this test, a product is defective if foreseeable risks of harm could have been reduced by adoption of a ***reasonable alternative design***, the omission of which renders the product not reasonably safe. This means that if the greater safety provided by an alternative design outweighs its disadvantages (*e.g.*, more costly, less attractive), the defendant's design is defective. This reasonable alternative design test is quite similar to the risk/utility test, except that the risk/utility test does not require proof of an alternative design.

TESTS FOR DESIGN DEFECTS—A SUMMARY	gilbert
RISK/UTILITY TEST	A design is defective if its ***risks outweigh its utility***; in particular if it was possible to ***remove the danger without serious adverse impact*** on utility and price.
CONSUMER EXPECTATION TEST	A design is defective if the product did not perform ***as safely as an ordinary consumer would have expected*** (widely applied in food cases, but not applicable in some states in cases where a bystander is injured).
COMBINED APPROACH TEST	Recovery is permitted if ***either*** of the above tests is satisfied (but the consumer expectation prong may apply only in situations in which the everyday experience of consumers would allow a valid opinion regarding safety).
REASONABLE ALTERNATIVE DESIGN TEST (REST. 3D)	A design is defective if a ***reasonable alternative design*** would have reduced the foreseeable risks of harm posed by the product.

(d) **Dangers not foreseeable at time of marketing (scientifically unknowable risks) [§976]**

Whatever test of defect is used, a critical question is whether to weigh the factors as of the time of manufacture or as of the time of injury or trial. In negligence cases, the proper time to use is that of manufacture and release of the product, because the courts are explicitly judging the defendant's behavior. In so-called strict liability cases, the courts are rarely explicit about the relevant time because "negligence" is said not to be the test. In fact, however, in cases in which some crucial new information has been discovered ***after*** the product's release, the courts generally focus on the defendant's conduct ***after*** the crucial information appeared.

1) **Dominant approach—reasonable human skill [§977]**

The overwhelming view denies strict liability where the danger was something the manufacturer could not have guarded against "by the application of reasonable, developed human skill and foresight." [Rest. 2d §402A cmt. j; **Owens-Illinois, Inc. v. Zenobia,** 601 A.2d 633 (Md. 1992); **Feldman v. Lederle Laboratories,** 479 A.2d 374 (N.J. 1984), *retreating from* **Beshada v. Johns-Manville Products Corp.,** 447 A.2d 539 (N.J. 1982)—D was liable for risks unknowable at time of D's actions; *but see* **Johnson v. Raybestos-Manhattan, Inc.,** 740 P.2d 548 (Haw. 1987)—following *Beshada*]

(e) **Discovery of danger [§978]**

Even if the state does not impose liability for unknowable dangers, when the scientifically unknowable risk becomes discoverable, the manufacturer or supplier may be liable for negligence.

1) ***If the danger feasibly may be eliminated,*** the manufacturer must use due care to do so before continuing to market the product; otherwise it faces liability for selling a defective product. (*See supra,* §967.)

2) ***If the risk cannot be eliminated,*** the product is ***unavoidably unsafe.*** The manufacturer must then provide a suitable warning or, if the danger outweighs the benefits from the product, discontinue distribution altogether. (*See infra,* §983.)

3) ***A manufacturer is under a duty to take reasonable steps to warn earlier purchasers*** of already marketed products about defects that only recently became discoverable. [**Patton v. Hutchinson Wil-Rich Manufacturing Co.,** 861 P.2d 1299 (Kan. 1993)—duty imposed to use due care to warn about safety hazards discovered after sales; *but see* **Romero v. International Harvester Co.,** 979 F.2d 1444 (10th

Cir. 1992)—no duty to notify buyers of earlier model that new safety devices have been developed to handle a long-known safety problem]

(3) Inadequate warnings [§979]

In addition to the actual product itself, defects may arise from packaging and inadequate instructions, warnings, labels, etc. Inadequate warnings may make a product defective when the dangers are not apparent to consumers and users. [**Benedi v. McNeil-P.P.C., Inc.**, 66 F.3d 1378 (4th Cir. 1995)—must warn against danger of even moderate consumption of alcoholic beverages while taking Tylenol; **Davis v. Wyeth Laboratories, Inc.**, 399 F.2d 121 (9th Cir. 1968)—failure to warn user that polio vaccine gave polio to a certain number of recipients; **Emery v. Federated Foods, Inc.**, 863 P.2d 426 (Mont. 1993)—must warn against risk that young children may choke eating marshmallows]

(a) Unexpected dangers [§980]

The "danger" must be something that a reasonable user would have no reason to expect or anticipate in the product.

---

e.g. **Example:** The manufacturer of a flight of steps does not have a duty to warn of the dangers posed by use of the steps without handrails because those dangers are patently obvious. [**Lorfano v. Dura Stone Steps, Inc.**, 569 A.2d 195 (Me. 1990)]

---

e.g. **Example:** A manufacturer of an above-ground swimming pool has no duty to warn of the danger of diving into the pool if it reasonably perceives that the potential danger is readily apparent or would be disclosed by casual inspection. [**Glittenberg v. Doughboy Recreational Industries**, 491 N.W.2d 208 (Mich. 1992)]

---

e.g. **Example:** The danger of an unlocked pilot seat during the takeoff of aircraft is sufficiently obvious that the defendant manufacturer could not be held liable for failure to provide additional warning, especially where it had taken other safety precautions. [**Argubright v. Beech Aircraft Corp.**, 868 F.2d 764 (5th Cir.), *cert. denied,* 493 U.S. 934 (1989)]

---

cf. **Compare:** On the other hand, it may be reasonable to expect a martini olive to be pitted, so that strict liability might apply when a customer breaks her tooth while biting into that kind of olive.

---

1) Unexpected means of harm [§981]

Even where a product warns of a risk of harm, a court might require the warning to specify the ***means by which the harm would come about.***

---

e.g. **Example:** If a miter saw is protected by blade guards and contains a warning not to remove them, a plaintiff might argue that he reasonably thought the warnings were geared to protect inexperienced users from the danger of cutting themselves—not to protect from the danger of the blade flying from the spindle if the guards were not in place. [**Hood v. Ryobi America Corp.,** 181 F.3d 608 (4th Cir. 1999)—warning was adequate despite this argument]

---

2) **Unanticipated danger [§982]**
If the danger is also unexpected by the defendant because it could not be anticipated, most courts will analyze it as a ***negligence*** question, as with design defects, *supra*. Just as virtually no court expects manufacturers to design a product with unknowable risks in mind, virtually no court expects manufacturers to warn about the unknowable. [**Feldman v. Lederle Laboratories,** *supra*, §977; *but see* **Carlin v. Superior Court,** 13 Cal. 4th 1104 (1996)—attempting to identify a standard more demanding than negligence but less severe than strict liability in the case of an unknown danger]

(b) **Unavoidably unsafe products [§983]**
Many useful products are unavoidably unsafe (*e.g.,* knives), but this does not render them "defective"—because there is no safer way to make them.

1) **Relation to design defect [§984]**
It is clear that suppliers cannot avoid liability for a ***design*** defect by giving an adequate warning. In states that follow the risk/utility approach, an adequate warning may suffice to avoid liability only if the product's design is not defective under that test. [**Camacho v. Honda Motor Co.,** *supra,* §969]

---

e.g. **Example:** Strict liability has been imposed for marketing short-burning dynamite fuses without suitable warning, the danger from such fuses being one that would ***not*** be apparent to or expected by the normal user. [**Canifax v. Hercules Powder Co.,** 237 Cal. App. 2d 44 (1965)]

---

a) **Distinguish—consumer expectation test [§985]**
Under the consumer expectation test, however, the obviousness of a danger may well make the product nondefective. In such a situation, there would be no need to warn to avoid liability. [**Sterling Drug, Inc. v. Yarrow,** 408 F.2d 978 (8th Cir. 1969)—duty to warn patient's doctor about side effect]

(c) Testing the adequacy of warnings [§986]

A warning attached to an unreasonably dangerous product may be inadequate if, *e.g.*, it does not specify the risk the product presents, it is inconsistent with how the product is to be used, or it does not give the reason for the warning. [**MacDonald v. Ortho Pharmaceutical Corp.**, 475 N.E.2d 65 (Mass. 1985)—warning on oral contraceptive must include mention of "stroke"]

1) Limitation—special users [§987]

Although warnings usually must be written for the ordinary user [**Laaperi v. Sears, Roebuck & Co.**, 787 F.2d 726 (1st Cir. 1986)], a supplier may take into account the nature of a special clientele [**Mackowick v. Westinghouse Electric Corp.**, 575 A.2d 100 (Pa. 1990)—warning on electrical capacitor need not warn of dangers generally known to electricians].

2) Excessive warnings [§988]

Although it often seems virtually costless to add a marginal warning to a product [**Moran v. Faberge, Inc.**, 332 A.2d 11 (Md. 1975)—duty to warn of danger of pouring cologne over candle], courts are increasingly recognizing that excessive warnings may reduce the impact of important warnings [**Cotton v. Buckeye Gas Products Co.**, 840 F.2d 935 (D.C. Cir. 1988)—if every foreseeable danger needed a warning, the "list of foolish practices warned against would be so long, it would fill a volume"].

(d) Testing who must receive warning [§989]

Usually the warning must reach the person at risk from the danger. [**McCullock v. H.B. Fuller Co.**, 981 F.2d 656 (2d Cir. 1992)—supplier of glue to bookbinding plant must warn those workers who come in contact with the glue of its dangers; *but see* **Mazur v. Merck & Co.**, 964 F.2d 1348 (3d Cir. 1992)—manufacturer met its duty to warn by imposing such a duty in its contract with the distributor]

1) Learned intermediary exception [§990]

Most courts hold that in the case of pharmaceuticals, an adequate warning need reach only the prescribing physician. [**Felix v. Hoffmann-LaRoche, Inc.**, 540 So. 2d 102 (Fla. 1989); *but see* **MacDonald v. Ortho Pharmaceutical Corp.**, *supra*—warning required by FDA must reach patient] Some courts follow a similar rule as to the supplying of bulk products. [**Adams v. Union Carbide Corp.**, 737 F.2d 1453 (6th Cir.), *cert. denied,* 469 U.S. 1062 (1984); *but see* **Hunnings v. Texaco, Inc.**, 29 F.3d 1480 (11th Cir. 1994)—bulk supplier must try to assure that warnings on bulk container are repeated as product is subdivided into smaller containers]

DEFECTS CREATING STRICT LIABILITY—A SUMMARY	gilbert
MANUFACTURING DEFECTS	The product is ***not in the condition it was intended to be in*** when it leaves the defendant's control, such as a car that leaves the factory with a few lug nuts missing.
DESIGN DEFECTS	The product is in the condition intended when it leaves the defendant's control, but it was ***designed in such a way as to present an undue risk*** of harm in normal use, such as a car designed with only two lug nuts per wheel (the norm being four or five).
WARNING DEFECTS	The product is in the condition intended when it leaves the defendant's control, and it does not present an undue risk of danger when used normally, but its ***packaging or accompanying literature fails to warn of unexpected dangers from foreseeable misuses***, such as a car that becomes unstable at speeds in excess of 90 miles per hour and sold without warnings indicating this.

5. **Scope of Liability [§991]**
The developing case law has broadened the application of strict tort liability as follows. (*See infra,* §§1305-1312, for statutory limitations on strict tort liability.)

a. **Parties liable—commercial suppliers [§992]**
Any party who causes the product to "enter the stream of commerce" or "passes it on" in the stream of commerce—*i.e., all participants in the marketing* of the product—may be held strictly liable.

(1) **Applications**

(a) **Sellers [§993]**
The doctrine thus applies to ***retailers and distributors***, as well as manufacturers. Each is "an integral part of the marketing enterprise," and therefore must share the business risk with the manufacturer. [**Vandermark v. Ford Motor Co.,** 61 Cal. 2d 256 (1964)]

(b) **Lessors [§994]**
Likewise, the commercial ***bailor or lessor*** of a defective chattel may be held strictly liable for injuries caused by the defect. [**Price v. Shell Oil Co.,** *supra*, §761]

1) **Limitation—landlords [§995]**
Landlords are ***not*** treated as bailors or lessors of the furnishings or fixtures that come with a rental unit. [**Peterson v. Superior Court,** 10 Cal. 4th 1185 (1995)]

2) **Limitation—financiers [§996]**
When a financier of a commercial deal becomes a "lessor" to

protect a security interest, most courts refuse to apply strict liability. [**Nath v. National Equipment Leasing Corp.,** 439 A.2d 633 (Pa. 1981)]

(c) Assemblers of component parts [§997]

As in negligence cases (*see supra*, §940), the manufacturer is responsible for the safety of all component parts. Hence, although the manufacturer only assembles those parts into a finished product, she can be held strictly liable for ***defective components supplied by others.*** The seller of a defective component part, of course, also may be liable.

(d) Contractors [§998]

Although usually it is not negligent for a contractor to follow most specifications (*see supra*, §936), different considerations may apply in strict liability. Because the product is the issue, a contractor who provides a "defective" product may be liable. [**Michalko v. Cooke Color & Chemical Corp.,** 451 A.2d 179 (N.J. 1982)—liability imposed on contractor who rebuilt machine to specifications but without feasible safety devices and without warning about remaining nonobvious danger]

(e) Successors in interest to manufacturers of defective products [§999]

Normally, a company that has purchased the assets of a prior manufacturer, without expressly or impliedly assuming its liabilities, is not liable for injuries caused by defects in the predecessor's products. [**Lemire v. Garrard Drugs,** 291 N.W.2d 103 (Mich. 1980)—successor in interest to drugstore owner not liable for prior sale of defective drug] But most courts hold the new company strictly liable where: (i) the deal was a ***merger or continuation*** of the old corporation; (ii) the buying company ***agreed to assume*** the seller's liability; ***or*** (iii) the sale was a ***fraudulent attempt*** by the seller to escape liability. [**Nissen Corp. v. Miller,** 594 A.2d 564 (Md. 1991)]

(f) Sellers of used products [§1000]

Sellers of used products in some jurisdictions may be strictly liable for safety defects attributable to the design or manufacture if they conflict with the purchaser's reasonable expectations. In these cases an "as is" disclaimer does ***not*** shield the sellers from liability. [**Turner v. International Harvester Co.,** 336 A.2d 62 (N.J. 1975)—used truck; Rest. 3d-PL §8]

1) But note

Some courts bar strict liability against sellers of used products in the absence of representations of quality, because buyers of used products cannot reasonably expect the products to be free of defects. [**Grimes v. Axtell Ford Lincoln-Mercury,** 403 N.W.2d 781 (Iowa 1987)]

2) **Distinguish—modified or misused products [§1001]**
A separate question arises where the defect occurs not in the original design or manufacture but through modification, dilapidation, or misuse between the original and second sales. In such cases, strict liability is rarely imposed on the seller. [**LaRosa v. Superior Court,** 122 Cal. App. 3d 741 (1981)—used punch press sold 16 years after manufacture]

(g) **Franchisors [§1002]**
Even though franchisors do not normally provide the bulk of the goods sold by franchisees, they still may be liable for product defects, particularly when they retain some control over franchisees' behavior. [**Kosters v. Seven-Up Co.,** 595 F.2d 347 (6th Cir. 1979)]

(h) **Trademark licensors [§1003]**
A trademark licensor that participates in the process of designing and marketing the defective product may be strictly liable even if the licensor did not manufacture the product. [**Torres v. Goodyear Tire & Rubber Co.,** 786 P.2d 939 (Ariz. 1990)]

(2) **Distinguish—noncommercial suppliers [§1004]**
Strict liability applies only to persons ***regularly engaged*** in the ***business*** of manufacturing, selling, or leasing the product in question. Thus, persons who make only an ***occasional*** sale or bailment (*e.g.,* those who sell their own used car or lend it to another) would ***not*** be liable on this theory. [Rest. 2d §402A cmt. f; *and see* **Stiles v. Batavia Atomic Horseshoes, Inc.,** 81 N.Y.2d 950 (1993)—no strict liability for sale of used punch press where D's normal business was making horseshoes and it did not regularly sell used products]

(a) **Endorsers of products [§1005]**
Similarly, one who merely gives ***commercial endorsement*** to a product (*e.g.,* the "Good Housekeeping Seal of Approval") may be liable on a theory of ***negligent misrepresentation*** (*see infra,* §1655), but generally is ***not*** liable in warranty or strict liability in tort if the product proves defective. *Rationale:* The endorser has not put the defective product into the stream of commerce. [**Hanberry v. Hearst Corp.,** 276 Cal. App. 2d 680 (1969)]

(b) **Publishers of advertising [§1006]**
In the absence of a guaranty or warranty, a publisher is not strictly liable for defects in goods ***advertised*** in its publications. [**Yuhas v. Mudge,** 322 A.2d 824 (N.J. 1974)]

(c) **Auctioneers [§1007]**

Auctioneers are generally not held to be sellers for purposes of strict liability. [**Musser v. Vilsmeier Auction Co.,** 562 A.2d 279 (Pa. 1989)]

b. **Parties who may invoke liability**

(1) **Ultimate user or consumer [§1008]**

The ultimate user or consumer, as well as the purchaser, clearly may invoke the doctrine. Thus family members, employees, guests, etc., of the purchaser are protected. [**Alvarez v. Felker Manufacturing Co.,** 230 Cal. App. 2d 987 (1964); Rest. 2d §402A]

(a) **Note**

Passengers in a car, as well as the driver, are treated as "users."

(2) **Bystanders [§1009]**

Virtually all states hold that ***any person*** injured by a defective product can invoke strict tort liability—*e.g.,* pedestrian hit by a car whose brakes have failed. [**Codling v. Paglia,** 32 N.Y.2d 330 (1973)]

(a) **Rationale**

Bystanders should be entitled to at least as much protection as the purchaser or user of the product, because unlike the purchaser or user bystanders did not have an opportunity to inspect for defects prior to injury. Furthermore, because the manufacturer's losses can be covered by insurance or passed on to the public in the form of increased costs, there is no economic reason for treating bystanders worse than purchasers. [**Elmore v. American Motors Corp.,** 70 Cal. 2d 578 (1969)]

(3) **Rescuers [§1010]**

There is some case authority allowing recovery by persons injured while attempting to aid another who was imperiled by a defective product. [*See, e.g.,* **Guarino v. Mine Safety Appliance Co.,** 25 N.Y.2d 460 (1969)]

(4) **Business firms [§1011]**

Courts are split over whether business entities may recover from each other for property damage on the basis of strict liability. In most cases, where the parties in a commercial setting are of equal bargaining strength and have negotiated, tort actions, whether for strict liability or for negligence, have been foreclosed when the claim is solely for lost profits or other economic loss. [*See, e.g.,* **Spring Motors Distributors, Inc. v. Ford Motor Co.,** 489 A.2d 660 (N.J. 1985)] A few courts go further, barring tort actions even when the claim is for damage to property as well as economic loss. [*See, e.g.,* **Hapka v. Paquin Farms,** 458 N.W.2d 683 (Minn. 1990)—U.C.C. controls action for damage to commercial farmers' property from allegedly defective seeds]

c. **Liability extends only to "products" [§1012]**
Strict tort liability applies only where the injuries or damages have resulted from a defective "product." However, the courts have taken an expansive view of what constitutes a "product":

(1) **Products in natural state [§1013]**
Although most products are manufactured or processed in some way, this is not essential; strict liability may apply to products in their natural state (*e.g.*, sales of unprocessed, poisonous mushrooms). [Rest. 2d §402A cmt. e]

(2) **Real property as "product" [§1014]**
As originally formulated by the courts, the doctrine of strict tort liability applied only to defective ***goods***. However, courts have extended such liability to defects in the design or construction of mass-produced buildings (*i.e.*, tract homes). [**Del Mar Beach Club Owners Association v. Imperial Contracting Co.,** 123 Cal. App. 3d 898 (1981)—owners stated strict liability claim for design and construction of building complex on unstable bluff; **Schipper v. Levitt & Sons,** 207 A.2d 314 (N.J. 1965)—guest in home injured by boiler explosion]

(3) **"Products" vs. "services" [§1015]**
Strict tort liability does not apply to the rendition of services any more than does warranty liability (*see infra*, §1079). Thus, a passenger injured in an air crash cannot invoke strict liability if the cause of the crash was pilot error or improper repairs, but she can if the crash was due to a defect in the design or manufacture of the plane.

(a) **Negligent installation, service, or use of nondefective product [§1016]**
Courts refuse to apply strict liability where the product itself is not defective and the injury is caused by the manner in which the product has been ***installed, serviced, or used***. [**Hinojasa v. Automatic Elevator Co.,** 416 N.E.2d 45 (Ill. 1980)—nonmanufacturer-installer of elevator; **Hoover v. Montgomery Ward & Co.,** 528 P.2d 76 (Or. 1974)—tire dealer mounted nondefective tire on car]

(b) **Professional conduct [§1017]**
Strict liability does not apply to a physician's diagnosis or treatment [**Hoven v. Kelble,** 256 N.W.2d 379 (Wis. 1977)] or to a pharmacist's sale of prescription drugs [**Murphy v. E.R. Squibb & Sons,** 40 Cal. 3d 672 (1985)].

(c) **Hybrid conduct [§1018]**
If the defendant is providing services ***and*** a product, the courts look for the ***dominant aspect***. [**Newmark v. Gimbel's, Inc.,** 258 A.2d 697 (N.J. 1969)—strict liability against beauty salon that applied defective hair solution to customer's head]

(d) **Electricity [§1019]**

Electric current flowing through high voltage transmission lines is not a product for this purpose. [**Fuller v. Central Maine Power Co.,** 598 A.2d 457 (Me. 1991)]

(e) **Blood [§1020]**

Almost all states have passed statutes that bar courts from applying strict liability (or breach of warranty) in cases involving claimed defects (such as hepatitis virus or AIDS-related virus) in transfused blood. Plaintiffs in such cases must prove negligence. [*See, e.g.,* **Zichichi v. Middlesex Memorial Hospital,** 528 A.2d 805 (Conn. 1987)]

(4) **Product in stream of commerce [§1021]**

Remember that the "product" must have entered the stream of commerce to result in strict liability. Thus, where a plaintiff is injured by an experimental model of a machine that has been advertised but not yet sold, its manufacturer cannot be held strictly liable. [**Woods v. Luertzing Corp.,** 400 A.2d 562 (N.J. 1979)]

EXAM TIP **gilbert**

Remember that strict products liability ***applies only to products***. Thus, if you encounter an exam question in which the defendant is providing ***both a service and a product***, you must determine which is the ***dominant aspect***. If the product is provided ***incident to the service*** (*e.g.,* infected blood during an operation), there is no strict liability; the plaintiff must prove negligence. But if the service is provided ***incident to the product*** (*e.g.,* defective hair color solution applied by stylist), the defendant ***is subject to strict liability***.

d. **Liability extends only to "defective" products [§1022]**

The area of greatest difficulty is what makes a product "defective" for purposes of imposing strict liability. This in turn depends on two separate issues: (i) the types of defect, and (ii) the standard used to determine the defect. The first of these two—manufacturing defects, design defects, and defects due to lack of adequate warning—were discussed *supra,* §§959 *et seq.* The following sections consider the second issue, the standard to be applied.

(1) **Basic approaches**

(a) **Restatement approach—"defect" plus "unreasonable danger" [§1023]**

The Restatement recognizes a product as "defective" only if it is ***"unreasonably dangerous,"*** meaning that the defect that caused the plaintiff's injury must be something other than what a reasonable person would expect in normal use. [Rest. 2d §402A cmts. g, i]

1) **Latent vs. patent defects [§1024]**

This "consumer expectation" approach, literally applied, would insulate from liability any product that is patently dangerous.

a) **Modern view [§1025]**

However, as discussed *supra*, most courts no longer bar recovery simply because a defect was patent. [**Nichols v. Union Underwear Co.,** 602 S.W.2d 429 (Ky. 1980)—consumer knowledge only one of several factors that determine unreasonableness; *but see* **Curtis v. General Motors Corp.,** 649 F.2d 808 (10th Cir. 1981)—buyer of convertible vehicle cannot recover for rollover injuries even though available safety devices were not installed]

b) **Significance of modern view [§1026]**

Because most states follow either the "risk/utility" test (*supra*, §967) or the combined approach (*supra*, §972), they have implicitly rejected the narrow Restatement view that allowed recovery only for latent dangers. Note however that some of these states may still decide to adopt the Restatement's requirement that any alleged danger be "unreasonably dangerous" before finding the product "defective."

(b) **Alternative approach—"defect" alone [§1027]**

The California courts have led a strong movement that rejects the Restatement terminology of "unreasonable danger" because of possible confusion with the concept of "unreasonable" as used in negligence cases. Under this view, an action lies for injuries from a defect that may ***not*** be unreasonably dangerous in terms of foreseeability.

---

e.g. **Example:** When the racks in the back of a bakery truck came loose in a crash, hurling the driver through the windshield, the driver need only prove that defective metal clamps caused the dislodging in order to establish the required defect; he need not show that it was foreseeable that such clamps posed a risk of personal injury. [**Cronin v. J.B.E. Olson Corp.,** 8 Cal. 3d 121 (1972)]

---

(2) **Misuse [§1028]**

Regardless of what kind of "defect" is claimed, it must have arisen during the ***normal or foreseeable*** use of the product. A manufacturer is not to be held liable for ***all*** possible harms caused by its product, but only for harms caused through its intended or foreseeable use. [**Schemel v. General Motors Corp.,** 384 F.2d 802 (7th Cir. 1967)—no liability for car that went out of control at 115 m.p.h.; *but see* **Ellsworth v. Sherne Lingerie, Inc.,** 495 A.2d 348 (Md. 1985)—wearing nightgown inside out is foreseeable use]

(a) **"Normal use" [§1029]**

"Normal use" has a broader meaning than "intended use." A product may involve ***no*** risk of harm when used as intended but a serious risk when used for other purposes (*e.g.*, laundry products may be safe when used for cleaning purposes, but may contain caustic chemicals that could be fatal if swallowed by children). A manufacturer must ***foresee a certain amount of misuse or carelessness*** by customers, and thus must warn them of any dangers that could be created by such use, or must build into the product appropriate safety devices. To the extent unintended uses are reasonably foreseeable, the product may be adjudged "defective" if adequate warnings are not given or if feasible safety measures are not taken (*e.g.*, use of child-proof top). [**Gardner v. Q.H.S., Inc.**, 448 F.2d 238 (4th Cir. 1971)—strict liability imposed for failing to warn purchasers that hair rollers would explode if overheated; **Reid v. Spadone Machine Co.**, 404 A.2d 1094 (N.H. 1979)—strict liability for design change on guillotine-like cutting machine that encouraged dangerous use by two workers, rather than safe use by one worker at a time]

(b) Modifications by others [§1030]

If it is foreseeable that the buyer, after sale, will modify the chattel purchased in a dangerous way, the supplier may still be responsible for harm caused if the product "invited" such modification. [**Liriano v. Hobart Corp.**, 92 N.Y.2d 232 (1998)—plaintiff employee in grocery's meat department could sue for failure to warn of consequences of removing safety guard on meat grinder or working without a guard]

(c) Distinguish—extreme misuse [§1031]

In some cases, however, the misuse may be so extreme that the defendant need not make any warnings or take other safety precautions against it. [**Venezia v. Miller Brewing Co.**, 626 F.2d 188 (1st Cir. 1980)—eight-year-old child injured when he threw beer bottle against telephone pole and it shattered; no liability]

(3) Abnormal reactions [§1032]

Highly unusual reactions to a product do ***not*** render it "defective." However, this refers only to the situation where a plaintiff's reaction is so bizarre or unexpected that it could not reasonably have been anticipated or guarded against. [**Mountain v. Procter & Gamble Co.**, 312 F. Supp. 534 (E.D. Wis. 1970)—with over 200 million bottles of shampoo sold, only two confirmed allergic reactions before P's reaction]

(a) Distinguish—not highly unusual reaction [§1033]

On the other hand, if the reaction is shared by any significant number of potential users—even a small percentage—the manufacturer must guard against the risk by changing the product, warning of the danger, or suggesting methods by which users can safely determine their own reactions (*e.g.*, patch tests). [**Basko v. Sterling Drug, Inc.,** 416 F.2d 417 (2d Cir. 1969)]

(b) **Trend—duty to warn [§1034]**
Indeed, the growing view is that if there is a ***known*** risk of harm to ***any*** number of potential users, no matter how small, the manufacturer owes a duty to warn—particularly if a self-administered test is available to the user that would disclose his sensitivity to the product. Under such circumstances, the manufacturer's failure to warn renders the product defective. [*See* **Griggs v. Combe, Inc.,** 456 So. 2d 790 (Ala. 1984)—no liability where reaction unique; **Tiderman v. Fleetwood Homes,** 684 P.2d 1302 (Wash. 1984)—appreciable number]

WHEN PRODUCT IS DEFECTIVE—EXAMPLES **gilbert**

DEFECTIVE	NONDEFECTIVE
• Injures someone while being used properly	• Injures someone while being used properly but the injury is the result of a highly unusual and unanticipated reaction by the defendant
• Injures someone while being used in a foreseeable but improper manner (but carelessness may be a defense)	• Injures someone while being used in an extremely unusual manner
• Injures someone after being modified in a foreseeable manner even if modification contributes to injury	• Injures someone after product wears out after normal lifespan

e. **Proof required [§1035]**
The burden is on the plaintiff to prove (i) that the product ***was in fact "defective"*** when it left the defendant's control, and (ii) a ***causal relationship*** to the plaintiff's injuries. Often, expert witnesses are required. [**Friedman v. General Motors Corp.,** 331 N.E.2d 702 (Ohio 1975)]

(1) **Circumstantial evidence of "defect" [§1036]**
Even though the plaintiff cannot prove a specific defect in the product, some courts permit recovery if an inference that the relatively new product ***was*** defective can be drawn from proof that it ***functioned improperly in normal use.*** [**Greco v. Bucciconi Engineering Co.,** 407 F.2d 87 (3d Cir. 1969)]

(2) **Causation [§1037]**
The plaintiff must show that the injuries were caused ***by*** some defect in the product that ***existed*** at the time it was ***marketed by the defendant.*** [**Moerer v. Ford Motor Co.,** 57 Cal. App. 3d 114 (1976)]

(a) Defectiveness at time of marketing [§1038]

The plaintiff must show that the product was defective at the time it left the defendant's hands; *i.e.*, strict liability will not be imposed on the defendant if the defect is attributable to subsequent mishandling [**Williams v. Ford Motor Co.,** 494 S.W.2d 678 (Mo. 1973)] or to a dangerous and unforeseeable alteration in the product after it was purchased [**Jones v. Ryobi, Ltd.,** 37 F.3d 423 (8th Cir. 1994); *but see* **Liriano v. Hobart Corp.,** *supra,* §1030—if modification is foreseeable, liability may follow].

(b) Cause in fact (actual cause) [§1039]

It is sufficient that the defect was a ***substantial factor*** in causing the injury. [**Codling v. Paglia,** *supra,* §1009]

1) Warning cases [§1040]

In warning cases, the plaintiff must show that an adequate warning would have made a difference. [**Odom v. G.D. Searle & Co.,** 979 F.2d 1001 (4th Cir. 1992)—alleged lack of adequate warning irrelevant where physician testified that he knew of danger of IUD and would still have used same product even if it had contained more extensive warning; **Lussier v. Louisville Ladder Co.,** 938 F.2d 299 (1st Cir. 1991)—even though ladder may have lacked warnings against unsuitable uses and thus been a defective product, P used ladder in way he knew was unsuitable so that warning would not have mattered]

a) Application—the "heeding presumption" [§1041]

In an effort to encourage suppliers to use adequate warnings, some courts have developed a "heeding presumption" under which it is presumed that if an adequate warning had accompanied the product, the buyer/user would have heeded it—and not been hurt. [**Richter v. Limax International, Inc.,** 45 F.3d 1464 (10th Cir. 1995)—buyer need not persuade jury that she would have behaved differently if the missing warning had been present—causation was presumed; **Coffman v. Keene Corp.,** 628 A.2d 710 (N.J. 1993); *but see* **General Motors Corp. v. Saenz,** 873 S.W.2d 353 (Tex. 1993)—refusing to apply presumption in case where warning was given but was claimed to have been inadequate]

2) Lack of safety features [§1042]

A defendant manufacturer may be liable where it failed to provide safety features that decreased the severity of injuries from inevitable accidents—even where the product did not cause the accident. [**Tafoya v. Sears Roebuck & Co.,** 884 F.2d 1330 (10th

Cir. 1989)—riding lawnmower lacked "deadman device" that would have lessened severity of plaintiff's injuries when mower tipped over]

(c) **Proximate cause—effect of intervening causes [§1043]**
If other causes are proved, their effect on causation is determined by the same proximate cause tests applicable in negligence cases (*see supra*, §§442 *et seq.*).

---

e.g. **Example:** The defect that caused a truck to stall on a highway (where P later ran into it) was not a proximate cause of the crash because the driver had abandoned the truck, and for three hours before the accident, cars had safely avoided it. [**Peck v. Ford Motor Co.,** 603 F.2d 1240 (7th Cir. 1979)]

---

e.g. **Example:** The manufacturer of defective fire clothing is not liable for harm sustained by the sister of a burned firefighter who agreed to donate skin tissue for her brother's grafts. [**Bobka v. Cook County Hospital,** 422 N.E.2d 999 (Ill. 1981)]

---

1) **Injuries to third parties after supplier's adequate warning to purchaser [§1044]**
Under present case law, a supplier who has given ***adequate*** post-sale warning of a latent danger to the original purchaser of the product may not be liable for injuries later suffered by third persons. The original purchaser's ***failure to respond*** to the warning may be treated as a ***superseding cause*** of the injury.

a) **Application—auto recall cases [§1045]**
Auto Manufacturer recalls all cars sold by it for replacement of potentially dangerous steering control. Purchaser receives recall notice but fails to return the car for replacement of the defective part. Later, Purchaser sells the car to a third party, without advising of the recall. Purchaser's failure to return the car or warn the new owner about the steering control terminates Manufacturer's liability (but ***Purchaser*** may be liable to the new owner in a negligence case). [**Ford Motor Co. v. Wagoner,** 192 S.W.2d 840 (Tenn. 1946); *and see supra*, §947—retailer who knows about danger in a product]

b) **Application—prescription drugs [§1046]**
Similarly, the manufacturer of a new drug who has given ***adequate*** warning to prescribing physicians of the drug's potential hazards is not ordinarily strictly liable to a patient who suffers adverse reactions from the medication.

The physician's failure to disclose the hazards to the patient is regarded as a superseding cause of the injury. (But the patient may have a valid claim against the physician for lack of informed consent; *see supra*, §§112-113.)

1/ Exception—mass immunization [§1047]
Warning physicians may not be sufficient where the drug is the subject of mass immunization programs. Here, the manufacturer is required to warn the ***ultimate recipients*** or see to it that notice reaches such persons. *Rationale:* In these cases, there is no physician to provide the patient with an individualized balancing of the risks; hence, consumers must be given sufficient information to balance the benefits and risks themselves. [**Reyes v. Wyeth Laboratories,** 498 F.2d 1264 (5th Cir. 1974); Rest. 3d-PL §6]

f. Kinds of losses recoverable

(1) Personal injuries (or death) [§1048]
Pain and suffering caused by injury from the defective product are recoverable, together with all damages consequential thereto—medical expenses, loss of income, etc. And if the injury results in death, a wrongful death action will lie.

(2) Property damage [§1049]
Physical damage to other property is recoverable in almost all states. [**Vaughn v. General Motors Corp.,** 466 N.E.2d 195 (Ill. 1984); **John R. Dudley Construction, Inc. v. Drott Manufacturing Co.,** 66 A.D.2d 368 (1979)]

(3) Economic losses [§1050]
Most courts, however, do ***not*** allow recovery in tort for ***purely economic losses*** (*e.g.,* product does not perform well, and purchaser is deprived of profits she expected to make through its use or is forced to incur additional expenses to make it work, etc.). The purchaser's right to recover such losses is more of a "sales" problem than a "torts" problem, and she usually is limited to a contract action against the person who sold her the product (or, if there are warranties running from the manufacturer, against the manufacturer as well). [**East River Steamship Corp. v. Transamerica Delaval, Inc.,** 476 U.S. 858 (1986); **Danforth v. Acorn Structures, Inc.,** 608 A.2d 1194 (Del. 1992)] This approach applies even where the defect created a serious risk of personal injury that did not come to pass. [**Airport Rent-A-Car, Inc. v. Prevost Car, Inc.,** 660 So. 2d 628 (Fla. 1995); *but see* **Washington Water Power Co. v. Graybar Electric Co.,** 774 P.2d 1199 (Wash. 1989)—adopting a minority rule that permits recovery of pure economics loss where a risk of personal injury had been created]

(a) **Minority view [§1051]**
A minority has extended strict tort liability for defective products to purely economic losses. [*See, e.g.,* **Alaskan Oil, Inc. v. Central Flying Service, Inc.,** 975 F.2d 553 (8th Cir. 1992)]

(b) **Misrepresentation [§1052]**
In any event, if the product has been ***advertised*** or represented to perform according to certain specifications, there may be a possibility of recovery in tort for ***misrepresentation*** (*see infra,* §§1671-1674).

(c) **Part of other action [§1053]**
Moreover, if the plaintiff suffers personal injury or property loss, all states permit economic loss to be recovered in tort with the other damages under strict liability.

6. Defenses to Strict Tort Liability

a. Contributory negligence [§1054]
Whether contributory negligence is a valid defense depends on how this term is used:

(1) **Failure to discover or guard against danger [§1055]**
Contributory negligence in the sense of ***failing to exercise reasonable care to discover*** the danger ***or to guard against it*** traditionally was ***not a valid defense*** to a strict liability claim in most states. [Rest. 2d §402A cmt. n]

---

e.g. **Example:** D leased an airplane without oil in it to P, who took off without checking the oil level. D could not allege contributory negligence as a defense when the plane crashed shortly after takeoff. [**Rudisaile v. Hawk Aviation, Inc.,** 592 P.2d 175 (N.M. 1979)]

---

(2) **Unreasonable misuse [§1056]**
However, contributory negligence in the sense of ***unreasonable misuse*** of a defective product—in a manner or for a purpose for which no reasonable person would use it (*e.g.,* driving a passenger car at 150 m.p.h.)—traditionally ***did bar*** liability. [**McDevitt v. Standard Oil Co.,** 391 F.2d 364 (5th Cir. 1968)]

(a) **Note**
As previously discussed, the better analysis is that a product will not be found "defective" if it did not stand up under the plaintiff's ***unforeseeable*** misuse. (Remember, however, that a certain amount of product misuse may be considered "normal"; *see supra,* §1028.)

b. Comparative fault [§1057]
Most comparative negligence states reduce the plaintiff's recovery in strict liability cases by some amount to reflect the fact that the injury was caused in

part by the plaintiff's own carelessness. This avoids the need to distinguish between "knowing" and "unknowing" contributory fault. [**Daly v. General Motors Corp.,** 20 Cal. 3d 725 (1978); *but see* **Simpson v. General Motors Corp.,** 483 N.E.2d 1 (Ill. 1985)—contra]

(1) Comment

There is a theoretical inconsistency in talking about "comparative negligence" here because the defendant seller may not have been negligent at all; *i.e.,* his liability may arise regardless of any fault on his part. Still, it is thought anomalous to allow the defense where the claim is based on negligence and deny it where the claim is based on strict liability. Where contributory negligence is shown, these jurisdictions refuse to deprive the plaintiff of all recovery in strict liability. Therefore, courts recognizing comparative negligence in negligence cases apply a comparable notion here (sometimes called comparative "fault") that has the effect of reducing the plaintiff's recovery by an amount the jury deems appropriate. [**Suter v. San Angelo Foundry & Machine Co.,** 406 A.2d 140 (N.J. 1979); **Seay v. Chrysler Corp.,** 609 P.2d 1382 (Wash. 1980)]

(2) Note

Another approach is to compare the plaintiff's deviation from a reasonable standard and separately compare the deviation between the defendant's product and a good product—and then compare the two deviations. [*See* **Sandford v. Chevrolet Division of General Motors,** 642 P.2d 624 (Or. 1982)]

(3) Crashworthiness [§1058]

Where the plaintiff is hurt in a car accident that was totally his fault and then seeks to recover for enhanced injuries due to the lack of crashworthiness of the car's interior, most courts will reduce the plaintiff's recovery to reflect his fault in the original accident. [**Whitehead v. Toyota Motor Corp.,** 897 S.W.2d 684 (Tenn. 1995); *but see* **Reed v. Chrysler Corp.,** 494 N.W.2d 224 (Iowa 1992)—contra]

c. Assumption of the risk [§1059]

One who ***knows*** of the danger or risk involved, and ***unreasonably*** continues to use the product, may be held to have assumed the risk. This is a ***valid defense*** to strict liability. But this is more clearly understood in terms of lack of proximate causation—that the danger did not cause the injury because the victim, knowing fully of the danger, undertook to encounter it. Note that in cases of obvious dangers, the analysis parallels the "consumer expectation" approach to defects (*see supra,* §969)—but it extends beyond obvious dangers.

(1) Application—warning of latent danger [§1060]

Thus, even where the danger was not obvious, if the plaintiff has learned about it and still unreasonably continues to use the product, recovery may be barred. The analysis here may be similar to the analysis of actual cause, *supra,* §§1039-1040.

(a) **"Adequately" warned [§1061]**
The crucial issue, of course, is the ***adequacy*** of the warning given. Courts tend to be demanding in judging this factor, holding the warning inadequate if it was either incomplete (as where the manufacturer disclosed some but not all risks) or was "watered down" by the manufacturer's own aggressive sales promotion, which had the effect of persuading users to disregard the warnings given. [**Stevens v. Parke, Davis & Co.,** 9 Cal. 3d 51 (1973)]

(2) **Limitation—reasonable alternative required [§1062]**
There is no "voluntary" assumption of the risk where the plaintiff's continued use of the known defective product results from ***economic duress.*** [**Messick v. General Motors Corp.,** 460 F.2d 485 (5th Cir. 1972)—traveling salesman (P) had asked D repeatedly to repair defective steering, and was "forced" to continue driving car because D was unable to replace it]

(3) **Limitation—voluntary and knowing assumption of risk required [§1063]**
The injured party must actually have known of the particular danger involved and freely decided to face it.

---

e.g. **Example:** Where the injured party was run over and killed by a road grader, no assumption of risk defense lies. Deliberately confronting the machine would have been suicide, and the victim exhibited no such intention. [**West v. Caterpillar Tractor Co.,** 547 F.2d 885 (5th Cir. 1977)]

(a) **Note**
The relevant knowledge and voluntary decision to face the risk is that of the ***victim***, not that of the product's ***buyer***. [**Hammond v. International Harvester Co.,** 691 F.2d 646 (3d Cir. 1982)—manufacturer who removed safety device at request of knowledgeable buyer cannot argue that buyer's employee assumed the risk]

(4) **Rejection of assumed risk as complete defense [§1064]**
The impact of comparative negligence is felt in products cases as well. Certainly, as noted, a court that uses the risk/utility test will be less likely to find assumption of risk because the danger is more likely to be latent. But beyond that, most courts hold that if a dangerous situation confronts a person who unreasonably chooses to encounter it, the defense is not assumption of risk but rather comparative fault. [**Davenport v. Cotton Hope Plantation Horizontal Property Regime,** *supra,* §859]

d. **Disclaimers [§1065]**
Contractual disclaimers of liability generally have been held ***invalid as against public policy***—at least as to products liability claims involving personal injury arising out of ***consumer*** transactions. [**Vandermark v. Ford Motor Co.,** *supra,* §993]

(1) **Exception—parties of equal bargaining power [§1066]**
Courts may uphold contractual disclaimers as between two business concerns with relatively equal bargaining positions. [**Delta Air Lines, Inc. v. McDonnell Douglas Corp.,** 503 F.2d 239 (5th Cir. 1974)—upholding contract limiting liability for repair expenses due to defective nose gear] Note that the harm when commercial entities are involved is economic loss, not personal injury.

e. **Statute of limitations [§1067]**
The personal injury (tort) statute of limitations applies, rather than the contracts statute of limitations. (*But compare* "statutes of repose," *infra*, §1307.)

f. **Preemption [§1068]**
In a few situations, courts have concluded that federal legislation has impliedly preempted state tort law. [**Geier v. American Honda Motor Co.,** 529 U.S. 861 (2000)—National Transportation and Motor Vehicle Safety Act and administrative regulations issued under it preempt state tort action claiming that a 1987 car marketed without airbags was defectively designed; **Cipollone v. Liggett Group, Inc.,** 505 U.S. 504 (1992)—federal statute preempted state tort claims in cigarette cases based on failure to warn in advertising and promotion and neutralization of warnings by advertising, but did not preempt claims based on fraud, testing and research, or express warranty]

E. Liability Based on Breach of Warranty

1. **Introduction [§1069]**
Rather than relying on negligence or strict liability as the basis for liability, courts may impose liability for breach of warranty in a *contract* action.

2. **Express Warranties [§1070]**
Whatever a seller represents to a purchaser about the product involved (by advertising or otherwise) may be an express warranty, *i.e.*, a part of the contract. And if the warranty is breached (the product is not as represented), causing damage or injury to the purchaser relying on the representation, that purchaser has a direct action against the seller *on the contract.*

3. **Implied Warranties [§1071]**
However, most warranty actions are based on *implied* warranties—the assurance (implied in law) from the seller to the buyer that the product purchased will do no harm in normal use.

a. **U.C.C. provisions [§1072]**
The Uniform Commercial Code ("U.C.C.") implies two pertinent warranties:

(1) Fitness for particular purpose [§1073]

If the seller knows (or has reason to know) that the buyer is purchasing goods ***for a particular purpose***, and is ***relying on the seller's skill or judgment*** in supplying appropriate goods, there is an implied warranty that the goods sold are in fact fit for ***that*** purpose. [U.C.C. §2-315]

(2) Merchantability [§1074]

If goods are supplied by one who deals in goods of that kind, a warranty is implied that they are of at least "fair average" quality, *i.e.*, ***generally fit for ordinary purposes.*** [U.C.C. §2-314]

TYPES OF WARRANTIES — gilbert

TYPE	HOW ARISES	BY WHOM	DISCLAIMER
EXPRESS	By affirmation of fact, promise, description, model, or sample	Any seller	Extremely difficult to disclaim
IMPLIED			
• **WARRANTY OF MERCHANTABILITY (FIT FOR ORDINARY PURPOSES)**	By sale of goods of the kind regularly sold by the merchant	Merchant only	By disclaimer mentioning "merchantability" (if written disclaimer, it must be conspicuous).*
• **WARRANTY OF FITNESS FOR PARTICULAR PURPOSE (FIT FOR BUYER'S PARTICULAR PURPOSE)**	By sale of goods where seller has reason to know of particular purpose and of buyer's reliance on seller to choose suitable goods	Any seller	By conspicuous ***written*** disclaimer.* If there is no disclaimer, an attempt to limit consequential damages that may be recovered for defective consumer goods is prima facie unconscionable

*These warranties may also be disclaimed by language such as "as is."

(3) Distinguish—warranty and strict liability in tort [§1075]

Warranties under the U.C.C. are judged from the consumer expectation perspective. It is thus possible that a product might be defective in tort because of the existence of feasible alternatives while at the same time not breach either implied warranty. Similarly, a product might breach a warranty although it is not defective under tort analysis. [*See, e.g.,* **Castro v. QVC Network, Inc.,** 139 F.3d 114 (2d Cir. 1998)—roasting pan might not breach the risk/utility test, but it breached the warranty standard because unduly dangerous if used as advertised; **Denny v. Ford Motor Co.,** 87 N.Y.2d 248 (1995)—although plaintiff's Ford Bronco II passed the risk/utility test for off-road use, jury should be charged on warranty theory as well because Ford arguably improperly marketed the Bronco II as an "ordinary purpose" vehicle safe for daily driving]

b. Transactions covered [§1076]

The U.C.C. itself applies only to ***sales of goods*** (*i.e.,* personal property).

(1) Bailments [§1077]

Most courts, however, have implied similar warranties ("by analogy") in connection with the ***bailment*** or ***lease*** of personal property. [Gary D. Spivey, Annotation, Application of Warranty Provisions of Uniform Commercial Code to Bailments, 48 A.L.R.3d 668 (1973)]

(2) Sale of real property [§1078]

Some courts have held that a breach of warranty claim may exist in connection with the construction and sale of a ***new home.*** [**Caceci v. Di Canio Construction Corp.,** 72 N.Y.2d 52 (1988)]

(3) "Goods" vs. "services" [§1079]

But warranties will ***not*** be implied in contracts for ***services.*** Thus, a doctor does not "impliedly warrant" the safety or adequacy of the treatment furnished; a railroad does not warrant the fitness or safety of the transportation furnished; and a repair shop, in the absence of an express agreement, does not warrant the adequacy of its work. Any liability for injuries sustained as the result of improper services rendered must therefore be based on tort (or an explicit contract provision), not implied warranty. [**Dennis v. Allison,** 698 S.W.2d 94 (Tex. 1985)—no warranty in case of psychiatrist assaulting patient]

(a) Borderline cases [§1080]

Sometimes it is difficult to distinguish a "sale of goods" from "services rendered." This issue has frequently been encountered with regard to restaurants. Early cases concluded that no "sale of goods" was involved and hence no warranty implied. Virtually all courts now agree that even though a service is also provided, food served in restaurants is in fact "sold," so that the owner is subject to implied warranty liability. [**Arnaud's Restaurant v. Cotter,** 212 F.2d 883 (5th Cir. 1954)]

(b) Blood [§1081]

Almost all states have legislation barring warranty suits by persons who have received infected blood in a transfusion. [**Zichichi v. Middlesex Memorial Hospital,** *supra,* §1020]

(4) **Defendants must be dealers [§1082]**
Liability for implied warranties generally is imposed only on those who "deal" regularly in the product. Thus, *e.g.,* it generally does not apply to a person who sells his car or stereo system to a neighbor.

4. **Effect of Breach of Warranty [§1083]**
Liability for breach of warranty is really a form of ***strict liability.*** If the product is defective, the warranty is breached and the manufacturer is automatically liable—whether or not due care was exercised in its manufacture, or the manufacturer was otherwise "at fault."

5. **Requirement of "Privity of Contract" [§1084]**
The traditional problem with basing liability on breach of warranty is that it is a ***contract*** action, so that "privity of contract" between the injured party and the party sought to be held liable for the injuries normally must be shown.

a. **Former rule—implied warranties required pure privity [§1085]**
Because a seller's implied warranties ran only to the immediate buyer, a manufacturer's implied warranties normally would run only to its distributor or wholesaler. The ultimate ***purchaser*** or consumer of the goods had ***no direct action against the manufacturer,*** because there was no contract between them.

(1) **Result—multiplicity of suits [§1086]**
This led to a multiplicity of actions: Injured purchaser sued retailer, who in turn sought indemnity from wholesaler, who in turn sought indemnity from manufacturer. Moreover, if the retailer was insolvent, the purchaser might have had no effective remedy, in which case the manufacturer escaped liability.

(2) **Distinguish—express warranties [§1087]**
But the result was different if the manufacturer made an ***express*** warranty to the public (*e.g.,* in advertising) upon which the ultimate purchaser ***relied*** in acquiring the product. Here, in the event of breach, the purchaser (but not other users or injured bystanders) was allowed a direct action against the manufacturer. [**Hauter v. Zogarts,** 14 Cal. 3d 104 (1975)]

b. **Modern law—modified interpretation of privity [§1088]**
The privity rules still apply to retailers, manufacturers, and other commercial sellers, but the rules have been relaxed considerably and no longer distinguish between implied and express warranties.

(1) **U.C.C. provisions [§1089]**
The U.C.C. offered three ***alternative*** versions for the states to adopt. [U.C.C. §2-318] Thus, depending on the state, privity extends to:

(a) ***The family or guests of the immediate buyer*** when personally injured; ***or***

(b) ***Any individual who may reasonably be expected to use***, consume, or be affected by the goods and who suffers personal injury; ***or***

(c) ***Any person who may reasonably be expected to use,*** consume, or be affected by the goods and who is injured.

(2) Background [§1090]

These alternatives were not offered when the U.C.C. was first presented to the states, and therefore some states adopted no version of section 2-318 because the version initially offered was more restrictive than state law.

c. Abandonment of "privity" requirement as to dangerous products [§1091]

Aside from the U.C.C., courts struggling with warranty concepts have been chipping away at the old privity requirements in order to hold a manufacturer or supplier strictly liable to those hurt by use or consumption of its product.

(1) Former view—exceptions regarding specific products [§1092]

The earliest cases involved foodstuffs, medicines, firearms, etc. Because of the great potential harm involved, courts held the manufacturer liable in warranty to the ultimate ***user*** of such products (whether or not such person was the actual purchaser).

(2) Modern approach—"foreseeable scope of use" test [§1093]

Today, many courts have expanded this to encompass ***any dangerous product***, and hold that implied warranties arising from the sale thereof extend not only to the purchaser or user of such products, but also to all persons within the ***foreseeable scope of use***. [**Henningsen v. Bloomfield Motors, Inc.,** 161 A.2d 69 (N.J. 1960)—auto manufacturer held liable in warranty for injuries caused by a defective steering wheel, not only to ultimate purchaser of the car but also to foreseeable users (*e.g.*, passengers in car)]

d. Consumer protection statutes [§1094]

A few states have gone even further to abolish the requirement of "privity" between the manufacturer and purchaser of ***all consumer goods*** (whether or not generally thought of as dangerous). [*See, e.g.,* Cal. Civ. Code §§1790 *et seq.*]

e. Causation [§1095]

The defendant is not liable where, because of an independent superseding event, such as the plaintiff's assumption of risk, its breach is not the proximate cause of the damage.

(1) Limited to latent dangers [§1096]

The warranty approach is the source of the "consumer expectation" approach. This means that if the danger of the product is apparent to the ordinary buyer, there will be no liability for breach of any warranty, either because there is no breach or because there is no causation. In effect, this means that plaintiffs in warranty cases are often limited to latent dangers.

---

e.g. **Example:** Ps noticed sparks and smoke coming from their television set and called D for a service appointment. Before the repair, however, they turned on the set again and watched it for two hours, despite seeing more sparks and smoke. D was not liable for the resulting fire. [**Erdman v. Johnson Bros. Radio & Television Co.,** 271 A.2d 744 (Md. 1970)]

---

f. **Damages [§1097]**

Damages for breach of warranty are substantially the same as in a successful strict liability tort action—*i.e.,* all damages proximately caused by the breach (including personal injury, pain, and suffering). However, a few states bar damages for wrongful death (*see infra,* §§1156-1171) on a breach of warranty theory. [**Geohagan v. General Motors Corp.,** 279 So. 2d 436 (Ala. 1973)]

EXAM TIP gilbert

In products liability actions based on ***negligence*** or ***strict liability theories***, ***any foreseeable plaintiff***, including a bystander, can sue ***any commercial supplier*** in the chain of distribution ***regardless of*** the absence of a contractual relationship (privity) between them. However, ***breach of warranty*** is a contract action, which traditionally required privity between the plaintiff and the defendant. But under modern law, privity extends at least to the ***family or guests of the immediate buyer*** (and to others under alternative U.C.C. provisions). Thus, where a father purchases a six-pack of soda and one of the glass bottles explodes, injuring his daughter, the daughter may bring a breach of warranty action against the manufacturer of the bottle.

6. Defenses to Warranty Actions

a. **Contributory negligence [§1098]**

Although the plaintiff's contributory negligence is not formally a defense to a claim for breach of warranty [**Brown v. Chapman,** 304 F.2d 149 (9th Cir. 1962)], most courts have developed an analogous defense to parallel the tort developments [*see, e.g.,* **West v. Caterpillar Tractor Co.,** *supra,* §1063—comparative fault defense in warranty cases].

(1) **Distinguish—assumption of risk [§1099]**

If the plaintiff actually discovers a defect and unreasonably uses the product in its defective condition, assumption of the risk *is* a complete defense in warranty actions. Some courts might analyze this as a lack of causation (*see supra,* §1095).

b. Disclaimers [§1100]

By appropriate language, a manufacturer or seller may limit or exclude warranties that would otherwise arise from the sale of goods. [U.C.C. §2-316]

(1) Sufficient language [§1101]

If a chattel is conspicuously marked "as is," the "as is" language may be sufficient to exclude all warranty liability. Warranty liability may be disclaimed more specifically, too, such as by the following language: "No warranties, express or implied, are made as to the fitness or merchantability of this product beyond the description on the face hereof." [U.C.C. §2-316]

(2) Consumer goods [§1102]

However, some states now require much more specific language to disclaim warranties in the sale of consumer goods. [*See* Cal. Civ. Code §1792.4—requires such explicit warnings that few products could be sold on this basis]

(3) Limitation—"unconscionability" [§1103]

If there has been no valid disclaimer, an attempt to limit consequential damages that may be recovered after a breach is deemed "prima facie unconscionable" as to ***personal injuries*** arising out of the use of ***consumer goods.*** [U.C.C. §2-719(3)]

(4) Scope of disclaimers as effective defense—seller not insulated from liability [§1104]

Although the seller is able to successfully exclude warranties, disclaimers are binding only on the purchaser of the goods; they do not bar the claims of an injured third party who is ***not*** the purchaser. [**Ferragamo v. Massachusetts Bay Transportation Authority,** 481 N.E.2d 477 (Mass. 1985)]

c. Notice requirements [§1105]

Warranty actions may be barred if the injured purchaser fails to give the seller "timely notice" of breach. [U.C.C. §2-607(3)(a)]

d. Statute of limitations [§1106]

The usual warranty limitations period is four years, running from the delivery of the goods. [U.C.C. §2-725] Because the tort statute generally is shorter but runs only from the time of injury, a plaintiff may find that ***only*** tort (or warranty) is available in a specific case.

Chapter Five: Nuisance

CONTENTS

▶	Key Exam Issues	
A.	In General	§1107
B.	Plaintiff's Interest	§1114
C.	Defendant's Conduct	§1118
D.	Substantial and Unreasonable Harm to Plaintiff	§1122
E.	Causation	§1132
F.	Remedies	§1134
G.	Defenses	§1138

Key Exam Issues

If you see a nuisance question on your exam, consider the following issues:

1. Is this a ***public*** or ***private*** nuisance (*i.e.,* whose interest is being invaded)? This issue affects a party's standing to sue.

2. Is this a ***nuisance*** situation or a ***trespass to land***? The distinction between nuisance and trespass is very important. Nuisance protects the plaintiff against ***interference with the use or enjoyment*** of her land; trespass involves a ***physical invasion*** of the plaintiff's land. Consider the facts carefully to make this determination. And don't forget that a particular fact situation could be ***both*** a nuisance and a trespass to land.

3. Is the harm ***substantial and unreasonable***? In general, plaintiffs are accorded less protection against nuisance than against trespass. When someone has physically intruded onto your land either by entering it or by throwing rocks onto it, there are few defenses to their actions. But where the interference has involved something that is harder to keep contained, such as odor or noise, there is—out of necessity—less complete protection. This accounts for the introduction of questions of reasonableness, the nature of the neighborhood, etc. Therefore, it is particularly important to work carefully with the facts in determining whether a nuisance is present.

A. In General

1. Prima Facie Case [§1107]

Prima facie case:

- *Act by Defendant*
- *Nontrespassory Invasion of Plaintiff's Interest*
- *Intent, Negligence, or Strict Liability*
- *Substantial and Unreasonable Harm*
- *Causation*

2. Private Nuisance vs. Public Nuisance

a. Private nuisance defined [§1108]

A "private nuisance" is a nontrespassory interference with the plaintiff's interest in the ***use or enjoyment*** of her property.

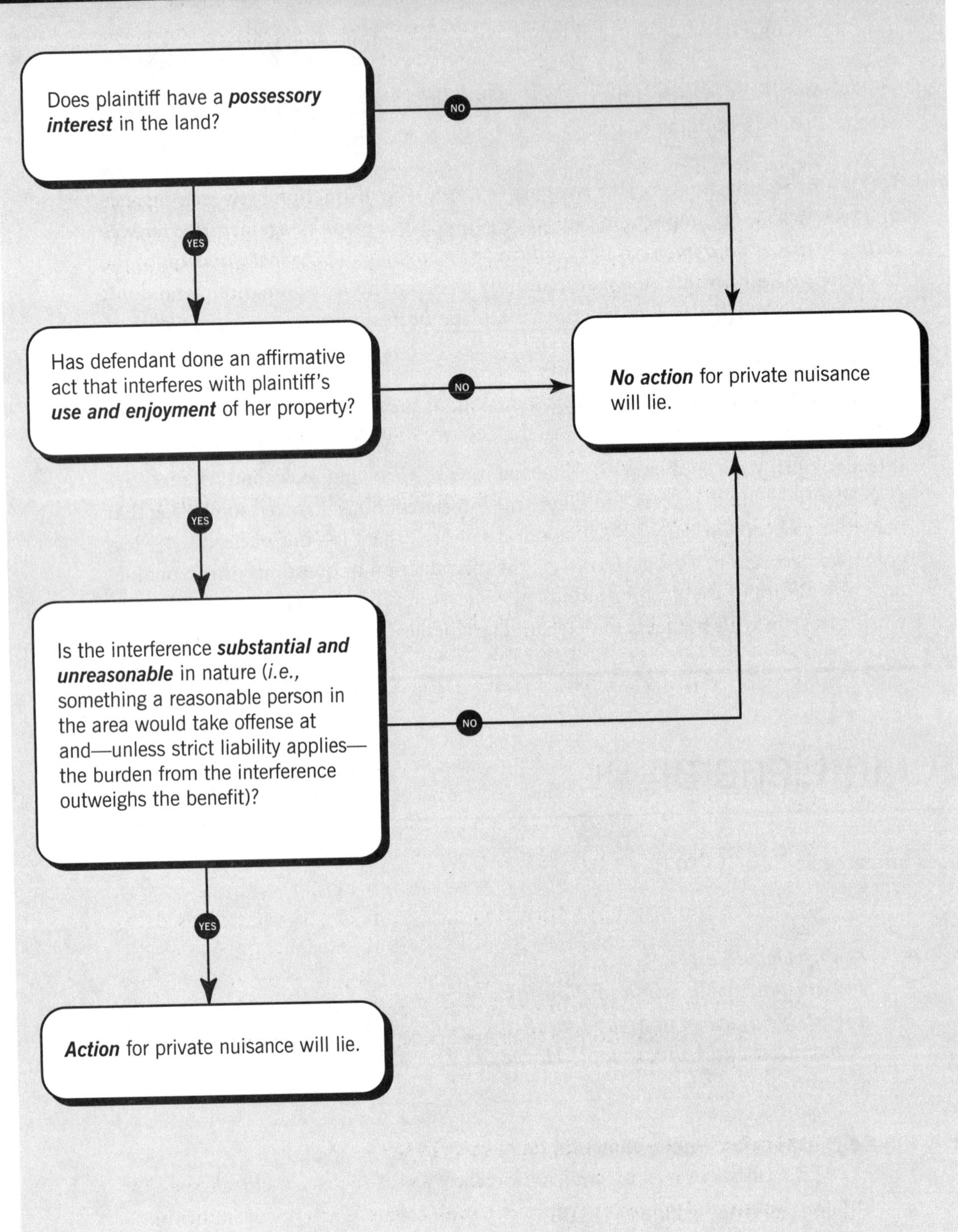
APPROACH TO DETERMINING PRESENCE OF A PRIVATE NUISANCE
gilbert
Does plaintiff have a possessory interest in the land?
NO
YES
Has defendant done an affirmative act that interferes with plaintiff's use and enjoyment of her property?
NO
No action for private nuisance will lie.
YES
Is the interference substantial and unreasonable in nature (i.e., something a reasonable person in the area would take offense at and—unless strict liability applies—the burden from the interference outweighs the benefit)?
NO
YES
Action for private nuisance will lie.

(1) **Distinguish—trespass [§1109]**

Many types of conduct may be ***both*** a trespass and a nuisance; *e.g.,* blasting on the defendant's land may unreasonably interfere with the plaintiff's enjoyment of her land because of the noise involved (and thus be a nuisance) and at the same time may throw rocks into the plaintiff's garden (and thus be a trespass). Similarly, the flooding of the plaintiff's land or seepage onto it may also constitute both a trespass and a nuisance.

---

e.g. **Example:** Although D's act in casting microscopic, undetectable particulates from its smelters onto P's land may be a trespass [**Bradley v. American Smelting & Refining Co.,** *supra,* §205], if the intrusion comes through noise waves, odor, or light, only nuisance will lie [**Wilson v. Interlake Steel Co.,** 32 Cal. 3d 229 (1982)].

---

b. **Public nuisance defined [§1110]**

A "public nuisance" is an act by a defendant that obstructs or causes ***inconvenience or damage to the public*** in the exercise of ***rights common to all,*** or in the enjoyment or use of common property. For a public nuisance, criminal as well as civil sanctions may be imposed. [**Armory Park Neighborhood Association v. Episcopal Community Services,** 712 P.2d 914 (Ariz. 1985)]

(1) **Standing to sue [§1111]**

Generally, only the state—acting through public officials—can redress a public nuisance; a private individual may maintain an action for a public nuisance ***only*** if she suffers an injury ***"peculiar in kind"***—*i.e.,* apart from that common to the public.

---

e.g. **Example:** An obstruction on a public road is a public nuisance, but it is a private nuisance as to P if it also blocks her driveway. [**Burgess v. M/V Tamano,** 370 F. Supp. 247 (D. Me. 1973)]

---

e.g. **Example:** During construction on D's building, a wall collapsed, resulting in street closures that disrupted P's business for five weeks. The court found that P's injury was greater in degree than others but not different in kind, and therefore was insufficient to sustain a public nuisance claim. [**532 Madison Avenue Gourmet Foods, Inc. v. Finlandia Center, Inc.,** 96 N.Y.2d 280 (2001)]

---

(2) **Application—environmental damage [§1112]**

This distinction is of vital importance where a private citizen sues for environmental pollution. At present, most courts limit a private individual's recovery to those damages that she ***personally*** sustains, on the rationale that pollution is a public problem with which courts cannot deal effectively in litigation between private parties. [**Boomer v. Atlantic Cement Co.,** 26 N.Y.2d 219 (1970)]

(3) **Application—handguns and fast food [§1113]**
In recent years, plaintiffs have attempted to use public nuisance doctrine as a broader public policy tool, particularly in the context of handguns and fast food. Courts have generally dismissed claims that the ***lawful sales of lawful products*** can create a public nuisance. [*See, e.g.,* **Camden County Board of Chosen Freeholders v. Beretta, U.S.A. Corp.,** 273 F.3d 536 (3d Cir. 2001)] With regard to handguns, suits of this sort were ended by a federal statute enacted in 2005 that bars tort liability for gun manufacturers in the absence of a ***defect*** in the gun. [Protection of Lawful Commerce in Arms Act, 15 U.S.C. §§7901 - 7903]

B. Plaintiff's Interest

1. **In General [§1114]**
The defendant's act must have resulted in a nontrespassory interference with the plaintiff's interest in the ***use or enjoyment of land.***

2. **Possessory Interest in Land Required [§1115]**
The plaintiff's interest must be either ***actual possession*** or the ***right to immediate possession.*** Thus, *e.g.,* a lessee or adverse possessor can recover, whereas a lessor cannot. [**Brink v. Moeschl Edwards Corrugating Co.,** 133 S.W. 1147 (Ky. 1911)]

a. **Who may sue [§1116]**
The plaintiff must be the one who has possession. Thus, an employee, a licensee, or even the spouse of the possessor does ***not*** have sufficient status to sue. [**Page v. Niagara Chemical Division,** 68 So. 2d 382 (Fla. 1953)]

3. **Expansion—Interference with Business Interest [§1117]**
Some courts have extended the tort of nuisance to interference with business interests, as well as use and enjoyment of land. For example, several cases have held that pollution of a lake or river is a private nuisance as to commercial fisheries operating on the river. [**Hampton v. North Carolina Pulp Co.,** 27 S.E.2d 538 (N.C. 1943)]

C. Defendant's Conduct

1. **Nature of Act [§1118]**
The defendant's act must be shown to have been (i) ***intentional,*** (ii) unintentional but ***negligent, or*** (iii) neither intentional nor negligent, but actionable under rules governing liability for abnormally dangerous activities (***strict liability***). [Rest. 2d §822; **Copart Industries, Inc. v. Consolidated Edison Co.,** 41 N.Y.2d 564 (1977)]

a. **Act is required [§1119]**
Some act is required because of the traditional view that a landowner has no duty to avoid harm to neighbors from natural conditions. [**Lichtman v. Nadler,** 74 A.D.2d 66 (1980)—no liability for mosquito infestation and unpleasant odors emanating from natural accumulation of water on D's land]

b. **Application [§1120]**
Of course, ***most nuisances are intentional*** because the plaintiff has usually complained to the defendant, and the defendant has ignored the complaints and continued his activities. [**Smith v. Staso Milling Co.,** 18 F.2d 736 (2d Cir. 1927)]

---

e.g. **Example—negligent nuisance:** In cases where D has failed to exercise due care to abate a condition under his control (*e.g.*, a stench, or fires on his property that blow smoke onto P's land), negligent nuisance is found.

---

e.g. **Example—strict liability nuisance:** A nuisance may be predicated on ***strict liability*** even where D has taken reasonable precautions to control the situation and is therefore not "at fault", as where D stores explosives in a residential neighborhood, or causes noise and fumes from oil well drilling. [**Cumberland Torpedo Co. v. Gaines,** 255 S.W. 1046 (Ky. 1923)] *But note:* Strict liability applies only where the nuisance results from an abnormally dangerous activity or from an animal. (*See supra*, §§881 *et seq.*)

---

2. **Why Does It Matter? [§1121]**
This distinction based on the defendant's conduct is of primary importance in determining what ***defenses*** are available. For example, contributory negligence is a defense to a nuisance predicated on negligence but not to intentional nuisances. [**McFarlane v. City of Niagara Falls,** 247 N.Y. 340 (1928)]

D. Substantial and Unreasonable Harm to Plaintiff

1. **In General [§1122]**
The nontrespassory invasion must result in ***substantial and unreasonable*** harm to the plaintiff's interest in the use and enjoyment of the land.

2. **"Substantial" [§1123]**
The term "substantial" refers to the quantitative aspect of the interference: It must be something that a ***reasonable person*** would take offense at, rather than a de minimis annoyance to which only a grouchy neighbor or unduly sensitive person would object. [**Dunlop v. Daigle,** 444 A.2d 519 (N.H. 1982)—kennel for 38 dogs four feet from P's rental unit]

3. "Unreasonable" [§1124]

If an intentional or negligent nuisance is alleged, the defendant's conduct must be unreasonable in the sense that, taking all the factors into consideration, the harm done by the interference ***outweighs*** justifications for the defendant's conduct. [**Antonik v. Chamberlain,** 78 N.E.2d 752 (Ohio 1947); *and see* Property Summary]

a. Factors to consider [§1125]

Important factors in determining whether the conduct is unreasonable are:

(i) The ***suitability*** of the invading use ***to the neighborhood*** where it takes place;

(ii) The ***values*** of the respective properties;

(iii) The ***cost*** to the defendant to eliminate the condition complained of; and

(iv) The ***social benefits*** from allowing the condition to continue (employment of others, etc.).

[Rest. 2d §828; *and see* Remedies Summary—doctrine of "balancing hardships" in deciding whether to enjoin a nuisance]

b. Aesthetic considerations [§1126]

Most courts have held that aesthetic considerations may not ordinarily create a nuisance if the activity is being run without unreasonable noise, odors, etc. [**Wernke v. Halas,** 600 N.E.2d 117 (Ind. 1992)—tasteless yard decorations involving toilet seat and unattractive and vulgar graffiti not actionable; *and see* **Adkins v. Thomas Solvent Co.,** 487 N.W.2d 715 (Mich. 1992)—property owner cannot recover for lost value due to erroneous public fear that defendant's pollution will some day reach plaintiff's property]

(1) Exception—funeral homes [§1127]

Many states have concluded that a funeral home, no matter how carefully and tastefully run, may be a nuisance if located in a residential district. [**Mitchell v. Bearden,** 503 S.W.2d 904 (Ark. 1974); **Travis v. Moore,** 377 So. 2d 609 (Miss. 1979)—properly run funeral home that caused "depressed feelings" to residents in residential neighborhood was a nuisance]

c. Prior occupation [§1128]

For some courts, a relevant question as to the reasonableness of a use is whether the use ***preceded the plaintiff's presence.*** [**McQuade v. Tucson Tiller Apartments, Ltd.,** 543 P.2d 150 (Ariz. 1975)] This is especially true where the use offended no one until the plaintiff moved in. [**Spur Industries, Inc. v. Del E. Webb Development Co.,** 494 P.2d 700 (Ariz. 1972)] On the other hand, this cannot be conclusive because the defendant's conduct might not have become "unreasonable" until persons moved onto surrounding land.

d. **Effect of zoning [§1129]**
Neither are zoning ordinances conclusive as to what is a "reasonable use," because activities permitted under zoning laws may still be unreasonable as to neighbors. [**Armory Park Neighborhood Association v. Episcopal Community Services,** *supra*, §1110—center that provided care for indigent people could be held a nuisance despite its compliance with zoning provisions]

(1) **But note**
A *few* states (*e.g.*, California and New York) provide that a zoning ordinance is a ***presumptive defense***; *i.e.*, if the use is permitted under local zoning ordinances, it is presumptively not a nuisance. (*See* Property Summary.)

4. **Minority Rule—Intentional Substantial Interference Enough [§1130]**
A growing minority of states now hold that in cases of ***intentional*** nuisance, the plaintiff need only show a substantial interference with the use and enjoyment of the land; *i.e.*, the defendant may be liable even if his conduct is reasonable. [**Jost v. Dairyland Power Cooperative,** 172 N.W.2d 647 (Wis. 1969)—very useful power plant provided much needed energy to area but also damaged crops on P's nearby land; even though benefits created by D outweighed harm, plant was held a nuisance]

a. **Restatement view [§1131]**
The Second Restatement provides that an intentional invasion is unreasonable "if the harm resulting from the invasion is severe and greater than the other should be required to bear without compensation." [Rest. 2d §829A]

E. Causation

1. **Intentional Nuisance [§1132]**
If the case is one of intentional nuisance, causation is basically the same as for battery (*see supra*, §17).

2. **Negligence or Strict Liability [§1133]**
If the nuisance is predicated on negligence or strict liability, the rules of causation are based on negligence standards (*see supra*, §§415 *et seq.*).

F. Remedies

1. **Judicial Relief [§1134]**
Compensatory ***damages*** may be awarded for the interference, and where the invasion is of a nonrecurring nature compensatory damages usually suffice. However, most nuisances are continuing in nature, and the remedy sought in such cases is usually an

injunction against future invasions together with damages for past invasions. [**Valasek v. Baer,** 401 N.W.2d 33 (Iowa 1987)—D enjoined from spreading hog manure on a section of his farmland close to P's home because of noxious odor] (For conditions governing injunctive relief, *see* Remedies Summary.)

a. **Continuing nuisances [§1135]**
If the nuisance is continuing but can be discontinued, the plaintiff may elect whether to sue once for all damages or sue periodically for past damages. [**Baker v. Burbank-Glendale-Pasadena Airport Authority,** 39 Cal. 3d 862 (1985)—D could stop airport nuisance at any time]

b. **Punitive damages [§1136]**
Punitive damages may be recovered if the defendant's conduct was willful and malicious. [**Atlas Chemical Industries, Inc. v. Anderson,** 524 S.W.2d 681 (Tex. 1975)]

2. **"Self-Help" [§1137]**
The plaintiff may also be entitled to the "self-help" remedy of ***abatement***—*i.e.,* entering the defendant's land to correct the nuisance. (*See* Property Summary.)

G. Defenses

1. **Contributory Negligence [§1138]**
Depending on the type of nuisance involved, the defendant may reduce or escape liability by proving that the plaintiff was negligent. [**Delaney v. Philhern Realty Holding Corp.,** 280 N.Y. 461 (1939)]

a. **Negligence [§1139]**
Where a nuisance results from negligence, contributory negligence is an available defense. [**Calder v. City & County of San Francisco,** 50 Cal. App. 2d 837 (1942)] The jurisdiction's normal rules of comparative negligence (or contributory negligence) are used. [**Nelson v. Hansen,** 102 N.W.2d 251 (Wis. 1960)]

b. **Intentional nuisance [§1140]**
However, where the nuisance is intentionally committed, contributory negligence is ***no defense.***

c. **Abnormally dangerous activity [§1141]**
Where the nuisance is based on an abnormally dangerous activity, ***comparative*** negligence is likely to apply (*see supra,* §921).

2. **Assumption of Risk [§1142]**
Whether a nuisance is intentional, negligent, or based on strict liability, assumption of risk ***is*** an available defense. [**Jacko v. City of Bridgeport,** 213 A.2d 452 (Conn. 1965)]

a. **Consent [§1143]**
If the plaintiff has consented to the building of structures by the defendant, knowing that they will create a nuisance, the plaintiff cannot recover for damages caused by that construction. [**Crawford v. Magnolia Petroleum Co.,** 62 S.W.2d 264 (Tex. 1933)]

b. **"Coming to" the nuisance [§1144]**
However, the mere fact that an activity creating a nuisance existed before the plaintiff came within its scope is ordinarily ***not*** a defense.

(1) **No knowledge of nuisance [§1145]**
If the plaintiff did not foresee the damage complained of, she is not precluded from seeking recovery for it. [**Weston Paper Co. v. Pope,** 57 N.E. 719 (Ind. 1900)]

(2) **Knowledge of nuisance [§1146]**
Even if the plaintiff knew of the nuisance, the majority holds that the knowledge is generally no defense, and the plaintiff may seek recovery. [**Kellogg v. Village of Viola,** 227 N.W.2d 55 (Wis. 1975)]

(a) **Prior occupation [§1147]**
These courts may still consider prior occupation as relevant to the reasonableness of the activity. (*See supra*, §1128.)

(b) **Plaintiff's purpose [§1148]**
Even in states following the majority position, if the plaintiff moved in solely to bring a lawsuit, recovery will be barred. [Rest. 2d §840D]

(c) **Minority view [§1149]**
A minority of courts deny recovery altogether when a plaintiff comes to a nuisance with knowledge of it. [**East St. Johns Shingle Co. v. City of Portland,** 246 P.2d 554 (Or. 1952)]

EXAM TIP **gilbert**

Coming to the nuisance is a popular exam ploy. Watch out for a fact pattern with a sympathetic defendant—such as a farmer whose family has been raising pigs on the same plot of land for generations without complaint from neighboring farmers, but who has been receiving complaints over the past five years from rich urban lawyers who have moved into country estates built by developers who bought out all of the farmer's neighbors. If the lawyers file a nuisance action, although some courts will take into account the plaintiffs' coming to the nuisance, ***in no court will that fact be determinative***—all other relevant factors will also be considered, such as the ***suitability*** of the farmer's use ***to the neighborhood***, the ***value*** of the properties in question, the ***costs*** of eliminating the condition complained of, and the ***social benefits*** of allowing the use to continue.

Chapter Six: Miscellaneous Factors Affecting Right to Sue

CONTENTS

▶	Key Exam Issues	
A.	Survival of Tort Actions	§1150
B.	Wrongful Death	§1156
C.	Injuries to Members of the Family	§1172
D.	Tort Immunity	§1211
E.	Release and Contribution Among Joint Tortfeasors	§1252
F.	Indemnity	§1262
G.	Statutes of Limitations	§1268

Key Exam Issues

The material in this chapter applies to ***every tort action*** considered in this Summary but is central to personal injury situations. It is rare that an exam question will build heavily on any part of this material, but on the other hand, it is quite common for these topics to be necessary to fill out your answer. Therefore, keep in mind the following:

1. Always check to see if anyone has died, because this will require you to address questions of ***survival*** and ***wrongful death***.

2. If any of the parties are related, look for ***new types of damage*** (such as loss of consortium), and consider ***intrafamily immunities*** if one tries to sue the other.

3. If more than one person has committed the tort, consider whether there may be ***contribution*** or ***indemnity***.

A. Survival of Tort Actions

1. Common Law—No "Survival" [§1150]

At common law, with few exceptions, there was a rule that tort actions did not "survive," meaning that the death of ***either*** the tortfeasor ***or*** the person injured terminated any existing tort cause of action and prevented any recovery by or against the estate.

2. Survival Statutes [§1151]

The common law rule has been changed to some extent by statute ("survival statutes") in almost every jurisdiction.

a. Personal injury and property damage [§1152]

These statutes allow survival of causes of action for personal injuries as well as property damage incurred up to the time of death.

(1) Pain and suffering [§1153]

There is a split of authority on whether a plaintiff may recover for a decedent's pain and suffering. The majority of jurisdictions allow such recovery [*see, e.g.,* **Beynon v. Montgomery Cablevision Ltd. Partnership,** *supra,* §525—$350,000 award for emotional distress suffered during two seconds before deadly automobile accident; **De Long v. County of Erie,** 60 N.Y.2d 296 (1983)—$200,000 for 12 minutes of terror before death], but some jurisdictions deny it [*see, e.g.,* Cal. Civ. Proc. Code §377.34—claim for pain and suffering damages does not survive victim's death; *but see* **Sullivan v. Delta Air Lines, Inc.,** 15 Cal. 4th 288 (1997)—statute does not apply where death occurs while plaintiff's trial court judgment is on appeal].

b. **Intangible personal interests [§1154]**
Most states do not allow actions to survive where the tort involves recovery of damages for the invasion of intangible personal interests—*e.g.,* defamation, right of privacy, malicious prosecutions, etc. [**Innes v. Howell Corp.,** 76 F.3d 702 (6th Cir. 1996); *but see* **Canino v. New York News, Inc.,** 475 A.2d 528 (N.J. 1984)—contra]

c. **No punitive damages [§1155]**
Even though a cause of action survives the death of the tortfeasor, it is generally recognized that the plaintiff ***cannot*** recover punitive damages against the estate of a deceased tortfeasor. [**Hofer v. Lavender,** 679 S.W.2d 470 (Tex. 1984); *but see* **G.J.D. v. Johnson,** 713 A.2d 1127 (Pa. 1998)—explicitly adopting minority position]

EXAM TIP **gilbert**

It is important to remember these, perhaps logically inconsistent, rules: While most survival statutes allow survivors to sue for the pain and suffering felt by the decedent before death, they do not allow victims to sue a deceased tortfeasor's estate for punitive damages.

B. Wrongful Death

1. **Common Law—No Cause of Action [§1156]**
At common law, no action could be brought for wrongfully causing the death of a human being; *i.e.,* the person responsible for the death could be held criminally, but not civilly, responsible. Thus, apart from the law against murder, it was cheaper for one to kill a victim than to scratch him!

2. **Wrongful Death Statutes [§1157]**
This situation was remedied in England by the passage of Lord Campbell's Act in 1846, essentially a "true" wrongful death statute (*see* below). Today, every American jurisdiction has some type of statutory remedy for wrongful death.

a. **Types of wrongful death statutes**

(1) **"Survival" type [§1158]**
Some statutes authorize the survival of any action that the ***decedent himself***

might have maintained, and enlarge it to include the damages ***sustained by his estate*** by reason of his death ("survival type").

---

e.g. **Example:** Damages recoverable under this type of statute therefore include the decedent's pain and suffering and medical expenses, together with loss of future net earnings or savings.

---

(2) "True" type [§1159]

Most jurisdictions have statutes that create a ***new cause of action*** for the benefit of particular ***surviving relatives*** (usually spouse, children, and parents), and permit recovery only of the ***pecuniary loss*** sustained by the relatives. [Cal. Civ. Proc. Code §§377.60 - .62; *but see* **Hopkins v. McBane,** 427 N.W.2d 85 (N.D. 1988)—allowing recovery of damages for survivors' mental anguish]

(a) No recovery for decedent's damages [§1160]

Under this type of statute, any claim that the victim would have had against the tortfeasor must be maintained in a ***separate survival action*** (by his estate), although the two actions are usually prosecuted concurrently and may ultimately benefit the same survivors. Thus, if the victim had incurred wage losses, medical expenses, etc., prior to his death, these are recoverable by his estate—as are pain and suffering in those states that permit survival of such claims (*see supra,* §1153).

(b) Measure of damage—pecuniary loss [§1161]

The measure of damages under the "true" type of wrongful death statute is the ***pecuniary loss*** suffered by the surviving relatives—*i.e.,* the loss of the value of the ***companionship, support, services, and contributions*** that they would have received from the victim had he not been killed. Even the value of lost inheritance is considered a pecuniary loss. [**Schaefer v. American Family Mutual Insurance Co.,** 531 N.W.2d 585 (Wis. 1995)] (Note that most states deny recovery for the survivors' grief or mental anguish caused by the wrongful death, although undoubtedly juries are influenced by this factor in evaluating the pecuniary loss. [*See, e.g.,* **Wardlow v. City of Keokuk,** 190 N.W.2d 439 (Iowa 1971)])

1) Computing pecuniary loss

a) Wage earners [§1162]

If the decedent was a wage earner, the damages to survivors are based on the estimated amount of ***earnings*** (less living expenses) over the remainder of the decedent's working expectancy and divided among the eligible survivors.

b) Children [§1163]

If the victim was a child, the earnings are likely to be purely speculative—as are any "contributions" or support that the parent might have received. Even so, courts uniformly permit recovery, instructing the jury to fix an award based on the "pecuniary value" of the loss of the child's life, including contributions that might have continued after majority. [*See, e.g.*, **Mitchell v. Buchheit,** 559 S.W.2d 528 (Mo. 1977)]

1/ Note

One way to calculate "pecuniary value" is to consider what the parents would otherwise have received in their expected later years from their (then) adult children, calculated in terms of what it would cost to obtain comparable care from nurses and comparable advice and counseling from advisers and therapists. [**Green v. Bittner,** 424 A.2d 210 (N.J. 1980)]

c) Non-wage earners [§1164]

If the victim was a spouse or parent with no earnings, courts generally permit recovery of an amount that would be required to ***replace the services*** performed in caring for the children and family. A non-wage earner's advice and companionship to the family are deemed lost "services," and hence substantial verdicts can be sustained as "pecuniary losses." Some courts do not require proof of the actual cost of replacing these services. [**Wentling v. Medical Anesthesia Services,** 701 P.2d 939 (Kan. 1985)—$786,166.64 to surviving husband and two children]

d) Retired persons [§1165]

Again, there is a problem in computing damages for the death of elderly parents because it is highly speculative what support or contributions the survivors could expect. But courts generally uphold reasonable awards on the theory that every life has ***some*** pecuniary value.

2) Effect of remarriage [§1166]

If the decedent was married, most courts bar evidence that the surviving spouse has remarried (for fear of discouraging remarriage) or may remarry (on the rationale that it is too "speculative" whether remarriage will better the surviving spouse's position financially). The jury thus assesses evidence on the assumption that the survivor will remain a widow(er) for the rest of her (or his) life. [**Groesbeck v. Napier,** 275 N.W.2d 388 (Iowa 1979)]

(c) **No punitive damages [§1167]**
The general rule is that even in cases where punitive damages could have been awarded against the defendant had the victim survived (*i.e.,* where the defendant acted "maliciously," etc.), punitive damages are not awardable in a wrongful death action. Courts have held that such a distinction is constitutional. [**Georgie Boy Manufacturing, Inc. v. Superior Court,** 115 Cal. App. 3d 217 (1981)]

b. **Defenses assertable**

(1) **Victim's negligence, etc. [§1168]**
Under either type of wrongful death statute, defenses that could have been asserted against the decedent had she survived may be set up as defenses in the wrongful death action. Thus, the victim's ***contributory negligence, assumption of the risk,*** etc., will all be held to bar maintenance of a wrongful death action by her survivors. (In comparative negligence states, the victim's negligence may ***reduce*** the damages recoverable.) [**Horwich v. Superior Court,** 21 Cal. 4th 272 (1999)—recognizing general rule imputing victim's negligence to those suing derivatively]

(2) **Victim's recovery inter vivos [§1169]**
Similarly, most courts hold that if the victim sued and ***recovered*** for the injury during her lifetime, the recovery ***precludes*** any action after death based on the same injury.

(3) **Beneficiary's negligence [§1170]**
In the majority of jurisdictions (*i.e.,* those having the "true" type of wrongful death statute), contributory negligence of the ***sole*** beneficiary in causing the accident that led to the victim's death is a bar to any recovery (or a basis for reducing recovery in a comparative negligence jurisdiction).

(a) **Multiple beneficiaries [§1171]**
If there are *several* beneficiaries under the statute, and only one was negligent, the damages recoverable are generally reduced proportionally (and the negligent beneficiary's recovery is reduced or barred). [**Lucas v. Mississippi Housing Authority,** 441 So. 2d 101 (Miss. 1983); *but see* **Teeter v. Missouri Highway & Transportation Commission,** 891 S.W.2d 817 (Mo. 1995)—allowing full recovery and requiring defendant to bring a contribution action against the negligent beneficiary]

"TRUE" TYPE WRONGFUL DEATH ACTIONS	gilbert
WHO MAY SUE?	In most states, a surviving spouse and surviving lineal relatives, such as children and parents of the decedent.
WHAT MAY BE RECOVERED?	Damages for the ***pecuniary loss*** the ***survivor*** has suffered as a result of the decedent's death, such as the value of lost companionship, support, services, and contribution.
WHAT MAY *NOT* BE RECOVERED?	Damages for the decedent's lost wages, medical expenses, pain and suffering, etc.; and in many states, damages for mental anguish caused by the victim's death and punitive damages.
WHAT DEFENSES MAY BE RAISED?	Defenses that could be raised against the decedent had the decedent survived (*e.g.,* the decedent's contributory negligence, assumption of risk, and/or comparative negligence); the decedent's recovery of damages for the injury while alive; and the beneficiary's negligence that contributed to the decedent's death.

C. Injuries to Members of the Family

1. Loss of Consortium and Services

a. Common law

(1) Husband's right—services and consortium [§1172]

The common law rule was that a husband had a right to the ***services and consortium*** (society and sexual relations) of his wife and was entitled to damages if deprived thereof. Thus, if a third person tortiously injured the wife, causing her illness or other bodily harm, the husband had his own ancillary cause of action against the tortfeasor for loss of his wife's services and consortium (together with the actual ***expenses*** he incurred for her care).

(2) Parent's right—services only [§1173]

Either parent (father or mother) having the custody and control of a minor child was deemed entitled to the child's ***labor***, and could maintain an independent action against any third person who injured the child for loss of the child's earnings or services of economic value (together with any ***expenses*** incurred by the parent for the child's care). But ***no*** action was permitted for loss of the child's consortium (filial affection and society).

(3) Distinguish—no wife's or child's right [§1174]

A wife was ***not*** deemed to have any right to the services ***or*** consortium of her husband; nor was a child deemed to have any right to the support of a parent. The result was that although a wife or child was protected under wrongful death statutes in the event the tortfeasor ***killed*** the victim, they had ***no*** protection if the victim survived.

b. Modern law

(1) Either spouse can recover for loss of services and consortium [§1175]
Most states today have changed the common law rule so as to permit ***either spouse*** to recover for loss of the other's services and consortium, on the ground that both spouses have equal rights in the marital relationship. [*See, e.g.,* **Rodriguez v. Bethlehem Steel Corp.,** 12 Cal. 3d 382 (1974)]

(a) What constitutes "loss of consortium" [§1176]
To establish loss of consortium, the plaintiff must show a ***complete*** loss of the companionship of and intercourse with the injured spouse for ***some definite period*** of time. Recovery is generally not permitted for injuries that merely put a "strain" on the marital relationship (*e.g.,* where injured spouse scarred or disfigured). [**Park v. Standard Chem Way Co.,** 60 Cal. App. 3d 47 (1976)]

1) Spouses only [§1177]
The relationship must be one of legal marriage. Thus, a long-term live-in lover may not recover for injuries suffered by his or her partner, neither may a person recover for injuries suffered by his or her prospective spouse during their engagement. [**Elden v. Sheldon,** *supra*, §774; *but see* **Dunphy v. Gregor,** *supra*, §774—contra]

a) No recovery against negligent spouse [§1178]
The deprived spouse has no cause of action for loss of consortium against the negligent injured spouse. [**McIntosh v. Barr,** 397 N.W.2d 516 (Iowa 1986)]

2) Distinguish—death of spouse [§1179]
If a spouse has been killed, the only remedies available to the surviving spouse are the survival and wrongful death statutes. Almost all courts have refused to create common law loss of consortium actions in such cases. [**Liff v. Schildkrout,** 49 N.Y.2d 622 (1980); *but see* **Gaudette v. Webb,** 284 N.E.2d 222 (Mass. 1972)—recovery for wrongful death has common law origin]

(b) Minority view [§1180]
Only Utah rejects consortium actions altogether. [**Boucher *ex rel.* Boucher v. Dixie Medical Center,** 850 P.2d 1179 (Utah 1992)]

(2) Parent can recover for loss of child's services and consortium [§1181]
Most states permit a parent to recover for loss of an injured child's consortium.

[*See, e.g.*, **United States v. Dempsey,** 635 So. 2d 961 (Fla. 1994); **Gallimore v. Children's Hospital Medical Center,** 617 N.E.2d 1052 (Ohio 1993); *but see* **Powell v. American Motors Corp.,** 834 S.W.2d 184 (Mo. 1992)—contra; **Estate of Wells v. Mount Sinai Medical Center,** 515 N.W.2d 705 (Wis. 1994)—no action by parent for loss of companionship of adult child]

(a) Damages [§1182]

The older rule limited the recovery to economic losses, but later cases extend recovery to loss of the child's society and comfort. [*See, e.g.*, **Howard Frank, M.D., P.C. v. Superior Court,** 722 P.2d 955 (Ariz. 1986)]

(b) Extent of harm [§1183]

For the parent to recover for loss of the child's consortium, the injury does ***not*** necessarily have to be the functional equivalent of death or be characterized as "catastrophic." [**Pierce v. Casas Adobes Baptist Church,** 782 P.2d 1162 (Ariz. 1989)—evidence of significant interference with child's capacity to interact with parents in a normally gratifying way may suffice]

(c) Limitation—minors [§1184]

Most states limit the action to injuries to minor children. A minority of states extend it to adult children. [*See, e.g.*, **Howard Frank, M.D., P.C. v. Superior Court,** *supra*]

(3) Child cannot recover for loss of parent's consortium [§1185]

Most states ***deny*** recovery when children sue for loss of the consortium of their injured parents. [*See, e.g.*, **Borer v. American Airlines, Inc.,** 19 Cal. 3d 441 (1977); *but see* **Villareal v. Arizona Department of Transportation,** 774 P.2d 213 (Ariz. 1989)—small minority contra]

c. Effect of victim's contributory negligence [§1186]

Most courts treat the spouse's or parent's claim for medical expenses and loss of consortium as "derivative" of the victim's claim. Thus, they hold that the victim's contributory negligence (or assumption of the risk or other valid defense) ***bars*** the spousal or parental claim as well (or, in comparative negligence states, reduces damages proportionately). [*See, e.g.*, **Blagg v. Illinois F.W.D. Truck & Equipment Co.,** 572 N.E.2d 920 (Ill. 1991)]

d. Joinder requirement [§1187]

To minimize the possibility of double recovery, the spouse's or parent's claim for loss of consortium must be joined in the same action with the victim's claim for personal injury. Thus, no consortium recovery is allowed if the victim has settled or already recovered. [**Schreiner v. Fruit,** 519 P.2d 462 (Alaska 1974)]

2. Prenatal Injuries to Child

a. Early view—no recovery [§1188]

Early cases denied a child any cause of action for injuries sustained prior to birth.

b. Modern view—recovery allowed by virtually all courts [§1189]

The modern view allows recovery by a child after birth for any prenatal injuries, provided the child was shown to have been *"viable"* (*i.e.*, capable of life apart from the mother) at the time of injury. [*See, e.g.*, **Williams v. Marion Rapid Transit,** 87 N.E.2d 334 (Ohio 1949)]

(1) Extension in a few states [§1190]

A small minority of courts has extended the cause of action to nonviable fetuses. [*See, e.g.*, **Santana v. Zilog, Inc.,** 95 F.3d 780 (9th Cir. 1996); **Farley v. Sartin,** 466 S.E.2d 522 (W. Va. 1995)]

(2) No recovery against negligent mother [§1191]

Even courts that permit an action for prenatal injuries against third parties deny an action by the child against the mother. The reasoning is that it would be against public policy to turn mother and fetus into legal adversaries. [**Stallman v. Youngquist,** 531 N.E.2d 355 (Ill. 1988)—no action by infant for mother's negligent driving while pregnant]

c. Wrongful death [§1192]

There is a split as to whether an action can be maintained for the wrongful death of an unborn child (miscarriage or stillbirth). Many states allow the action if the child was viable (capable of life apart from the mother). [**Volk v. Baldazo,** 651 P.2d 11 (Idaho 1982)] A number of states refuse to recognize a wrongful death action for miscarriage of a fetus or for a stillbirth, often on the basis that a fetus is not a "person" within the meaning of the wrongful death statute. [*See, e.g.*, **Justus v. Atchison,** 19 Cal. 3d 564 (1977)] However, these states generally allow the mother to recover for the physical and emotional injuries attending the stillbirth or miscarriage. [*See, e.g.*, **Modaber v. Kelley,** 348 S.E.2d 233 (Va. 1986)]

d. "Wrongful birth" [§1193]

Likewise, there is a split of authority as to whether plaintiff parents can recover against a negligent defendant for the costs of raising and educating an unwanted child (*e.g.*, where D physician negligently performs a vasectomy, or D pharmacy negligently sells diet tablets in place of oral contraceptives). Generally, recovery is permitted by the mother for pain and suffering during pregnancy and delivery, for related medical expenses, and for loss of consortium during this time. [*See, e.g.*, **Wilson v. Kuenzi,** 751 S.W.2d 741 (Mo.) (en banc), *cert. denied*, 488 U.S. 893 (1988)—no cause of action for wrongful birth, but listing 17 states recognizing such a cause of action; **Miller v. Johnson,** 343 S.E.2d 301 (Va. 1986)]

(1) Healthy children [§1194]

The modern trend is to permit recovery for the costs of raising an unwanted healthy child [**Zehr v. Haugen,** 871 P.2d 1006 (Or. 1994)—negligently performed sterilization makes surgeon liable for costs of child's upbringing where goal of family was to avoid added financial stress], but not all courts agree [*see, e.g.*, **O'Toole v. Greenberg,** 64 N.Y.2d 427 (1985)—denying upbringing costs]. States that do permit the action usually ***offset*** benefits of the birth against the recoverable expenses. [*See, e.g.*, **Burke v. Rivo,** 551 N.E.2d 1 (Mass. 1990); *but see* **Marciniak v. Lundborg,** 450 N.W.2d 243 (Wis. 1990)—emotional benefits of birth not set off against economic harm from birth]

(a) No duty to limit damages [§1195]

If recovery is allowed, plaintiffs do ***not*** have a duty to limit their damages (under the doctrine of avoidable consequences in tort or mitigation in a breach of contract action) by aborting the child. [**Johnson v. University Hospitals of Cleveland,** 540 N.E.2d 1370 (Ohio 1989)]

(b) Statutory limitation [§1196]

Some states have adopted legislation barring actions for the "wrongful birth" of healthy children. [**Edmonds v. Western Pennsylvania Hospital Radiology Associates,** 607 A.2d 1083 (Pa. 1992), *cert. denied,* 510 U.S. 814 (1993)—upholding such a statute against constitutional challenge]

(2) Unhealthy children [§1197]

Courts are split on what recoveries are available to parents who, through medical malpractice, conceive and bear children with genetic defects. The right to recover in such cases has been limited to parents. [**Michelman v. Ehrlich,** 709 A.2d 281 (N.J. 1998)—rejecting grandfather's suit for negligence that caused his grandson to be born with a neurological disease usually fatal before the age of five]

(a) Economic harm [§1198]

Most courts permit recovery for the extraordinary medical and related expenses due to the nature of the child's condition, but not for the usual child-rearing expenses that would have occurred had the child been normal. [*See, e.g.*, **Greco v. United States,** 893 P.2d 345 (Nev. 1995); **Schroeder v. Perkel,** 432 A.2d 834 (N.J. 1981); *but see* **McAllister v. Ha,** 496 S.E.2d 577 (N.C. 1998)—rejecting recovery of extraordinary expenses involved in raising an impaired child after doctor negligently failed to inform plaintiffs of test results showing they faced a one in four chance of having a child with sickle cell disease]

1) **Note**

Damages will include sums for expenses during the child's adult life as well as childhood expenses if the state requires parents to support disabled adult children. [**Smith v. Cote,** 513 A.2d 341 (N.H. 1986)]

(b) **Emotional distress [§1199]**

In many states, parents may recover for emotional distress caused by the birth of the unhealthy child. [**Greco v. United States,** *supra*; **Berman v. Allan,** 404 A.2d 8 (N.J. 1979)]

(c) **No "wrongful life" suit by child [§1200]**

Almost all states bar a suit by the unhealthy child. [*See, e.g.*, **Walker v. Mart,** 790 P.2d 735 (Ariz. 1990)—no "legally recognizable" injury; *but see* **Procanik v. Cillo,** 478 A.2d 755 (N.J. 1984)—child can recover extraordinary expenses for specialized treatment likely to be needed as an adult, but not general damages for being born in an unhealthy condition]

3. Intentional Interference with Family Relationships

a. Alienation of affections

(1) **Early view—recovery [§1201]**

At common law, and still in many states, a husband could sue a third party who had intentionally alienated the affections of his wife. Because the wife was considered an "asset" of her husband, the wife was allowed no similar action.

(2) **Modern view—split over spousal claim**

(a) **Action abolished [§1202]**

Most states have abolished the action by either judicial or legislative action. [**Russo v. Sutton,** 422 S.E.2d 750 (S.C. 1992)—listing 40 states; *but see* **Veeder v. Kennedy,** 589 N.W.2d 610 (S.D. 1999)—retaining cause of action and noting that of the states that have abandoned the alienation action, only five had done so by judicial decision]

(b) **Action preserved [§1203]**

Where the action has been preserved, *either* spouse may bring it. [*See, e.g.*, **Kline v. Ansell,** 414 A.2d 929 (Md. 1980); **Veeder v. Kennedy,** *supra*]

(3) **Modern view—parent-child claims rejected [§1204]**

When parents sue for alienation of a child's affections, or vice versa, the claim generally has been rejected because of fear of abuse and the potential impact on family relations. [**Wheeler v. Luhman,** 305 N.W.2d 466 (Iowa

1981)—child cannot recover for alienation of mother's affections; **Bock v. Lindquist,** 278 N.W.2d 326 (Minn. 1979)—father cannot recover for loss of 10-year-old child's affections]

(a) **Application—religious groups [§1205]**
Suits by parents against religious groups for the alienation of the affection of their adult children have also been rejected. [*See, e.g.*, **Schuppin v. Unification Church,** 435 F. Supp. 603 (D. Vt.), *aff'd without opinion,* 573 F.2d 1295 (2d Cir. 1977); **Radecki v. Schuckardt,** 361 N.E.2d 543 (Ohio 1976)]

(b) **Exception—child abduction [§1206]**
Some states recognize a cause of action against one who abducts or entices away a minor child. [**Silcott v. Oglesby,** 721 S.W.2d 290 (Tex. 1986)]

b. **Criminal conversation**

(1) **Early views [§1207]**
At early common law, a plaintiff could sue for damages for "criminal conversation" if he could prove that the defendant had had sexual relations with the plaintiff's wife. A few states did not require a showing of intercourse. In no state could the wife sue.

(2) **Modern view [§1208]**
Most states have ***abolished*** this action because of its potential for blackmail and doubt about its deterrent value. [**Thomas v. Siddiqui,** 869 S.W.2d 740 (Mo. 1994)]

c. **Intentional interference with custodial rights [§1209]**
In recent years, several states have recognized a cause of action for intentional interference with a parent-child custodial relationship, often arising in the context of a divorce or child custody suit. [Rest. 2d §700; *see, e.g.*, **D&D Fuller CATV Construction, Inc. v. Pace,** 780 P.2d 520 (Colo. 1989)—grandparents who aided father in kidnapping child from mother may be held liable; **Stone v. Wall,** 734 So. 2d 1038 (Fla. 1999)—in father's suit against members of ex-wife's family for having failed to return his child from a visit and then concealing the child, court recognized action for intentional interference with custodial relationship; *but see* **Larson v. Dunn,** 460 N.W.2d 39 (Minn. 1990)—rejecting tort claim against spouse for felony refusal to return child because tort not in child's best interest]

d. **Emotional distress claims [§1210]**
The courts are split over whether to permit an action for intentional infliction of emotional distress where the action closely resembles one for alienation of affections or criminal conversation that has been ***barred*** by the state. [*See, e.g.*,

Figueiredo-Torres v. Nickel, 584 A.2d 69 (Md. 1991)—despite abolition of actions for alienation of affections and criminal conversation, patient could sue psychologist for commencing romantic relationship with patient's wife while treating couple for marital problems; *but see* **Koestler v. Pollard,** 471 N.W.2d 7 (Wis. 1991)—state policy against actions for criminal conversation would be subverted if claim could be framed for emotional distress by alleging further facts]

D. Tort Immunity

1. Intrafamily Tort Immunity

a. Husband-wife

(1) Common law—absolute immunity between spouses [§1211]

The common law regarded the husband and wife as a single legal entity, and accordingly provided that a husband and wife could not sue each other for personal injury torts committed by one upon the other, whether before or during marriage. [**Thompson v. Thompson,** 218 U.S. 611 (1910)]

(2) Abolition of immunity in most states [§1212]

Virtually all jurisdictions today have ***rejected*** the doctrine of interspousal tort immunity entirely, rejecting the common law fiction of a single legal identity for husband and wife. Some have abolished the immunity only as to intentional torts, while others have abolished it as to ***all*** torts, intentional or negligent. [*See, e.g.,* **Beattie v. Beattie,** 630 A.2d 1096 (Del. 1993)]

(3) Immunity not applicable under respondeat superior [§1213]

Even where interspousal immunity has been retained, it does not shield an employer from liability where an employee injures his spouse while acting within the scope of the employment. The injured spouse can sue the employer under respondeat superior; and the employer may have no right to indemnity from the employee. (*See* Agency, Partnership & Limited Liability Companies Summary.)

b. Parent-child [§1214]

Although no such immunity was recognized under the English common law, the early American decisions held that a child could not sue his parents (nor a parent her child) for ***personal*** torts. *Rationale:* This rule was to preserve family harmony and parental authority. [**Hewellette v. George,** 9 So. 885 (Miss. 1891)]

(1) Limitation—no immunity for property torts [§1215]

The immunity was recognized ***only as to personal torts.*** It never applied to bar causes of action by a child against a parent for damage to the child's property.

(2) **Modern trend rejects immunity [§1216]**
Because of the obvious unfairness in many cases, the clear trend of authority today is to ***restrict or reject*** the concept of parent-child immunity. [*See, e.g.*, **Glaskox *ex rel.* Denton v. Glaskox,** 614 So. 2d 906 (Miss. 1992)—*overruling* **Hewellette v. George,** *supra*, and rejecting parent-child immunity]

(a) **Restricted to negligence [§1217]**
Most courts have confined any immunity to negligence cases, thus ***allowing*** a child to sue his parent, or vice versa, for willful torts. [*See* **Schlessinger v. Schlessinger,** 796 P.2d 1385 (Colo. 1990); **Crotta v. Home Depot, Inc.,** 732 A.2d 767 (Conn. 1999)]

(b) **Abolished [§1218]**
A growing number of states have abolished parent-child immunity entirely—on the ground that negligence actions are most likely to be brought only if ***liability insurance*** exists, so that there really is no "threat to family harmony." [**Anderson v. Stream,** 295 N.W.2d 595 (Minn. 1980)]

1) **Limited duty [§1219]**
Some states that have abolished the immunity nonetheless do not impose a full duty of due care in the parental situation. [**Zikely v. Zikely,** 98 A.D.2d 815 (1983), *affirmed on opinion below,* 62 N.Y.2d 907 (1984)—mother owes no duty of careful supervision over child who was scalded after being left unsupervised while tub was filling]

2) **Full duty [§1220]**
Other states have imposed a normal duty of due care on the parent with the fact of parentage being one of the factors going into the analysis. [**Broadbent v. Broadbent,** 907 P.2d 43 (Ariz. 1995)—test is what an ordinarily reasonable and prudent ***parent*** would have done in similar circumstances; **Hartman *ex rel.* Hartman v. Hartman,** 821 S.W.2d 852 (Mo. 1991)—same]

3) **Note**
Parental immunity may not be a bar to recovery where there are allegations of negligence arising ***apart*** from any duty to supervise the child. [**Cates v. Cates,** 619 N.E.2d 715 (Ill. 1993)—father driving negligently]

EXAM TIP **gilbert**

When writing an answer to a question involving a tort committed by one spouse against the other or by a parent against her child, it is best to mention the common law rule first and then explain that it has been abolished or modified. If you don't mention the common law immunity, you probably will not receive full credit for your answer.

c. **Other relationships [§1221]**
Even where still recognized, the doctrine of intrafamily tort immunity does not extend to relationships other than husband-wife and parent-child. Thus, *e.g.*, brothers and sisters can sue each other on any type of claim [**Midkiff v. Midkiff,** 113 S.E.2d 875 (Va. 1960)], although some states bar suit by one child for harm caused by a sibling's negligent supervision [*see, e.g.*, **Smith v. Sapienza,** 52 N.Y.2d 82 (1981)].

2. **Governmental Tort Immunity (Sovereign Immunity)**

a. **Traditional doctrine [§1222]**
At common law, when a plaintiff attempted to sue the State for a personal wrong, the State was held to be immune from tort liability. [**Russell v. Men of Devon,** 100 Eng. Rep. 359 (1788)]

(1) **State and federal [§1223]**
Following this doctrine, it is usually held that not only are state and federal governments immune from tort liability, but so also are various state and federal agencies (hospitals, schools, etc.).

(2) **Municipalities—no immunity for "proprietary" functions [§1224]**
A great deal of law has developed regarding the tort liability of municipal corporations. The law limits tort immunity to the ***"governmental"*** or "public" functions. A municipality's ***"proprietary"*** or "private" functions are ***not*** immune and may therefore result in tort liability.

(a) **"Governmental" vs. "proprietary" functions [§1225]**
The difficulty arises in attempting to determine which city functions are "governmental" and which are "proprietary":

1) **"Governmental" functions [§1226]**
"Governmental" functions are those functions that can be performed adequately ***only*** by the government—*i.e.*, police, fire, courts, etc.

2) **"Proprietary" functions [§1227]**
"Proprietary" functions are those functions that the city performs, but which ***could as well be provided by a private corporation,***

particularly where the city derives revenue from the operation—*e.g.,* water, gas, electricity, public halls, etc.

---

e.g. **Example:** The construction and maintenance of public streets, highways, sewers, or other public improvements are generally regarded as "proprietary" functions, but there is a minority view contra.

---

b. **Status of doctrine today [§1228]**

Many state courts have ***abolished*** the doctrine of sovereign immunity. [*See, e.g.,* **Muskopf v. Corning Hospital District,** 55 Cal. 2d 211 (1961); **Molitor v. Kaneland Community Unit District No. 302,** 163 N.E.2d 89 (Ill. 1959)]

(1) **Legislative response [§1229]**

State legislatures have often responded to judicial abolition by reenacting some limited form of governmental immunity. [*See* Cal. Gov't Code §§945 *et seq.*; **Harinek v. 161 North Clark Street Ltd. Partnership,** 692 N.E.2d 1177 (Ill. 1998)]

(2) **Equal protection not violated [§1230]**

Sovereign immunity does not violate equal protection of the laws. [**Martinez v. California,** 444 U.S. 277 (1980)—statutory denial of state's liability for parole decision is constitutional]

(3) **Federal Tort Claims Act [§1231]**

The Federal Tort Claims Act ("FTCA") abolishes tort immunity (*i.e.,* permits the federal government to be held liable) for "***negligent*** or wrongful act or omission" by government employees, plus most ***intentional*** torts by ***federal investigative or law enforcement*** officers. However, immunity is ***retained*** for other intentional torts, and for strict liability and ***"discretionary" acts*** by government employees. [28 U.S.C. §§1346, 2671 *et seq.*; **Deuser v. Vecera,** 139 F.3d 1190 (8th Cir. 1998)—holding that national park rangers' decision to release plaintiff without charging him with a crime was a discretionary function, and thus rangers were immune from liability when plaintiff subsequently wandered onto a highway and was struck and killed by a car]

(a) **Immunity for intentional tort of agent [§1232]**

If a government employee commits a battery, but the suit claim is based on the negligence of the government in hiring the employee, some courts hold that the claim is based on battery and thus barred. [*See, e.g.,* **Johnson v. United States,** 788 F.2d 845 (2d Cir.), *cert. denied,* 479 U.S. 914 (1986); *but see* **Doe v. United States,** 838 F.2d 220 (7th Cir. 1988)—contra]

(b) ***Feres* doctrine [§1233]**

Under a judicially created exception to the FTCA, members of the armed forces injured "in the course of activity incident to service" are ***denied tort recoveries*** against the government. [**Feres v. United States,** 340 U.S. 135 (1950)] The Supreme Court has expanded this restriction to injuries that occur outside the command structure [**United States v. Stanley,** 483 U.S. 669 (1987)—army officer given LSD without his knowledge during an experiment] and where the tort is committed by a federal civilian employee [**United States v. Johnson,** 481 U.S. 681 (1987)].

(c) Government contractor defense [§1234]

A government contractor may generally assert the federal government's immunity as a defense to a products liability claim where it can show that it followed reasonably precise government specifications, and that it warned the government about any patent errors in the design or use of the equipment. [**Boyle v. United Technologies Corp.,** 487 U.S. 500 (1988)]

c. Liability of governmental officers [§1235]

In addition to the government's immunity, government officers in their private capacity may also be immune.

(1) High-ranking officers [§1236]

Judges, legislators, and high-ranking members of the executive branch (*e.g.,* cabinet members and department heads) are ***completely immune*** from tort liability for acts carried out ***within the scope of their duties***, even if their conduct involves "malice" or "abuse of discretion." [**Barr v. Matteo,** 360 U.S. 564 (1959)—extending common law absolute privilege to acting director of a federal agency]

(2) Lower-level officers

(a) Federal law [§1237]

Lower-level administrative officers or employees are immune from claims of ***negligence*** under ***federal*** law; and some states also follow this position.

(b) Some states—no immunity for "ministerial" functions [§1238]

Other states retain the common law rule that granted immunity to lower-level governmental officers or employees only when performing "discretionary" (as opposed to "ministerial") functions.

1) "Discretionary" functions [§1239]

"Discretionary" functions are those in which the officer has some element of personal judgment or decisionmaking (*e.g.,* evaluating property for assessment purposes or designing or routing a highway). In carrying out these functions, the officer is granted immunity as long as she was acting ***in good faith.*** [*See* **Ross v. Consumers Power Co.,** 363 N.W.2d 641 (Mich. 1984)]

2) "Ministerial" functions [§1240]

"Ministerial" functions are those in which the officer is left no choice of her own; she is carrying out orders of others or established duties of her office (*e.g.,* repairing roads, driving vehicles). Here, there is no tort immunity. If the officer negligently fails to perform her required duties properly, she can be held personally liable for any damages resulting therefrom—even if she was acting in good faith. [*See, e.g.,* **Collins v. Kentucky Natural Resources & Environmental Protection Cabinet,** 10 S.W.3d 122 (Ky. 1999)—no immunity for negligent performance of coal mine inspection because that is ministerial duty]

(3) Statutory changes [§1241]

Under the Civil Rights Act of 1871 [42 U.S.C. §1983], a person acting under color of ***state law*** who deprives anyone of a ***federal*** constitutional right is subject to liability for damages.

(a) Basis of liability [§1242]

It now appears that liability will lie only if the deprivation was caused by intentional and malicious behavior or "deliberate indifference." [*See, e.g.,* **Wilson v. Seiter,** 501 U.S. 294 (1991); **Estelle v. Gamble,** 429 U.S. 97 (1976)—for a section 1983 action, failure to adequately treat prisoner's medical problems must be result of "deliberate indifference"; *but see* **County of Sacramento v. Lewis,** 523 U.S. 833 (1998)—in a police chase, the "shocks the conscience" standard is required and cannot be met by a mere showing of deliberate indifference]

(b) Interests protected [§1243]

Although it is clear that interests in physical well-being and freedom from improper incarceration are protected under section 1983 [*see, e.g.,* **Imbler v. Pachtman,** 424 U.S. 409 (1976)], beyond this the limits are not yet clear [*see, e.g.,* **Conn v. Gabbert,** 526 U.S. 286 (1999)—interest in practicing law not protected under Fourteenth Amendment as either "liberty" or "property"; **Siegert v. Gilley,** 500 U.S. 226 (1991)—interest in reputation not protected under Fourteenth Amendment].

(c) Defenses [§1244]

The statute is silent about defenses, and no general rules have emerged. Some officials have received absolute immunity from liability while others have been given only qualified immunity. [**Briscoe v. LaHue,** 460 U.S. 325 (1983)—police witness at trial has absolute immunity;

Wood v. Strickland, 420 U.S. 308 (1975)—school official has only qualified immunity, which requires reasonable behavior and good faith; **Scheuer v. Rhodes,** 416 U.S. 232 (1974)—state governor has only qualified immunity; **Pierson v. Ray,** 386 U.S. 547 (1967)—judge has absolute immunity against damage liability]

1) **Municipalities [§1245]**
When municipalities are sued under section 1983 (usually for failure to establish official guidelines to guide staff behavior), they have ***no immunity*** at all and may not rely on the good faith of the officials involved. [**Owen v. City of Independence,** 445 U.S. 622 (1980)]

(d) **Distinguish—federal agents [§1246]**
Although federal agents are not covered under section 1983 (because the statute applies only to persons acting under color of ***state*** law), analogous civil liability may still be imposed if their behavior violates federal constitutional rights. [**Bivens v. Six Unknown Named Agents,** 403 U.S. 388 (1971)—Fourth Amendment violation by FBI agents gives rise to damage action]

1) **Defenses [§1247]**
The defenses are also analogous to those under section 1983. [**Hunter v. Bryant,** 502 U.S. 224 (1991)—Secret Service agents have qualified immunity for arrest; **Cleavinger v. Saxner,** 474 U.S. 193 (1985)—members of federal prison disciplinary committee have qualified immunity]

3. Charitable Immunity

a. **Common law doctrine [§1248]**
A separate ground of tort immunity was recognized at common law for nongovernmental, charitable organizations and enterprises. [*See, e.g.*, **Parks v. Northwestern University,** 75 N.E. 991 (Ill. 1905)]

(1) **Rationale**
A rationale sometimes advanced for the doctrine of charitable immunity is that the funds upon which a charity operates are donated, and that subjecting such funds to the payment of tort claims would divert them from the purpose intended by the donor. [**Abernathy v. Sisters of St. Mary's,** 446 S.W.2d 599 (Mo. 1969); **Feoffees of Heriot's Hospital v. Ross,** 8 Eng. Rep. 1508 (1846)]

(2) **Application [§1249]**
Thus, it was held for many years that private charities—hospitals, schools,

community organizations (*e.g.*, YMCA)—were not liable for torts committed by their agents or employees.

b. Status today [§1250]

Almost all states have repudiated the doctrine, with courts finding that any interest in protecting a donor or a volunteer is ***outweighed*** by the need to provide compensation to victims of negligence. [*See, e.g.*, **Bing v. Thunig,** 2 N.Y.2d 656 (1957); *but see* **Moore v. Warren,** 463 S.E.2d 459 (Va. 1995)—volunteer was immune from liability because driving for charitable organization at time of accident]

(1) Middle ground [§1251]

Some states have legislation that makes charities liable in tort but only to a limited extent. [*See, e.g.*, **English v. New England Medical Center, Inc.,** 541 N.E.2d 329 (Mass. 1989), *cert. denied,* 493 U.S. 1056 (1990)—statute limiting size of judgments against charities to $20,000 is constitutional; *but see* **Hanvey v. Oconee Memorial Hospital,** 416 S.E.2d 623 (S.C. 1992)—statute limiting liability of charitable hospital to $100,000 violates state constitution's Equal Protection Clause]

E. Release and Contribution Among Joint Tortfeasors

1. Introduction [§1252]

Various rules evolved at common law to cover "joint tortfeasors"—*i.e.,* persons who have either (i) acted ***in concert*** (by agreement) for the purpose of causing the plaintiff's injury; ***or*** (ii) acted entirely independently but whose acts have caused a single ***indivisible injury*** to the plaintiff (*e.g.,* two negligent motorists who collide, causing a single injury to a pedestrian). Joint tortfeasors were traditionally ***jointly and severally liable*** for the harm they caused (*i.e.,* the plaintiff could sue any one or more and recover her full damages from the tortfeasor(s) sued). (*See supra,* §418.)

a. Indivisible injury—conduct need not be simultaneous [§1253]

Where there is an indivisible injury, simultaneous conduct may not be necessary to a finding of joint and several liability. [**Ravo *ex rel.* Ravo v. Rogatnick,** 70 N.Y.2d 305 (1987)—pediatrician whose negligent treatment of infant contributed to injury that infant suffered at birth due to negligence of obstetrician was jointly and severally liable for indivisible injury]

2. Judgment and Satisfaction [§1254]

An unsatisfied judgment against one of several joint tortfeasors does not bar the plaintiff's action against the others. [**Verhoeks v. Gillivan,** 221 N.W. 287 (Mich. 1928)] However, the ***satisfaction*** of a judgment against one tortfeasor extinguishes the cause of action and bars any later suit for a greater or additional amount against any of the others. *Rationale:* Satisfaction of the court-ordered amount is the equivalent of payment of the damages sustained.

3. Releases—Early Rule [§1255]

Some courts originally held that a claim or a judgment was extinguished if the plaintiff released one of several joint tortfeasors—*i.e.*, "release of one operates to release all"—and this held true regardless of the sufficiency of compensation paid for the release. [**Aljian v. Ben Schlossberg, Inc.,** 73 A.2d 290 (N.J. 1950)]

a. Rejection of early rule [§1256]

A growing number of states have by statute ***rejected*** this rule entirely. [*See, e.g.,* Cal. Civ. Proc. Code §877—release does not discharge other tortfeasors, but reduces claims against them; Unif. Comparative Fault Act §6]

b. Avoidance of early rule [§1257]

Many courts have circumvented the doctrine that a release of one releases all joint tortfeasors by upholding a release with reservation of rights (*i.e.,* a provision in the release that it will not prejudice the plaintiff's rights against other tortfeasors) or by permitting a ***covenant not to sue*** (or a covenant not to execute on a judgment) in lieu of a release. [*See, e.g.,* **Cox v. Pearl Investment Co.,** 450 P.2d 60 (Colo. 1969)] Other courts have held that a release discharges only those parties it specifically names. [*See, e.g.,* **Alsup v. Firestone Tire & Rubber Co.,** 461 N.E.2d 361 (Ill. 1984)]

4. Contribution

a. Common law—no contribution [§1258]

The common law rule was that "no contribution is allowed between joint tortfeasors," meaning that if a judgment was recovered and satisfied against one tortfeasor, he had no right to recover from the others their pro rata share. *Rationale:* A "wrongdoer" should not invoke the aid of the courts to force other wrongdoers to help him shoulder the load.

b. Modern view—contribution allowed in negligence cases [§1259]

Today, virtually all states permit contribution among ***negligent*** (but not intentional) joint tortfeasors. Thus, contribution is ***not*** allowed where punitive damages are awarded. [**Smith v. Lightning Bolt Productions, Inc.,** 861 F.2d 363 (2d Cir. 1988)—highly culpable defendant should not be allowed chance to escape payment of imposed penalty]

(1) But note

Contribution operates only in systems that apply joint and several liability. Many states have abolished that rule or restricted its application. (*See infra,* §1331.)

c. **Impact of comparative negligence [§1260]**
A number of states have retained the rule of joint and several liability among joint tortfeasors notwithstanding the adoption of comparative negligence. The purpose of comparative negligence is to protect negligent ***plaintiffs*** against the harshness of the "all or nothing" rule of contributory negligence, rather than to eliminate joint and several liability. [**Ravo *ex rel.* Ravo v. Rogatnick,** *supra,* §1253—each joint tortfeasor remains individually liable for all damages caused, but contribution allowed between them on ***comparative*** fault basis]

d. **Limitation [§1261]**
Joint and several liability may be inconsistent with the rationale of market share liability (*see supra,* §427) if the goal is to match an individual defendant's ***total*** liability to its market share. To prevent a manufacturer with a small market share from being held liable for damages of an insolvent manufacturer with a large market share, defendants are only ***severally*** liable for damages under most versions of market share liability theory. [**Brown v. Superior Court,** 44 Cal. 3d 1049 (1988)]

F. Indemnity

1. **Doctrine [§1262]**
A defendant who is only ***secondarily*** liable for the plaintiff's injury, but who is sued and forced to pay a judgment, is entitled to indemnification against the party who was ***primarily*** responsible for causing the injury. [*See, e.g.,* **White v. Quechee Lakes Landowners' Association,** 742 A.2d 734 (Vt. 1999)]

a. **Rationale**
Indemnity is an ***equitable*** remedy granted to ***prevent the unjust enrichment*** that would occur if one whose liability was merely secondary could be forced to bear the debts of the "real" wrongdoer.

b. **Application—vicarious liability cases [§1263]**
The most common application of the doctrine is where the responsibility for the plaintiff's injury lies entirely with one defendant, but another has been held ***vicariously*** liable for the injury.

---

e.g. **Example:** Employee E is negligent in driving Employer R's truck, resulting in injuries to P; P sues and recovers judgment against R on the basis of respondeat superior (*see supra,* §609). R is entitled to indemnification against E—whether or not P sued E.

---

e.g. **Example:** Similarly, a defendant is entitled to indemnification where she has been held liable under "permissive use" statutes or the family purpose doctrine (*see supra,* §§602-603), or for negligent performance of work by an independent contractor (*see supra,* §§616 *et seq.*).

c. **Distinguish—contribution [§1264]**

Contribution involves wrongdoers who are ***jointly and severally*** liable; it requires that each pay his ***proportionate share.*** Indemnity involves one who is ***primarily*** responsible for an injury; it shifts the ***entire*** loss to his shoulders from another who has been compelled to pay it because he was ***secondarily*** liable therefor.

EXAM TIP **gilbert**

To keep these two doctrines separate in your mind, recall that generally, for ***contribution*** to apply, both defendants must have a ***measurable degree*** of culpability for the tort, but ***indemnity*** usually applies when one of the parties is ***much more responsible*** than the other. The most extreme disparity in responsibility—and the clearest legal case for indemnity—occurs when a master has been held vicariously liable for the actions of a servant and is thus not at all personally at fault. It is important to note that under joint and several liability neither contribution nor indemnity affects how much the plaintiff receives. Rather, they deal with how much of the total award each defendant ultimately must pay.

2. **Differing Degrees of Culpability [§1265]**

In states with joint and several liability, indemnity is also available where the defendants are both directly liable to the plaintiff, but the ***degree*** of their culpability differs greatly. [**Builders Supply Co. v. McCabe,** 77 A.2d 368 (Pa. 1951)]

e.g. **Example:** A retailer who is held ***strictly liable*** for injuries caused by a defective product she sells may obtain indemnity against the manufacturer whose ***negligence*** (usually shown by the defect itself) caused the product to malfunction.

e.g. **Example:** Similarly, where the plaintiff has been injured as a result of concurrent acts, one negligent and one intentional, the defendant who was only negligent may be entitled to indemnity against the defendant who committed the intentional tort.

a. **Nonfeasance vs. misfeasance [§1266]**

In a few states, a defendant who was only ***"passively"*** negligent (*i.e.,* nonfeasance—such as failing to discover dangerous condition) may be entitled to indemnity from a defendant who was ***"actively"*** negligent (*i.e.,* misfeasance—such as creating a dangerous condition). [**Rossmoor Sanitation, Inc. v. Pylon, Inc.,** 13 Cal. 3d 622 (1975)]

3. **Aggravation Cases [§1267]**

If an original negligent tortfeasor has been held liable under proximate cause principles for a physician's negligent aggravation (*see supra,* §479), the original tortfeasor is entitled to indemnity from the physician for the aggravation damages.

a. **But note**
A minority view is contra. [**Stuart v. Hertz Corp.**, 351 So. 2d 703 (Fla. 1977)]

G. Statutes of Limitations

1. **Typical Duration for Negligence [§1268]**
A "statute of limitations" prescribes a bright-line time period during which a plaintiff may bring an action. The typical duration for negligence cases is ***two or three years***.

2. **Accrual Rule [§1269]**
The statutory period begins to run when the plaintiff's claim "accrues." In most states, a claim for negligence accrues after the defendant commits a negligent act and when the plaintiff suffers ***legally cognizable injury***. In some states, a claim accrues upon the defendant's act, without regard to the plaintiff's injury.

   a. **Common law—plaintiff's knowledge irrelevant [§1270]**
   At common law, the accrual rule barred a plaintiff's claim unless it was filed within the statutory period, regardless of whether the plaintiff knew about the defendant's negligent act, the injury, or the causal connection between the two.

   b. **Modern view—discovery rule [§1271]**
   Most states have amended their statutes of limitations to provide that the statutory clock does not begin to run until the plaintiff ***discovers*** that she is injured and that the defendant caused the injury (or facts sufficient to indicate that further investigation would reveal the defendant's connection to the injury). [*See, e.g.*, N.Y. C.P.L.R. 214-c; **Hymowitz v. Eli Lilly & Co.**, *supra*, §428]

Chapter Seven: Statutory Changes in Personal Injury Law

CONTENTS

▶ Key Exam Issues

A. Changes Targeting Specific Kinds of Tort Claims §1272

B. Changes Affecting Tort Claims Generally §1329

Key Exam Issues

Since 1900, pressure has repeatedly been brought to bear on state legislatures to change various aspects of traditional tort law. Motivations for change have varied from concerns about inadequate compensation or inefficiency in the system to concerns that damages awards had become excessive. Attempts at tort reform in response to these pressures highlight some of the basic policy problems in tort law. One example of the legislative response is comparative negligence (discussed *supra*, §§815 *et seq.*), which was instituted by the state legislatures in most states. As with comparative negligence, the legislative response has sometimes been directed at the entire tort system; sometimes it has targeted specific kinds of tort claims.

Your Torts class may not have covered some or any of these statutory changes. However, in answering a torts question on your exam, especially one involving joint tortfeasors or the amount of damages that a plaintiff can recover, you may need to include a discussion of the effect of relevant state statutes.

A. Changes Targeting Specific Kinds of Tort Claims

1. Workers' Compensation

a. Motivation [§1272]

With the industrial revolution came a steadily increasing number of injuries and deaths among workers. Under traditional tort principles, many workers were completely barred from recovery by their own ***contributory negligence***. In addition, two new tort principles emerged during this period: ***assumption of risk***, which barred recovery by any worker who perceived the dangers of his employment, and the ***fellow-servant*** doctrine, which provided that the employer could not be held vicariously liable for the negligence of a plaintiff's co-worker. In combination, the three doctrines made recovery by injured workers virtually impossible.

b. Response [§1273]

Early in the 20th century, the states removed from the tort system virtually all claims for personal injury by workers against their employers. The tort system was replaced with a comprehensive system of workers' compensation that now covers well over 80% of all workers, and is probably the most substantial statutory change in personal injury law to have occurred in the United States. (It is the subject of a separate course in many law schools.)

(1) **Operation of workers' compensation system**

(a) **Mandatory insurance [§1274]**
In almost every state, private employers are required to acquire workers' compensation insurance to cover their employees.

(b) **Scope of coverage [§1275]**
The insurance extends to all claims for personal injury that arise out of and in the course of the worker's employment, ***without regard to fault.***

(c) **Processing of claims [§1276]**
A worker who is not satisfied with the settlement offered by the insurance company may file an administrative claim. After the agency hearing, a dissatisfied party may appeal to an administrative board and then, in most states, to a state appellate court, but only on legal questions.

(d) **Amounts recoverable [§1277]**
Most workers recover all their medical expenses and up to two-thirds of their lost wages. Although traditional noneconomic damages, such as pain and suffering, are not available, all states provide lump sum payments for loss of bodily parts or functions.

EXAM TIP **gilbert**

It is important to remember that workers' compensation provides both a carrot and a stick for both employees and employers. If an employee is injured on the job and the injury is a covered injury, the employee is entitled to a specific recovery, ***regardless of fault*** and generally with no ifs, ands, or buts. On the other hand, by instituting workers' compensation laws, states have forced employees to give up their right to sue in tort and recover for the full extent of their injuries. Employers are benefited by workers' compensation laws because they are freed from the burden of being subject to potentially unlimited tort liability to injured employees—in most states employers need only pay mandatory insurance premiums. The cost to employers, however, is that even an employer who runs a safe workplace—where no one has ever been injured—is required to participate in the system and purchase the mandatory insurance.

(2) **Impact of workers' compensation on tort recovery**

(a) **Exclusive remedy against employer [§1278]**
A worker whose claim falls within the workers' compensation system cannot sue the employer in tort. Claims by family members are generally also barred, even though workers' compensation may provide no benefits to an injured worker's family.

1) **Application**
Even though the injury is covered, a particular harm suffered by

the worker (such as loss of smell) may not be compensable under the statute. Generally, no tort remedy is available to the worker in this situation. [*See, e.g.*, **Fetterhoff v. Western Block Co.,** 49 A.D.2d 1001 (1975)—no tort remedy for worker's noncompensable loss of sexual function]

2) **Exception—intentional tort [§1279]**
In some states, a worker may escape coverage of the workers' compensation system by showing that the injury resulted from the employer's commission of an intentional tort that was not suffered in the course of the employment. [**Magliulo v. Superior Court,** 47 Cal. App. 3d 760 (1975)—allowing tort action to waitress who alleged that she was injured when her employer hit her in anger and threw her down; *but see* **Livitsanos v. Superior Court,** 2 Cal. 4th 744 (1992)—no tort remedy for emotional distress intentionally or negligently inflicted by employer if occurrence was within the "normal risks" of the employment relationship, even if the compensation system offered no remedy because no disability had been suffered]

(b) **Claims against third parties allowed [§1280]**
In most states, workers can bring tort actions against third parties involved in the injury. For example, a worker can sue the manufacturer of a defective piece of equipment.

1) **Effect of compensation [§1281]**
A worker who accepts compensation does not waive the right to sue a third party in tort.

2) **Collateral sources rule [§1282]**
The collateral sources rule (*supra*, §539) generally ***prevents*** the third party from reducing its damages by proving that the plaintiff obtained compensation payments from the employer.

3) **Employer's right to reimbursement [§1283]**
The employer generally has a lien on the worker's tort recovery to cover the compensation payments it has made to the worker. In addition, if the worker fails to sue a third party, the employer can bring a tort action in the worker's name. [**Boldman v. Mt. Hood Chemical Corp.,** 602 P.2d 1072 (Or. 1979)] In some states, the amount recoverable by the employer is reduced if the employer's negligence has contributed to the injury.

4) **Third party's right to reimbursement [§1284]**
If the employer was also at fault in the worker's injury, most states

hold that the exclusivity of workers' compensation ***bars*** the third party from seeking contribution or indemnity from the employer. [Arthur Larson, Third-Party Action Over Against Workers' Compensation Employer, 1982 Duke L.J. 483]

2. "No-Fault" Auto Insurance

a. Motivation [§1285]

Because auto accidents are so numerous and include so many small claims, auto cases suffer particularly from many of the problems that critics identify with a fault-based system: delays in receiving payments from liability insurers, malapportionment of benefits by which small claims are treated very generously, inefficiency, high insurance premiums, and dishonesty.

b. Response [§1286]

Almost half the states have changed the handling of auto accident claims by adopting "no-fault" insurance plans.

(1) Operation of "no-fault" plans [§1287]

Although the plans adopted vary considerably, the following are the essential provisions:

(a) Mandatory insurance [§1288]

All car owners are required to obtain and keep in effect insurance to cover claims arising out of the operation of their cars.

(b) Scope of coverage [§1289]

The insurance extends to all claims of injury arising out of the use or operation of any motor vehicle, ***without regard to fault.***

1) Note

This includes claims allowed under traditional tort concepts, as well as certain claims not currently allowed—*e.g.*, claims by drivers who hurt themselves solely through their own fault.

(c) Claims handled on "first party" basis [§1290]

Injured car occupants usually make claims against the policy covering the cars they were riding in, so that in the typical two-car crash, the occupants of each car claim against the insurance covering that car. Pedestrians injured by autos generally make claims against the insurance covering the cars that struck them. (Under a few plans, though, pedestrians who own cars make a claim against their own insurers.)

1) Note

Because fault is immaterial, the claims procedure is relatively simple, and any disagreement between the policy holder and the insurance company as to the amount recoverable is subject to arbitration.

(d) Damages recoverable [§1291]

None of the statutes provides coverage for pain and suffering or disfigurement. Coverage is limited to economic losses (lost wages, medical bills, etc.). However, the plans vary considerably as to the maximum coverage, from $1,000 or $2,000 to as much as $50,000 and more.

(2) Impact of "no-fault" plans

(a) Curtailment of tort litigation [§1292]

The plans vary concerning the extent to which traditional negligence actions (with traditional "fault" principles) are still permitted.

1) "Partial" abolition [§1293]

All existing statutes allow tort actions in at least some situations.

a) Application

Under some plans, tort actions against other drivers can still be maintained for all but relatively minor cases. Thus, at one extreme, a plaintiff can sue for pain and suffering whenever medical expenses exceed $500. Under other plans, specifically those (*e.g.*, in Michigan, New York) with generous first-party benefits, only cases of serious injury can be pursued in court—*e.g.*, cases involving death, permanent injury or disfigurement, or inability to work for more than six consecutive months.

2) "Add-on" statutes [§1294]

Some states have simply added a no-fault system to the tort liability system already in place. Any auto victim who receives no-fault compensation can still sue in tort as before. The no-fault insurer has subrogation rights up to the amount it has paid to the victim under no-fault.

(b) Elimination of double recovery by injured persons [§1295]

Most plans prevent the injured party from obtaining a duplicate recovery for the same economic losses. This is usually accomplished by making no-fault insurance the primary source of benefits, or by providing for automatic subrogation for any payments made under any other insurance.

c. Future of no-fault [§1296]

The future of automobile no-fault insurance is somewhat uncertain. In recent years, a few states have returned to the fault system.

3. Medical Malpractice

a. Motivation [§1297]

In the mid-1970s, physicians and surgeons were faced with rapidly escalating malpractice insurance rates.

b. Response [§1298]

Virtually every state has since adopted legislation addressing the malpractice area. However, statutory provisions vary.

(1) Shortened statute of limitations [§1299]

The most common change is to shorten the statute of limitations. Minors are often required to sue within eight or 10 years of the infliction of injury, rather than being able to wait until they reach majority. [*But see* **Kenyon v. Hammer,** 688 P.2d 961 (Ariz. 1984)—three-year statute violates state Equal Protection Clause]

(2) Limits on pain and suffering [§1300]

A few states have placed limits on the amount that can be recovered for pain and suffering. Such limits have been challenged on grounds that they violate the separation of powers, the right to a jury trial, the right against takings of private property without just compensation, and the rights of procedural and substantive due process. [*See, e.g.*, **Fein v. Permanente Medical Group,** 38 Cal. 3d 137, *appeal dismissed*, 474 U.S. 892 (1985)—statute limiting pain and suffering recovery in malpractice cases to $250,000 is constitutional; **Pulliam v. Coastal Emergency Services,** 509 S.E.2d 307 (Va. 1999); *but see* **Carson v. Maurer,** 424 A.2d 825 (N.H. 1980)—cap on nonpecuniary damages violates state's Equal Protection Clause]

(3) Periodic payments [§1301]

Some states provide that if an award exceeds some minimum figure, the judge may or must require that it be paid periodically rather than in a single lump sum. If the victim dies before all payments are made, amounts still unpaid for pain and suffering and for expected future medical expenses need no longer be paid. [**American Bank & Trust Co. v. Community Hospital,** 36 Cal. 3d 359 (1984)]

(4) Legal fees [§1302]

In an effort to discourage attorneys from taking on frivolous cases, some states have set sliding scale limits on the size of contingent fees that lawyers may charge to represent victims in malpractice cases. The limits are lower than the rates generally prevailing. [*See, e.g.*, **Roa v. Lodi Medical Group, Inc.,** 37 Cal. 3d 920 (1985)—upholding limits; *but see* **Carson v. Maurer,** *supra*—limits violate equal protection]

(5) Collateral sources [§1303]

Some states have provided that if the plaintiff has received first party insurance benefits or other help in meeting the costs imposed by the defendant's malpractice, the trier may deduct these benefits from the award. [*See, e.g.*, **Barme v. Wood,** 37 Cal. 3d 174 (1984)—upholding provision; *but see* **Farley v. Engelken,** 740 P.2d 1058 (Kan. 1987)—preferential treatment to health care providers violates equal protection]

(6) **Malpractice panels [§1304]**
A few states have created three-member panels, consisting of a physician, an attorney, and a judge, to conduct a pretrial liability review. If the panel reaches a unanimous decision on the merits of the malpractice claim after an informal hearing, that determination is admissible as evidence in any later trial. [*See, e.g.*, **Treyball v. Clark,** 65 N.Y.2d 589 (1985)—statute does not violate party's right to jury trial or deny due process; *but see* **Bernier v. Burris,** 497 N.E.2d 763 (Ill. 1986)—statute impermissibly requires judge to share decisionmaking authority with panel members]

4. Products Liability

a. Motivation [§1305]
The common law development of products liability led groups of manufacturers and retailers to seek legislation to moderate the financial impact of the new decisions.

b. Response [§1306]
Despite calls for congressional action based on a need for national uniformity, federal legislation to enact comprehensive statutory changes to govern products liability claims has not been adopted. About half of the states, most of them nonindustrial states, have adopted legislation drawing back in some respects from the common law rules of strict liability.

(1) **Statutes of repose [§1307]**
The most common change has been the enactment of "statutes of repose," providing that no action may be brought on a defective product claim more than a certain number of years after the product's initial distribution. This might bar an action even before the victim has been hurt (*e.g.*, a defect in an airplane might not cause an injury until after the statute of repose has expired). The period adopted in most states is between 10 and 12 years. [*See, e.g.*, **Gibson v. West Virginia Department of Highways,** 406 S.E.2d 440 (W. Va. 1991)—10-year statutory limitation constitutional; *but see* **Berry v. Beech Aircraft Corp.,** 717 P.2d 670 (Utah 1985)—statute violates state constitution's guarantee of open courts]

(2) **State of the art [§1308]**
Some states provide that a manufacturer's compliance with industry custom will bar recovery on a defective product theory.

(3) **Compliance with federal standards [§1309]**
Some states provide that compliance with federal standards (*e.g.*, FDA regulations) may bar recovery, or may bar recovery of punitive damages.

(4) **Presumption of safety [§1310]**
Some states provide that if the product has not caused harm for a certain number of years, the plaintiff must present "clear and convincing" proof of a claimed defect.

(5) **Manufacturer primarily liable [§1311]**
Some statutes provide that a nonnegligent retailer or distributor may not be held liable, or may be held liable only if the manufacturer is insolvent. [**Baker v. Promark Products West, Inc.,** 692 S.W.2d 844 (Tenn. 1985)]

c. **Vaccines [§1312]**
Vaccines pose a special problem because of their importance and the tremendous liability risk of producing them. In 1986, Congress enacted a modified no-fault compensation scheme for injuries resulting from certain childhood vaccines. The victims are first offered generous no-fault compensation. If they reject the no-fault award, they may sue in tort, but the federal statute reduces the situations in which defendants may be found liable. [42 U.S.C. §§300aa-10 *et seq.*]

5. **Miscellaneous Statutory Changes to Personal Injury Law**

a. **Duty to rescue [§1313]**
A few states have passed criminal statutes requiring a person to render reasonable assistance to one exposed to grave physical harm unless the effort would endanger the person or interfere with important duties that person owes to others. [*See, e.g.*, 12 Vt. Stat. Ann. §519] None of these states had imposed a civil duty to rescue.

(1) **Use of incentives [§1314]**
Recall that almost all the other states have proceeded by legislating exceptions to the duty of due care so as to encourage physicians and others to volunteer aid (*see supra*, §566). [*See* Mass. Gen. Laws Ann. ch. 94, §305D—using good faith standard for restaurant employees to try to help choking customers; Volunteer Protection Act of 1997, 42 U.S.C. §§14501 *et seq.*—volunteers of nonprofit organizations and governmental entities are not liable for negligence; 42 U.S.C. §1791(c)(2)—good faith standard used for food suppliers who donate leftover food to nonprofit organizations; Cal. Civ. Code §1714.25(b)—same]

b. **Dram shop liability [§1315]**
A number of states have enacted restrictions on the liability of taverns and social hosts who serve alcohol to people who get drunk and injure third parties (*see supra*, §§636-649). [**Cory v. Shierloh,** 29 Cal. 3d 430 (1981)]

c. **Victims of violent crimes [§1316]**
To meet the problems of insolvent defendants, most states have adopted legislation to provide aid to some victims of violent crimes.

(1) **Common provisions [§1317]**
Common features include requirements that the victim report the crime quickly and cooperate with the police. Crimes within the family are usually excluded.

(2) **Financial hardship [§1318]**
States are split over whether all victims are eligible, or only those who would suffer financial hardship if uncompensated. [*See, e.g.*, **Regan v. Crime Victims Compensation Board,** 57 N.Y.2d 190 (1982)]

d. **International airplane crashes [§1319]**
To meet problems of international legal conflicts, many nations, including the United States, have joined the Warsaw Convention, which provides the victims of any international air mishap with a strict liability recovery of a limited amount of damages. [*See, e.g.*, **Eastern Airlines, Inc. v. Floyd,** 499 U.S. 530 (1991)—no recovery for emotional distress unaccompanied by physical injury; **Air France v. Saks,** 470 U.S. 392 (1985)]

(1) **Recovering beyond strict liability [§1320]**
Although the Convention has been modified several times to increase the amount recoverable without proof of fault, "willful misconduct" must be established in order to recover any additional amount. [*See* **Piamba Cortes v. American Airlines, Inc.,** 177 F.3d 1272 (11th Cir. 1999)]

(2) **Death on the High Seas Act [§1321]**
Because the Warsaw Convention does not specify what substantive law is to be used to determine what types of damages are recoverable, the courts must look elsewhere. In crashes over international waters, the federal Death on the High Seas Act ("DOHSA") provides the relevant American law. [**Zicherman v. Korean Air Lines Co.,** 516 U.S. 217 (1996)—DOHSA does not permit survivors of international plane crash to recover for lost society]

(a) **Application**
State law, not the DOHSA, applies to crashes within the 12-mile territorial limit. [***In re* Air Crash off Long Island, New York,** 209 F.3d 200 (2d Cir. 2000)—TWA 800 crash eight miles off shore did not occur on the "high seas" and thus is governed by state law]

e. **Nuclear accidents [§1322]**
Because of the inability of nuclear power plants to get adequate liability insurance, Congress enacted legislation to provide victims of nuclear accidents with

limited no-fault compensation. Damages in excess of an individual firm's liability insurance are to be paid out of a fund to which all federal nuclear licensees must contribute. [*See* **Duke Power Co. v. Carolina Environmental Study Group, Inc.,** 438 U.S. 59 (1978)]

f. **Black lung compensation [§1323]**
Because workers' compensation statutes often fail to compensate workers for occupational diseases, Congress has enacted legislation to provide no-fault compensatory payments to miners afflicted with black lung disease. [*See* 30 U.S.C. §801]

g. **September 11th victim compensation [§1324]**
Shortly after September 11, 2001, Congress enacted a statute providing for no-fault compensation for all personal injury victims and survivors of those killed in the attack. [49 U.S.C. §40101 note] The statute uniquely provides full compensation for those victims, rather than the more modest provisions in other no-fault schemes. Pursuant to this statute, some $7 billion was distributed to those eligible.

6. Federal Preemption of State Tort Claims

a. **Federal legislation and authority [§1325]**
Congress enacts legislation to regulate certain risks, such as those presented by prescription drugs, consumer products, or interstate railroads. In the course of doing so, Congress may displace the states from also regulating those areas because of the Supremacy Clause in the United States Constitution declaring federal law to be supreme to that of state law. [U.S. Const. art. VI, cl. 2]

b. **Express preemption [§1326]**
When Congress does write limitations on the authority of states to act in an area addressed in legislation, it expressly "preempts" state law. Such limitations may not only prevent the state from affirmatively adopting laws or regulations in the area, but also bar the state from permitting tort suits that are related to or inconsistent with the requirements imposed in the federal legislation. [**Cipollone v. Liggett Group, Inc.,** *supra,* §1068—1969 amendments to Federal Cigarette Labeling and Advertising Act, imposing required warnings of the dangers of smoking, preempted tort claims claiming manufacturers inadequately warned of the dangers of smoking]

(1) **"Requirement" [§1327]**
In a series of decisions, the Supreme Court has declared that when Congress provides in an express preemption clause that states may not impose certain "requirements," use of the word "requirement" includes tort law claims. [**Riegel v. Medtronic, Inc.,** 128 S. Ct. 999 (2008)—use of "requirement" in Medical Device Amendments of 1976 preempted state tort claims based on design or warnings defects in medical devices subject to full premarketing review by FDA]

c. **Implied preemption [§1328]**
Even when Congress has not included a provision expressly displacing state law, "implied preemption" may prevent a state from imposing tort liability when such liability would frustrate the objectives of federal legislation or impose obligations that would conflict with federal law. [**Geier v. American Honda Motor Co.**, *supra,* §1068—federal regulations requiring some form of passive restraint impliedly preempted state tort claim that automobile was defective for failing to employ one particular form of passive restraint (an airbag)]

B. Changes Affecting Tort Claims Generally

1. **Motivation [§1329]**
In the mid-1980s, many perceived the entire tort system to be in a state of crisis. Damages awards were skyrocketing. Some defendants who were jointly and severally liable had to pay amounts that were grossly disproportionate to their degree of fault. Insurance premiums soared. For an increasing number of entities, liability insurance became completely unavailable. In response, a large majority of the states have adopted legislation intended to deal with these problems. The most significant statutory provisions involve limitations on joint and several liability, on damages, and on the collateral sources rule.

2. **Joint and Several Liability [§1330]**
Some 40 states have enacted some form of limitation on joint and several liability (*see supra,* §§418, 1252-1266). [*See* **Coats v. Penrod Drilling Corp.**, 61 F.3d 1113 (5th Cir. 1995) (*en banc*)—summarizing state positions]

a. **Abolition [§1331]**
About 10 states have abolished joint and several liability entirely. Several more have abolished it for all ***noneconomic damages***, and several more have done so for all cases in which the plaintiff is found to have been ***comparatively negligent.***

b. **Limitations based on defendant's degree of fault [§1332]**
A number of states have decided that the fault percentages should control the abolition or restriction of joint and several liability. Thus, in cases in which the defendant's fault is less than the plaintiff's fault, or where the defendant's fault is less than a given percentage of the total fault, some states bar joint and several liability. In a few states, the defendants are jointly and severally liable, but a defendant's liability cannot exceed his fault by more than a certain percentage (*e.g.*, a defendant who is 10% at fault may be jointly and severally liable for no more than 20% of the plaintiff's damages).

c. **Exceptions based on nature of tort [§1333]**

Some states that have enacted legislation curtailing joint and several liability provide that it will still be available in cases involving certain kinds of torts. For example, a state may provide that joint and several liability applies only if the defendants acted with a common plan, if they committed an intentional tort, or if the action involves defective products, toxic substances, or hazardous waste. [*See, e.g.,* **Smith v. Department of Insurance,** 507 So. 2d 1080 (Fla. 1987)—upholding statute that abolishes joint and several liability with exceptions based on the defendant's relative fault, the nature of the tort, and the total amount of damages]

3. Limitations on Damages

a. **Noneconomic damages [§1334]**

More than a quarter of the states have enacted restrictions on noneconomic damages awards (*e.g.,* pain and suffering, emotional distress, loss of consortium). Usually these take the form of a cap on all noneconomic damages. [*See, e.g.,* **Murphy v. Edmonds,** 601 A.2d 102 (Md. 1992)—$50,000 cap on noneconomic damages constitutional] In a few states, the cap may apply to all noneconomic damages except those for disfigurement or physical pain and suffering. [*But see* **Smith v. Department of Insurance,** *supra*—cap on noneconomic damages violates Florida Constitution's guarantee of access to courts]

b. **Periodic payments [§1335]**

A number of states have provided that if a plaintiff's award includes substantial future damages, the defendant may be permitted to make periodic payments for these future damages instead of paying a lump sum at the time of judgment. In about half of these states, periodic payments are required; in the remainder, they are at the discretion of the court. In some states, the requirement to make periodic payments ceases with the death of the plaintiff; in others, at least some payments survive the plaintiff. [*See* Ralph Nader, The Corporate Drive to Restrict Their Victim's Rights, 22 Gonz. L. Rev. 15 (1986)]

c. **Punitive damages [§1336]**

Nearly half the states have enacted some form of restriction on punitive damages. [*See* S. Loyd Neal, Punitive Damages: Suggested Reform for an Insurance Problem, 18 St. Mary's L.J. 1019 (1987)] In addition, the Supreme Court has imposed federal constitutional limitations on punitive damages awards under the Due Process Clause of the Fourteenth Amendment. The Court established three factors to consider in determining excessiveness: (i) the degree of reprehensibility of the breach of duty, (ii) the disparity between the harm or potential harm suffered by the plaintiff and the punitive damages award, and (iii) the difference between the punitive damages awarded and the criminal penalties authorized or imposed in comparable cases. [**BMW of North America, Inc. v. Gore,** *supra,* §26]

(1) **Caps on damages awards [§1337]**
Half of these states have enacted caps on punitive damages awards. These may take the form of a flat cap (*e.g.*, $150,000), a cap based on some multiple of the compensatory damages awarded, or some combination of the two.

(2) **Heightened standard of proof [§1338]**
A number of states have provided that the plaintiff must prove by clear and convincing evidence, or even beyond a reasonable doubt, that punitive damages are warranted. [*See* **Linthicum v. Nationwide Life Insurance Co.,** 723 P.2d 675 (Ariz. 1986)]

(3) **Procedural reforms [§1339]**
Some states have called for bifurcated trials when punitive damages are sought. Others have prohibited plaintiffs from pleading punitive damages until after they have made a preliminary showing of the defendant's fault.

(4) **Recipients [§1340]**
Some states have required that a certain percentage of all punitive damages awards be paid to a state fund, usually either a general state fund or a victims' compensation fund. [*See, e.g.*, **Gordon v. State,** 608 So. 2d 800 (Fla. 1992)—statute giving state 60% of all punitive damages awards is constitutional; *but see* **Kirk v. Denver Publishing Co.,** 818 P.2d 262 (Colo. 1991)—statute giving state one-third of such awards is unconstitutional]

d. **Miscellaneous damages provisions**

(1) **Ad damnum clauses [§1341]**
A handful of states have barred plaintiffs from stating in the complaint the amount of damages sought.

(2) **Additur and remittitur [§1342]**
A few states have increased the courts' power to modify the damages award or to order a new trial where damages awarded by the jury are either inadequate or excessive.

(3) **Interest [§1343]**
A handful of states have acted either to adjust the interest rate on damages or to allow plaintiffs to recover interest for the period preceding the judgment. [*See, e.g.*, **Fleming v. Baptist General Convention,** 742 P.2d 1087 (Okla. 1987)]

4. Collateral Sources Rule [§1344]
More than a quarter of all the states have restricted the operation of the collateral sources rule (*see supra*, §539). [James L. Branton, The Collateral Source Rule, 18 St. Mary's L.J. 883 (1987)]

a. **Mandatory setoff [§1345]**
Half of these states require that the amount reimbursed by a collateral source be deducted from the plaintiff's damages award. [*See, e.g.,* **Ryan v. City of New York,** 79 N.Y.2d 792 (1991)—statute applies only to reduce tort recovery to extent of collateral sources received for pre-verdict harm]

b. **Discretionary setoff [§1346]**
In a few states, reduction of the plaintiff's award is at the discretion of the court or jury.

c. **Evidentiary rules [§1347]**
A few states simply provide that evidence that the plaintiff was reimbursed will be admissible at trial.

d. **Exceptions for certain kinds of sources [§1348]**
Generally, these statutes do not apply in cases in which the collateral source has a right of subrogation or where reimbursement was received from certain specified sources, such as life insurance.

5. **Miscellaneous General Changes**

a. **Regulation of attorneys' fees [§1349]**
A few states have set standards for the attorneys' disclosure of the fee structure. Several others have provided that attorneys' fees must be based on the amount actually recovered by the plaintiff (rather than on the amount awarded), or have made fees subject to a judicial review for reasonableness. [Charles P. Kindregan & Edward M. Swartz, The Assault on the Captive Consumer: Emasculating the Common Law of Torts in the Name of Reform, 18 St. Mary's L.J. 673 (1987)]

b. **Sanctions for frivolous claims [§1350]**
Nearly half the states have enacted sanctions for frivolous claims. These generally provide that the attorney or the party asserting the frivolous claim must pay the costs and fees associated with defending it.

c. **Alternative dispute resolution [§1351]**
A few states have required that claims below a certain minimum be submitted to arbitration.

Chapter Eight: Defamation

CONTENTS

▶	Key Exam Issues	
A.	In General	§1352
B.	Publication to a Third Party	§1357
C.	Harm to Reputation	§1380
D.	False Facts	§1409
E.	Causation	§1422
F.	Damages and Other Remedies	§1423
G.	Defenses	§1451
H.	Constitutional Privileges	§1503

Key Exam Issues

The common law of defamation has always been confusing because it is a mixture of political history, ecclesiastical law, and common law. It has always had a long prima facie case plus a long list of defenses and privileges. This alone made it hard to learn. But then the United States Supreme Court entered the field, complicating matters even more with its First Amendment rulings.

The common law operated on a principle of strict liability. The prima facie case did not include a requirement of fault. This meant that if a speaker hurt the reputation of the plaintiff by the recitation of some facts and those facts were not shown to be true, the speaker might be liable, despite a reasonable belief that the facts were true. The Supreme Court invalidated this rule of strict liability in most, but perhaps not all, cases.

This means that your specific concerns in answering a defamation question include the following:

1. Note that historically the plaintiff did ***not*** have to prove that the statement was false. Rather, the ***defendant*** had to prove that it was true. (It was generally held that the plaintiff had to allege falsity, but this was a matter of form and did not ease the burden on the defendant.)

   But note: If the statement is made about a matter of ***public concern***, constitutional limits ***require the plaintiff to prove falsity***.

   And note: If the statement is made about a ***public figure***, constitutional limitations require the plaintiff to ***prove knowledge*** that the defamatory statement was false ***or made in reckless disregard*** for its truth. If the statement is made about a ***private person*** and is about a matter of public concern, constitutional limitations require the plaintiff to prove that the falsity in the defamatory statement was attributable to at least ***negligence***.

2. Note too the curious role played by damages in this tort. In some situations, the plaintiff must show a certain type of damages (special damages) ***to recover any money at all***. At other times, that showing is not required. The type of damages suffered may control liability itself rather than simply measure the extent of the recovery.

3. Remember that various common law ***privileges*** survive the constitutionalization of defamation law and may prevent liability under state law.

4. ***Constitutional issues*** are especially important in many defamation questions. In analyzing constitutional issues, be sure to focus on the ***type of plaintiff***—whether the plaintiff

is properly called "public" or "private"—and then on the nature of the defamatory statement.

5. Also remember to consider the related torts of ***invasion of privacy*** and ***infliction of emotional distress.***

A. In General

1. Prima Facie Case [§1352]

Prima facie case at common law:

- *Publication to Third Person*
- *Understood as Defamatory of Plaintiff*
- *Allegation of Falsity*
- *Causation*
- *Damages*
- (*Falsity—see infra*, §§1409-1421)

2. At Common Law [§1353]

A prima facie case of defamation at common law required the ***publication*** to some ***third person*** of a statement that harmed the ***reputation*** of the ***plaintiff***, thereby ***causing*** the plaintiff to suffer ***damages***. Except for the defense of truth and for certain narrowly defined classes of ***privileged communications***, defamation was generally a ***strict liability*** tort.

3. Constitutional Considerations [§1354]

The Supreme Court has altered the common law framework in a series of cases holding that the ***First Amendment*** to the United States Constitution prohibits states from using strict liability because of the ***chilling effect*** such liability may have on ***freedom of speech.***

4. Importance of Common Law [§1355]

Despite the constitutional changes, the common law is still central to any analysis. Because the plaintiff's claim is based on state tort law, it must pass all state law tests before that state law has to be judged against constitutional standards.

5. Related Torts—Privacy and Emotional Distress [§1356]

For purposes of analysis, any problem that involves defamation may also involve an invasion of the right of ***privacy*** (*infra,* §§1544 *et seq.*) or the wrongful causing of ***emotional distress*** (*supra,* §§79 *et seq.*). Therefore, consideration should always be given to establishing liability for those torts as well as defamation.

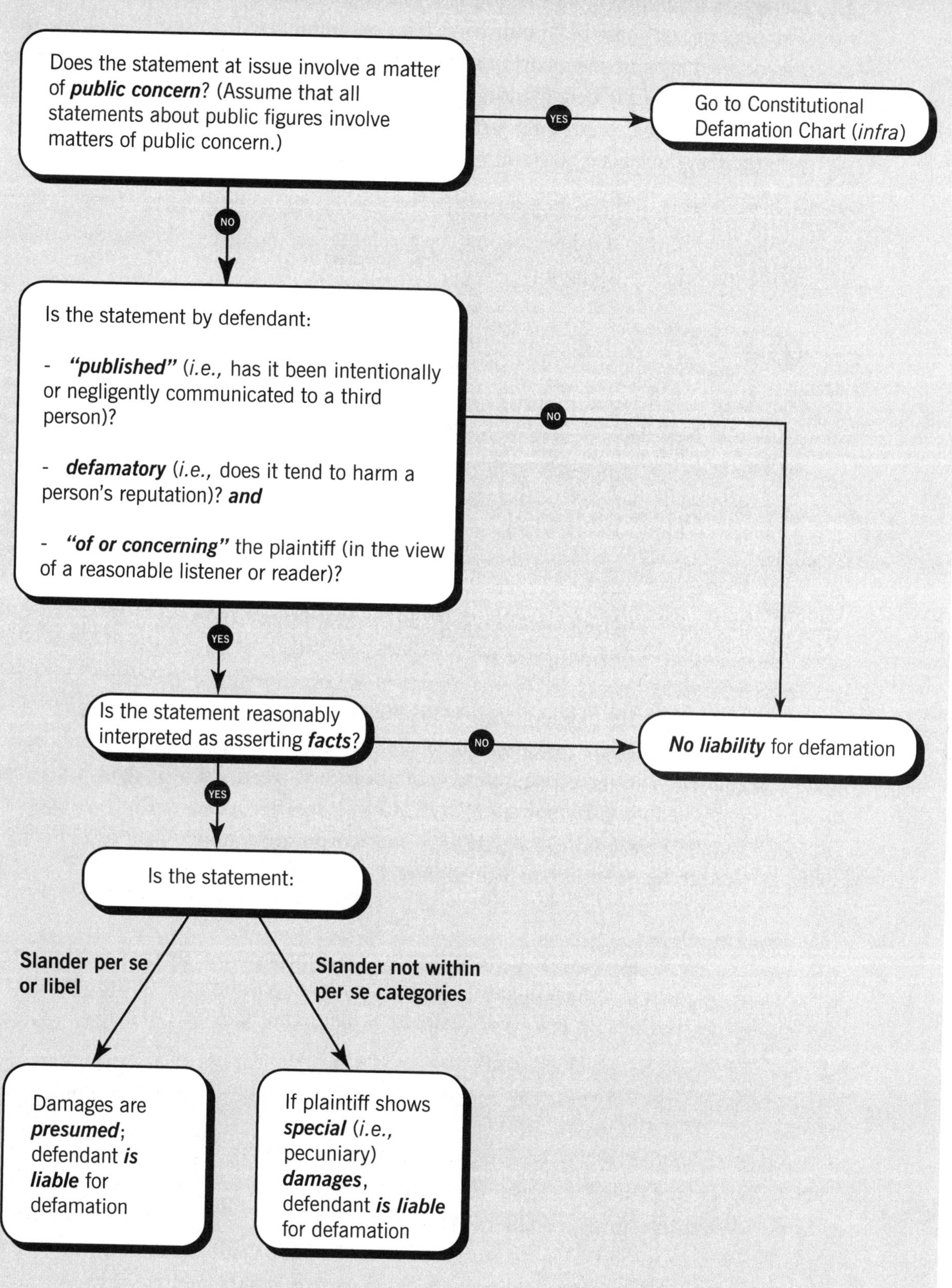
APPROACH TO COMMON LAW DEFAMATION
gilbert
Does the statement at issue involve a matter of ***public concern***? (Assume that all statements about public figures involve matters of public concern.)
YES
Go to Constitutional Defamation Chart (*infra*)
NO
Is the statement by defendant:
- ***"published"*** (*i.e.,* has it been intentionally or negligently communicated to a third person)?
- ***defamatory*** (*i.e.,* does it tend to harm a person's reputation)? ***and***
- ***"of or concerning"*** the plaintiff (in the view of a reasonable listener or reader)?
NO
YES
Is the statement reasonably interpreted as asserting ***facts***?
NO
No liability for defamation
YES
Is the statement:
Slander per se or libel
Slander not within per se categories
Damages are ***presumed***; defendant ***is liable*** for defamation
If plaintiff shows ***special*** (*i.e.,* pecuniary) ***damages***, defendant ***is liable*** for defamation

B. Publication to a Third Party

1. **Language Uttered Only to Plaintiff Not Actionable [§1357]**
   The defamation must be "published" (*i.e.*, communicated) to someone ***other than the plaintiff*** because the recovery is intended to remedy damage to ***reputation***. Statements uttered by the defendant directly to the plaintiff (in person, by phone, or by letter), and neither seen nor heard by anyone else, do not satisfy this requirement because there has been no harm to the plaintiff's reputation.

2. **Any Third Person Sufficient [§1358]**
   Publication to ***any*** third person may be a defamation, regardless of any relationship to the plaintiff or defendant.

---

e.g. **Example:** Remarks made by a supervisor to his superiors that defame the plaintiff-employee are "published" for purposes of defamation law, although they may be protected by privilege (*see infra*, §1468). [**Simpson v. Mars, Inc.,** 929 P.2d 966 (Nev. 1997)—coworker's defamatory statement to supervisor that plaintiff had sexually harassed her was considered published for purposes of establishing prima facie case, although defendant may try to show that the statement was privileged] Similarly, remarks to one's ***spouse*** are published but are privileged (*see infra*, §1461).

---

e.g. **Example:** Telephone callers' statements to husband that wife was having an affair and may have become pregnant by another man are considered published. [**Ellis v. Price,** 990 S.W.2d 543 (Ark. 1999)]

---

   a. **Intracorporate publication rule [§1359]**
      Most courts have adopted the Second Restatement position that publication can occur in intracorporate communications. [Rest. 2d §577 cmt. i; *and see, e.g.,* **Wallulis v. Dymowski,** 918 P.2d 755 (Or. 1996); *but see* **Dixon v. Economy Co.,** 477 So. 2d 353 (Ala. 1985)—intracorporate communications not considered to be published to a third party]

      (1) **Note**
      Even in courts that treat dictation as a publication, there is a strong argument that such dictation should be ***privileged***, because of the confidential relationship involved. [**Ostrowe v. Lee,** 256 N.Y. 36 (1931)]

3. **Manner of Publication [§1360]**
   Defamatory publications are not limited to statements that are printed and distributed. Because the gist of the tort is harm to reputation, ***any action*** by the defendant that causes the statement to be communicated to a third person is a "publication" of that statement.

   a. **Words, gestures, conduct [§1361]**
      Words are certainly the most common manner of publication, but they are not essential. Gestures or other conduct in public may suffice. [Rest. 2d §568 cmt. d]

Example: Marching customer P handcuffed through a store to its security office was a pantomime that published a defamation. [**K-Mart Corp. v. Washington,** 866 P.2d 274 (Nev. 1993)]

4. Publication Must Have Been Intentional or Negligent [§1362]

To hold the defendant liable, the plaintiff must allege and prove that the defamation was ***intentionally*** communicated by the defendant to some third person ***or*** that the communication resulted from the defendant's failure to exercise due care—*i.e.*, ***negligence*** (*e.g.*, leaving the writing where it could foreseeably be read by third persons).

a. Application—mass media [§1363]

This element will always be satisfied with publications by the media because those publications are ***intended*** to reach third persons.

b. Application—communication with plaintiff overheard [§1364]

The issue of ***negligence*** in publication arises most frequently where the defendant has communicated directly to the plaintiff, but some third person has seen or overheard the communication (*e.g.*, an accusation mailed by defendant to plaintiff, opened by plaintiff's spouse or secretary). In such cases, there is a negligent "publication to a third person" only if the defendant ***had reason to foresee*** that this would happen ***and*** a reasonable way to avoid it.

Examples: Mailing a defamatory letter to a blind person (foreseeable that she will ask another to read it to her) is publication, as is defamation printed on a postcard (foreseeable that mail carrier may read), or mailing a defamatory letter to P at her office, if D had reason to know that P's secretary usually opens her mail. [*See, e.g.,* **Barnes v. Clayton House Motel,** 435 S.W.2d 616 (Tex. 1968)]

c. Application—plaintiff compelled to repeat defamation [§1365]

If the defendant makes a defamatory statement to the plaintiff and the defendant has reason to believe that the plaintiff may be forced to repeat the statement (*e.g.*, where an employer (D) terminates an employee (P) for dishonesty and the employee will likely have to explain the reasons for discharge to future prospective employers [*see* **Churchey v. Adolph Coors Co.,** 759 P.2d 1336 (Colo. 1988)]), there is a split of authority as to whether a publication occurs at the time of the repetition. [*See* **Overcast v. Billings Mutual Insurance Co.,** 11 S.W.3d 62 (Mo. 2000)—insurer's registered letter to be delivered only to the insured saying that insurer refuses to pay for fire loss because the insured committed arson may provide the basis for defamation action because it is foreseeable that when the insured seeks new insurance he will have to explain the prior refusal to pay; *but see* **Sullivan v. Baptist Memorial Hospital,** 995 S.W.2d 569 (Tenn. 1999)—no publication when former employee repeats employer's statement]

5. Who Is a Publisher? [§1366]

Three separate types of defendants may utter defamations. Each is subject to different analysis:

a. Original publishers [§1367]

Anyone who has any part in the original publication is treated as an original publisher and is therefore potentially liable for the defamation. For example, in the case of a defamation appearing in a newspaper, the reporter, editor, and publisher may all be held liable. [*See* **Davis v. Hearst,** 160 Cal. 143 (1911)]

(1) Distributors [§1368]

Newspaper distributors and carriers might also be responsible for publication (*see* below).

(2) Principles of respondeat superior apply [§1369]

It need not be shown that a newspaper owner intended to publish the defamation or failed to exercise due care. All that need appear is that the elements be shown against someone for whom the owner is vicariously liable.

b. Republishers [§1370]

At common law, the republisher of a defamatory statement could be held liable equally with the original publisher. Thus, someone could be sued for accurately repeating someone else's defamatory statement. However, the common law rule is subject to certain exceptions for ***privileged communications***, discussed *infra,* §§1453 *et seq.*

(1) Rationale

The last utterance may do more harm than the first.

(2) Slander or libel [§1371]

If the original defamation is libel (generally, written defamation; *see infra*, §1424), any republication—even an oral recitation of the writing—is libel. And putting an oral defamation (slander; *see infra*, §1425) into writing makes the repetition libel.

EXAM TIP gilbert

Language is important to lawyers, and probably to your professor as well, so you don't want to use the wrong terminology in an essay answer dealing with defamation. To keep libel and slander straight, just remember the "S" mnemonic: **S**lander is **S**poken. (For further detail, *see infra*, §§1424-1426.)

(3) Basis for liability [§1372]

Like original publishers, republishers—***unless privileged***—are held to the same rules of strict liability on every element of the prima facie case except the manner of publication, which must be intentional or negligent.

(a) Failure to remove [§1373]

Failing to remove a defamation posted on one's premises by someone else may also constitute a negligent republication of the defamation by the owner of the premises. [*See, e.g.,* **Tacket v. General Motors Corp.,** 836 F.2d 1042 (7th Cir. 1987)—D employer allowed defamation of P worker to remain on plant wall for seven months despite complaints; **Hellar v. Bianco,** 111 Cal. App. 2d 424 (1952)—D tavernkeeper obligated to use due care to remove defamatory statement about P's chastity after learning that the words had been scrawled on the wall of the men's room]

(4) Effect of republication on liability of original publisher [§1374]

If there is a republication of the defamation, the original defamer's liability is increased by whatever harm the repetition causes ***if the republication was either:*** (i) ***intended*** by the original defamer, or (ii) ***reasonably foreseeable.*** [Rest. 2d §576; **Barnette v. Wilson,** 706 So. 2d 1164 (Ala. 1997)—police chief could be held responsible for republication of his press conference statement accusing former police officers of being "dirty cops"]

(5) Legal duty to republish [§1375]

One who has a legal duty to republish certain information has an ***absolute privilege*** to do so and may proceed even if the statement published would otherwise give rise to a defamation action, as in the case of an executor who is under a legal duty to probate a will even if it contains defamations.

c. Disseminators [§1376]

A disseminator is a type of republisher who circulates, sells, rents, or otherwise deals with the ***physical embodiment*** of defamatory matter (*i.e.*, libraries, dealers or distributors of books, newspapers, etc., that contain defamatory matter).

(1) Limited liability [§1377]

Disseminators are ***not*** held to the same standards of liability as the original publisher and other republishers. Rather, a disseminator is held only to a ***standard of due care.*** Thus, a disseminator who has no knowledge of the defamation contained in the material being handled and has no reason to know of the defamation is not liable for it. [Rest. 2d §581]

(2) Distinguish—printers [§1378]

Independent contract printers have ***no duty to inspect*** a publication for libelous content. [*See, e.g.,* **Maynard v. Port Publications, Inc.,** 297 N.W.2d 500 (Wis. 1980)]

(3) Distinguish—computer bulletin boards [§1379]

The majority view is that a congressional statute bars holding Internet service providers liable for the defamatory comments made by their subscribers. [47 U.S.C. §230; *and see* **Zeran v. America Online, Inc.,** 129 F.3d 327 (4th Cir. 1997), *cert. denied,* 524 U.S. 937 (1998)]

C. Harm to Reputation

1. Defamatory Meaning [§1380]

To be actionable, a statement must have the potential to ***injure the reputation*** of the plaintiff. There are two aspects to this inquiry: (i) whether the ***meaning*** alleged by the plaintiff is defamatory, and (ii) if so, whether the statement can be ***interpreted*** to carry that meaning.

a. Is the alleged meaning defamatory? [§1381]

To be defamatory, a statement must ***tend to lower the plaintiff's*** reputation in the estimation of the community where published ***or*** deter others from associating with the plaintiff. [Rest. 2d §559]

(1) Narrow view [§1382]

Some states insist that the meaning expose the plaintiff to "hatred, contempt, or ridicule" in order to be actionable. This is narrower than "lowering" the plaintiff's reputation in the estimation of the community.

---

e.g. **Example:** Under the narrow standard, a charge that P is insane might ***not*** be considered defamatory. [*See* **Grant v. Reader's Digest Association,** 151 F.2d 733 (2d Cir. 1945)]

---

(2) Community standards control [§1383]

Whichever standard of defamation is used, the question of whether a statement is defamatory generally depends on the attitudes and mores of the audience to whom it was communicated. To be actionable, a widely published statement must injure the plaintiff "in the eyes of a substantial and respectable minority" of the community. [*See* Rest. 2d §559 cmt. e]

(3) Defamatory effect [§1384]

In determining whether a meaning is defamatory, the focus is on ***how the words were reasonably understood*** by the third persons to whom it was published, ***not*** on what the speaker meant.

(a) Rationale

Unless someone understands the publication in a defamatory sense, the plaintiff's reputation is not harmed.

(b) Application—foreign language [§1385]

If the statement to a specific group of people is couched in a foreign language, the plaintiff must show that at least one group member understood the language. [**Economopoulos v. A.G. Pollard Co.,** 105 N.E. 896 (Mass. 1914)]

EXAM TIP **gilbert**

It is important to remember that a statement can be defamatory only if it is published to a ***third person*** (*i.e.,* someone other than the speaker and the defamed person) ***who understands it***. A classic exam ruse is a fact pattern involving persons speaking in a foreign language in front of someone else who doesn't (*e.g.,* Jacques accuses Michelle of cheating on her husband, while Michelle's butler, Hans, is present, but the accusation is in French and Hans does not speak French). If the third person did not understand what was being said, the statement cannot be defamatory.

(c) Who decides? [§1386]

If the effect is clear, the question of whether the meaning is defamatory may be answered by the judge; if the effect of the meaning is unclear, a jury decides.

---

e.g. **Example:** A statement that one committed a serious crime is defamatory on its face as a matter of law. [**Lawrence v. Bauer Publishing & Printing Ltd.,** 446 A.2d 469 (N.J.), *cert. denied*, 439 U.S. 999 (1982)]

---

e.g. **Example:** As a matter of law, a statement that one knows an imprisoned criminal and is interested in his well-being is not defamatory. [**Romaine v. Kallinger,** 537 A.2d 284 (N.J. 1988)]

---

e.g. **Example:** A suggestion that a lawyer asked a client to sign an affidavit that the lawyer knew was false might be found defamatory by a jury. [**Armstrong v. Simon & Schuster, Inc.,** 85 N.Y.2d 373 (1995)]

---

e.g. **Example:** Statements that an air show pilot had executed a maneuver "frowned upon" by the Federal Aviation Administration ("FAA") could not reasonably be interpreted to imply that the pilot violated FAA rules. [**Reesman v. Highfill,** 965 P.2d 1030 (Or. 1998)]

---

(4) "Libel-proof plaintiffs" [§1387]

At common law, some courts dismiss cases brought by persons whose reputations are so bad that a false statement could not hurt the reputation more than nominally. [**Jackson v. Longcope,** 476 N.E.2d 617 (Mass. 1985)—convicted murderer cannot sue over false report that he had also raped his victims]

(a) No constitutional basis [§1388]

The libel-proof plaintiff doctrine is ***not required by the First Amendment***. Thus, it is ***solely a matter of state law***, and states are free to accept or reject it without constitutional constraint. [**Masson v. New Yorker Magazine, Inc.,** 501 U.S. 496 (1991)]

b. Can the words carry the suggested meaning? [§1389]

In determining the meaning attached to a statement, courts look at the ***fair and natural meaning*** the statement will be given by ***reasonable persons of ordinary intelligence***. [**Romaine v. Kallinger,** *supra*]

(1) Context important [§1390]

Publications are generally read as a whole in light of the context in which the statement appears. [**Romaine v. Kallinger,** *supra*]

---

e.g. **Example:** Three sentences of a newspaper article about an arrest and assault did not say "alleged" although the other five did use that word. Viewed in its entirety, the publication could not reasonably be read as a charge by the newspaper that P committed the assault. [**Foley v. Lowell Sun Publishing Co.,** 533 N.E.2d 196 (Mass. 1989)]

(a) Exceptions—headlines and lengthy publications [§1391]

Although normally an article is to be read in its entirety for defamatory thrust, this rule may not apply to ***headlines*** [**Kaelin v. Globe Communications Corp.,** 162 F.3d 1036 (9th Cir. 1998)—headline after O.J. Simpson's murder trial—"Cops Think Kato Did It!"—could be defamatory even though article's text indicated headline referred to perjury charge], nor to ***very long*** articles where the defamatory thrust is at the outset but is not explained away until much later in the article [**Kunst v. New York World Telegram Corp.,** 28 A.D.2d 662 (1967)].

(b) Format relevant [§1392]

Typography and paragraphing may be crucial in determining a reasonable reader's reactions. [**Vandenburg v. Newsweek, Inc.,** 507 F.2d 1024 (5th Cir. 1975)]

---

e.g. **Example:** Where D writes that P was one of "several women described as 'associated' with" a slain executive, the use of quotation marks around "associated" permits a defamatory interpretation. [**Wildstein v. New York Post Corp.,** 40 Misc. 2d 586 (1963), *aff'd*, 24 A.D.2d 559 (1965)]

---

(2) Defamation by implication and insinuation [§1393]

The form of the language used by the defendant is not controlling, as long as third persons to whom it is published could ***reasonably*** interpret it in a sense defamatory to the plaintiff. [Rest. 2d §565 cmt. b; **Davis v. Ross,** 754 F.2d 80 (2d Cir. 1985); **Aronson v. Wiersma,** 65 N.Y.2d 592 (1985)]

---

e.g. **Example:** D newspaper reported that a man who had objected to YMCA policy had suffered a heart attack and died during a rally near a YMCA board meeting. The paper also reported that the man's family was upset because he was not treated quickly. The next paragraph stated that P, the president of the YMCA, was a doctor and was present at the meeting. The court held that a reasonable reader could draw a defamatory meaning from these two paragraphs. [**Healey v. New England Newspapers, Inc.,** 555 A.2d 321 (R.I.), *cert. denied*, 493 U.S. 814 (1989)]

---

e.g. **Example:** Sometimes asking a question may be defamatory if it implies that the speaker is asserting underlying facts. [**Chapin v. Knight-Ridder, Inc.,** 993 F.2d 1087 (4th Cir. 1993)—not defamatory to ask, "Who will benefit more from [a project to send gifts to soldiers]—GIs or [plaintiff]?"]

(a) Minority view—"possible innocent meaning" rule [§1394]
A very few states have taken the position that where the defamation appears only by implication or insinuation, it is not actionable if, in context, the statement is reasonably equivocal—*i.e.*, if it is plausible to give the statement a reasonable innocent meaning. [*See, e.g.,* **Chapski v. Copley Press,** 442 N.E.2d 195 (Ill. 1982)]

(3) Incomplete defamation [§1395]
If the defamatory meaning arises only when the words are combined with extrinsic facts not apparent on the face of the publication, the plaintiff must allege and prove the extrinsic facts (called the ***"inducement"***), that these facts were known to some third person who read or heard the statement, and that the implication (***"innuendo"***) of the statement, when combined with those facts, is defamatory. [*See* **Whitby v. Associates Discount Corp.,** 207 N.E.2d 482 (Ill. 1965)]

---

e.g. **Example:** D newspaper published a notice that P's wife had just given birth to twin sons. The statement on its face certainly was not defamatory, but it became so when tied to the extrinsic fact—presumably known to some readers—that P and his wife had been married only one month, the innuendo being that P and his wife had been unchaste prior to marriage. [**Morrison v. Ritchie & Co.,** 39 Scot. L. Rep. 432 (1902)]

---

2. "Of and Concerning" the Plaintiff [§1396]
For a statement to be actionable, some third person must have ***reasonably interpreted*** it to refer to the plaintiff.

a. Defamed person unnamed—colloquium [§1397]
A publication may clearly be defamatory of somebody, and yet on its face make no reference to the plaintiff (*e.g.,* "a certain well-known industrialist who lives on Queensbury Road is keeping company with prostitutes"). In such a case, the

plaintiff must establish the ***"colloquium"***—*i.e.*, that some persons to whom the statement was published ***reasonably interpreted*** it as applying to the plaintiff.

---

e.g. **Example:** A mother writes a letter to the editor attacking her child's teacher without naming the teacher. A jury might find that some readers knew that the speaker's only child was in third grade and that P was the only third grade teacher in that school. [**Zelik v. Daily News Publishing Co.,** 431 A.2d 1046 (Pa. 1981)]

EXAM TIP gilbert

Your professor may be a stickler for terminology. If so, be sure to remember the following technical terms that are used when the defamatory statement is not complete on its face.

- If a statement is not defamatory without some extrinsic facts, the plaintiff must plead and prove the ***additional facts as inducement*** to the trier of fact to find the statement defamatory. The defamatory implication of the statement plus the extrinsic facts is (the other "i word") ***innuendo***.

- On the other hand, if the statement is clearly defamatory, but it is ***not clear on the face of the statement who is being defamed*** (*e.g.*, a magazine article that starts out, "A certain former super model who grew up in DeKalb, Illinois . . ."), the plaintiff must establish the ***colloquium***—the facts that show that some people will understand that the statement was about the plaintiff.

---

(1) Fiction [§1398]

Depending on resemblances, a jury may be permitted to find that statements in a novel are of and concerning a real plaintiff. [**Bindrim v. Mitchell,** 92 Cal. App. 3d 61, *cert. denied*, 444 U.S. 984 (1979)]

(2) Distinguish—unintended but explicit use of plaintiff's name [§1399]

On the other hand, if the plaintiff's name *is* used, he may maintain an action for defamation even though the defendant was really referring to another person by the same name—provided some persons to whom the defamation was published reasonably interpreted it as applying to the plaintiff.

---

e.g. **Example:** D reports that "Artemus Jones," supposedly a fictitious person, was seen cavorting with a woman other than his wife. A real Artemus Jones satisfies this element if he can show that persons who read the article reasonably thought it referred to him. [**Hulton v. Jones,** 1910 A.C. 20] The same result would follow if D was referring to a real Artemus Jones but some reasonable readers understood it to refer to a different Artemus Jones.

---

b. Who may be defamed—in general [§1400]

Any living person, corporation, partnership, or other legally recognized entity may be the subject of a defamation and may bring an action therefor.

(1) Other groups [§1401]

Clubs, fraternities, and other unincorporated associations do not possess sufficient status as an entity to sue for defamation; however, individual members may sue if the matter clearly defames them (*see infra*). Some decisions, on the other hand, recognize the right of a labor union to sue ***as an entity***—comparable to the rights accorded a corporation or partnership. [**Daniels v. Sanitarium Association,** 59 Cal. 2d 602 (1963)]

(2) Deceased persons [§1402]

No action will lie for the defamation of one who is already dead. [**Keys v. Interstate Circuit, Inc.,** 468 S.W.2d 485 (Tex. 1971)—no action by heirs of "Bonnie and Clyde"]

(a) Distinguish—defamation of deceased reflecting upon living person [§1403]

Note, however, that certain defamations of a deceased person may also defame a living person, and hence may be actionable. [Rest. 2d §564 cmt. e]

---

e.g. **Example:** If D states to someone that Z, a deceased woman, had no legitimate children, this might defame Z's living children.

(b) Distinguish—survival of action [§1404]

Most states following the usual tort rule provide that when the plaintiff dies after being defamed but before suit or trial, the claim survives. A few states, however, hold that death before judgment destroys the defamation claim.

c. Individual claims arising from group defamations [§1405]

No individual member of a class defamed may bring an action unless the group is so small that the statement may reasonably be interpreted as applying to each member. [**Neiman-Marcus v. Lait,** 13 F.R.D. 311 (S.D.N.Y. 1952)] Thus, the ***size of the group*** is the key factor in determining whether an action will lie.

---

e.g. **Example:** The statement "all lawyers are shysters" cannot defame Attorney A unless other facts suggest that the recipients reasonably understood that A was being singled out (*e.g.*, the speaker pointed a finger at A while making the statement). [*See, e.g.*, **Thomas v. Jacksonville Television, Inc.,** 699 So. 2d 800 (Fla. 1997)—individual members of group of 436 commercial net fisherman could not sue for defamatory statements about group's fishing practices]

---

cf. **Compare:** If the statement was "the Election Board took bribes," the target group is smaller and, without more, the finger of defamation may point sufficiently at each individual member.

---

(1) **Minority view—"intensity of suspicion" test [§1406]**
Some courts hold that the size of the group is not the sole consideration. Other factors, such as definition of the group's composition, degree of cohesiveness, and prominence affect the intensity of suspicion that the defendant's statements cast on the group. [*See, e.g.,* **Brady v. Ottaway Newspapers, Inc.,** 84 A.D.2d 226 (1981)—fact question whether group of 53 police officers is too large a group to sue]

(2) **Reference to part of group [§1407]**
If the group is small enough, a charge against "some" may be a charge against all. [**Neiman-Marcus v. Lait,** *supra*—suit by 15 male salespersons over statement that "most" of 25 male salespersons on staff were "fairies"; **Gross v. Cantor,** 270 N.Y. 93 (1936)—group of 12]

3. **Strict Liability [§1408]**
Although the element of "publication" requires either an intentional or a negligent publication, the element of "harm to reputation" is based on ***strict liability***. This means that at common law it is irrelevant whether the defendant anticipated or should have anticipated that some readers would understand an article as it is now claimed they did, or whether the defendant should reasonably have realized that a supposedly fictitious name was used by some real person. However, constitutional law has restricted strict liability. (*See infra*, §1503.)

D. False Facts

1. **Falsity [§1409]**
At common law, plaintiffs have to allege falsity, but defendants bear the burden of proving that the statement was true. If the statement was true, any injury to reputation is not actionable.

a. **Knowledge of falsity [§1410]**
The traditional common law rule was that a defendant was ***strictly liable*** for defamatory statements—*i.e.*, liable without regard to the defendant's knowledge or even negligent failure to know of a statement's truth or falsity. This is still the rule in many jurisdictions, although some have moved to a negligence standard. Where the plaintiff is a ***public figure*** or official, however, or where the defamatory statement was a matter of ***public concern***, the United States Supreme Court has imposed stricter standards in light of the First Amendment. (*See infra*, §§1503-1543.)

b. **Truth is complete defense [§1411]**
The general view is that truth of the defamatory matter is a ***complete*** defense—even if the publication was made out of pure spite and even if the defendant did not believe the statement was true at the time it was made. [**Craig v. Wright,** 76 P.2d 248 (Okla. 1938)]

EXAM TIP **gilbert**

If a statement is true, the plaintiff has no cause of action for ***defamation***. However, if you see this type of statement in an essay question, consider whether the plaintiff may have a cause of action for ***intentional infliction of emotional distress*** (*supra,* §§79 *et seq.*) or ***invasion of right to privacy*** (*infra,* §§1544 *et seq.*) (unless plaintiff is a public figure).

(1) Sting of the charge must be proven [§1412]

The defendant need not prove the literal truth of the charge, but must only establish its "sting." Thus, a claim that the plaintiff robbed a bank of $50,000 may be shown to be true even if the amount taken was only $7,000. [*See, e.g.,* **Posadas v. City of Reno,** 851 P.2d 438 (Nev. 1993)—charge of "lying under oath" not shown to be true by showing that P police officer lied to two other officers who questioned him while he was not under oath, because lying under oath is a crime and the latter was not]

(2) Constitutional rule as to public officials [§1413]

Even if a state were to assert that truth alone was not enough, this view cannot apply where a ***public official*** has been attacked in her public capacity. Freedom of speech requirements in such cases dictate that truth alone must be a sufficient defense. [**Garrison v. Louisiana,** 379 U.S. 64 (1964)]

2. Plaintiff's Burden to Prove Falsity [§1414]

At least where the statement involves a ***matter of public concern***, the First Amendment requires ***all plaintiffs*** to bear the burden of proving that the statement is false. [**Philadelphia Newspapers, Inc. v. Hepps,** 475 U.S. 767 (1986)]

a. Summary judgment [§1415]

Even though plaintiffs must prove the defamatory statement false, it may be that, as a practical matter, any defendant who seeks summary judgment on falsity grounds must demonstrate that the statement is true—in order to show that the plaintiff will be unable to prove it false at trial.

3. Statement Cannot Be False Unless It Contains Assertions of Fact [§1416]

Only facts can be true or false. Thus, the alleged defamation must contain explicit statements of fact or implied unstated facts that were ***false***.

a. No automatic protection for "opinion" [§1417]

A statement generally characterized as an "opinion" may be defamatory if it can be ***reasonably interpreted*** by the recipients as implying underlying defamatory facts. [*See* **Milkovich v. Lorain Journal Co.,** 497 U.S. 1 (1990)]

(1) Note

States may choose to protect this type of speech to a greater extent than required by the First Amendment. [*See* **Immuno AG. v. Moor-Jankowski,** 77 N.Y.2d 235, *cert. denied*, 500 U.S. 954 (1991)—New York state constitution allows consideration of the "tone and apparent purpose" of the communication to greater extent than federal law in deciding whether D's statement is protected "opinion"]

b. Determining what speech is factual [§1418]

Whether under federal or state law, determining whether speech is factual is a very fact specific inquiry. Some representative cases follow:

---

e.g. **Example:** Mock advertisement published in Hustler Magazine suggesting that the Reverend Jerry Falwell's first sexual experience was a drunken tryst with his mother in an outhouse could not reasonably be perceived as a factual statement. [**Hustler Magazine v. Falwell,** *supra*, §96]

---

e.g. **Example:** Union official's statement that former union attorney was a "very poor lawyer" was mere expression of opinion. [**Sullivan v. Conway,** 157 F.3d 1092 (7th Cir. 1998)—statement too difficult to verify or refute in defamation suit]

---

e.g. **Example:** Calling a little-known version of the popular Broadway musical *Phantom of the Opera* a "Fake Phantom . . . thriving off the confusion created by the two productions . . . a rip-off, a fraud, a scandal, a snake-oil job" was nonactionable opinion. [**Phantom Touring, Inc. v. Affiliated Publications,** 953 F.2d 724 (1st Cir. 1992)]

---

e.g. **Example:** A newspaper story questioning the "hefty mark-ups" charged by a charity program selling gift packs for troops in the Persian Gulf did not allege factual statements. [**Chapin v. Knight-Ridder, Inc.,** *supra,* §1393]

---

e.g. **Example:** An accusation that a high school wrestling coach committed perjury while testifying at a hearing in an attempt to get his team taken off probation was "***sufficiently factual*** to be susceptible of being proved true or false." [**Milkovich v. Lorain Journal Co.,** *supra*]

---

e.g. **Example:** Calling P a "racist" is not actionable because the word is used so casually today that it has lost its core meaning. [**Stevens v. Tillman,** 855 F.2d 394 (7th Cir. 1988), *cert. denied*, 489 U.S. 1065 (1989)]

---

e.g. **Example:** Statement implying that land developer was a slumlord who had "done well through poorly maintained properties" was defamatory factual allegation. [**Ramunno v. Cawley,** 705 A.2d 1029 (Del. 1998)]

---

e.g. **Example:** Even though a false allegation of incest is defamatory, no reasonable person exposed to the invective of "motherf____" would conclude that speaker was actually accusing plaintiff of having sexual intercourse with his mother. [**Bullock v. Jeon,** 487 S.E.2d 692 (Ga. 1997)]

---

c. **Statement of opinion not genuinely held [§1419]**

As a result of the difficulty of proving the insincerity of an opinion, statements of opinion not genuinely held by the speaker are nevertheless generally protected. [**Moldea v. New York Times Co.,** 22 F.3d 310 (D.C. Cir. 1994)—"There simply is no viable way to distinguish between reviews written by those who honestly believe a book is bad, and those prompted solely by mischievous intent"]

d. **Hyperbole in public debate [§1420]**

A broad statement made in the course of ***public debate*** will usually be characterized as "mere hyperbole," which is not actionable because reasonable people could not interpret it as being an assertion of fact. *Rationale:* The audience expects a certain degree of name calling and overstatement in public debates and does not take broad statements literally. [**Gregory v. McDonnell Douglas Corp.,** 17 Cal. 3d 596 (1976)]

---

e.g. **Example:** A newspaper report of a "blackmail" charge hurled at a city council meeting against a real estate developer for refusing to sell his land to the city unless it gave him a zoning variance on other property was not actionable. This could not reasonably be understood as charging the crime of blackmail. At most it was a claim that P was a hard bargainer—an accusation that was not defamatory. [**Greenbelt Cooperative Publishing Association v. Bresler,** 398 U.S. 6 (1970)]

---

e.g. **Example:** The epithet "traitor" was not actionable when used in a union newspaper against an employee who refused to join the union. [**Old Dominion Branch No. 496, National Association of Letter Carriers v. Austin,** 418 U.S. 264 (1974)]

---

e.g. **Example:** Calling a woman "a bitch" at a public meeting is vituperation and abuse not meant to be taken seriously. [**Ward v. Zelikovsky,** 643 A.2d 972 (N.J. 1994)]

---

e. **Specificity of language [§1421]**

The more specific the language used, the more likely it is to be reasonably interpreted as either a statement of fact or a statement based on underlying facts.

---

e.g. **Example:** The accusation that a journalist has libeled others was held actionable, but not the charge that he ran an "openly fascist journal." [**Buckley v. Littell,** 539 F.2d 882 (2d Cir. 1976), *cert. denied*, 429 U.S. 1062 (1977)]

E. Causation

1. Cause in Fact and Proximate Cause [§1422]

The cause in fact and proximate cause requirements for defamation are the same as those for negligence (*see supra*, §§415-509). (Note, however, that recovery of special damages (below) is limited to ***foreseeable*** damages.)

F. Damages and Other Remedies

1. In General [§1423]

The scope of damages recoverable in a defamation action under common law rules depends on the ***form*** of the publication—whether it is libel or slander—and on the ***motives*** with which it was uttered. Recoverable damages are also constitutionally limited in several situations.

2. "Libel" and "Slander" Distinguished

a. "Libel" defined [§1424]

"Libel" is defamation usually appearing in some written or printed form, *i.e.*, reduced to some ***permanent, physical embodiment*** such as newspapers, letters, etc. Generally, representations to the ***eye*** are libel. Thus, words, pictures, signs, statues, films, and even certain conduct such as hanging the plaintiff in effigy may be libel. [**Whitby v. Associates Discount Corp.**, *supra*, §1395]

b. "Slander" defined [§1425]

"Slander" is usually ***oral*** defamation, *i.e.*, representations to the ***ear***. The principal characteristic is that the defamation is in less permanent and less physical form. Other examples include transitory gestures (*e.g.*, nod of head). [Rest. 2d §568 cmt. d]

c. Borderline cases—factors [§1426]

To decide whether a publication is libel or slander in difficult cases (*e.g.*, defamations contained on a phonograph record, or in a television or radio program), consider:

(i) The ***permanency*** of the form of publication;

(ii) The ***extent of dissemination***; and

(iii) Whether the publication was ***deliberate or premeditated.***

[**Shor v. Billingsley,** 4 Misc. 2d 857 (1956), *aff'd*, 4 A.D.2d 1017 (1957)—capacity for harm, including extent of dissemination, warrants treating extemporaneous remark on live television as libel]

(1) Broadcasting [§1427]

Under the newer view, all radio and television publications are considered libel, whether or not read from a manuscript. [**First Independent Baptist Church v. Southerland,** 373 So. 2d 647 (Ala. 1979); Rest. 2d §568A]

(a) **Statutory treatment [§1428]**
Some states categorize media by statute. [*See, e.g.*, Cal. Civ. Code §46—defamations by radio or television are slander even if written scripts are used]

3. Damages Rule for Slander [§1429]

Defamation in the form of slander is not actionable without a showing of ***special damages***, unless the slander is of a class that the law deems ***"actionable per se."***

a. Compensatory damages recoverable

(1) **Special damages [§1430]**
"Special damages" are those ***actually suffered by the plaintiff*** and not presumed by law—*e.g.*, loss of employment or business, or failure of any firm expectancy (even a gratuity, such as a vacation paid for by friends).

(2) **General damages [§1431]**
A plaintiff who proves some amount of special damages may ***also*** recover general damages, even if they far exceed the proven special damages.

(a) **"General damages" defined [§1432]**
General damages compensate for harm to the plaintiff's reputation. Their existence may be proven by such evidence as polls. But even if not provable, their existence may be presumed by the jury based on the likely effect of the defamation considering the number of people who learned of it, the nature of the charge, and the identity of the speaker and the plaintiff. Constitutional limits on the availability of general damages are discussed, *infra*, §§1540 *et seq.*

(3) **Emotional damages [§1433]**
In addition to special and general damages, many states allow recovery for emotional damages caused by the defamatory conduct. Due to the potential for overlapping recovery, however, other states limit recovery for emotional damages if the plaintiff also qualifies for presumed damages to reputation. [**Hustler Magazine v. Falwell**, *supra*, §1418]

b. Slander per se—special damages not required [§1434]

There are only four situations in which slanders are deemed ***"actionable per se"***—*i.e.*, where a showing of special damages is ***not*** required before the plaintiff may recover general damages. (Of course, if the plaintiff has suffered any special damages, they are recoverable; but in these four cases she can recover general damages to her reputation regardless.) The four "slander per se" categories include charges that the plaintiff has committed a ***serious crime***, has a ***loathsome disease***, is ***incompetent in her trade or profession***, or is ***unchaste***.

(1) **Crime [§1435]**
Where the defendant charges that the plaintiff has committed a ***serious***,

morally reprehensible crime, or has been incarcerated for such, the charge is slander per se.

(a) **Need not charge specific crime [§1436]**
A specific offense need not be charged, as long as the defendant clearly alleges that the plaintiff committed a fairly ***serious*** crime.

---

e.g. **Example:** The statement "you stole the money" has been held to be slander per se. [**Hruby v. Kalina,** 424 N.W.2d 130 (Neb. 1988); *but see* **Liberman v. Gelstein,** 80 N.Y.2d 429 (1992)—charge of bribing a police officer is sufficiently serious to be slander per se, but charge of the misdemeanor of harassment is not]

---

e.g. **Example:** A remark that P was a "faggot" was defamatory per se because it imputed act of sodomy, which was criminal under state law. [**Plumley v. Landmark Chevrolet, Inc.,** 122 F.3d 308 (5th Cir. 1997)] In other states, although sodomy is not criminal, the allegation of homosexuality may be actionable under "unchastity" analysis (*see infra,* §1442).

(b) **But note**
Charging that the plaintiff is a "crook" or a "thief" is generally not slander per se, absent some specific allegation of criminal misconduct. [**Hruby v. Kalina,** *supra*]

(2) **Disease [§1437]**
Statements imputing to the plaintiff a ***currently existing, loathsome, communicable disease*** are slander per se. This is generally limited to venereal disease and leprosy; imputations of insanity, tuberculosis, etc., do not qualify. [**Rade v. Press Publishing Co.,** 37 Misc. 254 (1902)]

(3) **Ineptitude in trade or profession [§1438]**
Statements imputing to the plaintiff ***conduct, characteristics, or associations incompatible with the proper performance of the plaintiff's business, trade, office, or profession*** are slander per se. These cases present the most frequent and difficult problems.

(a) **Rationale**
The law is willing to presume actual damages in these cases because charges that a person is incompetent in, or unsuitable for, her trade or profession is likely to harm her livelihood.

(b) **Defamation must be incompatible with business [§1439]**
Whatever defamation is charged must actually be incompatible with the plaintiff's business or profession. Thus, the effect of a given charge may depend on the nature of the plaintiff's occupation.

---

e.g. **Examples:** Calling a doctor a "butcher," a lawyer a "shyster," a teacher "immoral" or "insane," or a businessperson "uncreditworthy" may all be considered slanderous per se. [*See, e.g.*, **MacLeod v. Tribune Publishing Co.,** 52 Cal. 2d 536 (1959)]

---

cf. **Compare:** It is not actionable without a showing of special damages to charge that a physician has committed adultery, or that a gas company clerk has been consorting with prostitutes, because such imputations are not incompatible with their positions. [**Lumby v. Allday,** 148 Eng. Rep. 1434 (1831)]

---

(4) Unchastity [§1440]

Statements imputing unchastity are slander per se. Traditionally this category of slander per se has been limited to charges leveled against *female* plaintiffs, but some states have extended the law to include males as well.

(a) Impotency [§1441]

In a few states, imputation of impotency to a man is also actionable per se. [*See, e.g.*, Cal. Civ. Code §46] The general view is contra.

(b) Homosexuality [§1442]

Even in a state that has legalized all private sexual conduct between consenting adults, a false imputation of the commission of a homosexual act may be slanderous per se. [**Schomer v. Smidt,** 113 Cal. App. 3d 828 (1980); *but see* **Donovan v. Fiumara,** 442 S.E.2d 572 (N.C. 1994)—changing societal attitudes preclude false allegation of homosexuality from being defamatory in absence of proof of actual damages]

CATEGORIES OF SLANDER PER SE — **gilbert**

IT IS SLANDER PER SE WHEN PLAINTIFF IS ACCUSED OF:

- ☑ A ***serious, morally reprehensible crime*** (*e.g.*, murder, rape, robbery, embezzlement).
- ☑ ***Currently*** having a ***loathsome communicable disease*** (*e.g.*, venereal disease, leprosy).
- ☑ Being ***inept or unfit for trade or business***.
- ☑ Being ***unchaste*** (traditionally limited to female plaintiffs, but a few states have expanded this to include males as well).

4. Damages Rule for Libel [§1443]

If the defamation is in the form of libel *and* is clear on its face, most jurisdictions *presume general damages* from the fact that it was published. [*But see* **United Insurance**

Co. of America v. Murphy, 961 S.W.2d 752 (Ark. 1998)—joining a small group of states that have abolished the doctrine of presumed damages in defamation cases] The plaintiff ***need not show special damages*** to recover—although if she can show some, she can recover for these also. If clear on its face, the defamation need ***not*** fit within any of the slander per se categories.

a. **Rationale**

Because of the permanency of form, possible extent of dissemination, and other features of libel, there is a greater likelihood of harm; thus, general damages may be presumed. [Rest. 2d §569]

b. **Libel per quod [§1444]**

States disagree where the matter published is innocent on its face but becomes defamatory when linked up with certain extrinsic facts (*see supra*, §1395). Some follow the general libel rule and never require special damages. [*See, e.g.,* **Hearst Corp. v. Hughes,** 466 A.2d 486 (Md. 1983)] A second group presumes general damages only where the libel would have been actionable as one of the four types of "slander per se" (*see* above) if the words had been spoken. [*See, e.g.,* **Schlegel v. Ottumwa Courier,** 585 N.W.2d 217 (Iowa 1998)]

5. **Punitive Damages [§1445]**

Most states allow punitive damages if the defamation can be shown to have been uttered with ***common law malice***, such as hatred, ill will, or spite. [*See, e.g.,* **Norris v. Bangor Publishing Co.,** 53 F. Supp. 2d 495 (D. Me. 1999); *but see* **Le Marc's Management Corp. v. Valentin,** 709 A.2d 1222 (Md. 1998)—rejecting common law malice standard and requiring showing of actual knowledge of falsity]

a. **Federal constitutional restrictions [§1446]**

The First Amendment ***prohibits*** the imposition of punitive damages for defamations involving ***matters of public concern*** if the falsity is attributable only to ***negligence***. [**Gertz v. Robert Welch, Inc.,** 418 U.S. 323 (1974)] However, the Supreme Court has not ruled on whether the First Amendment provides any special protection against the imposition of punitive damages in libel cases. State courts have rejected this claim. [**DiSalle v. P.G. Publishing Co.,** 544 A.2d 1345 (Pa. 1988), *cert. denied*, 492 U.S. 906 (1989)]

(1) **What is a matter of public concern [§1447]**

The courts decide whether a statement is of public concern on a case-by-case basis, considering the content, form, and context of the publication. [**Dun & Bradstreet, Inc. v. Greenmoss Builders, Inc.,** 472 U.S. 749 (1985)]

---

e.g. **Example:** The Supreme Court has held that where the defamation involves a confidential report to five subscribers about a private plaintiff, it does ***not*** involve a matter of public concern and punitive damages ***may*** be recovered even for negligent defamations. [**Dun & Bradstreet, Inc. v. Greenmoss Builders, Inc.,** *supra*]

---

cf. **Compare:** If the local newspaper had published the same report, the ***context*** would have been very different, and the report presumably would have been covered by the *Gertz* rule.

---

b. **State constitutional restrictions [§1448]**

Some states disallow punitive damages under state constitutional law. [**Wheeler v. Green,** 593 P.2d 777 (Or. 1979)] Recall also the recent statutory limits on punitive damages generally, *supra*, §§1336 *et seq*.

6. **Retraction [§1449]**

Several states have adopted "retraction statutes," the effect of which is to limit the damages recoverable against specified media that publish defamations. Typically, these statutes provide that the named defendant cannot be held liable for ***general damages*** resulting from a defamatory publication unless it has failed to fairly and promptly publish a retraction of the defamation after a formal demand by the injured party to do so. Special damages may still be recovered, however. [*See, e.g.,* Cal. Civ. Code §48a]

7. **Injunctions [§1450]**

Courts traditionally have refused to enjoin defamatory speech because of First Amendment free speech concerns. [**Kramer v. Thompson,** 947 F.2d 666 (3d Cir. 1991)—refusal to enjoin client from continuing to defame attorney]

G. Defenses

1. **Consent [§1451]**

Consent is a defense to defamation under the same rules that make it a defense to an intentional tort. [*See, e.g.,* **Cox v. Nasche,** 70 F.3d 1030 (9th Cir. 1995)—release signed by job applicant protected former employer; **Live Oak Publishing Co. v. Cohagan,** 234 Cal. App. 3d 1277 (1991)]

2. **Truth [§1452]**

As discussed previously, truth is a ***complete*** defense to a charge of defamation in most jurisdictions (*see supra*, §1411). Beyond that, most states, either by constitutional mandate (*see supra*, §1414) or by common law, have imposed upon the plaintiff the burden of proving falsity in almost all cases.

3. **Common Law Absolute Privileges [§1453]**

Absolute privilege is a ***complete*** defense to any defamation action; *i.e.*, it is not affected by a showing of malice, lying, abuse, or excessive publication, as in the case of conditional privileges (*see infra*, §§1462 *et seq.*). Absolute privilege exists in the following situations:

a. **Participation in the processes of government**

(1) **Legislative privilege [§1454]**
All federal and state legislative members are absolutely privileged to utter defamations while on the floor of their legislatures or in committee sessions, etc. There is ***no requirement of relevancy*** to any matter at hand. [Rest. 2d §590] This protection is found in federal or state constitutional provisions. [*See, e.g.,* **Tenney v. Brandhove,** 341 U.S. 367 (1951)]

(a) **Inferior legislative bodies [§1455]**
The modern view is to accord inferior legislative bodies absolute privilege for statements made at meetings. [Rest. 2d §590 cmt. c; *and see* **Sanchez v. Coxon,** 854 P.2d 126 (Ariz. 1993)] However, some states are contra (*see infra*, §1463).

(2) **Judicial privilege [§1456]**
Any participant in a judicial proceeding is absolutely privileged to utter defamations in the course of the proceeding provided there is ***some relevancy*** (*i.e.*, a reasonable relationship) to the matter at hand. This includes the judge or any judicial officer, witnesses, attorneys, parties to the action, and jurors. [*See, e.g.,* **Irwin v. Ashurst,** 74 P.2d 1127 (Or. 1938); Rest. 2d §587; *but see* **Park Knoll Associates v. Schmidt,** 59 N.Y.2d 205 (1983)—no absolute privilege for organizer advising tenants applying for rent refunds]

(a) **"Course of judicial proceeding" [§1457]**
The defamation need not occur at the trial itself; it may be in a pretrial hearing, deposition, etc. Judicial proceedings are generally deemed to start ***when the complaint is filed***; hence defamations in the complaint or any document filed in conjunction with the complaint (*e.g.*, a lis pendens) are absolutely privileged. [**Theran v. Rokoff,** 602 N.E.2d 191 (Mass. 1992); Rest. 2d §586 cmt. a]

---

e.g. **Example:** An individual who writes a letter to the state bar complaining of an attorney's misconduct, but who makes no corresponding public announcement of the complaint is entitled to absolute immunity. [**Tobkin v. Jarboe,** 710 So. 2d 975 (Fla. 1998)]

---

e.g. **Example:** Statements about a company's lawyer made in a letter from a prospective employee to the company regarding the prospective employee's desire to settle a pending National Labor Relations Board proceeding were absolutely privileged. [**Price v. Armour,** 949 P.2d 1251 (Utah 1997)]

---

cf. **Compare:** Attorneys were not absolutely privileged to send local newspapers a copy of their demand letter because the newspapers were unconnected with the proposed lawsuit. [**Scott Fetzer Co. v. Williamson,** 101 F.3d 549 (8th Cir. 1996)]

---

cf. **Compare:** Lawyers who announce at a press conference the forthcoming filing of a lawsuit are not entitled to absolute privilege. [**Green Acres Trust v. London,** 688 P.2d 617 (Ariz. 1984); *and see* **Kennedy v. Zimmermann,** 601 N.W.2d 61 (Iowa 1999)—statements by attorney at press conference after filing suit are not absolutely privileged]

(b) "Relevancy" [§1458]

Statements made during judicial proceedings fall outside the absolute privilege only if they are so palpably irrelevant to the subject matter of the controversy that no reasonable person can doubt their irrelevancy or impropriety. [**McGranahan v. Dahar,** 408 A.2d 121 (N.H. 1979)]

e.g. **Example:** In a suit where a businessperson was not a party, a lawyer's suggestion that the businessperson was connected to organized crime was privileged. The businessperson's criminal activity was relevant to a determination of whether his partner knowingly participated in the securities fraud charged in the underlying lawsuit. [**Hugel v. Milberg, Weiss, Bershad, Hynes & Lerach, LLP,** 175 F.3d 14 (1st Cir. 1999); *but see* **Nguyen v. Proton Technology Corp.,** 69 Cal. App. 4th 140 (1999)—no privilege for pre-litigation letter from a law firm concerning potential unfair competition claims in which the firm states that the potential defendant's employee had been in prison for repeatedly assaulting his wife]

(c) Quasi-judicial proceedings [§1459]

Similarly, an absolute privilege applies in the case of quasi-judicial proceedings (*e.g.,* administrative hearings). [*See, e.g.,* **Miner v. Novotny,** 498 A.2d 269 (Md. 1985)—citizen's brutality complaint against deputy sheriff; **Pulkrabek v. Sletten,** 557 N.W.2d 225 (N.D. 1996)—letter to parole board]

(3) Executive privilege [§1460]

Absolute privilege is also provided for high-rank, ***policymaking*** executive officers (cabinet members, department heads, etc.) of state and federal governments when acting within the ***scope of their discretionary duties.*** However, as with judicial participants, there is a ***requirement of relevancy*** here. [Rest. 2d §591; *and see* **Barr v. Matteo,** *supra,* §1236; **Kilgore v. Younger,** 30 Cal. 3d 770 (1982)]

(a) Note

Some states extend this privilege to lower level executive officers. [*See, e.g.,* **City of Miami v. Wardlow,** 403 So. 2d 414 (Fla. 1981); **Williams v. Fischer,** 581 N.E.2d 744 (Ill. 1991)]

b. **Domestic privilege [§1461]**
Either spouse is absolutely privileged to utter defamations of third persons to the other ***spouse.*** A few courts extend this absolute privilege to communications among the immediate family (parent-child, etc.), but most treat the latter as only conditionally privileged (*see* below). [Rest. 2d §592]

4. **Common Law Conditional or Qualified Privileges [§1462]**
A "conditional" (also called "qualified") privilege exists when the potential speaker needs to be encouraged to speak—*i.e.*, needs protection from the strict liability that might otherwise inhibit the potential speaker from speaking. A conditional privilege, unlike an absolute privilege, can be lost through bad faith or abuse (*see infra*, §§1478 *et seq.*).

a. **Recognized conditional privileges**

(1) **Inferior legislative bodies, inferior executive and administrative officers [§1463]**
Although, as noted above (*supra*, §1455), the modern view is that inferior legislative bodies and executive officials have absolute privilege for their statements within the scope of their offices, some states accord such statements only conditional privilege.

(2) **Protection of private interests [§1464]**
A defendant is conditionally privileged to defame another, if the following conditions are met:

(a) **Protectable interest [§1465]**
The defendant must have a reasonable belief that some important interest in person or property is threatened; it can be ***his own interest***, that of the ***person to whom he publishes*** the defamation, or that of some ***third person***; and

(b) **Relevancy [§1466]**
The defamation published must bear some ***reasonable relevancy*** to the interest sought to be protected; and

(c) **Purpose to protect [§1467]**
The defendant must have published the defamation in the reasonable belief that the person to whom it was published was in a position to protect or assist in the lawful protection of the interest.

(d) **Volunteering information where relationship or common interest exists [§1468]**
Generally there must be some relationship between the publisher (the defendant) and the person to whom the information is published—either some family, business, or employment relationship—or a common interest in business affairs. If there is such a relationship, the

defendant may be privileged to ***volunteer*** defamatory information. [Rest. 2d §595(2)]

---

e.g. **Examples:** This covers the situation where a brother tells his sister, "Don't marry X; he has a venereal disease"; or an agent tells the principal, "Don't extend credit to X, she's a deadbeat"; or an employee tells his employer, "Don't believe anything that X has told you about me; he's a chronic liar." [**Weenig v. Wood,** 349 N.E.2d 235 (Ind. 1976)]

---

cf. **Compare:** P's immediate supervisor at P's place of employment is not privileged to relate to a customer the reason for P's discharge (the alleged defamation) because no common relationship or interest exists between the supervisor and the customer. [**Nelson v. Lapeyrouse Grain Corp.,** 534 So. 2d 1085 (Ala. 1988)]

(e) Answering request for information where no relationship exists [§1469]
If there is no such relationship or common interest, it usually must appear that the defamation was made in response to a ***request*** for information by the person to whom it was published, rather than volunteered by the defendant.

1) Credit agencies [§1470]
Frequently, a credit bureau asks a defendant for information regarding another person's credit. In this case, the defendant's response is privileged, but if the defendant had initiated the call to the credit bureau and volunteered the information, there would have been no privilege. [*See, e.g.,* **Stationers Corp. v. Dun & Bradstreet, Inc.,** 62 Cal. 2d 412 (1965)]

2) Prospective employers [§1471]
Some jurisdictions hold that former employers have a conditional privilege for responses (rather than volunteered statements) to the plaintiff's prospective employers where the prospective employers have a legitimate and obvious interest in the employee's qualifications. [*See, e.g.,* **Erickson v. Marsh & McLennan Co.,** 569 A.2d 793 (N.J. 1990); **Coclin v. Lane Press, Inc.,** 210 A.D.2d 98 (1994)]

(f) Self-defense [§1472]
A person is privileged to respond to others' attacks on her whether or not any prior relationship exists. [**Foretich v. Capital Cities/ABC, Inc.,** 37 F.3d 1541 (4th Cir. 1994)]

(3) Protection of public interest [§1473]
A person is conditionally privileged to defame another if he reasonably

believes his utterances are necessary to protect a legitimate public interest, and that the person to whom the statement is made is empowered to protect that interest.

 **Example:** D is conditionally privileged to run up to a police officer shouting, "There goes X—he just robbed the bank!"

(a) **Exception—media defendants [§1474]**
Mass media cannot claim the privilege of protecting the public interest for having published an article of general interest to the community—even though it warned the public against some asserted public problem. [*See, e.g.*, **Brown v. Kelly Broadcasting Co.,** 48 Cal. 3d 711 (1989)—consumer report broadcast about problems with licensed contractor was not privileged under common law]

TRADITIONAL ABSOLUTE AND CONDITIONAL PRIVILEGES — gilbert

ABSOLUTE PRIVILEGE	CONDITIONAL PRIVILEGE
• ***Legislators—anything*** uttered by legislator on floor of state or federal legislature or in committee; ***no relevancy*** requirement	• ***Inferior legislative bodies***—statements made by inferior legislative bodies (modern trend—absolute privilege)
• ***Policymaking executive officers***—statements made by high-rank, policymaking state or federal executive officers acting within scope of discretionary duties; ***must be relevant*** to duties	• ***Inferior executive and administrative officers***—statements made by lower-rank executive and administrative officers (modern trend—absolute privilege)
• ***Participants in judicial proceeding***—defamation uttered by ***anyone*** in the course of a judicial proceeding; ***must be relevant*** to the proceeding	• ***Public interests***—statements reasonably necessary to protect a legitimate public interest (*e.g.*, "X just robbed the bank!")
• ***Spouses***—defamations about third parties uttered by spouses to each other	• ***Private interests***—relevant statements protecting private interests (*e.g.*, truthful reviews of former employee when prospective employer calls)

b. **Conditional privilege may be lost through bad faith or abuse**

(1) **Lack of honest belief in truth of statements made [§1475]**
The general view is that the defendant must have an "actual, ***honest***" belief in the truth of the defamatory matter. Hence, there is no privilege if the defendant knows that the statements are unfounded.

(a) **Belief need not be reasonable [§1476]**
Even totally unreasonable statements may be found to be privileged, but lack of reasonableness is ***evidence*** that the defendant did not honestly believe the truth of his statement. [**Clark v. Molyneaux,** 3 Q.B.D. 237 (1877)] *But note:* Some courts hold that a speaker who seeks to ***protect the public interest*** must have ***reasonably*** believed his statement. [Rest. 2d §598]

(b) **Credit reports—honest and reasonable belief [§1477]**
A minority view asserts that the defendant must have ***both*** an honest and a reasonable belief in the truth of assertions made in credit standing cases, or the privilege is lost. [**Stationers Corp. v. Dun & Bradstreet, Inc.,** *supra,* §1470]

(2) **Malice in publication [§1478]**
The defendant's publication is privileged only if made, at least in part, in the public interest or in the protection of some lawful private interest. If it appears that the defendant was motivated ***solely*** by malice and an intent to injure the party defamed, whatever conditional privilege the defendant otherwise would have had is lost through abuse. [*See, e.g.,* **Sanborn v. Chronicle Publishing Co.,** 18 Cal. 3d 406 (1976); **Mihlovan v. Grozavu,** 72 N.Y.2d 506 (1988)]

(a) **"Malice" [§1479]**
The type of malice required here is the same as that required under state law for an award of punitive damages, *i.e.,* ***hatred, spite, or ill will.***

1) **But note**
A few courts have interpreted malice here to require "knowing or reckless disregard" for the truth—a focus on the defendant's attitude toward falsity rather than on the defendant's feelings toward the plaintiff. [*See, e.g.,* **Marchesi v. Franchino,** 387 A.2d 1129 (Md. 1978)] A few other states have held that the plaintiff can show abuse of conditional privilege by showing ***either*** type of malice. [*See, e.g.,* **Liberman v. Gelstein,** *supra,* §1436]

(3) **Excessive publication [§1480]**
Similarly, the defendant's publication must extend further than necessary to carry out the purposes for which the privilege is recognized. [**Coleman v. MacLennan,** 98 P. 281 (Kan. 1908)]

(a) **Effect—defendant placed under "duty of care" [§1481]**
For example, the defendant will lose the privilege if he speaks so loudly in a public place that he is overheard by persons other than those to whom the defamation is privileged. [**Kruse v. Rabe,** 79 A. 316 (N.J. 1910)]

(b) **Distinguish—incidental newspaper publication [§1482]**
If the publication is by a newspaper and the defamation is of a local person, the probability that the newspaper will be sent to persons out of state is not enough by itself to constitute an excessive publication. [**Coleman v. MacLennan,** *supra*; *but see* **Moyle v. Franz,** 293 N.Y. 842 (1944)—excessive publication by religious magazine with story about an internal matter where magazine sent to readers who were not interested in matter]

5. **Fair Comment Privilege [§1483]**
Courts have long protected critics who comment on the efforts of others—whether writers, entertainers, athletes, restaurants, or politicians. [**Cherry v. Des Moines Leader,** 86 N.W. 323 (Iowa 1901)] The common law developed two views on this privilege.

a. **Majority view [§1484]**
Under the majority view, the critic was protected if the comment was on a matter of public interest, was based on true facts, and expressed an honestly believed opinion. [**Post Publishing Co. v. Hallam,** 59 F. 530 (6th Cir. 1893)]

b. **Minority view [§1485]**
Under the minority view, the privilege existed even if the facts were incorrectly stated, as long as the critic honestly believed the version of the facts on which the criticism was based. [**Coleman v. MacLennan,** *supra*] This view played an important role in the constitutional developments discussed *infra*.

6. **Record Libel Privilege [§1486]**
Reports of ***judicial, legislative, or executive proceedings*** (so-called record libel) are privileged if ***fair and accurate***; *i.e.*, the reports must be either verbatim accounts or fair and impartial summaries of what happened. This privilege exists in all states either by statute or under the common law.

a. **Nonofficial proceedings [§1487]**
Although the paradigm situation involves a public and official meeting [Rest. 2d §611], some courts have extended the record libel privilege to reports of nongovernmental public meetings in which there is a ***general interest***, such as political or medical conventions [**Borg v. Boas,** 231 F.2d 788 (9th Cir. 1956)—mass meeting to urge grand jury investigation].

b. **Official but nonpublic document [§1488]**
Some courts have extended the privilege beyond meetings to government files or documents. [**Medico v. Time, Inc.,** 643 F.2d 134 (3d Cir.), *cert. denied*, 454 U.S. 836 (1981)—summary of FBI file]

c. **Reports of foreign governments [§1489]**
At least one court has refused to extend the privilege to reports from foreign governments, because they are not as open or reliable as domestic government

sources. [**Lee v. The Dong-A Ilbo,** 849 F.2d 876 (4th Cir. 1988), *cert. denied,* 489 U.S. 1067 (1989)]

d. How privilege is lost [§1490]

The record libel privilege is lost only when the defendant's report of what transpired is ***inaccurate***; traditionally, false or garbled accounts are not protected. (But note the impact of recent constitutional developments—some inaccurate reports may now be privileged; *see infra,* §§1532 *et seq.*)

(1) Distinguish—absolute privilege [§1491]

The privilege of record libel differs from absolute privilege in that the absolute privilege is available even to those who lie, whereas this privilege (at least in its common law form) is lost upon ***inaccuracy***, far short of lying.

(2) Distinguish—conditional privilege [§1492]

Unlike conditional privileges, which are lost if the publisher does not honestly believe the substance of his statement, the record libel privilege survives even if the reporter knows or strongly believes that one of the witnesses or officials who is being accurately quoted is in fact lying.

(a) Rationale

The explanation for these differences is that the record libel privilege is intended to permit the public to learn what is happening in government activities; this requires accuracy of reporting, and the harm to victims from accurate quotations—even of lying officials or witnesses—is outweighed by the importance attached to allowing the public to know what government officials are doing and what is being said in trials and hearings.

7. Federal Preemptive Privileges [§1493]

As discussed in connection with products liability (*see supra,* §1068), all state laws must be consistent with federal law under the Supremacy Clause. Preemption principles apply to defamation as well.

a. Defamations in campaign speech broadcasts [§1494]

Radio and television stations are ***not*** liable for broadcast defamations contained in campaign speeches by candidates for public office. [**Farmers Educational & Cooperative Union v. WDAY, Inc.,** 360 U.S. 525 (1959)]

(1) Rationale

Section 315 of the Federal Communications Act requires broadcasters to extend "equal opportunities" for all candidates for public office to use the station's facilities. [47 U.S.C. §315] This federal act ***preempts state laws*** that would impede its purposes—and state defamation laws would do so because stations fearful of being held liable for defamations in such broadcasts might refuse state and local candidates the right to use their facilities, in order to protect the stations from potential liability. (*Note:* Stations can no longer bar federal candidates from such access.)

(2) **Absolute immunity [§1495]**
The immunity here is absolute; it ***cannot be defeated*** by claims that the radio or television station knew that the statements to be uttered were false.

b. **Defamations in labor disputes [§1496]**
Likewise, federal labor laws are held to ***preempt*** state defamation law insofar as defamatory statements published during labor disputes are concerned. Federal labor laws set the limits on "free speech" in labor disputes, and state defamation laws cannot be applied to narrow these limits. [**Old Dominion Branch No. 496, National Association of Letter Carriers v. Austin,** *supra,* §1420]

c. **Petitions to government officials [§1497]**
Private letters to government officials arguing against the appointment of the plaintiff to a government post are protected under the *New York Times* rule (*infra,* §1503). They are ***not*** absolutely privileged under the Petitions Clause of the First Amendment. [**McDonald v. Smith,** 472 U.S. 479 (1985); *but see* **Imperial v. Drapeau,** 716 A.2d 244 (Md. 1998)—absolute privilege for doctor's letter sent to governor and member of Congress complaining about emergency medical technician's treatment of patient]

8. **Defenses of Republishers [§1498]**
A republisher cannot automatically rely on any defense or privilege the original publisher may have. Each republisher must establish its own privilege.

a. **Exception—intermediary [§1499]**
However, certain intermediaries are protected by a special privilege: One whose ***duty*** it is to dispatch messages (*e.g.,* a telegraph agent, perhaps a private secretary) is privileged to transmit a defamation, whether or not he believes it to be true. *Rationale:* Persons so employed have no authority or ability to check the accuracy of that which they are required to transmit. [Rest. 2d §612; *and see* **Mason v. Western Union Telegraph Co.,** 52 Cal. App. 3d 429 (1975)]

b. **Media reliance on usually reliable source [§1500]**
Because newspapers commonly must use information that is gathered by reporters outside of the publisher's control, most states have granted newspapers a ***conditional privilege*** to reprint wire service stories and syndicated features.

---

e.g. **Example:** Publication of allegedly defamatory, but facially consistent, story received over a wire service from a recognized reliable news source was privileged. [**Layne v. Tribune Co.,** 146 So. 234 (Fla. 1933)]

---

e.g. **Example:** A republisher is not negligent if it relies on a wire story from a reliable source, even if the story describes local events that could be easily verified by the republisher. [**Appleby v. Daily Hampshire Gazette,** 478 N.E.2d 721 (Mass. 1985)]

---

c. **Media reports of statements made by others [§1501]**
Some courts have granted media a ***constitutional privilege*** called "neutral reportage" to permit media to cover a story in which some important persons or groups are accusing others of improprieties. [**Edwards v. National Audubon Society, Inc.,** 556 F.2d 113 (2d Cir.), *cert. denied*, 434 U.S. 1002 (1977)—First Amendment prevents newspaper from being held liable for accurately ***reporting*** the false, libelous statements of a "responsible, prominent organization" because such statements are potentially ***newsworthy*** and thus important to readers; *but see* **Hogan v. Herald Co.,** 58 N.Y.2d 630 (1982)—rejecting the privilege] The articles in these cases may be seen as extensions of the fair and accurate report privilege because there is nothing official or public about the proceedings being reported upon.

9. **SLAPP Suits [§1502]**
In response to concern that some libel actions are brought to silence critics on public issues—so-called SLAPP suits (Strategic Lawsuits Against Public Participation)—some states have adopted legislation to help defendants terminate such cases at an early stage of the litigation. The legislation provides for striking the pleading unless the court concludes that there is a "probability" that the plaintiff will prevail. [*See, e.g.,* Cal. Civ. Proc. Code §425.16; **Briggs v. Eden Council for Hope & Opportunity,** 19 Cal. 4th 1106 (1999)—in libel claim by landlord against nonprofit organization that aided tenants, defendant need not show that statement at issue concerned an issue of public significance in order to take advantage of statute allowing it to seek early end to case]

H. Constitutional Privileges

1. **In General [§1503]**
The state has a legitimate interest in protecting the reputation of each citizen. But the threat of a defamation action is inevitably a curb on the freedom of speech and press guaranteed by the First Amendment of the United States Constitution: "Whatever is added to the field of libel is taken from the field of free debate." [**New York Times Co. v. Sullivan,** 376 U.S. 254 (1964)] In certain instances, the interest in freedom of expression is held to ***outweigh*** the interest in protecting reputations, and in these cases, defamations may be ***privileged as a matter of constitutional law*** (superseding any state law to the contrary). We have already discussed some constitutional developments in such areas as the need for a statement capable of being proven false (*see supra*, §1416) and the burden of proving falsity (*see supra*, §1414). We turn now to the major constitutional development—the ***rejection*** of the common law rule of strict liability.

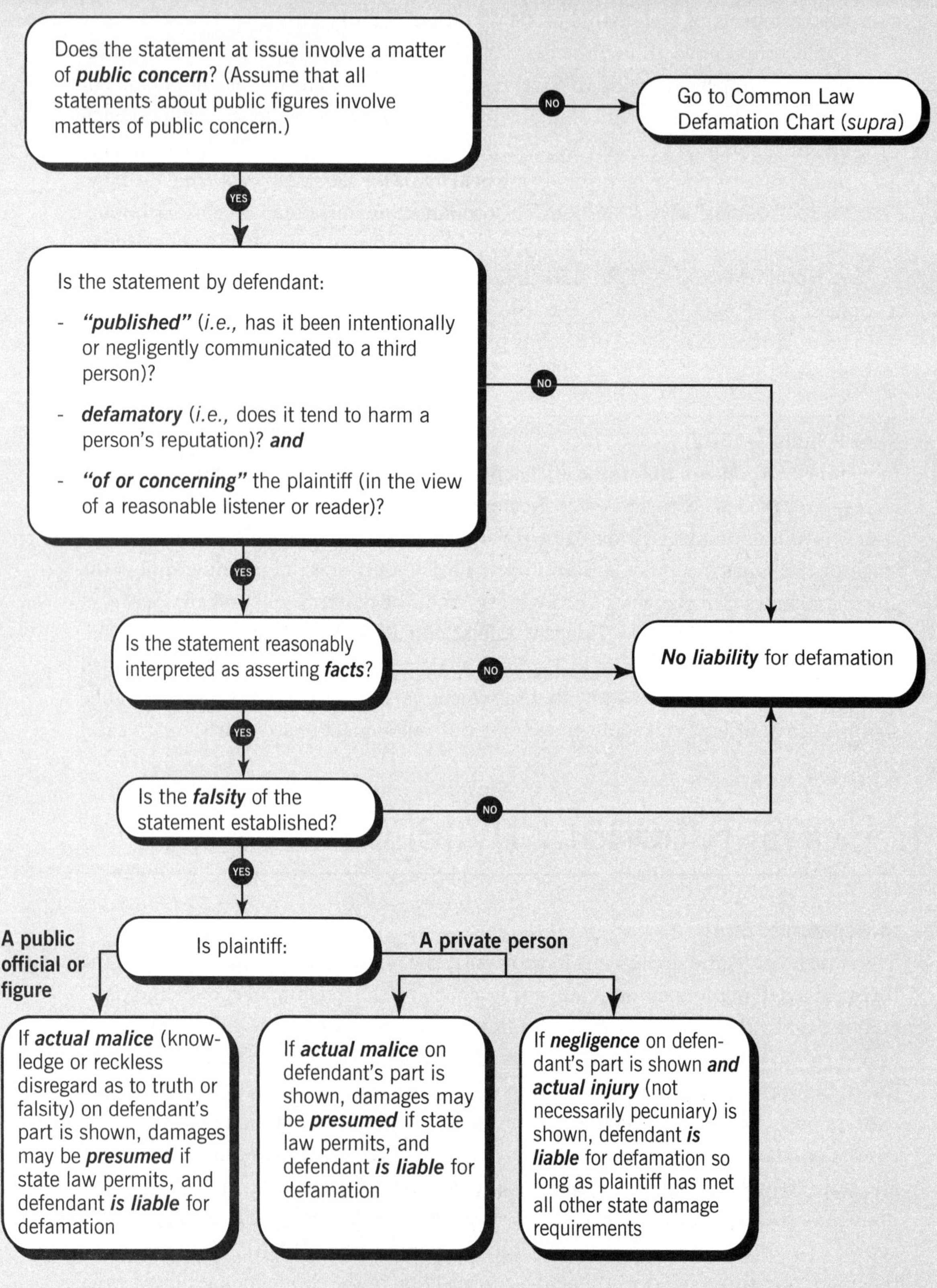
APPROACH TO CONSTITUTIONAL DEFAMATION
gilbert
Does the statement at issue involve a matter of *public concern*? (Assume that all statements about public figures involve matters of public concern.)
NO
Go to Common Law Defamation Chart (*supra*)
YES
Is the statement by defendant:
- ***"published"*** (*i.e.,* has it been intentionally or negligently communicated to a third person)?
- ***defamatory*** (*i.e.,* does it tend to harm a person's reputation)? ***and***
- ***"of or concerning"*** the plaintiff (in the view of a reasonable listener or reader)?
NO
YES
Is the statement reasonably interpreted as asserting ***facts***?
NO
No liability for defamation
YES
Is the ***falsity*** of the statement established?
NO
YES
Is plaintiff:
A public official or figure
A private person
If ***actual malice*** (knowledge or reckless disregard as to truth or falsity) on defendant's part is shown, damages may be ***presumed*** if state law permits, and defendant ***is liable*** for defamation
If ***actual malice*** on defendant's part is shown, damages may be ***presumed*** if state law permits, and defendant ***is liable*** for defamation
If ***negligence*** on defendant's part is shown ***and actual injury*** (not necessarily pecuniary) is shown, defendant ***is liable*** for defamation so long as plaintiff has met all other state damage requirements

a. **Status of plaintiff controls constitutional standard [§1504]**
The crucial step in determining the constitutional protection available in defamation cases depends on the *status* of the plaintiff. [**Gertz v. Robert Welch, Inc.,** *supra*, §1446; **New York Times Co. v. Sullivan,** *supra*]

(1) **Types of plaintiffs [§1505]**
For this constitutional analysis each plaintiff must be put into one of three categories: (i) public official, (ii) public figure, or (iii) private person.

(2) **Caveat—status of defendant [§1506]**
A few plurality Supreme Court opinions have suggested that the constitutional standards may also depend on the identity and status of the defendant speaker. [**Philadelphia Newspapers, Inc. v. Hepps,** *supra*, §1414] But this view has never commanded a majority in the Supreme Court and has been rejected by virtually all state courts and lower federal courts.

EXAM TIP — **gilbert**

Note that the status of the plaintiff (public figure or private person) is relevant ***only*** for the ***degree of fault*** required; the element of ***falsity*** must be proved regardless of the status of the plaintiff if a matter of public concern is involved (*see supra*, §1414), and you should assume that a matter of public concern is involved whenever the plaintiff is a public figure.

2. **Public Plaintiffs [§1507]**
The Supreme Court has granted its highest level of protection for statements concerning "public officials" or "public figures." Although the standard of protection for each group is identical, it is useful to keep the two groups distinct because of the way in which persons are placed into one or the other of these two categories.

a. **"Public officials" [§1508]**
Those persons within the hierarchy of government who have (or appear to have) ***substantial responsibility*** over government affairs have the status of public plaintiffs in defamation actions. [**Rosenblatt v. Baer,** 383 U.S. 75 (1966)]

(1) **Rationale**
It is important that members of the public be able to speak freely about—and criticize—the behavior of its public officials without running the risk of being held liable for every false defamatory statement. [**New York Times Co. v. Sullivan,** *supra*]

(2) **"Public official" not yet defined [§1509]**
The Supreme Court has not yet defined the term "public official." But it has said that the term does ***not*** encompass all public employees. [**Hutchinson v. Proxmire,** 443 U.S. 111 n.8 (1979); *and see* **Kassel v. Gannett Co.,** 875 F.2d 935 (1st Cir. 1989)]

(3) Police [§1510]

Because police officers are highly visible to the public and have considerable authority to act with force, virtually all courts have held even low ranking officers to be public officials. [*See, e.g.,* **Gray v. Udevitz,** 656 F.2d 588 (10th Cir. 1981); **Reed v. Northwestern Publishing Co.,** 530 N.E.2d 474 (Ill. 1988), *cert. denied*, 489 U.S. 1067 (1989)]

(4) Distinguish—principals and teachers [§1511]

Courts are split over whether principals and teachers are public officials. [*Compare* **Palmer v. Bennington School District,** 615 A.2d 498 (Vt. 1992)—principals are public, *with* **Ellerbee v. Mills,** 422 S.E.2d 539 (Ga. 1992), *cert. denied*, 507 U.S. 1025 (1993)—contra; *compare* **Richmond Newspapers, Inc. v. Lipscomb,** 362 S.E.2d 32 (Va. 1987), *cert. denied*, 486 U.S. 1023 (1988)—teachers are public, *with* **Kelley v. Bonney,** 606 A.2d 693 (Conn. 1992)—contra]

b. "Public figures" [§1512]

A person ("P") who is not a "public official" nonetheless may be deemed a "public figure" on one of two grounds: (i) P has achieved ***such pervasive fame or notoriety*** that P becomes a public figure for ***all*** purposes and contexts (*e.g.*, celebrity sports figure); or (ii) more commonly, P ***voluntarily*** enters or is drawn into a particular public controversy, and thereby becomes a "public figure" for that ***limited*** range of issues. [**Gertz v. Robert Welch, Inc.,** *supra*, §1504]

(1) Rationale

Although persons who are not in government do not have as direct a control over the lives and destinies of the public, there is much private power in this country that does exert great influence and that is not as easily scrutinized or removable by the electoral process. It is important that the public be able to comment freely on these persons as well. [**Curtis Publishing Co. v. Butts,** 388 U.S. 130 (1967)—opinion of Warren, C.J.]

(2) General public figures [§1513]

Plaintiffs who have been found to be general public figures include a famous journalist and political advocate [**Buckley v. Littell,** *supra*, §1421], and a well-known entertainer [**Carson v. Allied News Co.,** 529 F.2d 206 (7th Cir. 1976); *and see* **Waldbaum v. Fairchild Publications, Inc.,** 627 F.2d 1287 (D.C. Cir.), *cert. denied*, 449 U.S. 898 (1980)—a general public figure is a "well-known 'celebrity,' his name a 'household word.' The public recognizes him and follows his words and deeds . . . ."].

(3) Limited purpose public figures [§1514]

Lower courts have tended to use three steps in identifying "limited purpose" public figures: (i) the court isolates the public controversy involved in the particular case; (ii) the court decides if the plaintiff has voluntarily assumed a central role in that controversy; and (iii) the court must find the alleged defamation germane to the plaintiff's participation in the controversy. [**Foretich v. Capital Cities/ABC, Inc.,** *supra*, §1472—couple did not become public figures by responding publicly and often to assertions that they had abused their granddaughter; **Waldbaum v. Fairchild Publications, Inc.,** *supra*—outspoken chief executive officer of corporation was limited purpose public figure for media report on reasons for his dismissal]

(a) Application [§1515]

The Supreme Court has made it clear that not every person who seeks government aid or who draws attention by some voluntary behavior becomes a "public" plaintiff for libel purposes.

---

e.g. **Example:** A socially prominent woman does not become a "public figure" by seeking a divorce or by meeting with the press during the divorce trial. [**Time, Inc. v. Firestone,** 424 U.S. 448 (1976)]

---

e.g. **Example:** A scientist applying for a federal grant does not become a "public figure" by applying for the grant. [**Hutchinson v. Proxmire,** *supra*, §1509]

---

e.g. **Example:** A witness who refuses to testify before a grand jury does not thereby become a "public figure." [**Wolston v. Reader's Digest Association,** 443 U.S. 157 (1979)]

---

e.g. **Example:** State senator's wife who was a successful businessperson, who endorsed her husband's campaign and aided in it, and who participated in controversial minority business program was a public figure. [**Krueger v. Austad,** 545 N.W.2d 205 (S.D. 1996)]

(b) Involuntary public figures [§1516]

In *Gertz*, the Court indicated that it might be possible for people to become public figures through no purposeful action of their own, but thought such instances "exceedingly rare."

---

e.g. **Example:** An air traffic controller who happened to be on duty during a newsworthy airplane crash may be a public figure. [**Dameron v. Washington Magazine, Inc.,** 779 F.2d 736 (D.C. Cir. 1985), *cert. denied*, 476 U.S. 1141 (1986)]

---

c. Constitutional standard in cases involving public plaintiffs [§1517]

Plaintiffs who are either public officials or public figures for defamation purposes must prove that the false defamatory statement was published with what the Supreme Court has called ***"actual malice"—i.e., knowledge of the falsity*** of the defamatory statement or *reckless disregard for its truth*. [**New York Times Co. v. Sullivan,** *supra*, §1508]

(1) **Rationale**

The public interest in good faith debate regarding public persons outweighs the interest in protecting their reputations. But no public interest is served by a publication made with "knowing or reckless falsity," and hence there is no constitutional protection in such case. [**Garrison v. Louisiana,** *supra*, §1413]

(2) **What constitutes "knowing or reckless falsity" [§1518]**

The plaintiff must show that the defendant was ***subjectively aware*** that the statement was false or was subjectively reckless as to its truth when making the statement. [**New York Times Co. v. Sullivan,** *supra*]

(a) **Motive to harm insufficient [§1519]**

It is ***not*** enough that the defendant be shown to have acted with spite, hatred, ill will, or intent to injure the plaintiff. Unless "knowing or reckless falsity" is established, there is not the requisite "malice" for constitutional purposes. [**Rosenblatt v. Baer,** *supra*, §1508]

e.g. **Example:** Newspaper reporter's statements that he wanted to "get" the plaintiff were insufficient to establish actual malice. [**Margoles v. Hubbart,** 760 P.2d 324 (Wash. 1988)]

EXAM TIP **gilbert**

Although the Supreme Court has talked in terms of "actual malice," this is really a term of art referring to the requirement of ***deliberate falsity or reckless disregard for the truth*** of the information published. As such, it is quite different from the "malice" usually required under state tort law to support an award of ***punitive damages***—which requires a showing of hatred, spite, or ill will toward a plaintiff.

(b) **Negligence insufficient [§1520]**

"Reckless" conduct is ***not*** measured by a reasonable person standard or by whether a reasonable person would have investigated before publishing; *i.e.*, negligence is ***not*** enough. Rather, there must be a showing that the defendant ***in fact*** (subjectively) ***entertained serious doubts*** as to the truthfulness of the publication. [**St. Amant v. Thompson,** 390 U.S. 727 (1968)]

e.g. **Example:** If a scandal magazine completely fabricates a story about a celebrity, it necessarily entertained at least serious doubt as to the truth of the statements. [**Carson v. Allied News Co.,** *supra*, §1513]

1) **Freelance authors [§1521]**
The rule of respondeat superior does not apply in the case of authors who are not employees but rather are hired for single assignments or who submit proposed pieces. In such cases, the plaintiff must prove that the defendant publisher either knew that the freelancer was a deliberate liar or disbelieved the contents of the completed piece but published it anyway. [**Gertz v. Robert Welch, Inc.,** 680 F.2d 527 (7th Cir. 1982), *cert. denied*, 459 U.S. 1226 (1983)]

(3) **Proving "knowing or reckless falsity" [§1522]**
Because the standard of liability is ***subjective***, it is difficult to meet.

(a) **Burden of proof [§1523]**
In this type of case, the plaintiff must prove "actual malice" with ***convincing clarity***; *i.e.*, a mere preponderance is insufficient. [**New York Times Co. v. Sullivan,** *supra*]

---

e.g. **Example:** Where the only evidence in support of a jury verdict for the plaintiff involves conflicting accounts of key conversations, a court may conclude that actual malice was not demonstrated with convincing clarity. [**Long v. Arcell,** 618 F.2d 1145 (5th Cir. 1980), *cert. denied*, 449 U.S. 1083 (1981)]

---

1) **Note**
Under the Federal Rules of Civil Procedure, federal courts, when considering motions for summary judgment in libel cases, must hold the plaintiff to the standard of convincing clarity if that is the standard the plaintiff must meet at trial. [**Anderson v. Liberty Lobby, Inc.,** 477 U.S. 242 (1986)]

2) **And note**
Although the Supreme Court has required the plaintiff to prove falsity [**Philadelphia Newspapers, Inc. v. Hepps,** *supra*, §1506], whether the plaintiff must prove falsity with ***convincing clarity*** is an open question [**Harte-Hanks Communications, Inc. v. Connaughton,** 491 U.S. 657 (1989)].

(b) **Application**

1) **Extremely questionable source [§1524]**
A defendant may be found to have acted with actual malice where its source's credibility is seriously questioned by many other witnesses, where the defendant did not listen to taped conversations provided by the plaintiff to disprove the defendant's projected

story, where the defendant declined to interview a particular witness who could have verified the story, and where an earlier article by the defendant showed that it had already committed itself to attacking the plaintiff. [**Harte-Hanks Communications, Inc. v. Connaughton,** *supra*]

2) **Failure to investigate [§1525]**
But failure to investigate alone does not amount to actual malice. [**Sweeney v. Prisoners' Legal Services of New York, Inc.,** 84 N.Y.2d 786 (1995)]

3) **Publishing while knowing facts are incomplete [§1526]**
A newspaper that publishes an Associated Press wire service story, even though the Associated Press announced that more would soon follow, did not publish with actual malice because there was no showing that the staff did not believe the first story. [**Meisler v. Gannett Co.,** 12 F.3d 1026 (11th Cir. 1994)]

4) **Noting questionable veracity [§1527]**
Where a defendant newspaper carried an article defaming the plaintiff based on a source that the article noted had been called a liar by others, and the plaintiff sued for defamation, the article's attack on its own source was held to be a negation of actual malice rather than a showing of it. [**McFarlane v. Esquire Magazine,** 74 F.3d 1296 (D.C. Cir. 1996)]

(c) **Discovery [§1528]**
To prove the defendant's state of mind, the plaintiff may ask the defendant about it—even if the defendant is a reporter or editor. The First Amendment does not protect a journalist from discovery inquiries about his motives for reporting, belief in the accuracy of sources, the reason for pursuing some leads but not others, or the content of conversations among reporters and editors during the story's preparation. [**Herbert v. Lando,** 441 U.S. 153 (1979)]

(4) **Independent appellate review [§1529]**
Appellate courts, in determining whether the plaintiff has demonstrated convincing clarity, must undertake an independent review of the record, giving limited deference to trial court or jury findings. [**Bose Corp. v. Consumers Union,** 466 U.S. 485 (1984)] The Supreme Court has not yet decided whether independent appellate review must be applied to the jury's finding of falsity.

d. **Damages [§1530]**
Statements made with "knowing or reckless falsity" have no constitutional protection against defamation actions. So when a public person establishes the *New York Times* standard of liability against a media defendant, she may recover

whatever damages are permitted under ***state law*** (*see supra*, §§1429 *et seq.*), subject as always to constitutional limitations on such items as punitive damages (*see supra,* §§23, 1446).

3. Private Plaintiffs [§1531]

A plaintiff who is neither a public official nor a public figure is, for libel purposes, a private person. A lower constitutional standard applies in such cases because private persons are more vulnerable to injury from defamation because they lack the same opportunities for rebuttal as do public persons; and, unlike public persons, they did not voluntarily assume the risk of adverse comments. [**Gertz v. Robert Welch, Inc.,** *supra*, §1512]

a. Constitutional limitation [§1532]

However, to protect the freedom of speech and press guaranteed by the First Amendment, liability without fault ***cannot be imposed***, at least where a matter of public concern is involved. Where the statement published is such that substantial danger to the person's reputation would be ***apparent*** to a reasonably prudent editor or broadcaster, the plaintiff must prove that the publisher or broadcaster either ***knew*** that the defamatory words were false, ***was reckless*** as to truth, or ***was negligent*** as to their falsity. [**Gertz v. Robert Welch, Inc.,** *supra*]

(1) Limited damages [§1533]

Under the *Gertz* approach, a plaintiff who proves no more than falsity due to negligence may recover only "actual injury" damages (*see infra*, §1542).

(2) Caveat—matters of private concern [§1534]

Defamation actions brought by a private plaintiff may not be subject to constitutional limitations ***unless*** a matter of public concern is involved. If the defamation involves a matter of purely private concern, a private plaintiff may recover presumed and punitive damages without proving actual malice (*see supra*, §§1443-1448). [**Dun & Bradstreet, Inc. v. Greenmoss Builders, Inc.,** *supra*, §1447]

b. Applicable standard of liability [§1535]

In *Gertz,* the Supreme Court left it to the states to determine their own respective standards for liability to private individuals (in public concern cases), as long as they do ***not*** apply strict liability.

(1) Majority view—negligence [§1536]

Almost all states have accepted the *Gertz* invitation and have set the standard for liability at the level of negligence. [**Brown v. Kelly Broadcasting Co.,** *supra*, §1474]

(2) Minority view—deliberate or reckless falsity [§1537]

A few states have decided to adhere to the *New York Times* requirement (knowledge of falsity or reckless disregard for truth) in cases involving private plaintiffs in stories of general or public interest. [**Sisler v. Gannett Co.,** 516 A.2d 1083 (N.J. 1986)]

(3) New York view—grossly irresponsible manner [§1538]
New York has decided that when a story's content is "arguably within the sphere of legitimate public concern," a private plaintiff must prove that the publisher acted in a "grossly irresponsible manner without due consideration for the standards of information gathering and dissemination ordinarily followed by responsible parties." [**Gaeta v. New York News, Inc.,** 62 N.Y.2d 340 (1984)]

c. Burden of proving falsity [§1539]
A private plaintiff has the burden of proving falsity, at least where the speech is of public concern. The common law presumption of falsity has the potential to chill ***true*** speech on matters of public concern. [**Philadelphia Newspapers, Inc. v. Hepps,** *supra*, §1506]

d. Damages [§1540]
The First Amendment protects defendants in suits by private persons, if a matter of public concern is involved, by limiting the kinds of damages recoverable according to the degree of fault established by the plaintiff.

(1) If defendant's falsity due to negligence, but not deliberate or reckless [§1541]
Assuming the defendant was in fact negligent in ascertaining or reporting the truth of what it published—but had neither actual knowledge of the falsity nor reckless disregard for the truth—a private person ***can*** recover damages ***limited to the "actual injury"*** sustained. [**Gertz v. Robert Welch, Inc.,** *supra*, §1532]

(a) Rationale
Allowing recovery for damages ***not*** based on "actual injury" would not further an important state interest and would invite juries to punish unpopular defendants, which may in turn cause undue self-censorship and restrictions on free debate. [**Gertz v. Robert Welch, Inc.,** *supra*]

(b) "Actual injury" [§1542]
The Supreme Court has not defined what constitutes "actual injury," but has stated that it is ***not limited to out-of-pocket losses.*** It may include impairment of reputation and standing in the community, personal humiliation, and mental anguish and suffering. The important point is that there must be ***competent evidence*** of "actual" injury (no presumed damages), although there need not be evidence that assigns an actual dollar value to the injury. [**Time, Inc. v. Firestone,** *supra*, §1515]

(2) **If defamation deliberate or reckless [§1543]**

It follows that a private plaintiff who cannot prove "actual injury" by the publication cannot recover ***any*** damages—***unless*** she can show that the publication was made with knowledge of its falsity or with reckless disregard for the truth. In such a case, the plaintiff is entitled to whatever recovery is permitted under state law in such cases (*i.e.*, ***"presumed"*** and perhaps punitive damages). [**Gertz v. Robert Welch, Inc.**, *supra*]

(a) **Note**

A private plaintiff who wishes to obtain presumed or punitive damages in a case involving a matter of public concern must meet ***all*** of the requirements set by the *New York Times* rule for public plaintiffs, including proof with convincing clarity and independent appellate review (*supra*, §§1523-1529).

FAULT AND DAMAGES RULES IN CONSTITUTIONAL DEFAMATION ACTIONS gilbert

TYPE OF PLAINTIFF/ DEFAMATION	FAULT REQUIRED	DAMAGES RECOVERABLE
PUBLIC OFFICIAL OR PUBLIC FIGURE	***Actual malice*** (knowledge of falsity or reckless disregard as to truth or falsity)	Presumed damages under common law rules (and punitive damages where appropriate) if other state law damages requirements are met
PRIVATE PERSON/ MATTER OF PUBLIC CONCERN	***At least negligence*** as to statement's truth or falsity	Damages only for proved "actual injury" (if plaintiff proves actual malice, presumed and punitive damages may be available) if other state law damages requirements are met
PRIVATE PERSON/ MATTER OF PRIVATE CONCERN	***No fault*** as to truth or falsity need be proved	Presumed damages under common law rules (and punitive damages where appropriate) if other state law damages requirements are met

Chapter Nine: Wrongful Invasion of Privacy

CONTENTS

▶ Key Exam Issues

A. Intrusions into Plaintiff's Private Life or Affairs §1544

B. Public Disclosure of Private Facts §1562

C. Appropriation of Plaintiff's Name or Likeness §1590

D. Publicity Placing Plaintiff in a "False Light" §1602

E. Claims Involving Privacy of Third Persons §1612

F. Important—Related Torts §1619

Key Exam Issues

Recognition of the right of privacy in tort law and in other areas of law has come fairly recently. As a result, the tort actions do not have the historical baggage and complexity that we saw in defamation cases. This means that the prima facie cases and defenses are shorter and more coherent. On the other hand, because privacy is frequently invaded by words, First Amendment defenses are often raised in privacy torts, just as in defamation.

The four separate categories of invasion of privacy that you have to consider are:

1. ***An intrusion into plaintiff's private life***, usually done by the defendant secretly trying to learn something about the plaintiff;

2. ***A public disclosure of private facts*** about the plaintiff (this is perhaps the most famous privacy tort, derived from the famous Brandeis and Warren article, The Right to Privacy, 4 Harv. L. Rev. 193 (1890));

3. ***The use*** by defendant of the ***plaintiff's name or picture*** for commercial purposes; and

4. ***A publication placing the plaintiff in a "false light"*** (basically a weaker form of defamation).

Each type of "invasion" is sufficiently different that it is dangerous to lump them together. It is better to think of them as four separate torts, learning the prima facie case of each as you would for any other tort. But note that, occasionally, two or more may be involved in the same case.

Also, although this area of law is generally developing by common law, a few states, led by New York, have a limited statutory right, especially on the "public disclosure" tort, which would foreclose a common law action on this tort.

A. Intrusions into Plaintiff's Private Life or Affairs

1. Prima Facie Case [§1544]

To recover for this type of invasion of privacy, the plaintiff must prove:

- *Highly Offensive Intrusion by Defendant into Plaintiff's Private Life*
- *Intent or Negligence*
- *Causation*

2. Protected Area of Seclusion [§1545]

The law protects those areas of the plaintiff's life that the plaintiff can ***reasonably expect*** will not be intruded upon by one in the defendant's position. [**Pearson v. Dodd,** 410 F.2d 701 (D.C. Cir. 1969)]

---

e.g. **Example:** Wiretapping P's home would be a clear invasion of privacy. [**Hamberger v. Eastman,** 206 A.2d 239 (N.H. 1964)] But if P had sought a disability pension or filed a personal injury complaint, an investigator's efforts to photograph P in public would not intrude on reasonable expectations of privacy. [**Forster v. Manchester,** 189 A.2d 147 (Pa. 1963); **Jeffers v. City of Seattle,** 597 P.2d 899 (Wash. 1979)]

---

a. Distinguish—relationship between parties [§1546]

The ***relationship*** between the parties may convince some courts to deny recovery in what would otherwise give rise to an actionable invasion.

---

e.g. **Example:** Even though urine testing clearly intrudes upon legitimate expectations of privacy, where that testing is ordered by an employer to find employment-related information—*i.e.*, whether employees are reporting to work with drugs in their system—it does not invade employees' privacy. [**Baggs v. Eagle-Picher Industries, Inc.,** 957 F.2d 268 (6th Cir. 1992)]

---

e.g. **Example:** A husband's surveillance of his former wife and her lesbian partner in the course of a custody battle was not actionable by the partner because of a legitimate concern for the child's welfare. [**Plaxico v. Michael,** 735 So. 2d 1036 (Miss. 1999)]

---

b. Distinguish—no right of privacy for corporations [§1547]

Courts have uniformly denied a right to privacy for corporations, holding that they do not have traits of a highly personal and sensitive nature. [**Warner-Lambert Co. v. Execuquest Corp.,** 691 N.E.2d 545 (Mass. 1998)] This extends also to public disclosure of private facts, *infra.*

3. Types of Intrusion [§1548]

Any behavior that intrudes on the plaintiff's solitude may be actionable.

a. Intrusion onto plaintiff's property [§1549]

Invasions of privacy can occur when the defendant enters the plaintiff's property uninvited. Such intrusions can be tortious whether the defendant enters to obtain information (*e.g.*, an insurance investigator) or to convey information to the plaintiff.

(1) **Trespass [§1550]**

Invasions of privacy that involve entry onto the plaintiff's property are also likely to be actionable trespasses. *But note:* Some trespasses may not amount to invasions of privacy. [*See, e.g.,* **McLain v. Boise Cascade Corp.,** 533 P.2d 343 (Or. 1975)—trespass on periphery of P's land did not show unreasonable surveillance]

b. **Nonphysical intrusions [§1551]**

Nonproprietary impingements on the plaintiff's seclusion may also be tortious. [**Nader v. General Motors Corp.,** 25 N.Y.2d 560 (1970)]

---

e.g. **Example:** Owner of tanning salon secretly photographed a patron while she was undressing and nude in tanning room. [**Sabrina W. v. Willman,** 540 N.W.2d 364 (Neb. 1995)]

---

e.g. **Example:** From a hill some distance away, D used a high-powered telescope to look into P's upstairs bedroom, which could not otherwise be observed.

---

e.g. **Example:** Although P takes a risk that D will repeat P's statements, unauthorized recordings or films of the conversation intrude on P's right to control the range of his voice. [**Ribas v. Clark,** 38 Cal. 3d 355 (1985)]

---

e.g. **Example:** D impedes P's movements on public streets. [**Galella v. Onassis,** 487 F.2d 986 (2d Cir. 1973)]

---

e.g. **Example:** Taping conversations between a victim and emergency personnel at the site of a car wreck may be found actionable even if it occurred on public property, unless it can be shown that nearby bystanders also heard the conversations. [**Shulman v. Group W Productions, Inc.,** 18 Cal. 4th 200 (1998)]

---

4. **Intrusion Must Be Highly Offensive [§1552]**

For an intrusion into a plaintiff's solitude to be actionable, it must be ***highly offensive*** to a ***reasonable person.*** [Rest. 2d §652B]

---

e.g. **Example:** Hotel guests did not have to prove that someone ***actually*** watched them through the hole in their bathroom mirror; mere ***possibility*** of intrusion into privacy was sufficient. [**Carter v. Innisfree Hotel, Inc.,** 661 So. 2d 1174 (Ala. 1995)]

---

cf. **Compare:** P failed to state a claim for intrusion where D learned his information about P through voluntary first-hand interviews with P and others in the community, and P did not allege that D entered his home, searched through private papers, wiretapped his telephone, or eavesdropped on his conversations. [**Johnston v. Fuller,** 706 So. 2d 700 (Ala. 1997)]

---

5. **Intent [§1553]**
To satisfy the intent element, the plaintiff need only show that the defendant ***intended the intrusion*** into the plaintiff's affairs; the plaintiff need not show that the defendant intended to offend the plaintiff. [Rest. 2d §652B]

a. **Liability for acts of third parties [§1554]**
One court has held that a defendant who ***negligently*** permits a third party to intrude into the plaintiff's affairs is liable for that intrusion. [**LeCrone v. Ohio Bell Telephone Co.,** 201 N.E.2d 533 (Ohio 1963)—phone company gave husband phone number of estranged wife]

b. **Respondeat superior [§1555]**
A defendant whose employees were acting within the scope of their employment is liable in tort even though the employees' purpose had no relation to their duties. [**Doe v. B.P.S. Guard Services, Inc.,** 945 F.2d 1422 (8th Cir. 1991)—department store security guards videotaping models while they changed clothes during fashion show]

c. **Note**
The developing law of negligent infliction of emotional distress (*see supra*, §§762 *et seq.*) may apply here by analogy.

6. **No Publication Necessary [§1556]**
If the invasion of privacy consists of intrusion or eavesdropping (*e.g.*, by tapping phone wires), no publication is necessary because the interest protected here is the plaintiff's "right to be let alone" rather than his interest in not having the information disseminated. [**Rhodes v. Graham,** 37 S.W.2d 46 (Ky. 1931)]

7. **Causation [§1557]**
The defendant's conduct must have been the cause in fact and the proximate cause of the invasion of the plaintiff's interest in privacy and the ensuing damage.

8. **Defense—Consent [§1558]**
As with other torts, if the intrusion is authorized or permitted, there is no cause of action.

---

e.g. **Example:** There is no invasion of privacy where P gives a process server implied consent to enter her residence by backing up her wheelchair as the process server walks through the door. [**Harris v. Carbonneau,** 685 A.2d 296 (Vt. 1996)]

---

a. **Conduct must not exceed scope of consent [§1559]**
Consent is no defense, however, if the intrusions fall outside the plaintiff's actual or implied consent. [*See, e.g.,* **McDaniel v. Atlanta Coca-Cola Bottling Co.,** 2 S.E.2d 810 (Ga. 1939)—consent to investigators to investigate P's damages claim

did not authorize investigators to install secret monitoring device in P's hospital room]

(1) **Note**

The issues involving consent in trespass cases (*see supra,* §237) are also involved in intrusion cases. [**Dietemann v. Time, Inc.,** 449 F.2d 245 (9th Cir. 1971)—consent to enter given to reporter posing as patient did not extend to making secret recordings or photographs]

9. **Damages [§1560]**

Pure emotional distress and mental anguish ***are*** sufficient damages; thus, the plaintiff need not prove any special damages or pecuniary loss.

10. **Constitutional Protection [§1561]**

While state law may proscribe intrusion into the privacy of others, it may not impose liability on a third party who uses the fruits of that intrusion and publishes true statements that are of public interest. [**Bartnicki v. Vopper,** 532 U.S. 514 (2001)—radio commentator who discussed taped conversations obtained by another through illegal interception of cell phone conversations could not be held liable under state or federal statutes prohibiting such interceptions]

B. Public Disclosure of Private Facts

1. **Prima Facie Case [§1562]**

This action involves:

- *Highly Offensive Public Disclosure by Defendant of Private Facts about Plaintiff*
- *No Legitimate Public Interest*
- *Fault in Making the Disclosure*
- *Causation*

---

e.g. **Examples:** Motion picture discloses P's present identity and sordid details of her past life [**Melvin v. Reid,** 112 Cal. App. 285 (1931)]; P's doctor releases photos he has taken of P's anatomy or embarrassing information obtained in the course of treatment [**Horne v. Patton,** 287 So. 2d 824 (Ala. 1973)]. [*But see* **Anderson v. Fisher Broadcasting Cos.,** 712 P.2d 803 (Or. 1986)—requiring some additional element, such as violating a duty of confidentiality, or wrongful acquisition of the information]

---

2. **What Are "Private Facts"? [§1563]**

The disclosed facts must involve the plaintiff's private life, *i.e.,* those aspects of her life that have not already received some publicity and that are not left open to public observation or inspection.

e.g. **Examples:** Publication of the names and photographs of mentally retarded children is a disclosure of private information where the parents have kept private the mental capacities of their children. [**Deaton v. Delta Democrat Publishing Co.,** 326 So. 2d 471 (Miss. 1976)] So are the fact that P has a rare disease [**Barber v. Time, Inc.,** 159 S.W.2d 291 (Mo. 1942)], and that P was involuntarily sterilized [**Howard v. Des Moines Register & Tribune Co.,** 283 N.W.2d 289 (Iowa 1979)].

a. **Matters of public record [§1564]**

Facts that appear as a matter of public record do ***not*** fall in this category (*see infra*, §§1584-1586).

e.g. **Example:** P cannot complain about a publication of her age if this appears in birth records, or about publication of a dishonorable discharge if this appears in public records of P's military service. [**Stryker v. Republic Pictures,** 108 Cal. App. 2d 191 (1951)]

b. **Public occurrences [§1565]**

Facts that occur in public (*e.g.*, photos of the plaintiff taken in a public park or in a restaurant) are also outside this category. *Rationale:* Because anyone present would have observed the same thing, such facts are hardly "private."

e.g. **Example:** Marching in a public gay parade will make it much more difficult to argue that P's homosexuality is a private fact. [**Sipple v. Chronicle Publishing Co.,** 154 Cal. App. 3d 1040 (1984)]

cf. **Compare:** On the other hand, P's telling a group of friends and family that P has AIDS, with the understanding that it would be kept confidential, does not mean that the fact is no longer private. [**Multimedia WMAZ, Inc. v. Kubach,** 443 S.E.2d 491 (Ga. 1994)]

c. **Voluntary public figures [§1566]**

Persons who voluntarily come before the public eye, such as an actor or politician, have no right of privacy concerning reports of their public activities and appearances because these have not been kept private.

e.g. **Example:** A town's public disclosure that its former bookkeeper had left the town's books in disarray did not reveal any protectable private matters, notwithstanding the claim that the town had agreed to keep such matters private in exchange for the bookkeeper's resignation. [**Loe v. Town of Thomaston,** 600 A.2d 1090 (Me. 1991)]

(1) **Distinguish—involuntary public figure [§1567]**

Those involuntarily before the public eye, such as those accused of crimes or involved in catastrophes, have not opened any of their lives to the public.

If the facts disclosed did not occur before the public eye, reports may be considered to be of ***private*** matters. As discussed below, however, those disclosures are nonetheless privileged if they are newsworthy.

Example: While P is on trial for tax evasion for one year, D obtains I.R.S. records and publicizes the fact that P has paid no taxes in 10 years. Because the I.R.S. records are not public, the report discloses private facts—but it may nonetheless be privileged (*see infra,* §§1584-1586). Reports related to the trial are public facts even though P is involuntarily in the public eye.

---

3. Publication Must Be Highly Offensive [§1568]

Not every disclosure of the plaintiff's private affairs is actionable. Everyone must expect some observation by others of their comings and goings. So to prevail, the plaintiff must establish that the disclosure was such as would be ***highly offensive*** to a ***reasonable person.*** [**Sidis v. F-R Publishing Corp.,** 113 F.2d 806 (2d Cir. 1940)]

Example: A newspaper report that P is suffering from an embarrassing disease, had sex-change surgery, or is having an extramarital affair may well be highly offensive. [**Diaz v. Oakland Tribune, Inc.,** 139 Cal. App. 3d 118 (1983)—sex-change surgery]

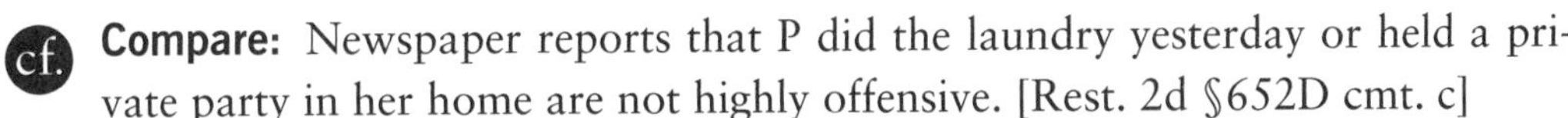

Compare: Newspaper reports that P did the laundry yesterday or held a private party in her home are not highly offensive. [Rest. 2d §652D cmt. c]

Compare: There is no actionable invasion where a magazine publisher, credit card issuer, etc., sells ***mailing lists*** of its subscribers to others. [**Shibley v. Time, Inc.,** 321 N.E.2d 791 (Ohio 1974)]

---

4. Must Be a "Public" Disclosure [§1569]

The element of a "public" disclosure requires ***more*** than publication in the defamation sense. The disclosure must involve publicity—communication either to the ***public at large*** or to ***enough individuals*** that it is likely to reach the general public.

Example: A single letter from a collection agency to P's employer disclosing that P has not paid her bills and requesting assistance in collection of P's debt is not an invasion of privacy. [**Timperley v. Chase Collection Service,** 272 Cal. App. 2d 697 (1969)] But disclosing that fact in a newspaper ad, or in a notice posted in a public place, is sufficient publicity to be actionable. [**Brents v. Morgan,** 299 S.W. 967 (Ky. 1927)]

Compare: Even without publicity, repeated letters or other unreasonable collection efforts may be actionable as intentional infliction of emotional distress (*see supra,* §§79 *et seq.*) or as an intrusion into private affairs (*see supra,* §§1544 *et seq.*).

---

e.g. **Example:** Disclosure to two co-workers that P has HIV does not satisfy the requirement of dissemination to the general public. [**Doe v. Methodist Hospital,** 690 N.E.2d 681 (Ind. 1997)]

---

e.g. **Example:** A lender's disclosure of a borrower's financial information to a third party is insufficient publicity to support an invasion of privacy claim. [**Swinton Creek Nursery v. Edisto Farm Credit,** 514 S.E.2d 126 (S.C. 1999)]

---

e.g. **Example:** Improper disclosure of P's school transcript to a state commission is not a public disclosure. [**Porten v. University of San Francisco,** 64 Cal. App. 3d 825 (1976)] *But note:* A few courts hold that a letter to a big government agency may be a "public" disclosure. [*See, e.g.,* **Beaumont v. Brown,** 257 N.W.2d 522 (Mich. 1977)]

---

5. No Public Interest ("Newsworthiness") [§1570]

If the defendant publicizes private facts about the plaintiff that are highly offensive, the plaintiff must show that the facts are not "newsworthy." [**Diaz v. Oakland Tribune, Inc.,** *supra*]

a. What is "newsworthy" [§1571]

Courts have generally given the term "newsworthy" a broad interpretation, holding it applicable to any matter as to which there is a ***"legitimate public interest."***

---

e.g. **Example:** The publication of P doctor's name and the report of her psychiatric and marital problems were newsworthy because they arguably related to the important public problem of medical malpractice. Additionally, the information added credibility to the story. [**Gilbert v. Medical Economics Co.,** 665 F.2d 305 (10th Cir. 1981)]

---

e.g. **Example:** P had foiled an assassination attempt on President Ford. D, in reporting about P, stated that P was a homosexual. The court found the item was newsworthy because it attempted to dispel the myth that gays were "timid and weak" and to raise the issue of whether the President's belated thanks displayed any discriminatory attitudes toward homosexuals. [**Sipple v. Chronicle Publishing Co.,** *supra*, §1565]

---

e.g. **Example:** Identifying the owner of a puppy as a runaway was in the public interest, given the publicity surrounding the puppy's brutal beating at the hands of a third party and the threats later made to the owner. [**J.C. v. WALA-TV, Inc.,** 675 So. 2d 360 (Ala. 1996)]

---

e.g. **Example:** Newspaper's reporting that P was the victim of a sexual assault while incarcerated was a matter of legitimate public interest. [**Doe v. Berkeley Publishers,** 496 S.E.2d 636 (S.C. 1998)]

---

(1) **Note**

If the published material involves a matter of legitimate public interest, the defendant will not be held liable, even if the material is in bad taste. [**Neff v. Time, Inc.,** 406 F. Supp. 858 (W.D. Pa. 1976)—photo of football fan posing with trousers unzipped]

b. **Application to voluntary public figures [§1572]**

Public interest in voluntary public figures often extends beyond their public appearances and activities. Disclosures of private facts concerning voluntary public figures are privileged if newsworthy.

---

e.g. **Examples:** D's disclosure that a member of Congress has taken bribes or has committed adultery is newsworthy. Similarly, if D reports that P, a famous singer, is losing her voice because of excessive drinking, that is newsworthy.

---

(1) **Limitation—matters not in legitimate public interest [§1573]**

Some aspects of a public figure's life may be so private or separate from her public life as to be beyond legitimate public interest. Publications of such private matters are ***not privileged.***

---

e.g. **Example:** If a newspaper invites readers to reveal their "unique love relationships" and then reports an entry from P's ex-husband that identifies P by first name as having had several abortions, as being unable to have children, and as having engaged in spouse swapping, a jury could find that this information was not of legitimate public interest. [**Winstead v. Sweeney,** 517 N.W.2d 874 (Mich. 1994)]

---

cf. **Compare:** A book revealing that P had once been a heavy-drinking ne'er-do-well who neglected his children and could not keep a job, was unfaithful, and left his wife for another woman was not actionable as a matter of law because the book was focused on the story of the woman P had left and was about the difficulties of urban migration. [**Haynes v. Alfred A. Knopf, Inc.,** 8 F.3d 1222 (7th Cir. 1993)]

(a) **Note**

The distinction between disclosure of matters of legitimate public interest and impermissible prying into private lives may depend on community attitudes and is often a jury question. [**Virgil v. Time, Inc.,** 527 F.2d 1122 (9th Cir. 1975), *cert. denied,* 425 U.S. 998 (1976); **Hawkins v. Multimedia, Inc.,** 344 S.E.2d 145 (S.C.), *cert. denied,* 479 U.S. 1012 (1986)—jury could find liability for story about teenage pregnancies that named P as a teenage father]

c. **Involuntary public figures [§1574]**

Just as with voluntary public figures, publishers may disclose private facts concerning involuntary public figures ***when they are newsworthy***, even though they go beyond the events that brought the plaintiff into the public eye.

 **Example:** Reports of P's past life and associations are privileged if P is on trial for murder. It does not matter if P is later acquitted.

---

(1) **Limitation—matters not in legitimate public interest [§1575]**

Again, some aspects of P's life may be so private as to be beyond legitimate public interest. Although protection does not depend on whether P is voluntarily or involuntarily public, courts may take that fact into consideration.

d. **"Current" public interest [§1576]**

The passage of time does not necessarily preclude a publication from being in the legitimate public interest. Thus, the life of one ***formerly*** in the public eye may be treated as "public property" and may be republished, although that individual is no longer in the public eye (*e.g.*, life history of former child prodigy; events from life of former prizefighter now retired; crimes committed in the past).

(1) **But note**

The passage of time is likely to indicate a lack of newsworthiness more quickly in the cases of involuntary public figures than of voluntary ones.

6. **Fault [§1577]**

Fault is an essential element of this tort because of its serious constitutional aspect. But the "fault" cannot be the same as in defamation (*supra*, §§1409 *et seq.*) because that was concerned with fault related to ***falsity*** and here the story is true. The fault element here instead is related to the action that gave rise to the highly offensive disclosure.

---

e.g. **Example:** A newspaper that runs a story about P's prior abortions, adultery, and sterility, where P is an ordinary private citizen, may be found to have known that its revelations would be highly offensive and lack legitimate public interest. [**Winstead v. Sweeney,** *supra*]

---

e.g. **Example:** A partner of a law firm who tells others in the office that an associate is a homosexual may be found to have acted with reckless disregard of the private nature of the facts disclosed. [**Robert C. Ozer, P.C. v. Borquez,** 940 P.2d 371 (Colo. 1997)]

---

a. **Note**

Although most revelations are intentional and are likely to be clear abuses of editorial discretion, a few actions may be based on negligence. [*See, e.g.,* **Multimedia WMAZ, Inc. v. Kubach,** *supra,* §1565—although D television station agreed to P's demand that his features be disguised by digitalization, a technician negligently failed to do so for seven seconds and P was identifiable]

7. Causation [§1578]

As with intrusions, causation is an essential element of the public disclosure claim. (*See supra,* §1557.)

8. Defenses

a. Truth is no defense [§1579]

Because the gist of the tort is embarrassment about public awareness of private facts, truth is irrelevant. [**Briscoe v. Reader's Digest Association,** 4 Cal. 3d 529 (1971)]

b. Consent [§1580]

As with intrusions, consent is a complete defense for public disclosures.

(1) Information disclosed by plaintiff to defendant [§1581]

Normally, the fact that the plaintiff has voluntarily divulged facts about herself to the defendant bars any later claim against the defendant for repeating this information to others—even if the defendant promised to keep it "in the strictest confidence." A person's failure to keep things secret is not yet deemed a tort. [**Wynne v. Orcutt Union School District,** 17 Cal. App. 3d 1108 (1971); *but see* **Robert C. Ozer, P.C. v. Borquez,** *supra*]

(a) Distinguish—breach of duty [§1582]

On the other hand, if the defendant was under a ***legal duty not to disclose*** the information without the plaintiff's consent (*e.g.,* doctor-patient, attorney-client, etc.), the defendant's doing so may be actionable as an invasion of privacy. [**Horne v. Patton,** *supra,* §1562]

(b) Distinguish—consent to disclosure withdrawn [§1583]

A magazine cannot rely on consent to publish embarrassing private facts elicited from a plaintiff during an interview if the plaintiff later changes his mind and, before publication, withdraws permission to print the story. [**Virgil v. Time, Inc.,** *supra,* §1573]

c. Constitutional privilege [§1584]

To assure freedom of speech and press, a constitutional privilege for the media has been recognized in the public disclosure area.

(1) Matters of public record—absolute privilege [§1585]

If the matters reported or published are taken from official court records and are accurately stated, the constitutional privilege is ***absolute.*** *Rationale:* The public interest in free reporting of such matters outweighs any interest in privacy on the part of those whose names appear in the records.

Example: A broadcaster who announces the name of a deceased rape victim obtained from court records is not liable for invasion of privacy of the victim's family. [**Cox Broadcasting Corp. v. Cohn,** 420 U.S. 469 (1975)]

Example: A newspaper's publication of facts contained in a 40-year-old court record about an individual involved in a child sexual abuse investigation did not create tort liability, even though the individual's name may not have been newsworthy. [**Uranga v. Federated Publications, Inc.,** 67 P.3d 29 (Idaho 2003)]

(2) Other matters—qualified privilege [§1586]
If the matter was ***lawfully obtained from the government,*** is truthful, and prohibition is not necessary to further a "state interest of the highest order," defendants are privileged to publish information.

Example: Publication of a rape victim's name that was obtained through inadvertent release by the police could not create civil (or criminal) liability. [**The Florida Star v. B.J.F.,** 491 U.S. 524 (1989)]

9. Damages [§1587]
The same rules for damages that apply to intrusions apply to public disclosure. (*See supra*, §1560.) The damages here are more likely to be based on the humiliation arising from the public disclosure.

10. Privacy Action Rejected [§1588]
A few states have rejected this type of privacy action where true facts are involved. These courts have expressed skepticism that the judiciary can develop adequate standards to determine what is highly offensive to a reasonable person and a fear that juries will second guess editorial judgments about truthful stories. [*See, e.g.,* **Hall v. Post,** 372 S.E.2d 711 (N.C. 1988); **Anderson v. Fisher Broadcasting Cos.,** *supra,* §1562]

a. New York statute [§1589]
Under a New York statute [N.Y. Civ. Rights Law §§50, 51], a true report about a person may be actionable only if published for "advertising purposes or for the purposes of trade"—which generally have been limited to advertisers—with the result that media stories are virtually never actionable. [**Finger v. Omni Publications International, Ltd.,** 77 N.Y.2d 138 (1990)]

C. Appropriation of Plaintiff's Name or Likeness

1. **Prima Facie Case [§1590]**

To recover for this type of invasion of privacy, the plaintiff must prove:

- *Unauthorized Use by Defendant of Plaintiff's Name or Likeness for a Commercial Purpose*
- *Causation*

EXAM TIP **gilbert**

Note that unlike the other privacy torts, an action for appropriation of a plaintiff's name or likeness does ***not*** require a showing that the invasion of privacy would be highly offensive to a reasonable person.

2. **Unauthorized Use [§1591]**

It is the ***unauthorized use*** of the plaintiff's name or likeness that is actionable. Therefore, it is no defense that the plaintiff is in fact a satisfied customer or user of the product involved. [**Fairfield v. American Photocopy Equipment Co.,** 138 Cal. App. 2d 82 (1955)]

a. **Distinguish—defamation [§1592]**

If the plaintiff is not a user of the product, and the advertisement hurts her reputation, it may also be defamation.

b. **Consent [§1593]**

A person who consents to the use of her likeness for a commercial purpose, and puts no limits on the nature of that use, cannot claim that her privacy has been invaded by the unforeseen manner in which her likeness was used. [**Miller v. American Sports Co.,** 467 N.W.2d 653 (Neb. 1991)—model in bath towel pictured in hot tub brochure beneath the letters "S E X"]

c. **Extension beyond name or likeness [§1594]**

Some cases have extended protection beyond the "name or likeness" to other features associated with the plaintiff's identity. [**Wendt v. Host International, Inc.,** 125 F.3d 806 (9th Cir. 1997), *cert. denied*, 531 U.S. 811 (2000)—actors who played roles in popular television series that took place in a bar had action for use in airport bars of robots that resembled the characters that they had played in the series; **White v. Samsung Electronics America, Inc.,** 971 F.2d 1395 (9th Cir. 1992), *cert. denied,* 508 U.S. 951 (1993)—advertiser's robot too closely evoked image of woman who performed role on television quiz show; **Carson v. Here's Johnny Portable Toilets, Inc.,** 698 F.2d 831 (6th Cir. 1983)—product's name too close to words used to introduce television performer at each show]

3. **Right of Publicity vs. Right of Privacy [§1595]**

If the plaintiff is a ***celebrity***, the use of her name clearly has commercial value so that she is entitled to damages not so much for invasion of privacy but rather for interference with her ***right of publicity*** (*i.e.*, her right to sell her endorsements to someone else). [**Haelan Laboratories, Inc. v. Topps Chewing Gum, Inc.,** 202 F.2d 866 (2d Cir.), *cert. denied*, 346 U.S. 816 (1953)]

a. **Distinguish—private person [§1596]**
On the other hand, if the plaintiff is an unknown person, the unauthorized use of her name is more clearly an invasion of ***privacy***; the plaintiff is entitled to compensation not for the commercial value of her name, but for interference with her "right to be let alone." [**Fairfield v. American Photocopy Equipment Co.,** *supra*]

4. **Causation [§1597]**
As with intrusion, causation is an essential element. (*See supra*, §1557.)

5. **Defense—Newsworthiness [§1598]**
If the plaintiff is a public figure or is a currently newsworthy figure, publication of the plaintiff's name or likeness is not actionable, as long as the use is not for the purposes of trade or advertising.

---

e.g. **Example:** Following a detective agency's investigation, P was convicted of the theft of bearer bonds. The agency published P's name and picture in its newsletter, which was distributed to law enforcement agencies and law firms. The court found that the main purpose of the article was noncommercial, and thus it was subject to the newsworthiness privilege. [**Joe Dickerson & Associates, LLC v. Dittmar,** 34 P.3d 995 (Colo. 2001)]

---

e.g. **Example:** A newspaper has a constitutional right to reprint action photos of a recently retired football star because they show newsworthy items of public interest. [**Montana v. San Jose Mercury News, Inc.,** 34 Cal. App. 4th 790 (1995)]

---

cf. **Compare:** A game manufacturer's use of a professional golfer's name in its product is actionable. [**Palmer v. Schonhorn Enterprises, Inc.,** 232 A.2d 458 (N.J. 1967)]

---

a. **No constitutional privilege for some noncommercial uses that destroy right of publicity [§1599]**
There is no First Amendment privilege allowing media to film or broadcast an ***entire*** commercial entertainment or performance (*e.g.*, sports event) without the consent of the participant. It may be of public interest, but this does not give the media any privilege to impair the performer's right of publicity—*i.e.*, the right to get paid for this use of the performance. This is comparable to media publication of an entire copyrighted work without the owner's consent. [**Zacchini v. Scripps-Howard Broadcasting Co.,** 433 U.S. 562 (1977)—unauthorized television news coverage of "human cannonball" act at county fair]

b. **Newsworthiness privilege inapplicable to promotional materials depicting noncurrent events [§1600]**
A promotional calendar distributed by a for-profit medical clinic where abortions were performed may not use an unaffiliated doctor's picture without her

consent, even if the photograph was from a past newsworthy event or the calendar's theme (the history of women's rights) was of undisputed public interest. [**Beverley v. Choices Women's Medical Center, Inc.,** 78 N.Y.2d 745 (1991)]

6. Damages [§1601]

For ***celebrity*** plaintiffs, the damages for appropriations include the reasonable value of the use of the plaintiff's name or likeness. Thus, the defendant does not profit from the unauthorized use, and the plaintiff is compensated for any loss sustained by being unable to sell her name, features, or act to some other company. For ***private*** plaintiffs, emotional harm is likely to be the main element.

D. Publicity Placing Plaintiff in a "False Light"

1. Prima Facie Case [§1602]

This action involves:

- *Publication by Defendant that Places Plaintiff in a False Light (Highly Offensive)*
- *Knowing or Reckless Falsity if "Newsworthy" Matter*
- *Causation*

a. Distinguish—appropriation of plaintiff's name or likeness [§1603]

This privacy action does not involve commercial appropriation; rather, it involves the unauthorized use of the plaintiff's name or likeness that places the plaintiff in a false light in the public eye. [**Cantrell v. Forest City Publishing Co.,** 419 U.S. 245 (1974)]

2. Publication [§1604]

For the plaintiff to suffer damages from a "false light" publication, dissemination to a reasonable number of third persons is required. [**Bernstein v. National Broadcasting Co.,** 129 F. Supp. 817 (D.D.C. 1955), *aff'd*, 232 F.2d 369 (D.C. Cir. 1956)]

3. Falsity Required [§1605]

The false light in which the plaintiff is placed must be ***highly offensive to a reasonable person***. [Rest. 2d §652E]

---

e.g. **Example—false light by association:** D published photographs of P in *Hustler* magazine without her permission. The court found that the implication that P was associated with the magazine could be highly offensive to a reasonable person. [**Douglass v. Hustler Magazine, Inc.,** 769 F.2d 1128 (7th Cir. 1985), *cert. denied*, 475 U.S. 1094 (1986)]

---

cf. **Compare:** Where D magazine includes photographs of P without her consent as a part of a book review, no association with the magazine is suggested. Thus, no false light privacy claim exists. [**Faloona v. Hustler Magazine, Inc.,** 799 F.2d 1000 (5th Cir. 1986), *cert. denied*, 479 U.S. 1088 (1987)]

---

cf. **Compare:** Ds (including a reporter and camera crew) conducted an "ambush interview" of P, with the film portraying P as unresponsive to charges of misconduct by P's company. The court found that the interview did not portray P in a false light because it was P's own conduct captured on film. [**Machleder v. Diaz,** 801 F.2d 46 (2d Cir. 1986), *cert. denied*, 479 U.S. 1088 (1987)]

---

4. **Distinguish—Defamation [§1606]**

If the "false light" would affect the plaintiff's reputation in the community, an action for defamation may also lie. Most states will prevent the plaintiffs from escaping the restrictions of defamation law simply by calling the action one for privacy. This would apply to such matters as the need for special damages. [**Fellows v. National Enquirer, Inc.,** 42 Cal. 3d 234 (1986)—applying state's libel retraction and special damages provisions to false light privacy action]

a. **Note**

A handful of states do not recognize the false light privacy cause of action precisely because a defamation action so closely relates to the false light cause of action that it suffices to protect a plaintiff's reputation and other interests. [*See, e.g.,* **Cain v. Hearst Corp.,** 878 S.W.2d 577 (Tex. 1994)]

5. **Fault [§1607]**

The First Amendment protects media (and other) defendants from liability for some "false light" publications.

a. **Newsworthy matters [§1608]**

Newsworthy statements by the media that put the plaintiff in a false light are not actionable unless the "knowing or reckless falsity" standard is met (*i.e.*, publisher knew or was blind to the fact that publication would place the plaintiff in highly offensive false light in the public eye). [**Time, Inc. v. Hill,** 385 U.S. 374 (1967)]

---

e.g. **Example:** A letter sent by a private individual to the state governor, attorney general, and members of the media charging a state board president's husband with improperly thrusting himself into state affairs did not give rise to a false light claim in the absence of clear and convincing evidence of actual malice. [**Dodson v. Dicker,** 812 S.W.2d 97 (Ark. 1991)—plaintiff must prove that the writer entertained actual doubts about the accuracy of the charges]

---

(1) **Distinguish—defamation [§1609]**

Should constitutional protections in this privacy area develop by analogy to the *Gertz* case in defamation (*see supra*, §1446), the media would not be shielded from liability for false light publications of private matters if they were negligent in not recognizing that a private person was portrayed in a false light. The Court has left the question open. [**Cantrell v. Forest City Publishing Co.,** *supra*] Some states have rejected the possibility of using negligence. [**Colbert v. World Publishing Co.,** 747 P.2d 286 (Okla. 1987)]

6. Causation [§1610]

As with intrusion, causation is an essential element. (*See supra*, §1557.)

7. Damages [§1611]

The plaintiff may recover for damages to reputation, for any emotional distress suffered, and for pecuniary damages.

FOUR CATEGORIES OF PRIVACY TORTS—A SUMMARY gilbert

PRIVACY TORT	DESCRIPTION	EXAMPLES
INTRUSION INTO PRIVATE LIFE	An ***intentional invasion*** into an area of plaintiff's life that plaintiff reasonably expects will not be intruded upon that would be ***highly offensive*** to a ***reasonable person***.	Secretly photographing nude tanning salon patron.
PUBLIC DISCLOSURE OF PRIVATE FACTS	An ***intentional publication*** of facts about plaintiff's life that have ***not*** already received some ***publicity***, are ***not*** a matter of ***public record***, are ***not newsworthy***, and publication of which would be ***highly offensive*** to a ***reasonable person***.	Newspaper article disclosing that the first female ever elected as student body president had a sex-change operation, where that fact had previously been disclosed only to a few friends and plaintiff's family.
APPROPRIATION OF PLAINTIFF'S NAME OR LIKENESS	An ***intentional unauthorized use*** of plaintiff's name or likeness for ***commercial purposes***.* * An action can be based on a ***noncommercial*** use if the use destroys the person's ***right of publicity*** (*e.g.,* broadcasting a singer's performance).	Using a picture of a celebrity in an advertisement without the celebrity's consent.
PUTTING PLAINTIFF IN A FALSE LIGHT	An ***intentional publication*** about plaintiff that gives a ***false impression*** that would be ***highly offensive*** to a ***reasonable person***.	Publishing in *Hustler* magazine a picture of a model who has not consented to the publication, where the photo implies that the model was associated with the magazine.

E. Claims Involving Privacy of Third Persons

1. **Publications Regarding Living Persons [§1612]**
Most courts hold that a plaintiff ***cannot*** recover for an invasion of privacy based on publicity concerning another living person no matter how close their relationship. [**Coverstone v. Davies,** *supra*, §167—father denied recovery for invasion of his privacy based on newspaper publicity concerning arrest of son]

2. **Publications Concerning a Dead Person [§1613]**
Neither can a cause of action ordinarily be maintained on account of publications regarding a person who is already dead.

 a. **Survivors' privacy claims [§1614]**
 Most courts hold that there is ***no*** "relational" right of privacy, so that a decedent's survivors (no matter how close) ***cannot*** complain of any invasion of ***their*** interests because of publicity concerning the decedent. [**Metter v. Los Angeles Examiner,** 35 Cal. App. 2d 304 (1939)—no recovery allowed for P's great anguish when D newspaper published photo of P's wife and lurid details of her suicide]

 b. **Decedent's claims [§1615]**
 And the ***decedent's*** right of privacy is a personal right that generally does not survive her death. Hence, no cause of action can be maintained on behalf of the decedent by her estate or heirs for publications ***after*** her death. [*See, e.g.,* **Maritote v. Desilu Productions, Inc.,** 345 F.2d 418 (7th Cir. 1965)—suit by heirs of Al Capone]

  (1) **Distinguish—publications during lifetime [§1616]**
  If the invasion occurred ***during*** the decedent's lifetime (rather than after death), clearly the decedent could have sued. Whether her estate can sue, however, depends on the survival statute in effect (*see supra*, §1151). If the statute is broad enough, an action can be maintained by the estate. [**Estate of Berthiaume v. Pratt,** 365 A.2d 792 (Me. 1976)—doctor took unauthorized pictures of dying cancer patient to show progression of illness; patient's estate allowed to sue for invasion of patient's privacy]

  (2) **Celebrity's right of publicity [§1617]**
  Most courts hold that whatever right a celebrity has to exploit her name and likeness must be exercised during the celebrity's life. If it is not, the heirs cannot inherit an exclusive right to that exploitation after death. [**Lugosi v. Universal Pictures,** 25 Cal. 3d 813 (1979); *but see* **Martin Luther King, Jr., Center for Social Change, Inc. v. American Heritage Products, Inc.,** 296 S.E.2d 697 (Ga. 1982)—contra]

(a) **Exploitation during life [§1618]**
At least where the right of exploitation was exercised during the celebrity's lifetime and then assigned to the plaintiff, it has been held to survive. [**Acme Circus Operating Co. v. Kuperstock,** 711 F.2d 1538 (11th Cir. 1983)]

F. Important—Related Torts

1. **Publication May Give Rise to Several Torts [§1619]**
It should be emphasized again that the torts of ***defamation***, ***wrongful infliction of emotional distress***, and ***wrongful invasion of privacy*** frequently occur concurrently, and accordingly each should be considered whenever any one of them appears to be involved.

2. **Breach of Confidential Relationship [§1620]**
If the parties have some preexisting relationship, courts may rely on that relationship instead of a privacy approach. [**Humphers v. First Interstate Bank of Oregon,** 696 P.2d 527 (Or. 1985)—physician who helped adopted person learn identity of her natural mother may have breached confidential relationship between physician and his former patient (the mother)]

3. **Limitation on Causes of Action Under Uniform Act [§1621]**
Under the Uniform Single Publication Act, in effect in some states [*e.g.*, Cal. Civ. Code §3425.3], only a single cause of action is allowed for damages arising from any single publication—whether for defamation, invasion of privacy, or any other tort founded on the publication. Recovery for one tort thus ***bars any other claim*** for damages ***arising out of the same publication***, anywhere. (Any issue of a book or magazine, any radio or television broadcast, or any one exhibition of a movie is regarded as a "single publication"—no matter how many persons heard it, read it, etc.)

Chapter Ten: Other Torts

CONTENTS

- ▶ Key Exam Issues
- A. Misrepresentation §1622
- B. Injurious Falsehood §1684
- C. Interference with Economic Relations §1710
- D. Unjustifiable Litigation §1758

Key Exam Issues

The list of torts discussed up to now is by no means all-inclusive, although it probably covers the torts you studied in your law school class. A number of other torts, however, have also been recognized. (Some are discussed in other Gilbert Summaries; *e.g.*, unfair competition and infringement of literary property are covered in the Remedies Summary.) Of the remaining recognized torts, the following are the most important for you to know:

1. ***Misrepresentation*** (based on intent, negligence, or strict liability);
2. ***Injurious falsehood*** (interference with the prospect of a sale or other advantageous relationship affecting the plaintiff's property);
3. ***Interference with economic relations*** (interference with contract or prospective economic advantage); and
4. ***Unjustifiable litigation*** (malicious prosecution, wrongful institution of a civil case, and abuse of process).

But also remember—there is ***no fixed, rigid number of torts***; facts that do not fit any particular "classic tort" pattern may still be actionable. And many new tort actions have been created by statute, such as those authorizing damages for discrimination and civil rights violations.

A. Misrepresentation

1. Introduction [§1622]

Misrepresentation—which protects the plaintiff's ***economic*** (not personal or physical) interests—may be predicated on any of the three bases of liability (intentional tort, negligence, or strict liability). However, with misrepresentation, there are substantial differences in the prima facie case and in the scope of liability, depending on which basis for liability is involved.

e.g. **Example:** D physician gave an incorrect opinion to P's attorney; as a result, P did not try to sue a negligent surgeon within the statute of limitations. P's suit against D was for the economic loss caused by the dismissal of that earlier lawsuit—and was properly brought for the misrepresentation. The loss is equivalent to what would have been recoverable in the personal injury case. [**Hart v. Browne,** 103 Cal. App. 3d 947 (1980)]

2. Intentional Misrepresentation ("Fraudulent Misrepresentation" or "Deceit") [§1623]

Prima facie case:

- *Misrepresentation by Defendant*
- *Scienter*
- *Intent to Induce Plaintiff's Reliance*
- *Causation—Actual Reliance*
- *Justifiable Reliance*
- *Damages*

a. Misrepresentation by defendant

(1) Affirmative misrepresentation [§1624]

Ordinarily, there must be a ***false, material*** representation of a past or present *fact*. However, in certain cases, false representations of opinion or law may also be actionable. (This is a question of justifiable reliance; *see infra,* §§1643-1653.)

(a) "Material" misrepresentation [§1625]

"Material" covers any representation that would have influenced a reasonable person in the plaintiff's position in this type of business dealing, as well as any representation that the defendant knew this specific plaintiff considered important.

(b) "Fact" [§1626]

A misrepresentation of a ***present state of mind or intention*** is treated as a misrepresentation of fact (*e.g.*, promises to perform that the promisor ***never intended*** to perform). "A man's state of mind or intention is as much a fact as his state of digestion." [**Lazar v. Superior Court,** 12 Cal. 4th 631 (1996); **Channel Master Corp. v. Aluminum Ltd. Sales, Inc.,** 4 N.Y.2d 403 (1958)]

1) Unauthorized promise [§1627]

A promise made by someone who knows he has no authority to make the promise is actionable as a misrepresentation. [**Boivin v. Jones & Vining, Inc.,** 578 A.2d 187 (Me. 1990)—company held liable for fraud after employee, who was promised lifetime employment by vice president, was fired]

(c) "Representation" [§1628]

The representation is usually by oral or written words, but it may be by conduct as well (*e.g.*, exhibiting a document, turning back the mileage indicator on a car offered for sale, etc.).

(2) Fraudulent concealment [§1629]

Even though no affirmative representation is made by the defendant, a fraudulent concealment of facts will be a sufficient "misrepresentation," ***except where***:

(a) ***The bill of sale or transaction is marked "as is"*** (minority view is contra); or

(b) ***Plaintiff is charged with some knowledge or notice*** of the facts concealed.

(3) Failure to disclose [§1630]

On the other hand, the defendant is ordinarily ***not*** under any ***duty to disclose*** facts. Thus, failure to disclose (as distinguished from active concealment) all the defendant knows is not a "misrepresentation." [Rest. 2d §551]

(a) Exceptions [§1631]

In the following cases, the defendant's failure to disclose ***will*** support an action for intentional misrepresentation.

1) Fiduciary relationship [§1632]

If the defendant and the plaintiff are in some special fiduciary relationship to each other (*e.g.*, trustee-beneficiary, guardian-ward), the defendant's failure to disclose will support an action for intentional misrepresentation.

2) "Half-truths" [§1633]

A defendant who has made an incomplete or ambiguous statement or half-truth, knowingly misleading, comes under a duty to clarify the statement and disclose the truth. [**Silva v. Stevens,** 589 A.2d 852 (Vt. 1991)—discussion of leaks that had been fixed created duty to warn about other leaks that had not been fixed, even absent duty to speak in the first place]

3) New information [§1634]

A defendant has a duty to disclose when he has made a statement believing it to be true but later finds out that it is false, or if the statement was true when made but material facts have changed, and the defendant knows that the plaintiff is relying on the first version.

4) Reliance [§1635]

If the defendant has made a statement knowing it is false but not intending that anyone rely on it, and then finds out that the plaintiff is about to act on it, the defendant also has a duty to disclose.

5) Sale of property [§1636]

Several states (modern trend) recognize an additional exception: In cases involving the sale of property, if certain material facts are known to the seller and are both ***unknown and not readily accessible to the buyer***, the seller is bound to disclose the facts to the buyer; the failure to do so constitutes misrepresentation actionable for damages or rescission. [*See, e.g.,* **Johnson v. Davis,** 480 So. 2d 625 (Fla. 1985); **Ollerman v. O'Rourke Co.,** 288 N.W.2d 95 (Wis. 1980)]

---

e.g. **Examples:** Actionable misrepresentation includes the failure to disclose that: the land sold was filled; the building sold was infested by termites; the house sold had a badly leaking roof when it rained; improvements on the property sold violated local building, health, or zoning ordinances or regulations; or litigation was pending involving the business or property sold. [*See, e.g.,* **Strawn v. Canuso,** 657 A.2d 420 (N.J. 1995)—duty on seller and broker to disclose existence of off-site closed landfill "not readily observable" by buyer]

---

b. **Scienter**

(1) **Defined [§1637]**
"Scienter" refers to the defendant's ***knowledge*** of the falsity of the representation made, or knowledge that he had an insufficient basis for determining the truth of the representation (*i.e.,* recklessness in making the statement). [**Derry v. Peek,** 14 A.C. 337 (1889); Rest. 2d §526]

(2) **Intent to deceive implied [§1638]**
Negligence alone is not sufficient for scienter; *i.e.,* the defendant's honest belief in the truth of the representation, even if based on unreasonable grounds, will ***not*** support an action for intentional misrepresentation. But the enormity of the unreasonable behavior ***may*** allow a jury to ***infer lack of honest belief***, which would suffice for scienter.

(3) **Burden of proof [§1639]**
Because it is relatively easy to claim fraud and often hard to disprove it, most courts demand that plaintiffs prove their claims of fraud by ***clear and convincing evidence***. [**Greycas, Inc. v. Proud,** 826 F.2d 1560 (7th Cir. 1987), *cert. denied*, 484 U.S. 1043 (1988)]

c. **Intent to induce reliance of plaintiff [§1640]**
The defendant must have intended to induce the reliance of the ***plaintiff***, ***or a class of persons*** to which the plaintiff belongs, in a particular transaction. [**Metric Investment, Inc. v. Patterson,** 244 A.2d 311 (N.J. 1968)]

(1) **Exception—ongoing deception [§1641]**
If the misrepresentation is a "continuous deception" (*e.g.,* the mislabeling of a product by its manufacturer, or a misrepresentation contained in a negotiable instrument), it is not necessary that the reliance of a particular plaintiff (or reliance in a particular transaction) be intended. Anyone who acquires the product or instrument may sue.

d. **Causation [§1642]**

It must be proven that the misrepresentation played a substantial part in inducing the plaintiff to act as she did—*i.e.*, ***actual*** reliance. The plaintiff's awareness of the falsity of the misrepresentation precludes reliance. [**Nader v. Allegheny Airlines, Inc.,** 626 F.2d 1031 (D.C. Cir. 1980)—P knew that airlines often "overbooked"]

(1) **Note**

The use of an "as is" clause will not prevent the plaintiff from proving fraud. [**Engels v. Ranger Bar, Inc.,** 604 N.W.2d 241 (S.D. 2000)—neither "as is" nor parol evidence rule bars plaintiff from proving existence of fraud]

e. **Justifiable reliance by plaintiff**

(1) **Plaintiff's reliance must be foreseeable [§1643]**

For the plaintiff's reliance to be "justified" it must have been ***intended*** by the defendant ***or reasonably foreseeable***. For example, a defendant would be liable to a plaintiff if the defendant made the misrepresentation to a third person but it is foreseeable that the misrepresentation will be communicated to the plaintiff. [Rest. 2d §533] On the other hand, if the plaintiff ***knows*** that she was not the person whose reliance was intended by the defendant (as where the plaintiff was an agent of a third person and the defendant made the representation to the plaintiff only for purpose of transmission to that person, and intending only that person to rely thereon), the plaintiff cannot justifiably rely thereon.

(2) **Whether reliance is "justified" depends on type of representation [§1644]**

Even assuming the plaintiff's reliance was intended or foreseeable, and that she did actually rely, the plaintiff's reliance on every type of representation made by the defendant may not be "justified."

(a) **Representations of fact [§1645]**

The plaintiff's unconditional reliance on ***material*** misrepresentations of ***fact*** (including misrepresentations of present state of mind and intention) is ***always justified***, except where the facts are obviously false. [*See* **Lockard v. Carson,** 287 N.W.2d 871 (Iowa 1980)]

1) **No duty to investigate [§1646]**

A plaintiff is under no duty to check the truth of the defendant's representations of fact, no matter how easy it would be to do so. [*See* **Belmac Hygiene, Inc. v. Belmac Corp.,** 121 F.3d 835 (2d Cir. 1997)—P's reliance on D's misrepresentation that FDA review was not needed to market medical product was sufficient to support claim even though further investigation would have revealed inaccuracy of statement; **Engels v. Ranger Bar, Inc.,** *supra*]

If the plaintiff does investigate, however, she cannot rely on representations that are inconsistent with the facts she discovered or reasonably should have discovered during such investigation.

(b) **Representations of opinion [§1647]**
A plaintiff is ordinarily ***not*** justified in relying on misrepresentations of ***opinion, value, or quality unless*** one of the following four exceptions applies:

1) **Superior knowledge [§1648]**
Where the defendant has superior knowledge not available to the plaintiff (*e.g.*, D is a jeweler, art dealer, etc., seeking to make a sale), the plaintiff may justifiably rely on the defendant's representations of opinion. The difficult problem is to determine when a dealer's "puffing" or bragging about his wares turns from "loose sales talk" into an actionable misrepresentation (*i.e.*, statements that can reasonably be interpreted as assurances of specific facts). [**Vulcan Metals Co. v. Simmons Manufacturing Co.,** 248 F. 853 (2d Cir. 1918)]

EXAM TIP **gilbert**

It is often difficult to distinguish sales "puff" from misrepresentation. If an exam question deals with a salesperson talking up her wares, discuss the ***specificity of the statement*** (*e.g.*, a "top-notch widget" vs. "voted the best widget in an independent poll of consumers") and the ***context of the transaction*** (*e.g.*, in a sales setting). Which side you come down on (*i.e.*, "puff" vs. "misrepresentation") should not be as important to your grade as the discussion, because often one court's "puff" is another court's misrepresentation.

2) **Fiduciary duty [§1649]**
The plaintiff may justifiably rely on the defendant's representations of opinion if the defendant owes some fiduciary duty to the plaintiff (*e.g.*, a trustee-beneficiary relationship).

3) **Special relationship [§1650]**
Where the defendant and the plaintiff are in some way affiliated or specially related, so that the defendant has ***"secured the confidence"*** of the plaintiff (*e.g.*, P and D are members of a family or common fraternal or religious organization), the plaintiff may justifiably rely on the defendant's representations of opinion.

4) **Undisclosed interest [§1651]**
The plaintiff may justifiably rely on the defendant's advice as to a transaction the plaintiff is contemplating with a third party where the defendant does not disclose his financial interest in the deal. [Rest. 2d §543]

---

e.g. **Example:** Bank president D recommends XYZ stock to customer P as a safe investment, without any reasonable grounds for believing this to be true and without disclosing that he has a financial interest in the sale of the stock. P's reliance on D's advice is justified.

(c) **Representations of law [§1652]**
A plaintiff's reliance on the defendant's representations of law is justified when the representation is in the nature of a *fact* (*e.g.*, "the Eighteenth Amendment was repealed yesterday"). However, if the representation constitutes an ***opinion*** (*e.g.*, "the city licensing ordinances should not affect your type of business"), reliance is justified only in the four situations discussed immediately above. [**National Conversion Corp. v. Cedar Building Corp.,** 23 N.Y.2d 621 (1969); Rest. 2d §545]

1) **Distinguish—regulations [§1653]**
There is no duty to disclose the existence of a regulation, because both parties have constructive knowledge of it. [**Baskin v. Collins,** 806 S.W.2d 3 (Ark. 1991)—no cause of action for nondisclosure of federal environmental regulations affecting gas station for sale]

f. **Damages [§1654]**
Unlike most intentional torts, ***proof of actual damages must be shown to obtain any recovery***. The measure of damages is discussed *infra*, §§1678-1683.

WHEN PLAINTIFF MAY RELY ON MISREPRESENTATIONS—A SUMMARY gilbert

TYPE OF REPRESENTATION	WHEN RELIANCE JUSTIFIED
OF FACT	Always justified, except where facts are obviously false.
OF OPINION	***Not*** justified ***unless***: (i) Defendant has a ***superior knowledge*** not available to plaintiff; (ii) Defendant owes plaintiff a ***fiduciary duty***; (iii) Defendant and plaintiff are ***closely related*** or affiliated; or (iv) Defendant ***offers advice*** to plaintiff as to plaintiff's transaction with a third party without disclosing defendant's interest in the deal.
OF LAW	Generally justified when in the nature of a fact, but not justified as to opinion, except as discussed above.

3. Negligent Misrepresentation [§1655]

Prima facie case:

- *Misrepresentation by Defendant*
- *Negligence Toward Particular Group*
- *Cause in Fact—Actual Reliance*
- *Justifiable Reliance*
- *Proximate Cause*
- *Damages*

a. Misrepresentation—made in business or professional capacity [§1656]

The same type of misrepresentation may serve as a basis for an action in negligent misrepresentation as for an action in intentional misrepresentation, above. *Note:* The negligent representation must normally be made ***by one in the business of supplying information for the guidance of others in business transactions*** (*e.g.*, accountants, lawyers, architects, surveyors, title abstractors, etc.). [**Ritter v. Custom Chemicides, Inc.,** 912 S.W.2d 128 (Tenn. 1995)—extending liability beyond statements by "professionals" to cover instructions for growing tomatoes]

---

e.g. **Example:** P is induced to withdraw from participation in a benefit program in reliance on negligent misrepresentation of insurance agent D. [**Florenzano v. Olson,** 387 N.W.2d 168 (Minn. 1986)]

---

(1) Distinguish—information volunteered under nonbusiness conditions [§1657]

If the representation is volunteered in a nonprofessional or noncommercial setting (*e.g.*, "curbstone advice" offered by a lawyer to a neighbor), liability will result only if the statements are ***not honestly made.***

(2) Distinguish—ordinary negligence [§1658]

If an attorney or other professional behaves carelessly, the resulting harm ***need not*** involve any reliance element. An attorney's failure to file suit before the statute of limitations expires, or the drafting of an invalid will that costs an intended legatee her inheritance, may cause harm without any negligent misrepresentation being made and relied on by the plaintiff. (*See infra*, §§1754-1755.)

b. Negligence toward particular plaintiff [§1659]

If the defendant provides information with the intent that the plaintiff rely on it in a business transaction or knows that such reliance is likely, the defendant is under a ***duty to exercise reasonable care*** to discover the truth or falsity of the representations made. [**International Products Co. v. Erie Railroad,** 244 N.Y. 331 (1927)] (Note how different this is from the scienter requirement in intentional misrepresentation, §1637, *supra.*)

(1) To whom duty owed [§1660]

A defendant owes a duty of care only to those persons to whom the representation was made or to those the defendant knew would rely upon it; *i.e.*, the ***defendant must have contemplated the reliance of a particular plaintiff*** or group of persons to which the plaintiff belongs. A duty to avoid negligent misrepresentation may also arise when a party volunteers information. [**Jackson v. Montana,** 956 P.2d 35 (Mont. 1998)—adoption agency assumed duty to refrain from making negligent misrepresentation when it began volunteering information to prospective adoptive parents]

(a) Distinguish—deceit [§1661]

If the action is for ***intentional misrepresentation***, the defendant is liable to any person whose reliance was intended or ***reasonably foreseeable*** (*see supra*, §1643).

(b) Privity of contract not required [§1662]

It is not essential that the plaintiff be in privity of contract with the defendant. Liability may be found where the defendant made a negligent representation to a third person (*e.g.*, client) ***with knowledge*** that the client intended to communicate the information to a ***specific individual or group*** for the purpose of inducing reliance thereon.

---

e.g. **Example:** Public weigher issued certificate to a seller it knew would sell goods to a particular purchaser who would purchase in reliance on the certificate. [**Glanzer v. Shepard,** 233 N.Y. 236 (1922); *but see* **Bronstein v. GZA GeoEnvironmental, Inc.,** 665 A.2d 369 (N.H. 1995)—agreement that report was prepared for exclusive use of only one named person barred others from suing in reliance on information contained in report]

---

(2) Professional liability [§1663]

Although professionals are always liable to clients for negligently prepared reports and documents (*e.g.*, financial statements), there is considerable disagreement as to how far liability may be extended to third parties.

(a) Traditional view [§1664]

Under the traditional view, an accountant was ***not liable to third parties*** for negligently prepared statements unless the relationship between the accountant and the third party was essentially one of privity. [*See* **Ultramares Corp. v. Touche,** 255 N.Y. 170 (1931)—accountants negligently certified corporation's financial statements, knowing that corporation intended to use the statements in dealing with creditors generally, but not knowing the nature of the dealings or identity of particular persons who would be shown the statements]

1) Rationale

The reason behind this limitation is the ***potential consequence*** of imposing a duty of care to third persons—*i.e.*, the concern that the defendant's thoughtless slip in dealing with one person (client) might expose him to "liability in an indeterminate amount for an indeterminate time to an indeterminate class" of other persons. [**Ultramares Corp. v. Touche,** *supra*]

(b) Modern views [§1665]

Recently, courts have become more willing to expand the scope of duty in *Ultramares*-type cases. Three different approaches have emerged:

1) New York ("linkage") view [§1666]

Before an accountant (defendant) may be liable for negligence to a noncontractual party (plaintiff), the defendant must be aware that a known party was intending to rely on the financial statement ***and*** some conduct must link the defendant to the plaintiff in a way that suggests the accountant's willingness to incur a duty to the creditor. [**Security Pacific Business Credit, Inc. v. Peat Marwick Main & Co.,** 79 N.Y.2d 695 (1992)—a single unsolicited phone call to the accountant does not create the needed linkage]

2) California ("specific foreseeability") view [§1667]

An accountant may be held liable if she knows that a specific third party plans to rely on the statement for a transaction whose nature and extent is known to the accountant. [**Bily v. Arthur Young & Co.,** 3 Cal. 4th 370 (1992)—similar to Rest. 2d §552]

3) New Jersey ("general foreseeability") view [§1668]

A very few states hold that an accountant may be liable if the third party (plaintiff) belongs to a class of people who could generally be foreseen to receive and rely on the statement. [**Citizens State Bank v. Timm, Schmidt & Co.,** 335 N.W.2d 361 (Wis. 1983)]

(c) Distinguish—liability based on statute [§1669]

Quite apart from common law negligence, liability to third persons may be based on a defendant's violation of ***statutory*** duties to provide accurate information. Such statutes create a duty to the general public; therefore, it is not necessary to show the defendant's knowledge that a particular plaintiff would rely.

---

e.g. **Example:** An accountant who negligently certifies a financial statement for a large corporate client may be held liable under S.E.C. Rule 10b-5 to any member of the public who purchases or sells the corporate shares in reliance thereon. (*See* Corporations Summary.)

---

c. **Cause in fact (actual reliance)**
See supra, §§415 *et seq.*

d. **Justifiable reliance [§1670]**
This is the same as in intentional misrepresentation (*see supra*, §§1643-1653), except that unreasonable failure to investigate may be ***contributory negligence***.

e. **Proximate cause**
See supra, §§442 *et seq.*

f. **Damages**
See discussion below.

4. **Misrepresentation Predicated on Strict Liability ("Innocent Misrepresentation") [§1671]**
Some courts also impose damages for certain misrepresentations in connection with the ***sale of land or chattels***—even if the falsity was neither known nor the result of negligence. [Rest. 2d §552C; *see, e.g.*, **Rosenau v. City of New Brunswick,** 238 A.2d 169 (N.J. 1968)]

a. **Nature of liability [§1672]**
The basis for liability here is very close to that for breach of express warranty (a contract theory); *i.e.*, having made a warranty as to the thing sold, the seller is bound thereby whether or not he had reason to know of its falsity. Another analogy is unjust enrichment—in which the defendant gets something from the plaintiff without justification.

(1) **But note**
This is clearly ***not*** a contract action; hence, contractual defenses such as the ***parol evidence rule*** (which often excludes verbal warranties made in connection with a written contract of sale) do ***not*** apply.

b. **Prima facie case [§1673]**
The prima facie case is the same as for negligent misrepresentation (*see supra*, §1655), except that there is ***no requirement of fault at all.*** All that need be shown is a ***false representation made with the intent to induce the plaintiff's reliance*** in a business transaction, and the plaintiff's ***justifiable reliance*** thereon to her ***financial detriment*** and to the defendant's gain.

(1) **Distinguish—products liability [§1674]**
Recovery for misrepresentation is limited to pecuniary damages to the plaintiff's ***business interests***. If physical harm has resulted from use or consumption of a product, consider the products liability rules (*see supra*, §§925 *et seq.*). [Rest. 3d-PL §9]

5. **Defenses**

a. **Contributory negligence [§1675]**
Contributory negligence is a defense to ***negligent*** misrepresentation, but ***not*** to

intentional misrepresentation or to misrepresentations pegged on strict liability. [*See, e.g.,* **FDIC v. W.R. Grace & Co.,** 877 F.2d 614 (7th Cir. 1989), *cert. denied*, 494 U.S. 1056 (1990)—contributory negligence not a defense to intentional fraud claim; **Otero v. Jordan Restaurant Enterprises,** 922 P.2d 569 (N.M. 1996)—comparative fault principles inapplicable to intentional misrepresentation claim]

(1) **Note**

Most states apply comparative negligence. [**Greycas, Inc. v. Proud,** *supra,* §1639; *but see* **Estate of Braswell v. People's Credit Union,** 602 A.2d 510 (R.I. 1992)—contra]

b. **Assumption of risk [§1676]**

Assumption of the risk is a defense to both ***strict liability*** misrepresentations and ***negligent*** misrepresentations.

c. **Exculpatory contracts [§1677]**

In most states, exculpatory contracts that seek to exempt one from ***fraud or intentional wrongdoing*** (*e.g.,* "buyer hereby waives any misrepresentations," etc.) are ***void.*** [*See, e.g.,* Cal. Civ. Code §1668; **Silva v. Stevens,** *supra,* §1633—"as is" provision in contract does not bar actions for fraud or for negligent misrepresentation]

(1) **But note**

In a few states, a contract that says the buyer is not relying on the seller's statement will bar a tort claim for fraud [*see, e.g.,* **Danann Realty Corp. v. Harris,** 5 N.Y.2d 317 (1959)], but a general merger clause will not [*see* **Hobart v. Schuler,** 55 N.Y.2d 1023 (1982)].

EXAM TIP **gilbert**

It might not be obvious from a casual reading of the material above, so be sure to note that in most states there are ***no defenses*** to intentional misrepresentation except for negating the existence of the required elements of this tort (*supra,* §1623).

6. **Measure of Damages [§1678]**

The courts are divided over the measure of damages to be awarded in misrepresentation cases, regardless of which basis for liability is involved:

a. **Benefit-of-bargain rule [§1679]**

The majority of courts hold that the plaintiff is entitled to the benefit of the bargain: the ***value*** of the property as ***contracted for*** (*i.e.,* had the representation been true) less the value of the property as it actually was. [*See, e.g.,* **Hartwell Corp. v. Bumb,** 345 F.2d 453 (9th Cir. 1965); **Rungee v. Cox,** 599 So. 2d 1151 (Ala. 1992)]

(1) **Note**

This is basically the same measure as applied in contract actions for breach of warranty. (*See* Contracts Summary.)

(2) **And note**

If the plaintiff is proceeding on an innocent misrepresentation theory, contract-based damages are ***not*** usually permitted because the action is thought of as one similar to restitution.

b. **Out-of-pocket loss rule [§1680]**

A minority view limits the plaintiff's recovery to out-of-pocket loss (the ***price paid*** less the value of the property received) which is a more typical tort measure of compensatory damage.

---

e.g. **Example:** D sells land to P for $10,000, falsely representing that the water well is adequate for irrigation purposes. Without adequate water, the land is worth no more than $7,000. With adequate water, it is realistically worth $15,000. Under the "benefit-of-bargain" rule, P recovers $8,000; whereas under the "out-of-pocket loss" rule, recovery is limited to $3,000.

---

c. **Middle ground positions [§1681]**

A few courts will apply ***either*** rule, making it a question of ***proof***: *i.e.*, if the value of the property as represented is proved to a ***reasonable certainty***, the plaintiff gets the benefit of the bargain; otherwise, the plaintiff can recover only out-of-pocket loss. [*See, e.g.,* **Hinkle v. Rockville Motor Co.,** 278 A.2d 42 (Md. 1971); **Zeliff v. Sabatino,** 104 A.2d 54 (N.J. 1954)]

d. **Emotional distress [§1682]**

Some states allow damages for emotional distress if it is a "natural and proximate" consequence of the misrepresentation. [*See, e.g.,* **Kilduff v. Adams, Inc.,** 593 A.2d 478 (Conn. 1991); *but see* **Jourdain v. Dineen,** 527 A.2d 1304 (Me. 1987)—contra] Some states also require that the emotional distress damages be severe in order to be recoverable. [*See, e.g.,* **Nelson v. Progressive Corp.,** 976 P.2d 859 (Alaska 1999)]

e. **Punitive damages [§1683]**

If the misrepresentation was intentional ***and*** made with "malice" (intent to harm), punitive damages may also be awarded.

(1) **Note**

In states that reject punitive damages, compensatory damages may be awarded "liberally" when the tortious act was "wanton, malicious, or oppressive." [**Crowley v. Global Realty, Inc.,** 474 A.2d 1056 (N.H. 1984)]

B. Injurious Falsehood

1. **Introduction [§1684]**

"Injurious falsehood" covers the tort commonly known as "disparagement," "slander of title," and "trade libel." The gist of this tort is ***interference with the prospect of sale*** or some other advantageous relationship with respect to the plaintiff's ***property***. The property involved may be real or personal, tangible or intangible (cases frequently involve the goodwill of the plaintiff's business). But, as will be seen, the interest protected goes well beyond property. Prima facie case:

- *False Statement by Defendant*
- *Publication to Others*
- *Statement Disparaging Business, Property, Financial Interests, Etc., of Plaintiff*
- *Intent*
- *Causation*
- *Special Damages*

2. False Statement [§1685]

First of all, the plaintiff must always prove that the defendant published the harmful statement and that the statement was in fact *false*.

3. Publication to Third Persons [§1686]

As in defamation cases, the defendant must publish the statement to others. (*See supra*, §§1357 *et seq.*)

a. Form [§1687]

Note that the disparaging statements may be ***oral or written***; *i.e.*, a "slander of title" may be in writing, and a "trade libel" may be oral.

4. Statement Disparaging Plaintiff's Business, Property, Etc. [§1688]

A statement is "disparaging" if it is ***reasonably likely to discourage others from dealing with the plaintiff*** or otherwise interferes with the plaintiff's relations with others to the plaintiff's disadvantage. (The interest in noncommercial expectancies, such as anticipation of a legacy, is discussed *infra,* §1748.)

a. Statements denying plaintiff's ownership ("slander of title") [§1689]

A statement that casts reasonable doubt on the validity or extent of the plaintiff's title is clearly a disparagement. These are the cases commonly known as ***"slanders of title."*** [**New England Oil & Pipe Line Co. v. Rogers,** 7 P.2d 638 (Okla. 1931); Rest. 2d §624]

---

e.g. **Examples:** These include recording a document falsely asserting an interest in P's property (thus denying that P has the entire ownership); or asserting that title to P's land is "clouded," or that anyone buying it is "buying a lawsuit." [**Phillips v. Glazer,** 94 Cal. App. 2d 673 (1949)]

---

b. Statements denying quality of plaintiff's property ("trade libel") [§1690]

Statements attacking the quality of the plaintiff's property (land, chattels, etc.), such that they would reasonably deter another from dealing with her, may be actionable as a disparagement. Such cases are commonly referred to as ***"trade libels."*** [Rest. 2d §626]

 **Examples:** Statements referring to P's merchandise as "seconds," "prison-made," or "defective" are disparaging statements of fact.

c. **Statements derogatory of plaintiff's business in general ("trade libel") [§1691]**
Cases often involve statements that are derogatory of the plaintiff's business or the manner in which it is conducted, without necessarily reflecting on the title or quality of any particular property (*e.g.*, statements that service in the plaintiff's restaurant is "poor," that its customers are "ruffians," etc.).

Example: A common case is the false assertion that the sale of the plaintiff's product infringes some patent or copyright. [**Dale System, Inc. v. Time, Inc.**, 116 F. Supp. 527 (D. Conn. 1953)—claiming D's business is "unique" is not sufficient for action by D's competitor]

d. **Statements interfering with nonbusiness relations [§1692]**
Several courts have permitted actions for injurious statements that did not affect any commercial enterprise.

Example: D may be liable for giving immigration officials false information about P's citizenship that results in efforts to deport P. [**Al Raschid v. News Syndicate Co.**, 265 N.Y. 1 (1934)]

e. **Statement need not be defamatory [§1693]**
The defendant's statement need not be defamatory as long as it is false.

Example: A false statement made to a potential customer that "P is dead (or out of business), so buy your goods from me" is not defamatory of P, but certainly is a trade libel—an "injurious falsehood."

(1) **Distinguish—defamatory statement [§1694]**
On the other hand, if the statement imputes fraud or dishonesty to the company manufacturing the product ("Ajax soap is a hoax; it isn't as pure as advertised"), it may be defamatory of the manufacturer (because harmful to reputation) as well as a trade libel.

(2) **Comment**
Although it can be argued that nearly every imputation against a business or its product implies some personal inefficiency or incompetence on the part of the manufacturer or owner of the business, thus suggesting defamation in every case, the courts refuse to go this far; *i.e.*, defamation is found only where the imputation is of fraud or dishonesty, rather than mere ignorance or negligence. [**Shaw Cleaners & Dyers, Inc. v. Des Moines Dress Club**, 245 N.W. 231 (Iowa 1932)—dry cleaner not defamed by charge that garments only "half-cleaned"]

5. **Intent [§1695]**

The general view requires simply an ***intent to disparage***—*i.e.*, to cast doubt on the plaintiff's property.

a. **Motive immaterial [§1696]**

It is not necessary to show that the defendant was motivated by malice or ill will toward the plaintiff, or was hoping to discourage some third person from dealing with the plaintiff. [**Gudger v. Manton,** 21 Cal. 2d 537 (1943); Rest. 2d §623A]

b. **Scienter [§1697]**

The modern view requires the plaintiff to show that the defendant knew that his statements were false, or that he did not have enough knowledge either way to make the statement. [Rest. 2d §623A(b)—D must "know" the statement is false or act in "reckless disregard of its truth or falsity"]

c. **Negligent falsity [§1698]**

Even though negligent falsity may not suffice here, note that such a statement may be actionable if it meets the negligent misrepresentation requirements (*see supra*, §1655).

6. **Causation and Damages [§1699]**

The usual requirement of actual and proximate causation exists. However, unlike defamation, where general damages are sometimes recoverable without a showing of pecuniary loss (*see supra*, §§1434, 1443), here the plaintiff must ***always*** prove proximately caused ***special damages***—actual, out-of-pocket, pecuniary damages.

a. **Slander of title [§1700]**

The usual damages in slander of title cases are ***loss of profits*** on a contemplated sale of property ***and*** costs of legal proceedings to remove the cloud on the plaintiff's title.

b. **Trade libel [§1701]**

Typical damages in trade libel cases are ***loss of profits*** from specific sales to identifiable customers rather than a general decline in business resulting from the falsehood. [**Waste Distillation Technology, Inc. v. Blasland & Bouck Engineers, P.C.,** 136 A.D.2d 633 (1988)—need special damages] Where this showing is impossible, courts may permit the plaintiff to recover on a showing of general decline in business. [**Dale System, Inc. v. Time, Inc.,** *supra*, §1691]

(1) **Note**

In most states, ***consequential damages*** (*e.g.*, loss of business that forced plaintiff to close her doors or go into bankruptcy) are ***not recoverable***. Neither are parasitic damages (*e.g.*, for mental distress). [**Collier County Publishing Co. v. Chapman,** 318 So. 2d 492 (Fla. 1975)—no damages for emotional distress]

7. Defenses

a. Consent [§1702]

Consent is a defense to injurious falsehood as with any intentional tort. (*See supra*, §100.)

b. Truth [§1703]

The falsity of the disparagement is an element of the prima facie case to be proved by the plaintiff. Hence, it is not necessary to consider truth as a defense, because unless the matter is shown to be false, the plaintiff has not proved a prima facie case. [Rest. 2d §634]

c. Privilege [§1704]

The ***same privileges to defamation*** are recognized as privileges to disparagement (*see supra*, §§1453 *et seq.*). [Rest. 2d §§635, 646A]

(1) Judicial proceedings [§1705]

The recording of a "lis pendens" (notice of lawsuit pending that may affect title to property) in the county recorder's office, which may cloud title to real property, is treated as part of the judicial proceeding and hence is absolutely privileged. [*See, e.g.,* **Zamarello v. Yale,** 514 P.2d 228 (Alaska 1973)]

(a) But note

If this is done maliciously, an action for malicious proceedings may lie (*see infra*, §§1778-1786).

(2) Protection of private interests [§1706]

A privilege of particular importance in disparagement cases is the ***conditional*** privilege to defame or disparage in protecting one's own interests or the interests of another.

(a) Privilege of competitors [§1707]

If the defendant and the plaintiff are competitors, the defendant is privileged to make general claims about ***his own*** product, even if false. However, the privilege does ***not*** extend to making specific false claims about the plaintiff's property or business. [Rest. 2d §649]

---

e.g. **Example:** D is privileged to claim that his product is "finer," of "higher quality" or performs "better than" P's—even if D does not honestly believe what he is saying. This is similar to the "puffing" discussed *supra*, §1648.

---

cf. **Compare:** There is no privilege if D falsely states that P's goods are "seconds," or "prison-made," or contain impurities. [*See, e.g.,* **National Refining Co. v. Benzo Gas Motor Fuel Co.,** 20 F.2d 763 (8th Cir. 1927)]

EXAM TIP **gilbert**

Be sure to remember the interesting difference depending on the subject of the lie: One may not lie about the quality of a competitor's goods, but one is privileged to lie or embellish characteristics of one's own goods (or at least such lies will not give rise to a ***competitor's*** action for injurious falsehood—it may, however, give customers an action for misrepresentation; *see supra*, §§1623 *et seq.*).

(b) **Noncompetitors [§1708]**

If the defendant and the plaintiff are ***not*** competitors, the defendant is generally protected if he honestly believes the truth of his statement and was speaking in any of the situations in which defamation would afford a privilege (*e.g.*, response to inquiry, protection of others, etc.). [Rest. 2d §646A]

e.g. **Examples:** Reports by a consumers' research organization commenting on new products on the market, or by doctors evaluating new drugs, are uniformly held to be privileged if made ***in good faith***.

1) **Constitutional protection [§1709]**

The constitutional privileges of libel law may apply here by analogy. [*See* **Bose Corp. v. Consumers Union**, *supra*, §1529]

C. Interference with Economic Relations

1. **Introduction [§1710]**

Tort liability has also been imposed for ***intentional*** interference with the plaintiff's existing or prospective economic relationship with third persons, thereby protecting the plaintiff's interest in stabilizing his contract relations and expectations. Note that this is an area of still-emerging principles; most of the cases are of recent origin, reflecting development of social and economic policies in these areas. Recently, negligence principles have begun to emerge in specific situations. The two generally recognized facets of this theory of liability are: interference with contract and interference with prospective advantage.

2. **Interference with Contract [§1711]**

Prima facie case:

- ***Defendant's Interference with Existing Contract***
- ***Intent***
- ***Causation***
- ***Special Damages***

a. **Nature of contract [§1712]**

This tort was first recognized in the master-servant relationship; *i.e.*, a third person who induced a servant to quit the master's employ might be held liable to the master in tort for loss of the servant's services. In the leading case of **Lumley v. Gye,** 118 Eng. Rep. 749 (1853), the doctrine was expanded to hold a defendant liable for inducing an opera star to breach her contract to sing at a particular opera house. Today, the tort can apply to ***any*** type of valid contract (except contracts to marry—as to which there generally is no tort liability for inducing breach). [*See, e.g.,* **Brown v. Glickstein,** 107 N.E.2d 267 (Ill. 1952); **Kenty v. Transamerica Premium Insurance Co.,** 650 N.E.2d 863 (Ohio 1995)—recognizing action against insurer; **Adler, Barish, Daniels, Levin & Creskoff v. Epstein,** 393 A.2d 1175 (Pa. 1978)—action by company against former employees seeking to enjoin them from luring away company's clients]

(1) **Illegal contracts [§1713]**

Contracts that are illegal or contrary to public policy do not qualify for protection because the law will not aid in upholding them. [*See, e.g.,* **Fairbanks, Morse & Co. v. Texas Electric Service Co.,** 63 F.2d 702 (5th Cir. 1933)—contract violative of antitrust laws]

(2) **Unenforceable contracts [§1714]**

However, the original contract need ***not*** have been enforceable by the plaintiff (or against him). The gist of the tort is the interference with the existing ***relationship***—not the contract.

---

e.g. **Example:** Tort liability has been imposed even where the original contract was unenforceable because of the Statute of Frauds, lack of consideration, lack of mutuality, or even uncertainty as to its terms. [*See, e.g.,* **Childress v. Abeles,** 84 S.E.2d 176 (N.C. 1954)]

(a) **But note**

A few courts refuse to protect some of these contracts. [*See, e.g.,* **Guard-Life Corp. v. S. Parker Hardware Manufacturing Corp.,** 50 N.Y.2d 183 (1980)—refusing to protect unenforceable exclusive dealership relation; **Travel Masters, Inc. v. Star Tours, Inc.,** 827 S.W.2d 830 (Tex. 1991)—covenant not to compete cannot form the basis of a tortious interference with contract claim if covenant was unenforceable]

(3) **Contracts terminable at will [§1715]**

Although some authorities refuse to impose tort liability for interfering with contracts that are terminable by either party at will, the general view is contrary. It is the ***relationship*** (rather than the particular contract) that is being interfered with, and the relationship might have continued ***but for*** the defendant's conduct. [*See, e.g.,* **Childress v. Abeles,** *supra*; **Sterner v. Marathon Oil Co.,** 767 S.W.2d 686 (Tex. 1989)]

(a) **Note**

The possibility of termination does bear upon the issue of the ***damages*** sustained, as well as the issue of defendant's ***privilege*** to interfere (*see* below). [**Scott v. Prudential Outfitting Co.,** 92 Misc. 195 (1915)]

b. **Defendant's interference [§1716]**

The defendant must play some ***active role*** in causing the interference. For example, it is not enough that the defendant accepted an offer from the party with whom the plaintiff had been dealing, even if the defendant had knowledge of the plaintiff's relationship with that party. [Rest. 2d §766]

(1) **Breach not required [§1717]**

Note that the defendant does not have to be shown to have induced a ***breach*** of the plaintiff's contract. All that must appear is that the defendant has prevented performance or made the performance more difficult and onerous.

---

e.g. **Examples:** D deliberately damages a highway that P is under contract to maintain and repair; D prevents X from performing his contract to supply P with goods by calling a strike among X's workers; D threatens P's employees with bodily harm if they continue working for P. [*See* **Snow v. West,** 440 P.2d 864 (Or. 1968)]

---

(2) **Collective action [§1718]**

A difficult case is the effect of ***concerted action*** by a number of individuals to do that which any one of them might be free to do alone (*e.g.*, refusal to deal, boycotts, etc.). This is the crux of the problem in collective refusals on the part of labor unions or trade associations to deal with the plaintiff, resulting in strikes, etc. (*See* Labor Law Summary.)

(3) **Whether defendant may be a party**

(a) **General rule—party not liable [§1719]**

No action for interference with contract lies against a ***party*** to that contract. [*See, e.g.,* **Morrow v. L.A. Goldschmidt Associates,** 492 N.E.2d 181 (Ill. 1986)]

(b) **Exceptions**

1) **Officer acting on own behalf [§1720]**

A corporate officer acting for his own benefit may be liable for inducing the corporation to breach its contract with the plaintiff. [*See, e.g.,* **Olympic Fish Products, Inc. v. Lloyd,** 611 P.2d 737 (Wash. 1980)]

2) Minority allows action for tortious breach of contract [§1721]
A few states permit one party to a contract to sue the other party in tort for a breach motivated by some interest other than the contract relationship, such as to help the defendant acquire a competitive benefit over the plaintiff in some other matter. [*See* **Charles v. Onondaga Community College,** 69 A.D.2d 144 (1979)]

a) Parties in fiduciary relationship [§1722]
Some states recognize a tort action for breach of implied covenant of good faith and fair dealing where there is a ***special relationship*** between the contracting parties, such as where an insurer unreasonably withholds payments from the insured [**Gruenberg v. Aetna Insurance Co.,** 9 Cal. 3d 566 (1973)]; or where an employer unreasonably withholds monthly payments from an elderly employee [**Wallis v. Superior Court,** 160 Cal. App. 3d 1109 (1984)]. Other states, however, disagree and will award damages only for breach of contract, even where there is a fiduciary relationship between the parties. [*See, e.g.,* **Farris v. United States Fidelity & Guaranty Co.,** 587 P.2d 1015 (Or. 1978)]

3) Majority allows suit for wrongful discharge [§1723]
The modern and majority view is that a tort action lies for discharging the plaintiff for an ***improper reason*** even though the hiring was at will. [*See, e.g.,* **Mapco, Inc. v. Payne,** 812 S.W.2d 483 (Ark. 1991)—employer liable for refusing to rehire employee after she filed for workers' compensation against employer; **Tameny v. Atlantic Richfield Co.,** 27 Cal. 3d 167 (1980)—firing P for refusal to participate in illegal price fixing scheme is actionable; **Gardner v. Loomis Armored Inc.,** 913 P.2d 377 (Wash. 1996)—employer could not terminate at-will driver of armored car who violated company policy by leaving car to save woman from life-threatening hostage situation; *but see* **DeMarco v. Publix Super Markets, Inc.,** 384 So. 2d 1253 (Fla. 1980)—firing P because a relative filed a personal injury suit against D is not actionable]

c. Intent [§1724]
It must be shown that the defendant acted with an awareness of the existing contract, and that she ***intended to cause the interference*** that proximately resulted from her conduct. The cases have refused to impose liability for mere ***negligent*** interference with contractual relationships. [*See, e.g.,* **Robins Dry Dock & Repair Co. v. Flint,** 275 U.S. 303 (1927)]

(1) Master-servant cases [§1725]
Although at common law, a master could recover for loss of the ***services of***

his servant if the servant had been injured by the defendant's negligence, most courts have rejected such an action. [*See, e.g.,* **Hartridge v. State Farm Mutual Automobile Insurance Co.,** 271 N.W.2d 598 (Wis. 1978)—clinic has no action for loss ***it*** suffered when its employee was negligently injured]

d. Causation and damages [§1726]

There is the usual requirement of actual and proximate causation and damages.

(1) Types of damages recoverable [§1727]

The modern view seems to allow recovery for all actual damages, consequential damages (unforeseen expenses), mental suffering, damage to reputation, and punitive damages in appropriate cases. [*See, e.g.,* **D'Andrea v. Calcagni,** 723 A.2d 276 (R.I. 1999)]

(2) Offset recovery for breach of contract [§1728]

The fact that the plaintiff may have an action against the party who breaches the contract does ***not*** bar the plaintiff's claim against the defendant for inducing the breach. The two are joint wrongdoers, and each may be liable for the loss (the defendant may be liable in tort, and the other in contract). However, any ***recovery*** against the breaching party must be offset against the damages recoverable from the defendant who induced the breach.

e. Defenses—privilege [§1729]

The principal defense to this tort is one of privilege; *i.e.*, the defendant will not be liable if there was ***proper justification*** for the interference ***and*** only ***reasonable methods*** were employed. This requires proof that ***both the ends and the means*** were justifiable.

(1) Ends [§1730]

The privilege may arise from acts undertaken for a social good or to protect the defendant's own interests.

(a) Furtherance of nonpersonal interests [§1731]

Claims of privilege are generally upheld if the defendant was acting for a social good (*e.g.*, D attempts to exclude a diseased youngster from school that her child attends), or to protect a third person's interest (*e.g.*, attorney's sincere advice to client not to deal with plaintiff). [*See, e.g.,* **Southwestern Bell Telephone Co. v. John Carlo Texas, Inc.,** 843 S.W.2d 470 (Tex. 1992)]

1) Mixed motive does not defeat privilege [§1732]

The defendant's privilege is not defeated where part of the defendant's motive for interference with the plaintiff's contractual relations is personal ill will, if the predominant motive is a legitimate safety concern. [*See, e.g.*, **Hatten v. Union Oil Co.**, 778 P.2d 1150 (Alaska 1989)]

(b) Furtherance of defendant's own financial interest [§1733]

If the defendant is acting to further her own interests, any claim of privilege will turn on whether she is seeking to protect ***existing*** economic interests or merely a ***prospective*** advantage.

1) Protecting present interest [§1734]

If the defendant has a present contract of her own with one of the parties, she is privileged to prevent the performance of another contract that threatens hers.

---

e.g. **Example:** If D induces debtor X to pay off the bills owed to D, thereby rendering X unable to perform X's contract with P, D is ***not*** liable for inducing breach of the P-X contract. [**Personal Preference Video, Inc. v. Home Box Office, Inc.**, 986 F.2d 110 (5th Cir. 1993)]

---

2) Protecting prospective advantage [§1735]

On the other hand, if the defendant has no existing relationship with either of the contracting parties and induces the breach solely to further her own business (*e.g.*, hiring away plaintiff's best employees, inducing plaintiff's suppliers not to supply, etc.), the defendant's purpose is ***not*** protected and generally no privilege is recognized.

a) Exception—contracts terminable at will [§1736]

The privilege to compete (and of employees to better themselves, etc.) takes precedence over the expectancy that an at-will contract will continue. Therefore, courts generally hold that one competitor ***is*** privileged to induce third persons (employees, suppliers, customers) to terminate contracts that they had with a competitor where such contracts were terminable at will. [*See, e.g.*, **Diodes, Inc. v. Franzen**, 260 Cal. App. 2d 244 (1968)]

(2) Means [§1737]

Even if the interference is for a justifiable purpose, the defendant is never privileged to use unethical or wrongful means. Thus, violence, lies, bribery, or extortion will defeat the privilege.

(a) Threats of "economic persuasion" [§1738]

Difficult cases involve threats of "economic persuasion"—*e.g.*, where

D threatens that she will not deal with X unless X severs all dealings with P. Such cases are generally analyzed on their own facts; *i.e.*, the more unreasonable and coercive the threat is under the circumstances, the more likely that it will defeat the privilege.

(b) **Other torts [§1739]**

If improper means are in fact used, always consider the possibility of other tort liability.

---

e.g. **Example:** If D induces X to discontinue dealing with P because "P's business is run by organized crime," D may be liable for defamation and injurious falsehood, as well as wrongful interference with P's contractual relations.

---

(3) **Burden of proof [§1740]**

Although most courts have held that the defendant must establish a proper justification for the challenged behavior [**Sterner v. Marathon Oil Co.,** *supra*, §1715], most courts have also held that the plaintiff must allege and prove that the defendant's conduct was "wrongful" by showing more than only the interference itself [**Della Penna v. Toyota Motor Sales, U.S.A., Inc.,** 11 Cal. 4th 376 (1995)].

3. **Intentional Interference with Prospective Economic Advantage [§1741]**

By analogy to interference with existing contractual relations, tort liability has been imposed for intentional interference with ***prospective*** economic advantage—*i.e.*, where there is no existing contract. [*See, e.g.,* **Los Angeles Airways, Inc. v. Davis,** 687 F.2d 321 (9th Cir. 1982)] The right being protected is the right to ***pursue*** business without unjustifiable interference. [**Printing Mart-Morristown v. Sharp Electronics Corp.,** 563 A.2d 31 (N.J. 1989)—tampering with bidding process so that plaintiff would not be awarded contract]

a. **Prima facie case [§1742]**

The prima facie case is virtually the same as with interference with contract (*see supra*, §1711), except that ***no existing contractual relationship*** need be shown.

(1) **Defendant's act [§1743]**

The interfering act consists of (i) inducing a third party not to enter into a prospective relationship with the plaintiff, or (ii) preventing the plaintiff from acquiring the prospective relationship. [Rest. 2d §766B] States disagree about whether the plaintiff must show that the interference was "wrongful" in addition to showing the interference itself. The modern view requires such a showing. [**Della Penna v. Toyota Motor Sales, U.S.A., Inc.,** *supra*]

(2) **Defendant not a party [§1744]**

As with interference with contract, the defendant need not be a party to the prospective economic relationship.

Example: An employee, acting to undermine the prospective relationship between his employer and the plaintiff, may be liable. [*See* **Printing Mart-Morristown v. Sharp Electronics Corp.,** *supra*—deferring question]

---

b. **Privilege [§1745]**
The chief difference between actions for interference with prospective advantage and interference with contract lies in recognition of ***more extensive privileges*** where the parties are competitors and there is no contract. (To the extent that courts insist that the plaintiff show an independent wrong as part of the prima facie case, *supra*, §1742, the role of privilege is reduced.)

Example: D is privileged to use any ***bona fide competitive means*** to solicit customers for herself before they enter into a contract with P.

---

(1) **Loss of privilege [§1746]**
As before, to the extent that the defendant uses unlawful or tortious means, she loses the privilege—and may be liable for unfair competition (*see* Remedies Summary). [*See, e.g.,* **Tuttle v. Buck,** 119 N.W. 946 (Minn. 1909)]

(a) **Exception—testimony [§1747]**
A special rule protects perjurers whose lies under oath are intended to and do cause harm to the plaintiff. To encourage witnesses to testify and to do so fully, they are absolutely protected against suits by unhappy litigants. [*See, e.g.,* **Cooper v. Parker-Hughey,** 894 P.2d 1096 (Okla. 1995)]

c. **Distinguish—interference with noncommercial expectancies (prospective gifts, etc.) [§1748]**
The modern trend is to allow recovery for wrongful interference with noncommercial expectancies—at least where there is a strong probability that they would have been realized. [Rest. 2d §774B]

Example: Tort recovery has been allowed where D, by use of fraud, ***induces a testator to disinherit P***—if there is strong evidence that the testator otherwise would not have done so. [*See, e.g.,* **Bohannon v. Wachovia Bank & Trust Co.,** 188 S.E. 390 (N.C. 1936)] The falsehood may either attack P or enhance D.

---

(1) **Action survives prospective donor's death [§1749]**
If the defendant fraudulently causes a donor to convey property to the defendant, and the donor intended the plaintiff to be a legatee of that property, the plaintiff may sue the defendant for wrongful interference with his intended legacy whether or not the donor is still alive. [*See, e.g.,* **Plimpton v. Gerrard,** 668 A.2d 882 (Me. 1995)]

(2) **No liability for interference with contest [§1750]**
Courts have refused to impose liability for interference in the context of sporting contests, such as horse racing. In addition to the difficulty of establishing a reasonable probability of winning, these sports are governed by other regulatory bodies, and allowance of claims would flood the courts with disgruntled losers. [*See, e.g.,* **Youst v. Longo,** 43 Cal. 3d 64 (1987)—no recovery against jockey who caused plaintiff's horse to break stride during race]

4. Negligent Interference with Prospective Economic Advantage [§1751]

Prima facie case:

- *Duty of Due Care*
- *Breach of Duty*
- *Causation*
- *Damages*

a. Duty [§1752]

Duty is the crucial issue. Generally, the plaintiff's interest in protection from economic harm has been considered too remote for the imposition of a duty of due care. [*See* **Robins Dry Dock & Repair Co. v. Flint,** *supra,* §1724]

(1) **Distinguish—misrepresentation [§1753]**
If the defendant's negligence has taken the form of misrepresentation upon which the plaintiff has relied, courts have imposed a duty on the defendants who are in the business of supplying information. (*See supra,* §1656.) Even there, however, the courts impose limits based on the nature of the transaction and the foreseeability that the plaintiff would rely. (*See supra,* §§1657, 1659 *et seq.*)

(2) **Modern trend [§1754]**
Because the defendant's negligence may cause economic harm to the plaintiff even though the plaintiff has never met or relied on the defendant, some courts are imposing a duty of care where the defendant can ***reasonably foresee*** harm to the specific plaintiff. [*See, e.g.,* **Simpson v. Calivas,** 650 A.2d 318 (N.H. 1994)—attorney cost P an inheritance by preparing T's will improperly]

(a) **Attorney liability [§1755]**
Most courts hold that attorneys may owe duties of due care to persons other than their clients in a negotiated deal. [*See, e.g.,* **Prudential Insurance Co. v. Dewey, Ballantine, Bushby, Palmer & Wood,** 80 N.Y.2d 377 (1992); *but see* **Goodman v. Kennedy,** 18 Cal. 3d 335 (1976)—attorney must provide undiluted advice to client and should not incur any duties toward those with whom client is dealing, even though they are identified]

(3) **Limitation [§1756]**

As in the professional cases (*supra*, §1663), courts here are concerned about extending a general duty of care to a large undefined group of plaintiffs. The result is the denial of a duty of care unless the defendant knows that her conduct will affect a pinpointed plaintiff. [*See, e.g.*, ***In re* Kinsman Transit Co. (No. 2)**, 388 F.2d 821 (2d Cir. 1968)—no liability after river accident to those who sustained solely economic burdens because damaged bridge made commercial activities more expensive; **Phoenix Professional Hockey Club, Inc. v. Hirmer,** 502 P.2d 164 (Ariz. 1972)—no liability on negligent driver who cost P money by running over P's hockey goalie; **Milliken & Co. v. Consolidated Edison Co.,** 84 N.Y.2d 469 (1994)—tenant lacking direct contractual relation with utility could not sue for economic losses suffered due to utility's negligence; *but see* **Union Oil Co. v. Oppen,** 501 F.2d 558 (9th Cir. 1974)—commercial fishermen may recover for income loss caused by D's oil spill; **People Express Airlines, Inc. v. Consolidated Rail Corp.,** *supra,* §789—airline may recover for damage caused by evacuation of terminal due to D's negligence]

b. **Other elements [§1757]**

Once duty is found, the other elements are analyzed as in regular negligence cases (*see supra*, §§276 *et seq.*). This may include the need for expert testimony to establish breach. [**Jim Mitchell & Jed Davis, P.A. v. Jackson,** 627 A.2d 1014 (Me. 1993), *cert. denied*, 510 U.S. 1081 (1994)—need expert where attorney refused to file complaint without having proof to support it]

D. Unjustifiable Litigation

1. **Introduction [§1758]**

Unjustifiable litigation includes several distinct torts involving the plaintiff's interest in freedom from unjustifiable legal proceedings.

2. **Malicious Prosecution [§1759]**

The tort of malicious prosecution concerns the wrongful institution of ***criminal proceedings*** by one private citizen against another, resulting in damage. Prima facie case:

- *Instigation of Criminal Proceedings by Defendant*
- *Proceedings Terminated Showing Plaintiff Not Guilty*
- *Lack of Probable Cause*
- *Improper Purpose*

a. **Distinguish—false imprisonment [§1760]**

Malicious prosecution must be distinguished from false imprisonment in several particulars. False imprisonment lies only where the ***arrest*** is "false"—in the sense that there was ***no valid process*** for the arrest (*i.e.*, no valid arrest warrant or no probable cause to arrest without a warrant). On the other hand, malicious prosecution lies where there has been a valid arrest but an ***improper purpose in instigating*** the criminal proceeding (*e.g.*, groundless charges by the defendant to the police, leading them to arrest the plaintiff). Furthermore, false imprisonment does not require any showing of malice or lack of probable cause to believe that the charges against the plaintiff are true; but these are essential elements of malicious prosecution.

b. Instigation of proceedings by defendant [§1761]

Criminal proceedings must be initiated by a charge made to the police or other public officials in such form as to cause the issuance of a warrant or indictment against the accused.

(1) Procuring another to institute proceedings [§1762]

One who procures or is instrumental in causing a third person (police) to institute a prosecution is liable just as if he instituted it himself. [Rest. 2d §653]

(2) Distinguish—merely providing information [§1763]

But one who provides full and truthful incriminating information to a public officer and leaves the decision to that officer has not initiated the proceeding. [**McHale v. W.B.S. Corp.,** 446 A.2d 815 (Conn. 1982)]

EXAM TIP **gilbert**

Remember this distinction: If you call the police, tell them you want your neighbor arrested, and make up some facts to encourage the police to make an arrest, you can be liable for malicious prosecution even though it is the police who make the arrest. On the other hand, if the police ***knock at your door***, ask you questions about your neighbor, and you provide them with ***truthful information*** that leads them to arrest your neighbor, no action for malicious prosecution will lie against you, even if your neighbor is found not guilty.

c. Proceedings terminated favorably to plaintiff [§1764]

A plaintiff must allege and prove that the criminal proceeding was terminated in a manner indicating his ***innocence***.

(1) Decisive termination [§1765]

This generally requires some sort of a decisive termination—*e.g.*, acquittal after trial, dismissal of the case by a magistrate at the preliminary hearing for lack of evidence, grand jury refusal to indict, etc. Conversely, a termination that is indecisive or consistent with guilt is not sufficient—*e.g.*, where the proceeding is dismissed on technical, procedural grounds or as an act of grace; or because of the impossibility of bringing the accused to trial; or a plea bargain. [Rest. 2d §660; *see, e.g.,* **Swick v. Liautaud,** 662

N.E.2d 1238 (Ill. 1996)—because dismissal of criminal case on nolle prosequi is ambiguous, plaintiff must show favorable termination; **Ward v. Silverberg,** 85 N.Y.2d 993 (1995)—termination in criminal defendant's favor where charges dismissed "on consent" after colloquy between court and counsel]

d. Lack of probable cause [§1766]

The plaintiff must also show that the defendant instituted the proceedings without probable cause—*i.e.*, that the defendant had ***no honest and reasonable belief*** in the truth of the charge.

(1) Objective standard [§1767]

Attorneys are not liable for malicious prosecution if they pursued a claim that a reasonable attorney would have considered tenable. Courts use this standard to avoid the chilling effect on reporting crime or bringing a civil claim that would follow from the use of a subjective standard. [*See, e.g.,* **Sheldon Appel Co. v. Albert & Oliker,** 47 Cal. 3d 863 (1989)]

(2) Proof—cannot be inferred from improper purpose [§1768]

Lack of probable cause must be proved ***independently*** from the improper purpose requirement (below), because even a person acting from improper motives may know of facts that give rise to a reasonable and honest belief of guilt.

(3) Application [§1769]

Because of its complex nature, the question of probable cause is usually decided by the court. [Rest. 2d 673(1)(c); *see, e.g.,* **Slade v. City of Phoenix,** 541 P.2d 550 (Ariz. 1975); *but see* **Hodges v. Gibson Products Co.,** 811 P.2d 151 (Utah 1991)—contra]

(a) Effect of indictment or commitment by magistrate [§1770]

The fact that the plaintiff was held to answer by the committing magistrate after a preliminary hearing, or was indicted by a grand jury, is ***prima facie evidence*** of probable cause. [Rest. 2d §663; *see, e.g.,* **Colon v. City of New York,** 60 N.Y.2d 78 (1983)—indictment creates presumption of probable cause rebuttable only by showing fraud, perjury, or suppression of evidence]

(b) Effect of conviction [§1771]

Where the plaintiff was actually convicted without fraud, perjury, or other corruption, probable cause is ***conclusively*** established—even if the conviction is later overturned on appeal. *Rationale:* If a jury or trial judge was satisfied of guilt beyond a reasonable doubt, it can hardly be denied that the accuser had reasonable grounds in making the charges. [*See, e.g.,* **Hanson v. City of Snohomish,** 852 P.2d 295 (Wash. 1993)]

1) **But note**

A minority view treats the conviction as creating only a ***presumption*** of probable cause. [*See, e.g.,* **MacRae v. Brant,** 230 A.2d 753 (N.H. 1967)]

(c) **Effect of advice of counsel [§1772]**

Reliance on advice of counsel will also ***conclusively*** establish probable cause, provided there was a ***full*** disclosure of the facts to the attorney and a resulting honest belief in the guilt of the injured party. [Rest. 2d §666; *see, e.g.,* **Boshell v. Walker County Sheriff,** 598 So. 2d 843 (Ala. 1992); **Kaarup v. St. Paul Fire & Marine Insurance Co.,** 485 N.W.2d 802 (S.D. 1992)]

e. **Improper purpose [§1773]**

It must appear that the defendant instituted the proceeding for some ***improper purpose***, some motive other than bringing a guilty person to justice. This is sometimes called "malice."

(1) **Proof—can be inferred from lack of probable cause [§1774]**

Although lack of probable cause cannot be inferred from improper purpose, improper purpose ***may*** be inferred from lack of probable cause. [Rest. 2d §669]

f. **Causation and damages [§1775]**

The plaintiff may recover all expenses incurred in defending against the criminal prosecution (*e.g.*, attorney's fees, investigative expenses, court costs, etc.). The plaintiff may also recover damages for mental suffering and embarrassment, harm to reputation, damage to business, etc., as well as punitive damages in appropriate cases.

g. **Defenses**

(1) **Plaintiff's guilt [§1776]**

Notwithstanding the termination of criminal proceedings favorable to the plaintiff, the defendant may show as a defense that the plaintiff really ***was*** guilty of the crime. The acquittal in the criminal proceedings only establishes that the state could not prove the plaintiff's guilt "beyond a reasonable doubt," whereas in the civil tort proceedings, the standard of proof is only a "preponderance of the evidence." [*See, e.g.,* **Shoemaker v. Selnes,** 349 P.2d 473 (Or. 1960); Rest. 2d §657]

EXAM TIP **gilbert**

It is important to remember that just because a person is found not guilty in a ***criminal trial*** does ***not*** mean that he can't be found liable in tort litigation. The different standards of proof required in the proceedings (proof beyond reasonable doubt in the criminal proceeding vs. a preponderance of the evidence in the civil proceeding) can make a difference in result.

(2) **Privilege [§1777]**
Judges, prosecutors, and various other law enforcement officers are ***absolutely privileged and immune*** from charges of malicious prosecution.

3. **Malicious Institution of Civil Proceedings [§1778]**
Many states extend the concept of malicious prosecution to ***civil proceedings*** as well. The basic elements are the same as those in actions based on malicious criminal proceedings, and the same types of damages may be recovered. [*See, e.g.,* **Cisson v. Pickens Savings & Loan Association,** 186 S.E.2d 822 (S.C. 1972)] However, a large minority rejects this action in order to encourage resort to the courts to settle disputes.

a. **Nature of proceedings [§1779]**
The tort extends to any form of noncriminal proceedings—including administrative hearings, insanity or narcotics commitment proceedings, etc.

(1) **Lis pendens [§1780]**
An action may be maintained for malicious institution of civil proceedings where the damage complained of results solely from the recordation of a lis pendens (notice of lawsuit pending that may affect title to property)—even though the notice itself would be absolutely ***privileged*** insofar as ***slander of title*** is concerned (*see supra*, §1705).

(2) **Small claims proceeding [§1781]**
A small claims court proceeding, even if maliciously instituted, may ***not*** be the basis of a suit. Such proceedings are too inexpensive and informal to cause any real damage. [*See, e.g.,* **Pace v. Hillcrest Motor Co.,** 101 Cal. App. 3d 476 (1980)]

(3) **Governmental entity may not maintain action [§1782]**
Governmental units may not be plaintiffs in this type of case after successfully defending a false arrest claim. [*See, e.g.,* **City of Long Beach v. Bozek,** 31 Cal. 3d 527 (1982)—absolute privilege to seek redress against government]

b. **Effect of prior verdict [§1783]**
Unlike the criminal acquittal in malicious prosecution cases (*see* above), a verdict for the plaintiff in the prior civil proceedings ***cannot*** be questioned in a subsequent action for malicious institution of those proceedings; *i.e.*, all material issues decided in the first suit are ***res judicata*** between the parties.

c. **Application—countersuits by physicians following malpractice actions [§1784]**
The most recent use of the malicious prosecution theory in civil cases has occurred in suits brought by physicians who have successfully defended malpractice actions. Virtually all such claims against patients and their attorneys have failed, some because the state rejects the action, others because lack of probable cause is much harder to prove in civil cases than in criminal cases. [*See, e.g.,* **Carroll v. Kalar,** 545 P.2d 411 (Ariz. 1976)]

d. **Causation and damages [§1785]**
The same causation rules apply as in the case of criminal prosecutions.

(1) **Minority rule [§1786]**
A minority of states hold that to recover when the unfounded case was a civil suit, the plaintiff must show ***special damages*** to person or property. Under this view, there is no claim when the plaintiff seeks to recover only attorney's fees. [**Johnson v. Calado,** 464 N.W.2d 647 (Wis. 1991)] However, special damages may include defense costs if a large number of suits are brought concurrently or consecutively. [*See, e.g.,* **Cult Awareness Network v. Church of Scientology International,** 685 N.E.2d 1347 (Ill. 1997)]

4. **Malicious Defense [§1787]**
A few states have recognized that a defendant's behavior in raising totally unjustified defenses may cause plaintiffs the same sort of harm that is produced by unjustified complaints. These states have created an action for malicious defense that mirrors the action for malicious institution of civil proceedings (*supra*). [*See, e.g.,* **Aranson v. Schroeder,** 671 A.2d 1023 (N.H. 1995)]

5. **Spoliation of Evidence [§1788]**
Some parties, rather than raising unjustifiable legal arguments, have sought to affect legal outcomes by hiding or destroying adverse evidence. Courts confronted with this conduct have generally created a new action for such destruction. [*See, e.g.,* **Coleman v. Eddy Potash, Inc.,** 905 P.2d 185 (N.M. 1995)—claim that employer D deliberately failed to preserve evidence crucial to P's action against a third party states claim for intentional spoliation by alleging (i) existence of a potential lawsuit; (ii) D's knowledge of it; (iii) destruction, mutilation, or substantial alteration of evidence; (iv) D's intent to disrupt or defeat the lawsuit; (v) a causal connection between the act and the inability to prove the lawsuit; and (vi) damages]

a. **Intentional spoliation during litigation [§1789]**
Although some courts allow a party to sue another party in litigation for destroying evidence, others conclude that this can adequately be handled by sanctions without the need to create a new tort action. [*See, e.g.,* **Cedars-Sinai Medical Center v. Superior Court,** 18 Cal. 4th 1 (1998)—no claim where spoliation discovered or reasonably discoverable during underlying litigation] Where third parties are concerned, however, sanctions will not deter them, so most courts have been persuaded to create actions. [*See, e.g.,* **Oliver v. Stimson Lumber Co.,** 993 P.2d 11 (Mont. 1999); *but see* **Temple Community Hospital v. Superior Court,** 20 Cal. 4th 464 (1999)—rejecting actions for spoliation, whether intentional or negligent, against any third party]

b. **Negligent spoliation [§1790]**
Occasionally the loss of the evidence is alleged to have resulted from negligence. In such cases, courts generally require some special circumstance (contract, agreement, or statute) to create a duty on the defendant to take care to preserve the evidence. [**Coleman v. Eddy Potash, Inc.,** *supra*—allegation that D "knew or should

have reasonably anticipated that" future litigation would occur does not impose duty to take due care to preserve such evidence]

6. Abuse of Process [§1791]

Abuse of process is a narrow tort committed by the misuse of process—civil or criminal—for some ulterior purpose. This means simply that defendant intentionally employed some court process (*e.g.*, attachment, execution, injunction, etc.) for a ***purpose other than that for which the process was designed.*** [Rest. 2d §682]

a. Prima facie case [§1792]

The prima facie case is made simply by showing an ***intentional misuse*** of process and resulting ***damage*** to the plaintiff. [*See, e.g.,* **Yaklevich v. Kemp, Schaeffer & Rowe Co.,** 626 N.E.2d 115 (Ohio 1994)—recognizing action]

---

e.g. **Example:** Attachment on property exempt from execution, or on an excessive amount of P's property, for the purpose of driving P into bankruptcy or forcing him to settle or dismiss his claims against D, is actionable as abuse of process. [**White Lighting Co. v. Wolfson,** 68 Cal. 2d 336 (1968)]

---

e.g. **Example:** A husband is guilty of abusing process in causing the sheriff to levy attachment on his wife's car, where it appeared this was done to harass her and pressure her to settle a pending divorce action. [**Spellens v. Spellens,** 49 Cal. 2d 210 (1957)]

---

(1) No showing of lack of probable cause [§1793]

Unlike the previous torts, the plaintiff does ***not*** have to show that the defendant lacked probable cause.

(2) No showing of favorable result [§1794]

Neither does the plaintiff have to show that the proceedings were terminated in his favor.

(3) Counterclaim [§1795]

In fact, where A has abused process in connection with an action instituted by him against B, B may ***counterclaim in the same action*** for damages arising from the abuse. [**White Lighting Co. v. Wolfson,** *supra*]

b. Who may sue [§1796]

The tort action may be maintained not merely by the other party to the abusive proceedings, but also by ***any third person whose property is injured thereby.***

---

e.g. **Example:** If D files suit against T, and to coerce payment causes an attachment to be levied against property owned by T's parents, D may be liable to the parents for abuse of process. [**Templeton Feed & Grain v. Ralston Purina Co.,** 69 Cal. 2d 461 (1968)]

Review Questions and Answers

Review Questions

FILL IN ANSWER

INTENTIONAL TORTS TO PERSONS

1. Donna is shopping at the supermarket with her children, when someone yells "Fire!" In a blind panic to save her children, Donna pushes her cart through a crowd of shoppers to reach the exit, injuring Paula.

   a. Has Donna "acted" so as to have committed a battery upon Paula? ________

   b. Did Donna have the requisite "intent" for a battery upon Paula? ________

2. As part of his nightclub act, Waldo hypnotizes volunteers from the audience. Horace volunteers and is hypnotized. Waldo directs Horace to pour a glass of water on Betty, another member of the audience, and Horace does so.

   a. Has Horace committed a battery on Betty? ________

   b. Has Waldo committed a battery on Betty? ________

3. David is invited to a party at Peggy's apartment. During the course of events, David engages in the following activities:

   a. To liven up the party, David secretly puts LSD into the punchbowl. Greta, one of the other guests, becomes violently ill as a result of drinking the punch. Has David committed any tort upon Greta? ________

   b. Next, David asks Peggy to dance with him, and while holding her very close, he makes an indecent proposal, which causes Peggy to burst into tears. Has David committed any tort on Peggy? ________

   c. Then David wanders into the bedroom where he finds his pal, Zeke, fast asleep. To get Zeke to join the party, David roughly shakes him awake. Zeke is unhurt, but is angered at being awakened. Has David committed a battery upon Zeke? ________

   d. Later, as part of the horseplay between himself and Zeke, David takes a dart off the dartboard and throws it at the wall near where Zeke is standing, intending to startle Zeke. Unfortunately, Beth walks in front of Zeke and is struck by the dart. Has David committed a battery on Beth? ________

4. Prudence is walking home by herself, late at night, when the following events occur:

a. Mildred, an elderly woman, observes Prudence walking in front of Mildred's house, and mistakes her for a prostitute. Mildred points a shotgun at Prudence, shouting, "Get off the streets, you hussy, or I'll fill you full of buckshot!" Has Mildred committed an assault on Prudence? ________

b. As a joke, Prudence's younger brother, George, sneaks up behind her and sets off a firecracker, frightening her severely. Has George committed an assault on Prudence? ________

c. Prudence turns to scold George and he responds by raising his fist as if to punch her. Prudence, however, is not frightened thereby because she knows that George is not strong enough to hurt her. Does George's raising his fist constitute an assault? ________

d. Later, Dominic approaches Prudence carrying what appears to be a knife, and demands that she submit to sexual intercourse with him immediately. Prudence is panicked thereby, although the "knife" in fact has a rubber blade, and Dominic is impotent. Has Dominic committed an assault on Prudence? ________

5. Tony was walking down the street when his enemy, Rocky, approached from behind and threw a knife at him, but missed. Tony's attention was diverted by traffic and he didn't know what had happened until Stranger yelled, "Watch out! That man is trying to kill you!" Tony whirled and saw Rocky being apprehended by a police officer, but nevertheless was shaken up by the realization that Rocky had made an attempt on his life.

   a. Is Rocky liable to Tony for any tort? ________

   b. Is Stranger liable to Tony for any tort? ________

6. As a prank, Doug puts a stocking mask over his face and points a water pistol at his best friend, Pete, saying, "I'm going to let you have it!" Any reasonable person in Pete's position would have realized that Doug was only joking, but Pete is abnormally sensitive and thinks the gun is real and that Doug is going to kill him. Is Doug liable to Pete for an assault? ________

7. Bob stripped naked for a physical exam in his doctor's office. While he was being examined by the doctor, the nurse took Bob's clothes and locked them in a closet. The nurse refused to return them until Bob agreed to pay a disputed bill from the doctor. Can Bob recover against the nurse for false imprisonment? ________

8. Law Student fell asleep at the law library after a hard day's study. Janitor tried to awaken him, but finally gave up and locked the library for the night.

   a. Assume Law Student slept through the night and was awakened only when Librarian opened the door the following morning. Is Janitor liable to Law Student for false imprisonment? ________

b. Assume Law Student awakened during the night and found the door locked but decided to relax and go back to sleep, thinking one of his buddies had locked him in as a prank. However, he became angered when Librarian arrived and told him it was Janitor. Is Janitor liable to Law Student for false imprisonment? ________

9. As part of his initiation rites into Fraternity, Neal is blindfolded and taken on a long ride. Fraternity brothers abandon him in the desert, 20 miles away from any settlement or highway. Can Neal recover from Fraternity brothers for false imprisonment? ________

10. During a bank robbery, cashier Pete is locked in the bank vault by the robbers. After the robbery, the bank president, Dan, is angry that Pete did not put up a fight; therefore, to punish Pete, Dan leaves the vault locked for a few hours.

    a. Can Pete recover from Dan for false imprisonment? ________

    b. Would it make any difference that Pete was unaware that he was being "punished" by Dan? ________

11. In response to labor strife at the XYZ Manufacturing Co., union members Able and Beetle place their autos across the driveway to the plant's only entrance, preventing those inside from driving their cars out, and preventing others from entering the plant.

    a. Can XYZ recover from Able and Beetle for false imprisonment? ________

    b. Can the workers in the plant who are unable to drive home recover from Able and Beetle for false imprisonment? ________

12. Virgil became suspicious that his neighbor, Homer, was engaged in selling narcotics. He reported his suspicions to the police, who arrested Homer. However, Homer was soon released because of lack of evidence. Can Homer recover from Virgil for false imprisonment? ________

13. Dick rented a police uniform for a costume party. While driving to the party, he became enraged at the way Phil, another driver, was operating his car. Dick made sure Phil could see the police uniform and then yelled, "Pull over there," intending to give Phil a stern lecture on his driving. Phil, believing Dick to be a police officer, pulled his car to the curb.

    a. Is Dick subject to liability to Phil for false imprisonment? ________

    b. Is it relevant that Phil's erratic driving constituted a crime for which even a private citizen would have had the ***privilege to arrest*** Phil? ________

14. Charley received a traffic ticket and paid the fine. However, by error, her payment was not recorded, and therefore a warrant was issued for her arrest.

a. Assume Sheriff called Charley on the telephone and told her about the warrant, and that she would have to come to court immediately, and Charley came. Could Charley later recover from Sheriff for false imprisonment? ________

b. Assume Sheriff went to Charley's house and told Charley that the only way she could avoid arrest would be to pay Sheriff the amount of the traffic fine again, plus $50 warrant costs, and Charley paid these. Could Charley later recover from Sheriff for false imprisonment? ________

c. Assume Sheriff went to Charley's house and showed Charley the warrant for her arrest, and Charley submitted to Sheriff's custody without telling Sheriff that she had already paid the traffic ticket. Could she later recover from Sheriff for false imprisonment? ________

15. Emil is badly injured in an automobile collision. He is on the "critical list" at the hospital, and under strict orders from his doctor to remain quiet; all visitors are warned not to upset him. Harvey, an insurance adjuster representing the driver of the other car, barges into Emil's room, and after attempting to force a settlement, accuses Emil of being a "phony, a faker, and a cheat!" Emil becomes angered and suffers a heart attack.

a. Is Harvey subject to liability to Emil for the intentional infliction of emotional distress? ________

b. Assume Emil had become angered and upset at Harvey but had ***not*** suffered the heart attack. Would this bar Emil's claim against Harvey for intentional infliction of emotional distress? ________

DEFENSES

16. As passengers line up to board an Acme Airliner, they are informed that there has been a bomb threat and that everyone has to be searched. Ernesta is abnormally sensitive to being touched by anyone, but she is anxious to reach her destination and therefore says nothing while the airline personnel conduct a "patdown" over her clothing. Can she later sue the airline for battery? ________

17. In the course of a free-swinging hockey match, Daniel strikes Pierre on the head with a hockey stick; and George, one of the fans, throws a beer bottle that hits Pierre on the back.

a. Is Daniel liable to Pierre for a battery? ________

b. Is George liable to Pierre for a battery? ________

18. Barbara goes to her doctor, complaining of stomach pains. After routine tests, Doctor recommends exploratory surgery, and Barbara enters the hospital for the operation.

a. Assume that Doctor was called out of town on an emergency, and therefore arranged to have Specialist perform the operation without Barbara's knowledge. Assume further that the surgery was skillfully performed and was entirely successful. Would either Doctor or Specialist be subject to liability for a battery? ________

b. Assume that Doctor performed the operation carefully and properly, but that as a result of the surgery, the skin over Barbara's stomach was badly scarred, which interfered with her career as a swimsuit model. Could Barbara recover from Doctor for a battery? ________

c. Assume that during the course of surgery, Doctor discovered that the cause of Barbara's stomach pain was an ulcer which if not removed would grow progressively worse and could threaten her life. Doctor therefore removed the ulcerated portion of Barbara's stomach by careful surgical procedures. If Barbara had not expressly consented to the removal of any body organ, would Doctor be liable for a battery? ________

19. Myrna is cited for reckless driving by Police Officer. Police Officer offers to tear up the ticket if she will go to bed with him. Myrna reluctantly agrees because she has already had several tickets and this citation would cause her to lose her driver's license. If Police Officer goes back on his word and turns in Myrna's traffic citation, can she hold him liable for a battery? ________

20. After Barney and his wife, Betty, had an expensive dinner at Restaurant, Barney found that he had left his wallet at home. Restaurant Owner insisted that Betty remain at Restaurant while Barney went to get his wallet. During his absence, Owner threatened to have his bartender beat up Barney when he returned unless Betty submitted to certain sexual acts with Owner, which she did.

a. Is Restaurant Owner liable to Betty for false imprisonment? ________

b. Is Restaurant Owner liable to Betty for battery? ________

21. During the course of a heated political discussion, Archie invites Rob outside to "settle the matter." Rob obliges, and a fist fight ensues, which is broken up only when both men are arrested for breach of the peace. Is either liable to the other for battery? ________

22. Arlene throws a stone at Buford, striking him in the leg. Buford picks up the same stone and hurls it back, hitting Arlene on the head. If Arlene sues for battery, has Buford a valid claim of self-defense? ________

23. Charlie had threatened to kill Bob unless he stayed away from Charlie's wife, but Bob had not done so. As Bob was walking down the street, he saw Charlie approaching with his fist raised toward Bob. Which, if any, of the following statements is true? ________

(A) Bob would be privileged to shoot Charlie based on the threats Charlie had made on his life.

(B) Bob would be privileged to strike Charlie without waiting for Charlie to hit him first.

(C) Bob would be under a duty to retreat as an alternative to striking Charlie.

(D) Bob would not be privileged to use any force against Charlie, if in fact Charlie had only raised his fist as a joke.

24. Bruno is wearing brass knuckles that cannot be seen because they are concealed by a large glove. He raises his fist as if to strike Carl, who responds by stabbing Bruno with a knife. Can Carl successfully claim the privilege of self-defense? __________

25. Raoul is showing off by juggling a hand grenade at a party at Ling's house. Suddenly, he draws his arm back as if he is going to throw the grenade at Ling. Which, if any, of the following statements is true? __________

(A) Ling is under a duty to retreat as an alternative to using deadly force against Raoul.

(B) Ling is not entitled to use ***any*** force against Raoul if she realizes that the safety pin is still in place so that the grenade could not explode.

(C) Ling would be entitled to shoot Raoul, to prevent his throwing the grenade, if she ***honestly*** believed that Raoul was about to kill her, even though a reasonable person would have realized that Raoul was only joking and that the "grenade" was a toy.

(D) If a reasonable person would have regarded Raoul's threat as real, Ling would be privileged to use deadly force against him, even though her doing so might endanger others at the party.

26. Frank is walking down the street, carrying a long fishing pole in front of him. As he approaches Mildred, she becomes alarmed because the tip of the pole is whipping about and Frank is paying no attention. Which, if any, of the following statements is true? __________

(A) Mildred is under a duty to retreat as an alternative to using ***any*** force against Frank.

(B) Mildred would not be privileged to use ***any*** force against Frank if she realized that he was merely negligent and intended her no harm.

(C) If Mildred could not otherwise get out of the way, she would be privileged to draw a gun from her purse and yell at Frank, "Watch out where you're going, or I'll shoot you!"

27. In the midst of a barroom argument, Alex points a gun at Bruno and threatens to shoot. Bruno pulls out his own gun and fires at Alex, who ducks so that the bullet misses. The bullet travels out the window, across the street, and through a wall, hitting Clara. Assuming the risk to Clara was not foreseeable, can she recover from Bruno? __________

28. Mildred is visiting at the home of her favorite nephew, Phil. She enters the kitchen and finds Phil struggling with a stranger, Don. In fear for Phil's life, Mildred picks up a knife and plunges it into Don's back. Which, if any, of the following statements is true? __________

    (A) If Phil had been the aggressor and hence not entitled to defend himself, Mildred was not privileged to use any force on his behalf.

    (B) Mildred's conduct was not privileged if Phil's life was not actually in danger.

    (C) Mildred's conduct was not privileged because she was not a member of Phil's immediate family or household.

29. Dude drives up to the gate across Farmer's driveway and asks for permission to enter and do a little hunting. Farmer responds by brandishing a shotgun at Dude, and cocking it as if to fire.

    a. Was Farmer's conduct privileged? __________

    b. Assume Dude ignores Farmer, and drives right through Farmer's gate. Although no warning is posted, the gate is electrically charged and Dude receives a severe shock. Is Farmer liable to Dude for a battery? __________

30. Knowing that Hussein was going to Europe for the summer, Laurence stole the key to Hussein's apartment and moved in. The owner of the building discovered what Laurence had done, and demanded that Laurence vacate, but he refused to do so. Is the owner privileged to use force to evict Laurence? __________

31. Shifty rents a car from Apex Car Rentals, establishing credit by using a phony credit card. Shifty fails to return the car as agreed. One week later, Apex catches up with Shifty and demands return of the car. If Shifty refuses, is Apex privileged to use reasonable force against Shifty to take back the car? __________

32. Pierre loans a famous painting for exhibition at Don's Gallery. After the exhibition, Don takes the painting home and hangs it on his wall. Pierre finds out and demands return of the painting, but Don refuses. Is Pierre privileged to use reasonable force against Don to effect recapture of the painting? __________

33. Employer suspects that one of many employees is stealing merchandise from the store, but has no reason to suspect one employee over any other. After store hours, Employer locks all doors and refuses to allow the employees to leave until each submits to a personal search. Is Employer's conduct privileged? __________

34. Store Detective observes a customer, Maude, slip a small bottle of perfume into her purse and walk out the door.

   a. Assume that Detective apprehends Maude on the street outside the store, and asks her to come back into the store to be questioned, but she refuses. Is Detective privileged to use force to detain Maude? ________

   b. Assume that the perfume bottle belonged to Maude all along and that Detective made a reasonable mistake in thinking that she was stealing from Store. Is Detective still privileged to use reasonable force to detain Maude? ________

   c. Assume further that Detective asked Maude to allow him to hold onto the bottle while the matter was being investigated, but she refused (the bottle in fact belonging to her). Is Detective privileged to use reasonable force to take the bottle from Maude? ________

35. The FBI posts a "wanted" bulletin for a certain person for murder. George reads the bulletin, and reasonably concludes from the description therein that his neighbor, Ned, is the wanted man. George thereupon arrests Ned without any warrant.

   a. Assume George is a private citizen (not a police officer). Was the arrest privileged if it turns out that Ned is ***not*** the wanted man? ________

   b. Assume George is a police officer. Was the arrest privileged if it turns out not only that Ned was ***not*** the wanted man, but also that ***no felony*** had actually been committed (*e.g.*, the "murder victim" was actually a suicide)? ________

36. The police are called to quell student riots at University. They arrest Bob, Carol, Ted, and Alice on charges of disorderly conduct, a misdemeanor. Although all four were present at the scene, only Bob was a participant in the rioting. Are the arrests all privileged? ________

37. Sheriff has a warrant for the arrest of Tony on a charge of murder. He apprehends Tony's twin brother, Sam, thinking he is Tony. Sam resists arrest, and in order to subdue him, Sheriff shoots Sam in the leg. Can Sam recover for battery? ________

INTENTIONAL TORTS TO PROPERTY

38. To clear some boulders out of her field, Farmer sets off dynamite charges. Unexpectedly, the explosion causes vibrations that extend to Neighbor's land, damaging a water well. Can Neighbor recover for trespass? ________

39. Rancher grants permission to Telephone Co. to erect and maintain telephone poles and wires across a portion of his land for a 10-year period. At the expiration of the 10 years, Rancher demands removal of the poles and wires, but Telephone Co. fails to comply.

a. Can Rancher recover from Telephone Co. for trespass? ________

b. Assume that Telephone Co. removed all of its poles, but later strung a telephone wire across one corner of Rancher's property from poles ***outside*** his land. Is this a trespass? ________

40. Jones has been dumping dirt on a corner of his property for years, to fill in a low spot. Without Jones's knowledge or consent, an adjoining landowner, Smith, throws a small amount of dirt on the same spot. Is Smith liable to Jones for trespass? ________

41. Audi owns a parcel of land leased to Beetle for 99 years. However, both Audi and Beetle reside elsewhere, and Chevy has gone into adverse possession of the parcel. Dodge trespasses. To whom, if anyone, is Dodge subject to liability? ________

42. Bookworm carries home a rare book from the library, inadvertently forgetting to check it out at the library counter.

a. Is Bookworm subject to liability for trespass to chattels? ________

b. Is Bookworm subject to liability for conversion? ________

43. A rare book is in the display case at the library, under a "Do Not Touch" sign. Nevertheless, Bookworm reaches into the case to examine the book, accidentally tearing one page.

a. Is Bookworm subject to liability for trespass to chattels? ________

b. Is Bookworm subject to liability for conversion? ________

44. As a prank, Randy turns up the heat in Richard's wine cellar, causing many bottles of wine to sour. Is Randy subject to liability either for trespass to chattels or conversion? ________

45. Angel buys a used car from Hood, believing Hood to be the owner. In fact, Hood stole the car.

a. Is Angel subject to liability for either trespass to chattels or conversion at the time he purchased the car? ________

b. If Owner later claims the car but Angel refuses to turn it over (honestly thinking he owns it), does his refusal constitute a conversion? ________

46. Being desperate for money, Sylvia pawns her fur coat at Benny's Pawnshop for a $500 loan. In which of the following cases could Sylvia recover against Benny for conversion of the coat? ________

(A) Before repaying the loan, Sylvia demanded return of her coat so that she could wear it to a party. Benny refused to give it back.

(B) A burglar broke into the pawnshop and stole Sylvia's coat.

(C) Benny forgot to put moth crystals in the closet where the coat was hanging, and it was destroyed by moths.

(D) Benny allowed his wife, Wilma, to wear the fur coat to a party one night; Sylvia was at the party and was very upset thereby.

(E) Same facts as in (D), except that someone spilled a drink on the fur, causing a stain that cannot be removed.

(F) At midnight, Sylvia telephoned Benny saying she wanted to repay the loan and for him to open up the store and give her back her coat. Benny told her to come in the next morning. Unfortunately, a fire occurred during the interim, destroying the coat.

47. Sucker purchases 100 shares of Goldray Uranium for $10 each through his stockbroker, Fastbuck. The shares are retained in Fastbuck's brokerage account. When the shares go up to $15 each, Fastbuck—without authority from Sucker—sells the shares and pockets the proceeds. Within a few weeks, the shares go up to $50 each, but then fraud is discovered and the company goes bankrupt so that the shares are now worthless. If Sucker sues Fastbuck for conversion, how much, if anything, will he recover? __________

PRIVILEGED INVASIONS OF PROPERTY

48. Because his own tractor is broken, Buford goes onto Clem's land and "borrows" Clem's tractor.

    a. Assume that Clem returns and sees his tractor sitting in Buford's field. Is Clem privileged to go onto Buford's land to reclaim his tractor without asking for Buford's permission? __________

    b. Assume that Clem asks for his tractor back, but Buford refuses and attempts to bar Clem's entry. Thereupon, Clem shoves Buford aside and drives his tractor off the land, doing some damage to Buford's crops in the process. Is Clem liable to Buford either for battery or for damage to Buford's crops? __________

49. Wilbur's poodle ran away from home and entered Mary's yard. Mary fell in love with the dog and put a leash on it. When Wilbur came looking for his poodle, Mary refused to return it and locked the gate to her property.

    a. Is Wilbur privileged to break down Mary's gate if necessary to enter her land to reclaim his dog? __________

    b. If Wilbur is privileged to break Mary's gate, must he pay for the damage? __________

    c. Is Wilbur privileged to break and enter Mary's front door if Mary has taken the dog inside the house? __________

d. Would it make any difference that the dog had run away several times previously, and Wilbur was negligent in not putting a leash on the dog? ________

50. Because of a gasoline shortage, Sinclair has hoarded almost 1,000 gallons of gasoline in his garage, located in a densely populated residential neighborhood. Neighbor has unsuccessfully complained to Sinclair about the potential fire hazard, which is apparent because the containers in which the gasoline is stored are not airtight, and occasionally leak. While Sinclair and his family are away on vacation, a savage lightning storm develops. Neighbor knows there is no lightning rod on Sinclair's garage and fears that a bolt of lightning may ignite the gasoline. Therefore, he breaks into the garage and pours the gasoline down the sewer.

   a. Was Neighbor's conduct privileged? ________

   b. Assume there was no lightning storm, but Neighbor simply decided to enter the garage and get rid of the gasoline in Sinclair's absence because Sinclair had ignored his requests to do so. Would Neighbor's conduct be privileged in such a case? ________

51. Wife is a diabetic, requiring insulin shots to survive. While on a vacation trip, Wife runs out of insulin and goes into a coma. Husband runs to the only drugstore in town to get insulin syringes, but Druggist refuses to sell him any because Husband did not bring a prescription. Husband thereupon goes behind the counter and forcibly takes the insulin from Druggist, after a violent struggle.

   a. If Druggist is injured thereby, is Husband subject to liability? ________

   b. Is Husband subject to liability to Druggist for damage to the drugstore counter caused in the struggle between Husband and Druggist? ________

   c. Is Husband subject to liability to Druggist for the value of the insulin taken? ________

NEGLIGENCE

52. Pedro sues Napoleon for negligence arising out of an intersection accident. Pedro proves that Napoleon did not slow down as he entered the intersection, notwithstanding a yellow "Caution" sign. Which of the following evidence, if any, offered by Napoleon in defense, ***conclusively proves*** (as a matter of law) that he was ***not*** negligent? ________

   (A) Undisputed testimony by Napoleon that he did not see the "Caution" sign at the intersection, because it was obstructed by a tree.

   (B) Undisputed testimony by others in the community that it was customary to enter this particular intersection without stopping, even though there was a "Caution" sign.

   (C) A city ordinance expressly provides that a driver is not required to stop or slow down at an intersection where the "Caution" sign is not fully visible.

53. Paula sues Donna for negligence arising out of an auto accident. Which of the following facts, if any, offered by Donna in defense, is ***relevant to show*** that she acted as a reasonable person under the circumstances and hence was not negligent? ________

(A) Donna's eyesight is so poor that she did not see Paula's car coming.

(B) Donna is mentally retarded, having the mentality of a 10-year-old.

(C) Donna had been drinking "Ripple" all morning and was slightly intoxicated so that she did not see Paula's car until too late to avoid the impact.

(D) Donna was not an experienced driver; she had just obtained a learner's permit, and had been driving for only a few weeks.

54. Martha is a 10-year-old child, but is unusually bright and very mature for her age.

a. Assume a neighbor asks Martha to babysit and a claim for negligence arises from her so doing. Is Martha's conduct to be judged according to ***her own*** superior intelligence (rather than the lesser abilities of the average 10-year-old child)? ________

b. Assume Martha drives the family car to the grocery store and is involved in an accident. Is her age a factor to be considered in determining whether she was negligent? ________

55. Dudley employs Attorney to represent him in a civil lawsuit. Which, if any, of the following statements is true in determining the standard of care owed by Attorney to Dudley? ________

(A) It makes no difference that Attorney has just passed the bar exam and that Dudley is her first client.

(B) It makes no difference that Attorney advised Dudley that this was her first case.

(C) If Attorney was in fact a trial specialist, she would owe a higher standard of care than would a nonspecialist, regardless of whether Dudley was aware of Attorney's special skill.

56. While driving her car in heavy traffic, Gabby is distracted by a discussion she is having with her passenger, Peggy, and as a result strikes a truck being driven by Felix.

a. If Felix is injured, can he base a claim for negligence against Gabby ***solely*** on the basis that she wasn't watching where she was going? ________

b. Assume that Felix's truck contained jet rocket fuel, and the collision set off an explosion, injuring Phillip, a pedestrian on the street. Is Gabby subject to liability for Phillip's injuries? ________

c. Assume that the same explosion knocked some bottles off a shelf in a medical laboratory nearby. The bottles shattered, and a worker, Wilma, was cut by the flying glass. Is Gabby subject to liability for Wilma's injury? ________

d. Assume that Gabby herself was injured and rendered unconscious in the collision, and her car set on fire. Assume further that a passerby, Sam, saw her predicament and rushed to her aid, but injured himself in so doing. Is Gabby subject to liability for Sam's injuries? ________

57. Alma buys a wrapped loaf of bread baked by Beetley. She takes it home, opens the sealed wrapper, eats a slice, and is injured by a piece of glass imbedded therein. Alma sues Beetley for negligence.

a. If Alma proves only the foregoing facts, has she made out a prima facie case of negligence? ________

b. If Beetley fails to put on any defense, is Alma entitled to a judgment against Beetley? ________

58. Should an inference of negligence by the defendant be drawn in any of the following cases?

a. Allen leaves his new Corvette parked on the side of a hill; 15 minutes later, the car rolls down the hill and crashes into Francesca's house. ________

b. Trans-Global Flight 02, on which Amelia was a passenger, disappears and no trace is ever found. Amelia's heirs sue Trans-Global and produce the following known facts with regard to the flight: good flying weather at the time of flight; flat terrain from take-off to destination; and all luggage examined by electronic equipment for bombs or weapons. ________

c. Alpha's store premises are damaged by water escaping from a main under the street. The water main had been installed by Beta Co., but the City was in charge of inspecting and maintaining the pipes. Alpha sues both Beta and City. An expert testifies that the water mains could have broken *either* because they were improperly installed or improperly maintained; but he can't tell which. ________

d. While filling her car with gas at the Ajax self-service station, Dominica is killed by an explosion at the pump. The cause of the explosion is unknown. Dominica's heirs sue both Ajax and the manufacturer of the pump. ________

59. In response to a gasoline shortage, a statute is enacted prohibiting auto travel on Sundays except for emergencies. Notwithstanding, Driver drives his car on Sunday to play golf. On the way back, he strikes Pedestrian, causing severe injuries. Can Pedestrian recover based solely on a showing that Driver violated the statute banning Sunday driving? ________

60. A statute makes it a crime to drive a vehicle after dusk unless both front and rear lights are lit. At night, Pedestrian is struck and injured by a car driven by Driver with its lights out.

   a. Would Pedestrian establish a prima facie case of negligence against Driver merely by showing that Driver had violated the statute? ________

   b. Would Driver be permitted to introduce evidence that even though her lights were out, she was driving carefully and maintaining a proper lookout on the road ahead? ________

   c. Would Driver be permitted to introduce evidence that her lights had failed just prior to impact with Pedestrian and that she had no opportunity to pull over to the side of the road? ________

61. Amy is a passenger on a bus operated by Bus Co. The bus collides with a car driven by Chris, due to the negligence of both the bus driver and Chris. Amy is injured in the collision.

   a. Was Chris's negligence the "cause in fact" of Amy's injuries? Was the bus driver's? ________

   b. Assume that moments after the accident, the bus is struck again because of Denny's negligent driving. Within hours, Amy is paralyzed but it is impossible to determine whether the paralysis was caused by the first or second impact, or as the result of the combined impacts. Can Amy recover against Bus Co., Chris, or Denny? ________

62. City fails to properly maintain a sidewalk, causing irregularities in the pavement. Property Owner is under a duty to keep the walk in front of her property free of debris and ice. After a storm, Pedestrian slips and falls on the sidewalk on which ice has accumulated. It cannot be determined whether the fall was due to the sidewalk irregularities *or* to the ice. Can Pedestrian prove a prima facie case of negligence against *either* City or Property Owner? ________

63. Abdul negligently operates his car so that it strikes a power line pole.

   a. Assume that the pole falls on a car being driven by Theo, causing him severe personal injuries. Is Abdul liable to Theo? ________

   b. Suppose that Theo has a heart condition and that the accident causes a severe attack resulting in Theo's death. A healthy person probably would not have died. Can Theo's heirs prevail in a wrongful death action? ________

   c. Assume that the impact with the pole cuts off power in a wide area and turns off all traffic signals and street lights. Several blocks away, two cars collide at an intersection because of the blackout. Is Abdul liable for injuries and property damages sustained in this second collision? ________

64. While operating his lawn mower in a careless manner, Andy strikes and seriously injures Bill's dog. In a frenzy, the dog runs into the house and bites Bill. Is Andy liable to Bill? ________

65. Al negligently drives his car so as to endanger Ben, walking in a crosswalk. To escape being hit, Ben jumps out of the way, in the process knocking down Cindy, who suffers injuries. Is Al liable to Cindy? ________

66. Don, a service station operator, negligently fails to replace the cap on the gasoline tank on Paul's new car. Later, Paul's neighbor, Norbert, notices that the gas cap is missing and throws a lighted match into Paul's gas tank. Is Don liable for the resulting destruction of Paul's car? ________

67. As Oscar is walking across the highway at night, he is struck and rendered unconscious by a car negligently driven by Felix. Felix hurriedly drives away, leaving Oscar lying helpless in the middle of the road.

    a. Assume that Oscar is run over by another car, driven by Phoebe; and that had Phoebe been paying attention to where she was going she could have avoided hitting Oscar. Is Felix liable for the additional injuries suffered by Oscar as the result of being run over by Phoebe's car? ________

    b. Assume that another motorist, Max, sees Oscar unconscious in the road, realizes that Oscar is helpless, and proceeds to "mug" him, stealing Oscar's wallet and gold watch. Is Felix liable to Oscar for the loss of the wallet and watch? ________

    c. Assume that while Oscar is still unconscious in the middle of the road a storm develops, and Oscar is struck by a bolt of lightning. Is Felix liable for the additional injuries suffered by Oscar as the result of being struck by lightning? ________

68. Contractor excavates a deep pit next to a public sidewalk, and fails to place barriers or warning lamps around it. Pedestrian falls into the pit, and cuts his head. His cries of help are heard by Neighbor, who could have summoned help, but it was late at night and Neighbor chose not to "get involved." As a result, Pedestrian bleeds to death.

    a. Is Contractor liable for Pedestrian's death? ________

    b. Is Neighbor liable for Pedestrian's death? ________

69. Dwight negligently causes an auto accident in which the other driver, Pam, sustains a small cut on her arm. Pam neglects to obtain medical treatment for the cut, and as a result, infection sets in and the wound becomes gangrenous, necessitating amputation of her arm. Is Dwight subject to liability for the loss of Pam's arm? ________

70. Dwight negligently causes an auto accident in which the other driver, Phyllis, sustains personal injuries. The cost of hospital and medical treatment for her injuries is $2,500, all of which is covered by her group insurance. Is Phyllis entitled to recover against Dwight for the medical and hospital bills, even though these bills were in fact paid by Phyllis's insurance? ________

NEGLIGENCE—SPECIAL DUTY QUESTIONS

71. Rich is driving his new Rolls Royce when he strikes Barbara, knocking her to the ground and causing her serious injuries.

    a. If the accident was not Rich's fault (*e.g.*, Barbara was negligent in stepping in front of his car), is Rich under any duty at common law to stop and render aid to Barbara? ________

    b. Assume Rich stopped his car and agreed to drive Barbara home. However, as he approached her house, the road was unpaved, and Rich refused to drive his new Rolls Royce further. Therefore, Barbara was forced to walk the remaining mile in the rain, aggravating her original injuries. Is Rich liable at common law to Barbara for the aggravation of her injuries? ________

72. Acme Airlines Flight 020 is hijacked in mid-air by a person who demands that the flight be diverted to Cuba, which is within the plane's cruising range. The pilot attempts to disarm the hijacker, but a gunfight ensues in which Hijacker shoots Passenger. Is Acme subject to liability to Passenger on a negligence theory? ________

73. Because his foot was burned, Michael cannot drive his car. He therefore asks Dwight to drive him to the doctor in Michael's car. En route, Michael notices that Dwight is driving recklessly, but he says nothing.

    a. Assume that immediately thereafter, Dwight negligently collides with a car driven by Jim. In the absence of a statute, is Michael liable for Jim's injury? ________

    b. Assume that the collision occurred after Dwight had dropped Michael off at the doctor's office. In the absence of a statute, would Michael be liable for Jim's injury? ________

74. Stanley, a truck driver for Widget Co., is driving back to the factory after making his last delivery of the day. On the way, he negligently causes a collision with a car driven by Stella, injuring her.

    a. Can Stella recover damages from Widget Co., even though Widget Co. was not negligent in hiring or supervising Stanley? ________

    b. If Stanley and Stella got into an argument as to whose fault the accident was, and Stanley punched Stella in the nose, could Stella recover against Widget Co. for injury to her nose? ________

c. Assume that Widget Co. was ***not*** otherwise liable for Stanley's punching Stella in the nose. Could Stella recover against Widget Co. by showing that when it employed Stanley, he had a police record for committing batteries and Widget Co. was aware of this record? ________

75. Trans-Global Airlines engages Aero Repair Co. to overhaul the engine in one of Trans-Global's planes. The job is done negligently by Aero. As a result, the plane crashes, injuring Passenger. Passenger sues Trans-Global.

a. Assume that Trans-Global was ***not*** negligent in selecting Aero Repair to do the work. Is Trans-Global liable for Aero's negligence? ________

b. Assume that Trans-Global ***is*** otherwise liable for Aero's negligence. Can it defend by showing that, under the repair contract, Aero assumed liability for injuries to others caused by its negligence? ________

76. Lars and Astrid form a carpool to drive to work, the understanding being that each will take his or her car on alternate days. Lars is driving on his day and negligently causes a collision with a car driven by Phyllis.

a. If Astrid is injured in the accident, can she recover against Lars under a typical "guest statute"? ________

b. If ***Phyllis*** is injured in the accident, can she recover from ***Astrid*** on a "joint enterprise" theory? ________

77. Mother employs Babysitter to care for Junior, age eight. Mother fails to advise Babysitter that Junior is proficient in karate. Babysitter engages in horseplay with Junior and is felled by a karate chop. Is Mother subject to liability for Babysitter's injuries? ________

78. In a state with a typical "Dram Shop Act," Norm gets drunk at Tavern. Shortly thereafter, he drives his car into a telephone pole, fracturing his neck. Can Norm recover against Tavern for his injuries? ________

79. Is the following jury instruction a correct statement of the law? "Every occupier of land owes to persons coming onto his land a duty to exercise reasonable care with respect to any condition or activity on his land that involves a foreseeable risk of harm." ________

80. Pedestrian is walking on a city sidewalk adjoining Owner's property.

a. Assume that Pedestrian is struck by a branch falling from a native tree located on Owner's property. If Owner has never inspected the tree to make sure it is safe, is Owner subject to liability for any injuries resulting to Pedestrian? ________

b. If Pedestrian is struck on the head by a baseball hit in a game being played on Owner's land, is Owner subject to liability therefor? ________

81. Thief was attempting to burglarize (at night) Rich's home in Bellaire, when he fell into Rich's partially completed swimming pool and was severely injured. If Rich had failed to erect any fence or post any warning or lights around the pool, is he subject to liability for Thief's injuries? ________

82. Philpott owns a large sandy lot adjacent to a public beach. He knows that beach users often park their cars on his lot, notwithstanding a large "No Trespassing" sign. To discourage this use, Philpott strews broken bottles in the sand where they park. One of the beach users, Beachbum, cuts his foot on the broken glass.

a. Is Philpott subject to liability therefor? ________

b. Would Philpott be subject to liability if the broken glass had been carelessly strewn ***by other beach users*** (rather than by Philpott), and Philpott had taken no action to clean it up? ________

83. Cement Co. maintains large piles of sand on its premises for use in making concrete. The sand is impure and often contains sharp pebbles and bits of glass. Over the weekend, the premises are unattended, although a fence and "no trespassing" signs have been erected. A group of 10-year-olds climb through the fence one weekend and are cut while playing in the sandpiles. Is Cement Co. subject to liability for their injuries? ________

84. Tamura raises goldfish in a small pond on his property, which is located next door to a nursery school for preschool age children. Tamura knows that sometimes children from the nursery school trespass onto his property to look at his fish, but he does nothing to prevent this because he enjoys having the children come onto his property. One day, in his absence, a three-year-old child from the nursery school trespasses, falls into the pond, hits her head, and is rendered unconscious and drowns in the water. Is Tamura liable for the child's death even though he never realized there was any risk of harm to the children? ________

85. Seymour, a door-to-door salesman, suffers a broken leg when he trips on a broken stair of Owner's front porch. Owner was not at home at the time, but he knew that the stair needed repair and that the danger was not readily visible. Is Owner liable for Seymour's injuries? ________

86. Claire owns a coffee shop. One of her customers inadvertently spilled a lot of water in the men's room, making the entrance very slippery. However, no one complained to Claire about the condition until several hours later, when Carter slipped and fell, hurting his back. Carter was not a customer of the coffee shop, but rather a 12-year-old child on his way home from school. Is Claire subject to liability for Carter's injuries? ________

87. Benny operates a gasoline service station. While Benny was servicing a car on the lube rack, some oil leaked onto the ground, making the surrounding area quite slippery. Before noticing the oil, Benny was called to the pumps to attend to a customer. While Benny was not looking, Larry, a 12-year-old on his way home from school, walked into the lube area, slipped, and fell. Is Benny subject to liability for Larry's injuries? ________

88. Rich and his friend, Winston, went hunting on Rich's rural estate. Terrance was trespassing across one of the fields. Neither Rich nor Winston saw Terrance because they were engrossed in conversation.

    a. If Rich negligently fired his gun without keeping a proper lookout and thereby wounded Terrance, would Rich be subject to liability to Terrance? ________

    b. If Winston negligently fired his gun without keeping a proper lookout and thereby wounded Terrance, would Winston be subject to liability to Terrance? ________

89. Larry is the owner of a house, which he leases to Tricia. Larry knows, but forgets to mention to Tricia, that the faucet on the bathtub does not work properly. When Tricia goes to turn it on the first time, it comes off in her hand, and she is scalded by hot water.

    a. Is Larry subject to liability for Tricia's injuries? ________

    b. Suppose it was Tricia's fiance, Bob, who was injured by the defective hot water faucet. Would Larry be subject to liability for Bob's injuries? ________

90. Leonard is the owner of an apartment house. Is he subject to liability for the following injuries?

    a. Tenant #1 is injured by an electric shock from a light switch that Leonard had negligently repaired. ________

    b. Tenant #2 is injured by an electric shock from a light switch that Leonard had failed to repair, notwithstanding a lease obligation and request from the tenant to do so. ________

    c. Visitor to Tenant #2 is injured by an electric shock from the same light switch referred to in "b." ________

    d. Tenant #3 is injured when she falls in the apartment house elevator, as the result of a broken floor tile that caught the heel of her shoe; the broken floor tile had been reported to Leonard, but he had forgotten to fix it. ________

    e. Visitor to Tenant #3 is injured when he falls in the elevator as the result of the same broken floor tile. ________

91. Mother is preparing lunch in her kitchen while her five-year-old daughter, Child, is playing outdoors. Mother hears the screeching of brakes and runs outside; she

sees Child lying in the gutter—having been struck by a car negligently operated by Drunk. Mother's emotional distress at this sight results in her suffering a heart attack. Is Mother entitled to recover against Drunk for the heart attack? ________

92. Edith is seated on a curbside bench waiting for a bus, when a car negligently driven by Archie roars past her at high speed.

  a. Assume that Archie's car splatters mud and debris from the gutter all over Edith's dress, causing her extreme embarrassment and anguish. Is Archie subject to liability for negligent infliction of emotional distress to Edith? ________

  b. Assume that Archie's car appeared to be careening out of control toward Edith herself, but swerved away at the last moment, and Edith fainted out of fright, but otherwise sustained no injury. Is Archie subject to liability for negligently causing emotional distress to Edith? ________

DEFENSES TO NEGLIGENCE

93. Don drove his car into an intersection without stopping at a posted stop sign. He broadsided a car being driven by Paula, causing her severe injuries.

  a. Assume that Paula was at fault in failing to keep a proper lookout on the road ahead of her, so that she was unable to avoid the impact. Assume further, however, that Paula's carelessness was slight as compared to Don's. Is Don excused from liability because of Paula's relatively slight negligence? ________

  b. Assume that Paula was not at all negligent in causing the accident, but thereafter carelessly failed to obtain medical attention for her injuries, causing aggravation thereof. Is Don excused from liability because of Paula's careless failure to obtain medical aid? ________

94. Able rushes into the street to rescue a child in the direct path of Beetle's negligently driven car. Able failed to see another car coming from a different direction, negligently driven by Charlie, and is struck and injured thereby.

  a. Is Charlie excused from liability because of Able's failure to look both ways before dashing into the street? ________

  b. Is Beetle subject to liability for Able's injuries? ________

  c. Assume that the child was Able's son, and that the ***child was negligent*** in wandering into the street, so that in some jurisdictions the child could not have recovered against either Beetle or Charlie. Is this a valid defense to Able's cause of action against either defendant? ________

95. In a ***contributory negligence*** state, Pedestrian entered the crosswalk at an intersection while reading a newspaper. He did not realize that he was walking against the traffic signal and into the path of oncoming traffic.

a. Brenda was driving down the street at an excessive speed. She would have been able to avoid Pedestrian, but for the fact that she glanced away from the road while lighting a cigarette. As a result, her car hit Pedestrian and knocked him unconscious. Assume that had Pedestrian looked up he would have seen Brenda's car coming and would have been able to get out of the way until just before the impact. Is Brenda subject to liability to Pedestrian? ________

b. Same facts as in the previous paragraph, except assume that Brenda was traveling so fast, and the street was so narrow, that even if Pedestrian had looked up he would ***not*** have been able to get out of the way in time. Under those circumstances would Brenda be subject to liability to Pedestrian? ________

96. Virginia and Georgia have a carpool for riding to work, the agreement being that Georgia will reimburse Virginia for half the expenses incurred in driving, parking, etc. On the way to work one day, a collision occurs between Virginia's car and another car driven by Florida in which both drivers were negligent. Georgia is the only one injured.

a. If Georgia sues Florida, will she be barred from recovery because Virginia was contributorily negligent in causing the collision? ________

b. Assume that, instead of a carpool, Virginia was in fact Georgia's chauffeur. In such a case, would Georgia be barred from recovering against Florida because of Virginia's negligence? ________

97. In a ***comparative negligence*** jurisdiction, Plaintiff proves that he sustained $8,000 damages, while Defendant proves that she sustained $2,000 damages, as the result of an accident in which both were equally at fault. How much is Plaintiff entitled to recover against Defendant? ________

(A) $8,000

(B) 8/10 of $8,000 (*i.e.*, $6,400)

(C) $4,000

(D) Zero

98. Louise is a passenger on a bus operated by Bus Co. The driver of the bus operates it at an excessive speed, causing it to go off the road and crash. Louise is seriously injured in the crash and sues Bus Co. Which of the following, if any, constitutes an assumption of the risk? ________

(A) The ticket that Louise purchased expressly provided that Bus Co. would not be liable for personal injuries to passengers regardless of cause, and a large sign at the bus station provided the same.

(B) Louise was aware when she got on the bus that the driver had been drinking.

(C) Louise sat right behind the bus driver, saw that he was speeding, and laughingly encouraged him to go "faster, faster!"

99. Interstate Oil Company fails to maintain properly its oil pipelines; as a result, one of the lines ruptures and spreads crude oil over a busy highway. The highway becomes so slippery as to be impassable. Harry is driving to work, sees the condition of the highway, and knows that the only available detour will cause him to be one-half hour late to work. Rather than risk his job, he decides to drive carefully through the oil spill. However, his car goes out of control and crashes, and he is injured. Has Harry assumed the risk? ________

STRICT LIABILITY

100. One of Farmer's cattle escapes from his farm, wanders onto Neighbor's land, and tramples her flowers. Neighbor attempts to drive the cow off of her land but the cow resists, knocking her down. Neighbor breaks her arm in the fall. For which of the following, if any, is Farmer subject to liability to Neighbor in the absence of any showing of negligence? ________

(A) Trespass

(B) Damage to the flowers

(C) Broken arm

101. Buckeroo operates a riding stable at a summer resort. One of the horses has a habit of breaking into a gallop on his own, but most riders are able to handle this. Buckeroo rents this horse to Tenderfoot, after warning him that the horse was likely to gallop. Tenderfoot is thrown when the horse breaks into a gallop.

a. Is Buckeroo subject to liability for Tenderfoot's injuries in the absence of a showing of negligence? ________

b. Is Buckeroo subject to liability on a negligence theory? ________

c. Assume that the horse Buckeroo rents to Tenderfoot is very gentle, but the horse throws and injures Tenderfoot because it is "spooked" by a rattlesnake. The snake is actually a pet kept in a cage in Buckeroo's office as a visitor's attraction. The snake had escaped from the cage, but was incapable of harming anyone as it had been defanged. Is Buckeroo subject to liability for Tenderfoot's injuries in the absence of any showing of negligence? ________

102. Priscilla keeps a Doberman Pinscher as a watchdog. It has never attacked anyone, but Priscilla knows that Dobermans as a breed are characteristically ferocious toward strangers.

a. One night, Elvis, the next door neighbor, comes home drunk and tries to crawl in the window of Priscilla's house, thinking it is his own. Elvis is attacked and severely bitten by the Doberman. Is Priscilla subject to liability therefor in the absence of any showing of negligence? ________

b. The following morning, the Doberman playfully trips the mail carrier on the front porch, causing her severe injuries. Is Priscilla subject to liability in the absence of any showing of negligence? ________

c. That afternoon, while the Doberman is sitting on the front porch, a bill collector comes to knock on the door. The Doberman growls menacingly, but the bill collector ignores him and keeps coming. Finally, the Doberman attacks and severely injures the bill collector. Is Priscilla subject to liability in the absence of any showing of negligence on her part? ________

103. Which, if any, of the following activities should be regarded as "abnormally dangerous" for purposes of imposing strict liability for harms caused thereby? ________

(A) Firing a shotgun at birds to prevent them from roosting in a residential neighborhood.

(B) Fumigating a house with cyanide gas to kill termites.

(C) Storing a large quantity of "cherry bombs" (firecrackers containing gunpowder) in a garage in a residential neighborhood.

104. Contractor is blasting rock at a remote desert quarry. Unexpectedly, the vibrations trigger an underground avalanche, resulting in a shifting of subsurface formations miles away, which knocks out Farmer's water well. Assuming no negligence, is Contractor liable for the damage to Farmer's well? ________

PRODUCTS LIABILITY

105. Duro Drugs markets a new eye medicine after having been warned by its laboratory staff that there is a strong likelihood of an adverse side effect (potential blindness) to users. Pamela purchases and uses the drug and suffers blindness as a result thereof.

a. Can Pamela recover for a battery? ________

b. Assuming Pamela could otherwise recover for a battery, could Duro defend on the ground that Pamela was contributorily negligent in failing to read the label on the medicine that warned of possible adverse side effects? ________

106. Retailer sells a shotgun to Sport. The shotgun has a "hair trigger" (not common for this type of gun), but Retailer neglects to warn Sport about this. While Sport is using the shotgun, it discharges prematurely due to the "hair trigger," resulting in injuries to Child.

a. Is Retailer liable to Child for negligence? __________

b. Is Retailer liable to Child under strict liability? __________

107. Dealer sells and installs in Archie's house a water heater manufactured by Biltrite Water Heater Co. Shortly after installation, the water heater explodes. Archie sues Biltrite for ***negligence***. Which of the following would be a valid defense? __________

(A) The water heater exploded because of poor design, rather than as a result of carelessness in the manufacturing process.

(B) The cause of the explosion was a defective valve manufactured by another company (and merely assembled by Biltrite into its heater).

(C) Biltrite had warned all of its dealers that the particular model was potentially dangerous. Dealer was negligent in selling and installing the water heater in Archie's house after having received such warning.

(D) The damage done by the explosion was only property damage (ruined floors, etc.), and not personal injuries.

108. Dealer purchases a closeout on dynamite caps from a company that is going out of business. Dealer has had no previous knowledge or dealings with that company or its products. Dealer sells some of the dynamite caps to Contractor. The caps prove defective in use, causing injury to Bystander.

a. If Dealer had no prior knowledge that the caps were defective, is Dealer liable in ***negligence*** for Bystander's injuries? __________

b. If Dealer had warned Contractor that the dynamite caps were a "closeout" and could not be guaranteed in any way, would Dealer be liable in ***negligence*** for Bystander's injuries? __________

109. Nhu purchases a new mattress from Ben's Furniture Store. The mattress had been manufactured by Sleeptite Co., a reputable company. When Nhu gets the mattress home, she flops down on it. Unfortunately, one of the inner springs had broken inside the mattress and a sharp wire pierces her back.

a. Assume Nhu sues Ben for ***negligence***. Is she entitled to recover if she can show that Ben made absolutely no inspection of the mattress, and that if he had, the dangerous wire would have been disclosed and her injury prevented? __________

b. Assume Nhu sues Ben on a ***warranty*** theory. Is she entitled to recover even if she cannot show that Ben had any reason to know that the mattress was dangerous? __________

c. Assume Nhu sues ***Sleeptite*** on a warranty theory. Can she recover? __________

110. Shawn purchases a new Duro power lawn mower from Gus's Hardware Store, choosing the Duro because of its nationwide advertising as "engineered for safety." While using the lawn mower, Shawn is struck in the eye by a small pebble kicked up by the Duro and which passed through a gap in the safety guard surrounding the blades.

a. Can Shawn recover from Duro on a ***negligence*** theory? ________

b. Can he recover from Duro on a ***warranty*** theory? ________

c. Assume another small pebble struck ***Bystander*** in the eye. Can Bystander recover from Duro on a negligence theory? ________

d. Assume the tag on the lawn mower recites that it is sold "without any warranty express or implied," and Shawn read this when he bought the Duro. If Shawn's child, Son, is struck in the eye by a pebble which passed through a gap in the safety guard on the mower, can Son recover against Gus's on a warranty theory? ________

111. Rider purchases a motorcycle from Dealer and soon discovers that a jumper wire that automatically turns on the headlamp is defective. While driving his motorcycle one evening, Rider is injured when Driver, who does not see Rider, strikes him with her car. Can Rider recover from Dealer on a negligence theory? ________

112. Andy manufactures and packs a can of barbecued beans, which he sells to wholesaler, Beth. Beth in turn sells the beans to jobber, Carl, who resells to retail grocer, Diane. Minnie buys the can of beans, takes it home and consumes the contents, and in so doing breaks her tooth on a small pebble which was of the same size, shape, and color as the beans in the can. Assume that no reasonable inspection could have revealed the pebble, and further that the beans were sold with an ***effective*** disclaimer against all warranty liability.

a. Minnie sues Andy, Beth, Carl, and Diane. Is she entitled to recover against any of them on any theory? ________

b. Assume that it was Minnie's friend, Pearl, who ate the beans and broke her tooth. Can Pearl recover ***against Minnie*** on any theory? ________

c. Could Pearl recover from Andy, Beth, Carl, or Diane on any theory? ________

113. No-Pest manufactures a garden insecticide packaged in a push-button spray can that is produced by Container Co. George buys a can of the spray to use on his roses, and is injured when, on pushing the spray button, the insecticide sprays back into his face and eyes due to a defect in the spray mechanism. Can George recover on a strict products liability theory against ***both*** No-Pest and Container Co.? ________

114. Father purchases a bicycle manufactured by Whizzo Co. as a birthday present for Son. Unbeknownst to anyone, the bicycle has defective handbrakes, which cause Son to lose control of the bicycle and injure Pedestrian who is crossing the street.

a. If Pedestrian is unable to prove any negligence on the part of Whizzo, can Pedestrian recover from Whizzo for his injuries? ________

b. Assume that Samaritan attempted to go to the aid of the injured Pedestrian, but was struck by a passing car, negligently driven by Bankrupt. Can Samaritan recover against Whizzo for his injuries? ________

115. Loveless Products markets a new face cream that Thelma purchases and uses as per the instructions. However, it causes serious inflammation and discoloration of her facial skin. Without further evidence, can Thelma recover from Loveless on a strict products liability theory? ________

116. Loveless Products markets a new hair dye that is safe when used on the scalp, but contains certain chemicals that could cause burns to the eyes. The label on the dye states that it is intended solely for use on the scalp, but no specific warning is made about the hazard to the eyes. Betty purchases the dye, uses it on her eyebrows, and a drop gets into her eye, causing severe injury. Can Betty recover from Loveless on a strict liability theory? ________

117. National Refrigerator Co. ships its appliances in heavy cardboard cartons. These cartons are normally thrown away when the appliances are sold. However, Employer keeps some of the cartons in his warehouse and uses them to store bedding materials that he also sells. Employee is injured while climbing on one of these cartons when it collapses. Can Employee recover against National Refrigerator Co. on a strict liability theory? ________

118. Bob was injured while driving his new sports car manufactured by Kamikaze Motors, Inc. In which of the following cases could Bob recover against Kamikaze on either a negligence or strict products liability theory? ________

(A) Bob's injuries were caused when the steering in his Kamikaze failed as he was driving straight down the highway at 110 m.p.h.

(B) Bob's injuries were caused by his Kamikaze rolling over when he slammed on the brakes at 55 m.p.h. to avoid a freeway crash ahead of him.

(C) Bob's injuries were caused by the lack of any side braces or supports to shield him from the impact when his car was broadsided by another car.

119. Presto Glue Co. manufactures a pleasant-smelling liquid glue used in industrial plants. Archie has been employed for over 20 years at an industrial plant at which such glue is used. A government-sponsored research study discloses that prolonged inhalation of fumes from the type of glue manufactured by Presto can cause brain

damage. Archie sues Presto for damage to his brain, claiming such inhalation. Can he recover on a strict liability theory? __________

120. Chris was injured when his new Kamikaze sports car crashed into a highway barrier. Chris testified that he was traveling at the legal speed limit, he attempted to turn the steering wheel while rounding a curve and heard something crack, and thereafter the wheels would not turn and the car went out of control and crashed.

    a. Without any further evidence, could Chris recover against Kamikaze on a negligence theory? __________

    b. Without any further evidence, could Chris recover against Kamikaze on a strict products liability theory? __________

    c. Assume that Chris had purchased the Kamikaze as a used car, and that it had about 50,000 miles on it at the time of purchase. Would this alter your answer to either "a." or "b." above? __________

121. Kara is injured when the brakes fail on her new Kamikaze sports car, causing it to crash. Which of the following is a valid defense to a strict liability claim by Kara against Kamikaze? __________

    (A) Kamikaze had warned all dealers of a potential hazard in the braking system, and had asked that all cars sold be checked for this hazard, but the dealer who sold the car to Kara neglected to do so.

    (B) Kamikaze had notified Kara a week before the accident that there was a potential hazard in the braking system, but Kara failed to bring her car in for inspection and repair.

    (C) Kara had attempted to repair the brakes himself, but performed the job incorrectly and thereby increased the risk of failure.

122. Pete purchases a new truck from Motorco. The truck's suspension system is defectively designed so that when fully loaded the weight shifts and the truck rolls over. Pete escapes injury, but the truck and load are seriously damaged.

    a. Can Pete recover from Motorco for the damage to his truck and load on a theory of strict liability? __________

    b. Can Pete recover, on a strict liability theory, damages based on the fact that even after repair, Pete cannot operate the truck fully loaded, and therefore it is not worth what he paid for it? __________

NUISANCE

123. Ajax Chemical Co. discharges certain chemical residues into a stream adjoining its manufacturing plant. These residues render the water unfit for human consumption but do not prevent its use for agricultural or other industrial purposes.

a. Al, who is active in the ecology movement, sues Ajax for damages to all residents of the state on a nuisance theory. Can Al recover? __________

b. Tipper, who owns land downstream from Ajax, sues Ajax for damages to the water supply on a nuisance theory. Can Tipper recover? __________

124. Archie installs an air conditioning unit on the roof of his house. When the unit is turned on, it emits a very loud motor noise. The noise is particularly bothersome to Archie's neighbor, Tom, whose lot is located on a hillside immediately above Archie's lot; the noise makes it difficult for Tom and his family to sleep, to enjoy normal conversation, etc.

a. Does the maintenance of the air conditioning unit on top of Archie's roof constitute a sufficient interference with Tom's enjoyment of his property to constitute an actionable nuisance? __________

b. If Archie had no reason to know or foresee the annoyance to Tom, and did not intend to cause such annoyance, will a nuisance action lie? __________

c. Assume Tom asked Archie to modify the air conditioning unit so as to reduce the noise output, and Archie refused. If Archie continues to run the air conditioner, is it legally possible for a court to award ***punitive*** damages to Tom? __________

d. Suppose Archie proved that he had installed and used the air conditioner on his roof long before Tom moved into the neighborhood, and that Tom should have been aware of the noise problem when he bought his house. Is this a valid defense to Tom's nuisance action? __________

e. Assuming an actionable nuisance exists, can Tom recover ***both*** damages and an injunction requiring Archie to modify the air conditioner so as to abate the noise? __________

LIMITATIONS ON RIGHT TO SUE

125. Morgan is seriously injured in an auto accident as a result of Paparazzo's negligence. Morgan files suit for property damage, loss of earnings, medical expenses, and pain and suffering.

a. Assume Morgan dies prior to trial. Can the executor of his estate recover for any of the damages sued for by Morgan? __________

b. If Morgan's executor recovers a judgment in the action filed by Morgan, does this affect the right of Morgan's wife and children to sue for wrongful death? __________

c. Assume Morgan's wife and children are permitted to maintain a wrongful death action. Is it a valid defense to such an action that Morgan was contributorily negligent in the action that caused his death? _________

d. Is it a valid defense to the wrongful death action brought by Morgan's wife and children that ***Morgan's wife*** was negligent in the accident that caused Morgan's death? _________

126. Luigi is seriously injured in an auto accident as a result of Mario's negligence. Luigi ultimately recovers from the accident, however.

a. Can ***Luigi's wife*** recover against Mario for the loss of Luigi's services and company during the time he was incapacitated by his injuries? _________

b. Can ***Luigi's children*** recover against Mario for the loss of Luigi's services and company during the time he was incapacitated by his injuries? _________

127. Husband is seriously injured in an auto accident as a result of Wife's negligent operation of the family car. Assume no guest statute is in effect.

a. Can Husband recover against Wife for his injuries? _________

b. Assume that the parties' child, Son, was also injured in the same accident. Can Son recover for his injury against his mother? _________

c. Assume that Husband's father, Grandpa, was injured in the same accident. Can Grandpa recover for his injuries against his son's wife? _________

128. In responding to an emergency call, Police Officer drives her police car negligently and strikes Pedestrian.

a. Is Police Officer subject to liability for Pedestrian's injuries? _________

b. Is City (which employs Police Officer) subject to liability for Pedestrian's injuries? _________

129. Tom and Jerry are both negligent in operating their cars, causing a collision that results in a piece of debris striking and injuring pedestrian, Pat.

a. Assume Pat sues and obtains a judgment against Tom. Can Pat thereafter file a separate action against Jerry to recover more money for the same injury? _________

b. Assume Pat entered into a settlement with Tom for $100. Would this bar Pat from thereafter recovering more money from Jerry? _________

c. Assume Pat obtained a judgment against Tom for $1,000, and Tom paid this judgment. Could ***Tom*** thereafter recover $500 from Jerry (half the judgment paid to Pat)? _________

d. Assume Pat obtained a judgment against Tom for $1,000, which Tom paid. Assume further that Tom had been working for Employer at the time of the accident. Is Tom entitled to ***indemnity*** against Employer for the amount of the judgment? ________

DEFAMATION

130. After a heated conversation, Editor goes back to her office and dictates to her secretary a letter to Agent, in which she calls Agent "an incompetent fool" and "unfit to represent authors."

    a. Is Editor subject to defamation based on her dictation of the remarks to her secretary? ________

    b. If Agent then angrily shows Editor's letter to Author, is Editor subject to liability to Agent for defamation? ________

131. Eager, a reporter for the *Daily Tribune*, writes a story accusing Warden of inhumane treatment of prisoners in a local jail. The story is published in the *Tribune*, having a total circulation of 10,000 readers. However, the following week, *Newsbeat Magazine*, having a nationwide circulation, repeats the story, carefully stating its source. The entire story is untrue, and both the newspaper and magazine were negligent in publishing it. (Assume Warden is not a "public official.")

    a. Is the owner of the *Daily Tribune* subject to liability even if she reasonably believed Eager's story was accurate when she published it? ________

    b. Is *Newsbeat Magazine* subject to liability even though it carefully ascribed the story to the *Daily Tribune*? ________

    c. Assuming *Newsbeat Magazine* is subject to liability, are the news dealers and distributors who handle the magazine also subject to such liability? ________

132. Could a defamation action be successfully based on any of the following published statements?

    a. "Angela's father [now deceased] was a convicted murderer." ________

    b. "Police officers in the 54th Precinct have been taking payoffs from local vice lords for years." (Angela is an officer in the Precinct.) ________

    c. "Angela has been having a torrid love affair with Dwight." (Angela is married to Andy.) ________

    d. "Angela has been spending an awful lot of time with Dwight." (Angela is married to Andy.) ________

133. Secretary Amy has told many of her friends, "All of my jobs were fun except for one where the boss was a pervert." Most of her friends do not know to whom she is

referring, but a few interpret this to apply to Waldo, the only employer to ever fire Amy. Actually, Amy was referring to a different person. Is Amy liable to Waldo for defamation? ________

134. The *Daily Tribune* publishes a report that "Engelbert Q. Schultz was arrested last night in a narcotics raid." Actually, there are two men by that name. Is the *Tribune* subject to liability for defamation to the Engelbert Q. Schultz who was not arrested if his friends read the report and think it referred to him? ________

135. In the course of a live television broadcast of a football game, the cameras pan over the huge crowd. A picture is transmitted showing several members of the crowd carrying a large banner reading, "No wonder we lose . . . Coach Jones spends all his time chasing college girls!"

   a. Assuming Coach Jones is not a public personage, is the television station subject to liability to Coach Jones for defamation? ________

   b. Assume that the television station was subject to liability for defamation based on the picture shown. Would Coach Jones be entitled to recover without proof of actual damages? ________

136. After losing a jury trial, Lawyer asks to speak to Judge in chambers. Lawyer tells Judge that he is a "prejudiced boob" and "unfit to sit on the bench." Judge had been expecting some sort of outburst from Lawyer, and therefore had left open his intercom line, and Lawyer's remarks were overheard by Clerk.

   a. Is Lawyer subject to liability for defamation because Clerk overheard Lawyer's remarks to Judge? ________

   b. Assume Lawyer is otherwise subject to liability for defamation. Were his remarks privileged? ________

   c. Assume Lawyer is otherwise subject to liability for defamation. Is Judge entitled to recover without proof of any damages? ________

137. Which, if any, of the following ***oral*** statements would be actionable without proof of any actual damages suffered by the person defamed—assuming the defendant deliberately lied? ________

   (A) "Patty is a dirty crook!"

   (B) "Peter chases everything in skirts!"

   (C) "Paula sleeps with every man in town!"

   (D) "Father Mulcahy [a clergyman] was seen in the company of prostitutes."

(E) "Dentist Smith was seen in the company of prostitutes."

(F) "Phillip is being investigated for the murder of his wife."

138. Which, if any, of the statements listed in the preceding paragraph would be actionable without proof of any actual damages, if they were published ***in writing***? ________

139. The *Daily Tribune* prints in its "Letters to the Editor" column a letter from Teller accusing Banker of misusing Bank funds. This letter is widely read, and Banker is summarily dismissed by Bank. Because there is a "retraction statute" in effect, Banker demands and receives a retraction from the *Daily Tribune*.

   a. Does the published retraction affect Banker's right to recover loss of income in a defamation suit against the *Tribune*? ________

   b. Does the published retraction affect Banker's right to recover general damages from Teller? ________

140. Snitch and Sterling are young executives at Acme Manufacturing, competing for a promotion. To prevent Sterling from getting ahead of her, Snitch tells Acme's president that Sterling uses narcotics. This is in fact ***true***, although Snitch was merely making an educated guess about it when she informed the president; and she did so with the intent of injuring Sterling's business career. Can Sterling recover against Snitch for defamation? ________

141. Partner Ernie sues Partner Bert for dissolution of their partnership. Ernie sets forth in his complaint as grounds for dissolution irreconcilable business differences with Bert, and that Bert was a member of the Mafia. This latter statement is untrue. Is Ernie subject to liability for defamation? ________

142. During the recess of a jury trial, Judge remarks to Clerk, "Plaintiff's attorney is absolutely incompetent—he is either drunk, or stupid, or both!" Is Judge subject to liability for defamation? ________

143. A Senate Investigating Committee is looking into cost overruns on a highway construction project. An auditor for one of the contractors is subpoenaed as a witness and volunteers testimony that his boss, Contractor, is a "card-carrying communist."

   a. Is Auditor subject to liability for defamation? ________

   b. Senator interjects, "Yes, we know that Contractor is a communist, but that is irrelevant to the issue here." Is Senator subject to liability for defamation? ________

   c. That evening, the *Daily Tribune* carries a report of the committee proceedings, which includes the statement that "The only interesting thing that happened all day was the accusation by Auditor that Contractor was a 'card-carrying communist'." Assume the *Daily Tribune* had reason to doubt the accuracy of Auditor's charge. Is the *Daily Tribune* subject to liability for defamation? ________

d. The following day, several reporters asked the Attorney General if he had seen the reports that Contractor was a "card-carrying communist." He replied: "Yes, I have. This is hardly new information, however. I've known Contractor was a 'commie' for many years." Is Attorney General subject to liability for defamation? ________

144. Stalwart and Sterling are young executives competing for a promotion at Acme Insurance Co. The president of Acme interviews each of them in turn. In the course of the interview, Stalwart says, "I just want to make sure you have all the facts on Sterling. Are you aware that he smokes marijuana regularly?" This is in fact untrue, although Stalwart reasonably believed what he said was true. Is Stalwart subject to liability for defamation? ________

145. Stalwart and Sterling are young executives competing for a promotion at Acme Insurance Co. Although neither is requested to obtain letters of recommendation, Stalwart thinks it would be a good idea to do so. Therefore, he asks one of his friends, Pompous, to write a letter to Acme's president, recommending Stalwart for the promotion. In the course of the letter, Pompous writes, "In any case, make sure you don't give the job to that no-good, pot-smoking Sterling." Pompous reasonably believed what he wrote about Sterling was true, but it was not. Is Pompous subject to liability for defamation? ________

146. Coward Hosell, the famous sports broadcaster, states on the air that the reason that Quarterback has "slowed down so much" this season is that he is "spending all his energy chasing dames." Quarterback is happily married and is not a woman-chaser. Assume Hosell had ***no information*** one way or the other on Quarterback's sex life when he made the statement. Is Hosell subject to liability for defamation? ________

147. In a heated election campaign for City Clerk, Candidate charges Incumbent with having committed statutory rape many years ago. This is in fact untrue, but Candidate honestly believed what he said, having received inaccurate information from one of his staff. Is Candidate subject to liability for defamation? ________

148. In the midst of an energy crisis, the *Daily Tribune* publishes an editorial containing the following statement: "It is perfectly obvious that the federal energy administrator, Jones, has been conspiring with the president of our local private power company, Smith, to drive up the cost of electricity to the public." This is in fact untrue, and the editor was negligent in making these charges.

a. Is the *Daily Tribune* subject to liability to Jones (the federal energy administrator)? ________

b. Is the *Daily Tribune* subject to liability to Smith (the president of the local private corporation)? ________

149. *Newsbeat Magazine* publishes a feature article on Senator Claghorn. The article falsely states that Claghorn is a "compulsive gambler."

a. Does this statement fall within the scope of the constitutional privilege? ________

b. Assume *Newsbeat* based its article on a sworn statement given by Claghorn's ex-secretary, but *Newsbeat* did nothing to verify the statement because it was on a vendetta to "get" Claghorn and wanted to publish the information as soon as possible. Is this sufficient "malice" to defeat any claim of privilege? ________

INVASION OF PRIVACY

150. The *Daily Tribune* prints a story captioned, "The Mini-Skirt Survives!", accompanied by a photo showing local women wearing minis on the streets. One of the photos is of Ranka, and it is rather unflattering of her. Ranka gave no permission to the *Daily Tribune* to take or publish her photograph. Can she recover for an invasion of her privacy? ________

151. In an effort to discourage local screening of sex films, Police Chief stations a police photographer next to the box office of a movie theatre showing such films, with instructions to take the picture of every person entering the theatre. Eager purchases a ticket and has his picture taken by the police photographer. Without any further use or publication of Eager's photo, is Police Chief subject to liability for invasion of Eager's privacy? ________

152. Actress Amy is very sensitive about her age, and has been passing herself off for years as "39 or so." Rona Rumor, the Hollywood columnist, publishes the following item: "Thought you'd like to know . . . the Hall of Records showed me Amy's birth certificate . . . the poor girl is only 62 this year. Amazing!"

a. Is Rona Rumor subject to liability for invasion of privacy as to Amy? ________

b. Assume Rona Rumor's column went on to state that Amy has had three face lifts in the past few years from Dr. Patchum, plus silicone injections in her buttocks. Would such disclosures be actionable invasions of Amy's privacy? ________

153. The *San Francisco Daily News* publishes a series of articles dealing with the psychology of those who commit suicide by jumping off the Golden Gate Bridge. As a "typical" suicide, they focus on Jumper, who leapt to his death 10 years ago. The story sets forth details of Jumper's life, including the fact that he was despondent because his wife, Portia, had left him for another man. Accompanying the article is a picture of Jumper's corpse after it was retrieved from the water.

a. Is the *Daily News* subject to liability to Jumper's estate for an invasion of his right to privacy? ________

b. Is the *Daily News* subject to liability to Jumper's heirs (children) for the embarrassment and anguish of seeing the picture of Jumper's corpse in the newspaper? __________

c. Is the *Daily News* subject to liability to Portia for publication of the facts of her life (*i.e.*, that she left Jumper for another man)? __________

d. Assume that the *Daily News* inadvertently got the facts wrong, and that Portia had been a faithful wife all along. Would its error preclude the *Daily News* from claiming that its publication was privileged as "newsworthy"? __________

154. Smirnup Vodka markets a new canned cocktail called "The Businessman's Pickup." To publicize their product, they hire a sexy female model to stand in a doorway on a public street, and then, with a concealed camera, they capture the glances from men passing by. One of these photos shows a portly businessman named Pompous ogling the model; he was totally unaware that his picture was being taken. This photo is used by Smirnup in its national advertising campaign.

a. If Pompous sues for an invasion of privacy, is it a valid defense that Smirnup merely publicized what had occurred on a public street? __________

b. If Pompous is otherwise entitled to recover for an invasion of privacy, must he prove some special damages as a result of the publicity? __________

MISREPRESENTATION

155. Patrick purchases an expensive home in Belleaire from Debbie. Prior to signing, Patrick asks Debbie if the roof leaks. Is there an actionable misrepresentation in any of the following responses by Debbie?

a. Debbie replied that she had recently obtained an inspection report showing no visible leaks in the roof. In fact, no such report had been obtained; and, unbeknownst to Debbie, the roof leaks. __________

b. Debbie replied that there were no leaks in the roof, because she had never seen evidence of any, but afterwards, just to check, she went into the attic and found water damage. She decided not to tell Patrick about this because he had not asked her to investigate and report back to him. __________

c. Debbie made no reply to Patrick's inquiry, but knew that the roof leaked. __________

d. Debbie's only reply to Patrick's inquiry was that the house was being sold "as is," while all along Debbie knew that the roof leaked. __________

156. Pamela purchases an expensive home in Belleaire. Prior to signing, Pamela asks Dudley if the house is free of termite infestation, and he replies that it is. It turns out, however, that the house is termite-infested. Is Dudley subject to liability for misrepresentation in any of the following cases?

a. Dudley honestly believed that there were no termites when he said so, having made a careful inspection of the premises himself recently, and having seen none. ________

b. Dudley made his statement in reliance on a report by a reputable pest control company that had conducted a recent inspection of the premises, and reported to him no infestation. ________

c. Dudley had never seen any termites, but on the other hand, he had never made an inspection of the premises to check for termite infestation. ________

d. Dudley was not the seller of the house, but rather a licensed pest control inspector whom Pamela had hired to inspect the property, and he simply did a poor job, overlooking the infestation. ________

157. Flako Enterprises, Inc., applies to Bank for a loan and submits a financial statement certified by Accountant. The statement contains several material misrepresentations, known by Flako to be false.

a. Assume that Bank turns down the loan application, but Bank's lending officer reads the financial statement and decides to invest personally in Flako stock. If he later discovers the financial statements were false, can he sue Flako for fraud? ________

b. Assume that Bank granted the loan on the basis of the financial statements submitted, without doing any independent checking of Flako's credit. If Bank later discovered that the financial statements were false, could Flako defend a fraud suit on the ground that Bank was imprudent in relying exclusively on the statements submitted? ________

c. Assume that Bank granted the loan on the basis of the financial statements certified by Accountant. If Flako subsequently went bankrupt, and the falsity of the financial statements was then discovered, could Bank recover from Accountant the amount of its loss? ________

d. Assume that Bank had made an independent credit check on Flako, and realized that the financial statements submitted were not accurate. Would this bar Bank's misrepresentation action against Flako and Accountant? ________

158. As part of the negotiations leading up to the sale of an apartment house, Seller made the following representations to Buyer, each of which was false. Which of these representations would subject Seller to liability for misrepresentation if relied upon by Buyer? ________

(A) "This property is worth at least $150,000, but I'll sell it to you for $120,000."

(B) "I have not previously offered this property for sale."

(C) "I don't think anything in the City Building Code will prevent you from splitting the larger apartments into smaller ones, if you want to, thereby increasing the rents."

159. While playing golf at the country club, Swinger tells his friend, Duffer, that he is considering making a loan to a company called Flako Enterprises, and asks Duffer if he knows the company. Duffer replies that he does, and that he considers it "a fine company with great business prospects." Actually, Flako Enterprises is on the verge of bankruptcy, and Duffer knows this because he is its major stockholder (a fact he does not disclose to Swinger).

a. If Swinger makes the loan in reliance on Duffer's assurances, and Flako later goes bankrupt, can Swinger recover from Duffer for misrepresentation? __________

b. Assume that Flako did ***not*** go bankrupt, and actually repaid the loan when due. Could Swinger sue Duffer for fraud on the theory that Duffer had deceived him into making a loan that Swinger otherwise would not have made? __________

160. Fastbuck advertises lots for sale in Golden Years Subdivision, which consists of undeveloped desert acreage. Eager visits the subdivision, and asks what improvements are planned. Fastbuck tells Eager all about planned swimming pools, shopping centers, etc., and relying thereon Eager buys one of the lots for $5,000. The swimming pools, shopping centers, etc., are never built.

a. Assume that Fastbuck never had the funds to build the promised swimming pools, etc., and never had ***any reasonable prospects*** of being able to do so. Can Eager recover damages for misrepresentation? __________

b. Assume that Eager is entitled to recover damages for misrepresentation. Assume further that the lot he purchased for $5,000 would have been worth $10,000 if the promised improvements had been completed, but that, as is, the lot is not worth more than $2,000. What is the proper measure of recovery to which Eager is entitled? __________

OTHER TORTS

161. Pioneer Aviation Co. and Aerospace Industries, Inc. are competing to obtain a government contract. Pioneer's sales manager tells the government procurement officer, "Be careful about accepting any bids from Aerospace . . . they're in real hot water with their creditors . . . they could be in bankruptcy any day now." If Aerospace files a tort action against Pioneer based on the foregoing statement, which of the following statements, if any, is true? __________

(A) No cause of action for disparagement lies because Pioneer's sales manager was only expressing her opinion.

(B) If the statements made are actionable as disparagement, the burden is on Pioneer to prove as a defense that the sales manager's statements were true.

(C) No action for disparagement lies unless malice toward the defendant is established.

(D) If the statements made are otherwise actionable as disparagement, Aerospace can recover against Pioneer even if Aerospace ends up with the government contract.

162. Sly opens a hamburger stand across the street from a stand operated by Fry. Sly tells people in the neighborhood, "Be careful about eating at Fry's; his so-called '100% beefburgers' are actually horsemeat!" Sly's statements are untrue. Can Fry recover against Sly ***in the absence of special damages***? ________

163. Wiley filed an action against Bright, claiming an interest in certain land to which Bright held title. Concurrently with filing the lawsuit, Wiley recorded a lis pendens, which put all persons on notice of the action, and effectively clouded Bright's title. Bright eventually won the lawsuit. If Wiley filed the suit without a good faith belief in its merits, can Bright recover for a ***slander of title*** based on the filing of the lis pendens? ________

164. Vera is the national sales manager for Loveless Cosmetics, and is employed at a salary of $5,000 per month. Regal, a competitor of Loveless, offers to double Vera's salary if she will come to work for them; she accepts. Which if any of the following statements is true? ________

(A) An action for inducing breach of contract cannot be maintained because Vera's employment was terminable by her at will.

(B) The fact that Vera's contract was terminable at will is relevant to the measure of damages, if Loveless is entitled to recover.

(C) Regal was privileged to induce Vera to terminate her contract with Loveless.

165. National Motors is negotiating with Sparko Batteries for the purchase of one million auto batteries. Sparko purchases its battery cases exclusively from Case. National Motors tells Sparko if it wants to do business with National, it will have to purchase all battery cases from another supplier. Can Case recover against National Motors for interference with its contractual relationship with Sparko? ________

166. Employer finds her cash drawer rifled and accuses Employee of having taken the money. Employee denies it. Employer thereupon calls the police and has Employee arrested on a theft charge. However, the charges against Employee are subsequently dismissed for insufficient evidence. Employee thereupon files an action against Employer for malicious prosecution. Which of the following statements, if any, is true? ________

(A) The action will not lie because Employee was not acquitted of the criminal charges against him.

(B) The burden is on Employee to prove that Employer instituted the action against him for some purpose other than bringing a guilty person to justice.

(C) The burden is on Employee to prove that Employer had no honest or reasonable belief in Employee's guilt when she called the police.

(D) Employer may prove as a defense that Employee actually took the money from the cash drawer.

(E) If Employee is entitled to recover, he may recover damages to his reputation in addition to the actual costs incurred in defending against the criminal charge.

Answers to Review Questions

1.a. **YES** — Any volitional act suffices. Donna may have acted in a panic, but she was in command of her senses, and hence her act was "volitional." [§§2, 4]

b. **YES** — All that is required is that Donna believed a harmful touching of one of the shoppers was substantially certain to occur. No hatred or ill will need be shown. [§§6-9]

2.a. **NO** — For two reasons: Because Horace was under hypnosis, there was no ***"voluntary"*** act; and there was ***no intent*** to inflict such a touching. [§§3, 6]

b. **YES** — Although there was no direct touching, Waldo ***set in motion the forces*** that caused the touching (Horace and the water). He will be deemed to have intended that which was ***substantially certain*** to happen. [§17]

3.a. **YES** — He committed a battery. David intended to cause a "harmful touching" (intoxication) of everyone at the party. This act was a substantial factor in bringing about the result that occurred (Greta's illness), and hence causation is established. Again, even without any direct "touching" of Greta, David set in motion the force that caused the touching, and that is sufficient. [§§7, 17]

b. **PROBABLY NOT** — No battery because the touching (by dancing) was consented to. [§100] No assault because words by themselves are usually not sufficient to create apprehension of ***immediate*** harmful or offensive touching. [§29] And probably no liability for intentional infliction of emotional distress because David did not intend to inflict such on Peggy (although arguably David was "reckless" in this regard). [§86]

c. **DEPENDS** — On whether a ***reasonable person*** in Zeke's position would have been offended by the shaking. (The fact that Zeke was offended is not conclusive, unless David knew that Zeke was particularly sensitive about being shaken.) Because they were "pals," there may be some latitude in what a reasonable person would regard as "offensive." [§§14-15]

d. **YES** — Under the ***transferred intent*** doctrine, David is liable for a battery even though he intended only an assault (to frighten Zeke), and even though the person struck was not the person he intended to frighten. Even though David and Zeke were "pals," and therefore it is arguable that there was some sort of consent to horseplay between them, Zeke's "consent" would not apply to Beth's cause of action. [§10]

4.a. **YES** — If Prudence heard it and was placed in apprehension of an immediate harmful touching thereby. The fact that the threat was ***conditional*** ("get off the streets or else") is immaterial, because the command was not one that Mildred was privileged to make. [§§35-46]

b. **YES** It is immaterial that George was only "joking" or that he had no intent to actually harm his sister. He intended to place her in apprehension of an imminent contact and that is sufficient. [§32] (*Note:* Intrafamily tort immunity does ***not*** apply to claims between brothers and sisters.) [§1221]

c. **YES** It is sufficient that she be in apprehension of a ***touching.*** She need not be frightened. [§§48-49]

d. **YES** *Apparent* ability is all that is required for the tort of assault. (The rule is contra under many criminal statutes.) [§§50-51]

5.a. **PROBABLY NOT** No battery because no actual touching. [§11] No assault because Tony was ***unaware*** of Rocky's attempt at the time thereof; and by the time he turned, Rocky was under arrest so no apprehension of further danger. [§§35-37] (And probably no liability for intentional infliction of emotional distress, because this was not what Rocky was intending—although again, arguably, Rocky was "reckless" in this regard.) [§§86-88] (*Compare:* Rocky could be ***criminally*** prosecuted in many states for an attempted battery.)

b. **NO** While Stranger intentionally placed Tony in apprehension of harm from Rocky, his doing so was probably ***privileged.*** [§103]

6. **YES** If Doug was intending to put Pete in apprehension, and such apprehension actually resulted from Doug's acts, it makes no difference that a "reasonable" person would not have been apprehensive. ***The test is subjective.*** [§§32, 49]

7. **YES** There was as much a confinement as if Bob had been locked in the office. A plaintiff is not required to escape by means that would offend a reasonable sense of personal dignity. No damages need be shown. [§§62-63, 71, 77]

8.a. **NO** There must be ***knowledge*** of the confinement ***at the time*** thereof. [§64]

b. **YES** It is ***not*** necessary that a person know by whom he was confined, as long as he realized he ***was*** confined during the confinement. Janitor is liable even though he had no intent to harm Law Student; it is sufficient that he took action (locking up) that he knew would result in confinement. [§§57-60, 64]

9. **PROBABLY NOT** He cannot recover on the basis of being driven in the car because he apparently consented to this (as part of fraternity initiation). [§100] Whether he can recover based on his being abandoned in the desert depends on whether this was a "confinement." If "reasonable" means of escape are available, there is no confinement; and it would seem that for a young man to walk the 20 miles is not an unreasonable means of escape. (Of course, the result would be contra if Neal was disabled ***and*** Fraternity brothers ***knew*** it.) [§§62, 71]

10.a. **YES** Failure to release a person when under a ***legal duty*** to come to his aid (employer-employee) constitutes a sufficient "act" of confinement. [§§72-73]

b. **NO** As long as Pete was conscious that he was being confined by someone (the robbers), it is not necessary that he know by whom else (Dan). [§§60, 64]

11.a. **NO** The obstruction of a private driveway is ***not*** a "confinement." [§§61-63] (*Compare:* XYZ may recover on a theory of private nuisance.) [§§1107 ***et seq.***]

b. **NO** False imprisonment relates to confinement of one's person, not one's car. (Result could be contra, however, if the plant was so remotely situated that auto transportation is the only way out, in which event depriving the workers of auto transportation might "confine" them personally.) [§§60-63]

12. **NO** Because Virgil took no part in the decision to make an arrest or in the actual arrest, he is not liable for false imprisonment. [§75] (*Compare:* He might be liable for ***malicious prosecution*** however, ***if*** Homer can show that Virgil acted without probable cause.) [§§1759 ***et seq.***]

13.a. **YES** Dick was asserting legal authority, and Phil submitted thereto. [§74]

b. **NO** Because Dick was not intending to take Phil before any court; he was intending only to "lecture" him. Hence, not a proper exercise of citizen's privilege of arrest. [§§166-167]

14.a. **NO** Because a submission to authority must be in the ***presence*** of the person asserting the authority (not over the telephone). [Rest. 2d §41 cmt. f] [§74]

b. **NO** Because ***no submission*** to Sheriff's custody. Compliance with Sheriff's demands—even if illegal—is not a submission to arrest. Hence, no false imprisonment. [§74]

c. **NO** But not because she did not tell Sheriff about paying the traffic ticket. Rather, because Sheriff is ***privileged*** in taking a person into custody under any warrant that is ***fair on its face***—even though it may have been issued in error. [§§168-169]

15.a. **PROBABLY** The intent or recklessness required for the intentional tort can be inferred where the defendant knows that the plaintiff is particularly susceptible to emotional distress (the fact that Harvey had been warned ["all visitors"] not to upset Emil is certainly evidentiary). If intent is found, then Harvey's conduct could be viewed as so extreme and outrageous that liability ***would*** be imposed. [§§86-87] *Note:* ***Words alone*** may constitute sufficient "outrageous conduct" for imposition of liability for intentional infliction of emotional distress. [§80]

b. **SPLIT** The older view requires demonstrable ***physical*** injuries; mere shock or anger is not enough. [§90] But the modern trend is contra—*i.e.,* where the defendant ***intends*** to cause severe emotional distress in the plaintiff, the outrageous nature of the defendant's conduct is deemed a more reliable indication of damage than physical injury. [§91]

16. **NO** By failing to object, she has manifested her apparent consent to being searched. The fact that she was "anxious to reach her destination" does ***not*** constitute "duress" so as to vitiate the consent given. [§§102, 108]

17.a. **PROBABLY NOT** There is implied consent to all physical contacts that are a ***normal*** part of the sport, and being hit with a hockey stick is probably not abnormal for the game. [§102]

b. **PROBABLY** Pierre's consent would extend only to touchings by those with whom contact was foreseeable (*i.e.,* other players). Unless violence from the fans is found to be a customary part of the sport, Pierre's consent would not extend to George's acts. [§§102, 105]

18.a. **YES** Specialist would be. Barbara's consent to a touching by Doctor is not effective as to anyone else, no matter how skillful, and even though the operation was successful. [§105]

b. **POSSIBLY** The issue would be whether Barbara's consent was sufficiently ***"informed."*** If Doctor failed to advise her as to the size and location of possible scars, her consent would not be effective (particularly if Doctor was aware of Barbara's modeling career). She might have chosen to forgo the operation rather than suffer the scars. [§113]

c. **NO** First of all, this is an unusual situation because except in emergencies, doctors generally insist on an express consent (including right to remove diseased organs) before they operate. Even without this, however, most courts would probably hold that the consent given here (to determine ***cause*** of stomach pains) would be broad enough to justify removal of whatever was causing the pain. Alternately, a court might find ***"implied consent"*** based on the fact that the removal was ultimately necessary to protect her life. [§§103-105]

19. **NO** The "fraud" goes to a ***collateral matter*** (disposition of the traffic ticket) rather than to the act (sexual intercourse) to which she consented. And, threat of loss of one's driver's license does not constitute "duress" so as to vitiate the consent given. [§§106-108]

20.a. **PROBABLY NOT** There was no actual force, and Owner's "insisting" that Betty remain probably did not constitute duress, because there was no threat of ***unlawful*** conduct. [§§66-68, 108]

b. **YES** Threats of harm to a spouse (Barney) ***are*** sufficient duress to negate her consent to the sexual acts. [§108]

21. **YES (most courts)** Most courts hold that where ***breach of the peace*** is involved, public interest requires that participants be held liable civilly, as well as criminally; and hence, their "consent" is not effective to prevent tort liability. Some courts hold a plaintiff's consent effective in any case, thus barring later claims based on the fight. [§§116-117]

22. **NO** When Buford acted, there apparently was ***no further threat*** from Arlene; *i.e.*, Buford acted in retaliation, not in self-defense. (Of course, the result might be contra if Buford could show that Arlene was about to throw another stone.) [**§§120, 131**]

23. **(B)** (A) is false because there is no privilege to use deadly force in self-defense where the only present threat is of nondeadly force. [**§124**]

(B) is true so long as a reasonable person (objective test) would believe he was in danger of imminent battery. [**§§120, 136**]

(C) is false because there is generally ***no*** duty to retreat before using ***nondeadly*** force. [**§122**]

(D) is false because Bob is entitled to rely on the ***apparent*** threat, regardless of Charlie's actual intentions. [**§120**]

24. **NO** If the only apparent threat of harm is ***nonserious*** (fist), Carl would be privileged to use only ***nonserious*** force. It makes no difference that serious bodily harm (brass knuckles) was in fact being threatened, because Carl was ignorant of the danger. [**§§124, 136**]

25. **(D)** (A) is false because even in jurisdictions that recognize the duty to retreat, it does not apply where the actor (Ling) is in her own home. [**§§125-128**]

(B) is false because even though the grenade might not kill Ling, it still would be a battery (harmful or offensive touching), and she would be entitled to use nondeadly force to prevent same. [**§120**]

(C) is false because the privilege of self-defense is conditioned on a ***reasonable*** belief (objective standard). [**§136**]

(D) is true insofar as Ling's liability ***to Raoul.*** But, of course, the fact that Ling's acts are privileged as to Raoul would not insulate her from liability (for negligence, if not battery) to anyone else foreseeably injured thereby. [**§§134-135**]

26. **(A) AND (C)** (A) is true. Because Frank's conduct appears to be negligent, rather than intentional, there is a duty to retreat. [**§122**]

(B) is false. There is a privilege to use reasonable force to prevent even a negligent touching. [**§120**]

(C) is true. A person is entitled to ***threaten*** more force than he would be privileged to inflict. [**§129**]

27. **NO** Because his act was neither intentional nor negligent as to her (risk unforeseeable), and was otherwise reasonable conduct in self-defense. [**§§135, 470**]

28. **(A) AND (B)**

(A) is true (under the traditional view, at least) because Mildred must "stand in the shoes" of Phil, and hence would not be privileged unless Phil was ***actually*** privileged. (The modern view is that Mildred would be privileged to defend Phil if it ***reasonably appeared*** that he was privileged to defend himself.) [**§§139-141**]

(B) is true (under either view) because Mildred was privileged to use only the means of defense that Phil was privileged to use. [**§§139-141**]

(C) is false because under modern law, any third person may be defended. [**§138**]

29.a. **NO**

While deadly force ***may*** be ***threatened*** to prevent a trespass upon his land, no force or threat is privileged unless it is ***reasonably necessary*** to prevent the intrusion, and a ***demand*** to leave has been ignored. The latter conditions have not been met here. [**§142**]

b. **YES**

A landowner is not privileged to use mechanical devices to prevent a trespass, unless the use thereof is reasonable under the circumstances. ***Adequate warning*** of any hidden danger is an essential element of "reasonableness." [**§143**]

30. **NO**

Most courts today hold there is ***no*** privilege to use force to recover possession of land, regardless of how possession was lost. A few courts allow the land occupier to use force if he was "tortiously dispossessed" (but that would not apply here, because ***Hussein***, not Laurence, was the land occupier who was dispossessed). [**§§146-149**]

31. **DEPENDS**

On when Apex discovered the fraud (the credit card being phony). No force is privileged unless Apex acted ***promptly*** on discovering that it had been tortiously dispossessed. (*Compare:* But Apex would still be entitled to ***reclaim the car itself,*** if this could be done ***without*** using any force on Shifty.) [**§§150-153**]

32. **NO**

Because Pierre loaned the painting to Don originally; hence, no tortious dispossession. (Arguably contra if Don was intending all along to take the painting.) [**§156**]

33. **PROBABLY NOT**

A privilege to detain for investigation is recognized where the actor has reasonable grounds to suspect ***the person detained.*** It is doubtful that courts would extend this to allow a search of a group of people. [**§§158-163**]

34.a. **YES**

Reasonable force is permitted under the "shopkeeper's privilege." Some courts would deny the privilege where (as here) the customer was apprehended ***outside*** of the store; but the better view is contra because until then, she could always claim she intended to pay. [**§§158-163**]

b. **YES**

Privilege to detain for investigation applies where the actor had ***reasonable grounds*** to suspect tortious dispossession. [**§§161, 164**]

c. **NO**	Unlike the privilege to detain for investigation (above), there is ***no*** privilege to use force ***to retake possession*** of a chattel unless the actor is ***in fact*** entitled to such possession (reasonable belief is not enough). [§151]
35.a. **YES**	A private citizen is privileged to arrest for a felony that has ***in fact*** been committed, if he reasonably suspects the person arrested committed it. [§165]
b. **YES**	A police officer (unlike a private citizen) is privileged to arrest on the basis of ***reasonable suspicion*** that a felony has been committed. [§165]
36. **NO (most courts)**	Most courts hold ***no*** police privilege to arrest those who are innocent of a misdemeanor charge, no matter how reasonable the police mistake. A minority is contra, extending the privilege to cover such mistakes. [§§166-167]
37. **YES (most courts)**	There is no privilege of arrest under a warrant, unless the person arrested is the person named therein. (A few states extend the privilege to cover reasonable mistakes, as here.) *Note:* In some states, it is a ***crime to resist arrest by a police officer***—regardless of the validity of the arrest—in which case because Sam's conduct was illegal, Sheriff would be privileged to use force to overcome. [§§168, 180]
38. **NO**	Trespass is usually limited to ***physical*** intrusions. Nonphysical intrusions such as vibrations are usually treated as a nuisance rather than a trespass. [§§188-189]
39.a. **YES**	Although the initial entry was consented to, the intentional failure to remove the poles within a reasonable period after the expiration of the license constitutes a trespass. [§188]
b. **YES**	An intrusion into the space immediately above land is treated the same as an intrusion on the surface. [§§196-200]
40. **YES**	Unless consented to, any intentional intrusion onto Jones's land is a trespass. No damages need be shown. [§§188, 204] (And no privilege here because entry was not "necessary" to protect a landowner's interests.) [§§263-264]
41. **CHEVY**	The person in ***actual*** possession is the only one who can sue (even if his right to possession could be terminated by another). [§§190-193]
42.a. **YES**	The only intent required is to deal with the chattel as he did; no intent to steal or dispossess the library is required. And the taking without the library's consent ***was*** a dispossession. [§§208-211]
b. **YES**	A dispossession is actionable either as trespass to chattels or conversion. [§§211, 220]
43.a. **YES**	Any ***intermeddling*** with the chattels of another is actionable as trespass. [§212]

b. **NO** Tearing one page would probably not amount to a destruction of the book; and a mere intermeddling is not a conversion. [§§221-222]

44. **YES** Randy is liable for ***conversion.*** He intentionally did an act that caused a ***material alteration*** (if not outright destruction) of the chattel. No intent to injure or direct touching is required. (No trespass to chattels, however, because ***no physical contact*** with the wine.) [§§210-212, 222]

45.a. **YES** Angel is liable for ***either*** trespass to chattels or conversion. Again, the only intent required is to deal with the chattel as he did; honest mistake of fact as to ownership is immaterial. [§§208, 218, 224]

b. **YES** Such refusal is a separate act of conversion (again, no matter how bona fide Angel's belief that he was entitled to possession). *Compare:* A ***qualified*** refusal (*e.g.*, to give Angel time to investigate Owner's claim) would ***not*** be actionable. [§§227-229]

46. **ONLY (E)** (A) is not a conversion because by pawning the coat Sylvia gave up the right to possession until the loan is repaid. [§230]

(B) is not a conversion by Benny because he did not intend to cause loss; a bailee is not an insurer. [§§217-218]

(C) is not a conversion for the same reason; but Benny might be liable for ***negligence.*** [§218]

(D) is not a conversion (in most courts) because—even though no right to use the coat was given—the single unauthorized use caused no harm to the chattel (regardless of Sylvia's feelings) and hence was not a "material" breach of the bailment contract. [§223]

(E) ***is*** a conversion because if any ***harm*** comes to the chattel during the unauthorized use, it constitutes a conversion, ***regardless of whose fault*** it is. [§223]

(F) is not a conversion because a bailee's obligation to return the chattel is based on a ***reasonable*** demand (and opening up at midnight would seem unreasonable). Destruction by fire is not a conversion because no intent by Benny (again, consider negligence). [§§218, 227]

47. **SPLIT** Fastbuck's selling his client's stock without authority was the act of conversion. Some courts limit recovery to the value of the stock at that time ($15 per share), the amount he pocketed. Others permit recovery of the ***highest value*** ($50 per share) between the date of conversion and the time of trial particularly where, as here, Fastbuck was apparently intending to swindle his client. [§235]

48.a. **NO** Even though he has been tortiously dispossessed, the chattel owner must ordinarily make demand for permission to enter, unless such demand would be futile, etc. Nothing here indicates demand would be futile; hence demand is a prerequisite to the right to enter. [§§239-240]

b. **NO** — Because the chattel is on Buford's land through Buford's (landowner's) own fault, Clem's privilege is ***complete***—he is not liable for damage to property in the ***reasonable*** exercise of the privilege. And he is permitted to use ***reasonable force*** against Buford as long as he is in "fresh pursuit" of his tractor. [§§242-244]

49.a. **YES** — Provided Wilbur was ***not negligent*** in allowing the dog to escape or come onto Mary's land. [§§245-246, 249]

b. **YES** — Because the privilege is ***incomplete***—the dog got onto the land without the fault of Wilbur ***or*** Mary. [§247]

c. **NO** — The privilege does not extend to breaking into dwellings. [§248]

d. **YES** — If Wilbur ***was at fault*** in the dog's coming onto Mary's land, then he would have ***no privilege*** to enter. If he wanted the dog back, he would have to sue for it (replevin, etc.). [§§245, 249]

50.a. **PROBABLY** — On either of two theories: If it ***reasonably appeared*** that disposal of the gasoline down the sewer was necessary to prevent an "imminent public disaster" (residential neighborhood), the trespass to land and conversion of the gasoline would be privileged as a ***public necessity.*** [§254] Alternatively, if the only apparent threat was to Neighbor and other immediate neighbors, such conduct might be privileged as a ***private necessity.*** [§§263-266]

b. **DEPENDS** — If the storage of gasoline in a residential neighborhood posed an ***unreasonable*** interference (threat) to Neighbor's use and enjoyment of his own land, he would be privileged to enter and ***abate a private nuisance.*** This also would be a ***complete*** privilege (although pouring the gasoline down the drain probably would ***not*** be privileged; only its removal to a safe place). [§§268-272]

51.a. **NO** — If it reasonably appeared that Wife's life was endangered, Husband was privileged to take the insulin (private necessity—to save Wife's life), and Druggist's resistance was ***not*** privileged. Therefore, Husband was ***privileged to use reasonable force to overcome*** Druggist's (nonprivileged) resistance. [§§263-265, 267]

b. **NO** — Husband's privilege to overcome Druggist's nonprivileged interference is a ***complete*** privilege. [Rest. 2d §197 cmt. k] [§267]

c. **YES** — Husband's privilege to take the insulin was ***incomplete*** because Husband was acting to protect his own interests or those of a third person (here, Wife). [§266]

52. **NONE** — While all of the evidence offered is ***admissible*** on the issue of negligence, none of it by itself disproves negligence as a matter of law. The legal standard is the amount

of care that a ***reasonable*** person would have exercised under the circumstances. [§§281-282]

(A) is not conclusive because a reasonable person might have seen the "Caution" sign even though Napoleon did not. [§284]

(B) is not conclusive because a reasonable person might have exercised a higher degree of care than was "customary" in the community. [§§385-392]

(C) is not conclusive because a reasonable person might still have slowed down or stopped even though not required by statute to do so. [§393]

53. **NONE** None of the evidence would affect the duty of care owed by Donna under the circumstances.

(A) A person's physical disability normally is relevant in determining the standard of care owed, ***but not*** where he knowingly engages in any activity (driving a car) that a reasonable person with such disability would not have attempted. [§§295-296]

(B) A person's mental deficiency is disregarded in determining the standard of care owed. [§299]

(C) The standard of care owed is the reasonable person standard; her intoxication is not relevant in this regard. [§298]

(D) Learners or beginners in any activity involving a known risk to others (driving a car) are held to the same standards as experienced persons. [§§291, 302]

54.a. **YES** The standard of care required of children is that of a reasonable person of ***like age, intelligence, and experience.*** However, if a child has superior intelligence, etc., she is to be judged according to ***her own*** (not the "average") intelligence. [§§291, 301]

b. **NO** The restricted standard of care afforded to children (above) generally does ***not*** apply where the child engages in adult activities (driving a car). [§294]

55. **ALL** (A) A professional is held to certain minimum standards even though not personally possessing the skills required. [§§301-304]

(B) A warning of lack of skill does ***not*** change the standard of care required. [*See* Rest. 2d §301] [§303]

(C) A person possessing ***superior*** competence in any field is required to perform accordingly. [§301]

56.a. **YES** Inattentiveness by the driver of an automobile in heavy traffic may be enough in itself to violate the reasonable person standard. [§§281-284]

b. **YES** Under the "Cardozo view," Gabby owed a duty of due care to all persons within the ***"zone of danger"*** (*i.e.,* foreseeable plaintiffs); and pedestrians on the sidewalk would fall in this category, even though the ***manner*** of the injury was not foreseeable. [§322] Under the "Andrews view," Gabby's duty was owed to all persons injured as a ***proximate result*** of her acts—regardless of the foreseeability of the risk of harm. [§321]

c. **SPLIT** *Not* under the "Cardozo view," because Wilma was not a foreseeable plaintiff. But, under the "Andrews view," Gabby might be held liable because Wilma's injuries were the direct and proximate result of Gabby's negligent act. [§§321-322]

d. **YES** Under either the "Andrews" or "Cardozo" views, the duty of care extends to ***rescuers***. If a rescue attempt is foolhardy under the circumstances, the defendant may not be liable for the resulting injuries. [§§327-328, 331]

57.a. **YES** The doctrine of res ipsa loquitur permits a plaintiff to prove the negligent act (*i.e.,* breach of duty) through circumstantial evidence, and thereby raises an inference or presumption that the defendant was at fault. To bring the doctrine into play, the plaintiff must establish ***three factors:*** (i) that the event would not occur in the absence of someone's negligence; (ii) that the negligence can be attributed to the defendant because the injury to the plaintiff is one which the defendant owed a duty to guard against; and (iii) that neither the plaintiff nor any third person contributed to the injury sustained. All three elements appear here: Glass would not normally be found in a loaf of bread but for someone's negligence because the package was sealed when Alma purchased the bread; Bakery is the indicated source of such negligence and owed a duty to guard against glass in its bread; and because the package was sealed, neither Alma nor any third person contributed to the injury. [§§363-378]

b. **SPLIT** Most courts treat res ipsa as raising only an ***inference*** of negligence that the trier of fact may accept or reject. [§382] However, a few courts treat it as a ***rebuttable presumption*** that shifts the burden of proof to the defendant. If the defendant fails to rebut the presumption by a ***preponderance*** of the evidence, the trier of fact is then bound by the presumption of negligence. [§383] In other states, res ipsa is a presumption that can be dispelled by ***any*** counterevidence. [§384]

58.a. **YES** Where the period of time is relatively short (here, only 15 minutes), and no other explanation appears for the car rolling downhill, the driver's negligence in parking the car can be inferred from the mere happening of the accident. (*Note:* A few courts are contra on this, holding that the lapse of any appreciable period of time suggests at least the possibility of other causes—*e.g.,* third persons tinkering with the car—which is enough to take the case out of res ipsa.) [§§363-378]

b. **YES** Because aviation has become a common mode of transportation, courts will probably infer negligence by the airline on a res ipsa theory where other possible causes have been eliminated. [§365]

c. **YES (most courts)** Even though Alpha is unable to establish ***which*** of the two defendants working on the same enterprise was negligent, res ipsa has been extended to situations where all of the defendants owed a duty to the plaintiff. [§§**373-375**]

d. **NO** No inference of negligence by a defendant can be drawn until the plaintiff's own conduct is eliminated as a responsible cause. Here, the fact that Dominica was at the gas pump filling her car precludes the inference that the accident was ***necessarily*** the fault of Ajax or the pump manufacturer (*i.e.,* it is possible that Dominica was lighting a cigarette, etc.). However, if there is ***other evidence*** to eliminate Dominica's conduct as a cause of the explosion, the inference of negligence could be drawn. [§§**376-377**]

59. **NO** Violation of a statute establishes duty and breach only where (i) the statute was enacted for the ***purpose*** of preventing the type of harm suffered by the plaintiff; and (ii) the plaintiff is a ***member of the class*** sought to be protected by the statute. Neither of these conditions appears here; the statute was enacted for the apparent purpose of conserving gasoline, not protecting pedestrians against highway injuries. [§§**398-402**]

60.a. **NO** Under the majority view, violation of a criminal statute (which was enacted for the purpose of preventing this type of injury, and providing the plaintiff is a member of the class sought to be protected) establishes only that the duty of care has been ***breached.*** It is still up to the plaintiff to prove the other requisite elements (duty, causation, and damages). [§§**396, 409**]

b. **NO (most states)** Showing such violation establishes a ***conclusive presumption***—meaning that it cannot be rebutted by evidence that Driver was acting carefully. (Some states are contra on this.) [§§**408-411**]

c. **YES (most states)** Even when the conclusive presumption applies, most courts recognize "exceptions" (or "excused violations" in Restatement terminology) to cover cases where the violation is in fact excused or justified. [§§**412-414**]

61.a. **YES (both)** Where an injury was caused by the ***concurrent*** negligent acts of two or more defendants, ***both*** are liable to the plaintiff—*i.e.,* if the accident would not have occurred "but for" the negligent acts of ***both*** Bus Co. and Chris, Amy can recover from both. [§**418**]

b. **YES** If each of the negligent acts was a ***"substantial factor"*** in causing the injury, each defendant is equally liable to the plaintiff—unless any one of the ***defendants can prove*** that the ultimate injuries were the result of the other defendant's negligence (*i.e.,* the burden of proof is shifted to the defendants). [§§**420-421**]

62. **YES** Because either City ***or*** Property Owner caused Pedestrian's injuries, he would not be able to establish "but for" cause against either of them. In recognition of this problem, courts generally shift the burden to each defendant to prove that

the injuries sustained by Pedestrian were ***not*** caused by negligence of that defendant. [**§§423-432**]

63.a. **YES** Abdul's negligence is the direct cause of Theo's injuries, and the injuries are of the type reasonably foreseeable. Hence, Abdul's conduct is the actual and proximate cause of Theo's injuries. [**§§453, 461-463**]

b. **YES** Although Theo's death might not be foreseeable (especially from a heart attack), Abdul's negligent conduct aggravated a preexisting condition and he is therefore liable for the ultimate injuries. The victim's abnormal sensitivities do ***not*** limit the tortfeasor's liability. "A tortfeasor takes his victim as he finds him." [**§§471-472**]

c. **PROBABLY NOT** Although it can be shown that the injuries sustained were a direct result of Abdul's negligence, some courts limit the extent of liability on the theory that they were ***too remote and unforeseeable.*** Note that under the "Cardozo view," these plaintiffs would not be in the "zone of danger"; hence one would not get past the "duty" element of a plaintiff's prima facie case. Under the "Andrews view," however, there ***is*** a duty owed to the plaintiffs that ***may*** be limited because of the unforeseeability of the injuries (*i.e.,* no proximate cause). [**§§467-470**]

64. **PROBABLY** The dog's actions constitute an intervening force between the defendant's act and the plaintiff's injury. However, if the intervening act is a ***normal response*** to the defendant's act, it will be deemed a ***dependent intervening force***—meaning it will ordinarily not break the chain of causation. Here, it is arguable that the dog's actions ***were*** a normal response to Andy's acts (pain causing the dog to act in frenzy), and hence he would be liable for the resultant injuries. [**§§478-484**]

65. **YES** Attempts to escape threatened harm are usually deemed normal responses even if the escape injures others. Thus, Al's liability to Cindy would not be cut off by Ben's act. (***Abnormal*** escape attempts, however, are treated as superseding causes.) [**§482**]

66. **NO** Even though the defendant's (Don's) negligence created the opportunity for the third person (Norbert) to act, the third person's intentionally tortious or criminal conduct is generally held to be a ***superseding cause*** of the harm (an unforeseeable, independent intervening force). (*Compare:* Result could be contra if Don ***had reason to foresee*** that Norbert might avail himself of the opportunity to set Paul's car on fire.) [**§§486, 490-491**]

67.a. **YES** Ordinarily, the negligent acts of a third person are held foreseeable intervening forces, and hence ***not*** superseding causes. By placing Oscar in a position where another's negligence could aggravate his injuries, Felix becomes liable therefor. [**§488**]

b. **NO** Again, the intentional or criminal acts of a third person are usually held to be unforeseeable intervening forces—hence, superseding causes. (Arguably contra if it was in a high-crime area, where such acts could be foreseen; in which event, Felix could be held liable for leaving Oscar in a helpless condition in such an area.) [§§486, 490-491]

c. **NO** — Injuries sustained as a result of storms (acts of God) are treated as superseding causes where they cause a ***result different*** than that threatened by the defendant's original negligence. Here, being struck by lightning would probably be regarded as a different result than being struck by a negligently driven car. (Again, arguably contra if the lightning storm was raging ***at the time*** of the original impact; in such event, the injuries to Oscar might be held foreseeable.) [§489]

68.a. **YES** — Generally, the inaction of a third party (even one under a duty to act) does not affect causation. It is ***not*** so extraordinary or unforeseeable as to constitute a superseding cause. [§494]

b. **NO** — Negligence ***cannot*** be based on nonfeasance (failure to act) unless there was an ***affirmative duty to act***; and there is no duty to go to the aid of another in this case. [§§339, 494, 551]

69. **NO** — The doctrine of avoidable consequences excuses Dwight from liability for those consequences that Pam ***could have avoided*** in the exercise of due care. (Dwight would still be liable for the cut, however.) [§§531-533]

70. **YES** — Dwight's liability is not reduced by the fact that Phyllis was covered by insurance ("collateral sources rule"). Note, however, that her insurance company may be entitled to ***subrogation*** as to such recovery. [§§539-544]

71.a. **NO** — Not at common law, if the accident was not his fault. (Many states are contra by statute, imposing a duty to aid any person injured by the driver's car, regardless of fault.) [§§551-556]

b. **YES** — If Rich's forcing her to walk home in the rain put her in a ***worse position*** than if he had not acted at all. Even though Rich was under no duty to aid her originally (*see* above), once having undertaken to do so, he owed a duty to act with reasonable care. [§§560-564]

72. **PROBABLY** — A common carrier owes the duty to choose the course of action ***least likely*** to expose its passengers to a risk of harm. (Landing in Cuba would probably be less likely a risk than shooting it out in mid-air.) [§§582-586]

73.a. **YES** — The bailor of a car owes a ***duty to control*** erratic driving of his car by another, where such occurs ***in his presence***. The risk of harm to third persons is clearly foreseeable. [§§593-596]

b. **PROBABLY** — On a "negligent entrustment" theory; *i.e.*, knowing that Dwight had been driving carelessly, Michael was probably negligent in allowing Dwight to drive the car. [§§597-598]

74.a. **YES** Under the doctrine of respondeat superior, Widget Co. is ***vicariously*** liable for torts committed by Stanley within the scope of his employment (driving truck) regardless of any showing of negligence on the part of the employer, Widget Co. [**§§609-613**]

b. **NO** Batteries and intentional torts by an employee are usually considered outside the scope of employment where the employment does not otherwise involve the employee using physical force on others. [**§611**]

c. **POSSIBLY** On the theory that the employer failed to exercise reasonable care in hiring, and thereby exposed persons coming into contact with such employee to a foreseeable risk of harm. [**§607**]

75.a. **YES** Ordinarily, the negligence of an independent contractor is not imputed to the person who employs him. But the result is different where—as here—the work contracted out involves a ***high risk of harm to members of the public*** if not carefully performed. In such cases, the employer cannot shield himself from liability by engaging an independent contractor to do the job. [*See* Rest. 2d §425] [**§625**]

b. **NO** Such an agreement (indemnification) merely fixes rights as between the contracting parties (Trans-Global and Aero). It does not affect the rights of third parties (Passenger), and hence is not a defense to suit by Passenger. [**§626**]

76.a. **YES** Most courts treat carpools involving the sharing of expenses as rides for ***consideration***, thus giving riders "passenger" status. [**§§589-590**]

b. **NO** Because a business purpose or joint ***control*** is required to establish the joint enterprise theory. Mere sharing of expenses is not enough. [**§§628-632**]

77. **POSSIBLY** Ordinarily, a parent is not liable for a child's torts (negligent or intentional). But if the parent knows or has reason to know that the child is ***likely to inflict harm*** to others, recovery may be allowed because of the parent's own negligence. Here, knowledge that the child is "proficient in karate" is not enough by itself to create liability; there would also have to be a showing that Mother knew that Junior was likely to ***use*** his karate on unsuspecting adults. [**§§633-635**]

78. **NO** Under typical "Dram Shop Acts," generally only third parties (and ***not*** the intoxicated patron) can recover. [**§639**]

79. **NO (most states)** The "reasonable person" standard does ***not*** apply in most cases. Rather, a land occupier's duty to persons coming onto his land is ***limited*** to specific standards of care that in many cases may be ***less*** than what a "reasonable person" would have done. (Some modern courts are contra, however, and would apply the "reasonable person" standard in every case.) [**§§650, 718**]

80.a. **YES** — A landowner generally owes no duty of care regarding natural conditions on his land. But an exception is recognized as to native trees in urban areas—the owner has a duty of reasonable care including inspection. **[§§653-655]**

b. **DEPENDS** — On whether a risk of harm to passersby was ***foreseeable***. The ***reasonable person*** standard applies where a person outside the land is injured by activities on the land. **[§659]**

81. **NO** — A land occupier owes ***no duty*** to ***unknown*** adult trespassers. (*Compare:* If Rich had ***seen*** Thief enter his land, he would have owed a duty to warn of dangerous conditions that Thief would be ***unlikely to discover***; and the pool excavation at night probably would qualify.) **[§§660-665]**

82.a. **YES** — If a land occupier knows that there are constant trespassers upon a limited area ("CTULAs"), he owes a duty to warn them of any artificial condition created by him involving a risk of death or ***serious bodily harm*** and that is not apparent to them. (Broken glass in sand would apparently pose such a risk.) **[§§666-673]**

b. **NO (most courts)** — A land occupier's liability here is limited to conditions ***for which he is responsible***. Foreseeability of harm to trespassers is not the test. [Rest. 2d §335 cmt. d] **[§§669-673]**

83. **DEPENDS** — On whether Cement Co. knew or had ***reason to know*** that children were likely to trespass, notwithstanding the fence and signs. If it did, then Cement Co. is probably liable because the sharp pebbles and bits of glass are not the ***kind of risk*** children would expect in a pile of sand. **[§§674-682, 685]**

84. **PROBABLY** — Whether Tamura personally foresaw any risk to the children is not the test. The test is whether a "reasonable person" would realize that the pond posed any risk of harm to such young children, whether the child who trespassed was old enough to appreciate the risk, and whether the risk to the children outweighed the burden of eliminating the danger (by fences, gates, etc.). **[§§678-682]**

85. **YES** — Door-to-door salespeople are usually treated as licensees (coming onto the land with the "implied" permission of the land occupier). As such, a land occupier owes a duty to make safe any ***known*** dangerous condition on his property. **[§§689-695]** (*Compare:* The result would be different if Owner had posted a large "No Solicitors" sign. In such a case, door-to-door salespeople would be regarded as ***trespassers***, to whom ***no duty*** is owed.) **[§690]**

86. **YES** — Even though Carter was not a customer, the premises were apparently open for public admission, and hence Carter would be treated as an ***invitee***. A land occupier owes to invitees a duty to use due care to ***inspect and discover*** dangerous conditions on her premises and to ***make them safe***. Because the accident occurred "several hours later," Claire apparently had time to discover the condition and remedy it. **[§§696-702, 704]**

87. **NO** The service area in a gasoline station would probably be regarded as an area into which the public is ***not*** invited. Hence, Larry would not be regarded as an invitee; at most, he was a licensee. As such, Benny owed a duty to warn or make safe any ***known*** dangerous conditions (and here, the spilled oil was not yet known). [§§692-697]

88.a. **NO** Because a land occupier owes ***no duty*** to adult trespassers of whose presence he is not actually aware. [§661]

b. **YES (most courts)** Because a licensee on another's land is ***not entitled to*** the land occupier's restricted scope of liability. Rather, he owes the same standard of care to others (*i.e.,* trespasser Terrance) as if they were both in some neutral place, and here the facts stipulate that Winston was negligent. [§§722-724]

89.a. **YES** A landlord owes a duty to his tenant to remedy or warn of dangerous conditions known by the landlord at the time the tenant takes possession. [§§735-736]

b. **SPLIT** The older view is that a landlord's duty is limited to those with whom he is in "privity"; no privity exists with guests of a tenant, and hence no liability. However, the Second Restatement and modern trend are contra, holding that a landlord owes the same duty to a tenant's guest as to the tenant. [§§745-748]

90.a. **YES** Where a landlord undertakes repairs (whether obligated by lease or not), he owes a duty of care. [§738]

b. **YES** Failure to repair ***when under a duty*** to repair (here, by lease) is a basis for negligence liability as well as breach of contract under modern law. [§§739-743]

c. **SPLIT** *See* answer to "89.b.," above. [§§745-748]

d. **YES** A landlord is treated as the ***land occupier*** of common areas (elevators, stairways, etc.). As to those areas he is liable ***both*** to tenants and their visitors (no "privity" necessary). [§751]

e. **YES** For reasons stated in answer to "d.," above. [§751]

91. **NO (most courts)** Where the defendant's conduct is only negligent, most courts retain the requirement that the plaintiff (Mother) must have been subjected to ***actual impact or threat*** thereof. [§§764-771] Some jurisdictions have relaxed this requirement where, as here, the plaintiff is a close family member of the one imperiled by the defendant's conduct, and suffers ***contemporaneous*** emotional distress (and resulting physical manifestation) from observing such peril. In such jurisdictions, Mother might recover even though she did not actually observe the accident, but came upon the scene immediately thereafter. [§§772-777] *Note:* Even in such jurisdictions, however, Mother might be denied recovery if Child had been contributorily negligent (*e.g.,* playing in the street), as Mother's cause of action is viewed as ***derivative*** in nature. [§779]

92.a.	**NO (most courts)**	Most courts would deny recovery where the emotional distress is attributable solely to property damage, and the plaintiff suffers no tangible physical manifestation. [§§780-784]
b.	**PROBABLY NOT**	Where the defendant's conduct is negligent, most courts would deny recovery in the absence of ***tangible physical manifestation.*** (However, shock to the nervous system would be a sufficient allegation of physical manifestation.) [§782] *Note:* If Archie was acting intentionally, most courts would be willing to impose liability in a case of this type (*i.e.,* by finding Archie's conduct to be "extreme and outrageous"). [§91]
93.a.	**NO (most states)**	Almost all states reject the notion that contributory negligence is a complete defense. Most states have adopted ***comparative negligence*** laws, which allow the plaintiff to recover even though she was at fault. [§§802-803, 815]
b.	**NO**	He remains liable for her original injuries. Under the doctrine of ***avoidable consequences***, however, Don is not liable for the aggravation thereof caused by Paula's carelessness. [§§531, 791]
94.a.	**PROBABLY NOT**	In a comparative negligence jurisdiction, a person's own negligence does not bar recovery. [§815] Even in a contributory negligence jurisdiction, the standard of care owed by the plaintiff for his own protection is that which a reasonable person would exercise under the circumstances—***including emergencies.*** If a reasonable person would have dashed into the street to save the child, Able's doing so is ***not*** contributory negligence. [§§793-794]
b.	**YES**	On the theory that "danger invites rescue," and that negligent acts of others are ***foreseeable*** intervening forces. [§§327-328, 492]
c.	**SPLIT**	One person's contributory negligence is ***not imputed*** to another who reasonably comes to his rescue (regardless of the relationship between them). [§807] On the other hand, the availability of comparative negligence has led some courts to permit imputation of negligence. [§§834-835]
95.a.	**NO**	Pedestrian placed himself in a position of ***inattentive peril*** (he would have been able to get out of the way had he looked up). In such cases, Pedestrian is barred by his contributory negligence unless the defendant had ***actual knowledge*** of the plaintiff's peril. Brenda did not, and hence the last clear chance doctrine does ***not*** apply. [§§804, 806]
b.	**YES (most courts)**	Here, Pedestrian would be in a position of ***helpless peril*** (could not escape even by exercise of due care). In such cases, most courts hold the defendant ***liable*** if he had actual knowledge of the plaintiff's peril or should have had such knowledge. (Minority view still requires actual knowledge, however.) [§§804-805]

96.a. **NO** The carpool did not create a "joint enterprise" (no mutuality of control). Hence, there is no basis for imputing Virginia's negligence—or contributory negligence—to Georgia. [§§628-632, 807, 809]

b. **YES** On the theory of ***respondeat superior***, Virginia's negligence—or contributory negligence—would be imputed to her employer (Georgia). [§808]

97. **SPLIT** Many comparative negligence jurisdictions ***deny any recovery***—(D)—where the plaintiff was ***equally (or more)*** at fault than the defendant. Others are contra (allowing the plaintiff to recover even if he was more at fault than the defendant), and would permit a recovery based on the ***degree*** of his fault; in this case (C)—one-half of the damages proved. [§§817-820]

98. **NONE** (A) does not constitute an assumption of the risk because such clauses in public transportation contracts (ticket) ***violate public policy***. Thus, there is no effective assumption of risk by contract. [§§842-848]

(B) does not constitute an assumption of the risk because there is no assumption of risk by conduct unless it is shown that the plaintiff was aware and voluntarily assumed the ***particular risk*** that caused her injury. Here, the fact that Louise knew that the driver had been drinking does not establish that she knew he would drive at an excessive speed. Also, on public policy grounds, companies furnishing public services are generally not allowed to claim that a member of the public assumed the risk in seeking to use those services. [Rest. 2d §496B cmt. j] [§§850-854]

(C) is probably not an assumption of the risk because there is no showing that Louise was aware of the ***particular risk*** (*i.e.,* that the driver's going "faster, faster" would result in the bus going off the road). [§§850-854]

99. **PROBABLY** The issue is whether Harry's assumption was a "voluntary" one. This boils down to whether he had ***any reasonable alternative*** to driving through, which means ***balancing the harm threatened*** by the delay (potential loss of job, etc.) versus the ***harm to which he exposed himself.*** Unless it is absolutely clear that being a half-hour late would forfeit his job (that the employer would not accept any excuses, etc.), it would seem that taking the detour was a more reasonable alternative, and hence that in driving through the oil spill he assumed the risk. [§§855-857]

100. **ALL** The possessor of livestock (cow) trespassing on the land of another is strictly liable for the trespass itself ***and any harm*** done by the trespass. [§§882-883]

101.a. **NO** The horse's propensity to gallop would probably ***not*** be regarded as "abnormally dangerous" because most riders were able to handle it. Hence, there is no basis for strict liability. [§§884-886]

b. **POSSIBLY** Merely warning Tenderfoot of the horse's propensity to gallop may not have been enough to discharge a bailor's duty of care with respect to the condition of the bailed chattel. Buckeroo owes a duty to exercise reasonable care to ascertain ***whether the chattel was likely to cause harm to the bailee***; here, this would probably include a ***duty to ascertain whether Tenderfoot was capable*** of handling the horse in the first place. [§§760-761]

c. **YES** Even though defanged, the rattlesnake was a wild animal with a dangerous propensity—that of ***instilling fear*** in other animals (or even humans) if it escaped. Accordingly, Buckeroo is strictly liable for any harm caused thereby, even though the snake escaped without any fault on Buckeroo's part. As to causation, the horse's rearing and throwing Tenderfoot must be regarded as a foreseeable intervening force (normal reaction), and hence not affecting the chain of causation. [§§889-890]

102.a. **POSSIBLY** Although a land occupier ordinarily owes ***no duty to unknown trespassers*** (even innocent ones), strict liability may be imposed for injuries inflicted by a ***vicious*** watchdog. Thus, if Priscilla's Doberman is regarded as a domestic animal with a ***known*** dangerous propensity, she would be liable—even though the dog had never previously bitten anyone. (*Distinguish:* Not every dog would be so regarded; the breed here might be distinguished by its reputation.) [§§885-886, 895-896] However, if the Doberman's reputation is ***not*** enough to constitute a "known dangerous propensity," Priscilla would not be strictly liable, because in most courts "every previously well-behaved dog is entitled to one free bite." [§887]

b. **NO** Business visitors (mail carriers) ***can*** invoke strict liability. [§894] However, the injury here was ***not*** the result of the animal's "dangerous propensity" (biting, etc.). Consequently, no strict liability would attach. Negligence is ruled out by the facts. [§886]

c. **YES** A bill collector is normally treated as a licensee, and hence ***can*** invoke strict liability. [§894] The possessor of an animal ***with a known*** dangerous propensity (either by its reputation or the fact it had bitten Elvis) is strictly liable for harm done thereby, even where (as here) the plaintiff may have been guilty of conduct that might be regarded as ***contributory negligence***. [§§884-886, 920] (*Compare:* However, if the bill collector had deliberately provoked the animal, ***knowing*** the danger, a court might find assumption of the risk, which ***is*** a valid defense to strict liability as well as to negligence.) [§922]

103. **(B) AND (C)** Whether an activity is "abnormally dangerous" is a legal conclusion based on the following factors: whether the activity is one of ***"common usage"*** in the community; the ***value*** of the activity to the community; the ***appropriateness*** of the activity to its location; the ***degree of risk*** involved in the activity; the ***gravity*** of the risk of harm; and the extent to which the risk could have been ***avoided or guarded against***. [§903]

(A) Firing a weapon—even in a city—is generally regarded as a matter of common usage. Hence, there is no liability in the absence of negligence. [§903]

(B) is probably "abnormally dangerous," because fumigating with cyanide involves risks that cannot be effectively guarded against, and is not a matter of common usage in most communities. [§903]

(C) is "abnormally dangerous" because it is neither a common nor an appropriate use of the property, and of no apparent value to the community (same activity in the desert might be treated differently). [§§903-904]

104. **NO (most courts)** The blasting would be regarded as an abnormally dangerous activity. However, most courts follow the "foreseeable plaintiff" test for proximate cause (unlike negligence), and therefore hold ***no*** strict liability where the particular harm that occurred was not reasonably foreseeable. (Minority view is contra, on the basis that strict liability extends to all harm ***directly*** caused by the abnormally dangerous activity.) [§§915-917]

105.a. **POSSIBLY** Battery requires a showing of ***intent to inflict*** a harmful touching. If Duro was "***substantially certain***" that users would suffer adverse side effects, it will be deemed to have ***intended*** those results. If it simply did not believe the lab reports, etc. (even if a reasonable person would have), or thought the risk was exaggerated, there is not sufficient intent for battery. [§929]

b. **NO** Contributory negligence is ***no defense*** to battery. [§803]

106.a. **YES** Retailer has a duty to warn about the dangerous characteristics of his goods. This duty is owed not only to the purchaser, but to all persons within the foreseeable ***scope of use*** of the goods (*i.e.*, no privity is required). So Child, a bystander and foreseeable victim, may recover for Retailer's negligent failure to warn of the "hair trigger" or make it safe. [§§932-933, 945]

b. **YES (most jurisdictions)** The "hair trigger" made the gun defective and unreasonably dangerous. Virtually all states hold that any person injured by a defective product can invoke strict tort liability. [§§952, 1009]

107. **POSSIBLY (C)** (A) is no defense because a ***design*** may be as negligent as lack of care in manufacturing. [§935]

(B) is no defense because Biltrite's duty of care extends to all components; some courts say that by assembling another company's components into its product, the other company's carelessness is ***imputed*** to Biltrite. [§§940-941]

(C) If the dealer actually knew that the water heater was ***defective and dangerous***, but sold it without a warning anyway, the sale will be treated as an unforeseeable intervening force, relieving the manufacturer of liability. [§947] However, if the dealer did not actually know of the defect or the danger, the manufacturer remains liable. [§946]

(D) is no defense because negligence liability extends to property damage as well as personal injuries (as long as risk of harm to property was foreseeable). [§938]

108.a. **PROBABLY** A highly dangerous product (dynamite caps) purchased from an unknown supplier should be regarded as inherently dangerous—meaning Dealer is under a duty of care to inspect, or at least to warn the purchaser that the product comes from an uncertain source of supply. [§945]

b. **PROBABLY NOT** Dealer's duty to warn has apparently been discharged; therefore, Dealer is not liable in negligence. Contractor now would owe a duty to test or inspect; and failing to do so, his negligence would be regarded as the superseding cause of injury to Bystander. [§§943-947]

109.a. **NO** A mattress cannot be regarded as an inherently dangerous product, and therefore the dealer generally owes no duty to inspect or test same prior to sale (at least where dealing in goods of a reputable manufacturer). [§944]

b. **YES** Regardless of whether or not a product is tested, and regardless of whether the dealer's not testing it was negligence, every seller ***impliedly*** warrants the fitness of the product sold for its normally intended use. [§§1074-1075]

c. **YES** In all but a very few states, privity requirements have been relaxed so that a manufacturer's implied warranty extends beyond its immediate purchaser (usually a distributor or retailer) at least as far as the consumer. [§§1085-1089]

110.a. **PROBABLY** The failure of the safety guard to screen out pebbles should be regarded as a design defect, and the manufacturer's duty extends to defects in design as well as in the manufacturing process. [§935]

b. **YES** The nationwide advertising should be regarded as an ***express warranty*** by the manufacturer that runs to all potential customers. The language is specific enough so as not to be mere "puffing" by the manufacturer. [§§1070, 1087]

c. **YES** The manufacturer's duty of care extends to all persons within the ***foreseeable scope of use*** of the product. [§937]

d. **YES** The manufacturer's and retailer's implied warranties extend ***at least*** to members of the consumer's family. (In most jurisdictions, they extend to anyone foreseeably injured by the product.) Even if the warranty disclaimer is valid—and disclaimer requirements for consumer goods are especially strict—it does not apply to nonpurchasers. [§§1089, 1104]

111. **NO** Because Rider voluntarily assumed the risk of driving his motorcycle without a working headlamp, he cannot recover for his injuries. [§§850-855, 951]

112.a. **YES (modern courts)** She is entitled to recover against ***all*** of them on a ***strict liability*** theory. All persons who participate in the ***marketing*** of a defective and unreasonably dangerous product are liable for injuries caused thereby—without any showing of negligence or privity (warranty), and regardless of warranty disclaimers. [§§952-957, 992-996, 1084-1089]

b. **NO** No liability in negligence because Minnie had no reason to know of the danger. And no warranty or strict liability because Minnie was a host, ***not a commercial supplier*** of the beans. [§1004]

c. **YES** Pearl can recover from all of them on an ***implied warranty*** theory. As a guest of the purchaser, she is in sufficient privity with the defendants to benefit from the implied warranty of merchantability, and the disclaimer does not apply to her. [§1089] Alternatively, Pearl could recover on a ***strict liability*** theory. The ultimate user or consumer of a product can invoke strict liability, as well as the actual purchaser. [§1008]

113. **YES** Strict liability is imposed against ***all*** persons placing the defective product in the stream of commerce, regardless of which person is actually responsible for the defect. Thus, dangers inherent in the packaging of a product are attributable to the manufacturer even though the defective packaging (container) was obtained from another. [§§992-993]

114.a. **YES** All persons within the foreseeable scope of use of an unreasonably dangerous and defective product can invoke strict liability for injuries caused by the defect. *Rationale:* The purchaser (Father) or user (Son) could certainly recover if they were the ones injured; and bystanders have even less opportunity to inspect the product for defects. [§1009] *Note:* Most states permit bystanders to recover under the manufacturer's implied warranty as well. [§§1091-1094]

b. **UNCLEAR** A ***few*** courts have extended the "danger invites rescue" rationale of negligence cases to products liability cases so that anyone going to the aid of someone imperiled by a defective product can invoke the same liability as the person imperiled. But the law is still unsettled. [§1010]

115. **NO** She would also have to prove that the product was "defective"—meaning that it would be harmful in normal use to a ***reasonable number*** of persons (*i.e.*, injury to Thelma not enough in itself to prove product "defective"). Stated differently, Thelma must prove that her adverse reaction was ***not*** a "one in a million" situation. [§§1022-1027, 1032-1034]

116. **PROBABLY** Even though Betty's use on her eyebrows may not have been the intended use of the product, it probably would be held foreseeable. And the doctrine of strict liability extends both to normal (intended) ***and foreseeable*** uses of the product. [§§1028-1029]

117. **NO** Strict products liability applies to a product's packaging as well as to the product itself. But it does not apply where the injury results from an ***unintended or unforeseeable use.*** Here, the cartons were clearly not intended to be used for supporting

a person's weight after being emptied, and it is doubtful that such a use would be held foreseeable. [§§1028-1029]

118. **ALL**

(A) Because Kamikaze built the car to go 110 m.p.h., it was foreseeable that someone would drive it that fast; Kamikaze cannot claim that doing so was an unforeseeable use. Because a defect apparently caused the car to go out of control, Kamikaze will be strictly liable. However, it can defend on a theory of comparative fault or, in some jurisdictions, contributory negligence. [§§980-982, 1028-1029, 1054-1057] Kamikaze may also be liable for negligence depending upon what caused the steering failure, and Bob's negligence might be relevant. [§§935, 951]

(B) The car's failure under emergency conditions (foreseeable in normal use) would be regarded as a design defect; *i.e.,* the manufacturer was under a duty to anticipate (hence, negligence liability as well). [§§961-968]

(C) It is foreseeable that an automobile will be involved in a highway accident, and Kamikaze will be strictly liable for not providing the protection to the car's occupants that consumers could reasonably expect. (This does not mean, of course, that Kamikaze must build a crash-proof car because no consumer could expect total protection in the event of a serious accident.) [§§965, 1023]

119. **PROBABLY NOT**

Most courts to date limit strict products liability to cases in which the danger involved was ***reasonably foreseeable*** at the time the product was manufactured. Hence, unless Presto had reason to know of the danger ***prior to the government research study,*** most courts would not impose strict liability. [§§976-978] (*But note:* Continuing to market the glue ***after*** the government study would be basis for strict liability or negligence, unless ***adequate warnings are given.***) [§§978-979]

120.a. **YES**

By invoking ***res ipsa loquitur***: The steering mechanism on a new car is not likely to fail in the absence of negligence; Kamikaze is the indicated source of that negligence; and Chris's testimony indicates that he did not cause or contribute to the causation of the failure. (Of course, res ipsa raises at most a ***presumption*** of negligence, and Kamikaze would be free to rebut by evidence showing that it had exercised due care in the car's manufacture.) [§§363-364, 942]

b. **YES (most courts)**

The same factors that create res ipsa in a negligence case create at least an ***inference*** of "defectiveness" for strict products liability purposes. (Again, this is ***not*** conclusive; Kamikaze is free to introduce evidence showing that the mechanism was not defective or that it failed for some other reason.) [§§942, 1035-1036]

c. **YES**

Where other causes for failure are apparent (wear and tear, etc.), no inference of negligence or defectiveness can be drawn from the mere fact that the mechanism failed in use (*i.e.,* after 50,000 miles usage, reasonable persons can conceive other causes as being responsible). [§§1037-1042]

121. **(B) AND (C)**	(A) is not a defense to strict liability because a third person's (dealer's) foreseeable negligence does not cut off the manufacturer's liability. [§§991-993] (However, the dealer's failure to inspect after Kamikaze's warning may relieve the manufacturer of negligence liability.) [§§944, 946-947] (B) is a valid defense, because by receiving such warning and failing to respond, Kara may be deemed to have assumed the risk. [§§1059-1061] (C) is a defense (or more accurately, it negates proximate cause) because any "substantial" change in the condition of the car terminates the manufacturer's liability; and here, Kara's repair work increased the risk of failure. [§§1030, 1035-1038, 1056-1057]
122.a. **YES**	Physical damage to the product itself or other property (as well as personal injuries), caused by a defect in the product, is recoverable under a strict products liability theory. [§1049]
b. **NO (most courts)**	Economic losses alone are compensable in a "sales" or contract action, but not in tort. [§§1050-1051]
123.a. **NO (most states)**	Most courts do not permit a private individual to maintain an action for a public nuisance, unless it is shown that the nuisance has caused him some injury peculiar in kind. (Such actions must be prosecuted by the state, not a private citizen.) [§§1110-1112]
b. **YES**	Adjoining riparian owners would have sustained damage to the extent the water supply was diminished in quality (fact that certain uses—drinking—could no longer be made of the water). Tipper might even be permitted to maintain a class action on behalf of all downstream riparian owners. [§§1110-1112]
124.a. **PROBABLY**	To constitute a nuisance, the interference with the plaintiff's use of his land must be "substantial" and "unreasonable." Running an air conditioning system is not necessarily an unreasonable use by Archie of his land, but it may become such because of the disproportionate interference with Tom's use of his land. The controlling issue is likely to be whether Archie can abate the noise without unreasonable expense, as compared to the harm to Tom's use of his land if the noise continues unabated. [§§1122-1125]
b. **YES**	Nuisance liability arises from the harm done—not the actor's state of mind; *i.e.*, a nuisance can be predicated on either intent, negligence, or strict liability. [§1118]
c. **YES**	The actor's refusal to abate a nuisance, after a request to do so, makes his continued interference with his neighbor's property an ***intentional*** tort. Hence, if sufficient "malice" (intent to injure) can be inferred from the continued operation of the air conditioner, it is legally possible for the court to award punitive damages to Tom. [§§1118, 1120, 1136]

d. **NO** The fact that the condition existed in advance is ***not*** enough ***by itself*** to show that it was reasonable. [§**1128**]

e. **YES** Tom can recover damages for the interference to date, and an injunction to prevent future interference. Damages alone would not be an effective remedy because it would require Tom to sue again in the future; an injunction alone would not compensate for past interference. [§**1134**]

125.a. **YES** A decedent's estate can be substituted as the plaintiff and recover for all of the damages claimed by Morgan, ***except*** that some states do not permit recovery for the decedent's ***pain and suffering***. [§§**1151-1153**]

b. **NO (most states)** Most states by statute recognize a ***new cause of action*** in the decedent's relatives for his wrongful death. The damages recoverable are distinct from those recoverable by the decedent's estate (above). Rather, the heirs are entitled to recover for their loss of ***support and companionship*** by the decedent's death. [§§**1158-1161**]

c. **YES** Any defense that could have been asserted against the decedent, had he brought an action during his lifetime, can be set up as a defense against an action for wrongful death filed by his heirs. [§**1168**]

d. **PARTIALLY** Most courts will reduce the amount of any wrongful death award by the negligent beneficiary's ***share*** thereof (or degree of fault in a comparative negligence jurisdiction). To this extent, therefore, it is a valid defense. [§§**1170-1171**]

126.a. **YES (modern law)** The common law rule is that a wife has ***no action*** for loss of her husband's consortium. But most modern states are contra, giving wives the same rights as husbands to recover against third persons causing injury to their spouse. [§§**1174-1179**]

b. **NO** At least where Mario's conduct was merely negligent, no cause of action is recognized in favor of a child for loss of a parent's consortium. [§**1185**]

127.a. **YES (most courts)** Intrafamily tort immunity was the rule at common law, but it has been rejected in virtually all jurisdictions today. The common law rule was based on the notion that it was essential to preserve "domestic tranquility," but modern courts recognize the reality that most of these cases are covered by insurance, so that there is no danger of marital disruption. [§§**1211-1212**]

b. **SPLIT** More courts retain parent-child immunity than husband-wife immunity. Again, the modern trend is to reject it entirely. [§§**1214-1218**]

c. **YES** Intrafamily tort immunity never extended beyond the immediate family relationships. [§**1221**]

128.a. **YES** Most courts hold that employees or agents of the government are personally liable for the torts they commit while performing "ministerial" (required) duties. [§§**1238-1240**]

b. **NO (most courts)**

Governmental tort immunity has been retained in most jurisdictions. Where a municipality is involved, it is limited to "governmental" (as opposed to "proprietary") functions. Police functions are clearly classified as "governmental" because they can be performed adequately only by the government. Hence, the City is immune from suit. (The modern trend, however, is to limit or abrogate governmental tort immunity.) [§§1224-1230]

129.a. **DEPENDS**

On whether the judgment against Tom was ***satisfied*** (paid) or not. If it was, then Pat cannot sue again on the same cause of action. [§1254]

b. **NO (most courts)**

A few courts hold that the ***release*** of one tortfeasor releases them all. But most courts today are contra, although the amount received from one (here, $100) ***reduces*** the claims against the others. [§§1255-1257]

c. **YES (most courts)**

The common law rule was that there is ***no contribution*** between joint tortfeasors. But today, virtually all states permit contribution, at least where only negligent conduct is involved. [§§1258-1259]

d. **NO**

Indemnity is available only in favor of a party who has been held ***vicariously*** liable for the acts of another. It does ***not*** apply where, as here, the party ***primarily*** liable (Tom) is the one who has had to pay the judgment. There's no reason to allow Tom to shift any portion of his loss to Employer. [§§1262-1264]

130.a. **SPLIT**

Most courts hold that publication to ***any*** third person, even in intracorporate communications, may be a defamation but may also be privileged. A few courts are contra. [§§1358-1359]

b. **NO**

Not unless Agent's showing the letter to Author was intended by Editor or reasonably foreseeable. Again, no publication ***by Editor***. [§1362]

131.a. **YES**

On a respondeat superior theory. The employer is liable for the intentional or negligent acts of employees (Eager) committed within the course and scope of employment. [§1369]

b. **YES**

Every republication of a defamation (unless privileged) is treated as a ***new publication***. A republisher ***cannot*** limit liability by stating its source. The republication may well do more harm than the original (here, it was nationwide). [§§1370-1374]

c. **NO**

One who merely distributes or sells (rather than publishes) is treated as a "***disseminator***," and is held only to a standard of due care. In the absence of knowledge or reason to know that the story was false, there would be no liability. [§§1376-1377]

132.a. **POSSIBLY**

No action can be brought on behalf of the father, because defamation actions cannot be brought on behalf of those who are already dead (their reputations are not protectable). However, ***if*** the statement would cause a substantial minority of the community ***to defer from association with Angela*** (as the child of a murderer), it could be regarded as defamatory of Angela. [§§1402-1403]

b. **DEPENDS** On whether the statement can reasonably be interpreted as applying to any particular police officer in the precinct. If the group is small enough that a reasonable person would regard it as applying to ***each*** police officer in the unit, then any of them could sue; however, if it is a large enough group, none of them can claim to have been individually defamed. [§§**1405-1407**]

c. **YES** While the statement that Angela has been having a "torrid love affair" is probably not defamatory on its face, it becomes defamatory (capable of lowering Angela's reputation in the community) when coupled with other facts not apparent on the face of the publication—here, that Angela is a married woman, and hence apparently guilty of adultery. (So-called defamation per quod cases.) [§§**1393-1395**]

d. **YES** It is enough that the statement is ***capable*** of defamatory interpretation by a reasonable person; defamation can be committed ***by insinuation and implication*** as well as outright statements. (One or two courts cling to the so-called possible innocent meaning rule.) [§§**1393-1395**]

133. **DEPENDS** All that is required is that ***some*** third person ***reasonably*** interpret it as applying to the plaintiff, Waldo. Hence, if the few who interpreted the statement as applying to Waldo did so ***reasonably,*** Amy is liable, even though in fact she had someone else in mind (and even though most of her friends did not know about whom she was speaking). The burden of proving this "colloquium" is on Waldo. [§§**1396-1397**]

134. **YES** All that is required is that some third person reasonably interpret it as applying to the plaintiff—even though the reference was unintended, and the *Tribune* report really was referring to another person by the same name. [§**1399**] (But it will have to be shown that the *Tribune* was ***negligent*** in not knowing there were several persons in the community by the same name. News media cannot be held liable unless published defamations were at least negligent.) [§**1532**]

135.a. **NO** It is essential that a defamation be ***intentionally or negligently*** published (this is the one element where strict liability does ***not*** apply). [§§**1362-1363**] Moreover, where news media are involved, ***all*** elements of the prima facie case must be based on ***at least negligence*** (no strict liability). [§§**1535-1538**]

b. **NO** A private person's recovery for a defamation by the news media is limited to damages for actual injury unless more than negligence is shown. [§§**1540-1542**]

136.a. **PROBABLY NOT** There is no liability for defamation unless the publication to a third person was intended or negligent. Unless Lawyer had reason to foresee that someone else could hear, ***defamatory remarks uttered in private are not actionable.*** [§**1364**]

b. **NO** Participants in "judicial proceedings" are absolutely privileged to utter defamations related to the matter at hand. But they must occur at some stage of the proceeding itself; conversations in corridors or chambers are not within the scope of the privilege. [§§**1456-1458**]

c. **YES** Calling a judge a "prejudiced boob" certainly imputes conduct incompatible with his office, and thus is "actionable per se" (without proof of actual damages). [**§§1434, 1438-1439**]

137. **(C) AND (D)** (A) is not actionable per se because it does not sufficiently charge Patty with a "serious offense." [**§§1435-1436**]

Neither is (B) because, traditionally, imputation of unchastity to a ***man*** is not actionable per se in most courts. The rule is the opposite as to women; *see* (C). [**§1440**]

(D) ***is*** actionable per se because it imputes to Father Mulcahy a characteristic (consorting) that is incompatible with his profession, the priesthood. But the result is contra where the profession does not demand the same moral standards; *e.g.,* the dentist, *see* (E). [**§§1438-1439**]

(F) is not actionable per se because it does not charge Phillip with the ***commission*** of the crime; it only indicates that he is under suspicion. [**§§1435-1436**]

138. **ALL** Any defamation in written form (libel) is actionable without proof of special damages. (Possible exception as to libel per quod cases.) [**§§1443-1444**]

139.a. **NO** In states having retraction statutes, an adequate retraction cuts off only the right to recover ***general*** damages; it does not affect the right to recover actual (special) damages. (And in states not having such statutes, a retraction has no effect on liability.) [**§1449**] *But remember:* In an action against news media, ***negligence*** must be proved; *i.e.,* it would have to be shown that the *Tribune* was at least negligent in publishing a letter containing such charges. [**§§1532, 1536**]

b. **NO** In states having retraction statutes, an adequate retraction limits the action only ***against the newspaper*** and its employees, not any other defendants. [**§1449**]

140. **NO (most states)** Truth is an absolute defense in most states—even where, as here, the defamatory remark was published maliciously and without certainty that the matter was true. [**§§1411-1413, 1452**]

141. **PROBABLY NOT** Statements published in the course of a judicial proceeding (complaint filed) are absolutely privileged, as long as they bear a "reasonable relationship" to the matter at hand. Here, a partner's underworld (Mafia) connections, if true, would reflect adversely on the partnership and hence it would seem sufficiently related to be absolutely privileged. [**§§1456-1457**]

142. **PROBABLY** Statements uttered during recess are not protected under the judicial proceedings privilege; that privilege extends only to utterances during the course of the proceedings themselves. [**§§1456-1457**]

143.a. **YES** Statements made by a ***witness*** in legislative hearings are protected to the same extent as in judicial proceedings (above)—*i.e.,* there is a requirement of reasonable *relevancy*. Here, Contractor's political beliefs or activities would seem unrelated to whether he has overcharged on the highway project. [§§1456-1459]

b. **NO** Defamations uttered by a ***legislative member*** are absolutely privileged—there is ***no requirement of relevancy*** to the matter at hand. [§1454]

c. **NO** Having reason to doubt the accuracy of the charge, the *Tribune* could ***not*** escape liability on the theory that publication was nonnegligent. However, it could rely on the so-called ***privilege of "record libel"—i.e.,*** the right to publish ***"full and fair"*** reports of proceedings in which there is a public interest. [§§1486-1492]

d. **DEPENDS** On whether the defamation was somehow related to the discharge of Attorney General's official duties. Top-grade cabinet officers are absolutely privileged to utter defamations, but there is a ***requirement of relevancy*** here. (Arguably, keeping track of "commies" is part of the Attorney General's official duties, and if so, this would be privileged.) [§1460]

144. **NO** Defamations uttered in an effort to advance one's own interests (or the interests of any third persons) are conditionally privileged if uttered in the reasonable belief that they are true, and relevant to a matter involving the person to whom uttered. ***No request*** for the information need be made where a sufficient ***relationship*** exists between the person uttering the defamation and the person to whom made (here, employer-employee). [§§1464-1468]

145. **YES** Because there was ***no relationship*** between Pompous and Acme's president. In the absence of such a relationship, defamations are conditionally privileged only where there was a prior ***request*** for the information by the person to whom the defamation was published. Here, no such request was made by Acme's president. [§1469]

146. **NO** Quarterback is probably a "public figure" so that Hosell's statements are constitutionally privileged as long as no actual malice (knowing or reckless falsity) is shown. Malice is ***not*** established merely by proof that Hosell did not know what he was talking about; it would have to be shown that he in fact entertained serious doubts as to the truth of what he said. [§§1512-1520]

147. **NO** The statement was constitutionally privileged. Charges of ***criminal*** conduct involving a candidate for ***any*** elected office (even a minor city post) are ***never considered irrelevant*** to the candidate's fitness for office, no matter how remote in time or place. Absent some showing of ***"actual malice"*** (reckless disregard for truth, or intentional falsehood), the constitutional privilege applies. [§1517]

148.a. **NO** The constitutional privilege protects defamatory remarks about ***public officials*** respecting matters of public concern. [§§1507-1509] The privilege applies unless "malice" is shown (intentional falsehood, or ***reckless disregard*** for the truth). But simple inaccuracy or even negligence in ascertaining the facts is ***not*** enough to establish "malice." [§§1517-1520]

b. **UNCLEAR** If Smith is ***not*** a "public figure"—either because he is not a celebrity or because he has not voluntarily injected himself into the limelight—he will win in most states. Accordingly, the statements regarding him would ***not*** be protected by constitutional privilege; and, because the *Tribune* was ***negligent*** in making such charges, it would be liable for defamation. But if Smith turns out to be a public figure, he will lose. [**§§1512-1516, 1520, 1531-1538**]

149.a. **YES** Senator Claghorn is a public official and his illegal gambling probably would be relevant to his official conduct. [**§1508**]

b. **NO** The constitutional privilege is defeated only by a showing that the defendant either ***knew*** that the statement was false, or published it with such ***reckless disregard*** for the truth that the defendant must have subjectively entertained serious doubts as to its truth. Negligence or unprofessionalism is not enough to establish "malice." [**§§1518-1520**]

150. **NO** Normally, unauthorized publication of a photograph taken ***in public*** is not actionable; it does nothing more than expose what anyone then present would have been free to see. [**§1565**] (*Compare:* The result is different where ***commercial advantage*** is taken.) [**§§1595-1596**]

151. **PROBABLY** Normally, merely ***taking*** another's picture is not actionable; some publication thereof is required. But this is not always essential. Certain intrusions into one's privacy are so "unreasonable" that the intrusion itself is actionable. Here, the interference is for a ***constitutionally impermissible purpose*** (to inhibit sex films not necessarily "obscene"), and to impair Eager's right to attend anonymously. Because no legitimate purpose is served thereby, it would probably be deemed an "unreasonable" intrusion. [**§§1545, 1552, 1563, 1568**]

152.a. **NO** There is ***no*** right of action where the facts disclosed are already ***public*** facts (here, birth records). There is no invasion of privacy in such a case. [**§1564**]

b. **YES** These are clearly ***not*** public facts. The issue here is whether the disclosure was privileged as "newsworthy." A few cases hold that ***anything*** affecting a celebrity is newsworthy. But the better view is that such intimate details of a celebrity's life are ***not*** "fair game." Hence, Rona can be held liable for their disclosure, even though true. [**§§1566, 1572-1573**]

153.a. **NO** The right of privacy is strictly a personal right. It does ***not*** survive; and hence no cause of action can be maintained by a decedent's estate or heirs. [**§1615**]

b. **NO** Most courts have held that a decedent's survivors, no matter how close, cannot complain of any invasion of their interests because of the publicity concerning a decedent. [**§1614**]

c. **PROBABLY NOT** The issue here is ***newsworthiness.*** If there is a "legitimate" public interest in the details of the life of one who committed suicide 10 years ago, then it would seem that the reasons for his killing himself are also within the public interest. Mere passage of time does not by itself negate newsworthiness. [**§§1570-1571, 1574-1576**]

d. **NO** The newsworthiness privilege is lost only where the defendant published with knowledge of falsity or ***reckless disregard*** for the truth. Inadvertent errors do not defeat the privilege. [**§§1607-1609**]

154.a. **NO** The defendant is not entitled to take ***commercial advantage*** of the plaintiff's appearance. Its unauthorized use of the plaintiff's picture is actionable—whether based on the plaintiff's appearance in public or otherwise. [**§§1591-1596**]

b. **NO** No pecuniary loss or other special damages need be shown. Mere embarrassment or anguish are sufficient damages. And where, as here, commercial advantage is taken, the value of the use made by the defendant is evidentiary of the damages to be awarded. [**§§1562, 1601**]

155.a. **YES** A false statement of a ***material*** fact is an actionable misrepresentation. A roof inspection report is a "material" fact because Debbie knew Patrick considered it important, and it is the kind of factor upon which reasonable persons customarily rely in buying houses. *Note:* It is not required that Debbie have knowledge that the roof leaked; it is sufficient that she made a false statement of fact (inspection report). (*Compare:* If the roof did ***not*** leak, the false statement might not be deemed "material.") [**§§1624-1628, 1636-1641**]

b. **YES** Having made a statement that she believed to be true, and knowing Patrick was relying thereon, Debbie came under a duty to disclose facts ***later acquired*** that made her earlier statement untrue. [**§1634**]

c. **SPLIT** Traditionally, there is ***no duty to disclose*** facts in a sale transaction unless there is a special relationship between the parties, or the defendant has made a prior statement that requires correction (as in "b." above). However, several states now require disclosure of facts known to the seller and both unknown and ***not readily accessible*** to the buyer. In these states, Debbie's failure to disclose would be actionable. [**§§1630, 1636**]

d. **NO** If the parties agree that the property is being sold "as is," or the plaintiff is charged with notice that facts are being withheld, the seller is not liable for failing to disclose. [**§1629**]

156.a. **NO** No scienter or intent to deceive where the defendant honestly and reasonably believes his statement was true. [**§§1637-1638**]

b. **NO** Again, no scienter or intent to deceive where the defendant honestly believed his statement to be true. It makes no difference that his belief was based on reports from third persons, as long as the belief was honestly entertained. (*Compare:* Result could be contra if Dudley had ***reason to doubt*** the accuracy of the inspection report; in such a case, his doubts might color whether he ***honestly*** believed the premises were termite free when he so stated to Pamela.) [§§1637-1638]

c. **PROBABLY** Knowledge by a defendant that he did not know one way or the other as to the truth of the matter is sufficient to establish scienter. Hence, if Dudley ***knew*** he did not know whether there were any termites, and he said there were none, he is subject to liability. [§1637]

d. **PROBABLY** On a theory of ***negligent misrepresentation*** by a person in the business of supplying information for the guidance of others in a business transaction. In such cases, many courts recognize a duty of care in gathering and reporting the facts, and impose liability for innocent, but negligent, misrepresentations. [§§1655-1656, 1659-1663]

157.a. **NO** Most courts deny recovery to a plaintiff who was not a member of the class of persons whom the defendant intended to influence. Here, Flako's financial statement was submitted to induce Bank's reliance in making a loan, rather than to entice the lending officer to purchase Flako stock. [§1643]

b. **NO** Reliance on a false statement of ***fact*** is always justified; the plaintiff is not required (insofar as the defendant is concerned) to check the accuracy of the statement before relying thereon. [§§1645-1646] Moreover, even if Bank's conduct constituted contributory negligence, this is no defense to a fraud suit. (But it may be a defense to negligent misrepresentation; *see* below.) [§1675]

c. **POSSIBLY** On a theory of ***negligent*** misrepresentation, if it was shown that Accountant was negligent in not discovering the falsity of the statements it certified. Most courts, however, have limited liability by requiring that the reliance of a ***particular*** plaintiff must have been intended or foreseen. Hence, it would have to be shown that Accountant knew or contemplated that Flako was going to use the statements to obtain a loan from Bank. [§§1656, 1659-1660, 1663-1669] (*Note:* Bank's failure to make any independent check of Flako's credit might be regarded as ***contributory negligence***, which would be a valid defense by Accountant to Bank's claim against him for negligent misrepresentation.) [§1675]

d. **YES** Because ***justifiable*** reliance is an essential element in either suit, and Bank cannot justifiably rely on a statement that it knows to be false. (Of course, this would not bar enforcement of the loan itself.) [§1642]

158. **NONE** (A) is a mere representation of value or quality and the buyer's reliance thereon is not deemed justified (in the absence of some special relationship, etc.). [§§1647-1651]

(B) Reliance is justified only on ***material*** misrepresentations of fact. It is a question of whether a reasonable person's investment decision would have been affected by the misrepresentation. This seems doubtful here because, whether or not offered for the first time, the investment decision would seem to be based on price and terms. [§1625]

(C) is an apparent misrepresentation of *law,* and reliance thereon by the plaintiff is not justified, absent special circumstances that do not appear here. **[§§1652-1653]**

159.a. **PROBABLY**

Because Duffer knew the condition of the company, he was apparently intending to deceive Swinger—hence, sufficient ***scienter.*** The real issue is whether Swinger can show ***justifiable reliance*** on Duffer's assurances that Flako had "great business prospects." Normally, reliance on representations of opinion or value is ***not justified.*** But a different rule applies where, as here, there is a special relationship between the parties, and one of the parties ***conceals his interest*** in the transaction about which he is offering apparently disinterested advice. (Duffer's interest as a stockholder stood to be wiped out in bankruptcy if the loan was not obtained.) **[§§1637-1638, 1643-1651]**

b. **NO**

Because unless ***damages*** are proved, no action lies for misrepresentation (unlike the rule as to other intentional torts). **[§1654]**

160.a. **NOT NECESSARILY**

Broken promises by themselves are not bases for fraud claims. However, if the promises were made ***without the intent to perform*** them, they will be treated as misrepresentations of the promisor's state of mind. The "reasonableness" of the promisor's prospect of being able to perform is evidentiary of his state of mind but is ***not conclusive*** (*i.e.,* a good faith intent to perform may exist notwithstanding lack of reasonable prospects). **[§§1626, 1638]**

b. **SPLIT**

Most courts award the defrauded plaintiff the benefit of his bargain—the difference between the value of that which he was promised ($10,000) and that which he received ($2,000); here, $8,000. **[§1679]** *Note:* The minority rule awards only out-of-pocket loss—the difference between the value paid ($5,000) and the value received ($2,000); here $3,000. **[§1680]**

161. **NONE**

(A) is untrue because ***dishonest*** expressions of opinion are as actionable as false statements of fact in a disparagement action. **[§1688]**

(B) is untrue because the burden is on the ***plaintiff*** in a disparagement action to prove the falsity of the facts or opinion expressed. **[§1685]**

(C) is untrue because the only intent required is the intent to disparage (and a dishonest expression of facts or opinion would suffice). **[§§1695-1698]**

(D) is untrue because the action cannot be maintained in the absence of special damages (out-of-pocket losses); and if Aerospace obtained the contract, it probably could not show any such damages. **[§1699]**

162. **YES**

On a theory of ***defamation,*** rather than disparagement. Not every trade libel is defamatory of the product manufacturer. However, where the disparaging statement also impairs the ***reputation*** of the manufacturer, either action will lie. Here, Sly's statement in effect accuses Fry of ***fraud*** (passing off horsemeat as beef). Such an imputation is ***defamatory per se***—actionable even without proof of special damages. [**§§1691, 1693-1694**]

163. **NO** The same privileges are recognized in disparagement actions as in defamation actions. One of these is an ***absolute*** privilege for statements filed as part of a judicial proceeding. And, a lis pendens is generally so regarded. [**§1705**] *Compare:* If Bright can prove that Wiley filed the lis pendens for an ***ulterior purpose*** (unrelated to the lawsuit), he may be able to recover for ***abuse of civil process*** (below). [**§§1791-1792**]

164. **(B) AND (C)** (A) is not true because the tort lies for interference with the ***relationship*** that exists—*i.e.,* it might have continued but for the interference. [**§1715**]

(B) is true; the possibility that Vera may have terminated anyhow must be taken into consideration in assessing damages. [**§1715**]

(C) is true. A defendant is privileged to interfere with an existing contract even though he was acting for his own selfish interests, where the contract is terminable at will. The privilege to compete takes precedence over a mere expectancy that such a contract will continue. [**§1736**]

165. **DEPENDS** On National's motives. Where the interference is ***justified***, there can be no recovery. Thus, there is no recovery if National has acted to protect its own interests (*e.g.,* in obtaining quality products, or in directing business to what it considers a more reliable supplier). On the other hand, if National was acting for an improper purpose (*e.g.,* solely to harm Case) the conduct would be actionable. [**§§1729-1736**]

166. **ALL EXCEPT (A)** (A) is false; it is only required that the proceedings be "terminated favorably" as to the plaintiff; and a dismissal for insufficient evidence is so regarded. [**§§1764-1765**]

(B) and (C) are both true. The plaintiff in a malicious prosecution must prove ***both*** that there was ***no probable cause*** for the criminal charge and that it was filed for an improper purpose. [**§§1766-1774**]

(D) is true. The dismissal (or even an actual acquittal) in the criminal proceedings only means that the prosecution was unable to prove Employee guilty "beyond a reasonable doubt." But a ***lesser standard of proof***—a mere "preponderance" of the evidence—suffices in civil cases. Thus, Employer may defend on the ground that Employee was in fact guilty all along. [**§1776**]

(E) is true. A successful plaintiff is entitled to recover all damages proximately caused by the institution of the criminal charge. [**§1775**]

Exam Questions and Answers

QUESTION I

Adam, a retired merchant, was driving his car in a careful manner when suddenly it swerved to the left across the center line and crashed into Brenda's parked car. Brenda had parked in the wrong direction on the left-hand side of the street in violation of a local ordinance. Just prior to the accident, Adam had taken his car for repairs to Smith's Garage. The car swerved because Smith had negligently assembled the steering apparatus after working on the car. As a result of the collision, both cars were badly damaged, Adam received a severe blow on the head, and a bottle of liquor that Adam had purchased fell from the seat and broke.

While extricating himself from his car, Adam felt and acted distinctly groggy because of the blow to his head. Brenda, drawn from her house by the noise, smelled the odor of whiskey occasioned by the broken liquor bottle, noted Adam's groggy behavior, and assumed Adam was intoxicated. In the presence of a group of persons who had gathered, she said, "I'll take this drunk to the police station." Then, despite Adam's protestations, she grabbed Adam by the arm and forcibly compelled him to go to the police station a block away. There Adam was examined by a physician and pronounced sober. He was released approximately a half hour after the accident had occurred.

Adam was greatly humiliated both by Brenda's reference to him as a drunkard and by his being compelled to go to the police station at Brenda's insistence, but he suffered no special damages on that account.

What are the rights of the various parties? Discuss.

QUESTION II

Tom, Bill, and Harry were riding in Tom's convertible bound for a football game. Tom was driving, Bill agreed to pay for the gasoline, and Harry purchased all three tickets as his contribution to the excursion. Due to the joint negligence of Tom and one Smith, who was driving his sedan, an accident occurred. As a result of the collision, the two cars were damaged and both Bill and Harry were injured.

After the accident, Tom and Smith became engaged in a heated argument as to who was responsible for the collision. Finally, Smith challenged Tom to a fight, Tom accepted the challenge, and both men removed their coats and proceeded to fight. They stopped only after Smith had knocked out two of Tom's front teeth. At that point, a reporter for the *Evening Chronicle* arrived at the scene and snapped a picture showing Tom bleeding at the mouth and holding a tooth in his hand. Realizing he had been photographed in this embarrassing position, Tom turned to the reporter and said, "I don't want you to publish that picture." Nonetheless, the picture was published in the *Evening Chronicle* along with an appropriate news item.

In due course, Tom had Dr. Todd, a reputable dentist, perform the necessary dental work and sent the dentist's bill to Smith, demanding payment. Smith replied by letter saying, "I won't pay this bill, and besides, I'm surprised that you would go to such a quack dentist as Dr. Todd." Smith, when writing Tom, had in good faith confused Dr. Todd with Dr. Dott, the latter being a truly disreputable dentist.

What are the rights and liabilities of the various parties? Discuss.

QUESTION III

Davis was the owner of a three-story brick building abutting the sidewalk. The first floor was rented to a chiropodist who used it for an office and sometimes spent the night there. The second floor was used by Davis himself as a storage space for his fine art collection. The third floor was occupied by Tenet and his family as a dwelling.

Davis employed Wasser, a window cleaner, to clean the windows in the building, giving him a belt attached to a stout rope with instructions to wear the belt around his waist and to tie the other end of the rope to the radiators under the second and third floor windows while he was cleaning them. Wasser neglected to do this, choosing instead to stand on the eight-inch ledge below the windows, holding on to an awning hook with one hand while he washed the windows with the other. While standing in this position outside the second floor window, Wasser was startled when a lighted cigarette fell on his bald head from the apartment on the third floor, where Tenet and his wife were entertaining guests at a cocktail party. Losing his hold on the awning hook and thereafter his balance, Wasser fell to the sidewalk below and was severely injured.

While the ambulance was taking Wasser to the hospital, Davis telephoned Mrs. Wasser, who—to his knowledge—was seriously afflicted with heart trouble, to tell her that her husband had fallen from the second floor and had been badly hurt. Mrs. Wasser fell over in a faint, struck her head against a doorknob, and died a month later from the head injury.

A state statute required owners of "multiple-dwelling" buildings to provide "approved" safety devices for window cleaners. The rope device provided by Davis had not been approved. The devices that had been approved could not be used on Davis's building because it lacked the proper hooks in the wall; it would not have been as effective in preventing falls as the rope and belt that Davis had supplied.

Discuss the rights of the parties. Assume that Wasser is not covered by workers' compensation laws.

QUESTION IV

Nerv was an extremely nervous person. He discussed his problems with his friend Phil, a licensed pharmacist who owned and operated a drugstore. Phil recommended "Dreamy," a new tranquilizer manufactured by Drugco that did not require a prescription. Dreamy had been extensively tested by Drugco and four months previously had been approved for sale to the public without prescription by the Federal Food and Drug Administration ("FDA"). Nerv purchased a bottle of Dreamy and began taking it in accordance with the instructions. The label on the bottle stated, "Normal dosage two pills every 12 hours—safe for adult use—not habit-forming."

The day after the purchase, Nerv took two Dreamy pills upon arising, had breakfast, and then got in his car and headed for the golf course. While driving on a public street, Nerv suddenly became dizzy and lost control of his car. The car swerved onto the sidewalk, hit Ima, seriously injuring her, and then ran into a pole, seriously injuring Nerv.

Subsequent analysis revealed that Nerv's dizziness was caused by an allergic reaction to Dreamy, but that only five persons out of 10,000 would have such a reaction. None of this had been discovered during the extensive premarketing tests that led to approval by the FDA. It was also learned that during the four months since Dreamy was first marketed, two other persons had reactions similar to those of Nerv, and Drugco had been so informed. As a result, Drugco had conducted further tests and had ordered new labels that would contain the following message: "CAUTION—Dizziness may result from normal dosage."

What are the rights of Ima against Nerv and Drugco? Discuss.

What are the rights of Nerv against Phil and Drugco? Discuss.

QUESTION V

Mower Company ("Mower") manufactures a 12-horsepower cub tractor with a riding seat and a rotary cutter. The cutter is advertised as capable of cutting through brush with stalks up to one inch in diameter. Park purchased one of Mower's tractors from Retail Company ("Retail") on the condition that it could be returned anytime during the first week if it was not performing properly. The entire price of $1,200 was paid at the time of delivery. Before delivery, Retail inspected and serviced the vehicle.

During the first week, Park noted that the cutter would not cut through brush of slightly less than one inch. When he used it over very rough terrain, he thought he noticed an increasing vibration and that the cutter was cutting closer on one side than on the other. Because he was enjoying its use, however, he made no attempt to return it to Retail. At the end of the first month, the vibration increased considerably, but then the first snow came and the tractor was put in the barn for the winter.

The following spring, Park got the tractor out to demonstrate it to a neighbor, Smith, who was interested in the purchase of one. Smith, an amateur mechanic of considerable ability, offered to fix the vibration by a simple adjustment of the nut that held the rotary cutter. Smith adjusted the nut. Subsequently, each took turns driving the cutter over very rough, stony, and brushy ground. The vibration continued but was not as great as before. While Smith was riding the tractor, the rotary cutter came off, broke through its housing, and severed the left foot of Park. The evidence showed a crack in the nut that held the cutter.

Park sued Mower and Retail for damages due to the tractor's failure to cut one-inch brush, for the damages to the equipment, and for his physical injuries.

What result? Discuss. Include in your discussion all possible theories of liability and defenses available to Mower and Retail.

QUESTION VI

The four-story law school building of University, a private institution, had a defective elevator that frequently stopped between floors. The elevator had an alarm button which, if pressed, would ring a bell in the hallway and thus alert persons in the building to the fact that the elevator had stopped between floors, with passengers inside it. The defective condition did not create any danger that the elevator might fall or otherwise physically injure any passenger.

Elco, an elevator maintenance company, had a contract with University to inspect, service, and maintain the elevator.

One night, Prof, a law teacher, and his administrative assistant, Prim, had been working late in Prof's office on the fourth floor of the building on an overdue manuscript. They entered the elevator to leave at about 11:20 p.m. The official closing hour for the building was 11 p.m., but there were exit doors from the building that could be opened from the inside. Both Prof and Prim knew that the elevator frequently stopped between floors.

The elevator stopped between the second and third floors. Prof pressed the alarm button, and the bell could be heard ringing in the hallway. Jones, a law student, was the only other person still in the building. He heard the alarm bell and realized that someone was trapped in the elevator. He thought this was very funny, and he deliberately did not call the campus maintenance staff.

Prof and Prim were not discovered and released until 8 a.m. the next day.

Prof suffered from high blood pressure. This condition and his fright at being confined in the elevator caused him to sustain a heart attack after two hours in the elevator.

Prim suffered severe nervous shock due to being confined in the elevator and her fear that Prof was dying. She was subsequently embarrassed and humiliated by remarks of students who suggested that perhaps some amorous activity in the elevator might have caused Prof's heart attack.

What rights do Prof and Prim each have against Jones, Elco, and University? Discuss.

QUESTION VII

Alana, while in a department store owned by Bernard, noticed a sign on the wall reading "FREE—PLEASE TAKE ONE," below which was a box of MP3 players. Alana put one of the players in her pocket and walked out of the store. Bernard rushed out of the store after Alana shouting, "Come back here with that player, you thief!" The street was crowded, and Alana, humiliated by the accusation, eluded Bernard and ran home.

Later that day, Carla, a customer who resembled Alana, went into the restroom of Bernard's store. Bernard, thinking Carla was Alana, locked the restroom door and called the police. There was an open window in the restroom. Carla mounted a chair, planning to climb out the window. As she put her weight on the back of the chair, it tipped. Carla fell to the floor and broke her leg.

Alana learned later that the "FREE—PLEASE TAKE ONE" sign referred to advertising flyers that were usually beneath the sign and not to the MP3 players. She offered to return the player, but Bernard refused to accept it.

Discuss the rights of Alana and Bernard against each other and the rights of Carla against Bernard.

QUESTION VIII

Twenty years ago Resco erected a building in what was then an unsettled area. Resco conducts experimental work in connection with cattle virus diseases in that building. The area surrounding the Resco property has now become a thriving cattle and dairy district.

Cattle ranchers in the area tried to induce Zoe, a cattle auctioneer, to establish a local market. Zoe was reluctant to do so because of her fear that a virus might escape from Resco's property and infect cattle.

Some of the ranchers called on Prex, the president of Resco. They told Prex of their desire to establish a market in the area and asked him to make a statement that would dispel Zoe's fears.

Prex called a conference and, without having made any investigation and without naming Zoe, stated that there was "no danger at all" of any virus escaping from the Resco premises, and that only a "driveling idiot" could conclude otherwise. This statement was printed in the *News*, a local newspaper, and received wide attention. As a result, Zoe was frequently referred to in the community as a "driveling idiot." This caused her considerable embarrassment.

In the belief that Prex's statement concerning the safety of the Resco operation was correct and to escape further embarrassment, Zoe established a market in the area for the auction of cattle. Shortly thereafter, without negligence on the part of Resco, a virus escaped from Resco's premises and infected cattle in the area.

To stop the spread of the infection, public authorities ordered the slaughter of all infected or exposed cattle, and Zoe had to abandon her market with consequent financial loss to her.

What are Zoe's rights against Resco? Prex? the *News*? Discuss all issues.

QUESTION IX

Transit operates buses in a city. One morning Driver, a Transit driver, awoke with a bad cold. He consulted the yellow pages of the telephone directory and called Dr. Ard, a physician listed under the category, "Physicians & Surgeons—M.D.—Eye, Ear, Nose & Throat." Driver told Dr. Ard that he had a bad cold and was scheduled to report for work at noon that day. Dr. Ard listened to Driver describe his symptoms, said he could not give Driver an appointment, and told him to buy a bottle of "Pyrib" at a drugstore and to use its contents as directed on the label. Pyrib is a cold remedy antihistamine prepared and marketed by Drugco. Driver obtained the Pyrib from a drugstore, took the first dosage called for on the label, and reported for work at noon.

At 1:30 p.m. that day, while driving his bus, Driver felt drowsy. However, he continued driving and shortly thereafter fell asleep. The bus jumped a curb and hit a pole. Pat, a paying passenger on the bus, was injured.

Pyrib is known to cause drowsiness and sleep in about 20% of the persons who take it. Dr. Ard did not warn Driver that the medication prescribed might cause drowsiness and sleep, and the label on the bottle did not contain any such warning.

Discuss Pat's rights against Drugco, Transit, and Dr. Ard.

QUESTION X

Twenty years ago, Phil worked in the research department of Bomm-Bay, a private armaments manufacturer doing substantial business with the government. At that time, Phil and his colleagues were testing a newly developed strain of bacteria for use in germ warfare. From tests on animals, they found the agent to be effective, and it has since been incorporated into weapons sold to the government. The strain of bacteria has never been used in combat and has never been tested on humans. However, because of inadequate safety mechanisms at Bomm-Bay's laboratories, Phil was accidentally exposed to the bacteria.

The exposure was very brief and Phil did not suffer immediate harm, but his health has gradually deteriorated. It recently became so poor that he checked into a hospital. Doctors quickly traced his maladies to the bacteria, but cannot cure him.

Roy, a reporter for the *Yellow Journal*, learned of Phil's condition and entered Phil's hospital room wearing a white coat and stethoscope. Phil, thinking Roy was a doctor, disclosed that his mental capacities were impaired, that a lung and a kidney were no longer functioning, that he wore a wig because all his hair had fallen out, and that he was now impotent.

The next day Roy published a story attacking the use of inhumane weapons by the government and the lack of safety precautions used by local arms manufacturers such as Bomm-Bay. The story included Phil's name, an account of his accident 20 years ago, and a description of the symptoms Phil had disclosed to Roy. In addition, the story falsely stated that Phil's son, born a year after the accident, was mentally retarded, and that Phil experienced temporary seizures during which he became uncontrollably violent, once even beating his wife and child. Roy had no reason to think these false statements were true, and included them because he felt entitled to a certain poetic license as to assertions that cast no personal blame on Phil.

Discuss Phil's rights against the *Yellow Journal*.

ANSWER TO QUESTION I

Brenda v. Smith

Brenda will bring a negligence action against Smith for the damage to her car. Smith, as an automobile repairer undertaking to service a car, owes a general duty of care—and this is particularly true when the work affects parts of the car that could cause injury if not properly repaired, such as the steering apparatus in this case. Breach of duty is given in the facts by use of the word "negligently." Actual causation is present because but for Smith's negligent reassembly, there would not have been a steering difficulty and Adam's car would not have crashed into Brenda's. Proximate cause is established by the fact that a foreseeable result (crash) occurred in a quite foreseeable manner (car swerving from faulty steering apparatus). And because both cars were "badly damaged," the prima facie case of negligence is complete.

Smith might allege that Brenda was contributorily negligent in parking her car in violation of an ordinance. However, this argument will fail because the ordinance undoubtedly is meant to protect against danger to oncoming traffic created by drivers who pull across the street to a parking space facing the wrong direction and then pull out again and try to merge with the proper flow of traffic. But here Brenda's car was already parked, and it posed no danger to oncoming traffic. Hence, it cannot be said that the purpose of the ordinance was to avoid the kind of harm that in fact occurred, and the violation of the ordinance is therefore irrelevant. (Note that even if Brenda's car had been properly parked in the space in question, it would still have been hit by Adam's car.)

Because the facts do not raise any other possible defense, it appears that Brenda will prevail in a negligence action against Smith.

(Smith cannot be held strictly liable here because he did not distribute a product, but simply rendered a service.)

Brenda v. Adam

Brenda will not meet with equal success in a negligence action against Adam for the damage to her car. The problem here is that although Adam—as a driver on the road and as owner of a car—owed a duty of due care to those who might foreseeably be hurt by his carelessness, there is no evidence that Adam breached that duty. In other words, there is no reason to believe that Adam knew that the car was defective before the episode occurred, and hence no indication that he acted unreasonably.

Adam v. Brenda

Property damage and personal injury: Brenda cannot be held liable to Adam for property damage and personal injury arising out of the crash itself, because there is no showing of any negligence on her part with respect to the occurrence of the accident. Her only misbehavior prior to the crash was parking in the wrong direction but, as discussed above, violation of the parking ordinance cannot be used to establish liability for this type of accident.

On the other hand, Adam has several possible bases for recovery against Brenda for harm suffered after the crash. First, by grabbing hold of Adam's arm (a "touching"), Brenda committed a battery. Second, an action for assault may lie—arguably Brenda's behavior led Adam reasonably to believe that if he were to try to break away or refuse to accompany Brenda to the station, he would be subject to further physical violence. Finally, a prima facie case is made out for false imprisonment, by the fact that Brenda restrained Adam through fear of force.

The crucial issue is whether there is a valid defense or privilege to the three intentional torts. Brenda will argue that she was arresting someone she reasonably believed to be guilty of drunk driving, so that her conduct was privileged. However, the general common law regarding arrests by private citizens without a warrant (even if drunk driving is considered a felony) is that despite the citizen's reasonable belief that a crime has been committed, the privilege is lost if in fact no crime was committed. Because the facts indicate that Adam did not commit a crime, Brenda's reasonable belief to the contrary will not protect her from liability for the intentional torts.

Therefore, Adam can recover at least nominal damages for all three torts, as well as compensatory damages for the half-hour detention.

Defamation: Arguably, Adam was slandered when Brenda referred to him as a "drunk." There was an intentional publication of words that would tend to damage Adam's reputation in the community. However, because we are told that he suffered no special damages, he can recover only upon a showing that Brenda's statement was "slander per se." It seems doubtful that the accusation of committing the crime of drunk driving or of being a public drunkard comes within one of the four categories of "slander per se." Even as a crime, such behavior probably lacks sufficient moral turpitude to support a slander per se recovery; and because Adam is retired, it is quite unlikely that the statement can be regarded as imputing conduct incompatible with his profession for purposes of a slander per se recovery. Being that the other two categories for recovery, a loathsome disease and unchastity of a woman, are not even arguably on point, an action for defamation will most probably fail.

Emotional distress: A claim for intentional infliction of emotional distress is also unlikely to succeed because it would be difficult to characterize Brenda's conduct as "extreme" or "outrageous." Brenda had reason to believe that drunk driving occurred, and there is no basis for inferring that she was acting for any other motive or in any way committing a practical joke.

Adam v. Smith

Smith will be liable to Adam for property damage (car and liquor bottle) as well as for personal injury occasioned by Smith's negligence. Adam's case in this regard is at least as strong as Brenda's case against Smith (above), and there are no apparent defenses against Adam.

A further question, however, is whether Smith is liable for the harm and humiliation that Adam suffered after the crash because of Brenda's behavior. Certainly Smith's negligence was an actual cause of what transpired, but it is unlikely to be considered a proximate cause. The foreseeable result of Smith's negligence involved personal injury but not the likelihood that the person injured would have a broken liquor bottle in the car and be mistakenly assumed to be drunk by someone else who would take the law into her own hands. In that sense, Brenda became an unforeseeable intervening force for which Smith is not responsible. (Some courts, however, might allow recovery because of the proximity in time and space between the crash and the subsequent harm—an Andrews analysis.)

Adam would also have an action for breach of the repair contract, Smith's negligence being the breach. But again, the damages would not extend beyond those suffered in the accident because recovery in contract is limited to foreseeable damages.

ANSWER TO QUESTION II

Bill and Harry v. Smith

Smith, as a driver, owed a general duty of care to those in and around the road who might foreseeably be injured by his carelessness. Bill and Harry, as passengers in another car, were within the zone of foreseeability and hence were owed that duty of care. The facts stipulate that Smith violated that duty by acting negligently. And because Smith's negligence was the actual and proximate cause of the harm Bill and Harry suffered (their injury being a foreseeable result), the prima facie case is complete.

Moreover, there are no apparent defenses. The fact that Tom was also negligent would be a defense only if negligence could be imputed to Bill and Harry on a joint enterprise theory. However, in this case the parties were not engaged in a joint enterprise: Although sharing expenses may remove Bill and Harry from "guest" status (below), it alone does not give them joint enterprise status. A joint enterprise also requires an equal right to control its operation, and here the facts do not indicate that the three had common control of the vehicle. The car was Tom's, he was driving, and he was apparently in control of how to drive, the route to take, etc.

Bill and Harry v. Tom

Bill and Harry have an action against Tom because of his negligent driving. At common law, a driver owes others in the car a duty of due care while driving. This duty has been breached, and that breach is the actual and proximate cause of the harm. Furthermore, no defenses are evident from the facts.

However, should the state be one of the few having a guest statute, the problem is more difficult. If Bill and Harry are considered "guests," these statutes require proof that Tom's driving was "wanton" or "grossly negligent," rather than simply negligent. Here the facts do not support such a showing (it is only stated that Tom was "negligent"). Nonetheless,

Bill and Harry could escape from this situation. They can argue that they are "passengers," not "guests"—on the theory that there was an agreement to share expenses. Generally, for a rider to be characterized as a "passenger," there must be some payment that motivates the driver to furnish the ride. Because Bill bought gas and Harry purchased the tickets, they will probably be deemed passengers and thus will succeed in their common law actions.

Smith v. Tom

The likelihood of Smith succeeding in a suit against Tom for the damage to his car will depend on whether the jurisdiction has adopted comparative negligence. If not, then his own negligence completely bars any action against Tom. On the other hand, if comparative negligence principles do apply, then the outcome depends on what type of comparative negligence is followed ("pure" or "partial") and the degree to which Smith and Tom were each at fault.

Tom also apparently assaulted and battered Smith during the fight and would be liable for nominal damages but for the fact that these actions are barred in some states by reason of Smith's consent to the fight (discussed further below).

Tom v. Smith

So far as damage to Tom's car is concerned, the analysis here is identical to the one discussed above in Smith's action against Tom (*i.e.,* the issue turns on applicability of comparative negligence).

Tom will also sue for battery to recover damages sustained in the fight. The prima facie case is made out because Smith intentionally hit Tom and it may be assumed that it was meant to be a harmful touching. Additionally, there may be a cause of action for assault, because Tom was undoubtedly apprehensive (and properly so) of Smith's efforts to hit him during the fight.

The obvious defense to the above two actions would be consent. By accepting Smith's challenge, Tom consented to a fight, and it appears that Smith did nothing to go beyond the consent or otherwise vitiate it. Tom, however, will argue that the consent was invalid—on the theory that one cannot effectively consent to a breach of the peace. The courts are split on this question, but in most states such consent is invalid (as a deterrence to fighting), and Tom would be permitted to recover for the harm to his teeth and related injuries.

Tom v. *Evening Chronicle*

A common law action for invasion of privacy lies for the mass circulation of private facts. The problem here, however, is that even though the picture of Tom was unauthorized, the event occurred in public in full view of all those who happened to be around. Moreover, one who undertakes to fight in public may not subsequently complain about the embarrassment that ensues simply because a photographer happened to come upon the scene. The point is not necessarily that the photograph was newsworthy—which is a defense—but rather that because there was no publication of ***private*** facts that would offend a reasonable person, there was no prima facie case for invasion of privacy in the first place. (Note that in the unlikely event that a prima facie case could be made out, consent would not be available as a defense because it was explicitly withdrawn by Tom before any publication occurred.)

Dr. Todd v. Smith

Smith's letter to Tom is an intentional publication of a libel concerning Dr. Todd, and the libel is apparent on its face because it holds him up to ridicule and contempt as an incompetent dentist. Where a defamatory publication takes the form of libel and is clear on its face, no state requires a showing of special damages. Hence, the prima facie case is complete.

The issue then is whether there is an applicable defense. Because the statement is not true, the only apparent defense under state law would be one of qualified privilege. But is this an occasion that calls for a conditional privilege? There seemingly is no common interest between Smith and Tom that would justify Smith's statement. On the other hand, Smith probably is concerned with his own financial interests should he be held liable to Tom—it may well be that Smith is afraid that Tom's going to an incompetent dentist will subject him to excessive dental bills. Had there been remaining dental work to be done, this theory might support a finding of a conditional privilege and Smith's "good faith" would protect him. Unfortunately for Smith, however, it appears that all necessary dental work has been completed so that there is nothing to be gained by Smith's telling Tom after the fact what he believes about Dr. Todd. Thus, there do not appear to be any state privileges on point.

It is highly doubtful whether the *Gertz* privilege would apply in this suit by a private citizen against another private citizen over a private communication. If it were to apply, Dr. Todd would have to prove negligence on the part of Smith to recover actual injury damages. Although Smith was writing in good faith, the facts do not seem to support the notion that he was acting reasonably in making such a clear mistake between Todd and Dott. If this is so, Smith was indeed negligent and *Gertz* would not stand in the way of Dr. Todd's recovery of actual injury damages, but Smith's good faith belief in the truth of what he wrote would prevent Todd's recovery of general damages.

ANSWER TO QUESTION III

Wasser v. Davis

One who employs another to perform tasks owes a duty of due care to provide reasonably safe working conditions. Here, Wasser would claim that Davis breached that duty by failing to supply the approved safety mechanism required by statute. Arguably Davis's brick building was not a "multiple dwelling" within the meaning of the statute—because only one floor was regularly used as a dwelling unit. If this is so, it cannot be said that Davis breached his duty by reason of a statutory violation. However, assuming the building is a "multiple dwelling" (perhaps because adaptable to such purposes), the result favors Wasser. The purpose of the statute undoubtedly is to prevent accidents of the sort that occurred here—*i.e.,* something causing the window cleaner to lose his balance and fall—and Wasser, being a window cleaner, is clearly within the class of persons to be protected. Therefore, Davis's failure to furnish the requisite safety device will be considered "negligence per se" in most states, as long as his violation is unexcused. Here the infraction does not appear to be excusable: There is no indication that Davis could not have refit his building to allow for use of the approved devices; indeed, he should have delayed the window washing until the necessary accommodations could have been made. It follows then that Davis's statutory violation sufficiently establishes breach for a negligence action.

Actual cause presents two problems for Wasser. First, even though Davis violated the statute without excuse, he nevertheless gave Wasser a safety mechanism that would have been more effective than an "approved" device. In other words, Wasser was not put in a more dangerous position because of the statutory infraction. (Note that this factor could also be analyzed under the breach discussion, arguing that Davis's violation was not contemplated by the statute because the statute was only meant to preclude use of safety devices that were more dangerous than the approved ones.) The second problem relates to Wasser's failure to use the device that Davis gave him—*i.e.,* even if Davis had provided the approved device, would Wasser have used it? This is unclear from the facts; hence, the actual cause issue cannot clearly be resolved.

On the issue of proximate cause, Davis may argue that the cigarette falling on Wasser's head was an unforeseeable intervening force that should terminate his liability. However, this contention is weak at best, because the statutory purpose is to protect the window cleaner from losing his balance no matter what the reason. It is therefore irrelevant that in this case the fall was occasioned by an unusual event. Moreover, there is clearly a foreseeable result—loss of balance and subsequent fall. Thus, there most probably is a sufficient showing of proximate cause. (Perhaps the result would be different had the intervening force amounted to a malicious tort or crime, but the facts do not indicate that such was the case.)

Assuming Wasser can overcome the actual cause problem, his injury completes the prima facie case. However, Davis appears to have a good defense. Wasser should have realized that any number of factors could have caused him to lose his balance. Such being the case, his failure to use any safety device casts serious doubt on the reasonableness of his behavior. If it was unreasonable, in a contributory negligence state, Wasser's conduct will completely bar his recovery; and in a comparative negligence jurisdiction, Wasser's recovery will at least be reduced (if not barred altogether)—the result turning on the type of comparative negligence adopted and the degree to which Wasser and Davis were each at fault.

(In some cases, a statute is perceived to have been enacted for the benefit of a group unable to protect itself, and the failure of a member of that group to behave reasonably has been totally disregarded. This most often applies to children and to workers on dangerous jobs who are told to undertake a hazardous task with the risk of being fired if they refuse. However, this is not the case here because Wasser was given safety equipment to use but nonetheless failed to use it—apparently unreasonably.)

Wasser v. Tenet, *et al.*

Wasser will claim that Tenet behaved negligently, either by tossing a lighted cigarette out the window or by allowing his guest to do so. The major problem, however, is proving who in fact dropped the cigarette (all we know is that Tenet and his wife were having a cocktail party—from the facts given, anyone could have been responsible). Assuming Wasser can gather proof that Tenet or his wife was at fault, a prima facie case will not be difficult to establish. Persons in apartments abutting public sidewalks must exercise due care so as not to endanger persons outside. Tenet might contend that under the Cardozo view Wasser was owed no duty because he was not a foreseeable plaintiff, being a window washer (possibly unexpected) and not a passerby on the sidewalk below. However, Tenet is unlikely to succeed with this argument—even Cardozo would agree that it would be ludicrous to restrict the class of foreseeable plaintiffs to those passing on the sidewalk. A window washer part way down is even more clearly in the zone of danger than are others on the street below. Hence, the better conclusion would be that Wasser was owed a duty of due care. Moreover, there is no problem with causation: But for the incident, Wasser would not have lost his balance and been hurt—hence, actual cause. Assuming Wasser is a foreseeable plaintiff, his injury was a foreseeable direct result of the cigarette hitting his head. Thus, proximate cause is present.

Liability would therefore seem to follow except for the fact that Tenet can rely on the same defense analysis as discussed in the suit against Davis—*i.e.,* contributory negligence or comparative negligence may well bar (or at least reduce) Wasser's recovery.

Going back to the issue raised earlier, if Wasser cannot show that Tenet or his wife was at fault, the likelihood of his making out a prima facie case greatly diminishes. An effort to hold Tenet vicariously liable for the misbehavior of whomever dropped the cigarette is unlikely to succeed because the relationship of host and guest does not give rise to imputed liability. Neither can there be primary negligence unless the host has some reason to know that one of his guests is creating unreasonable risks toward others. Absent such a showing, Wasser will have to identify the particular individual who dropped the cigarette; however, this is virtually impossible from the facts given. Wasser might try to rely on a res ipsa claim against everyone in the apartment, invoking *Ybarra v. Spangard* principles. However, the likelihood of his succeeding is dubious—the cocktail party seems to be entirely different from *Ybarra*, where it was known that each defendant had some contact with the plaintiff.

Mrs. Wasser v. Davis

A duty is owed to exercise due care so as not to subject others to a foreseeable risk of physical injury, through physical impact or threat thereof, that might foreseeably result from emotional distress. The problem here is that although Davis's conduct (phone conversation) was directed at Mrs. Wasser, there was no "threat of physical impact." Hence, these facts are far removed from the typical case. Nonetheless, arguably Davis's knowledge of Mrs. Wasser's heart trouble may well have subjected him to a duty not to impose an unreasonable emotional burden on her. If such is the case, the outcome turns on whether he in fact acted unreasonably in making the phone call, taking into consideration the frantic state of events. Would a reasonable person under similar circumstances have found a more gentle way to handle the situation? This is debatable. Should it be decided that Davis was negligent, he will be liable to Mrs. Wasser's estate for her injury and for expenses attending her subsequent death. Additionally, a wrongful death action may lie; although, should Wasser be a beneficiary in such an action, recovery would be barred or reduced because of his own negligence that occasioned Davis's call in the first place.

ANSWER TO QUESTION IV

Ima v. Nerv

Ima's claim against Nerv will be based on a negligence theory. Nerv owes a duty to those in and around the road to exercise due care while driving and while preparing himself to drive. The problem here, however, is that there is no clear breach of that duty—*i.e.,* the facts do not indicate that Nerv could have anticipated his allergic reaction. Arguably Nerv was negligent in driving after taking a tranquilizer whose strength and effect he had not previously determined, but seeing that the label raised no suspicion of side effects, and given the reality that persons often take medication before driving unless warned otherwise, this theory is not strongly supported by the facts.

Actual causation is present because, but for Nerv's having taken the drug, he would not have sustained the allergic reaction and would not have hurt Ima. On the other hand, proximate cause raises a problem because although the foreseeable risks undoubtedly included drowsiness, Nerv should have had time to pull over to the side of the road. But here he "suddenly" became dizzy and lost control of the car. Even though attributable to his taking the pills, the suddenness of the reaction arguably was not the risk reasonably to be anticipated. Hence, many courts would hold this to be an unforeseeable result, precluding a finding of proximate cause. Others, however, might hold that losing control of the car was the foreseeable risk involved and that it did in fact occur—although through unexpected dizziness rather than predictable drowsiness. Damages are given and there are no apparent defenses so that if the problems of breach and proximate cause can be overcome, Nerv will be liable to Ima.

Ima v. Drugco

Ima may pursue several theories against Drugco. First, strict liability in tort is possible, but Ima faces the problem that she is a "bystander." Almost all states allow any person injured by a defective product to invoke strict liability, on the theory that bystanders are in need of even greater protection than users or consumers. Thus, the case turns on whether the product was "defective." Here we are dealing with a claim of design defect because the entire batch can potentially cause allergic reactions. The question, however, is whether a product that is perfectly safe for 9,995 persons out of 10,000 is defectively designed because of the danger to the others. Given the fact that extensive premarketing tests had not disclosed the danger, most courts would probably treat the side effect as a scientifically unknowable risk, thus precluding a finding of design defect. However, under the growing trend if there is a known risk of harm to any number of potential users, no matter how small, the manufacturer owes a duty to warn, and its failure to do so renders the product defective. Thus, Drugco's failure to warn of Dreamy's potential, albeit slight, side effects after two prior allergic reactions were reported renders the product defective.

Should Ima attempt an action for breach of implied warranty of merchantability, she would run into the dilemma that she was not in privity with Drugco, the manufacturer. The Uniform Commercial Code offers several alternatives to the traditional strict privity requirement. States adopting the narrowest provision would not allow recovery, but those following the broader provisions might well find for Ima as a person reasonably to be expected to be affected by the product. Arguably Dreamy is not fit for normal use and hence, unmerchantable.

Another possible theory is breach of express warranty—because the label states that the drug is "safe for adult use." However, Ima faces the same privity problem as she does in the implied warranty action.

A strict liability action for innocent misrepresentation would be futile because there was no reliance by Ima on the label's representation.

Turning to negligence theories, it is clear that under the expanded interpretation of *MacPherson v. Buick Motor Co.*, Drugco owes a duty of due care to anyone who might be adversely affected by its products. The negligence here is apparently not in the failure to discover the allergic danger, because we are told that extensive testing—including testing by the FDA—did not reveal the defect. And it is unlikely that the testing was performed unreasonably. Rather, the negligence may be in the failure to respond faster once Drugco learned that others were having adverse reactions. Although further tests had been conducted and new labels ordered, perhaps the reasonable course of behavior would have been to inform all pharmacists immediately that potential problems were being reported and studied. If this had been done, a jury might well find that Phil would not have recommended the potentially dangerous tranquilizer to his friend Nerv. Causation would be present because an earlier warning of sudden dizziness might very well have avoided the harm that occurred here.

Nerv v. Phil

Strict liability applies only in the sale of a product; it does not apply to rendition of services. A pharmacist's sale of prescription drugs has been held to constitute professional services rather than the sale of goods. Although the drug in issue here was nonprescription, because Phil was asked to recommend a remedy, he might very well be treated as rendering a service here rather than as the seller of goods. Hence, even assuming the drug was "defective," a strict liability suit against Phil would probably fail.

On the other hand, arguably there should be liability for breach of the implied warranty of fitness for a particular purpose, because having discussed his problems with Phil, Nerv probably relied on Phil's judgment as a licensed pharmacist to supply appropriate medication. In that sense, Phil is no different from any retailer who selects a product in response to a customer's requirements—if the product does not work properly, it is at the risk of the one who selected it.

A negligence action probably would not be successful because there is no showing that Phil behaved unreasonably. Although he chose Dreamy, he had no reason to know that there was any problem, and the product had been adequately tested and certified for sale by the FDA.

Nerv v. Drugco

Nerv may have several actions against Drugco. In a strict liability in tort action, he will have to show that the product was "defective" (*e.g.*, under the Restatement approach, that the drug was "unreasonably dangerous"). As noted earlier, Drugco's failure to warn of a known risk of harm renders Dreamy defective.

Breach of the implied warranty of merchantability is available here if Nerv can surmount the privity problem—being that he bought the product from Phil. Again, states differ on this.

An express warranty theory would also be available, assuming Nerv had read the label "safe for adult use" before he bought the drug (or at least before he used it). The fact that it was Nerv's idiosyncrasy that made the product unsafe for him is irrelevant because the label gave no reason to believe that allergic reactions might follow; hence, Nerv had no reason to doubt the safety of the drug.

Drugco may also be liable on a strict tort liability theory for innocent misrepresentation. [Rest. 3d-PL §9] Actual and justifiable reliance on the label's representation can probably be shown.

Finally, Nerv has a negligence action against Drugco similar to that discussed above in "Ima v. Drugco"—*i.e.*, unreasonable delay in alerting the public of the drug's potential dangers. Had there been a timely warning, it is likely that Nerv would have taken appropriate precautions, thereby avoiding the result in this case. Thus, causation is present, and because there are no apparent defenses, liability should follow.

ANSWER TO QUESTION V

Personal Injury Claims by Park v. Mower

Negligence: Mower as a supplier of chattels owes a duty of due care in the manufacture and design of its cub tractors. This duty extends to buyers, users of the product, and "bystanders"—a category Park may fit into in this case because, at the time, he was watching Smith use the tractor. The apparent cause of the accident was a crack in the nut that held the rotary cutter (although this must be proven). From what we know at this point, if the evidence should suggest that this type of crack (assuming cause can be shown) is one that more often than not is attributable to negligence in the selection of metal for the nut or in the manufacture of the nut, then Park may be able to establish breach of duty by the use of res ipsa loquitur. If the defect was in fact visible and should have been found through the inspection process before leaving Mower's plant, then that would be another approach that Park may take to showing breach of duty. If the evidence supports the notion that this defect could as plausibly have occurred after the product left Mower's control and that Mower was in no way responsible for what subsequently happened (Retail's inspection or Smith's adjustment), then Park would be unable to use res ipsa loquitur and would have to show some specific negligence that occurred while the product was under Mower's control.

A final negligence theory might be that Mower negligently failed to design a housing sufficiently strong to prevent the escape of a detached cutter. More facts are needed here.

If Park can meet the negligence showing, then on the question of proximate cause, Park may lose if it is shown that Retail did in fact discover the defects but marketed the product anyway in callous disregard of the rights of consumers or that Smith did something unexpected in his efforts to tighten what appeared to be a loose nut.

No apparent defenses can be asserted against Park. It is true that he knew the product was not cutting evenly and not cutting one-inch branches, but there is no reason to think that he had unreasonably failed to perceive a danger to his physical security from the way the tractor had been performing. Assumption of the risk is absent here because Park seems not to have been aware of any particular danger from the machine. Even in comparative negligence jurisdictions, it is difficult to see what conduct on Park's part a jury might consider in reducing the recovery against Mower.

Strict liability: If Park should sue Mower on a strict products liability theory, Park would have to establish that the cutter was defective when it left Mower's control and that the defect was the cause of the accident. If the cracked nut existed at the time the product left Mower's control, then the defective nature of the product and the unreasonable danger created for users and bystanders are quite clear. The bystander's case is somewhat more difficult here, but Park might get around that if the state is one of almost all that has extended strict liability to bystanders or if Park can establish that he was a user who was only temporarily not in control of the product. If the product cannot be shown to have had the defect at the time it left Mower's control, then a strict liability case will fail for lack of the showing of the marketing of a defective product.

On proximate cause, Mower might again try to argue that Smith's repair was an unforeseeable misuse of the product. But the facts indicate that all he did was tighten a loose nut—and there is no showing that he was aware of the danger but nonetheless failed to warn Park. (The same may be said of any claim that Retail found the defect but failed to notify customers.) Neither can Mower defend on the ground that Park put the product to an abnormal use by riding it over rough terrain. It was marketed for the clearing of brush and its use, even if not exactly what the manufacturer expected, was certainly within the range of foreseeable uses.

So far as defenses are concerned, there appears to be no contributory negligence. But if the court should rule that a jury could find some contributory negligence on Park's part, a growing number of states will allow that to reduce his recovery against Mower on a strict liability theory.

Warranty: It is not clear who advertised that the product would cut one-inch brush. But in any event, this seems not proximately related to the claim for personal injury (*see* below). But the implied warranties under the Uniform Commercial Code would be available in Park's action against Mower for breach of the implied warranty of merchantability unless the most restrictive privity version of section 2-318 (limited to family members and "guests") is enforced. But even then some courts have expanded upon that statute to allow warranty recoveries for personal injury beyond its terms. If Mower argues that the one-week return provision was a permissible limitation on the remedy for breach of warranty, then Park may respond that section 2-719(3) declares that limitations of warranties against personal injury are prima facie unconscionable. Another answer may well be that this limitation was offered only by Retail and cannot help Mower.

If there are defenses, the trend is to use comparative fault here.

Personal Injury Claims by Park v. Retail

Negligence: Park's negligence action here must be based on the fact that Retail created the defect while the tractor was in Retail's control or that Retail negligently failed to find the defect that was previously there as a result of defective manufacture. The first claim seems unlikely from the facts. The second possibility, failure to discover, will depend on whether the crack was visible and whether the inspection and service that Retail did in this case, if done reasonably, should have disclosed the problem of the nut. The proximate cause problem of Smith and the defenses would be the same as in Park's case against Mower.

Strict liability: The claim here would be easier because the presence of the defect at the time it left Retail's hands is apparently clear from the facts and nothing that Smith did in tightening the nut was likely to have created the defect. Thus, we have Retail marketing a defective product, and traditional products liability law will apply because this product was certainly unreasonably and unexpectedly dangerous to the buyer. Again the defense questions would be the same.

Warranty action against Retail: Here there are no privity problems and the implied warranty of merchantability existed and was breached by this product. If any defenses are available, they would be a form of contributory negligence—as to which some states now use comparative fault and will reduce Park's warranty recovery. The one-week return privilege cannot serve to bar Park's action for personal injuries because of section 2-719(3) (discussed earlier).

Action for Damage to the Tractor

Park's action against both Mower and Retail for damage to the tractor would be analyzed the same way as a personal injury action as far as the negligence claim is concerned. Under a strict liability theory, however, some states have not allowed an action in the absence of privity for harm to the product itself, which is what happened in this case. The jurisdictions are split. The claim for product loss in warranty would likely be analyzed the same as the personal injury action above. If the jurisdiction allows Mower to be liable for breach of warranty under section 2-318, then that liability should extend to both the personal injury and the product. So far as defenses are concerned, however, Park may not have the advantage of section 2-719(3) because that applies only to personal injury claims and not to property damage claims. Nonetheless, the one-week return situation seemed to apply only to a customer who was dissatisfied because the product would not perform properly. It seemed not to contemplate a limitation on an action involving destruction of property.

Failure to Cut One-Inch Thick Brush

This is purely economic loss, and most courts would not recognize a negligence action for failure of a product to perform its function leading only to economic disappointment. The same seems to be true in strict liability, although here again the states are split. The best way to pursue this claim is an action for breach of express warranty. This warranty does not require privity; therefore, an action should be available against both Mower and Retail. The only possible defense is the one-week provision, and the question would then be whether that condition written into the contract serves to exclude all other remedies for failure to cut the one-inch brush.

Even so, Park cannot recover damages for both the destroyed tractor and for its failure to cut the brush in this case, because recovery of the $1,200 for loss of the tractor would cover Park's loss from the failure to cut.

ANSWER TO QUESTION VI

Prof and Prim v. Jones

Jones was not an employee of University and bore no special relationship to Prof or Prim. He did not cause the plaintiffs' predicament and so was under no obligation to attempt a rescue or to call for help. Because no duty existed, none was breached, and no negligence action lies. Other theories of liability do not apply.

Prof and Prim v. Elco

By not repairing a well-known defect in the elevator, Elco breached its contract with University. Even if the plaintiffs are able to sue as third-party beneficiaries, damages for breach of contract are limited to those reasonably contemplated by the parties when the contract was made. Because the facts state that no danger of falling or physical injury existed, the harm in this case was probably beyond the parties' contemplation when the contract was signed.

Because it does not appear that Elco sold or installed the elevator, negligence is the only available tort theory. In some states, if Elco never began to perform its contract, its conduct would be called nonfeasance, and no tort action would lie. Even though the elevator often stopped between floors and needed a maintenance worker to start it again, this restarting did not go to the defect and may not be misfeasance.

If Elco committed misfeasance by trying to fix the defect, all states would find liability a close question. The physical harm suffered by the plaintiffs was foreseeable; Elco's failure to do the repairs properly would be unreasonable. Prof's harm may be foreseeable in tort even though not recoverable in contract. His damages would be medical expenses and economic losses incurred as a result of the heart attack plus pain and suffering. Prim suffered "severe nervous shock" from her confinement and fear. Some states would call this purely emotional harm and bar recovery. In addition, her chances of getting damages for her embarrassment are small. Elco could not reasonably have foreseen this type of harm coming from its misfeasance.

Elco may claim that the plaintiffs were contributorily negligent in using the elevator after the building was closed, knowing of the defect. Even though it had an alarm bell, the likelihood that it would not be heard should have been considered. In comparative negligence states, there would be no complete bar in any event.

A second defense is assumption of the risk. Both plaintiffs were aware that the elevator often stopped between floors and should have foreseen the possibility of delayed rescue late at night. Unless Prof did not know of his high blood pressure, he may have voluntarily assumed the risk of a heart attack. The assumption of risk defense is less strong against Prim because she may not have known of the danger to Prof.

Prof and Prim v. University

If University was negligent in hiring Elco, then University may be liable for its own negligence. However, nothing in the facts suggests that Elco was not an appropriate company to hire for elevator maintenance.

In any case, University may be liable for Elco's negligence because the duties assumed by Elco were nondelegable. Maintaining elevators in the law school was part of University's duty to provide a safe place to work for employees. It might also go toward keeping public premises safe for visitors, but it is not clear that the law school was open to the public.

Damages and defenses are the same as discussed above. However, workers' compensation may bar suit against University.

ANSWER TO QUESTION VII

Bernard v. Alana

Bernard could bring an action against Alana for conversion. The main issue here is whether Alana has any defenses.

At common law, to recover for conversion, a plaintiff must show: (i) an act by the defendant that substantially interferes with the plaintiff's right to possess a chattel; (ii) intent to perform the act; and (iii) causation. The normal remedy for conversion is damages measured by the value of the chattel plus any damages that result from the dispossession. Here, Bernard can make out a prima facie case. Alana took an MP3 player that Bernard owned (and therefore had the right to possess); she intended to take the player; and her taking caused Bernard's dispossession. Thus, Bernard can make out a prima facie case for recovery.

Although Bernard can make out a prima facie case, Alana may raise a few defenses. The first defense that she should raise is consent. A plaintiff's consent to the taking operates as a complete defense to an action for conversion. Here, Alana will claim that she took the MP3 player because Bernard had posted a sign above the box of players that read: "FREE—PLEASE TAKE ONE." Bernard, of course, will argue that he did not consent to the taking of the player; the consent was meant for advertisements that normally are where the players were, and that the mistake should have been obvious to Alana. The outcome of either party's argument turns on the reasonableness of the mistake and facts not given (*e.g.*, were these high-end MP3 players or cheap players with little memory; did the store ever give free samples and, if so, did Alana know this, etc.). This determination would be made by the trier of fact.

Even if there was a technical conversion, Alana could successfully limit her damages somewhat. An offer by the defendant to return the chattel mitigates damages and limits the plaintiff to the basic remedy if the defendant acquired the chattel innocently and the chattel was not impaired in value or condition during the dispossession. Here, Alana offered to return the MP3 player to Bernard once she discovered the mistake. Thus, if the trier of fact finds her mistake to be innocent, she will probably not have to pay damages for consequences that occurred after she made her offer to return the player.

Alana v. Bernard

Alana could bring an action against Bernard for defamation. The main issue here is whether Alana must prove damages to recover.

A defamation case is established if there is a publication to a third person of a statement understood as defamatory of the plaintiff that causes damages to the plaintiff's reputation. The type of damage that the plaintiff must prove depends on whether the defamation constitutes libel or slander. Libel is the written or printed publication of defamatory language wherein the plaintiff does not need to prove special damages and general damages are presumed. Slander is spoken defamation wherein the plaintiff must prove special (*i.e.*, pecuniary) damages unless the defamation falls within a slander per se category. There are four slander per se categories: (i) serious crime, (ii) loathsome disease, (iii) incompetency in trade or profession, and (iv) unchastity.

Publicly accusing Alana of being a thief was a defamation by Bernard. The statement was made intentionally, in the presence of many people, and would tend to lower the reputation of Alana in their eyes. The defamation was a slander which Alana will argue is actionable per se. Although calling one a "thief" generally is not slander per se, Bernard's adding, "Come back here with that player!" is a specific allegation of shoplifting (a serious crime), and thus constitutes slander per se. Therefore, Alana need not prove special damages and will recover general damages.

Bernard may attempt to raise truth as a defense. Truth generally is a defense to an action for defamation. However, this defense will be unsuccessful—Alana was not in fact or law a thief, because she lacked criminal intent.

A stronger defense would be that Bernard enjoyed a conditional privilege to defame Alana to protect his own property. A defendant is conditionally privileged to defame another if the defendant had a reasonable belief that some important interest of the defendant was being threatened and the defamatory statement was made to protect that interest. However, such a privilege may be lost through bad faith, excessive publication, or the like. Here, Bernard saw Alana take his MP3 player and was merely trying to stop her from walking away with it. However, the "publication" may have been unreasonably excessive given the circumstances, which include the fact that Alana was walking away and not running. Otherwise, honest belief will sustain the privilege. If Bernard did not realize the ambiguity of his sign, a jury might well find he honestly believed a theft had occurred.

Carla v. Bernard

Carla may bring an action against Bernard for false imprisonment. The main issue here is whether Bernard may successfully assert the "shopkeeper's privilege."

To establish a prima facie case of false imprisonment, a plaintiff must show: (i) an act or omission to act on the part of the defendant that confines or restrains the plaintiff to a bounded area; (ii) intent on the part of the defendant to confine or restrain the plaintiff to the bounded area; and (iii) causation. In addition to any damages directly resulting from the imprisonment, the plaintiff is entitled to recover for any injuries sustained in making a reasonable attempt to escape.

Here, Bernard locked Carla in the store's restroom. The act was intentional and temporarily succeeded in confining Carla to a specific area, because Carla knew of the imprisonment and was not aware of a means of escape beforehand. Even if the possibility of climbing through the window was immediately apparent, it was not so simple and safe an escape as to negate the confinement. Not only did Carla have to stand on a chair to get to the window, she had to step on its back, and she was under no duty to take the risk of such a maneuver. Thus, Carla is entitled to recover any actual damages resulting from the detention. In addition, she can get damages for her broken leg, because injuries suffered in a reasonable attempt to escape false imprisonment are recoverable. Even if Carla were deemed negligent for trying to escape as she did, such negligence would not be a defense to an intentional tort.

Bernard may raise the shopkeeper's privilege as a defense. Most states give shopkeepers a privilege to detain temporarily for investigation anyone whom they reasonably suspect of having tortiously taken their goods. The detention must be effected in the store or nearby, the shopkeeper must have reasonable grounds to suspect the person detained, only reasonable force may be used, and the detention may only be for a reasonable time and must be conducted in a reasonable manner. Where these conditions are met, the shopkeeper is immune from liability for false arrest, battery, etc.

Here, Bernard detained Carla on the premises of his store. He also had reason to suspect Carla, because she looked like Alana and Bernard had seen Alana take an MP3 player earlier in the day. Moreover, Bernard did not use excessive force in detaining Carla. The only real question is whether the detention was conducted in a reasonable manner. Nothing here indicates that Bernard told Carla who he was or why he was locking her in the restroom. Indeed, nothing indicates that Bernard informed Carla that she was being intentionally confined. It might also be argued that a restroom is an odd place to confine a suspect. As a result, this defense likely will fail.

No other defense will work either. For example, recapture of chattels is limited to situations where the defendant is in fresh pursuit of the person who took his chattel, the defendant must have made a demand on the plaintiff to return the chattel, and the recapture must be from the person who tortiously took the chattel. None of these conditions is met here. Neither can Bernard argue that the confinement was pursuant to a citizen's arrest. First of all, Bernard never actually made an arrest. He did not even tell Carla that she was being held. Calling the police does not constitute an arrest. In addition, Bernard did not enjoy the privilege to arrest for a misdemeanor because he was not in fresh pursuit and had the wrong person. At common law, the privilege is not given to a citizen who mistakenly arrests the wrong person.

ANSWER TO QUESTION VIII

Zoe v. Resco

In this case it appears that Prex was acting in the scope of his employment to further Resco's relations with the community and that his actions will be chargeable to Resco.

Defamation: Prex intentionally published to third persons a statement that hurt Zoe's reputation in the community. This was not simply name-calling in a fit of anger. In this situation, the words used conveyed the idea that anyone who believed that Resco's operation created a danger of an escaping virus was an ignorant person whose intellectual abilities were far below normal. This would be enough to lower Zoe's reputation in the eyes of a substantial segment of the community. The fact that Zoe was not named is irrelevant. She can readily prove that hearers and readers understood that she was being referred to by Prex. Finally, Prex's assertion was one of fact because he had access to secret information that apparently induced him to condemn the intellect of disbelievers.

The next critical question is whether Zoe must show special damages. Because the damage occurred through the publication in the *News*, Zoe will argue that Prex committed libel even though he only spoke the words. Resco and Prex will argue a slander theory. If slander is the conclusion, this may not be slander per se because it does not suggest that Zoe is incompetent in her trade or profession—unless cattle auctioneers are expected to be familiar with the risks of experimental research involving cattle viruses. If this is part of the knowledge demanded of auctioneers, then Zoe has an action for slander per se.

If the claim is considered libel—a more likely result given Prex's effort to obtain widespread dissemination through the press—it is not a libel clear on its face. In such cases, some states follow the general libel rule and do not require a showing of special damages. In others, special damages are always required. In still other states, special damages are required unless the words, if spoken, would have been slander per se. That will depend on the slander analysis above. If special damages are required, the financial loss Zoe suffered will not suffice because it was not the result of public reaction to the defamation.

As to defenses, Resco may argue it has the qualified privilege to speak to protect its reputation as a safe activity in the community. But even if such a privilege were accorded, it would be lost if Prex did not have an actual, honest belief in the truth of the defamatory matter.

Because Zoe has not voluntarily thrust herself into this controversy, she will be a private person under the *Gertz* case. However, a majority of the Supreme Court Justices would apply *Gertz* to nonmedia defendants if the defamation regarded a matter of public concern. In this case, a matter of public concern is definitely involved (*i.e.,* safety of cattle virus research in a cattle and dairy district). *Gertz* probably applies; Zoe may recover actual injury damages—which may include the financial loss here and proven emotional distress and embarrassment—upon proof of negligence. That should be easy here given the lack of any investigation before speaking. If Zoe wants general damages, she must prove deliberate falsity or reckless disregard for the truth under the *New York Times* test. In a few states, private plaintiffs must prove this to recover any damages at all.

To the extent damages are attributable to the republication of the statement by the *News*, Resco will be responsible because the republication was both intended and foreseeable.

Intentional infliction of emotional distress: Can calling Zoe a "driveling idiot" (without any basis in fact) be considered extreme and outrageous behavior? On the one hand, Prex was trying to embarrass Zoe into taking action—and succeeded. The language itself seems to fit more comfortably into the nonactionable insult category. Yet this was a premeditated effort to humiliate Zoe, which might warrant liability—even though Prex was trying to achieve something for himself in the process, not simply playing the practical joker.

Zoe's "considerable embarrassment" appears serious enough to be actionable. (There is no requirement of physical injury.)

False light privacy: Some states permit actions when the defendant has placed the plaintiff in a false, but not necessarily defamatory, light in the eyes of the community. If an actionable defamation exists, this action adds little. But if no defamation was found because of lack of an actionable defamation or special damages, this action might help Zoe. She was falsely portrayed in the community as an ignorant person. Although a constitutional privilege might exist, Prex has forfeited it by being recklessly responsible for the falsity by speaking without having made any investigation. A jury could find that he knew he did not know the truth of the statements he was making.

Misrepresentation: Resco, through Prex, falsely stated that "no danger at all" existed from the plant. This statement was made recklessly, with knowledge that Prex did not know the truth, and with intent to induce Zoe to take certain steps in reliance. Even though the reliance was not to benefit Resco directly, that is not required with fraud. Zoe actually relied (although motivated in part by other reasons), and this appeared justifiable because nothing signalled that the statement was obviously false. Resco's argument that the statement was only one of opinion will be rejected because the words were spoken by one claiming to have special knowledge about secret experimental work. Zoe's economic losses were caused by her reliance—whether the cattle died from the virus or were killed to prevent its spread. The latter was a foreseeable result of the reckless statement.

Strict liability for abnormally dangerous activity: Resco's operation seems to qualify as an activity that should give rise to strict liability because of its dangerous and uncontrollable nature. Zoe's damages were actually and proximately caused by the miscarriage of the activity because the destruction of the cattle was a foreseeable result of the escape of the virus.

The major problem with this claim is that the type of loss suffered—financial—is not the personal injury or property damage claim usually brought in these cases. As with the law of defective products, the reasons that motivated the development of strict liability for these losses may not extend to pure economic loss. On the other hand, some courts might conclude that one who maintains a dangerous activity should be liable for all types of losses caused by its dangerous features, particularly when, as in this case, some victims sustained serious property damage.

If the action can be established, Zoe would not be barred by her own conduct. She did not assume the risk because she did not know about the danger. Because her behavior seems entirely reasonable in the situation, she was not negligent in any way.

Nuisance: This action is brought for interference with the use and enjoyment of one's land. It may be based on strict liability if the manner of interference is one that results from an abnormally dangerous activity—as in this case. The problem with nuisance here is that Zoe's loss was not caused by any inability to use her land. The land was usable—it was her business that was hurt by the lack of cattle in the area. Whether or not the virus invaded her land, her loss was peculiarly the result of the harm to others in the community rather than a possessor of land.

Zoe v. Prex

Prex is personally liable for the torts discussed in the foregoing discussion—except for strict liability for abnormally dangerous activity and nuisance, as to which Resco alone bears any liability.

Zoe v. the *News*

Defamation: The prima facie case against the *News* will be the same as that against Resco and Prex—except that now we clearly are dealing with libel. The privilege situation is quite different. The *News* may assert the state common law privilege of record libel. Although most courts limit this to accurate reports of governmental proceedings, some states do extend it to accurate reports of general open meetings—and they might be persuaded to extend it another step to any openly made statement about a matter of public concern. Such an extension might be based in part on reliance on the constitutional privilege of "neutral reportage" that protects press reports on both sides of an ongoing dispute of public concern. However, the privilege does not easily cover this case because here we are not dealing with an ongoing controversy or with two sides to a debate—or even with a public person.

In any event, the *News* has the *Gertz* privilege for reasons already discussed. Zoe must prove falsity due to negligence. If the *News* did not know and had no reason to know that the statements were aimed at Zoe before it published the story, then the *News* can defend on the ground that it cannot be liable because the statement did not show that damage to reputation was likely to result. Even if the *News* knew about the goal of the statement, it may have had no reason to doubt what Prex was saying—and thus was not negligent for printing the story without further investigation. On the other hand, the known self-interest of Prex might have alerted the *News* to the need for further research before printing the story. If Zoe proves negligence, she may recover actual injury damages.

The only constitutional privilege that avoids concern with negligent falsity would be an expansion of the neutral reportage approach—in which it is irrelevant whether the *News* believed that Prex was speaking accurately.

Intentional infliction of emotional distress: The *News* cannot be shown to have engaged in extreme and outrageous conduct by reporting Prex's statement. A showing of negligence would be insufficient for liability.

False light privacy: Even if a prima facie case can be established, Zoe will have to show that the *News* was reckless in making its error in its report of a story of public interest. At most, negligence seems likely.

Misrepresentation: A claim for misrepresentation will fail whether Zoe alleges intentional or negligent misrepresentation. The *News* reported the representation of another, and presumably credited to Prex his appraisal of the danger of a virus infection. The only representation of the *News* was that it reported accurately what was said. Zoe, therefore, did not rely on any representation of the *News*.

Even if the *News* claimed on its own that no danger existed, Zoe will not likely recover. The *News* did not intend to deceive anyone, had no knowledge that a danger existed, and did not mean for Zoe to rely on its statement, so it committed no intentional misrepresentation. The *News* may have been negligent in not investigating the claim, but probably did not intend that Zoe should rely on it in a business transaction, so it should not be liable for a negligent misrepresentation.

ANSWER TO QUESTION IX

Pat v. Drugco

Strict liability: Pat's most promising action against Drugco is for strict liability. Although Pat is not in privity with Drugco, virtually all states have abandoned privity requirements in strict liability actions and permit even injured bystanders to recover.

Pat may allege that failure to warn users that Pyrib often induces drowsiness made the drug unreasonably dangerous. For purposes of strict liability, a product may be defective not only in manufacture and design, but also in the warnings or instructions needed to make it safe. Pyrib was defective because, in the absence of a warning of the drug's side effects, a consumer could reasonably expect his alertness to remain unaffected. A specific caution against driving was also called for, because Drugco should have foreseen the special dangers posed to drivers who may fall asleep.

Pat should be able to show that the lack of warnings caused her injuries because Driver, if warned, either would not have taken Pyrib or would have stayed home. Driver's conduct was foreseeable, so even if it was negligent, the defective product remains a proximate cause. Dr. Ard's failure to warn Driver, even if negligent, does not supersede Drugco's liability.

Drugco has no defenses to a strict liability action, and Pat may recover for all of her damages.

Negligence: Because Pyrib is known to have the side effect, Pat should be able to make out a negligence action by the same showing as above. The only differences are that Pat must show that the danger created by the inadequate label was one that Drugco should reasonably have anticipated, and that the label could easily have been made adequate.

Pat v. Transit

Pat's action against Transit is for negligence. Transit is a common carrier, so it owes Pat, a passenger, a ***high*** standard of care. Pat can argue that Transit breached its duty in several ways: (i) that it failed to observe Driver's condition; (ii) that it failed to warn its bus drivers not to drive after taking medication; and (iii) that it failed to provide a doctor to treat its drivers without endangering passengers. "But for" each of these failures, the accident apparently would not have occurred, so each failure could have been an actual cause of Pat's injuries. The crash was foreseeable as a result of each failure, so if any of the three was an actual cause, it was also a proximate cause. Should the jury find that Transit breached its duty of care, and that the breach caused the accident, Pat may recover for all of her damages. Transit has no defenses.

Pat may also hold Transit liable for any negligence of Driver. Especially in light of the high duty of care owed to passengers, Driver appears to have been negligent in continuing to drive after he began feeling drowsy. Stopping and getting a replacement, or calling in to the office for advice, would have prevented the accident; thus, Driver's negligence was an actual and proximate cause of Pat's injuries. His negligence may be ***imputed*** to Transit under the doctrine of respondeat superior. Again, Transit has no defenses, but it may seek ***indemnity*** from Driver.

Pat v. Dr. Ard

In treating his patients, Dr. Ard owes a duty of care to third persons who will be affected by that treatment—at least to Pat because she was a foreseeable plaintiff. Whether he breached that duty is a jury question, and will largely depend on whether he knew that Driver was a bus driver or that Pyrib did not come with a warning of its side effects. If Dr. Ard knew either of these facts, he was probably negligent in not warning Driver that Pyrib might make him drowsy. Moreover, because most people drive, Dr. Ard may be negligent for failing to warn about potential drowsiness even if he thought the Pyrib label mentioned the risk. Pat can show that the failure to warn was an actual and proximate cause of her injuries. (Driver's own negligence, if any, would not exonerate Dr. Ard because it was foreseeable.) Dr. Ard has no defenses, and Pat may recover for all of her damages.

ANSWER TO QUESTION X

Under agency rules and the doctrine of respondeat superior, the *Yellow Journal* is liable for the torts committed by Roy because the reporter was acting within the scope of his employment.

Defamation

Roy's false statements could be found by a jury to lower Phil's reputation in the community. Even though the statements do not charge Phil with acts that reflect badly on his character or integrity, the law holds that defamation may be found in statements that lead others to think less well of Phil, such as charges that Phil was of illegitimate birth or is insane. The charges in this case are of the same sort—suffering a seizure and hurting others during the seizure. Fathering a retarded child might be read to suggest that Phil was suffering from some genetic problem that might lead others to shun or avoid him. If the jury finds the statements actionable, there is no question about their falsity (although Phil has the burden of proof on this issue). (Note that Phil has no cause of action for defamation of his son.)

Because this story involves a matter of public concern, Phil must prove more than the fact that he was defamed. The standard of liability Phil must establish depends on whether he is a public person. Because Phil was never a government employee, he cannot be a public official. Although the public may be interested in the work he did for Bomm-Bay and in the accident he had there, Phil has never voluntarily brought himself to the public's attention or injected himself into a public controversy; thus, he is not a public figure for defamation purposes.

As a private plaintiff, Phil is constitutionally required to prove only that Roy and the *Yellow Journal* were negligent in not recognizing the falsity of their statements. Because Roy invented the defamatory portions of his story, negligence can be easily proven. Phil may therefore recover for any "actual injury" that he can prove to the jury. His damages may include harm to his reputation, humiliation, or other emotional distress, and any monetary injuries he suffered. But because the action is for defamation, he may recover only for those injuries caused by the defamatory portions of the story—above and beyond the embarrassment and ostracism occasioned by the true revelations.

Besides negligence, Phil should be able to show that Roy published the story with knowing or reckless falsity. Although Roy did not ***know*** the defamatory statements were false, he did not honestly believe they were true. This amounts to recklessness. Statements published with knowing or reckless falsity receive no constitutional protection; thus, Phil's damages, if he can meet this standard of liability, will not be limited to "actual injuries." He may recover any damages the state law permits, including presumed and punitive damages.

Privacy

Public disclosure of private facts: A number of the facts included in the article were intimate details of Phil's life, and he should have no trouble establishing a prima facie case that they were wrongfully disclosed. Phil's impotence, loss of hair, and other impairments are private facts—even though some persons may already know about each. A jury could conclude that a reasonable person would find public disclosure of such facts—particularly facts involving medical or sexual details—highly offensive. The fact of the accident itself may be a private fact because it took place in a private area, but disclosure would not normally be highly offensive and so is not actionable.

The *Yellow Journal* will point out in its defense that Phil voluntarily disclosed all the intimate details being sued on. (The false statements in the article, although they concern private matters, are not actionable as disclosures of private facts. Phil may recover damages caused by them in a defamation or a "false light" action.) Normally, voluntary disclosure bars any action, even when the defendant has misrepresented his identity or promised confidentiality. An individual assumes some risk that a person he confides in is not who he seems. In this case, however, Phil reasonably believed that his statements were made under the legally binding doctor-patient privilege. Had Roy actually been a doctor, Roy's disclosure would have been actionable. Because Roy intentionally caused and knew of Phil's misapprehension, the consent defense fails.

The *Yellow Journal* will also contend that its story is privileged because it is newsworthy. Under privacy rules, an accident involving a bacteria warfare agent is of legitimate public interest, even when it has not been discovered for 20 years. Although Phil in no way acted intentionally to attract public attention, his involvement in the accident makes him a public figure (for ***privacy*** action purposes) because of its newsworthiness. Similarly, the disabilities that Phil has developed are of public concern. Phil is apparently the only human ever to be exposed to the bacteria, and the public is understandably interested in discovering the effects of a powerful weapon in its government's arsenal.

The problem is that Phil's identity does not involve the same level of public interest. The disclosure of newsworthy information would not have been any less effective if the *Yellow Journal* had protected Phil's anonymity. Normally the disclosure of a name is not actionable. Although many personal and embarrassing details of Phil's life were published, most courts would probably deny a privacy action on the ground that use of names adds credibility and impact to the story and should be a matter for editorial judgment alone.

If the newsworthiness defense is rejected, the *Yellow Journal* would try to extend the limited constitutional holding in *Cox Broadcasting Corp. v. Cohn* from public records to matters of public interest. This question was explicitly left open in *Cox*.

If Phil establishes liability, he may recover for any emotional distress or other damages incurred because of the public disclosures.

False light privacy: The false disclosures about Phil, especially concerning his temperament, placed him in a "false light." The statements were not simply minor inaccuracies but were so central as to make their disclosure highly offensive to a reasonable person. The "false light" statements were disseminated to a large number of third persons, so Phil can make out a prima facie case.

Again, the newsworthiness defense is the *Yellow Journal*'s best chance for success. The statements that turned out to be false nonetheless involve newsworthy information because they purport to describe effects of the bacteria. However, Phil may defeat the defense by showing that the disclosures were made with knowing or reckless falsity because the First Amendment affords no protection to such statements in tort cases. As discussed above, Phil should be able to meet this standard because Roy did not believe the statements to be true.

Phil may recover whatever damages the state law permits.

Wrongful intrusion of privacy: An intentional, highly offensive intrusion into an individual's privacy is actionable. In this case, Roy did not enter onto Phil's own property, but he did gain access to an area in which Phil had a reasonable expectation of privacy. The nature of the intrusion, with Roy falsely representing himself to be a doctor, would be highly offensive to a reasonable person. The intrusion would be no less serious than if Roy had bugged Phil's room and listened in on the private conversations between Phil and his doctors.

The only relevant defense here is consent, but as discussed above, it is likely to fail because Roy knew that Phil was mistakenly relying on Roy's deceptive appearance.

Although publication is not required to recover for a wrongful intrusion, some courts allow Phil to recover damages suffered from the newspaper article as consequential damages of Roy's tortious intrusion. Phil may therefore recover for any physical or emotional injury from the initial intrusion as well as for any monetary damages incurred. Courts disagree over whether damages from the publication of the article are recoverable when the facts were tortiously obtained. Because of the sensitive First Amendment aspects, it seems preferable to require Phil to show an actionable publication before being allowed to recover such damages.

Table of Citations

CITATIONS TO RESTATEMENT (SECOND) OF TORTS

Section	Text Reference	Section	Text Reference	Section	Text Reference
2	§2	102	§150	289(b)	§301
13	§§17, 18	103	§150	291	§352
13(a)	§6	104	§150	295A	§§385, 389
18	§§11, 16	105	§150	296	§286
19	§14	106	§150	299	§302
22	§36	119	§165	299A	§§303, 304
24	§48	120A	§158	316	§635
25	§41	121	§165	321	§555
26	§38	131	§173	324	§563
27	§§15, 49, 50	136	§179	330	§689
29(2)	§43	146	§181	332	§696
30	§45	147	§181	333	§662
31	§§29, 30	157	§191	334	§671
36	§62	158	§188	335	§671
38	§71	159(2)	§199	336	§662
39	§66	163	§204	337	§662
40	§68	195	§258	338	§662
40A	§§67, 69	196	§254	339	§§674, 678, 683, 687
41	§74	197	§263	341	§692
42	§64	198	§§241, 247, 250	341A	§704
45	§72	200	§245	342	§§692, 693
46	§§80, 82, 91	201	§§271, 272	343	§704
60	§117	204	§178	343A(1)	§721
62	§103	214(1)	§274	345	§§714, 715
63	§119	214(2)	§275	345(1)	§712
65	§§123, 127	217	§210	353	§755
65(2)	§128	228	§223	353(2)	§749
70(2)	§129	229	§224	357	§§740, 742
71	§132	237	§227	358	§748
72	§133	239	§228	363	§653
73	§134	244	§218	368	§658
76	§141	260	§252	370	§657
77	§142	263	§263	383	§724
81	§145	267	§617	384	§724
84	§143	281(b)	§322	385	§724
85	§144	283	§281	386	§724
88	§149	283B	§299	387	§724
89	§147	283C	§§295, 298	390	§597
91	§147	288B	§409	400	§940
101	§150	288C	§394	401	§945

Section	Text Reference	Section	Text Reference	Section	Text Reference
402	§904	512	§897	611	§1487
402A	§§952, 977, 1004, 1008, 1013, 1023, 1055	516	§896	612	§1499
416	§625	517	§892	623A	§§1696, 1697
424	§618	519	§§898, 902	624	§1689
431	§§422, 448	520	§903	626	§1690
432	§422	520A	§907	634	§1703
433	§422	521	§909	635	§1704
433A	§422	526	§1637	646A	§§1704, 1708
433B(3)	§425	533	§1643	649	§1707
435(2)	§464	543	§1651	652B	§§1552, 1553
436A	§782	545	§1652	652D	§1568
442B	§485	551	§1630	652E	§1605
445	§481	552	§1667	653	§1762
447(b)	§492	552(C)	§1671	657	§1776
448	§491	559	§§1381, 1383	660	§1765
449	§643	564	§1403	663	§1770
452	§§494, 495	565	§1393	666	§1772
463	§791	568	§§1361, 1425	669	§1774
467	§802	568A	§1427	673(1)(c)	§1769
469	§799	569	§1443	682	§1791
485	§807	576	§1374	700	§1209
487	§§150, 812	577	§1359	766	§1716
491	§809	581	§1377	766B	§1743
494	§810	586	§1457	774B	§1748
496B	§847	587	§1456	822	§1118
496F	§858	590	§§1454, 1455	828	§1125
504	§882	591	§1460	829A	§1131
509	§§884, 885	592	§1461	840D	§1148
511	§895	595(2)	§1468	876	§419
		598	§1476	892	§109
				922	§236

CITATIONS TO RESTATEMENT (THIRD) OF TORTS

APPORTIONMENT OF LIABILITY

Section	Text Reference
14	§828

LIABILITY FOR PHYSICAL HARM

Section	Text Reference
6	§339
7	§§321, 339
7(a)	§281
15	§405
17	§378
20	§905
21	§889
29	§447
34	§496
38	§550
44	§564

PRODUCTS LIABILITY

Section	Text Reference
2	§975
6	§1047
8	§1000
9	§1674

Table of Cases

532 Madison Avenue Gourmet Foods, Inc. v. Finlandia Center, Inc. - **§1111**

A

Abbott v. Page Airways, Inc. - **§380**
Abernathy v. Sisters of St. Mary's - **§1248**
Acme Circus Operating Co. v. Kuperstock - **§1618**
Acosta v. Southern California Rapid Transit District - **§582**
Adams v. Union Carbide Corp. - **§990**
Addis v. Steele - **§491**
Adkins v. Thomas Solvent Co. - **§1126**
Adler, Barish, Daniels, Levin & Creskoff v. Epstein - **§1712**
Aetna Insurance Co. v. Stringham - **§688**
Air Crash off Long Island, New York, *In re* - **§1321**
Air France v. Saks - **§1319**
Airport Rent-A-Car, Inc. v. Prevost Car, Inc. - **§1050**
Alaskan Oil, Inc. v. Central Flying Service, Inc. - **§1051**
Albala v. City of New York - **§337**
Alberts v. Schultz - **§437**
Alcorn v. Anbro Engineering, Inc. - **§91**
Alexander v. Sandoval - **§549**
Aljian v. Ben Schlossberg, Inc. - **§1255**
Allen v. Hannaford - **§50**
Allen v. Toledo - **§597**
Allison v. Fiscus - **§143**
Al Raschid v. News Syndicate Co. - **§1692**
Alsup v. Firestone Tire & Rubber Co. - **§1257**
Alteiri v. Colasso - **§10**
Alvarez v. Felker Manufacturing Co. - **§1008**
Amblo's Administratrix v. Vermont Associated Petroleum Corp. - **§661**
American Bank & Trust Co. v. Community Hospital - **§1301**
American Motorcycle Association v. Superior Court - **§822**
Anderson v. Fisher Broadcasting Cos. - **§§1562, 1588**
Anderson v. Liberty Lobby, Inc. - **§1523**
Anderson v. Minneapolis, St. Paul & Sault Ste. Marie Railway - **§421**
Anderson v. Service Merchandise Co. - **§364**
Anderson v. Stream - **§1218**
Anderson v. Theisen - **§401**
Anglin v. Kleeman - **§622**
Antonik v. Chamberlain - **§1124**
Appleby v. Daily Hampshire Gazette - **§1500**
Aranson v. Schroeder - **§1787**
Arena v. Gingrich - **§318**
Argubright v. Beech Aircraft Corp. - **§980**
Arlowski v. Foglio - **§244**
Armory Park Neighborhood Association v. Episcopal Community Services - **§§1110, 1129**
Armstrong v. Simon & Schuster, Inc. - **§1386**
Arnaud's Restaurant v. Cotter - **§1080**
Aronson v. Wiersma - **§1393**
Atherton v. Devine - **§479**
Atlas Chemical Industries, Inc. v. Anderson - **§1136**

B

BMW of North America, Inc. v. Gore - **§§26, 1336**
B.N. v. K.K. - **§80**
Baer v. Slater - **§226**
Baggs v. Eagle-Picher Industries, Inc. - **§1546**
Baisley v. Missisquoi Cemetery Association - **§659**
Baker v. B.F. Goodrich Co. - **§372**
Baker v. Burbank-Glendale-Pasadena Airport Authority - **§1135**
Baker v. Coon - **§75**
Baker v. Promark Products West, Inc. - **§1311**
Baker v. Shymkiv - **§203**
Baldinger v. Banks - **§7**
Baldwin v. City of Waterloo - **§822**
Baltimore & Ohio Railroad v. Goodman - **§360**
Bandel v. Friedrich - **§539**
Baptist Memorial Hospital System v. Sampson - **§621**
Barber v. Time, Inc. - **§1563**
Bardessono v. Michels - **§367**
Barker v. Kallash - **§830**
Barker v. Lull Engineering Co. - **§968**
Barme v. Wood - **§1303**
Barmore v. Elmore - **§689**
Barnes v. Clayton House Motel - **§1364**
Barnes v. New Hampshire Karting Association - **§842**
Barnette v. Wilson - **§1374**
Barnhill v. Davis - **§776**
Barr v. County of Albany - **§170**
Barr v. Matteo - **§§1236, 1460**

Table of Cases

Bartell v. State - **§106**
Bartnicki v. Vopper - **§1561**
Bartz v. Wheat - **§811**
Baskin v. Collins - **§1653**
Basko v. Sterling Drug, Inc. - **§1033**
Battalla v. State - **§§762, 764**
Batts v. Tow-Motor Forklift Co. - **§970**
Bauer v. J.B. Hunt Transport, Inc. - **§382**
Bauer v. Johnson - **§595**
Bauman v. Crawford - **§397**
Beattie v. Beattie - **§1212**
Beaulieu v. Elliott - **§521**
Beaumont v. Brown - **§1569**
Beck v. Bel Air Properties, Inc. - **§901**
Belmac Hygiene, Inc. v. Belmac Corp. - **§1646**
Bencosme v. Kokoras - **§952**
Benedi v. McNeil-P.P.C., Inc. - **§979**
Benn v. Thomas - **§471**
Berman v. Allan - **§1199**
Bernier v. Burris - **§1304**
Bernstein v. National Broadcasting Co. - **§1604**
Berry v. Beech Aircraft Corp. - **§1307**
Berthiaume, Estate of v. Pratt - **§1616**
Beshada v. Johns-Manville Products Corp. - **§977**
Bethel v. New York City Transit Authority - **§§290, 582**
Bevan v. Vassar Farms, Inc. - **§819**
Beverley v. Choices Women's Medical Center, Inc. - **§1600**
Beynon v. Montgomery Cablevision Ltd. Partnership - **§§525, 1153**
Bierczynski v. Rogers - **§419**
Billingsley v. Westrac Co. - **§826**
Bily v. Arthur Young & Co. - **§1667**
Bindrim v. Mitchell - **§1398**
Bing v. Thunig - **§1250**
Bird v. Jones - **§61**
Bishop v. Chicago - **§551**
Bivens v. Six Unknown Named Agents - **§1246**
Blagg v. Illinois F.W.D. Truck & Equipment Co. - **§1186**
Blakely v. Camp Ondessonk - **§660**
Bobka v. Cook County Hospital - **§1043**
Bock v. Lindquist - **§1204**
Boeing Airplane Co. v. Brown - **§935**
Bohannon v. Wachovia Bank & Trust Co. - **§1748**
Boivin v. Jones & Vining, Inc. - **§1627**
Bokhoven v. Klinker - **§824**
Boldman v. Mt. Hood Chemical Corp. - **§1283**
Bonpua v. Fagan - **§826**
Boomer v. Atlantic Cement Co. - **§1112**
Borders v. Roseberry - **§§725, 749**
Borer v. American Airlines, Inc. - **§1185**
Borg v. Boas - **§1487**
Bose Corp. v. Consumers Union - **§§1529, 1709**
Boshell v. Walker County Sheriff - **§1772**
Both v. Harband - **§§371, 728**
Boucher *ex rel.* Boucher v. Dixie Medical Center - **§1180**
Bovsun v. Sanperi - **§§771, 785**
Bowen v. Lumbermens Mutual Casualty Co. - **§783**
Bowman v. Barnes - **§822**
Boyle v. United Technologies Corp. - **§1234**
Bozanich v. Kenney - **§590**
Bradley v. American Smelting & Refining Co. - **§§205, 1109**
Brady v. Ottaway Newspapers, Inc. - **§1406**
Brannon v. Wood - **§365**
Brant v. Bockholt - **§520**
Braswell, Estate of v. Peoples Credit Union - **§1675**
Brawn v. Lyford - **§572**
Brents v. Morgan - **§1569**
Breunig v. American Family Insurance Co. - **§299**
Bridges v. Bentley - **§331**
Briggs v. Eden Council for Hope & Opportunity - **§1502**
Brink v. Moeschl Edwards Corrugating Co. - **§1115**
Briscoe v. LaHue - **§1244**
Briscoe v. Reader's Digest Association - **§1579**
Broadbent v. Broadbent - **§1220**
Broadwater v. Dorsey - **§597**
Brockett v. Kitchen Boyd Motor Co. - **§647**
Bronstein v. GZA GeoEnvironmental, Inc. - **§1662**
Brotherton v. Day & Night Fuel Co. - **§406**
Brower v. Ackerley - **§43**
Brown v. Chapman - **§1098**
Brown v. City of Clewiston - **§176**
Brown v. Glickstein - **§1712**
Brown v. Kelly Broadcasting Co. - **§§1474, 1536**
Brown v. Kendall - **§281**
Brown v. Lundell - **§111**
Brown v. San Francisco Ball Club - **§860**
Brown v. Shyne - **§403**
Brown v. Superior Court - **§§430, 1261**
Brown v. Wal-Mart Discount Cities - **§822**
Browning-Ferris Industries of Vermont, Inc. v. Kelco Disposal, Inc. - **§26**
Brzoska v. Olson - **§§14, 768**
Buckley v. Littell - **§§1421, 1513**
Builders Supply Co. v. McCabe - **§1265**
Bullock v. Jeon - **§1418**
Burgess v. M/V Tamano - **§1111**
Burgess v. Perdue - **§80**
Burke v. Fischer - **§920**
Burke v. Rivo - **§1194**
Burkett v. Freedom Arms, Inc. - **§910**
Busby v. Municipality of Anchorage - **§570**
Bush, People v. - **§126**
Bussard v. Minimed, Inc. - **§610**
Buzzell v. Jones - **§703**
Byrne v. Boadle - **§365**

C

Caceci v. Di Canio Construction Corp. - **§1078**
Cain v. Hearst Corp. - **§1606**

Calder v. City & County of San Francisco - **§1139**
Caldwell v. Haynes - **§515**
Camacho v. Honda Motor Co. - **§§965, 969, 984**
Camden County Board of Chosen Freeholders v. Beretta, U.S.A. Corp. - **§1112**
Campbell v. Animal Quarantine Station - **§781**
Canifax v. Hercules Powder Co. - **§984**
Canino v. New York News, Inc. - **§1154**
Canterbury v. Spence - **§§311, 315**
Cantrell v. Forest City Publishing Co. - **§§1603, 1609**
Carey v. Davis - **§553**
Carlin v. Superior Court - **§982**
Carnes v. Thompson - **§10**
Carroll v. Kalar - **§1784**
Carroll Towing Co., United States v. - **§§352, 353, 354, 355**
Carson v. Allied News Co. - **§§1513, 1520**
Carson v. Here's Johnny Portable Toilets, Inc. - **§1594**
Carson v. Maurer - **§§1300, 1302**
Carter v. Innisfree Hotel, Inc. - **§1552**
Carter v. Kinney - **§§689, 718**
Castro v. QVC Network, Inc. - **§1075**
Cates v. Cates - **§1220**
Catlin v. Union Oil Co. - **§945**
Causby, United States v. - **§§197, 199**
Cedars-Sinai Medical Center v. Superior Court - **§1789**
Chainani v. Board of Education - **§801**
Chamberlaine & Flowers, Inc. v. Smith Contracting, Inc. - **§92**
Chaney v. Smithkline Beckman Corp. - **§416**
Channel Master Corp. v. Aluminum Ltd. Sales, Inc. - **§1626**
Chapin v. Knight-Ridder, Inc. - **§§1393, 1418**
Chapski v. Copley Press - **§1394**
Charles v. Onondaga Community College - **§1721**
Charles v. Seigfried - **§647**
Chatkin v. Talarski - **§702**
Cherry v. DesMoines Leader - **§1483**
Childress v. Abeles - **§§1714, 1715**
Christensen v. Swenson - **§610**
Christians v. Homestake Enterprises, Ltd. - **§686**
Churchey v. Adolf Coors Co. - **§1365**
Cipollone v. Liggett Group, Inc. - **§§1068, 1326**
Cisson v. Pickens Savings & Loan Association - **§1778**
Citizens State Bank v. Timm, Schmidt & Co. - **§1668**
City of - *see* name of city
Clark v. Associated Retail Credit Men - **§90**
Clark v. Molyneaux - **§1476**
Clark v. Moore Memorial United Methodist Church - **§699**
Clark v. Ziedonis - **§141**
Clarke v. Hoek - **§557**
Cleavinger v. Saxner - **§1247**
Clevenger v. Haling - **§578**
Clift v. Nelson - **§375**
Clinkscales v. Carver - **§393**
Coats v. Penrod Drilling Corp. - **§1330**
Cobbs v. Grant - **§113**
Coclin v. Lane Press, Inc. - **§1471**
Codling v. Paglia - **§§1009, 1039**
Coffman v. Keene Corp. - **§1041**
Cohen v. Groman Mortuary, Inc. - **§770**
Cohen v. St. Regis Paper Co. - **§796**
Colbert v. World Publishing Co. - **§1609**
Coleman v. Eddy Potash, Inc. - **§§1788, 1790**
Coleman v. MacLennan - **§§1480, 1482, 1485**
Collette v. Boston & Manchester Railroad - **§4**
Collette v. Page - **§760**
Collier County Publishing Co. v. Chapman - **§1701**
Collins v. Kentucky Natural Resources & Environmental Protection Cabinet - **§1240**
Collyer v. S.H. Kress - **§159**
Colon v. City of New York - **§1770**
CompuServe Inc. v. Cyber Promotions, Inc. - **§207**
Comunale v. Traders & General Insurance Co. - **§§872, 873**
Conder v. Wood - **§765**
Conn v. Gabbert - **§1243**
Connors v. University Associates - **§367**
Conroy v. Briley - **§857**
Cooper v. Parker-Hughey - **§1747**
Copart Industries, Inc. v. Consolidated Edison Co. - **§1118**
Copeland v. Hubbard Broadcasting, Inc. - **§237**
Corcoran v. Banner Super Market, Inc. - **§372**
Corey v. Havener - **§421**
Corgan v. Muehling - **§§769, 787**
Corn v. Sheppard - **§10**
Corso v. Merrill - **§776**
Cory v. Shierloh - **§1315**
Cote v. Palmer - **§856**
Cotton v. Buckeye Gas Products Co. - **§988**
County of - *see* name of county
Coverstone v. Davies - **§§167, 1612**
Cowden v. Bear Country, Inc. - **§892**
Cox v. Nasche - **§1451**
Cox v. Pearl Investment Co. - **§1257**
Cox Broadcasting Corp. v. Cohn - **§1585**
Craig v. Wright - **§1411**
Cram v. Howell - **§557**
Crawford v. Halkovics - **§800**
Crawford v. Magnolia Petroleum Co. - **§1143**
Crawn v. Campo - **§863**
Crisci v. Security Insurance Co. - **§§873, 874**
Critz v. Farmers Insurance Group - **§875**
Cronin v. J.B.E. Olson Corp. - **§1027**
Crosby v. Cox Aircraft Co. - **§907**
Cross v. Wells Fargo Alarm Services - **§568**
Crotta v. Home Depot, Inc. - **§1217**
Crow v. Colson - **§482**
Crowley v. Global Realty, Inc. - **§1683**
Cruz v. Middlekautt Lincoln-Mercury, Inc. - **§599**
Cullison v. Medley - **§29**
Cult Awareness Network v. Church of Scientology International - **§1786**

Cumberland Torpedo Co. v. Gaines - **§1120**
Curtis v. General Motors Corp. - **§1025**
Curtis Publishing Co. v. Butts - **§1512**

D

D&D Fuller CATV Construction, Inc. v. Pace - **§1209**
Dahl v. Bayerische Motoren Werke - **§832**
Dahlstrom v. Shrum - **§502**
Dale System, Inc. v. Time, Inc. - **§§1691, 1701**
Daluiso v. Boone - **§146**
Dalury v. S-K-I, Ltd. - **§848**
Daly v. General Motors Corp. - **§1057**
Dameron v. Washington Magazine, Inc. - **§1516**
Danann Realty Corp. v. Harris - **§1677**
D'Andrea v. Calcagni - **§1727**
Danforth v. Acorn Structures, Inc. - **§1050**
Daniels v. Brunton - **§741**
Daniels v. Dillard Department Stores, Inc. - **§142**
Daniels v. Sanitarium Association - **§1401**
Darmento v. Pacific Molasses Co. - **§401**
Davenport v. Cotton Hope Plantation Horizontal Property Regime - **§§859, 864, 1064**
Davidson v. City of Westminster - **§569**
Davies v. Mann - **§804**
Davis v. Davis - **§590**
Davis v. Hearst - **§1367**
Davis v. Ross - **§1393**
Davis v. Wyeth Laboratories, Inc. - **§979**
Davis & Allcott Co. v. Boozer - **§62**
Dawson v. Chrysler Corp. - **§§967, 968**
Day v. Caslowitz - **§841**
Day v. Montana Power Co. - **§784**
Deaton v. Delta Democrat Publishing Co. - **§1563**
DeBurkarte v. Louvar - **§438**
Delair v. McAdoo - **§301**
Delaney v. Philhern Realty Holding Corp. - **§1138**
Della Penna v. Toyota Motor Sales, U.S.A., Inc. - **§§1740, 1743**
Dellwo v. Pearson - **§302**
Del Mar Beach Club Owners Association v. Imperial Contracting Co. - **§1014**
De Long v. County of Erie (1982) - **§570**
De Long v. County of Erie (1983) - **§1153**
Delta Air Lines, Inc. v. McDonnell Douglas Corp. - **§1065**
Delta Tau Delta v. Johnson - **§707**
Delvaux v. Vanden Langenberg - **§821**
DeMarco v. Publix Super Markets, Inc. - **§1723**
Dempsey, United States v. - **§1181**
Dennis v. Allison - **§1079**
Denny v. Ford Motor Co. - **§1075**
Derby v. Public Service Co. - **§756**
Derry v. Peek - **§1637**
Desnick v. American Broadcasting Cos. - **§§107, 237**
Deuser v. Vecera - **§1231**
Diaz v. Oakland Tribune, Inc. - **§§1568, 1570**
Dickau v. Rafala - **§701**
Dietemann v. Time, Inc. - **§1559**
Dillard v. Little League Baseball Inc. - **§850**
Dillon v. Legg - **§§772, 779**
Dini v. Naiditch - **§715**
Diodes, Inc. v. Franzen - **§1736**
Di Ponzio v. Riordan - **§401**
DiSalle v. P.G. Publishing Co. - **§1446**
District of Columbia v. Peters - **§483**
Ditto v. McCurdy - **§316**
Dixon v. Economy Co. - **§1359**
Dodson v. Dicker - **§1608**
Doe v. B.P.S. Guard Services, Inc. - **§1555**
Doe v. Berkeley Publishers - **§1571**
Doe v. Manheimer - **§§447, 448**
Doe v. Methodist Hospital - **§1569**
Doe v. United States - **§1232**
Donaldson v. YWCA - **§553**
Donovan v. Fiumara - **§1442**
Doss v. Town of Big Stone Gap - **§498**
Douglass v. Hustler Magazine, Inc. - **§1605**
Dowd v. Portsmouth Hospital - **§697**
Dragna v. White - **§179**
Dreisonstok v. Volkswagenwerk, A.G. - **§968**
Duke Power Co. v. Carolina Environmental Study Group, Inc. - **§1322**
Dun & Bradstreet, Inc. v. Greenmoss Builders, Inc. - **§§1447, 1534**
Dunahoo v. Bess - **§770**
Dunlop v. Daigle - **§1123**
Dunn v. Ralston Purina Co. - **§938**
Dunphy v. Gregor - **§§774, 1177**

E

East River Steamship Corp. v. Transamerica Delaval, Inc. - **§1050**
East St. John's Shingle Co. v. City of Portland - **§1149**
Eastern Airlines, Inc. v. Floyd - **§1319**
Eckert v. Long Island Railroad - **§794**
Economopoulos v. A.G. Pollard Co. - **§1385**
Edmonds v. Western Pennsylvania Hospital Radiology Associates - **§1196**
Edwards v. National Audubon Society, Inc. - **§1501**
Elden v. Sheldon - **§§774, 1177**
Elder v. Orluck - **§821**
Ellerbee v. Mills - **§1511**
Ellis v. D'Angelo - **§635**
Ellis v. Lindmark - **§946**
Ellis v. Price - **§1358**
Ellis v. State - **§133**
Ellsworth v. Sherne Lingerie, Inc. - **§1028**
Elmore v. American Motors Corp. - **§1009**
Emery v. Federated Foods, Inc. - **§979**
Engels v. Ranger Bar, Inc. - **§§1642, 1646**
England v. Tasker - **§841**

English v. New England Medical Center, Inc. - **§1251**
English, United States v. - **§518**
Enis v. Ba-Call Building Corp. - **§497**
Erdman v. Johnson Bros. Radio & Television Co. - **§1096**
Erickson v. Kongsli - **§402**
Erickson v. Marsh & MacLennan Co. - **§1471**
Erlich v. Menezes - **§780**
Espinoza v. Elgin, Joliet & Eastern Railway - **§394**
Estate of - *see* name of party
Estelle v. Gamble - **§1242**
Estrada, People v. - **§126**
Ewart v. Southern California Gas Co. - **§494**
Ewen v. McLean Trucking Co. - **§970**

F

FDIC v. W.R. Grace & Co. - **§1675**
Faber v. Creswick - **§740**
Fackler v. Genetzky - **§781**
Fairbanks, Morse & Co. v. Texas Electric Service Co. - **§1713**
Fairfield v. American Photocopy Equipment Co. - **§§1591, 1595**
Faloona v. Hustler Magazine, Inc. - **§1605**
Falzone v. Busch - **§764**
Faniel v. Chesapeake & Potomac Telephone Co. - **§70**
Fantozzi v. Sandusky Cement Products Co. - **§526**
Farina v. Pan American World Airlines, Inc. - **§382**
Farley v. Engelken - **§1303**
Farley v. Sartin - **§1190**
Farmers Educational & Cooperative Union v. WDAY, Inc. - **§1494**
Farris v. United States Fidelity & Guaranty Co. - **§1722**
Farwell v. Keaton - **§§343, 553**
Faya v. Almaraz - **§768**
Fein v. Permanente Medical Group - **§1300**
Feldman v. Lederle Laboratories - **§§977, 982**
Felix v. Hoffman-LaRoche, Inc. - **§990**
Fellows v. National Enquirer, Inc. - **§1606**
Fennell v. Southern Maryland Hospital Center, Inc. - **§437**
Feoffees of Heriot's Hospital v. Ross - **§1248**
Feres v. United States - **§1233**
Ferragamo v. Massachusetts Bay Transportation Authority - **§1104**
Ferreira v. Strack - **§648**
Ferriter v. Daniel O'Connell's Sons, Inc. - **§778**
Fetterhoff v. Western Block Co. - **§1278**
Feuerherm v. Ertelt - **§641**
Fields v. Synthetic Ropes, Inc. - **§613**
Figueiredo-Torres v. Nickel - **§§80, 1210**
Finger v. Omni Publications International, Ltd. - **§1589**
Fireman's Fund American Insurance Cos. v. Knobbe - **§374**
Firman v. Sacia - **§502**
First Independent Baptist Church v. Southerland - **§1427**
Fischer v. Johns-Manville Corp. - **§950**
Fisher v. Carrousel Motor Hotel, Inc. - **§11**
Fleming v. Arrington - **§704**
Fleming v. Baptist General Convention - **§1343**
Fletcher v. Western National Life Insurance Co. - **§80**
Flies v. Fox Bros. Buick - **§937**
Flint & Walling Manufacturing Co. v. Beckett - **§577**
Florenzano v. Olson - **§1656**
Florida Star, The v. B.J.F. - **§1586**
Foley v. Lowell Sun Publishing Co. - **§1390**
Ford Motor Co. v. Mathis - **§941**
Ford Motor Co. v. Wagoner - **§1045**
Foretich v. Capital Cities/ABC, Inc. - **§§1472, 1514**
Forster v. Manchester - **§1545**
Foster v. Preston Mill Co. - **§917**
Franklin v. Gwinnett County Public Schools - **§84**
Fraser v. United States - **§557**
French v. Willman - **§411**
Frey v. Kouf - **§7**
Freyermuth v. Lufty - **§471**
Friedman v. General Motors Corp. - **§1035**
Frobig v. Gordon - **§753**
Fuller v. Central Maine Power Co. - **§1019**
Fuller v. Preis - **§483**
Fuller v. Standard Stations, Inc. - **§598**
Funeral Services by Gregory, Inc. v. Bluefield Community Hospital - **§14**
Furey v. Thomas Jefferson University Hospital - **§310**

G

G.J.D. v. Johnson - **§1155**
Gaeta v. New York News, Inc. - **§1538**
Gala v. Hamilton - **§310**
Galella v. Onassis - **§1551**
Gallick v. Barto - **§753**
Gallimore v. Children's Hospital Medical Center - **§1181**
Gammon v. Osteopathic Hospital of Maine, Inc. - **§770**
Garcia v. Joseph Vince Co. - **§426**
Gardner v. Boston Elevated Railway - **§582**
Gardner v. Coca-Cola Bottling Co. - **§382**
Gardner v. Loomis Armored Inc. - **§1723**
Gardner v. Q.H.S., Inc. - **§1029**
Garratt v. Dailey - **§7**
Garrison v. Louisiana - **§§1413, 1517**
Gaudette v. Webb - **§1179**
Gehrts v. Batteen - **§887**
Geier v. American Honda Motor Co. - **§§1068, 1328**
General Motors Corp. v. Saenz - **§1041**
Geohagan v. General Motors Corp. - **§1097**
George v. Parke-Davis - **§429**
Georgie Boy Manufacturing, Inc. v. Superior Court - **§1167**
Germolus v. Sausser - **§131**
Gertz v. Robert Welch, Inc. (1974) - **§§1446, 1504, 1512, 1531, 1532, 1541, 1543**
Gertz v. Robert Welch, Inc. (1982) - **§1521**
Gibson v. Garcia - **§492**

Gibson v. West Virginia Department of Highways - **§1307**
Gilbert v. Medical Economics Co. - **§1571**
Giles v. City of New Haven - **§837**
Gipson v. Kasey - **§321**
Girard v. Anderson - **§157**
Glanzer v. Shepard - **§1662**
Glaskox *ex rel.* Denton v. Glaskox - **§1216**
Glidden v. Szybiak - **§215**
Glittenberg v. Doughboy Recreational Industries - **§980**
Glorioso v. YMCA - **§795**
Goff v. Taylor - **§5**
Golden v. Amory - **§919**
Goldman v. Johns-Manville Sales Corp. - **§432**
Gonzalez v. Garcia - **§859**
Goodman v. Kennedy - **§1755**
Gordon v. State - **§1340**
Grainy v. Campbell - **§486**
Grant v. Reader's Digest Association - **§1382**
Gray v. Grunnagle - **§112**
Gray v. Udevitz - **§1510**
Greco v. Bucciconi Engineering Co. - **§1036**
Greco v. United States - **§§1198, 1199**
Greeley v. Jameson - **§886**
Green v. Bittner - **§1163**
Green Acres Trust v. London - **§1457**
Green Valley School, Inc. v. Cowles Florida Broadcasting, Inc. - **§262**
Greenbelt Cooperative Publishing Association v. Bresler - **§1420**
Greenman v. Yuba Power Products, Inc. - **§§952, 954**
Green-Wheeler Shoe Co. v. Chicago Rock Island & Pacific Railway - **§499**
Gregory v. McDonnell Douglas Corp. - **§1420**
Greycas, Inc. v. Proud - **§§1639, 1675**
Griffin v. Hustis - **§482**
Griggs v. Combe, Inc. - **§1034**
Grimes v. Axtell Ford Lincoln-Mercury - **§1000**
Grimsby v. Samson - **§85**
Grimshaw v. Ford Motor Co. - **§359**
Groesbeck v. Napier - **§1166**
Gross v. Cantor - **§1407**
Grover v. Eli Lilly & Co. - **§337**
Gruenberg v. Aetna Insurance Co. - **§§877, 1722**
Guard-Life Corp. v. S. Parker Hardware Manufacturing Corp. - **§1714**
Guarino v. Mine Safety Appliance Co. - **§1010**
Gudger v. Manton - **§1696**

H

H.B. & S.B. v. Whittemore - **§553**
H.E. Butt Grocery Co. v. Bilotto - **§833**
H.R. Moch Co. v. Rensselaer Water Co. - **§581**
Hackett v. Perron - **§619**
Haelan Laboratories, Inc. v. Topps Chewing Gum, Inc. - **§1595**
Haft v. Lone Palm Hotel - **§440**
Hale v. Allstate Insurance Co. - **§596**
Haley v. Pan American World Airways, Inc. - **§525**
Hall v. Duke - **§690**
Hall v. Dumitru - **§533**
Hall v. Post - **§1588**
Halliday v. Sturm, Ruger & Co. - **§974**
Hamberger v. Eastman - **§1545**
Hamman v. County of Maricopa - **§557**
Hammond v. International Harvester Co. - **§1063**
Hammontree v. Jenner - **§297**
Hampton v. North Carolina Pulp Co. - **§1117**
Hanberry v. Hearst Corp. - **§1005**
Hanke v. Global Van Lines, Inc. - **§§80, 87**
Hanson v. City of Snohomish - **§1771**
Hanvey v. Oconee Memorial Hospital - **§1251**
Hapka v. Paquin Farms - **§1011**
Harinek v. 161 North Clark Street Ltd. Partnership - **§1229**
Harper v. Herman - **§§342, 567**
Harrell v. Travelers Indemnity Co. - **§869**
Harris v. Carbonneau - **§1558**
Harris v. Jones - **§92**
Hart v. Browne - **§1622**
Hart v. Geysel - **§117**
Harte-Hanks Communications, Inc. v. Connaughton - **§§1523, 1524**
Hartke v. McKelway - **§312**
Hartley v. Floyd - **§574**
Hartman *ex rel.* Hartman v. Hartman - **§1220**
Hartridge v. State Farm Mutual Automobile Insurance Co. - **§1725**
Hartwell Corp. v. Bumb - **§1679**
Hastie v. Handeland - **§485**
Hatten v. Union Oil Co. - **§1732**
Hauter v. Zogarts - **§1087**
Hawkins v. Multimedia, Inc. - **§1573**
Hawkins v. Pizzaro - **§557**
Haynes v. Alfred A. Knopf, Inc. - **§1573**
Healy v. New England Newspapers, Inc. - **§1393**
Hearst Corp. v. Hughes - **§1444**
Heath v. Swift Wings, Inc. - **§303**
Heil Valley Ranch, Inc. v. Simkin - **§843**
Heimer v. Privratsky - **§309**
Helfend v. Southern California Rapid Transit District - **§539**
Hellar v. Bianco - **§1373**
Helms v. Harris - **§135**
Henningsen v. Bloomfield Motors, Inc. - **§1093**
Henry v. Brown - **§888**
Herbert v. Lando - **§1528**
Hewellette v. George - **§§1214, 1216**
Higgins v. Mason - **§588**
Hightower-Warren v. Silk - **§367**
Hildebrand v. Minyard - **§851**
Hill v. City of Glenwood - **§295**
Hill v. Edmonds - **§418**

Hill v. Thompson - **§371**
Hills v. Lyons Plumbing & Heating Co. - **§759**
Hines v. Garrett - **§486**
Hinkle v. Rockville Motor Co. - **§1681**
Hinojasa v. Automatic Elevator Co. - **§1016**
Hirpa v. IHC Hospitals, Inc. - **§566**
Hobart v. Schuler - **§1677**
Hodges v. Gibson Products Co. - **§1769**
Hofer v. Lavender - **§1155**
Hogan v. Herald Co. - **§1501**
Hogle v. H.H. Franklin Manufacturing Co. - **§606**
Holland v. Baltimore & Ohio Railroad - **§685**
Hollerud v. Malamis - **§114**
Holzhauer v. Saks & Co. - **§371**
Holzheimer v. Johannesen - **§701**
Hood v. Ryobi America Corp. - **§981**
Hoover v. Montgomery Ward & Co. - **§1016**
Hopkins v. Fox & Lazo Realtors - **§334**
Hopkins v. McBane - **§1159**
Horn v. General Motors Corp. - **§965**
Horne v. Patton - **§§1562, 1582**
Horwich v. Superior Court - **§1168**
Hoven v. Kelble - **§1017**
Hoven v. Rice Memorial Hospital - **§373**
Howard v. Des Moines Register & Tribune Co. - **§1563**
Howard Frank, M.D., P.C. v. Superior Court - **§§1182, 1184**
Howe v. Stubbs - **§706**
Hruby v. Kalina - **§1436**
Hudson v. Craft - **§118**
Huffman & Wright Logging Co. v. Wade - **§99**
Hugel v. Milberg, Weiss, Bershad, Hynes & Lerach, LLP - **§1458**
Hull v. L. & A. Montagnard Social Club, Inc. - **§364**
Hulton v. Jones - **§1399**
Humphers v. First Interstate Bank of Oregon - **§1620**
Hunnings v. Texaco, Inc. - **§990**
Hunt v. Blasius - **§936**
Hunter v. Bryant - **§1247**
Huset v. J.I. Case Threshing Machine Co. - **§929**
Hustler Magazine v. Falwell - **§§96, 1418, 1433**
Hutcherson v. City of Phoenix - **§829**
Hutchinson v. Proxmire - **§§1509, 1515**
Hymowitz v. Eli Lilly & Co. - **§§428, 1271**

I

Imbler v. Pachtman - **§1243**
Immuno AG. v. Moor-Jankowski - **§1417**
Imperial v. Drapeau - **§1497**
In re - *see* name of party
Indiana Harbor Belt Railroad v. American Cyanamid Co. - **§903**
Indianapolis Street Railway v. Dawson - **§692**
Innes v. Howell Corp. - **§1154**
International Products Co. v. Erie Railroad - **§1659**
Irwin v. Ashurst - **§1456**

J

J. v. Victory Tabernacle Baptist Church - **§607**
J.C. v. WALA-TV, Inc. - **§1571**
J.C. Penney Casualty Insurance Co. v. M.K. - **§869**
J.S. v. R.T.H. - **§550**
Jacko v. City of Bridgeport - **§1142**
Jackson v. City of Kansas City - **§570**
Jackson v. Longcope - **§1387**
Jackson v. Montana - **§1660**
Jackson v. Nestle-Beich, Inc. - **§971**
Jacobson v. Leventhal - **§739**
Jeffers v. City of Seattle - **§1545**
Jensen v. Chicago & Western Indiana Railroad - **§235**
Jim Mitchell & Jed Davis, P.A. v. Jackson - **§1757**
Jividen v. Law - **§887**
Joe Dickerson & Associates, LLC v. Dittmar - **§1598**
John A. Artukovich & Sons, Inc. v. Reliance Truck Co. - **§213**
John R. Dudley Construction, Inc. v. Drott Manufacturing Co. - **§1049**
Johnson v. Bathey - **§675**
Johnson v. Calado - **§1786**
Johnson v. Davis - **§1636**
Johnson v. Kosmos Portland Cement Co. - **§489**
Johnson v. Manhattan & Bronx Surface Transit Operating Authority - **§515**
Johnson v. Raybestos-Manhattan, Inc. - **§977**
Johnson v. Rogers - **§530**
Johnson v. Ruark Obstetrics & Gynecology Associates - **§783**
Johnson v. State - **§770**
Johnson v. United Parcel Services - **§70**
Johnson v. United States - **§1232**
Johnson v. University Hospitals of Cleveland - **§1195**
Johnson, United States v. - **§1233**
Johnson's Estate, *In re* - **§105**
Johnston v. Fuller - **§1552**
Jones v. Hansen - **§718**
Jones v. Robbins - **§341**
Jones v. Ryobi, Ltd. - **§1038**
Jones & Laughlin Steel Corp. v. Pfeifer - **§519**
Josephson v. Meyers - **§394**
Jost v. Dairyland Power Cooperative - **§1130**
Jourdain v. Dineen - **§1682**
Judson v. Giant Powder Co. - **§379**
Juiditta v. Bethlehem Steel Corp. - **§523**
Justus v. Atchison - **§1192**

K

K.A.C. v. Benson - **§768**

K-Mart Corp. v. Washington - **§1361**
Kaarup v. St. Paul Fire & Marine Insurance Co. - **§1772**
Kaelin v. Globe Communications Corp. - **§1391**
Kahlenberg v. Goldstein - **§597**
Kambat v. St. Francis Hospital - **§367**
Kassel v. Gannett Co. - **§1509**
Katko v. Briney - **§144**
Kearns v. Smith - **§734**
Kelley v. Bonney - **§1511**
Kelley v. R.G. Industries, Inc. - **§§911, 964**
Kelley, Estate of v. Moguls, Inc. - **§836**
Kellogg v. Village of Viola - **§1146**
Kelly v. Gwinnell - **§648**
Kelly v. Henry Muhs Co. - **§402**
Kelly, Estate of v. Falin - **§836**
Kelman v. Wilen - **§193**
Kennedy v. Providence Hockey Club, Inc. - **§851**
Kennedy v. Zimmermann - **§1457**
Kentucky Fried Chicken v. Superior Court - **§709**
Kenty v. Transamerica Premium Insurance Co. - **§1712**
Kenyon v. Hammer - **§1299**
Kerr v. Corning Glass Works - **§957**
Keys v. Interstate Circuit, Inc. - **§1402**
Kilduff v. Adams, Inc. - **§1682**
Kilgore v. Younger - **§1460**
Kindt v. Kauffman - **§645**
Kingsland v. Erie County Agricultural Society - **§495**
Kinsman Transit Co. (No. 1), *In re* - **§§497, 507**
Kinsman Transit Co. (No. 2), *In re* - **§1756**
Kiriluk v. Cohn - **§639**
Kirk v. Denver Publishing Co. - **§1340**
Kirk v. Stineway Drug Store Co. - **§944**
Kitchen v. K-Mart Corp. - **§597**
Klein v. Beeten - **§366**
Klein v. Pyrodyne Corp. - **§901**
Klein v. Raysinger - **§646**
Kline v. 1500 Massachusetts Avenue Apartment Corp. - **§752**
Kline v. Ansell - **§1203**
Knight v. Jewett - **§863**
Knoll v. Board of Regents - **§334**
Koestler v. Pollard - **§§94, 1210**
Kolakowski v. Voris - **§373**
Koonce, State v. - **§180**
Koos v. Roth - **§904**
Korman v. Mallin - **§312**
Kosters v. Seven-Up Co. - **§1002**
Kozicki v. Dragon - **§599**
Kramer v. Lewisville Memorial Hospital - **§437**
Kramer v. Thompson - **§1450**
Krieger v. Ownership Corp. - **§750**
Krueger v. Austad - **§1515**
Kruse v. Rabe - **§1481**
Kuhns v. Brugger - **§635**
Kunst v. New York World Telegram Corp. - **§1391**

L

L.S. Ayres & Co. v. Hicks - **§279**
Laaperi v. Sears, Roebuck & Co. - **§987**
LaBier v. Pelletier - **§807**
Landreth v. Reed - **§523**
Langan v. Valicopters, Inc. - **§903**
Langford v. Shu - **§33**
Largey v. Rothman - **§317**
LaRosa v. Superior Court - **§1001**
La Rossa v. Scientific Design Co. - **§955**
Larsen v. General Motors Corp. - **§965**
Larson v. Dunn - **§1209**
LaVallee v. Vermont Motor Inns, Inc. - **§391**
Lawrence v. Bauer Publishing & Printing Ltd. - **§1386**
Lawton v. Great Southwest Fire Insurance Co. - **§877**
Layne v. Tribune Co. - **§1500**
Lazar v. Superior Court - **§1626**
LeCrone v. Ohio Bell Telephone Co. - **§1554**
Lee v. Colorado Department of Health - **§810**
Lee v. Dong-A Ilbo, The - **§1489**
Lehnhard v. Robertson's Administratix - **§922**
Leiker v. Gafford - **§526**
Le Marc's Management Corp. v. Valentin - **§1445**
Lemire v. Garrard Drugs - **§999**
Le Mistral, Inc. v. Columbia Broadcasting System - **§262**
Leong v. Takasaki - **§774**
Lesniak v. County of Bergen - **§517**
Lester v. Sayles - **§795**
Lestina v. West Bend Mutual Insurance Co. - **§863**
Levey v. DeNardo - **§287**
Levine v. Russell Blaine Co. - **§392**
Li v. Yellow Cab Co. - **§815**
Libbey v. Hampton Water Works Co. - **§581**
Liberman v. Gelstein - **§§1436, 1479**
Lichtman v. Nadler - **§1119**
Liff v. Schildkrout - **§1179**
Linder v. Bidner - **§635**
Linthicum v. Nationwide Life Insurance Co. - **§1338**
Liriano v. Hobart Corp. - **§§1030, 1038**
Live Oak Publishing Co. v. Cohagan - **§1451**
Livitsanos v. Superior Court - **§1279**
Lobert v. Pack - **§3**
Lockard v. Carson - **§1645**
Loe v. Lenhardt - **§908**
Loe v. Town of Thomaston - **§1566**
Logan v. Old Enterprise Farms, Ltd. - **§675**
Loney v. McPhillips - **§687**
Long v. Arcell - **§1523**
Long Beach, City of v. Bozek - **§1782**
Lopez v. Southern California Rapid Transit District - **§584**
Lorfano v. Dura Stone Steps, Inc. - **§980**
Los Angeles Airways, Inc. v. Davis - **§1741**
Louisville & Nashville Railroad v. Spinks - **§576**

Louisville & Nashville Railroad v. Spoonamore's Administrator - **§666**
Low v. Park Price Co. - **§391**
Lowrey v. Horvath - **§330**
Lucas v. Mississippi Housing Authority - **§1171**
Lugosi v. Universal Pictures - **§1617**
Lumby v. Allday - **§1439**
Lumley v. Gye - **§1712**
Lussier v. Louisville Ladder Co. - **§1040**
Lynch v. Rosenthal - **§300**
Lyons v. Midnight Sun Transportation Services, Inc. - **§287**

M

MacDonald v. Ortho Pharmaceutical Corp. - **§§986, 990**
MacLeod v. Tribune Publishing Co. - **§1439**
MacPherson v. Buick Motor Co. - **§§933, 934, 937, 939**
MacRae v. Brant - **§1771**
McAllister v. Ha - **§1198**
McCahill v. New York Transportation Co. - **§471**
McCarty v. Pheasant Run, Inc. - **§356**
McCullock v. H.B. Fuller Co. - **§989**
McCutcheon v. United Homes Corp. - **§848**
McDaniel v. Atlanta Coca-Cola Bottling Co. - **§1559**
McDevitt v. Standard Oil Co. - **§1056**
McDonald v. Smith - **§1497**
McDougald v. Garber - **§§524, 526**
McDougald v. Perry - **§365**
McFarlane v. Esquire Magazine - **§1527**
McFarlane v. City of Niagara Falls - **§1121**
McGettigan v. Bay Area Rapid Transit District - **§586**
McGranahan v. Dahar - **§1458**
McGrane v. Cline - **§599**
McGuire v. Almy - **§5**
McHale v. W.B.S. Corp. - **§1763**
McIntosh v. Barr - **§1178**
McKenzie v. Cheetham - **§746**
McKiddy v. Des Moines Electric Co. - **§674**
McLain v. Boise Cascade Corp. - **§1550**
McLane v. Northwest Natural Gas Co. - **§894**
McLaughlin v. Mine Safety Appliances Co. - **§491**
McQuade v. Tuscon Tiller Apartments, Ltd. - **§1128**
Machleder v. Diaz - **§1605**
Mackowick v. Westinghouse Electric Corp. - **§987**
Maddox v. City of New York - **§851**
Magliulo v. Superior Court - **§1279**
Maldonado v. Southern Pacific Transportation Co. - **§342**
Malloy v. Commonwealth Highland Theatres, Inc. - **§381**
Maloney v. Rath - **§619**
Maltman v. Sauer - **§332**
Malvicini v. Stratfield Motor Hotel, Inc. - **§371**
Mapco, Inc. v. Payne - **§1723**
Marchesi v. Franchino - **§1479**
Marciniak v. Lundborg - **§1194**
Marek v. Professional Health Services, Inc. - **§621**
Margoles v. Hubbart - **§1519**
Maritote v. Desilu Productions, Inc. - **§1615**
Marshall v. Ranne - **§924**
Marshall & Michel Grain Co. v. Kansas City, Ft. Scott & Memphis Railroad - **§226**
Martin v. Abbott Laboratories - **§429**
Martin v. Herzog - **§409**
Martin v. Houck - **§§56, 74**
Martin v. Reynolds Metals Co. - **§189**
Martin Luther King, Jr., Center for Social Change, Inc. v. American Heritage Products, Inc. - **§1617**
Martinez v. California - **§1230**
Martinez v. Lazaroff - **§497**
Mason v. Western Union Telegraph Co. - **§1499**
Masson v. New Yorker Magazine, Inc. - **§1388**
Mastland, Inc. v. Evans Furniture, Inc. - **§292**
Matomco Oil Co. v. Arctic Mechanical, Inc. - **§401**
Matthews v. Lawnlite Co. - **§962**
Matthies v. Mastromonaco - **§311**
Mauro v. Raymark Industries, Inc. - **§§433, 439**
Maynard v. Port Publications, Inc. - **§1378**
Mazur v. Merck & Co. - **§989**
Medico v. Time, Inc. - **§1488**
Meiers v. Fred Koch Brewery - **§716**
Meisler v. Gannett Co. - **§1526**
Meistrich v. Casino Arena Attractions, Inc. - **§860**
Melville v. Southward - **§308**
Melvin v. Reid - **§1562**
Merchants Mutual Bonding Co., United States v. - **§235**
Meritor Savings Bank v. Vinson - **§84**
Merrill v. Central Maine Power Co. - **§682**
Merritt v. Nickelson - **§651**
Messick v. General Motors Corp. - **§1062**
Metric Investment, Inc. v. Patterson - **§1640**
Metro-North Commuter Railroad v. Buckley - **§767**
Metter v. Los Angeles Examiner - **§1614**
Metz v. United Technologies Corp. - **§520**
Mexicali Rose v. Superior Court - **§971**
Meyers v. Delaney - **§654**
Miami, City of v. Wardlow - **§1460**
Michalko v. Cooke Color & Chemical Corp. - **§998**
Michelman v. Ehrlich - **§1197**
Mickle v. Blackmon - **§965**
Micromanolis v. The Woods School, Inc. - **§661**
Midkiff v. Midkiff - **§1221**
Mieske v. Bartell Drug Co. - **§528**
Mihlovan v. Grozavu - **§1478**
Milkovich v. Lorain Journal Co. - **§§1417, 1418**
Miller v. American Sports Co. - **§1593**
Miller v. Arnal Corp. - **§561**
Miller v. Johnson - **§1193**
Miller v. Rhode Island Hospital - **§103**
Milliken & Co. v. Consolidated Edison Co. - **§1756**
Miner v. Novotny - **§1459**
Mist v. Westin Hotels, Inc. - **§834**

Mitchell v. Bearden - **§1127**
Mitchell v. Buchheit - **§1163**
Mitchell v. Churches - **§597**
Modaber v. Kelley - **§1192**
Moerer v. Ford Motor Co. - **§1037**
Moldea v. New York Times Co. - **§1419**
Molitor v. Kaneland Community Unit District No. 302 - **§1228**
Molko v. Holy Spirit Association for the Unification of World Christianity - **§97**
Monreal v. Tobin - **§571**
Montana v. San Jose Mercury News, Inc. - **§1598**
Montgomery Ward & Co. v. Anderson - **§539**
Moody v. Haymarket Associates - **§351**
Moore v. Hart - **§800**
Moore v. Warren - **§1250**
Moradi-Shalal v. Fireman's Fund Insurance Cos. - **§876**
Morales v. City of New York - **§401**
Moran v. Faberge, Inc. - **§988**
Morgan v. Yuba County - **§574**
Morrison v. Ritchie & Co. - **§1395**
Morrow v. L.A. Goldschmidt Associates - **§1719**
Mountain v. Procter & Gamble Co. - **§1032**
Moyle v. Franz - **§1482**
Muchow v. Lindblad - **§782**
Muldovan v. McEachern - **§859**
Multimedia WMAZ, Inc. v. Kubach - **§§1565, 1577**
Munley v. ISC Financial House, Inc. - **§80**
Murphy v. E.R. Squibb & Sons - **§1017**
Murphy v. Edmonds - **§1334**
Murphy v. International Society for Krishna Consciousness of New England - **§97**
Murrell v. Trio Towing Service, Inc. - **§218**
Musch v. H-D Electric Cooperative, Inc. - **§§718, 723**
Muskopf v. Corning Hospital District - **§1228**
Musser v. Vilsmeier Auction Co. - **§1007**
Mussivand v. David - **§322**

N

Nabozny v. Barnhill - **§853**
Nader v. Allegheny Airlines, Inc. - **§1642**
Nader v. General Motors Corp. - **§1551**
Nallan v. Helmsley-Spear, Inc. - **§568**
Nancy P. v. D'Amato - **§782**
Nanda v. Ford Motor Co. - **§965**
Narsh v. Zirbser Bros. - **§757**
Nath v. National Equipment Leasing Corp. - **§996**
National Conversion Corp. v. Cedar Building Corp. - **§1652**
National Refining Co. v. Benzo Gas Motor Fuel Co. - **§1707**
National Steel Service Center, Inc. v. Gibbons - **§909**
Nazareno v. Urie - **§642**
Neff v. Time, Inc. - **§1571**
Negri v. Stop and Shop, Inc. - **§350**
Neibuhr v. Gage - **§108**
Neiman-Marcus v. Lait - **§§1405, 1407**
Nelson v. Hansen - **§1139**
Nelson v. Johnson - **§602**
Nelson v. Lapeyrouse Grain Corp. - **§1468**
Nelson v. Progressive Corp. - **§1682**
Nephi Processing Plant, Inc. v. Talbott - **§235**
Nestle v. City of Santa Monica - **§201**
New England Oil & Pipe Line Co. v. Rogers - **§1689**
New Meadows Holding Co. v. Washington Water Power Co. - **§904**
New York Times Co. v. Sullivan - **§§1503, 1504, 1508, 1517, 1518, 1523**
Newman v. Golden - **§736**
Newmark v. Gimbel's, Inc. - **§1018**
Ney v. Yellow Cab Co. - **§401**
Nguyen v. Proton Technology Corp. - **§1458**
Nichols v. Sukaro Kennels - **§781**
Nichols v. Union Underwear Co. - **§1025**
Nissen Corp. v. Miller - **§999**
Noback v. Town of Montclair - **§171**
Norfolk & Western Railway v. Liepelt - **§514**
Norris v. Bangor Publishing Co. - **§1445**
Nova Southeastern University v. Gross - **§567**

O

O'Brien v. Cunard Steam-Ship Co. - **§102**
O'Brien v. Western Union Telegraph Co. - **§770**
Odom v. G.D. Searle & Co. - **§1040**
O'Keefe v. South End Rowing Club - **§676**
Old Dominion Branch No. 496, National Association of Letter Carriers v. Austin - **§§1420, 1496**
Old Island Fumigation, Inc. v. Barbee - **§901**
O'Leary v. Coenen - **§720**
Oliver v. Stimson Lumber Co. - **§1789**
Ollerman v. O'Rourke Co. - **§1636**
Olympic Fish Products, Inc. v. Lloyd - **§1720**
Ornelas v. Randolph - **§717**
Osborn v. City of Whittier - **§466**
Osborne v. McMasters - **§396**
Ostrowe v. Lee - **§1359**
Ostrowski v. Azzara - **§831**
Otero v. Jordan Restaurant Enterprises - **§1675**
O'Toole v. Greenberg - **§1194**
Ouellette v. Carde - **§835**
Outwater v. Miller - **§945**
Overcast v. Billings Mutual Insurance Co. - **§1365**
Owen v. City of Independence - **§1245**
Owens-Illinois, Inc. v. Zenobia - **§977**

P

Pace v. Hillcrest Motor Co. - **§1781**
Page v. Niagara Chemical Division - **§1116**

Pagelsdorf v. Safeco Insurance Co. - **§§719, 744**
Palmer v. Bennington School District - **§1511**
Palmer v. Schonhorn Enterprises, Inc. - **§1598**
Palsgraf v. Long Island Railroad - **§§320, 321, 322, 323, 501, 502, 503, 508**
Park v. Standard Chem Way Co. - **§1176**
Park Knoll Associates v. Schmidt - **§1456**
Parks v. Northwestern University - **§1248**
Parness v. City of Tempe - **§460**
Parvi v. City of Kingston - **§563**
Pate v. Threlkel - **§§558, 559**
Patton v. Hutchinson Wil-Rich Manufacturing Co. - **§978**
Paul v. Watchtower Bible & Tract Society - **§97**
Pavia v. State Farm Mutual Automobile Insurance Co. - **§871**
Pearson v. Dodd - **§1545**
Pease v. Sinclair Refining Co. - **§357**
Peck v. Ford Motor Co. - **§1043**
Pendry v. Barnes - **§401**
People v. - *see* name of party
People Express Airlines, Inc. v. Consolidated Rail Corp. - **§§789, 1756**
Perham v. Coney - **§223**
Perry v. S.N. - **§547**
Personal Preference Video, Inc. v. Home Box Office, Inc. - **§1734**
Peterson v. City of Long Beach - **§174**
Peterson v. Romine - **§700**
Peterson v. Superior Court - **§995**
Peterson v. Taylor - **§291**
Petriello v. Kalman - **§435**
Petrovich v. Share Health Plan of Illinois, Inc. - **§617**
Phantom Touring, Inc. v. Affiliated Publications - **§1418**
Phennah v. Whalen - **§420**
Philadelphia Newspapers, Inc. v. Hepps - **§§1414, 1506, 1523, 1539**
Phillips v. Glazer - **§1689**
Phillips v. Kimwood Machine Co. - **§967**
Phoenix Professional Hockey Club, Inc. v. Hirmer - **§1756**
Piamba Cortes v. American Airlines, Inc. - **§1320**
Pierce v. Casas Adobes Baptist Church - **§1183**
Pierson v. Ray - **§1244**
Plaxico v. Michael - **§1546**
Plimpton v. Gerrard - **§1749**
Ploof v. Putnam - **§267**
Plumley v. Landmark Chevrolet, Inc. - **§1436**
Pokora v. Wabash Railway - **§361**
Polemis, *In re* - **§§446, 469, 470, 472, 497, 507, 509**
Porten v. University of San Francisco - **§1569**
Posadas v. City of Reno - **§1412**
Posecai v. Wal-Mart Stores, Inc. - **§708**
Poskus v. Lombardo's of Randolph, Inc. - **§599**
Post Publishing Co. v. Hallam - **§1484**
Potter v. Firestone Tire & Rubber Co. - **§§439, 767**
Powell v. American Motors Corp. - **§1181**
Praesel v. Johnson - **§558**
Prentiss v. Evergreen Presbyterian Church - **§690**
Preston v. Goldman - **§754**
Price v. Armour - **§1457**
Price v. Kitsap Transit - **§795**
Price v. Shell Oil Co. - **§§761, 994**
Priewe v. Bartz - **§649**
Printing Mart-Morristown v. Sharp Electronics Corp. - **§§1741, 1744**
Procanik v. Cillo - **§1200**
Proffitt v. Ricci - **§35**
Prudential Insurance Co. v. Dewey, Ballantine, Bushby, Palmer & Wood - **§1755**
Pulkrabek v. Sletten - **§1459**
Pulliam v. Coastal Emergency Services - **§1300**

Q

Quinlan v. City of Philadelphia - **§483**
Quinnett v. Newman - **§636**

R

Rade v. Press Publishing Co. - **§1437**
Radecki v. Schuckardt - **§1205**
Ramunno v. Cawley - **§1418**
Randi W. v. Muroc Joint Unified School District - **§§334, 344**
Rappaport v. Nichols - **§643**
Rasmussen v. Benson - **§780**
Ratlif v. Schiber Truck Co. - **§571**
Ravi v. Coates - **§622**
Ravo *ex rel.* Ravo v. Rogatnick - **§§1253, 1260**
Reed v. Chrysler Corp. - **§1058**
Reed v. Northwestern Publishing Co. - **§1510**
Reesman v. Highfill - **§1386**
Regan v. Crime Victims Compensation Board - **§1318**
Reichert v. Atler - **§829**
Reid v. Spadone Machine Co. - **§1029**
Reikes v. Martin - **§317**
Reilly v. United States - **§782**
Reminga v. United States - **§573**
Rennick v. Fruehauf Corp. - **§942**
Renslow v. Mennonite Hospital - **§337**
Reyes v. Wyeth Laboratories - **§1047**
Reynolds v. Willson - **§§682, 685**
Rhodes v. Graham - **§1556**
Ribas v. Clark - **§1551**
Richards v. Soucy - **§635**
Richmond Newspapers, Inc. v. Lipscomb - **§1511**
Richter v. Limax International, Inc. - **§1041**
Riegel v. Medtronic, Inc. - **§1327**
Riss v. City of New York - **§569**
Ritter v. Custom Chemicides, Inc. - **§1656**
Rivera v. New York City Transit Authority - **§286**
Roa v. Lodi Medical Group, Inc. - **§1302**
Robbins v. Footer - **§307**

Robbins v. Minute Tapioca Co. - **§723**
Robert C. Ozer, P.C. v. Borquez - **§§1577, 1581**
Roberts v. Ring - **§296**
Robins Dry Dock & Repair Co. v. Flint - **§§1724, 1752**
Robinson v. Butler - **§493**
Robinson v. District of Columbia - **§406**
Robinson v. Lindsay - **§294**
Rodrigues v. State - **§784**
Rodriguez v. Bethlehem Steel Corp. - **§1175**
Rodriguez v. Johnson - **§181**
Roessler v. Novak - **§617**
Rogers v. Board of Road Commissioners - **§188**
Rogers v. Kabakoff - **§150**
Roling v. Daily - **§765**
Romaine v. Kallinger - **§§1386, 1389, 1390**
Rome, City of v. Jordan - **§569**
Romero v. International Harvester Co. - **§978**
Rose v. Pennsylvania Railroad - **§466**
Rosenau v. City of New Brunswick - **§1671**
Rosenblatt v. Baer - **§§1508, 1519**
Ross v. Cheema - **§765**
Ross v. Consumers Power Co. - **§1239**
Rossmoor Sanitation, Inc. v. Pylon, Inc. - **§1266**
Rowe v. State Bank of Lombard - **§752**
Rowland v. Christian - **§718**
Rudeck v. Wright - **§622**
Rudisaile v. Hawk Aviation, Inc. - **§1055**
Rungee v. Cox - **§1679**
Russell v. Men of Devon - **§1222**
Russell-Vaughn Ford, Inc. v. Rouse - **§220**
Russo v. Sutton - **§1202**
Russo v. White - **§80**
Rutter v. Northeastern Beaver County School District - **§860**
Ruttger Hotel Corp. v. Wagner - **§765**
Ryan v. City of New York - **§1345**
Ryan v. New York Central Railroad - **§466**
Rylands v. Fletcher - **§900**

S

Sabrina W. v. Willman - **§1551**
Sacramento, County of v. Lewis - **§1242**
Safer v. Estate of Pack - **§559**
St. Amant v. Thompson - **§1520**
St. Clair v. Denny - **§525**
St. Luke's Episcopal Hospital v. Agbor - **§623**
Sanborn v. Chronicle Publishing Co. - **§1478**
Sanchez v. Coxon - **§1455**
Sandford v. Chevrolet Division of General Motors - **§1057**
Santana v. Zilog, Inc. - **§1190**
Santiago v. Sherwin Williams Co. - **§432**
Satterlee v. Orange Glenn School District - **§410**
Savage v. Jacobsen Manufacturing Co. - **§963**
Sayadoff v. Warda - **§117**
Schaefer v. American Family Mutual Insurance Co. - **§1161**
Schemel v. General Motors Corp. - **§1028**
Scheuer v. Rhodes - **§1244**
Schipper v. Levitt & Sons - **§1014**
Schlegel v. Ottumwa Courier - **§1444**
Schlessinger v. Schlessinger - **§1217**
Scholey v. Steele - **§748**
Schomer v. Smidt - **§1442**
Schreiber v. Physicians Insurance Co. of Wisconsin - **§319**
Schreiner v. Fruit - **§1187**
Schroeder v. Perkel - **§1198**
Schuppin v. Unification Church - **§1205**
Scott v. Bradford - **§318**
Scott v. Prudential Outfitting Co. - **§1715**
Scott Fetzer Co. v. Williamson - **§1457**
Seay v. Chrysler Corp. - **§1057**
Security Pacific Business Credit, Inc. v. Peat Marwick Main & Co. - **§1666**
Seigneur v. National Fitness Institute, Inc. - **§848**
Shaw Cleaners & Dyers, Inc. v. Des Moines Dress Club - **§1694**
Sheeley v. Memorial Hospital - **§307**
Sheets v. Ritt, Ritt & Ritt, Inc. - **§720**
Sheldon Appel Co. v. Albert & Oliker - **§1767**
Sherman v. Field Clinic - **§80**
Shibley v. Time, Inc. - **§1568**
Shine v. Vega - **§315**
Shoemaker v. Selnes - **§1776**
Shor v. Billingsley - **§1426**
Shorter v. Shelton - **§147**
Shulman v. Group W Productions, Inc. - **§1551**
Sidis v. F-R Publishing Corp. - **§1568**
Siegert v. Gilley - **§1243**
Silcott v. Oglesby - **§1206**
Silva v. Stevens - **§§1633, 1677**
Simmons v. Pacor, Inc. - **§434**
Simonian v. Patterson - **§218**
Simpson v. Calivas - **§1754**
Simpson v. General Motors Corp. - **§1057**
Simpson v. Mars, Inc. - **§1358**
Sindell v. Abbott Laboratories - **§§430, 441**
Sindle v. New York City Transit Authority - **§78**
Sipple v. Chronicle Publishing Co. - **§§1565, 1571**
Sisler v. Gannett Co. - **§1537**
Slade v. City of Phoenix - **§1769**
Slicer v. Quigley - **§647**
Smalich v. Westfall - **§808**
Smith v. Arbaugh's Restaurant, Inc. - **§718**
Smith v. Cote - **§1198**
Smith v. Cutter Biological, Inc. - **§432**
Smith v. Department of Insurance - **§§1333, 1334**
Smith v. Eli Lilly & Co. - **§431**
Smith v. Green - **§735**
Smith v. Lightning Bolt Productions, Inc. - **§1259**

Smith v. Sapienza - **§1221**
Smith v. Shannon - **§312**
Smith v. Staso Milling Co. - **§1120**
Smoot v. Mazda Motors of America, Inc. - **§378**
Snellenberger v. Rodriguez - **§481**
Snow v. West - **§1717**
Solgaard v. Guy F. Atkinson Co. - **§793**
Sommer v. Federal Signal Corp. - **§849**
Sorensen v. Allred - **§825**
Sorichetti v. City of New York - **§570**
Soronen v. Olde Milford Inn, Inc. - **§645**
Soule v. General Motors Corp. - **§974**
South Dakota Department of Health v. Heim - **§254**
Southwestern Bell Telephone Co. v. John Carlo Texas, Inc. - **§1731**
Spalt v. Eaton - **§583**
Spellens v. Spellens - **§1792**
Spencer v. Aetna Life & Casualty Insurance Co. - **§877**
Spier v. Barker - **§536**
Sporting Goods Distributors, Inc. v. Whitney - **§227**
Sprecher v. Adamson Cos. - **§655**
Spring Motors Distributors, Inc. v. Ford Motor Co. - **§1011**
Spur Industries, Inc. v. Del E. Webb Development Co. - **§1128**
Stagl v. Delta Airlines, Inc. (1995) - **§352**
Stagl v. Delta Airlines, Inc. (1997) - **§390**
Stallman v. Youngquist - **§1191**
Stallworth v. Doss - **§157**
Stanley, United States v. - **§1233**
State v. - *see* name of party
State Farm Mutual Automobile Insurance Co. v. Campbell - **§26**
State Rubbish Collectors Association v. Siliznoff - **§91**
Stationers Corp. v. Dun & Bradstreet, Inc. - **§§1470, 1477**
Steinhauser v. Hertz Corp. - **§471**
Sterling Drug, Inc. v. Yarrow - **§985**
Sterner v. Marathon Oil Co. - **§§1715, 1740**
Stevens v. Parke, Davis & Co. - **§1061**
Stevens v. Tillman - **§1418**
Stevens v. Veenstra - **§§294, 302**
Stewart v. Motts - **§285**
Stiles v. Batavia Atomic Horseshoes, Inc. - **§1004**
Stockdale v. Baba - **§93**
Stockdale v. Bird & Son, Inc. - **§778**
Stone v. Wall - **§1209**
Strauss v. Belle Realty Co. - **§336**
Strawn v. Canuso - **§1636**
Strever, Estate of v. Cline - **§599**
Strubhart v. Perry Memorial Hospital Trust Authority - **§623**
Stryker v. Republic Pictures - **§1564**
Stuart v. Hertz Corp. - **§1267**
Student, The - **§710**
Stultz v. Benson Lumber Co. - **§947**
Suess v. Arrowhead Steel Products Co. - **§858**
Suiter v. Epperson - **§597**
Sullivan v. Baptist Memorial Hospital - **§1365**
Sullivan v. Conway - **§1418**
Sullivan v. Delta Air Lines, Inc. - **§1153**
Summers v. Tice - **§§425, 440**
Suter v. San Angelo Foundry & Machine Co. - **§1057**
Swajian v. General Motors Corp. - **§832**
Sweeney v. Prisoners' Legal Services of New York, Inc. - **§1525**
Swick v. Liautaud - **§1765**
Swinton Creek Nursery v. Edisto Farm Credit - **§1569**

T

T.J. Hooper, The - **§389**
Tacket v. General Motors Corp. - **§1373**
Taco Bell, Inc. v. Lannon - **§707**
Tafoya v. Sears Roebuck & Co. - **§1042**
Tallbull v. Whitney - **§306**
Tameny v. Atlantic Richfield Co. - **§1723**
Taneian v. Meghrigian - **§751**
Tarasoff v. Regents of the University of California - **§557**
Tavarez v. Lelakis - **§565**
Taylor v. Metzger - **§§80, 93**
Taylor v. Superior Court - **§530**
Tedla v. Ellman - **§406**
Teel v. May Department Stores Co. - **§§158, 164**
Teeter v. Missouri Highway & Transportation Commission - **§1171**
Teeters v. Frost - **§116**
Temple Community Hospital v. Superior Court - **§1789**
Templeton Feed & Grain v. Ralston Purina Co. - **§1796**
Tennessee v. Garner - **§175**
Tenney v. Brandhove - **§1454**
Tenuto v. Lederle Laboratories - **§557**
Texas & Pacific Railway v. Behymer - **§389**
Tharp v. Bunge Corp. - **§§705, 721**
Theran v. Rokoff - **§1457**
Thing v. La Chusa - **§§773, 775, 777**
Thomas v. Atlantic Coast Line Railroad - **§849**
Thomas v. Holliday - **§840**
Thomas v. Jacksonville Television, Inc. - **§1405**
Thomas v. Siddiqui - **§1208**
Thompson v. Fox - **§479**
Thompson v. McNeill - **§338**
Thompson v. Thompson - **§1211**
Thorne v. Deas - **§572**
Tiderman v. Fleetwood Homes - **§1034**
Time, Inc. v. Firestone - **§§1515, 1542**
Time, Inc. v. Hill - **§1608**
Timperley v. Chase Collection Service - **§1569**
Tobia v. Cooper Hospital University Medical Center - **§797**
Tobkin v. Jarboe - **§1457**
Toney v. Kawasaki Heavy Industries, Ltd. - **§969**
Torres v. Goodyear Tire & Rubber Co. - **§1003**
Trahan-Laroche v. Lockheed Sanders, Inc. - **§608**

Tratchel v. Essex Group, Inc. - **§803**
Travel Masters, Inc. v. Star Tours, Inc. - **§1714**
Travis v. Moore - **§1127**
Trentacost v. Brussel - **§486**
Treyball v. Clark - **§1304**
Triestram v. Way - **§284**
Trimarco v. Klein - **§387**
Tucker v. Marcus - **§838**
Tunkl v. Regents of the University of California - **§848**
Turner v. International Harvester Co. - **§1000**
Tuttle v. Buck - **§1746**
Tyler, City of v. Likes - **§780**

U

Uccello v. Laudenslayer - **§753**
Udseth v. United States - **§377**
Uhr v. East Greenbush Central School District - **§549**
Ultramares Corp. v. Touche - **§§1664, 1665**
Union Oil Co. v. Oppen - **§1756**
Union Park Memorial Chapel v. Hutt - **§565**
United Insurance Co. of America v. Murphy - **§1443**
United States v. - *see* name of party
Upham's Case - **§480**
Uranga v. Federated Publications, Inc. - **§1585**

V

Valasek v. Baer - **§1134**
Valenti v. NET Properties Management, Inc. - **§620**
Van Arsdale v. Hollinger - **§626**
Vandenburg v. Newsweek, Inc. - **§1392**
Vandermark v. Ford Motor Co. - **§§993, 1065**
Vaughan v. Menlove - **§282**
Vaughn v. General Motors Corp. - **§1049**
Veeder v. Kennedy - **§§1202, 1203**
Venezia v. Miller Brewing Co. - **§1031**
Verhoeks v. Gillivan - **§1254**
Vesely v. Sager - **§642**
Villareal v. Arizona Department of Transportation - **§1185**
Vince v. Wilson - **§§341, 598**
Vincent v. Lake Erie Transportation Co. - **§266**
Virgil v. Time, Inc. - **§§1573, 1583**
Volk v. Baldazo - **§1192**
Volkswagen of America, Inc. v. Young - **§968**
Voorhees v. Preferred Mutual Insurance Co. - **§866**
Vulcan Metals Co. v. Simmons Manufacturing Co. - **§1648**

WX

Wagenblast v. Odessa School District - **§848**
Wagner v. International Railway - **§328**
Wagon Mound No. 1 - **§§470, 471, 497, 507, 509**
Waldbaum v. Fairchild Publications, Inc. - **§§1513, 1514**
Walker v. Mart - **§1200**
Wallace v. Rosen - **§102**
Wallis v. Superior Court - **§1722**
Wallulis v. Dymowski - **§1359**
Ward v. Forrester Day Care, Inc. - **§380**
Ward v. Silverberg - **§1765**
Ward v. Zelikovsky - **§1420**
Wardlow v. City of Keokuk - **§1161**
Warner-Lambert Co. v. Execuquest Corp. - **§1547**
Washington Water Power Co. v. Graybar Electric Co. - **§1050**
Waste Distillation Technology, Inc. v. Blasland & Bouck Engineers, P.C. - **§1701**
Watson, United States v. - **§165**
Weenig v. Wood - **§1468**
Weinberg v. Dinger - **§581**
Weirum v. RKO General, Inc. - **§346**
Weiss v. Axler - **§383**
Welch v. Outboard Marine Corp. - **§972**
Welge v. Planters Lifesavers Co. - **§960**
Wells, Estate of v. Mount Sinai Medical Center - **§1181**
Wells v. Storey - **§311**
Welsh v. Bulger - **§607**
Wendland v. Sparks - **§437**
Wendt v. Host International, Inc. - **§1594**
Wentling v. Medical Anesthesia Services - **§1164**
Wernke v. Halas - **§1126**
West v. Caterpillar Tractor Co. - **§§1063, 1098**
Western Union Telegraph Co. v. Hill - **§29**
Weston Paper Co. v. Pope - **§1145**
Wheeler v. Bagley - **§833**
Wheeler v. Green - **§1448**
Wheeler v. Luhman - **§1204**
Wheeler v. Raybestos-Manhattan - **§432**
Whitby v. Associates Discount Corp. - **§§1395, 1424**
White v. Inbound Aviation - **§597**
White v. Quechee Lakes Landowners' Association - **§1262**
White v. Samsung Electronics America, Inc. - **§1594**
White Lighting Co. v. Wolfson - **§§1792, 1795**
Whitehead v. Food Max of Mississippi, Inc. - **§828**
Whitehead v. Toyota Motor Corp. - **§1058**
Whiteside v. Lukson - **§316**
Whitman v. Atchison Topeka & Santa Fe Railway - **§110**
Whitman Hotel Corp. v. Elliott & Watrous Engineering Co. - **§915**
Whitney v. Northwest Greyhound Lines, Inc. - **§371**
Whittaker v. Sandford - **§73**
Widmyer v. Southeast Skyways, Inc. - **§290**
Wildstein v. New York Post Corp. - **§1392**
Wilk v. Georges - **§705**
Wilkinson v. Downton - **§90**
Williams v. Baker - **§771**
Williams v. Cunningham Drug Stores, Inc. - **§707**
Williams v. Fischer - **§1460**
Williams v. Ford Motor Co. - **§1038**

Williams v. Marion Rapid Transit - **§1189**
Williams v. New York Rapid Transit - **§391**
Williams v. Steuart Motor Co. - **§945**
Williamson v. Waldman - **§768**
Wilson v. Interlake Steel Co. - **§1109**
Wilson v. Kuenzi - **§1193**
Wilson v. Seiter - **§1242**
Winslow v. Hammer - **§632**
Winstead v. Sweeney - **§§1573, 1577**
Winterbottom v. Wright - **§926**
Withrow v. Becker - **§531**
Wolston v. Reader's Digest Association - **§1515**
Womack v. Eldridge - **§86**
Wood v. Strickland - **§1244**
Woods v. Luertzing Corp. - **§1021**
Woolley v. Henderson - **§312**
Wright v. Creative Corp. - **§939**
Wright v. Moffitt - **§645**
Wynne v. Orcutt Union School District - **§1581**

Y

Yaklevich v. Kemp, Schaeffer & Rowe Co. - **§1792**
Ybarra v. Spangard - **§373**
York v. Day's, Inc. - **§811**
Younce v. Ferguson - **§718**
Young v. Paxton - **§690**
Youst v. Longo - **§1750**
Yuhas v. Mudge - **§1006**
Yukon Equipment, Inc. v. Fireman's Fund Insurance Co. - **§904**

Z

Zacchini v. Scripps-Howard Broadcasting Co. - **§1599**
Zamarello v. Yale - **§1705**
Zaslow v. Kroenert - **§221**
Zavala v. Regents of the University of California - **§830**
Zehr v. Haugen - **§1194**
Zelenko v. Gimbel Bros. - **§560**
Zeliff v. Sabatino - **§1681**
Zelik v. Daily News Publishing Co. - **§1397**
Zentz v. Coca-Cola Bottling Co. - **§372**
Zeran v. America Online, Inc. - **§1379**
Zicherman v. Korean Air Lines Co. - **§1321**
Zichichi v. Middlesex Memorial Hospital - **§§1020, 1081**
Zikely v. Zikely - **§1219**
Zimmerman v. Ausland - **§531**
Zuchowicz v. United States - **§416**
Zurla v. Hydel - **§338**

Index

A

ABATEMENT OF NUISANCE
See Nuisance

ABNORMALLY DANGEROUS ACTIVITIES
See Strict liability

ABUSE OF PROCESS, §§1791-1796. *See also* Malicious prosecution

ACT BY DEFENDANT
assault, **§§28-31**
battery, **§§2-5**
conversion, **§217**
defamation, **§§1360-1361**
extreme or outrageous conduct, **§§80-85**
false imprisonment, **§55**
in general, **§§2, 28, 55, 1118-1121**
misconduct, effect on privilege, **§§274-275**
misfeasance and nonfeasance, **§§339-346, 572**
misrepresentation, **§§1624-1636**
negligence, **§279**
nuisance, **§§1118-1119**
omission to act, **§279.** *See also* Negligence
reflex actions, **§4**
trespass to chattels, **§207**
trespass to land, **§183**
unconscious acts, **§3**
volition required, **§§2, 28, 183, 207, 211, 279**
words alone, **§§29-30, 56, 80.** *See also* Defamation

ACT OF GOD
as intervening force, **§§455, 485, 489**
carriers, negligence of concurring with, **§499**
chattels, movement of, **§§246-249**
threats of harm from, **§41**

ACTUAL CAUSE
alternative liability, **§§423-432**
    market share liability, **§§427-432**
"but for" rule, **§§416, 422**
cause in fact, **§415**
concurrent liability, **§§418-420, 422**
defamation, **§1422**
defendant's conduct as, **§§415-416**
jointly engaged tortfeasors, **§419**
multiple sufficient causes, **§§421-422**
plaintiff deprived of proof, **§§440-441**
probability of loss to plaintiff, **§§436-439**
risk of future harm, **§§433-435**
strict liability, **§918**
"substantial factor" rule, **§§421-422**
successive tortfeasors, **§420**

AERONAUTICS
international plane crashes, **§§1319-1321**
negligence may apply, **§907**
nuisance, flight through airspace, **§201**
res ipsa loquitur, **§382**
strict liability for ground damage, **§§906, 908**
trespass, flight through airspace, **§§196-201**

ALIENATION OF AFFECTIONS
See Interference with family relationships

ANIMALS
domestic, liability for, **§§882-888**
    known dangerous traits, **§§884, 886**
    normally dangerous animals, **§885**
    unknown dangerous traits, **§§887-888**
    vicious watchdogs, **§896**
invitees and licensees, injury to, **§894**
strict liability for, **§§882-884, 886**
trespassers, injury to, **§§895-897**
    foreseeable trespassers, **§897**
trespassing, **§882**
    consequences, liability for, **§§882, 891**
watchdog, defense of property by, **§896**
wild, strict liability for, **§§889-892**
    kept under a public duty, **§892**

ARREST
by private citizen, **§§165-166, 171, 173**
entry upon land to, **§178**
false. *See* False imprisonment
force in making, **§§171-177**
    deadly force, **§§172-177**
misconduct following, **§179**
resisting, **§180**
with a warrant, **§§168-170**
without a warrant
    for felony, **§165**

for misdemeanor, §§166-167

ASSAULT
See also Battery
apprehension of battery
apparent ability to touch, **§§50-51**
awareness of plaintiff, **§36**
harm, nature of, **§§38-40**
imminence of harm, **§§42-46**
in general, **§35**
nature of plaintiff's, **§§47-51**
source of harm, **§41**
threats, **§§29-31, 36-46.** *See also* Threats
battery distinguished, **§37**
causation, **§52**
character of defendant's act, **§§28-31.** *See also* Act by defendant
criminal assault distinguished, **§51**
damages, **§53**
emotional distress compared, **§§31, 39, 44, 89**
intent required, **§§32-33**
prima facie case, **§27**
transferred intent, **§§10, 32**

ASSUMPTION OF RISK
appreciation of danger, **§854**
comparative negligence, relation to, **§859**
consortium, loss of, as defense to, **§1186**
contributory negligence, relation to, **§§860-864**
exculpatory clauses, **§§842-849**
adhesion contracts, **§§845-848**
intentional torts, **§849**
public policy, **§§847-848**
express agreement, **§§842-849**
firefighter's rule, **§841**
general rule, **§§839-841**
implied acceptance of risk, **§§850-857**
abolition of, **§§860-864**
knowledge of risk, **§§851-854**
negligent misrepresentation, as defense to, **§1676**
nuisance, as defense to, **§§1142-1143**
primary and secondary—minority view, **§§862-864**
products liability, as defense to, **§§951, 1059-1064**
statutorily protected class, **§858**
strict liability
defense to, **§§922-924**
misrepresentation, defense to, **§1676**
voluntary acceptance of risk, **§§855-858**
warranty, as defense to breach of, **§1099**
wrongful death, as defense to, **§1168**

ATTRACTIVE NUISANCE DOCTRINE
See Trespassers

AUTOMOBILES
accident, duty to aid person involved in, **§556**
bailors' vicarious liability, **§§601-603**
"crashworthiness," **§965**
duty to maintain, **§619**
failure to wear seat belts in, **§§535-537, 832**
family purpose doctrine, **§602**
guests. *See also* Guest statutes
common law rule, **§588**
sharing expenses, **§590**
joint enterprise. *See* Joint enterprise
liability insurance. *See* Liability insurance, effect of
negligent entrustment, **§§597-599**
owner, vicarious liability of, **§§601-603, 619**
permissive use statutes, **§603**
recall cases, **§1045**

AVIATION
See Aeronautics

AVOIDABLE CONSEQUENCES
anticipatory, **§§534-537**
comparative negligence, under, **§831**
seat belts, failure to wear, **§§535-537, 832**
contributory negligence distinguished, **§791**
damages aggravated by, **§§531-538**

B

BAILMENTS
automobiles
family purpose doctrine, **§602**
permissive use statutes, **§603**
contributory negligence, imputed, **§811**
conversion, **§§223, 226-228**
negligence
chattels, defective, **§§604, 758**
commercial bailor, liability of, **§§760-761**
gratuitous bailor, liability of, **§759**
liability of bailor to bailee, **§604**
liability of bailor to third persons, **§§593-600, 598-599, 604**
negligent entrustment, **§§597-599**
strict liability, **§994**
trespass to chattels, action for, **§§210-211, 213-215**
warranties, **§1077**

BATTERY
See also Assault
causation, **§§17-18**
character of defendant's act, **§§2-5.** *See also* Act by defendant
damages, **§§19-26**
punitive damages factors, **§§23-26**
harmful or offensive touching, **§§11-16**
intent required, **§§6-10**
physicians and surgeons
consent, lack of, **§112**
plaintiff's awareness, **§16**
prima facie case, **§1**
products liability, **§§929-930**
transferred intent, **§10**

BURDEN OF PROOF
See Evidence

BUSINESS VISITORS
See Invitees

C

CARRIERS
See also Negligence
abnormally dangerous cargo, §**909**. *See also* Strict liability
duty of due care, §§**290, 582-586**
duty to aid passenger in peril, §§**553-555**
insult, liability for, §**83**
negligence concurring with act of God, §**499**

CAUSATION
See Actual cause; Proximate cause

CHARITIES
immunity from tort action, §§**1248-1251**

CHATTELS
See also Conversion; Products liability; Recapture of chattels; Trespass to chattels
privilege to exclude or evict trespassing, §§**252-253**

CHILDREN
See also Parent and child; Wrongful birth
consent to tort, incapacity to, §**114**
duty toward. *See* Trespassers, attractive nuisance doctrine
negligence
- engaging in adult activity, §**294**
- minimum age statutes, §§**292-293**
- standard of conduct for, §§**291-294**

prenatal injuries, §§**1188-1192**
trespassers. *See* Trespassers
wrongful birth, §§**1193-1200**
wrongful death, §§**1163, 1192**

CIVIL RIGHTS ACT OF 1871, §§1241-1247

COLLATERAL SOURCES RULE, §§539-544, 1303, 1344-1348

COMPARATIVE NEGLIGENCE
absent parties, §**822**
apportionment of damages, §§**815-822**
avoidable consequences under, §§**538, 831-832**
consortium, loss of, as defense to, §**1186**
effect on
- contribution, §**1260**
- drunk drivers, §**836**
- imputed negligence, §**834**
- jury instructions, §**833**
- rescuers, §**835**
- res ipsa loquitur, §**837**
- punitive damages, §**838**

in general, §**815**
last clear chance doctrine under, §**824**
multiple defendants, §**821**
nuisance, §**1141**
partial, §§**818-822**
products liability, as defense to, §§**951, 1057-1058**
pure, §**817**
strict liability, as defense to, §§**921, 1057-1058**
wanton or reckless conduct, effect of, §§**825-830**
- intentional act and other person's negligence, §§**827-829**
- intentional torts, §**826**
- reckless plaintiff, §**830**
- warranty, as defense to breach of, §**1098**

wrongful death, as defense to, §§**1168, 1170**

CONFINEMENT
See False imprisonment

CONSENT, AS DEFENSE TO INTENTIONAL TORTS
by conduct, §**102**
conduct or custom, implied by, §§**102-103, 237**
criminal acts, to, §§**115-118**
duress, effect of, §**108**
exceeding, §**105**
express, §**103**
fraud, effect of, §§**106-107**
incapacity to, §**114**
informed, §**113**
in general, §§**100, 237**
invasion of land and chattels, §**237**
lack of, §**100**
law, implied by, §**103**
mistake, §§**109-113**
surgery, §§**112-113**

CONSORTIUM
See Husband and wife

CONSTITUTIONAL PRIVILEGE
See Defamation; Privacy

CONTRACT
interference with. *See* Interference with contract
misfeasance, §§**577-579**
negligence
- breach of contract, relation to, §§**575-579**
- liability of contractor to third parties, §**580**

nonfeasance, §**576**
promise, breach of as negligence, §**578**
tort liability to third persons, §§**580-581**
warranty. *See* Warranty, liability based on breach of

CONTRIBUTION
See also Joint torts
indemnity distinguished, §**1264**
joint tortfeasors, §§**1258-1259**
- comparative negligence, impact of, §**1260**

negligence cases, §**1259**

CONTRIBUTORY NEGLIGENCE
assumption of risk, relation to, §§**859-861**
avoidable consequences distinguished, §**791**
common law—absolute bar, §§**802-803**
comparative negligence. *See* Comparative negligence
consortium, loss of, as defense to, §§**810, 1186**

defense only to negligence, **§803**
defined, **§791**
effect of, **§§802-803**
imputed, **§807**
bailments, **§811**
consortium, loss of, **§810**
employer and employee, **§808**
husband and wife, **§§812-814**
family purpose cases, **§811**
recovery as community property, **§814**
joint enterprise, **§809**
wrongful death, **§810**
intentional torts, no defense to, **§803**
last clear chance doctrine, **§§804-806**
helpless peril, **§805**
inattentive peril, **§806**
mentally disabled, standard of conduct, **§300**
negligent misrepresentation, as defense to, **§1675**
negligent nuisance, as defense to, **§1139**
prima facie case, **§§792-801**
products liability, as defense to, **§§951, 1057**
standards of care, **§§793-801**
children, **§795**
emergencies, **§794**
in general, **§793**
statutory, **§§798-801**
strict liability, no defense to, **§§920, 1054-1056**
violation of statute by plaintiff, **§§798-801**
wrongful death, as defense to, **§§810, 1168, 1170-1171**

CONVERSION

bailee
misdelivery, **§226**
unauthorized use, **§223**
causation, **§231**
character of defendant's act, **§217**. *See also* Act by defendant
damages, **§§233-236**
demand, requirement of, **§227**
destruction or alteration, **§222**
dispossession, **§220**
fraud, acquisition of chattel by, **§220**
intent, **§218**
invasion, sufficiency of, **§§219-229**
multiple conversions, **§229**
possession, necessity of, **§230**
prima facie case, **§216**
remedies, **§§232-236**
stolen property bought or sold, **§§224-225**
strict liability, **§218**
surrender, refusal to, **§§227-228**
trespass to chattels compared, **§§221, 236**

COVENANT NOT TO SUE, §1257
See also Joint torts

CRIME

foreseeable criminal acts, **§486**
proximate cause, intervening criminal acts, **§§486, 490-491**
victim compensation, **§§1316-1318**

CUSTOM

consent by, **§§102-103, 237**
effect of in negligence cases, **§§385-392**
physicians and surgeons, **§§303-310**

D

DAMAGES

ad damnum clauses, **§1341**
additur and remittitur, **§1342**
arbitration of, **§1351**
assault, **§53**
avoidable consequences, **§§531-538**
battery, **§§19-26**
collateral sources, **§§539-544, 1303, 1344-1348**
comparative negligence. *See* Comparative negligence
compensatory, **§§511, 1134**
conversion, **§§233-236**
defamation, **§§1423-1450, 1530, 1540-1543**
economic loss rule, **§§789-790**
emotional distress. *See* Emotional distress
false imprisonment, **§§77-78**
general
battery, **§21**
libel, **§1443**
negligence, **§§522-527**
slander, **§§1431-1432**
injurious falsehood, **§§1699-1701**
interference with contract, **§§1726-1728**
joint and several liability, **§§1330-1333**
joint torts, **§§1252-1261**
malicious prosecution, **§1775**
misrepresentation, **§§1654, 1678-1683**
modern limitations, **§§1334-1343**
negligence, **§§510-544**
nuisance, as remedy for, **§§1134-1136**
parasitic, **§763**
personal property, destruction of, **§528**
privacy, invasion of, **§§1560, 1587, 1601, 1611**
products liability
intentional acts, **§930**
negligence, **§§949-950**
strict liability, **§§1048-1053**
public nuisance, necessity of particular damages, **§§1110-1112**
punitive
assault, **§53**
battery, **§§23-26**
caps, **§§1337-1340**
constitutional limitation, **§1336**
defamation, **§§1445-1448, 1543**
free speech concerns, **§§98-99**
intent as basis of, **§9**

malicious prosecution, **§1775**
misrepresentation, **§1683**
negligence, not recoverable for, **§529**
nuisance, willful, **§1136**
products liability, **§§930, 950**
reckless conduct as basis of, **§530**
special
battery, **§22**
defamation, **§1430**
false imprisonment, **§§77-78**
injurious falsehood, **§§1699-1701**
insurer, against, **§874**
libel, **§§1443-1444**
negligence, **§§512-521**
privacy, invasion of, **§§1601, 1611**
slander, **§§1429-1430**
slander of title, **§1700**
slander per se, no proof required, **§§1434-1442**
trade libel, **§1701**
trespass
to chattels, **§215**
to land, **§§204-205**
tavernkeepers, **§§645-649**
warranty, breach of, **§1097**
wrongful death, **§§1158-1167**

DANGEROUS THINGS AND ACTIVITIES

See Strict liability

DEATH

See Survival of tort actions; Wrongful death

DECEIT

See Misrepresentation

DEFAMATION

basis for liability, **§§1353-1358**
broadcasting
libel or slander, **§1427**
political broadcast, **§§1494-1495**
burden of proof, **§§1414-1415, 1523, 1539**
causation, **§1422**
colloquium, **§§1397-1399**
community standards, **§1383**
consent as defense to, **§1451**
constitutional privileges
damages, limitations on, **§§1446-1448, 1530, 1540-1543**
First Amendment, **§§1354, 1388, 1410, 1413-1414, 1446, 1450, 1503, 1528**
Gertz v. Robert Welch, Inc., **§§1446, 1504, 1512, 1516, 1531-1536, 1541, 1543**
knowing or reckless falsity, **§§1479, 1517-1530, 1532, 1543**
New York Times Co. v. Sullivan, **§§1497, 1503-1504, 1508, 1517-1518, 1523, 1530, 1537, 1543**
officers and candidates, **§§1460, 1483, 1494-1495**
private persons, **§§1530-1543**
public concern, matters of, **§§1446, 1448, 1501-1502, 1532-1539**
public figures, **§§1505, 1512-1530**
public officials, **§§1413, 1508-1511, 1517-1530**
scope of, **§§1503-1543**
corporations, defamation of, **§1400**
damages
emotional, **§1433**
general, **§§1431-1432**
in general, **§1423**
libel, **§§1443-1448**
private persons, **§§1533-1534, 1540-1543**
public figures, **§1530**
punitive, **§§1445-1448, 1543**
slander, **§§1429-1442**
special, **§1430**
dead, defamation of the, **§§1402-1404**
defined, **§§1380-1395**
emotional distress, infliction of, interrelation with, **§§1356, 1433**
fact, statement of, **§§1416-1421**
falsity, **§§1409-1421**
burden of proof, plaintiff's, **§§1414-1415**
defendant's knowledge of, **§1410**
opinion vs. facts, **§§1416-1419**
public debate, **§1420**
truth is complete defense, **§§1411-1413, 1452**
group defamations, **§§1401, 1405-1407**
harm to reputation, **§§1380-1395**
"libel-proof plaintiffs," **§§1387-1388**
strict liability, **§1408**
implication and insinuation, **§§1393-1395**
inducement, **§1395**
innocent, **§1394**
innuendo, **§1395**
intent required, **§1362**
interpretation, **§§1389-1407**
labor disputes, **§1496**
libel
broadcasting, **§§1427-1428**
defined, **§1424**
per quod, **§1444**
proof of general damages not required, **§§1443-1444**
proof of special damages required, **§§1429, 1443-1444**
retraction, **§1449**
slander distinguished, **§§1425-1426**
negligence, liability based on, **§§1362, 1532, 1536**
"of and concerning" the plaintiff, **§§1396-1407**
opinion, statement of, **§§1417, 1419**
prima facie case, **§1352**
privacy, invasion of, interrelation with, **§1356**
privilege
absolute, **§§1453-1461**
abuse of conditional, **§§1475-1482**
conditional, **§§1462-1482**

consent, §**1451**
constitutional. *See* constitutional privileges, above
excessive publication, §§**1480-1482**
executive communication, §§**1460, 1463, 1486**
fair comment, §§**1483-1485**
federal preemption, §§**1493-1497**
husband and wife, §**1461**
judicial proceedings, §§**1456-1459**
labor disputes, §**1496**
legislative proceedings, §§**1454-1455**
loss of privilege, §§**1475-1482**
malice, §§**1445, 1453, 1478-1479, 1517-1530**
motive, §**1478**
political broadcasts, §§**1494-1495**
private protectable interests, §§**1464-1472**
public interest, §§**1473-1474**
records, §§**1486-1492**
self-defense, §**1470**
statutory, §§**1493-1497**
truth, §**1452**
publication
disseminators, §§**1376-1379**
distributors, §**1368**
intent or negligence, §**1362**
intracorporate publication rule, §**1359**
manner of, §§**1360-1361**
negligence, §§**1362-1365**
original publishers, §§**1367-1369**
overheard communication, §**1364**
republishers, §§**1370-1375**
defenses, §§**1498-1501**
legal duty to, §**1375**
to third person required, §§**1357-1359**
vicarious liability, §**1369**
related torts, §**1356**
retraction, §**1449**
slander
business, profession, or office, §§**1438-1439**
crime, imputation of, §§**1435-1436**
defined, §**1425**
disease, imputation of, §**1437**
emotional damages, §**1433**
general damages, §§**1431-1432**
impotency, imputation of, §**1441**
libel distinguished, §**1426**
per se, no proof of damages, §§**1434-1442**
retraction, §**1449**
special damages, §**1430**
unchastity, imputation of, §§**1440-1442**
SLAPP suits, §**1502**
strict liability, §**1408**
truth as defense to, §§**1411-1413, 1452**
Uniform Single Publication Act, §**1621**
unintended, §§**1364, 1399**
who may be defamed, §§**1400-1407**

DEFENSE OF OTHERS
force, use of, §§**137, 141**
mistake, §§**139-141**
privilege, in general, §**137**
who may be defended, §**138**

DEFENSE OF PROPERTY
See Property, defense of

DETENTION FOR INVESTIGATION
See Shopkeeper's privilege

DIRECT CAUSATION
See Proximate cause

DISCIPLINE, PRIVILEGE OF, §181

DISPARAGEMENT
See Injurious falsehood

DOGS
See Animals

DOMESTIC RELATIONS
See Husband and wife; Parent and child

DRAM SHOP ACTS, §§637-641, 1315
See also Intoxication; Negligence
Social hosts, §§**646-648**

DURESS, CONSENT OBTAINED UNDER, §108

DUTY
See Negligence

E

ECONOMIC RELATIONS
See Interference with economic relations

EMERGENCY
See also Necessity to invade land or chattels
effect of in negligence cases, §§**551-556**
medical treatment in, §§**314, 560-561, 566, 1314**

EMOTIONAL DISTRESS, INTENTIONAL INFLICTION OF
assault, distinguished from, §§**31, 39, 44, 89**
causation, §§**90-91**
character of defendant's act, §§**80-85**. *See also* Act by defendant
damages, §§**98-99**
defamation, interrelation with, §§**1356, 1433**
defenses, §§**94-97**
extreme or outrageous conduct, §§**80-85, 91**
harassment, claims of, §**84**
insult and indignity
carriers and public utilities, §**83**
general rule, §**80**
petty insults, §**82**
intent required, §§**86-89**
no transferred intent, §**88**
physical injury, requirement of, §§**90-91**
modern view—distress only, §**91**
prima facie case, §**79**
privacy, invasion of, interrelation with, §§**1356, 1619**
reckless conduct, §§**86-87**

severe emotional distress required, **§§92-93**
eggshell psyche rule, **§93**
special susceptibility of plaintiff, **§87**
third persons, liability to, **§85**
words may be sufficient, **§§31, 80**

EMOTIONAL DISTRESS, NEGLIGENT INFLICTION OF
acts directed at third person, **§§771-779**
bystander recovery, **§§771-779**
dead bodies, negligence toward, **§770**
false death reports, **§770**
impact, actual or threatened, **§§764-769**
AIDS cases, **§768**
mere exposure, **§767**
intentional infliction compared, **§766**
nature of duty owed, **§762**
parasitic damages for, **§763**
pet, death of, **§781**
physical manifestation, requirement of, **§§764-769, 782-784**
property, damage to, **§§779, 784**
recovery without impact, **§764**
severe emotional distress required, **§§785-788**
eggshell psyche rule, **§§786-788**

EMPLOYER AND EMPLOYEE
contributory negligence, imputed, **§§807-808**
duty of care to employee, **§553**
independent contractors. *See* Independent contractors
interference with relation. *See* Interference with contract
liability based on employer's negligence, **§§605-608**
vicarious liability
intentional torts, **§§611-612**
respondeat superior, **§§609-613**
scope of employment, **§§610-611**
workers' compensation, **§§1272-1284**

EVIDENCE
burden of proof
alternative liability, **§§423-432**
apportionment of damages, **§532**
colloquium, **§1397**
defamation per quod, **§1444**
plaintiff deprived of proof, **§§440-441**
products liability, **§§1035-1037**
causation in fact, proof, **§§415-441**
expert testimony, necessity of in malpractice, **§§367-368**
negligence
circumstantial evidence, **§§350-351**
direct evidence, **§§348-349**
presumptions, **§§382-384**
proof, **§§348-351**
res ipsa loquitur. *See* Res ipsa loquitur
spoilation of, **§§1788-1790**

F

FALSE IMPRISONMENT
arrest as, **§§74-75**
awareness of, **§64**
barriers to escape, **§§71-73**
causation, **§76**
character of defendant's act, **§55**. *See also* Act by defendant
confinement, **§§60-75**
elements constituting, **§§60-63**
how caused, **§§65-75**
damages, **§§77-78**
intent required, **§§57-59**
transferred intent, **§59**
means of escape available, **§§62-63**
prima facie case, **§54**
threats, **§§67-70**

FAMILY RELATIONS
See Husband and wife; Parent and child

FAULT
See Strict liability

FEDERAL TORT CLAIMS ACT, §§1231-1234. *See also* Immunities

"FIREFIGHTER'S RULE," §841
See also Assumption of risk

FORESEEABILITY
See Negligence; Proximate cause

FRAUD
See Misrepresentation

G

GOVERNMENTAL IMMUNITIES, §§1222-1247
See also Immunities

GUEST STATUTES, §§589-590
See also Negligence

H

HUSBAND AND WIFE
alienation of affections, **§§1201-1203**
automobiles, family purpose doctrine, **§602**
consortium, loss of, **§§1172-1187**
assumption of risk as defense to, **§1186**
common law, **§§1172-1174**
comparative negligence as defense to, **§1186**
contributory negligence
as defense to, **§1186**
imputed, **§810**
death of spouse compared, **§1179**
husband's action, **§§1172, 1175**
joinder requirement, **§1187**
negligent spouse, no recovery against, **§1178**
scope of, **§§1176-1179**
wife's action, **§§1174-1175**
contributory negligence, imputed, **§810**
criminal conversation, **§§1207-1208**

defamation, immunity in, **§1461**
emotional distress claims, **§1210**
immunity in tort actions between, **§§1211-1213**
loss of services. *See* consortium, loss of, above

I

IMMUNITIES
armed forces, **§1233**
charities, **§§1248-1251**
Federal Tort Claims Act, **§§1231-1234**
governmental, **§§1222-1247**
government contractors, **§1234**
husband and wife, **§§1211-1213**
liability insurance and, **§1218**
municipal corporations, **§§1224-1227**
  governmental functions, **§§1224, 1226**
  proprietary functions, **§§1224, 1227**
parent and child, **§§1214-1220**
public officers
  agents, **§§1232, 1246-1247**
  Civil Rights Act of 1871, **§§1241-1247**
  discretionary acts, **§1239**
  ministerial acts, **§§1238, 1240**
  sovereign, **§§1222, 1228**
  superior and inferior officers, **§§1236-1237**

IMPUTED NEGLIGENCE
See Contributory negligence; Vicarious liability

INCOMPETENTS
consent to tort, incapacity to, **§114**
contributory negligence of, **§300**
liability for acts by, **§5**
standard of conduct, **§§299-300**

INDEMNITY
See also Joint torts
contribution distinguished, **§1264**
culpability, differing degrees of, **§§1265-1266**
in general, **§1262**
physician's negligent aggravation, **§1267**
vicarious liability, applied to, **§1263**

INDEPENDENT CONTRACTORS
apparent authority, **§617**
assumption of liability by building contractor, **§626**
collateral negligence, **§627**
health care providers, **§§621-623**
inherently dangerous activities, **§625**
negligence of the employer, **§614**
nondelegable duties, **§§618-626**
vicarious liability for torts, **§§614-627**

INDIRECT CAUSATION
See Proximate cause, indirect causation

INDUCING BREACH OF CONTRACT
See Interference with contract

INFANTS
See Children

INJURIOUS FALSEHOOD
business interests, as to, **§§1688-1691**
causation, **§1699**
competition, **§§1706-1709**
consent as defense to, **§1702**
constitutional protection, **§1709**
damages, **§§1699-1701**
disparagement of property, **§§1688-1691**
  defamation distinguished, **§§1693-1694**
in general, **§1684**
intent, necessity of, **§§1695-1698**
judicial proceedings, **§1705**
motive immaterial, **§1696**
nonbusiness relations, **§1692**
prima facie case, **§1684**
privileges, **§§1704-1709**
proof of falsity, **§1685**
protection of defendant's interests, **§§1706-1709**
publication required, **§§1686-1687**
scienter, **§1697**
slander of title, **§§1689, 1700**
special damages required, **§1699**
trade libel, **§§1690-1691, 1701**
truth as defense to, **§1703**

INSANITY
See Incompetents

INSULTS
See also Emotional distress, intentional infliction of
carriers, **§83**
liability for, **§82**
public utilities, **§83**

INSURANCE
See Liability insurance, effect of

INTENT
abuse of process, **§1791**
assault, **§§32-34**
battery, **§§6-10**
consequences substantially certain to follow, **§7**
conversion, **§218**
emotional distress, **§§86-89**
false imprisonment, **§§57-59**
injurious falsehood, **§§1695-1698**
interference with contract, **§§1724-1725**
malice distinguished, **§9**
misrepresentation, **§§1637-1641**
motive immaterial to, **§9**
nuisance, **§§1118-1121**
privacy, invasion of, **§§1553-1555**
products liability, **§§929-930**
punitive damages based on, **§§9, 23**
test of, **§§7, 33**
transferred, **§§10, 34, 57, 88, 187, 209**
trespass to chattels, **§208**
trespass to land, **§§184, 187**

INTENTIONAL TORTS
See Assault; Battery; Conversion; Emotional distress, intentional infliction of; False imprisonment; Trespass to chattels; Trespass to land

INTERFERENCE WITH CONTRACT
breach not required, **§1717**
burden of proof, **§1740**
causation, **§1726**
collective action, **§1718**
damages, **§§1726-1728**
defendant's interest, protection of, **§§1733-1736**
employer and employee, **§§1722, 1725**
illegal contracts, **§1713**
illegal means, **§§1737-1739**
intent to interfere, **§§1716, 1724-1725**
nature of contract, **§1712**
negligent interference, **§1724**
prima facie case, **§1711**
privilege, **§§1729-1739**
public interest, action in, **§§1731-1732**
related actions, **§§1721-1723, 1739**
terminable at will, **§§1715, 1723, 1736**
unenforceable contracts, **§1714**
who may be sued, **§§1719-1723**

INTERFERENCE WITH ECONOMIC RELATIONS
See also Interference with contract; Interference with prospective advantage
in general, **§1710**
labor unions, **§1718**

INTERFERENCE WITH FAMILY RELATIONSHIPS
alienation of affections, **§§1201-1206**
  common law, **§1201**
  parent-child claims, **§§1204-1206**
criminal conversation, **§§1207-1208**
custodial rights, interference with, **§1209**

INTERFERENCE WITH PROSPECTIVE ADVANTAGE
in general, **§§1710, 1741**
intentional interference, **§§1741-1750**
  prima facie case, **§§1742-1743**
negligent interference, **§§1751-1757**
  prima facie case, **§1751**
noncommercial expectancies, **§§1748-1750**
privilege, **§§1745-1747**

INTERVENING FORCES
See Proximate cause

INTOXICATION
as negligence, **§§298, 530**
Dram Shop Acts, **§§637-642, 1315**
liability of social host, **§§646-648**
liability of tavernkeeper, **§§636-649**
  as land occupier, **§649**
  to patron, **§§636-645**
  to third parties, **§§636-644**
standard of conduct for voluntary, **§298**

INVASION OF PRIVACY
See Privacy

INVITEES
animals, strict liability for, **§887**
area of invitation, **§703**
business visitors, **§§701-703**
change of status, **§703**
chattels supplied to, **§710**
defined, **§§696-699**
duty required toward, **§§704-710**
duty to inspect, **§§704-706**
entrants on another's land, duty of, **§§722-724**
liability of occupier to, **§§696, 718**
liability of third person to, **§§722-723**
minority view—status irrelevant, **§§718-720**
obvious dangers, **§721**
protection against third person crime, **§§707-709**
public entrants, **§§711-716**
public invitees, **§§697-699**
recreational lands, **§717**
strict liability to, **§887**

J

JOINT ENTERPRISE
automobile trips, **§§630-632**
common purpose, **§629**
contributory negligence, imputed, **§809**
extension beyond business purposes, **§632**
mutual right of control, **§629**
vicarious liability, **§628**

JOINT TORTS
concurrent liability, **§§418-420, 422**
contribution, **§§1258-1261**
  comparative negligence, impact of, **§1260**
  indemnity distinguished, **§1264**
  negligence cases, **§1259**
covenant not to sue, **§1257**
indemnity, **§§1262-1266**
joint and several liability, **§§1330-1333**. *See also* Damages
joint tortfeasors, **§§1252-1253**
judgment, **§1254**
release of one releasing others, **§§1255-1257**
satisfaction, **§1254**

K

KNOWLEDGE
assumption of risk, **§851**
defamation. *See* Defamation
last clear chance doctrine, **§§804-806**
lessors of defective condition, **§743**
special knowledge and skills, **§§301-319**
special vulnerability of plaintiff, **§787**

L

LAND, OWNERS AND OCCUPIERS OF
See also Property, defense of; Recovery of land
animals, duty as to. *See* Animals
defined, **§651**
duty to persons outside land, **§§653-659**
foreseeable risk, **§652**
general rules, **§650**
invitees. *See* Invitees
landlord and tenant. *See* Landlord, duties of
licensees. *See* Licensees
minority view—reasonable person, **§§718-720**
obvious dangers, **§721**
public entrants, **§§711-716**
public premises, duty to maintain, **§620**
recreational lands, **§717**
sellers of land. *See* Sellers of land
straying from highway, liability to one, **§§258-261**
tavernkeepers, **§649**
trespass. *See* Trespass
trespassers. *See* Trespassers

LANDLORD, DUTIES OF
agreement to repair, **§§738-744, 750**
  negligent repair, **§738**
concealment of condition, **§732**
control of common areas, **§§725, 751-752**
  foreseeable criminal acts, **§752**
dangerous activity by tenant, **§753**
latent dangers, **§§735-736, 748-749**
liability to third persons, **§§745-750**
limited, **§725**
patent dangers, **§734**
trespass to land, action for, **§§194-195**
to lessee
  after transfer, **§§737-744**
  danger at transfer, **§§733-736**
to persons outside land, **§§726-732**

LAST CLEAR CHANCE
See Contributory negligence

LEGAL AUTHORITY
See Arrest

LIABILITY INSURANCE, EFFECT OF
collateral sources rule, **§§539-544**
  statutory restrictions, **§§1344-1348**
"no fault" insurance, **§§1285-1296**
  black lung compensation, **§1323**
  damages recoverable, **§1291**
  essential provisions, **§§1287-1290**
  "first-party" basis, **§§877-879, 1290**
  impact of, **§§1292-1295**
  international plane crashes, **§§1319-1321**
  nuclear accidents, **§1322**
  scope of coverage, **§1289**
recovery of damages and, **§§539-544**
subrogation, **§§541-544**
"third-party" system, **§§865-879**
  cooperation clauses, **§870**
  "first party" insurance compared, **§§877-879**
  in general, **§§865-866**
  insurer
    direct actions against, **§868**
    liability, **§§867-869**
    third persons, no duty to, **§876**
  reckless conduct, **§869**
  settlements, **§§871-875**
    breach of duty, **§§873-875**
    duty of good faith regarding, **§§871-872**

LIABILITY WITHOUT FAULT
See Strict liability

LIBEL
See Defamation

LICENSEES
animals, strict liability for, **§893**
automobile guests, **§588**
defined, **§§689-691**
disclosure of known dangerous conditions, **§§692-694**
duty required toward, **§§692-695**
liability of occupier to, **§§692-695, 719**
liability of third person to, **§§722-724**
minority view—status irrelevant, **§§718-720**
obvious dangers, **§721**
persons included, **§§690-691**
private entrants, **§712**
public entrants, **§§711, 713-716**
recreational lands, **§717**
social guests, **§690**
strict liability to, **§894**

LIMITATIONS, STATUTE OF
negligence, **§§1268-1271**
strict tort liability, **§1067**
warranty actions, **§1106**

LOSS OF CONSORTIUM
See Husband and wife; Parent and child

M

MALICE
assault, **§33**
defamation
  conditional privilege in, **§§1478-1479**
  meaning in, **§§1517-1521**
injurious falsehood, **§1696**
intent distinguished, **§9**
malicious civil proceedings, **§1778**
malicious prosecution, **§1773**
punitive damages in cases of, **§§9, 1445, 1519**

MALICIOUS PROSECUTION
abuse of process, **§§1791-1796**
  prima facie case, **§1792**

who may sue, §**1796**
causation, §**1775**
civil proceedings, §§**1778-1786**
nature of proceedings, §§**1779-1782**
prior verdict, §**1783**
damages, §**1775**
false imprisonment distinguished, §**1760**
guilt as defense to, §**1776**
improper purpose, §§**1768, 1773-1774**
in general, §**1759**
instigation of proceedings, §§**1761-1763**
malicious defense, §**1787**
prima facie case, §**1759**
privileges, §**1777**
probable cause, lack of, §§**1766-1772**
advice of counsel, §**1772**
disposition of case as evidence, §§**1769-1771**
improper purpose, §**1768**
objective standard, §**1767**
spoilation of evidence, §§**1788-1790**
termination in favor of plaintiff, §§**1764-1765**

MANUFACTURERS
See Products liability

MASS MEDIA
See Defamation; Privacy

MASTER AND SERVANT
See Employer and employee

MEDICAL MALPRACTICE, §§**1297-1304**

MENTAL DISTRESS
See Emotional distress

MISFEASANCE
See Act by defendant; Contract; Negligence

MISREPRESENTATION
advertisements, §**1052**
damages, measure of, §§**1654, 1678-1683**
deceit. *See* intentional misrepresentation, below
defenses, §§**1675-1677**
economic interests protected, §**1622**
exculpatory contracts, §**1677**
innocent. *See* strict liability for, below
intentional misrepresentation, §§**1623-1654**
burden of proof, §**1639**
by conduct, §**1628**
causation, §**1642**
concealment, active, §**1629**
continuous deception, §**1641**
damages, necessity of, §**1654**
failure to disclose as, §§**1630-1636**
intent to deceive, §§**1637-1641**
materiality, §§**1624-1627**
negligence distinguished, §**1659**
nondisclosure. *See* Nondisclosure
prima facie case, §**1623**
promises, §§**1626-1627**
punitive damages, §**1683**
reliance, §§**1640-1641, 1643-1653**
intent to induce, §**1640**
justifiable, §§**1643-1653**
on statements of fact, §§**1645-1646**
on statements of law, §§**1652-1653**
on statements of opinion, §§**1647-1651**
scienter, §§**1637-1638**
substantial factor, §**1642**
negligent misrepresentation, §§**1655-1670**. *See also* Actual cause; Negligence; Proximate cause
assumption of risk as defense to, §**1676**
business capacity, §§**1656, 1659**
causation, §§**1669-1670**
contributory negligence as defense to, §**1675**
deceit distinguished, §**1661**
duty of due care, §**1659**
exculpatory contracts as defense to, §**1677**
persons protected, §§**1659-1669**
prima facie case, §**1655**
reliance, justifiable, §**1670**
statutory duties, §**1669**
pecuniary damages, limited to, §§**1622, 1674**
strict liability for, §§**1671-1674**. *See also* Products liability; Strict liability
assumption of risk as defense to, §**1676**
express warranty, breach of, §**1672**. *See also* Warranty, liability based on breach of
physical injuries, §**1674**
prima facie case, §**1673**
products liability compared, §**1674**

MISTAKE
consent given under, §§**109-113**
defense of others under, §§**139-141**
recapture of chattels under, §**151**
self-defense under, §**120**
shopkeeper's mistake, §**164**
trespass to land, §§**243, 251**

MORAL RESPONSIBILITY
See Proximate cause

MOTIVE
in tort law, §**9**
injurious falsehood, §**1696**
nuisance, as factor in, §§**1118-1121**

MUNICIPAL CORPORATIONS
Civil Rights Act of 1871 governmental functions, §§**1225-1226, 1241-1247**
immunity, §§**1224-1230.** *See also* Immunities
proprietary functions, §§**1224, 1227**

N

NAMES, APPROPRIATION OF, §§1590-1601
See also Privacy

NECESSITY TO INVADE LAND OR CHATTELS
damages inflicted under
  private necessity, **§§266-267**
  public necessity, **§260**
force used under, **§§257, 265**
media not privileged, **§262**
private necessity, **§§263-267**
public necessity, **§§254-261**

NEGLIGENCE
See also Actual cause; Proximate cause; Vicarious liability
acts and omissions, **§§279, 347**
assumption of risk. *See* Assumption of risk
automobiles. *See also* Automobiles
  guests, **§§587-590**
bailments, **§§593-604**
  negligent entrustment, **§§597-599**
balancing risk against utility of conduct, **§§352-359**
beginners, standard of conduct, **§302**
breach of duty, **§347**
  determined by judge vs. jury, **§§360-362**
  proof of, **§§348-351**
  res ipsa loquitur, **§363-384**. *See also* Res ipsa loquitur
  unreasonable conduct, **§§352-359**
burden of proof. *See* Evidence
causation. *See* Actual cause; Proximate cause
children
  engaging in adult activity, **§294**
  minimum age, **§§292-293**
  standard of conduct, **§§291-294**
circumstantial evidence of, **§§350-351**
comparative. *See* Comparative negligence
contract
  interference with, **§§1724-1725**
  liability to third parties, **§§580-581**
  misfeasance, **§577**
  nonfeasance, **§576**
  relation to gratuitous promises, **§575**
contractual relationships, **§577**
contributory. *See* Contributory negligence
controlling conduct of others, **§§557, 567-571, 591-592**
custom, **§§385-392**
damages
  amount recoverable. *See* Damages
  necessity of, **§510**
direct evidence of, **§349**
duty of due care, general, **§277**
  beginners, **§302**
  dangerous substances or instrumentalities, **§341**
  determined by court, **§280**
  failure to warn, **§343**
  foreseeability of plaintiff, **§§320-332**
  limitations on, **§§333-338**
  misfeasance and nonfeasance, **§§339-346**
    act vs. omission, **§§339-340**
    creation of risk, **§342**
    negligent entrustment, **§341**
    negligent misrepresentation, **§§344-345**
  Palsgraf v. Long Island Railroad, **§§321-326**
  profession or trade, **§§303-319**
    community standard, **§304**
  proximate cause compared, **§509**
  reasonable person standard, **§§281-291**
    children, **§291**
    common carriers, **§290**
    emergencies, **§§286-287**
    objective test, **§§282-283**
  rescuers, **§§327-332, 343, 551**
  special duty distinguished, **§288**
  special relationships, **§§553, 557**
  to whom owed, **§§320-346**
  unforeseeable plaintiff, **§§320-332**
duty of due care, special, **§277**
  auto driver, liability to guest, **§§587-590**
  carriers, **§§290, 582**
    to aid passenger, **§553**
    to protect passengers from harm, **§§582-586**
  controlling conduct of others, **§§557, 567-571, 591-592**
    bailor-bailee, **§§593-604**
    independent contractors, **§§614-627**
    master-servant, **§§605-613**
    parent-child, **§§633-635**
    partners and joint venturers, **§§628-632**
    tavernkeepers, **§§636-649**
  emergency, **§§551-566**
  employer to employee, **§553**
  family, **§553**
  general duty, in addition to, **§545**
  Good Samaritan obligation, **§§560-566, 1314**
  governmental entities, **§§569-570**
  landowners and occupiers. *See* Land, owners and occupiers of
  peril, to aid those in, **§§551-566, 1313**
  prevention of harm, **§§567-570**
  private enforcement action, **§§548-549**
  promise to aid, **§§560-566, 572-574**
    abandonment, **§561**
  statute, imposed by, **§§546-550, 556-557, 566, 570, 1313-1315**. *See also* Statute, violation of
  tavernkeepers, **§§636-649, 1315**
  voluntary assumption of care, **§568**
emergency, **§§286-287, 551-566**
employers. *See* Employer and employee
employers of independent contractors, **§§614-627**. *See also* Vicarious liability
gratuitous promises, **§§572-574**
in general, **§§276-277**
intoxication. *See* Intoxication
invitees. *See* Invitees

joint enterprises, **§§628-632**
landlord and tenant. *See* Landlord, duties of
lessors, repairs made by, **§738**
licensees. *See* Licensees
mental deficiency, standard of conduct, **§§299-300**
misfeasance, liability for, **§§339-346, 572-573, 577-580**
misrepresentation. *See* Misrepresentation
nonfeasance, liability for, **§§339-346, 572, 576**
nuisance predicated on, **§§1118-1120**
parental liability, **§§633-635**. *See also* Vicarious liability
per se, **§§395, 546-550, 644**. *See also* Statute, violation of
physically disabled, standard of conduct, **§§295-298**
voluntary intoxication compared, **§298**
physicians and surgeons
community standard, **§§306, 308-309**
consent in medical treatment, lack of informed, **§§311-319**
exceptions, **§§313-316**
failure to warn, **§§558-559**
Good Samaritan statutes, **§§560-566, 1314**
national standard, **§307**
statute of limitations, **§§1268-1271**
prenatal injuries, liability for, **§§1188-1200**
prima facie case, **§278**
products liability. *See* Products liability
proof, **§§348-351**
proximate cause. *See* Proximate cause
recklessness. *See* Reckless conduct
rescuers, duty owed to, **§§327-332**
res ipsa loquitur. *See* Res ipsa loquitur
special knowledge and skills, **§§301-319**
standard of conduct, **§§279-288**
beginners, **§302**
children, **§§291-294**
circumstances considered, **§284**
custom, effect of, **§§385-392**
intoxication, voluntary, **§298**
mentally impaired, **§§299-300**
physically disabled, **§§295-298**
statute, compliance with as due care, **§§393-414, 545**. *See also* Statute, violation of
statute of limitations, **§§1268-1271**
trespass to land, **§185**
trespassers. *See* Trespassers
vicarious liability. *See* Vicarious liability
violation of statute. *See* Statute, violation of
voluntary aid, **§§560-566, 568**
willful and wanton conduct. *See* Reckless conduct

NEWSPAPERS
See Defamation; Privacy

NONDISCLOSURE
See also Misrepresentation
ambiguous statements, **§1633**
confidential relation, **§1632**
duty to disclose, physicians', **§§311-319, 557-559**
lessors, **§§728, 735, 747**
new information, **§1634**
reliance, **§1635**
vendors, **§1636**

NONFEASANCE
See Act by defendant; Contract; Negligence

NUISANCE
abatement, **§§268-273, 1137**
abnormally dangerous activity as, **§§1120, 1141**
aesthetic considerations, **§§1126-1127**
funeral homes, **§1127**
assumption of risk as defense to, **§§1142-1149**
balancing harm vs. interests, **§1124**
business interest, interference with, **§1117**
causation, **§§1132-1133**
character of defendant's act, **§§1118-1121**. *See also* Act by defendant
coming to the nuisance, **§§1128, 1144-1149**
comparative negligence, **§1141**
consent, **§1143**
contributory negligence, **§§1121, 1138-1141**
damages as remedy for, **§§1134-1136**
continuing nuisance, **§1135**
injunction, relief by, **§1134**
negligence and, **§1120**
possession, necessity of, **§§1115-1116**
prima facie case, **§1107**
private nuisance, **§1108**
trespass distinguished, **§1109**
privilege to abate, **§§268-273, 1137**
demand required, **§270**
extent of, **§272**
owner or possessor, **§269**
public nuisance compared, **§273**
self-help, **§1137**
public nuisance, **§§1110-1112**
abatement of, **§273**
environmental damage, **§1112**
fast food, **§1113**
handguns, **§1113**
standing to sue, **§1111**
reasonable use, **§§1123-1125, 1130-1131**
aesthetics, **§§1126-1127**
coming to the nuisance, **§1128**
factors affecting, **§1125**
zoning ordinances, **§1129**
remedies, **§§1134-1137**
self-help, **§1137**
strict liability and, **§1120**
substantial interference, **§§1122-1123, 1130-1131**
unreasonable interference, **§§1122, 1124-1129**
zoning, effect of, **§1129**

O

OFFICERS
See also Arrest
defamation, privileges in
executive communications, **§1460**
judicial proceedings, **§§1456-1459**
legislative proceedings, **§§1454-1455**
Federal Tort Claims Act, **§§1231-1234**
immunities of
arrests, **§§165-168, 178**
Civil Rights Act of 1871, **§§1241-1247**
discretionary acts, **§1239**
ministerial acts, **§§1238, 1240**
superior and inferior officers, **§§1236-1240**
invitees, **§§711-716, 718-719**
licensees, **§§713-716, 718-719**
trespass ab initio, **§178**

OWNERS AND OCCUPIERS OF LAND
See Land, owners and occupiers of

PQ

PARENT AND CHILD
alienation of affections, **§§1204-1206**
automobiles, family purpose doctrine, **§602**
consortium, loss of, **§§1173-1174, 1181-1187**
child cannot recover, **§§1174, 1185**
defenses to, **§1186**
joinder requirement, **§1187**
custody, intentional interference with, **§1209**
discipline, **§181**
duty to control conduct of child, **§§633-634**
immunity in tort actions between, **§§1214-1220**
injury to parent, **§§1174, 1185**
loss of services. *See* consortium, loss of, above
negligence of parent, **§635**
vicarious liability for torts, **§§633-634**
wrongful birth, **§§1193-1200**
wrongful death, **§§1163, 1192**

PERIL
See also Negligence
contributory negligence and, **§794**
duty to aid those in, **§§327-332, 553-571, 1313**
emotional distress at peril to another, **§§771-779**
"helpless," **§805**
"inattentive," **§806**

PHYSICIANS AND SURGEONS
battery, **§§112, 311-319**
duty to disclose, **§§311-319, 1046-1047**
prescriptions, **§§1046-1047**
duty to warn others, **§§557-559**
emergency, Good Samaritan statutes, **§§560-566**
indemnity from, **§§1265-1266**
informed consent, **§§311-318**
malicious prosecution theory, **§1784**
malpractice
in general, **§§1297-1304**
statute of limitations, **§1299**
mass immunization, product liability, **§1047**
negligence, **§§305-319**
statute of limitations, **§§1268-1271, 1299**
negligent aggravation, **§1267**

POSSESSION
conversion, **§230**
trespass to chattels, **§213**
trespass to land, **§§190-200**

PRESUMPTIONS
negligence, **§§409-414**
res ipsa loquitur. *See* Res ipsa loquitur

PRIVACY
appropriation of name or likeness, **§§1590-1601**
celebrity's right of publicity, **§§1595-1596, 1617-1618**
consent as defense, **§1593**
damages, **§1601**
extension of protection, **§1594**
newsworthiness as defense, **§§1598-1600**
prima facie case, **§1590**
unauthorized use, **§§1591-1594**
constitutional privilege, **§§1561, 1584-1586, 1599**
dead persons, **§§1613-1618**
emotional distress, infliction of, interrelation with, **§§1569, 1619**
false light, **§§1602-1611**
damages, **§1611**
defamation compared, **§§1606, 1609**
falsity, **§1605**
newsworthiness as defense, **§§1607-1609**
prima facie case, **§1602**
publication required, **§1604**
intrusions into private life or affairs, **§§1544-1561**
consent as defense, **§§1558-1559**
constitutional protection, **§1561**
corporations, no right to, **§1547**
damages, **§1560**
highly offensive, **§1552**
intent, **§§1553-1555**
prima facie case, **§1544**
protected areas, **§§1545-1547**
trespass compared, **§1550**
private facts, **§§1562-1589**
consent as defense, **§§1580-1583**
damages, **§1587**
fault, **§1577**
highly offensive publication, **§1568**
involuntary public figures, **§§1567, 1574-1575**
media privilege, **§§1584-1586**
newsworthiness as defense, **§§1570-1576**
prima facie case, **§1562**
private facts defined, **§§1563-1567**

public disclosure required, **§1569**
voluntary public figures, **§§1566, 1572-1573**
related torts, **§§1619-1621**
survival of action, **§§1613-1618**
third persons, privacy rights of, **§§1612-1618**
Uniform Single Publication Act, **§1621**

PRIVILEGED INVASIONS OF PERSONAL INTERESTS
See Arrest; Consent; Defense of others; Property, defense of; Recapture of chattels wrongfully withheld; Recovery of land; Self-defense; Shopkeeper's privilege

PRIVILEGED INVASIONS OF PROPERTY
See also Necessity to invade land or chattels; Recapture of chattels as defense to invasion of property; Trespass, chattels trespassing
defendant's misconduct, effect of, **§§274-275**

PRIVITY
See Products liability; Warranty, liability based on breach of

PRODUCTS LIABILITY
in general, **§925**
intentional acts, liability based on, **§§929-930**
damages, **§930**
market share liability, **§§427-432**
negligence, liability based on
assumption of the risk as defense to, **§951**
builders, **§§936, 939**
bystanders, **§937**
care required, **§§943-948**
comparative negligence as defense to, **§951**
concealment of known defects, **§947**
concurrent duties, **§§943-948**
contributory negligence as defense to, **§951**
damages, **§§949-950**
dealer. *See* intermediate party, below, this section
defects
design, **§§935-936**
manufacturing, **§§925-926**
defendants liable, **§§925, 943-948**
foreseeability of harm, **§933**
in general, **§§925-928, 932**
intermediate party
duty to inspect, **§§944-947**
negligence of, effect, **§946**
omission to act, **§§947-948**
MacPherson v. Buick Motor Co., **§§933-934**
privity, **§§932-934**
products made by others, **§§940-941**
property damage, **§938**
proving negligence, **§942**
real property, defects in, **§939**
res ipsa loquitur, **§942**
scope of, **§§934-942**
strict liability in tort
abnormal reactions, **§§1032-1034**
advertisers, **§1006**
assemblers of parts, **§997**
assumption of risk as defense to, **§§1059-1064**
auctioneers, **§1007**
bailors, **§§994-995**
burden of proof, **§§1035-1036**
causation, **§§1037-1047**
circumstantial evidence of "defect," **§1036**
comparative negligence as defense to, **§§1057-1058, 1064**
contractors, **§§998, 1014**
contributory negligence as defense to, **§§1054-1056**
"crashworthiness," **§965**
"danger," natural vs. unnatural, **§§980-982**
defects
approaches, **§966**
consumer expectation, **§§969-975, 985, 1023-1026**
"defect" alone, **§1027**
risk/utility test, **§§967-968, 972-974, 984, 1026**
unreasonable danger, **§§1023-1026**
requirement of, **§§957-958, 1022**
types
design, **§§961-978**
manufacturing, **§960**
warnings, inadequate, **§§979-990**
defendants liable
commercial suppliers, **§§992-1003**
franchisors, **§1002**
noncommercial suppliers, **§§1004-1007**
successors, **§999**
disclaimers, effect of, **§§1065-1066**
economic losses, recovery for, **§§1050-1053**
elements of, **§957**
federal preemption, **§1068**
foreseeability of harm, **§§976-977**
handguns, **§§964, 974**
inadequate warning, **§§979-990**
in general, **§952**
intervening causes, effect of, **§§1043-1047**
latent defects, **§§1024-1026, 1060-1064**
lessors, **§§994-996**
liability not absolute, **§§957-958**
misrepresentation, **§1052**
misuse, **§§1028-1029, 1031, 1056**
modifications, **§1030**
patent defects, **§§1024-1026**
personal injuries or death, recovery for, **§1048**
plaintiffs protected, **§§1008-1011**
prescription drugs, **§§986, 990, 1046**
"products"
blood exception, **§1020**
defective only, **§§957-958, 1022**

defined, **§1012**
in their natural state, **§1013**
manufactured by others, **§997**
services and, **§§1015-1021**
stream of commerce, **§1021**
proof, **§§1035-1047**
property damage, recovery for, **§1049**
protected parties
business entities, **§1011**
bystanders, **§1009**
consumer or ultimate users, **§1008**
passengers, **§1008**
rescuers, **§1010**
public policy, **§§953-956**
real property, defects in, **§1014**
recalls, **§1045**
scope of, **§§991-1053**
sellers of, **§§993-996**
used products, **§§1000-1001**
services, **§§1015-1021**
statute of limitations, **§1067**
statute of repose, **§1307**
statutory limitations on, **§§1305-1312**
successors to manufacturers of defective products, **§999**
unavoidably dangerous products, **§§983-988**
unforeseeable danger of harm, **§§976-977**
discovery of danger, **§978**
vaccines, **§§1047, 1312**
warnings, **§§979-990, 1044-1047**
assumption of the risk, **§§1060-1061**
bulk suppliers, **§990**
inadequate, **§§979-990**
third parties, injuries to, **§§1044-1047**
who must receive, **§§989-990**
warranty, liability based on breach of. *See* Warranty, liability based on breach of

PROPERTY, DEFENSE OF

See also Recapture of chattels as defense to invasion of property; Recovery of land
apparent necessity, **§142**
mechanical devices, **§§143-144**
nondeadly force only, **§142**
privilege of, in general, **§142**
threats privileged, **§145**

PROXIMATE CAUSE

See also Damages; Negligence
Andrews factors, **§449**
burden of proof. *See* Evidence
contributory negligence distinguished, **§456**
defamation, **§1422**
direct causation, **§§453, 461-472**
defined, **§453**
foreseeable results, **§§461-466**
indirect causation distinguished, **§§454-456**
no intervening forces, **§§453, 457-459**
unforeseeable results, **§§467-472**
directness/remoteness test, **§446**
duty of care compared, **§§451, 509**
foreseeability. *See* intervening forces; unforeseeable consequences; both below
foreseeability test, **§445**
highly extraordinary consequences, **§§464-466, 485, 489-493, 505**
indirect causation, **§§454-460, 473-500**. *See also* intervening forces, below
defined, **§454**
direct causation distinguished, **§453**
in general, **§§473-476**
intervening forces
act of God, **§§455, 485, 489**
acts not constituting, **§§457-459**
contributory negligence distinguished, **§456**
criminal acts, **§§486, 490-491, 506**
defined, **§455**
foreseeability, **§§444-449, 460, 463-469, 478-486, 488, 497, 500, 504-509**
foreseeable results of unforeseeable, **§§474-475, 488-496**
unforeseeable results of foreseeable, **§497**
unforeseeable results of unforeseeable, **§§498-499**
intervening forces, dependent
checking forces, **§§479-480**
escape forces, **§482**
in general, **§478**
normal responses, **§§479-484**
rescue forces, **§§481, 493**
response forces, **§483**
suicide, **§483**
intervening forces, independent
criminal acts, **§§486, 490-491, 506**
foreseeability, **§§485-486**
negligent acts, **§487**
risk rule, **§447**
strict liability, **§919**
substantial factor test, **§448**
tavernkeepers, **§§642-643**
third person's omission to act, **§§494-496**
unforeseeable consequences
direct causation, **§§462-466**
in general, **§§442-451**
limitation of liability to risk, **§§464-466**
Polemis case, **§469**
"thin-skulled plaintiffs," **§§471-472**
unforeseeable results, **§§467-472, 497-500**
unusual sequences, **§§464-466, 468-470**
Wagon Mound case, **§470**
unforeseeable plaintiff, **§§501-509**

PUBLIC OFFICERS

See Officers

PUNITIVE DAMAGES

See Damages

R

RECAPTURE OF CHATTELS AS DEFENSE TO INVASION OF PROPERTY
See also Property, defense of
act of God, **§§246-249**
chattel owner at fault, **§§238, 245, 251**
defendant's misconduct, effect of, **§§274-275**
landowner at fault, **§§238-244, 251**
  demand required, **§240**
  extent of privilege, **§§242-244**
  force, use of, **§244**
  mistake, **§§243, 251**
  reasonable entry, **§241**
mistake, **§251**
third party at fault, **§§238, 250**

RECAPTURE OF CHATTELS WRONGFULLY WITHHELD
See also Shopkeeper's privilege
no tortious dispossession, **§§156-157**
  conditional sales contract, **§157**
privilege of, in general, **§§150, 156**
tortious dispossession, **§§150-155**
  demand, **§152**
  fresh pursuit, **§153**
  mistake, **§151**
  nondeadly force, **§150**
  right to immediate possession, **§151**
  transfer to innocent person, **§155**

RECKLESS CONDUCT
as intervening force, **§480**
emotional distress, intentional causing of, **§§86-88**
liability for under guest statutes, **§589**
punitive damages, as basis for, **§530**
rescuers, **§§331, 493**

RECOVERY OF LAND
See also Property, defense of
no force, majority view, **§146**
reasonable nondeadly force, minority view, **§§147-149**
  tortious vs. other dispossessions, **§§148-149**

RELATIONAL INTERESTS
See Interference with family relationships; Husband and wife; Parent and child

RELEASE
See also Joint torts
covenant not to sue, **§1257**
joint tortfeasors, **§1252**
  effect of release of one, **§§1255-1257**
  indivisible injury, **§1253**
  satisfaction, **§1254**

RES IPSA LOQUITUR
airplane accidents, **§382**
burden of proof, **§§382-384**
bursting bottle cases, **§372**
defendant's duty, **§§369-375**
eliminating plaintiff as causal factor, **§376**
  contributory negligence distinguished, **§377**
evidence, accessibility of, **§379**
exclusive control in defendant, **§§370-372**
expert testimony, necessity of, **§367**
inference from facts, **§382**
inference that defendant was negligent, **§§363-364, 378**
inference that someone was negligent, **§§365-368**
multiple defendants, **§§373-375**
nature of accident, **§§365-368**
physicians and surgeons, **§373**
presumptions
  disappearing, **§384**
  permissible inference, **§382**
  rebuttable, **§383**
products liability negligence of manufacturer, **§942**
proving specific acts, effect of, **§§380-381**
Third Restatement approach, **§378**
three-part test, **§364**

RESCUERS
duty owed to, **§§327-328**
duty to rescue, statutory, **§§1313-1314**
foolhardy, **§§331, 493**
harm by, **§329**
professional, **§332**
proximate cause, **§§481, 493**

RESPONDEAT SUPERIOR, §§609-612. *See also* Employer and employee; Vicarious liability

RIGHT OF PRIVACY
See Privacy

S

SALES
See Products liability; Warranty, liability based on breach of

SATISFACTION
See Release

SCIENTER
dangerous animals, **§§890-891**
deceit, **§§1637-1638**
injurious falsehood, **§1697**

SELF-DEFENSE
See also Defense of others
apprehension of immediate contact, **§124**
deadly force, **§§123-128**
force, use of, **§§121, 129, 131-132**
limitations on right, **§§130-135**
mistake, **§§120, 122**
nondeadly force, **§§119-122**
privilege in general, **§§119-123, 133**
reasonableness test, **§136**

retreat, duty to, **§§122, 125-128**
threats, privilege to make, **§129**

SELLERS OF LAND
duration of liability, **§757**
known concealed dangers, **§755**
liability after transfer, **§754**
persons outside premises, duty to, **§756**

SHOPKEEPER'S PRIVILEGE
force, use of, **§162**
mistake, **§164**
reasonable suspicion, **§161**
temporary detention of suspected thief, **§§158-164**

SLANDER
See Defamation

SLANDER OF TITLE
See Injurious falsehood

STATES
Civil Rights Act of 1871, **§§1241-1247**
immunity of, **§1223**. *See also* Immunities

STATUTE, VIOLATION OF
class of persons protected, **§402**
community custom, **§§385-392**
Dram Shop Acts, **§§637-649**
effect of, **§§408-414**
evidence of negligence, **§§408-414**
excused violations, **§§404-407, 412-414**
negligence per se, **§§395, 396-402, 404, 406-407**
presumptions, **§§410-411**
prevention of particular harm, **§401**
standard of conduct, statutory, **§399**
type of risk covered, **§§400-401**

STATUTES
alternative dispute resolution, **§1351**
attorneys' fees regulation, **§1349**
automobiles
  family purpose doctrine, **§602**
  guest statutes, **§§589-590**
  no-fault insurance, **§§1285-1296**
  permissive use statutes, **§603**
black lung compensation, **§1323**
charities, **§1251**
Civil Rights Act of 1871, **§§1241-1247**
collateral sources rule, limitations on, **§§1344-1348**
compliance with as due care, **§§393, 549**
consortium, loss of, **§§1175-1187**
crime victims, **§§1316-1318**
damages, limitations on, **§§1334-1343**
Dram Shop Acts, **§§637-641, 1315**. *See also* Negligence
federal preemption, **§§1325-1328**
Federal Tort Claims Act, **§§1231-1234**
frivolous claim sanctions, **§1350**
Good Samaritan acts, **§§560-566, 1314**
international plane crashes, **§§1319-1321**
joint and several liability, limitations on, **§§1330-1333**
medical malpractice, **§§1297-1304**
no fault, **§§1285-1296, 1319-1321**. *See also* Liability insurance, effect of
nuclear accidents, **§1322**
officers, liability of governmental, **§§1241-1247**
permissive use, **§603**
products liability, **§§1305-1312**. *See also* Products liability
rescue, duty to, **§§1313-1314**
September 11 victim compensation, **§1324**
survival of actions, **§§1151-1153**
vicarious liability, extension by, **§634**
workers' compensation, **§§1272-1284**
wrongful death acts, **§§1157-1171**

STRICT LIABILITY
See also Animals; Products liability
abnormally dangerous activities, **§§898-913**
  defined, **§§899-902**
  determinative factors, **§903**
  relation to surroundings, **§§904-905**
airplanes, ground damage from, **§§906-908**
animals. *See* Animals
assumption of risk, **§§922-924**
blasting, **§§901, 917**
common carriers, **§909**
comparative negligence, **§921**
consent as defense to, **§923**
contributory negligence, **§920**
extent of liability, **§§914-919**
  foreseeable hazards, **§917**
  foreseeable plaintiffs, **§§915-916**
handguns, **§§910-911**
in general, **§880**
international plane crashes, **§§1319-1321**
negligence compared, **§916**
nonnatural use of land, **§900**
prima facie case, **§881**
products liability compared, **§§912-913**
proximate cause, **§919**
Rylands v. Fletcher, **§900**
ultrahazardous activities, **§901**
vicarious liability. *See* Vicarious liability
warranty. *See* Warranty, liability based on breach of

SUPPLIERS OF CHATTELS
See Products liability

SURVIVAL OF TORT ACTIONS
common law rules, **§1150**
pain and suffering, **§1153**
personal torts, **§§1152-1154**
  intangible interests, **§1154**
privacy, invasion of, **§§1613-1618**
property torts, **§1155**
punitive damages not recoverable, **§1155**
statutory provisions, **§§1151-1154**

T

TENANT
See Landlord, duties of

THREATS
assault, basis for, **§§29-31, 36-46**
emotional distress, infliction of, **§§31, 80**
plaintiff's awareness required for assault, **§36**
privileged in defense of property, **§145**
privileged in self-defense, **§129**
when sufficient for confinement, **§§67-70**

TOUCHING
See Battery

TRADE LIBEL
See Injurious falsehood

TRANSFERRED INTENT
See Intent, transferred

TRESPASS
ab initio, **§275**
chattels trespassing, privilege to exclude or evict, **§§252-253**
common law action of, **§10**

TRESPASS TO CHATTELS
bailment cases. *See* Bailments
causation, **§214**
character of defendant's act, **§207**. *See also* Act by defendant
consent as defense to, **§237**
damages, **§215**
intent, **§§208-209**
invasion of chattel interest, **§§210-212**
  dispossession, **§211**
  intermeddling, **§212**
negligence compared, **§208**
possession, necessity of, **§213**
prima facie case, **§206**
strict liability compared, **§208**
transferred intent, **§209**

TRESPASS TO LAND
airspace, **§§196-200**
causation, **§§202-203**
character of defendant's act, **§183**. *See also* Act by defendant
consent as defense to, **§237**
damages, **§§204-205**
defendant's intrusion, **§§188-189**
  by intangibles, **§189**
intent, **§§184-187**
landlord and tenant, **§§194-195**. *See also* Landlord, duties of
leased property, **§§194-195**
negligence compared, **§185**
nuisance distinguished, **§201**
possession, necessity of, **§§190-200**
prima facie case, **§182**
privilege to exclude trespassing chattels, **§§252-253**
privilege to reclaim chattels. *See* Recapture of chattels as defense to invasion of property
strict liability compared, **§186**
transferred intent, **§187**

TRESPASSERS
attractive nuisance doctrine, **§§674-688**
  age of child, **§676**
  artificial conditions, **§§678-686**
  balancing risk against utility, **§681**
  child's appreciation of danger, **§§678-687**
  dangerous activities, **§683**
  defense, as a, **§688**
  discover, duty to child, **§677**
  foreseeability of trespass, **§679**
  natural conditions, **§687**
  ordinary risks, **§685**
  risk of injury, foreseeable, **§680**
children. *See* attractive nuisance doctrine, above
conditions, dangerous, **§§662, 671-673, 721**
constant trespassers upon a limited area, **§§664-673**
dangerous activities, **§§662, 664, 671**
discovered, **§§662, 665**
habitual intruders, **§§666-673**
in peril, duty to, **§663**
liability of occupiers to, **§§661-665**
liability of third person to, **§§722-724**
minority view—status irrelevant, **§§718-720**
ordinary, **§§660-665**
privilege of to abate nuisance, **§§268-273**
straying from highway, **§§258-261**

U

UNITED STATES
Federal Tort Claims Act, **§§1231-1234**
immunity of, **§§1222-1223**. *See also* Immunities

V

VICARIOUS LIABILITY
automobiles, liability of owners, **§§594-597, 601-603**
  family purpose doctrine, **§602**
  negligent entrustment, **§§594-597**
  permissive use statutes, **§603**
bailors and bailees, **§§592, 597-598, 600-603**
defamation, **§1369**
direct liability distinguished, **§592**
employer and employees, **§§605-613**. *See also* Employer and employee
  intentional torts, **§610**
  negligent supervision, **§608**
employer and independent contractors
  collateral negligence, **§627**
  dangerous activities, **§§625-626**

health care providers, **§§621-623**
negligence of employer, **§§614-626**
no liability rule, **§615**
nondelegable duties, **§§618-626**
indemnity, **§1263**
joint enterprise. *See* Joint enterprise
parent and child, **§§633-634**
stolen property, **§599**

VIOLATION OF STATUTE
See Statute, violation of

WXYZ

WARRANTY, LIABILITY BASED ON BREACH OF
assumption of risk as defense to, **§§1095, 1099**
causation, **§§1095-1096**
consumer protection statutes, **§1094**
contributory negligence no defense, **§1098**
damages, **§1097**
disclaimers as defense to, **§§1100-1104**
effect of, **§1083**
express warranties, **§§1070, 1087**
extension beyond sellers of chattel, **§§1076-1082**
bailments, **§1077**
dealer requirement, **§1082**
leases, **§1077**
new homes, **§1078**
goods vs. services, **§§1079-1081**
blood, **§1081**
implied warranties, **§§1071-1082**
fitness for particular purpose, **§1073**
merchantability, **§1074**
manufacturers or suppliers, **§§1084-1090**
notice of breach, **§1185**
plaintiffs protected, **§§1084-1094**
privity requirement, **§§1084-1094**
dangerous products excepted, **§§1091-1093**
latent dangers only, **§1096**
statute of limitations, **§1100**
strict liability in tort, **§§1075, 1083**
U.C.C. provisions, **§§1072-1082**
privity, **§§1089-1090**
sale of goods only, **§1076**
strict liability in tort compared, **§1075**

WILLFUL AND WANTON MISCONDUCT
See Reckless conduct

WORKERS' COMPENSATION, §§1272-1284

WRONGFUL BIRTH
healthy child, **§§1194-1196**
in general, **§1193**
no suit by child, **§1200**
unhealthy child, **§§1197-1200**
emotional distress, **§1199**

WRONGFUL DEATH
assumption of risk as defense to, **§1168**
beneficiary's negligence as defense, **§§1170-1171**
common law, **§1156**
comparative negligence as defense to, **§§1168, 1170**
contributory negligence
as defense to, **§§1168, 1170**
imputed, **§810**
damages
measure of, **§§1161-1167**
no punitive, **§1167**
recoverable, **§§1158-1160**
decedent's recovery inter vivos as defense, **§1169**
prenatal injuries, **§1192**
statutes, types of, **§1157-1167**

Notes

Notes

Notes

Notes